Futility Ending in Disaster

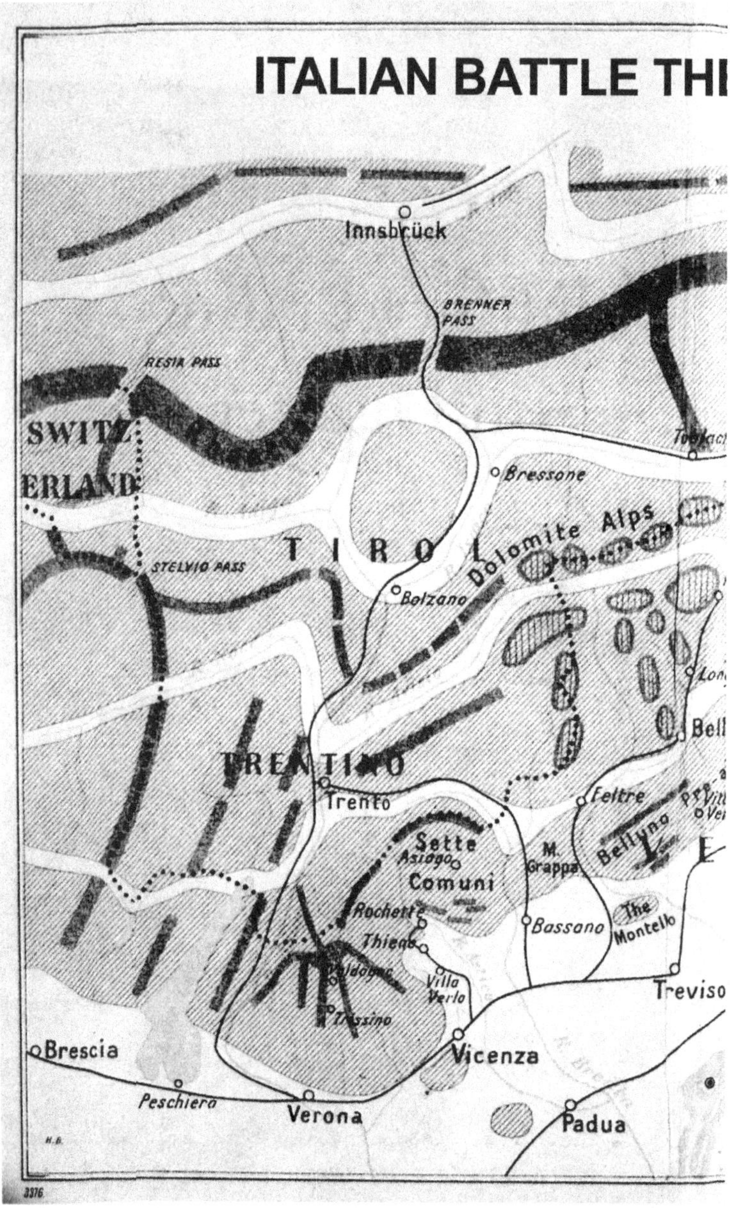

ITALIAN BATTLE THE
Innsbrück
BRENNER PASS
RESIA PASS
SWITZERLAND
Bressone
Dolomite Alps
TIROL
STELVIO PASS
Bolzano
TRENTINO
Trento
Feltre
Belluno
Sette Comuni
Asiago
M. Grappa
Rochette
Thiene
Bassano
The Montello
Valdagno
Villa Verla
Treviso
Trissino
Brescia
Vicenza
Peschiera
Verona
Padua

EATRE, 1915 - 1918

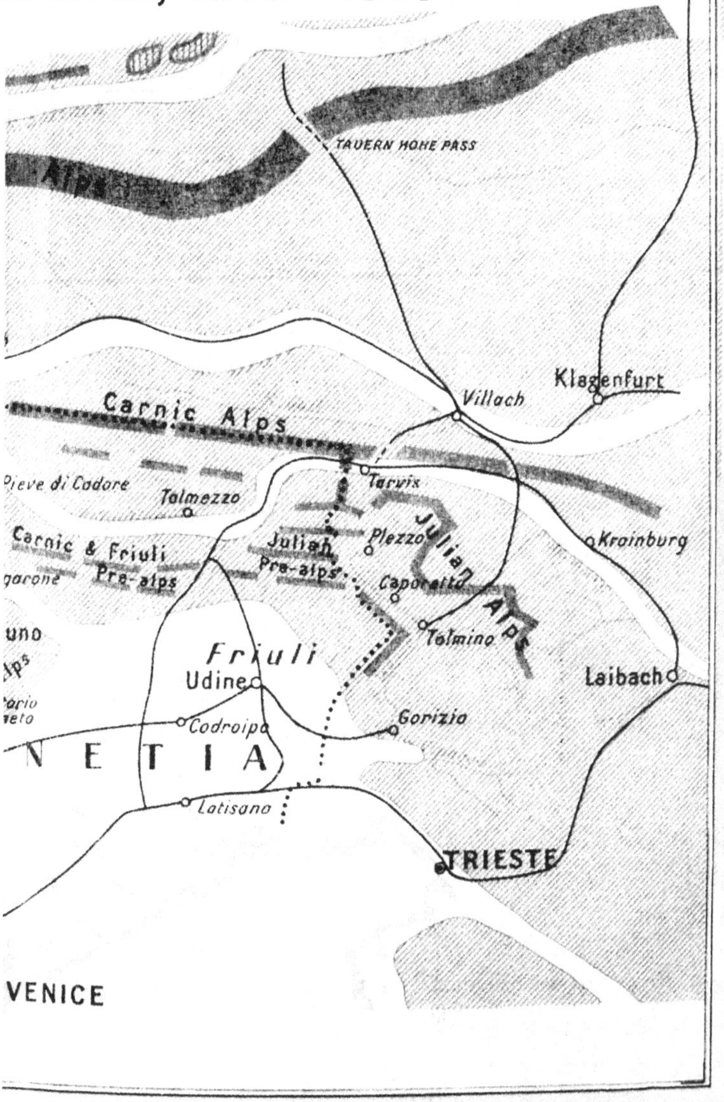

Library of Congress Control Number: 2004093504
ISBN: Hardcover 978-1-4134-5742-1
Softcover 978-1-4134-5741-4

This book was printed in the United States of America.

To order additional copies of this book, contact:
Xlibris Corporation
1-888-795-4274
www.Xlibris.com
Orders@Xlibris.com
19968

OTHER BOOKS BY GAETANO V. CAVALLARO

THE BEGINNING OF FUTILITY
DISASTER ENDING IN FINAL VICTORY

Futility Ending in Disaster

Diplomatic, Military, Aviation and Social Events in the First World War on the Austro-Italian Front 1917

Volume II

Gaetano V. Cavallaro

CONTENTS

To the *Fanti* that died
And to Those Who Rose to Repel the Invader.

List of Maps (Edited)

INTRODUCTION

As noted in *The Beginning of Futility*, in the various Isonzo battles, the *grigioverde* assaulting mountains one at a time slowly advanced against the enemy. Realizing that it was running out of defensive positions with Vienna itself in danger the A.O.K. decided to go on the offensive. With Czarist Russia disintegrating Vienna could now afford to send many troops to its last combat front but nonetheless requested German assistance. Aware of the enemy's intentions (but not all his intentions), General Cadorna notified the allies he was going on the defensive resulting in their request for the return of artillery mouths which had been loaned to the Italian Army. Ludendorff was reluctant to give aid feeling that the Italian Front was a secondary concern. Instead Hindenburg sent a mountain warfare expert (Lt. Gen. Konrad Krafft von Dellmengsingen) to reconnoiter the sector. A daring and risky attack using new tactics (Blitzkrieg) theretofore unknown on the Italian Front was proposed which if successful would yield great rewards. Used were the divisions of the German Strategic Reserve whose tactics confused the Comando Supremo similar to how in May 1940 the German assault in France confused the Anglo-French forces. Slowly the Austro-Germans went into place so that by the middle of October, they had achieved a *Strategic Surprise*. On October 24, 1917 in a surprise assault against the bewildered *fanti* the Austro-Germans sliced through Italian defenses like a hot knife through butter. The loaned allied artillery enroute to France now had to backtrack and return to the Italian Front. In a brilliant maneuver penetrating Italian lines a short distance Austro-German forces caused the withdrawal of over one million Italian troops which were lucky to find salvation west of the Piave River. Moving a division in the roadless mountains would take one month for a short distance.

At the outbreak of the conflict Italian men enlisted hearing the words *Dulce et decorum est, pro patria mori* (It is sweet and proper to die for one's country). Upset by their terrible treatment under Cadorna some of the illiterate infantry surrendered *en masse* others were easily taken prisoner,still others deserted intending to go home to help with the harvest. In less than three weeks the Austro-Germans reached the Piave (one hundred miles away), bewildering Italian staff officers as well as the peasant *fanti* who had decided that the war was over. By the middle of November, the Comando Supremo had three defensive bulwarks, the Asiago Plateau, M. Grappa and the Piave River.

Suddenly for reasons unknown to this day the combativeness of the *fanti* on the Grappa and the Asiago Plateau changed to a devil-may care fight to the death attitude. The Austro-Germans were stopped as their slogan noted "Victorious but dead." Cadorna desperately called for allied military manpower which was grudgingly sent by Gen. Robertson, Chief of the Imperial General Staff while the French immediately sent two divisions. London and Paris were haunted by the specter of a conquered Italy freeing up millions of enemy combat-hardened troops for the French Front. Exhausted allied armies on the Western Front would not be able to handle the Austro-German onslaught. Anglo-French troops initially were afraid of fighting along side Italian troops fearing that they would flee exposing them to danger an attitude which soon changed. Italian military wrote some of the best pages of their history defending on the Asiago Plateau and M. Grappa. Many of the *fanti* had never seen snow nor experienced the bitter cold of their mountain positions but they did not yield. To the bewilderment of many at Caporetto Gen. Badoglio had to change his headquarters five times. Finally the reason has been found in German literature. Reading and researching after many years one realized that aviation had become an important part in the war's offensive and defensive actions. A chapter is therefore included on aviation activity on the Austro-Italian Front. Although not their war many American citizens fought in the *Regia Aeronautica.* Rare photos have been introduced as well as graphically illustrated maps. Many maps originally scheduled to be only in Volume III of this (*Disaster With Final Victory*) work are also in this volume. Often there are two maps for one site as the mountains are dotted with many tiny strategic villages which could not be easily noted on one map. The second map is also often noted to give an overall view of the battle. Originally this was supposed to be the final volume, but due to computer limitations (yes computer) it has been divided into the second and third (final) volume of this work.

Independence Day, 2001

ACKNOWLEDGEMENTS

In this second volume, I am indebted to Mr. Stephen Noble of the House of Lords Library in London as well as Col. Antonio Santini of the *Commissariato Generale in Onoranza dei Caduti in Guerra. Dott.ssa* L. Romaniello of the *Museo del Risorgimento* in Milano assisted me in obtaining important documents. Signora Antonella Baldo of the *Ufficio Storico dello Stato Maggiore* in Rome was of great help. I am indebted to His Honor the Mayor of Asiago Avvocato Francesco Gattolin for allowing me to use photographs from the Asiago Collection. Among the many who aided me in my research in Italy were dear cousins Signora Carmen Fratto and Domenico Gagliardi. Great thanks are due to Hofrat Dr. Christoph Tepperberg *Direktor der Kriegsarchiv*, Vienna for his generous assistance as well as to Gen. Micheli, commander of the Italian III Army for his assistance. Signora Giovanna (who refused to give me her last name) of the *Museo Storico della Guerra* (Rovereto) was a great help. Many years ago *Signor* Guido Bertello did some magnificent color drawings which I have saved to use on the cover of my texts. Despite valiant efforts I have not been able to track him down. Perhaps this work will result in my efforts bearing fruit. I am indebted to Herr Wolf Albrecht Kainz for allowing me to use photos from his collection as well as Signor Marco Rech who assisted me greatly in my Caporetto research. Mr. Antony Richards of the Imperial War Museum, London is owed a debt as from that distant post he assisted me in tracking down the author of some American poetry. Ms. Cybele Cappelli of the Adriance Memorial Library (Poughkeepsie, New York) was tireless in her efforts to obtain data for me. Univ.-Doz. Dr. Meinrad Pizzinini of the Tiroler Landesmuseum Ferdinandeum (Innsbruck) helped me greatly with some important documents. Signora Igea Muraro is owed a debt of thanks for allowing me to use photographs from her late husband's book. Italian authors Enrico Acerbi, Alessandro Massignani, Maurizio Longoni also contributed greatly. I am indebted to Mr. Robert Shoop and Mr. Robert Repich for material on the aviation chapter. Thanks are due Mr. Bruce Robertson for allowing me to use one of his photos from his magnificent collection. Prof. Glen Steinberg of New Jersey University assisted me in outlining the House of Savoy family tree. I am grateful to Reverend Armando Padula OFM for his help with the Catholic Encyclopedia and Ms. Eva DiGregorio for helping me translate Hungarian documents. Finally I am indebted to my loving wife Linda Miele-Cavallaro for her patience in enduring my long absences for research on this work.

VOLUME II

GLOSSARY TERMS SPECIFIC TO VOLUME II

Alemagna Road	road going along the Piave Valley up to Tai di Cadore, then eastward to Cortina d'Ampezzo to Villach where it joined the roadway of Val Pusteria
Linea dell'Armata	a primitive Italian Army defensive line called outdated by the British Army
Siamo Perduti	(We are lost); description of Savoia Pomilio planes by pilots
Sepultura per due	(A grave for two) description of SP2 Savoia-Pomilio planes by crews
Trentino	mountainous area around city of Trento in northwest sector of Austro-Italian Front.
Yellow Road	false defensive line eighteen miles behind the front lines. Its northern end was near Pieve di Cadore at Fortezza Cadore Maé
Imboscati	Italian military from wealthy families who were given cushy jobs far from harm's way

Further rank and unit denominations in Italian, Austro-Hungarian and German military

Aufklärungskompagnien	—Reconnaissance and artillery spotting air unit
Fliegerabteilung	(FAA) Also used for artillery spotting
Fliegerkompagnie	(FLIK) Austro-Hungarian air unit usually six planes
Insegna	Ensign in the Italian Navy

Feldwebel	Company Sergeant Major
Grigioverde	Color of Italian infantry uniform
Jagdkompagnien	—Fighting scout units with sixteen to twenty airplanes
Kampf Einsitzer Staffel	(KEST) Single seater squadron
Offizierstellvertreter	Acting officer
SchutzStaffel	(SCHUSTA) Escort Squadron
Vizefeldwebel	Vice Sergeant Major

For further information see Glossary Volume I

CHAPTER I

DAY ONE, THE DISASTER BEGAN October 24, 1917

On October 24, 1917, after a short furious gas and shell barrage, the Austro-Germans broke through Italian lines at Plezzo and Tolmino.[1] Using heretofore unknown attack tactics on the Italian front, the Austro-Germans infiltrated the IV Corps attacking it from the rear, while the VII Corps was enveloped. There were no long attack lines but relatively small units attacking without a regular scheme. It was no accident that attacking troups consisted of the best Jäger units as well as elite mountain forces which the A.O.K. contributed. There was confusion throughout the defending trenches. Italian infantry had not been trained in maneuver warfare which included redeploying and attacking while staff officers could not handle the logistics. For the first time troops would advance not worrying about their flanks. Favored by fog new infiltration tactics were used to assault the weak point of the Italian defenses. A German air umbrella had prohibited any Italian air reconnaissance. The Saga Gorge west of Caporetto was abandoned while both sides of the Isonzo and all the Italian positions east of the Stol, including Caporetto were taken.[2]

Then forward, valiant fighters!
And forward, German riders!
And when the heart grows cold,
Let each his love infold.

Charles Theodore Körner, The Sword Song
Translated from German by Charles T. Brooks

IT HAD BEEN raining for three weeks. Trenches had been used in the American Civil, the Boer, and the Russo-Japanese Wars, but only the Germans had learned anything from these experiences. Now another type of warfare would be attempted, the multipronged blitz. An attempt will be made to place all in chronological and sequential order via graphically illustrated maps and notes. As Krafft had noted in his talk to the General Staff (see Vol. I), weather would be a factor. In this battle, there would be four different simultaneous weather reports including snow, fog, rain, and sun, all on the same geographic point depending on the altitude of the troop location. One would ask why would the Plezzo-Tolmino sector be used for the offensive. Studies by the A.O.K. felt that crashing through the Isonzo at that point would be easier as Italian defenses there were not strong so proceeding southwest after the breakthrough attacking troops would enfilade the whole network of Italian defenses on the lower Isonzo.[3] Well-equipped, well-trained and well-led German troops in a maneuver warfare mode would assault ill-trained, ill-equipped and poorly led Italian troops which the latter knew nothing about. Illiterate Italian troops could not handle the tactics of the Austro-Germans. The *fanti* were only familiar with the *attacco frontale.* The assault would not be predicated on Schlieffen's dictum of a twenty-nine kilometers (17.4 miles) advance using a single column through a single road.[4] It would be across bad roads and bad mountains hoping for bad weather.

At 0200, under light rain and fog, the attackers started shelling Italian positions using poison gas and explosives.[5] Shelling tactics used were those learned at the mountain artillery school in Sonthofen.[6] Krafft wrote, "In the enemy camps, we saw lights coming into action, checking our advance positions and followed by small and medium Italian artillery shelling. To our amazement the much feared destructive type of shelling of our assembly points did not take place." One by one, the flood lights went out.[7] The attackers had been practicing for about two weeks against specific targets, but firing very little lest their guns be discovered. When the time came, they could fire in the dark with such precision that Krafft later wrote about that day, "Today I would not wish to be Italian." Austro-German infantry 500 yds. from Italian trenches on the level ground or fifty yards above on the slope trenches were getting ready to make their move.

Comando Supremo

0500

Daily at this time, Cadorna arose, had breakfast and wrote to his family. On this day, writing to his daughter, he indicated that he had made adequate preparations and was tranquil about the outcome.[8]

0600

Cadorna met with his colonels, Melchiade Gabba his Operations Chief and Riccardo Calcagno of the Situation Office. Previously, the Operations Chief had been Col. Brig. Roberto Bencivenga who had been imprisoned after a quarrel with him. The Generalissimo had to answer to no one for his command actions. Only the king could dismiss him but as has been noted Vittorio Emanuele reigned but did not govern. Calcagno stated the phrase that he liked "Much smoke but little meat." indicating that the Austro-Germans were feinting in the Isonzo but would attack in the Trentino. Cadorna's whole staff always agreed with him making even Intelligence information conform with his opinions.[9] To constantly disagree resulted in being transferred away from such a cushy staff job. At 0800, he met with Lt. Gen. Carlo Porro, Vice Chief of Staff, who commented, "They are shelling, shelling, but they shall not fool us."[10] This was the same Porro who, at Rapallo a few weeks later, so disturbed Foch and British Prime Minister Lloyd George by his lack of information and comprehension, that both insisted that he be replaced.[11] Luigi Barzini of the *Corriere della Sera* had written an article headlined "Austrian hopes" in which he noted that Vienna might sue for a separate peace.[12] (The statement shall be adequately discussed in Chapter XV).

0900

Cadorna telegraphed the II Army reminding them to hold the line Jeza-Globocak (Map 14). Still concerned about an attack on the III Army, he telegraphed at 1035 and 1215 to find out how many guns the II Army could send to the III Army.[13]

Events at II Army Headquarters

Information regarding the Austro-German attack first arrived at the II Army from forward artillery observers not individual units. By 1030 Capello already had been informed that the enemy had broken through the lines of the XXVII Corps and so informed Caviglia (XXIV Corps).[14] He noted that the enemy had reached Cemponi and Costa Duole (Map 20). The II Army commander also heard that there was no counterbattery fire, which disturbed him. To stop any enemy advance, he sent the *Vicenza* to the Stupizza Strait in the Val Natisone west of Caporetto (Map 13). A new command of the left wing of the II Army under Lt. Gen. Luca Montuori, consisting of the VII, XXXVII and IV Corps was created. At 1300, headquarters was notified that the enemy had occupied Plezzo (IV Corps, Fiftieth Division sector), and was proceeding toward Saga (Map 15). The Forty-sixth Division had been pierced with the enemy proceeding past Selisce (Map 14).[15] Enemy shelling had started at 0200 mostly on the positions of the IV and XXVII Corps, the left wing of the XXIV and the right wing of the XII in V. Raccolana & V. Dogna. It ceased at 0530 to restart in a destructive pattern from 0630 to 0800 on the IV and XXVII Corps positions. Advancing in the valley floor was a big gamble for the Austro-Germans as they could have been pounded by Italian artillery. Later in the day, Capello visited Cadorna who noting he looked pale and sick took his pulse which was 130 or almost twice the normal. He was persuaded by a medical officer to be hospitalized. The II Army commander had a history of chronic renal disease and had been intermittently hospitalized in the past. His replacement was Montuori. Telegrams now went out at 1800 to all commands notifying them of the change confusing the the II Army command structure.

In the past when Capello was sick he was still giving orders from his bed at II Army headquarters. Montuori was *Commandante Interinale,* or provisional commander. Officers arriving to discuss business would go to see Capello, noted he was ill, and would not discuss II Army business with anyone else causing defense details to be overlooked. A major one was the lack of deployment of the XXVII Corps on the right side of the Isonzo. Toward evening Capello left Udine and proceeded to Cividale, on his way to the hospital at Padua. Arriving at Cividale where stragglers were already arriving, he was informed of the loss of Caporetto, Saga Strait, as well as lack of news from the Nineteenth Infantry Division. Leaving it he proceeded to Monte Maggiore which was the hinge of the linkup with the Zona Carnia Command (Maps 19, 22). The *VII Gruppo Alpini* passing through Cividale was to proceed to Nimis and place itself at the disposal of the XXX Corps, which was to block all valley entrances with the *Ferrara, Avellino, Messina* and *Ionio.* The XXIV and II Corps were to withdraw to new defensive lines.

Isonzo Valley with roadways on both sides.

The Isonzo Valley between Tolmino and Caporetto.
To the left is the Stol, on the right is M. Plezia, to the rear is the Polovnik and further to the rear is M. Canin.

German truck convoy east of Tolmino approaching the Caporetto Front, Oct. 1917

Photo of fog on mountains in the Isonzo River Valley taken on October 24, 1999 by Prof. Zelko Cimpric of the *Kobariski Musej* per request of the author.

Troops of the 58th Infantry Division (*Armée Isonzo*) marching through Gorizia on October 29, 1917.
Courtesy Kriegsarchiv, Vienna

6

View of the Jeza and Ciginj on the Isonzo Front
Courtesy Kriegsarchiv Vienna

7

Lt. Gen. Otto von Below commander of the
German XIV Army at Caporetto

Lt. Gen. Eric Ludendorff,
German Army First Quartermaster or
German Army Vice Chief of the General Staff

Lt. Gen. Krafft von Dellmensingen,
architect of the Caporetto breakthrough

GdI Alfred Krauss, commander of the Austro-Hungarian I Corps at Caporetto

Gen. Armando Diaz, Italian Army Chief of the General Staff after Nov. 9, 1917 *Courtesy USSME*

Gen. Andrea Graziani, commander of the Italian 45th Div. on the Pasubio and Inspector General during the Caporetto debacle.

Lt. Gen. Pietro Badoglio After committing many errors at Caporetto was appointed Vice Chief of the Italian Army General Staff after Nov. 9, 1917

Lt. Gen. Gaetano Giardino Italian War Minister and commander of the *Armata del Grappa*

Lt. Gen. Enrico Caviglia, commander of XXIV Corps at Caporetto and VIII Army at Vittorio Veneto

Emperor Charles I of Habsburg, *Courtesy Kreigsarchiv*

Lt. Gen. the Earl of Cavan, commander of the British XIV Corps and Anglo-Italian X Army on the Italian Front

Archduke Josef of Habsburg, commander of Austro-Hungarian Sixth Army on the Montello.

Krauss Group[16]

The I Corps commander was the only Habsburg officer the Germans allowed to command such an important group. Krauss would become the premier Habsburg tactician on the Italian Front always writing of the invincibility of German (German-speaking people's) arms. With classic mixups some of his men had received summer uniforms while he had not received adequate munitions or gasoline deficiencies which were soon corrected. So respected was he that when Germany invaded Austria in 1938, Krauss was made a General of Infantry in the German Army. Constantly looking at his maps he pondered for a long time the tactics to be used in the assault. He noted that the Plezzo basin was formed by the junction of the Isonzo River and Coritenza Creek and surrounded by high mountains (Map 14). Assaulting those slopes would be time-consuming and cost many casualties giving the enemy time to reorganize his forces. Therefore he decided to attack through the bottom of the basin with a massive force crashing through three enemy defensive lines proceeding southwest and arrive at the Stol (Map 17). The Rombon the highest mountain in the sector would also be neutralized. North of the Isonzo infantry would be used only in mopping up operations. He discussed his plan with Below who commented, "I understand, you intend to overcome the Italians and not give them time to halt and reorganize." Krauss would not guarantee the northern wing of the XIV Army's assault in the classic sense of occupying the mountain passes. He would attempt to crash through and create a breach between Italian troops in the Carnia region to the north (known as the Zona Carnia Command) and the Italian II Army (Map 40). A linkup with the Austro-Hungarian Tenth Army would occur in the Fella Valley near Gemona (Map 35). The I Corps combat sector borders were delineated as Passo-Predil-Rombon-Fella Valley to Gemona on the right while M. Nero (excluded) Ladra, Caporetto and Kred on the left (Maps 14,35). Looking at I Corps maps Below noted many black dots on the slopes of the Rombon. Asking what they were he received the reply that they represented the eighty Italian artillery positions within caves which dominated the basin. Each cave would be shelled by a single gun. Testing had shown that two out of ten shells would precisely hit the target thus neutralizing all enemy artillery. In other sectors as will be noted specially equipped German mountain troops would climb the slopes and capture the enemy guns. The XIV Army commander approved and allowed Krauss to proceed on his own without any interference. Prior to the assault, he issued the following bulletin to his men : "Soldiers of the I Corps. For the second time in this war, we go on the offensive against Italy. Your motto shall be 'No rest, no stopping until the Italians are cut into pieces.' God be with us. Forward!" His was the most difficult task in the whole attack. Extra pack trains and over one thousand laborers were assigned to get supplies over road-less mountains and to move the heavy caliber artillery toward the attack sector. Liaison to this unit from the XIV Austro-German

Army was Capt. Hans Gunther von Kluge, future Second World War Field Marshall who committed suicide after the July, 1944 attempt on Hitler. Krauss ordered his men to move forward ever forward and not halt for orders. This was a new military doctrine in the Austro-Hungarian Army. The best description of the action in this sector is by Col. Hermanny-Miksch, commander of a battalion in the I Kaiserschützen.[17] For weeks his assault troops had been practicing their assault. To the right was the Third Division also known as the *Edelweiss* Division made up of the Mountain 14° and 59°. On May 2, 1915, it had been officially named *Edelweiss* (Star of the Alps). The 14° troops were men from Linz in Upper Austria, while the 59° were men from the Salzburg area, all knowledgeable in mountain climbing and fighting. Included with these units was the infamous 28° (Prague) which had gone over to the Russians in 1915 (see Vol. I, chapter XII, The Second Battle) but here would attack the *Gruppo Alpini Rombon*. Krauss was worried about occupying M. Ursig and obtained the services of Lt. Mlaker (a noted mining expert), from the Tyrol Army Group. Sappers under this officer's command had detonated a large bomb under under M. Cimone in 1916. In the center the fez-wearing Twenty-Second Schützen (Vol. I, chapter XXXIII) along with a German chemical warfare unit attacked the two depleted regiments of the *Friuli*.[18] To the left between Krasij and the Vrata, proceeding toward M. Nero, were the Fifty-fifth and Twenty-sixth Divisions, 38 *Gebirgs* who overran the *Genova* (Map 14). Krafft felt that gas was necessary to hit the Italian artillery positions nestled in caves on the slopes which would be nigh impossible to attack due to their location. He counted on the morale problem inflicted because the Italians had had little training in gas warfare. Krauss as noted had his own methods of neutralizing the guns. From the first, Austro-German shelling hit warehouses, troop concentrations, command centers, and all communication centers to create disturbances in the Italian rear. At 0200, the XXXV German Gas Warfare Battalion electrically ignited 900 phosgene bombs and launched them from Ravelnik, one half mile east of Plezzo (Map 15). Fired were shells containing diphenylchlorarsine and diphenylcyanarsine sternutators and irritants to the eyes and respiratory lining also inducing vomiting. These gases was called *Blaukreuz* (Blue Cross) due to the markings on the shells. Also fired were phosgene shells marked with a green cross (*Grünkreuz*) which was a vesicant penetrating the skin and attacking the eyes and respiratory linings. It was a tremendous lung irritant incapacitating or killing in doses as small as 200 parts per ten million. There was no defense against it except a total body uniform. Another type of shell contained dichlorethylsulfide known as mustard gas (Yellow Cross) produced burning and blisters on exposed body surfaces blinding the troops and remaining in the area for a long time holding off any troop advance. The rationale for gas was multipurpose.[19] First, the artillery men in the mountains would have to wear gas masks which would make their task more difficult. Blue Cross shells caused persistent coughing and sneezing making it impossible to keep a gas mask on. Secondly, it was aimed to kill the crews before they could wreck havoc on advancing infantry. Death rode the wind. The poisonous cloud sailed slowly to the southeast pulled by the currents over the Isonzo, then westward in direction of Cezsoca (Map 16). Present at the launching and inventor of this horrible weapon was Capt. Fritz Haber, a German chemist with I.G. Farben who had synthesized ammonia for the first time and would eventually go on to synthesize other lethal chemicals. The destructive shelling of the attackers was a disaster for the Italian defenders. Heavy fog produced two results. First it enveloped the Austro-Germans advancing along valley floors unseen by Italian garrisons on the mountain summits who could have called in artillery support. Secondly it prohibited aerial reconnaissance. Cadorna is quoted in the OBARI as stating that subjected to the gas attack troops of the IV Corps panicked. Using inadequate equipment subjected to a burning throat, lungs and eyes, who would not panic? This demonstrates how far removed he was from the actual situation on the battle front.

The Rombon sector had about four feet of snow and plenty of ice on the valley floor. It was defended by the *Alpini* Dronero,

Saluzzo, and Borgo S. Dalmazzo Battalions, which had been in the trenches for ten months. Collectively they were called the *Gruppo Alpini Rombon.* Assaulting it was the Austro-Hungarian Rombon Group with its *Edelweiss* Division whose objective as the right wing of the assault was to proceed along Val Uccea to Gemona, then Passo Tanamea (Maps 28,23,35). Many of these troops came from the Altipiano of Folgaria in the Trentino. There were also troops who spoke the Salzburg dialect of upper Austria (59°). Four times the Cuklja was assaulted and four times defenders repulsed the attackers. A company of elite *Hochgebirgskompagnie* attempted to assault the rear of the Rombon but was forced to withdraw due to a severe snow storm. Even the attack by the LIX Mountain Brigade (X Army) in the Rio del Lago Valley ended in failure. Finally the *Edelweiss* took the hamlet of Pluzna thus effectively blocking the mule path that supplied the Rombon's 5,000 defenders (Map 14). Cut off from supplies, Col. Alfredo Cantoni the *Gruppo's* commander ordered a circuitous retreat toward Sella Prevala to the west arriving with only about 500 men including sick and wounded in Val Raccolana in the rear echelons of the XII Corps.[20] This would be only a temporary reprieve as shall soon be noted. Periodically the glacier of the area gives up a preserved body with full documents.[21] The withdrawal was in freezing rain, thousands of feet above sea level. Stopping for a wound or tiredness was a death sentence. The lucky Italians were taken prisoners with only about sixty men per battalion returning home after the war when no one was aware of their ordeal. Apparently in the chaos of the retreat the loss of a few battalions did not matter. The Twenty-second Schützen encountered little resistance due to the effect of gas on the *Friuli* deployed in Cezsoca. Passing these positions the next day, troops of the Kaiserschützen noted the great silence in the whole sector. There were cadavers throughout. The officer mess had cadavers at the table, and cookies ready to be served.[22] The men still had their rifles between their knees with uniforms and armaments intact. No gas alarm had been given.[23]

German infantry soldier. The spike on his helmet was abandoned in 1916

Two captured Italian officers taken at Caporetto with the confused look of despair classic of blitzkrieg victims.
Courtesy Wolf-Albrecht Kainz

21

One of the tunnels recovered from an escarpment of the roadway Plezzo-Cezsoca. This became the tomb of hundreds of Italian soldiers of the *Friuli* on Oct. 24, 1917. The village of Plezzo (now Bovec) has restored the tunnel.

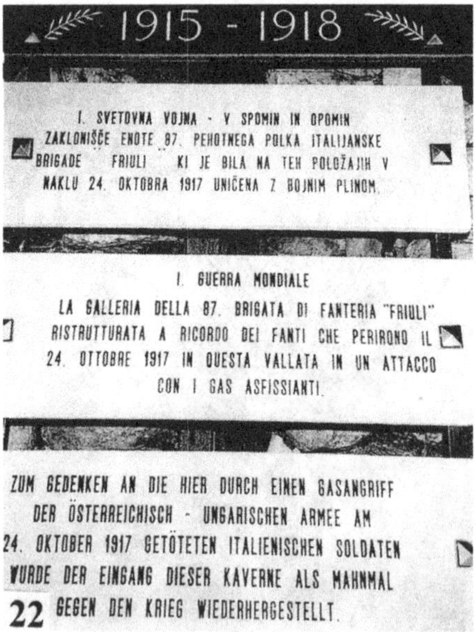

22

A multi language tablet within the tunnel.
The German language inscription erroneously blames the Austro-Hungarians for the gas attack instead of the Germans

German Sturmtroopers on the attack on the Western Front.
Units like these trained for the Battle of Caporetto.
Around their neck were bags full of grenades,
carbines with some men carrying sub-machine guns.

A photo of Caporetto taken a few minutes before the
arrival of the German Twelfth Silesian Division.
Everyone here was taken prisoner.

Fearing encirclement Italian III Army troops withdrawing due to the collapse of the Italian II Army.

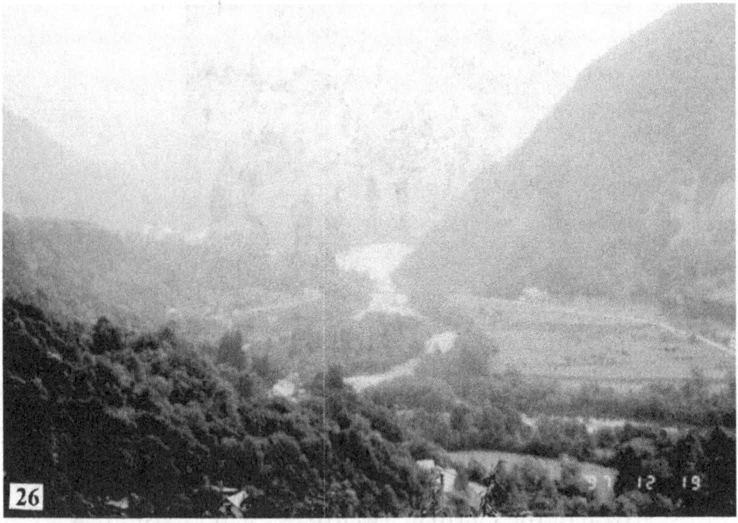

Photo of the Saga Strait taken by the author

M. Rosso after the Austro-Hungarians exploded a bomb under it on Oct. 24, 1917

Italian generals thought that gas would be ineffective in the mountains, with the winds carrying it down to the valley floor. Badoglio and Cavaciocchi had been heard to state this when it was brought up at staff meetings.[24] Meanwhile as if nothing had happened, the Italian Fiftieth Infantry Division, signaled the IV Corps that the effects of the gas had been minimal and that the masks worked very well. Instead the forward observation post at Maritza reported that after firing red flares, the Austrians were coming out of their trenches and advancing toward the Italian lines. At 0940, it signaled again that the enemy had broken through, and was advancing along the valley floor from Plezzo.[25] A counterattack was ordered, but who was supposed to do this? Krafft later wrote, "The troops in the trenches and artillery crews had fled their posts confronted with the lethal effects of the gas."

Today the village of Plezzo (now Bovec), has groups that climb the overlooking Rombon (over 7,000 feet) which still casts a shadow on the town. There is also a private museum, *Zbirka iz I. Svetovne Vojne* "87.Polk"(First World War Collection of "87 Regiment").

The Twenty-second Schützen which had its path cleared by the gas attack on the *Friuli* marched quickly toward the Saga Strait. Its objective was to occupy the Stol as quickly as possible. Toward evening, it attacked and occupied Podcela near the overflowing Boka River (Map 15). Bivouacking near a waterfall, it awaited the dawn. On the morrow, the bridge across the river which was supposed to have been destroyed, was noted to be passable. Some units of the *Edelweiss* and Twenty-second Schützen were sent to take Planina Goricjca assaulting the rear of the Cuklja. The left wing of the Twenty-second met serious resistance trying to climb the Slatnica Valley toward Jama Planina and the crest of Prihovec-Veliki Vrh in order to run over onto the opposite side into the Isonzo Valley (Map 15). By 1000, the "camel's hump," had been occupied by Major Buol's III/26° Schützen. By 1300 they had pierced the second Italian defensive line.

Due to ice and snow, the Fifty-fifth Imperial Division (Maj. Gen. Prince Schwarzenberg), did not attack in the M. Nero sector until 0930. It was to occupy Italian lines east of the Polovnik as the Sella Za Kraju and M. Vrsic from which it would descend onto the Dreznica Basin, behind the crest Vrata-M. Nero (Map 14). From Dreznica the road to Caporetto would be open. Linkups would be at Borjana with the Schützen and with the III (Bavarian) Corps at the Matajur (Maps 17,23). Troops entrusted with these tasks had a hard time due to Italian resistance and heavy snows. Its right wing (XXVI Mountain Brigade) proceeding from Javorscek and Lipnik proceeded along the northern slopes of Krasji Vrh, reached Jana Planina and then the northern slopes of the Polovnik (Map 14). At 10:30, the Italian Forty-third Infantry Division telephoned corps headquarters that the situation was serious due to the threat on Krasji Vrh. It had been feverishly working to bolster its defensives.[26] To salvage the situation it requested and received the two battalions of 9° Bersaglieri in reserve at Dreznica. By the end of the day, the Krauss Group had experienced great success. Krauss reported in his excellent text that he had taken fifty four officers and 2,518 men of the 87°, 88°, 97° 224° and some from the 280°.[27] An eyewitness account was given in a newspaper in 1961.[28] "We were fighting in the sector known as the lower Ursig (*M. Vrisic to the Slovenians)*, to the left of M. Nero, and the summit known as Camperi. These positions were garrisoned by the *Genova* (97° and 98°). The defenses were beautifully located, so that we almost could defend them using only rocks. We saw no enemy approaching in front of us. All of a sudden the enemy was in our rear and there was only one choice, raise our arms and surrender. Our artillery had fired very few salvos."

As Col. Brig. Boccacci, Chief of Staff of the IV Corps listened to the telephoned reports, he thought that he was listening to men who were hallucinating. He was receiving reports that the enemy was at Dreznica, then at Caporetto. Only when an ambulance arrived from there with bullet holes in its sides, did he believe it. Bands of stragglers started to roam the countryside some of whom would eventually become prisoners of war.

German aviation furnished great help for these well-organized thrusts. There were six fighter squadrons, one reconnaissance squadron plus a tremendous amount of anti-aircraft guns. The whole objective was to at least halt any Italian air reconnaissance or photography of the sector between Plezzo and Canale (Maps 12, 17).

The Italian defenses along the Isonzo River shall now be examined. They are best summarized as "organized confusion." On the left bank to protect Gabrje were two companies of the 156° (*Alessandria*) (Map 21). There was nothing more for three miles when we found the III/155° deployed on the slopes. Twelve hundred feet to the rear was the III/156° while the II/147° was one half mile to the rear and I/156° was at S. Lorenzo. On the right bank there was a big surprise. Two companies of the *Taro*

(208°), were on an observation line at Volzana, a platoon of the II/147° at Osteria, and *then nothing until Caporetto.* To compensate for this there were sixty medium and heavy caliber guns on the northern slopes of the Kolovrat aiming at Slieme, Mrzli, Caporetto, Monte Nero and Monte Rosso. However, *since the guns could not be depressed* they guns could not fire on the roadways along the Isonzo. A machine gun company (Forty-sixth Infantry Division), had been deployed along the southern bank of the Isonzo to give flanking fire to the two companies of the 156° but it had been ordered elsewhere. The Caporetto Inquiry Commission never found out who gave the order to redeploy it. The *Napoli* (XXVII Corps), which was to have garrisoned the sector, Plezia-Foni-Isonzo, had been withdrawn, with one battalion sent to M. Plezia, and one company from Foni to the Isonzo but not touching the river.[29] Its deployment was high up on a mountain slope facing the river, but not extending to the river. Thus when the Twelfth Silesian walked along the banks of the Isonzo River, there was no one there to stop them. The reserves of the VII and XXVII Corps were not deployed in depth but were on the Kolovrat looking down onto the "Volzana trap sector." This was an erroneous Italian military doctrine which held that invading Austro-Hungarian infantry should be allowed to enter the Isonzo Valley via Volzana (Maps 16-18). Proceeding up the valley, they would be destroyed by Italian guns nestled high up in the mountains on both sides. As noted above, this was impossible due to the fact that the guns could not be depressed to fire into the valley below. The 281° and 282° were proceeding through the rain and fog along the river toward Caporetto. As dawn approached they were on the left bank north of the iron bridge (Map 21). Later the C.O. Col. Brig. Francesco Pisani received new orders. The 282° would proceed to Saga to seal the breach opening up in the Fiftieth Infantry Division sector, while the 281° would remain where it was. As the 282° was crossing the river and climbing the opposite bank, new orders arrived. Arrighi felt that he could handle the breach without further troops. The 282° received another order that it was to cross the river to the left bank and proceed post-haste to place itself at the disposal of the Forty-sixth Infantry Division which intended to counterattack. If this was not possible it was to deploy at Ladra sending a battalion across the river, but remain always in contact with the 281°. Again the ping-pong ball situation.

So what had happened to the reserves of the IV Corps? The *Foggia,* the 2°, 9° Bersaglieri, the *Alpini* battalions were all employed elsewhere, while the *Potenza* and *Massa Carrara* as well as the VII *Gruppo Alpini* were all far away. The IV Corps felt secure in its deployment as it was behind two defense lines, the Nineteenth Infantry Division, plus the *Napoli* (so it thought), with the VII Army Corps up in the hills like a wildcat ready to pounce down into the valley. Chaos reigned along the river valley. Reinforcements could not proceed on the road from M. Nero to Dreznica as trucks and cars were trying to climb as others were descending. By 1300 the head of the 282° column was at Ladra, while the tail had not yet passed the bridge (Map 16). Suddenly as refugees approached from the south, the words "The Germans are at Idersko" were heard causing panic and confusion among the troops.

The Stein Group

At 0630, its artillery and mine launchers started to furiously shell the Italian lines. There was no Italian artillery response, which Krafft described as Italian paralysis. Its principal objective was the Matajur a 5,000 ft. mountain. As was noted in the orders of October 10, Cadorna had specifically and clearly ordered a *contropreparazione* shelling, which was diluted to an artillery barrage, by the time it got down to the subordinate commanders. As noted, deserters had made known to the Italians, that there would be two shelling periods, from 0200 to-0600 and from 0630-0800. During the first shelling period, the Austro-Germans were not disturbed by Italian shelling which only went into action during the second period, by which time the assembled Austro-German infantry had left its positions and was advancing, assisted by fog, rain, and darkness. *The defending Italians shelled empty enemy positions.* As noted in the OIR, one must pay attention to Badoglio's Order No. 3267 of October 22, 1917 to his troops, which really shattered Cadorna's orders of October 10.

The K.u.k. Fiftieth Infantry Division's right wing had the most difficult task which was to proceed toward Caporetto along a line between Dolje and M. Nero (Maps 16, 18). It slowly descended through the snow from M. Rosso to Vodil on the left bank of the Isonzo and proceeded toward Caporetto. A mine planted weeks before under M. Rosso weeks before, was now detonated, burying hundreds of Italian soldiers. Comforting to the defenders was the presence of the two Bersaglieri regiments at Dreznica. Multiple attempts made to take M. Nero from the Italians, met with failure, but by bypassing it, the Austro-Hungarians rendered it tactically insignificant. During the night its defenders could see flames all about them, at Caporetto, Staroselo, and along the Isonzo (Map 16). Seeing this the *fanti* started to think "If the enemy is behind us what are we doing here?" Next day cut off from supplies, troops on M. Nero surrendered.

The III Mountain Brigade (Col. Tlaskal) of the Fiftieth Inf. Division's right wing proceeded toward Planina Leskovica where it ran into the *Etna* which put up a fierce resistance. Col. Brig. Odoardo Famea its commander did not know that the Forty-third Infantry Division's commander had been captured as shall soon be noted. With no clear cut orders, he kept fighting, did not retreat, was cut off and captured. Soon most troops of the Italian Forty-third and Forty-sixth Infantry Divisions were in the same predicament. By 1100, the III Mountain Brigade's left wing was able to descend onto the village of Krn, and then proceed to the Italian second line of defense, deployed from M. Kozljak (5000 feet) to the valley floor, south of Vrsno Map 14).

During the previous year these men had constructed the Church of the Holy Ghost east of the Mrzli at Javorca, 3,500 feet above sea level. To arrive there one needs a fearless driver with steel nerves proceeding along one-lane mountain roads with no guard rail and deep ravines arriving via an unpaved road to a cattle pasture where there are few visitors. The base is made of stone, topped by dark wood onto which are painted the coats of arms of the provinces of the empire. Inside is the "Book of the Dead," with the name of every soldier who fell fighting for the Mrzli ridge. Most of the men of the III Mountain Brigade (mostly Poles) killed in action are buried in a cemetery east of Tolmino at Loèe which contains about 7,000 dead. Some graves have family-purchased headstones which happened after the fall of communism in Eastern Bloc countries.

The XV Mountain Brigade (Fiftieth Infantry Division) broke through the Italian positions between Slieme and Mrzli despite the energetic resistance of the *Caltanisetta*. To its left was the II/ 18° which rapidly proceeded toward Gabrje and made possible the advance of the right column of the Twelfth Silesian Division by attacking the left flank and rear of some units of the *Alessandria* deployed there opposing German units attempting to advance westward. Descending from the Vodil Habsburg mountain troops reached the village of Gabrje along the roadway on the left bank of the Isonzo arriving to the rear of other *Alessandria* units at Dolje which were opposing the right column of the Twelfth Silesian advancing from Tolmino (See German 63° this chapter). Completely surrounded the Italians surrendered. An easily available excellent eyewitness account of this event describes many *fanti* declaring that the war was over. So disheartened were the troops that they needed no guards as they marched toward the rear of the Austro-German lines.[30]

Commanding the II/147° (*Caltanisetta)*, was Col. Maurizio Piscicelli. From M. Nero all morning he had been looking down into the valley from his mountain position, noting it was very quiet. Through the fog, he noted what he thought were prisoners of war, captured by the Nineteenth Division marching in columns of four to the Italian rear. About noon as the fog lifted, Piscicelli got a good look at the columns marching just before Kamno (Map 16). Noting the capes of the officers he realized that they were German. These men were the 63° of the Twelfth Silesian Division enveloped and protected by the fog. Piscicelli emplaced his machine guns and opened fire. The columns melted and advanced toward him. He was asked to surrender but refused. He died at his machine gun. Posthumously, he was awarded the *Medaglia d'Oro al Valore Militare.* At the award ceremony, the quotation read:

> "Col. Maurizio Piscicelli, of the Aosta Lancers:
>
> Having assumed the command of an infantry battalion, in the tragic hours of a desperate resistance he was attacked by superior enemy forces. Surrounded and asked to surrender, he intensified his fire. Mortally wounded he fell on one machine gun exclaiming *Viva l'Italia.*"

After overcoming the II/147° the Silesian 63° attacked the headquarters of the 147° capturing the wounded commander Col. Orazio Raimondo. Most of his men were taken prisoner.

1100

Knowing that the enemy would attack from Tolmino, Badoglio nonetheless ordered the Nineteenth Infantry Division to leave the right bank of the Isonzo unprotected. As previously noted, the plan was to shell the advancing infantry with the guns nested in the mountains on both sides and then counterattack with this division. Ever obedient to the orders, the artillery crews awaited for the order to fire that never came. First, this was because of Badoglio's order; later it was because of the destruction of communication equipment due to enemy shelling. Using ten foot metal ladders which they nailed to the mountain walls as they climbed, German mountain troops went up the mountainsides up to 300 feet with the hammering noise being drowned out by gunfire. By now Koschak's XV Brigade was near Caporetto, while the Tlaskal (III Brigade), Detachment proceeded beyond Caporetto where it was to link up with the Fifty-fifth Division (Map 18). The Fiftieth Infantry Division had already taken 7,000 prisoners and 90 cannons. Men of its Koschak Detachment proceeded along the valley floor toward Selisce and north to Vrsno (Map 16). It was only a matter of time before the Italian troops in the mountains would become prisoners.

The Twelfth Silesian Infantry Division was compressed like canned sardines in the Tolmino bridgehead behind the Alpenkorps (Map 21). German troops were literally shoulder to shoulder in the bridgehead. An Italian-speaking soldier enrolled in the Austro-Hungarian Army told the captured Lt. Guido Sironi of the *Arno* that should the Italians have shelled that sector, there would have been a massacre.

The Germans would mix troops of two different units to perform special tasks, therefore in reports one unit would seem to be in two different places simultaneously. Units of a battalion would be reported as completing the special task as well as the original task assigned to most of the battalion in a far away location. Due to the overflowing and rapidly flowing Isonzo, the 63° and the I/23° were unable to cross and were held at Dolje and Pan di Zucchero (Map 16). The II and III/23° were sent to use a gangway south of Tolmino as they followed the Alpenkorps along the right bank. The 62° arrived late due to a traffic jam. At exactly 0800, units of the 63° attacked and broke through on the left bank of the Isonzo (Map 18). At 0930 white rockets (unable to be seen due to the fog) signaled that they were halfway between Gabrje and Volarje. Fearing friendly fire casualties, the infantry halted until the artillery was notified. Simultaneously the I/23° broke through at S. Daniele and advanced on the right protected on its left flank (Map 18) by units of the Bavarian *Leibregiment* (Body Guards). Speed in the advance was of the essence. By 1100 troops at Selisce advancing three miles in as many hours gained visual contact across the river with troops at Foni. The second line of defense was from Foni to Selisce which was pierced by the I/63° and the II and III/23°. Supposedly deployed at Foni was the *Napoli* (Map 16). As the the 63° and I/23° proceeded along the left bank, the I/23° crossed the Volarje gangway to join the other two battalions of the 23° on the right side and proceed toward Caporetto, where the *Foggia* was supposed to be deployed.

The Italian confusion continued. Of the *Foggia's* two regiments one had been sent to protect the Dreznica Basin, the other to the Saga Strait, and later to Selisce. There were no forces to defend Caporetto. By 1300 units of the German II/23° had reached Idersko. The *Foggia* was destroyed piece meal while Pisani was taken prisoner. The 63° reached Kamno capturing many Italians who were coming down from the mountains. Units of the I/23° (Maj. Hermann Eicholz von Eischorn) took three hours to climb the steep northeastern slopes of the Kolovrat reaching the roadway Idersko-Luico at a point north of the hamlet of Golobi (Map 17). By 1530 at Luico they surprised and took many prisoners. Along the roadway they were reinforced by the II/62° and III/23°.

By 1400, the Germans were at Ladra controlling both sides of the river (Map 16). Visiting this sector in 1920, Capello noted that *chevaux de frise* intended to block the roadway were still along the sides of the road. Looking upward, he noted still intact trenches and barbed wire fences denoting that the troops had fled. Indicative of the confusion of the times when captured by mountain-climbing German infantry some guns were still firing even though having been strictly forbidden to do any shelling until so ordered. Krafft reported that the crews resisted some even with pistols but were quickly overcome.[31] At 1530 units of the 23° entered Caporetto from the east, taking two thousand prisoners. As Krafft noted, "The splendid progress of the Twelfth Silesian was extraordinarily favored by the bad weather which hid it from the enemy until the Germans were in the center of enemy positions. Naturally, the aggressive spirit of the troops contributed a great deal."[32]

Today Caporetto (now Kobarid in the Republic of Slovenia) retains its eighteenth century charm overlooked on all sides by steep mountains. Eastward is M. Krn (over 7,000 feet), to the southwest is M. Matajur. Northward is the Charnel House on top of St. Anthony's Hill containing the remains of over 7,000 Italian dead who fell between the Rombon and Tolmino. Names of known dead are inscribed in green serpentine. Built by the Italians, it was dedicated in 1938 by Benito Mussolini. On top of the hill is the church of St. Anthony consecrated a long time ago in 1696. Since 1990 the town now boasts a museum which in 1993 received the European Community award for European Museum of the year. Prof Zelko Cimpric assists in running the museum and is very helpful in organizing displays of uniforms and weapons. If notified in advance he will also provide a guide service. In Tolmino which was never taken by the Italians there is a beautiful German ossuary built about twenty years after the end of the war. Buried here are the remains of German dead fighting in the Twelfth Battle. Often noted are German teenagers visiting to commemorate the long-ago death of a relative on duty for the Fatherland.

The Silesian advance divided Italian forces. On M. Nero were two divisions of the IV Corps, while on the Kolovrat was the VII Corps (Map 16). Meanwhile, thousands of Italian soldiers came down from the mountains ready to surrender. With Italian troop morale hitting rock-bottom, Krafft summarized it succinctly when he wrote, "Deprived of commanders, part happy, part troubled, the prisoners walked toward Tolmino, waving white handkerchiefs and crying *Eviva Germania* with the intention of finding safety as soon as possible." Boccacci later noted "It was a tranquil march of tranquil men. There was not a face which showed shame or desperation, nor an eye which was not serene. There was no sign of rowdiness, or revolution, actually even a sign of respect toward me as I passed by."[33] The mentality of the illiterate peasant infantry now took over. Cries of "The war is over," or "Long live Russia," were heard as the men gave up and started to walk home.[34] Not knowing what Italy was or stood for, the men were anxious to get home to help their families with the harvest. Since there was no social assistance in Italy at the time, if one did not produce, one did not eat. The troops wanted to provide help to their families in any which way they could. Socialist propaganda had indoctrinated them, telling them since the war was now over, it was time to stop fighting and go home to help with the harvest. Caviglia noted deserters from the XXVII Corps moving along the right side of the Isonzo walking homeward.[35]

In the darkness, the II/23° and 63° (which had arrived from the left bank), met stiff resistance at Staroselo. At 2230, they occupied Robic (the old border town), at the entrance of the middle V. Natisone, and the village of Kred, former headquarters of the Italian IV Corps which had withdrawn (Maps 14,15). Weather had been a factor in the attack, but one must admire the skill, imagination and daring of the German troops. Maj. Gen. Lequis was immediately awaited the *Pour le Mérite* by the Kaiser. Often not noticed in the glory of the victory was the fact that in the War Diary of the Twelfth Silesian he not only noted the victory, but also the fact that his men had seized three chickens declaring this to be the "height of human felicity." Austro-German troops had to live off the land. By the end of the day the Twelfth Silesians had taken 15,000 prisoners and 100 guns with the K.u.k. Fiftieth Infantry Division having taken 7,000 prisoners and 50 guns.[36]

AlpenKorps

Attached to this unit was the Württemberg Mountain Battalion (Major Theodor Sproesser) which really had the armaments of a regiment. It had crossed the Isonzo at S. Daniele and climbed the Hlevnik on the north east slope, going around it to arrive at Foni. Fighting in it and commanding two companies was Lt. Erwin Rommel of future fame and tragic end.[37] For several centuries the Prussian throne had been served by a hereditary caste, but now with the German Empire and all kings and dukes owing allegiance to the Kaiser the expanded army necessitated that men of the middle class enter the Officer Corps. Rommel, the son of a schoolmaster had tried to enlist in the more prestigious artillery or engineers but was turned down. In July, 1910 he joined the *Infanterie-Regiment Nr. 124.* The following March he was sent to the *Königliche Kriegsschule* in Danzig graduating in January 1912 after which he rejoined his regiment. With the advent of the war he fought at Verdun, the Argonne, Romania, where he was wounded and Macedonia. Foni was taken by nightfall. The booty consisted of many large caliber cannons. Krafft stated little about Foni. He simply stated that shortly after 1100 the I/63° near Selisce, and north of Foni joined up with the II and III/ 23° capturing many prisoners.[38]

Uniting with the Bavarian Guards, the Württembergers descended and took Hlevnik. The Guards had climbed the spur of Costa Raunza reaching Leisce by 1400, then Hlevnik and its western undefended slope (Map 16). The German troops kept climbing to reach the military road on the opposite side of the Kolovrat. Serving as the 12 company commander was Lt. Ferdinand Schörner who along with Rommel would earn the *Pour Le Mérite* during this battle.[39] As darkness approached, an opening in the barbed wire of the Podklabuc defenses was noted. By 1730, it was in German hands along with 400 prisoners. The Württembergers were ordered to the Podklabuc to meet an expected Italian counterattack. Krafft later wrote, "An almost impossible task was realized, so that by the first day, the most important stronghold, the cornerstone of the Kolovrat defenses, had fallen." Having occupied Volce, the 1° Jåger of the AlpenKorps climbed the spur of Costa Duole ending the Stein Group's operations on the first day of the battle. We shall now follow the events on the Italian side of the barbed wire, especially in rear positions.

Italian IV Corps

Lt. Giorgio Bini-Cima, commander of a company in the *Alpini* Val d'Adige Battalion heard the enemy shelling start at 0100. Soon after, it started to center on his position and later the odor of poison gas was noted. This produced heavy losses as reported in German newspapers.[40] . The dead were all piled up like a cord of wood. The *Alpini* Morbengo Battalion was attacked at 0800 and had to retreat together with the Monte Berico into the Val Doblar. At 1100, the Val d'Adige was ordered to redeploy onto M. Jeza and report to the commander of the Nineteenth Division. Reaching Villani, he was ordered to linkup with the *Taro* and *Spezia* and obtain munitions from them. Instead these units had already withdrawn or disappeared. Only three companies of his battalion had arrived on the Jeza. Deploying on *Albero Bello* he was assaulted by German forces. The battalion commander Major Michel with about fifty men succeeded in withdrawing to Clabuzzaro linking up with the Nineteenth Infantry Division. Bini-Cima was captured and sent to prison at Celle. In classic *blitzkrieg* fashion illustrating the "mailed fist attack," the Italian Forty-third and Nineteenth Infantry Divisions deployed from M. Nero to Doblar had been attacked by five enemy divisions.[41]

By 1300, Cavaciocchi had informed the II Army headquarters at Cividale that the enemy had broken through at Plezzo and had forced its way past the V.Slatnica to arrive near Sella Za Kraju. With the loss of Mrzli, Gabrje, and Selisce defenses, the line of Kamno-Vrsno-Plece-Kozljak was attacked (Maps 15,16). Meanwhile the garrison at Caporetto communicated that the Germans were at Idersko. The IV Corps would have to be described as the "forgotten corps," because it was always left out of conferences, and really was not up to good standards in performance or morale.[42] Boccacci ordered the Alessandria Cavalry to slow down the enemy advance as much as possible. He also requested the VII Corps to garrison the *linea d'armata* line between Luico and Idersko to attack the advancing Germans in the flank. Bongiovanni responded by stating that the mentioned sector was not his responsibility. Cavaciocchi now realized that he had not placed enough troops in the Saga Gorge as requested by Cadorna. Only an incomplete 280° was there. The 281° and the 282° were now assigned to the Fiftieth Infantry Division to assist in the garrisoning of the Saga Gorge.[43] Units of the 282° coming from Ladra crossed the wooden bridge to assist the cavalry but were mauled by the Silesians and had to withdraw to Staroselo. By 1300, Capello had already been informed that the Forty-sixth and Forty-third Divisions had been overcome. In a first on the Italian Front, motorized patrols were used to inform the Silesians of Italian deployments. At 1530 the Caporetto Iron Bridge connecting both river banks near Caporetto which was to be demolished only on personal orders of Cavaciocchi was blown per orders of a Capt. Platania causing the entrapment of thousands of Italian troops. The *Caltanisetta, Alessandria,* and troops deployed north of the river would now be taken prisoner. A particular prisoner was Lt. Gen. Angelo Farisoglio, commander of the Forty-third Infantry Division who was at Caporetto for a meeting. Instead, he was dispatched to the *Kriegsgefangenenlager* at Ellwangen. Faldella made a tragicomical comment of this event, noting that Farisoglio was not only the first Italian general captured, but the first one in his division to be taken prisoner.[44] With this information, the few defenders of Caporetto who were lucky to escape, withdrew to Potoki, east of Kred, leaving the Passo di Staroselo unprotected.

Entrusted with the defense of the road going west from Caporetto had been the Fiftieth Infantry Division. Late in the a.m. Cavaciocchi felt that he did not have enough forces for the task. He assigned it the 281° and 282° which were refused by Lt. Gen. Arrighi, its commander who felt he had enough troops.[45] The 281° was assigned to the Forty-third Infantry Division which was in trouble, while the 282 ° went to the Forty-sixth Infantry Division.[46] Again to be noted is that the Thirty-fourth Division was without troops. This oft-moving about of troops was later severely criticized by Allied troop comanders in Dec. 1917.[47] Simultaneously, Lt. Gen. Giulio Amadei (Forty-sixth Division), arrived at Kred, while the headquarters of the IV Corps was transferred to Breginj, i.e. in the basin which formed the beginning of V. Natisone. German troops arriving at Kred found the documents of Lt. Maxim (see Vol. I, p. 494) which had not even been looked at by the Italians. Also found was a list of Italian agents operating in

Habsburg territories which kept the execution squads of Duke Ulrich of the Württemberg very busy. German generals noted the lack of Italian counter-battery fire. Having entered Caporetto at 1530, the Silesians were now in a position to assist the Krauss Group assaulting the Saga and Stol.[48]

When moving about among his troops, to be easily recognized Arrighi always wore a white scarf. The *Gruppo Rombon* was holding, as were the *Alpini* Argentera and the 88° on the southern bank of the Isonzo. Nevertheless, he felt depressed at the slightest bad news. Older literature (Bencivenga), had severely criticized him for withdrawing from the Saga Gorge, but with the publication of the Official Italian Army Report (*Relazione Ufficiale)*, much of the confusion has been eliminated. Previous authors did not have the full facts available to them. Its publication had been stopped during the 1930s during the Fascist regime. No one wanted to openly criticize the military hierarchy which Mussolini courted to stay in power. At 1600 Montuori visited the IV Corps headquarters, issuing orders that the Fiftieth Infantry Division should withdraw from the Saga Gorge to the Val Uccea, thus denying the enemy the road to the west (Map 23). Orders were immediately sent out at 1600 but did not reach Fiftieth Infantry Division headquarters until after midnight.[49] However, Arrighi concerned that his troops would be attacked in the rear by enemy troops advancing westward from Caporetto sent a staff officer, Major Piazzoni via auto over the Stol to Breginj to discuss this with corps headquarters. There he discussed the situation with Boccacci who showed him Montuori's orders. Upon his return, he reported to Arrighi who gave the order to withdraw starting at 1800 resulting in troop withdrawals before receiving official orders. By the a.m. units were deployed in the Val Uccea. Later, interviewed by L. Albertini, Krafft was very critical of this, stating that a simple machine gun could have held up any advance for hours. Ordering the abandonment of the Saga Strait by 1800, put the men on the Rombon, the southern banks of the Isonzo, as well as most of the Italian Forty-third Infantry Division in grave danger. It led to the loss of the IV Corps which now had no means of escape as the bridges at Caporetto and Serpenizza had been blown. Arrighi was simply prematurely following orders which would arrive later. By the end of the day, the Forty-sixth Infantry Division had been destroyed by the K. u. k. Fiftieth Infantry Division which had attacked it from higher up on the slopes where it was deployed, as well as to its rear after entering Caporetto. The Italian Forty-third Division which had been ordered by Farisoglio to attack from the valley floor, was wiped out. The Italian Fiftieth and Nineteenth Infantry Divisions were in bad shape. *A fifteen mile breach had now developed in the northern wing of the II Army deployment.*

Italian VII Corps

Composed of the Third and Sixty-second Infantry Divisions, this corps would relate a long tale of woe.[50] The Sixty-second had been called from the Trentino arriving at Cividale on October 23. In the week preceding the enemy offensive it had been assigned to successive army corps. During the first day, the Sixty-second deployed and attempted to strengthen its defenses. By evening, the *Elba* was deployed west of the Jeza, the *Arno* on the southern slopes of the Kolovrat, the *Salerno* on the Matajur, the *Firenze* in reserve at Drenchia and the IV Bersaglieri at Luico (Map 17). During the day Bongiovanni received many panicky reports. He was told that the Germans had climbed the slopes of the Kolovrat, taken all the artillery at Golobi, bivouacking near the Bersaglieri. At 2230 Bongiovanni notified Cividale that he was getting ready for an offensive.

The War Diary of the VII Corps noted that King Vittorio Emanuele III was at the command center, and had telephoned Badoglio at his headquarters asking what was happening receiving the response that there had been heavy shelling which now had decreased. He had received no notice of any infantry attack nor was there now any enemy shelling. *The Austro-Germans were not shelling his positions for fear of hitting their own men who had already arrived at his positions. He did not know that his forward infantry positions were being invaded because his communications had been destroyed.* Years later, Caviglia noted in his book that the king told him that when he arrived at VII Corps headquarters, "All the officers were not only ignorant of the battle, but acted as if they were out of the war itself."[51]

Lt. Guido Sironi of the *Arno* (Third Infantry Division, VII Corps), was guiding his unit to the crest of the Kolovrat (Maps 16,17,18). Barbed wire which had been requisitioned months before had finally arrived on October 23. It simply had to be stretched out in front of the trenches or artillery positions. He wrote, "There was a dense darkness as one climbed but saw nothing. Climbing in the mud, one finally reached the roadway on the crest which goes from Passo Zagradan to Kuk and Luico *(Map 16).* We saw many 270 mm. and 149 mm. mortars all lined up on the crest, all surrounded by ammunition." Taking his unit to their cavern, Sironi went to check for stragglers. It was 0200. All of a sudden, there was a tremendous amount of enemy shelling of his positions. Soon there was a cry, *Maschera!* as the gas alarm was sounded. About 0600 hrs, there was a pause in the shelling, then it restarted, stopping at 0800. Communication lines had been destroyed. Italian artillery crews fearing hitting Italian infantry, did not fire. At 0700 the unit was ordered to attack the oncoming Austro-Germans. At 1500 hrs., realizing that the company was surrounded, the company commander surrendered.[52] The enemy officer asked him *Nicht Weiss Brot?.*[53] For Lt. Sironi, the long trip to the *Kriegsgefangenenlager* in Austria or Germany had started.

At noon, hundreds of artillery crews carrying obturators in their hands, arrived down from the mountains screaming "The Austrians! the Austrians!" They had been stationed on Bukovna Jeza (Maps 13, 16). Plans now called for the 213° (*Arno),* to race up and deploy on M. Piatto adjacent to it. Arriving at the summit they realized that the Germans were already there. However, no need to worry there was a plan for the *Firenze* to come to the rescue. There in the distance appeared the brigade to the rescue. However, as the proverb states, "When things go badly, they do get worse." Arriving at the Clabuzzaro fork in the road, the rescuing brigade took the road not to M. Piatto, lightly defended by the Germans, but against the Podklabuc which was already occupied by the enemy and had no Italian troops to lend a hand. Shelling puffs of black smoke from enemy artillery appeared on the slopes of the Podklabuc resulting in holes in the advancing Italian infantry formations which kept advancing until the machine guns opened up.

As soon as the II Army command found out that Selisce had been occupied by the enemy, it ordered the two divisions of the VII Corps (Third and Sixty-second Infantry Divisions plus artillery), to assume the previously mentioned deployment at noon.[54] Bongiovanni moved his headquarters to Prapotnizza (Map 18). The Sixty-second Infantry Division was ordered to linkup with the IV Corps (which never happened) and to stand fast at Sella di Luico. At 1900, he ordered the division to attack the Silesians in their left flank as they proceeded up the Isonzo, not knowing that the enemy had reached Caporetto by 1530 (Order No. 11176). This order was impossible to convey via phone as the operators at Luico had disabled the phones and fled. Bongiovanni next notified headquarters that on the morrow, he would counterattack toward Hlevnik and Jeza requesting more troops. He also stated that the Passo Zagradan was in his hands, with a large reserve available. Again poor communications were involved as he did not know that both the Passo Zagradan and the Podklabuc were in enemy hands.

On the opposite end of Lt. Sironi's unit's (213°) deployment was Felice Troiani who held the rank of *Ufficiale Aspirante*.[55] Eleven years later he was in the polar expedition of Umberto Nobile and fell with the dirigible *Italia* north of the Spitsbergen Islands. He had one month's experience at the front, and was the commander of an infantry company deployed on M. Kuk overlooking the Isonzo. Suddenly, his company was under fire by by small caliber artillery, and machine gun fire. Under a white flag, an enemy officer approached and announced *Nichts zu machen, alles kaputt. Wir haben schon Cividale besetz.*[56] He later wrote of his experiences declaring that his soldiers happily left the trench ready to be prisoners. Not being able to resist alone, he surrendered his pistol. He had been in the war for twenty two days and had not fired a shot. His men attempted to talk to their German captors, who gave them the cold shoulder.[57] Assigned to defend the Saga Gorge was the Thirty-fourth Infantry Division which was a division in name only. On October 24, 1917, it had been assigned to the IV Corps. Men and officers did not know each other. The regiments had been severely mauled on S. Gabriele and had been recuperating. Marching toward Caporetto, they had stopped at Suzit, then proceeded to destination arriving at 0400 on October 24. Bongiovanni sent another telegram to headquarters stating that the Twenty-second and Sixty-second Infantry Divisions were counterattacking at Golobi and had taken the eleven artillery pieces of 105 mm. which they had lost that afternoon, while from the Matajur, the *Salerno* would assist the action. Actually, the Sixty-second Infantry Division communicated that the IV Bersaglieri Brigade would assault Golobi, move along the spurs, but not descend into the valley.[58] The Bersaglieri had been sent via train from the Trentino to arrive at Cividale on the day prior to the enemy offensive then deployed the next day.[59]

An example of the mentality that pervaded the military hierarchy may be noted in the tale of the *Ionio.* At 23.30 it was ordered to garrison a certain area five miles away by 0130. In complete darkness troops would have to walk up and down road-less mountains to reach their objective. Instead of going with his troops to the new sector (Torreano two miles from Cividale as the crow flies), its commander Lt. Gen. Vittorio Magliano, proceeded to headquarters to explain why he would be late getting to his new position (Map 13). Fearing dismissal, he was anxious to explain that his troops had been informed late, and thus would arrive late.[60] Midnight found the *Napoli, Arno,* and *Firenze* on the crest of the Kolovrat, with the *Napoli* at Passo Zagradan, all threatened by the loss of the Podklabuc. To the south, the *Elba* failed in attempting to link up with the

XXVII Corps while the *Salerno* occupied the Matajur (Map 17). These moves were important as the advances of the Berrer Group are discussed.

Austro-German Berrer Group (Hofacker)

The Two Hundredth Infantry Division was deployed, with its 4° Jäger on the right, the 3° Jäger on the left and the 5° Jäger as a reserve. Each had four battalions. The Twenty-sixth Division was in the Tolmino bridgehead, somewhat in the rear due to heavy traffic. At 0745, the vanguard troops started to cross the depression in front of Cighinj (Map 19). Up to this point, the Italians did not know of imminent attacks in this sector. Without casualties, the Twenty-sixth reached Ciginj (Map 19). After a brief battle the 4° Jäger climbed the eastern slopes of the Jeza-Varda Vrh-Krad Vrh system reaching aroad (at 2500 ft.) and proceeded to Cappella Slieme. From Ciginj the 3° Jäger arrived at Jeseniak, then climbed to the summit of Hill 631 from which they could see Italians, military and civilians, fleeing. Not knowing that the summit was in friendly hands, Austro-German artillery kept shelling it, so the regiment had to withdraw. Later it was occupied by the I/3° Jäger. By 1115, units of the II/3° Jäger had occupied the "False Jeza.," (2800 feet) which is 1500 feet to the east of the real Jeza. After a failed counterattack, fearing a gas attack, the Italian commander surrendered. Soon after, the Jeza was taken by units of the IV/3°and II/3° Jäger. After the Jeza, the German units divided, aiming for the Globocak and the Kolovrat, while the Italians had no available reserves to stop them.

Italian XXVII Corps

By 1100 advancing Austro-German troops had rendered the Volzana trap plan useless. Badoglio had ordered Villani (Nineteenth Infantry Division on the Jeza), to leave about one mile of his front unguarded, hoping to entice enemy infantry into the trap so Italian guns positioned in the hills would fire on them while Villani counterattacked. Known as the hinge of Italian defenses the Jeza was a prime target of the attackers. Maximum numbers of guns were trained on it and the Kolovrat to stop any reinforcements from arriving. There had been no Italian counter-battery fire per personal orders of Badoglio. With no communications, Villani did not know that the right bank was void of Italian troops nor that the *Napoli* was deployed high up on the hills and not on the valley floor at the river bank where it could have halted any enemy advance. His troops (Nineteenth Infantry Division, *X Gruppo Alpini),* were deployed from M. Plezia along the Isonzo then proceeded up to the Bainsizza Plateau a distance of seven miles. Attacking troops infiltrated his defense positions penetrating to his rear. The first attack wave consisted of thirty battalions of the Alpenkorps, the Two Hundredth German Infantry and the Austro-Hungarian First Infantry Division against five battalions of the *Taro (*207° and 208°), five of the *Spezia* (125° and 126°) and three of the *X Gruppo Alpini.* A subsequent assault wave consisted of men of the Twelfth Silesian. Wave after wave of attackers hit the Jeza (Map 14). By noon, Villani decided to call up the *Alpini* Val d'Adige Battalion the only reserve he had to assist in the defense of his center. Holding off the 4° Jäger, the *Taro* was refused artillery support with the Volzana trap being quoted. Here on the Cemponi, the *Spezia* held off the 3° Jäger until 1400 when the *Albero Bello* was lost (Map 20). This was a small summit near the Jeza summit which had only one tree, hence the name "beautiful tree." The danger to the Nineteenth Infantry Division was not in the center, but in the wings. Climbing the undefended northern slopes of Costa Raunza, the combined Bavarian Guards-AlpenKorps, the Württemberg Mountain Battalion and the 23° of the Twelfth Silesian arrived at Foni by 1300, then veered left toward Passo Zagradan (Map 16). By 1630 M. Piatto fell, as the attackers prepared to attack the Podklabuk. Southward, the *X Gruppo Alpini* yielded the Cukli Vrh. Soon the presence of enemy troops to its rear on the Kolovrat and attackers to its front forced it to withdraw. The *Spezia* withdrew to line Vogrinski-Ostri Kras (the ridge that separated the Doblar Valley from the Iudrio River Valley (Map 20). At 1600 Villani decided to take the *Napoli* from Passo Zagradan. As units of the brigade (75°) proceeded toward Casoni Solarie and Bukovna Jeza, Italian troops coming down the slopes of Casoni Solarie advised the *Napoli* that all the Italian cannons on the slopes were in enemy hands (Map 16). *These were the very guns which Badoglio had wanted to use to destroy advancing enemy infantry.* Seeing the *Napoli* being destroyed piecemeal, at 1800 Villani withdrew westward to Clabuzzaro. On the way he stopped at Passo Zagradan and realized that the enemy was already there (Map 18). Assessing the situation with only 1300 effectives, Villani realized that the Volzana trap had sprung in reverse. At 2000 he notified Badoglio that he was at Clabuzzaro with no artillery and few troops placing himself under the command of the VII Corps. This explains why authors have stated that his division was reported as having been swallowed up by the earth. It certainly was, having been engulfed and sent to the Prisoner of War camps.

The OIR cited a report sent to the *Relazione della Commissione d'Inchiesta Dall'Isonzo al Piave,* on February 26, 1918. In it, Badoglio noted that the enemy shelling started to decrease about 0500. It has already been noted that in a conversation with the king he had stated that there had been neither shelling nor enemy infantry assaults in his sector. With his communications knocked out by enemy shelling he received no information concerning enemy infantry advances while enemy gunners did not fire fearing hitting their own men. Moreover he felt that atmospheric conditions were unsuitable for gas shelling. At 1520 Badoglio from Cave Kambresko reported that in the Nineteenth Infantry Division sector, the enemy had taken the spur of Cemponi below Varda (Map 20). Asking for more troops he noted that he was on the Globocak with the *Puglie,* attempting to hold the enemy on the line Pusno-Jazna.[61] Forty minutes later, Badoglio again telegraphed the II Army, that he had received news neither from the Nineteenth Infantry Division, nor the Forty-sixth Infantry Division (IV Corps), on his left. The *Puglie* deployed blocking the Judrio Creek and between Srednje and Cicer. He intended to defend the Jeza, ending his message that he was incommunicado at Cave Kambresko.[62]

Capt. A. Sforza liaison from the Comando Supremo to the XXVII Corps noted that Badoglio left his headquarters and visited the areas under attack, so there was no way to contact him, should any information arrive at his headquarters at Ostry Kras. From there, Badoglio who was completely in the dark regarding the situation of troops under his command went to Kambresko to learn as much as he could. At 1100 he was able to get through to the VII Corps noting that all was calm in his sector which was due to his lack of communications as already noted. His subordinates had begged for artillery support but all artillery mouths were under orders not to fire until personally ordered by Badoglio. When he was ready to give orders, all communications had been destroyed. Sforza (brother of the diplomat), on December 17, 1917, reported that Badoglio intended to open fire at the initiation of the second phase of the enemy' s shelling, an impossible move due to destruction of communications. Dispatch couriers had a hard time getting through to their destinations. When they did arrive, the situation had changed making their carried orders useless. During his telephone and radio conversations, with the II Army headquarters as well as the Comando Supremo he was authorized to withdraw as far as Cividale if needed. Listening in on these conversations was the Austro-German XIV Army. On this day, Badoglio changed his headquarters five times going to Liga, Ostry Kras, Cave Kambresko, Kosi and Pusno (Map 20). Having no communication with Ostry-Kras (XXVII Corps Artillery headquarters), at 0800, Badoglio sent Major Cantatore a staff officer to investigate. The major was not authorized to order the artillery to open fire but simply to make contact. As he proceeded at 1200 he noted enemy troops (VII Mountain Brigade, First Habsburg Mountain Division) had already crossed the dorsum of Varda Vrh. Approaching too close to enemy troops on his way to report to Badoglio he was wounded in a hand by enemy fire. Going along mountain paths through fog and shell smoke he ran into the *Puglie* (Major General Tullio Papini). Reporting this situation to Papini, they both decided to deploy the *Puglie* along the line of Pusno-Globocak to block the enemy's entrance into the Judrio Valley (Map 20). Later Badoglio sent orders via staff officer Major Freguglia to Lt. Gen. V. Fiorone (Sixty-fourth Infantry Division) to also assume command of the Twenty-second and Sixty-fifth Infantry Divisions deployed on the left bank and transfer them to the right bank protecting the Isonzo bridges at Doblar as well as Cicer Vrh. The orders read : "The enemy has broken through the line of Cemponi, stop. I do not have information on the rest of the Nineteenth Division which I hope still occupies Jeza, stop. With the *Puglia* Brigade which I have in reserve, I shall attempt to dam the enemy advance, deploying from M. Kum-Srednje-Globocak, stop (*Maps 17,20).* Your Excellency will assume command of the troops on the left of the Isonzo and attempt to block the enemy from proceeding west of the Subjuk, stop. I am at the Kambresko Caves, stop. Signed, Badoglio.[63] Kambresko was a quarry, hence the name Cave. This move would result in the left flank of the right wing of the XXIV Corps waving in the breeze and in contact with no one.

All day the Italian Twenty-second, Sixty-fifth and Sixty-fourth Infantry Divisions fought off the attackers taking one thousand prisoners (Maps 13, 20).[64] However toward the day's end they were almost surrounded and from the Lom heights could see enemy troops on Krad Vrh (Map 12 for geography). In the evening, the 47° Bersaglieri arrived and was placed under the command of the XXVII Corps. As the Caporetto Inquiry Commission noted, "It was the intention of the XXVII to attack the line Srednje-Ostry Kras with the two brigades of Bersaglieri *(Map 20).* They would be assisted by the VII Corps, while the *Treviso (*115° &116°) would occupy Cicer Sobink." Since the VII Corps (Third Infantry Division), could not assist, the plan was abandoned.

As Krafft later wrote, "After the Podklabuc, the second Italian defensive pillar on the Kolovrat was taken. Now, one could consider the German breakthrough a *fait accompli.*" Previously considerations had been given to an attack on two fronts, Isonzo and Tyrol, but the latter had been discarded due to insufficient troops and too long a preparation time.[65] The 3° Jäger spent the night on the Jeza full of pride and satisfaction while the 4° Jäger who were to have conquered the Jeza but did not, spent the night on the lower slopes.

Austro-German Scotti Group

This unit had twenty battalions of elite mountain troops deployed in the area since 1915 knowing the sector well. The Austro-Hungarian First Infantry Division starting from the southern sector of the Tolmino bridgehead moved in two directions. Following it was the Fifth Brandenburg Division which was to follow it westward from the slopes of Cemponi and eventually aid it to capture the Globocak. The VII Mountain Brigade deployed on the right, took the Varda Vrh, the Cemponi Spur, Varda Vrh, Scuole di Rutte, Zible Vrh, and the Cukli Vrh (Map 20). The latter was situated on a spur that from Krad Vrh descended onto Podselo at the big bend in the Isonzo near Tolmino and S. Lucia. By now, except for the Krad Vrh, the whole dorsum from M. Jeza projecting southward to the junction of the Doblar and Isonzo Rivers was in Austro-German hands. Defending the two mile front around the Velik Vrh was the *X Gruppo Alpini* consisting of the Morbengo, Monte Berico, Vicenza and Val d'Adige Battalions, three in all with one in reserve to oppose the twenty enemy battalions (Map 15). The *X Gruppo Alpini* movements illustrated a curious Italian method of moving troops at the time. When the Comando Supremo wanted to send an *Alpini* group to Dreznica it would have been easy to send troops from the general reserve. Instead the *V Gruppo Alpini* deployed on Krad Vrh was picked and replaced by the *X Gruppo Alpini* taken from the Bainsizza, which was replaced by the *Roma.* Thus three defense positions were manned by troops newly arrived on location and not aware of their surroundings allowing easy infiltration of Italian positions. Survivors of the Morbengo and Monte Berico Battalions withdrew to Val Doblar while the Vicenza was isolated on Krad Vrh. At 1100 the *Alpini* Val d'Adige Battalion went looking for the Nineteenth Infantry Division which had almost disappeared. Three of its companies had been sent elsewhere, the 258 to *Albero Bello* the 256 to the Jeza and the 257 to the Jeza summit. With constant German infantry attacks, their commander realized that they would soon be surrounded. As darkness arrived, with a bayonet charge they broke through the German lines reaching Clabuzzaro and the survivors of the Nineteenth Infantry Division. There were now no opposing forces against the First Imperial Division. The Doblar Gorge would have to be crossed, beyond which start the slopes of the Jeza which then descend onto the Isonzo toward Ronzina. From Ostry-Kras to the Globocak, the troops could protect the V. Judrio to the rear (Map 20). By 1530, the attackers had crossed the Doblar Gorge arriving at the villages of Auska and Bizjak. By nightfall, they arrived at the Doblar-Judrio Rivers watershed. Having accomplished this, they had isolated the Globocak removing the last obstacle on the way to Cividale. The First Imperial Division took 4,600 prisoners, seventy cannons, thirty two machine guns and much material. Its left wing (XXII Mountain Brigade) proceeded toward the hamlet of Javor and the Krad Vrh.

Italian IV Corps

By afternoon, this corps had dissolved resulting in a large breach developing in the northern extremity of the Italian II Army between it and the Zona Carnia troops.

Italian VII Corps

At 1805, Bongiovanni (VII Italian Corps), received an order from Capello to attack along the valley floor toward Caporetto which had fallen three hours prior. To put things in perspective, the VII Corps was the only unit still intact on the upper Isonzo as the IV Corps (left bank) and the XXVII Corps (right bank) no longer existed. Terrifying news-grams, one after another, arrived at headquarters. Bongiovanni seemed paralyzed, remaining in his office for hours not communicating with anyone. The next day, at 0825, he issued the (in) famous bulletin to his division commanders. "The enemy troops are only weak detachments of troops, etc." Perhaps he had heard this from Capello. Later, testifying at the Caporetto Inquiry Commission hearing, he stated that he had no knowledge of his troops being routed the first morning of the battle. After the debacle he was put in command of aviation squadrons.

Italian XXVII Corps

At 1755, Badoglio received news from his Artillery Chief, Col. Alfredo Cannoniere stationed at Ostry Kras. The colonel had sent a message at 1420 stating that Villani had sent an officer to check who learned that the line Jesenjak-Cemponi-Zible Vrh had been pierced, forcing him to retreat to the line M. Jeza-Ostry Kras-Pusno (Map 20). With communications out there was no news from Krad Vrh. At 1820 Badoglio notified Capello what he had just learned stating that he would hold the line at Jeza-Pusno with the Sixty-fourth Infantry Division and the *Puglie*, deploying them on either side of the Isonzo River to block the enemy advance. He also described the mission of Major Freguglia. At 2000, while everyone thought that the Nineteenth Infantry Division was retreating as explained, two battalions of the 72° (*Puglie*), were surprised by enemy troops near Pusno and were heavily mauled, losing one company. These units were on the way to strengthen the line at Jeza-Pusno. He now moved his headquarters from Kambresko to Liga, a village of about five km. (three miles), in direct flight to the south west on the left of the Judrio River. So frustrated was Badoglio that at one point he asked for messenger pigeons, so "my messages will get through."[66] At Liga, he was able to have telephone communications with

Capello, who confirmed to him that at 1820 he had been assigned the I Bersaglieri Brigade. Badoglio did not know anything about this yet, being officially notified at 2340. Capello also notified him that he was taking the V Bersaglieri Brigade from the VII Corps and assigning it to him and also asked about his plans concerning the well-known counterattack on M. Jeza or Tolmino. Badoglio responded that he would counterattack in the a.m. in the direction of Ostry-Kras-Globocak with these four regiments, but had no artillery. His "silent" artillery had all been captured by advancing Austro-German troops. In reality the Globocak was still in Italian hands.[67]

The OIR noted, with all these communications back and forth, no one seemed to mention the fact that the enemy had breached the defensive positions of the XXVII Corps and was aiming for Caporetto. Its troops deployed on the left side of the Isonzo were isolated by attacks of the Koschak Group (*II Armée Isonzo*) and the XIV Army and subjected to heavy bombardment resulting in enemy troops arriving to the headwaters of the Avscek River (Map 12, Vol. I for geography). Habsburg forces had as their objective the borders between the two countries northwest of the Korada-M. Santo chain. Enemy units had broken through to the head of the Avscek River. As the OAR noted, "The Koschak Group had less luck." The Sixtieth Infantry Division crossed the Italian trenches in the lower Isonzo, while the Thirty-fifth crossed the first lines south of Hoje. However, the Sixtieth was counterattacked by the Italian Sixty-fifth Infantry Division and had to retreat while the *Belluno* fought valiantly at the Vogercek Gorge but had to yield.[68]

The 4° Jäger reached a road going to Capella Slieme but was halted by fierce Italian resistance. At 1700, the IV/3 Jäger arrived to reinforce those present and soon they attacked the Jeza conquering it in a few hours. The OIR really did not believe the War Diary of the XXVII Corps concerning the events of these days. Thirteen pages of the diary were torn from the book and not available to the Caporetto Inquiry Commission. This was done per order of the king who after the debacle had pushed for

Badoglio's appointment as Vice-Chief of the General Staff, not knowing the what really happened to the XXVII Corps. Nonetheless, it reported that orders had been given to seal the breach at V. Judrio at Pusno and to occupy the line Pusno-Globocak-Kambresko with the *Puglie.* We already know that decision was made by Maj. Cantatore and Gen. Papini.

The II Army War Diary, bears no news from the Nineteenth Infantry Division on this date, nor from the troops deployed on the left of the Isonzo. Incidentally, it should be noted that at Kambresko, Badoglio *could not communicate with anyone.* With the tight command structure in the Italian Army, how were subordinate commanders to maneuver? Initiative had been stifled. It was a corps commander's duty to communicate with his subordinate commanders as best as he could. (Results and effects of Badoglio's peregrinations on this day are fully discussed in chapter XIV, Critique). By nightfall, the few survivors of the *X Gruppo Alpini* were on the southern slopes of Krad Vrh near Robarje. Like Badoglio all of Villani's communications equipment had been destroyed while dispatch couriers got lost so he had no idea of the situation developing. Prior to arriving at Clabuzzaro he sent a message to the telephone station there to relay to Badoglio. He noted his precarious condition and few survivors. He collected survivors from the *Spezia* and *Taro* and as noted, placed all including himself under the command of the VII Corps. An officer sent to Villani, had learned that the defense line Jesionek-Cemponi-Zible Vrh was lost, and therefore it was necessary to redeploy on the line M. Jeza-Ostry Kras-Pusno (Map 20). Badoglio also told the II Army that he would counterattack on the morrow in the direction of Ostry-Kras-Globocak.

Receiving his orders Fiorone ordered the Sixty-fifth Infantry Division and the *Roma* to remain in the line beyond the Isonzo.[69] The Sixty-fourth and Twenty-second Divisions would go to the right bank of the river, occupy the spur of Cicer Vrh-Subjuk and make contact with the garrison on the Globocak. In doing this, the deployment would be extended to the area of the junction of the Doblar and Isonzo Rivers, thus protecting the bridges further south in the rear of the XXIV Corps (Map 12 for geography). Before any of these orders could be carried out, an order arrived via the Forty-ninth Infantry Division that the divisions of the XXVII Corps were now under the command of the XXIV Corps.[70] This move was at the instigation of its commander Lt. Gen. Enrico Caviglia who felt it necessary to have one commander for the area of Globocak, Bainsizza, Lom and the lower Isonzo (Map 12 for geography). After he had already ordered the withdrawal of his divisions about 2300 he became aware of the isolation of divisions of the XXVII Corps. Thus under his *own initiative* rare in Italian officers, he led the divisions on the Lom to safety, sacrificing his Forty-ninth Infantry Division on the left (Lt. Gen. Alessandro Vigliani) and saving all the troops he could.

By the end of the day, the XXVII command was reduced to the *Puglie* and the I and V Brigate Bersaglieri recently assigned it by the II Army. The War Diary of the II Army stated that at 0930 the Comando Supremo had issued orders that there be adequate forces on the line at Matajur-Jeza-Globocak, to assure the protection of the origin of the V. Judrio. Headquarters assigned this to five brigades of the VII Corps which also received the V Bersaglieri Brigade. After Major Cantatore's visit the latter unit had been detached to the XXVII Corps to take part in the counterattack on the Jeza which never happened as has been explained in previous paragraphs.

As the events unfolded the Comando Supremo sent the reserve Fifty-third Division to fortify the area of V. Natisone between Stupizza and Brischis (Map 22). As previously noted, a unified command had been instituted for the IV and VII Corps in the left wing of the II Army with the command being assigned to Lt. Gen. Luca Montuori who left Cividale at 1300 for Kred to assume command. Along the way, he met Lt. Gen. Costantino Bruno walking alone. When Montuori asked him what his command was, the response was *Brigata Alessandria.* Another question, "Where is it?" The laconic answer was "It has melted."[71]

Near Stupizza, his auto was blocked by the fleeing civilians, so he had to proceed on foot. He reached his destination just as Cavaciocchi was leaving to go to Breginj (Map 23). After talking with Capello via telephone, he assured the latter, that he would use the three regiments of the *Potenza* to block the enemy advance. Just before leaving for Breginj, he met their commander, Col. Brig. Luigi Amantea, gave the necessary orders and left for Cividale via an alternative route via Nimis. Visiting the VII Corps headquarters, he then proceeded to II Army headquarters. Along the way he noted thousands of troops, mostly bombardiers and gunners. They had neither helmets nor rifles, but had kept their gas masks. Many years ago the author interviewed some Italian artillery Caporetto veterans who were deployed in caves high up on mountain slopes some of whom had been taken prisoners, as well as some who had fled. The former firing their piece emplaced in a cave high up on a road-less mountainous slope, were suddenly confronted by enemy mountain troops at the mouth of the cave who threatened to throw grenades into their habitat. The latter seeing enemy troops climbing toward them and no infantry to defend them disabled their pieces and fled.

By 1600 Montuori felt that the Fiftieth Infantry Division was not needed to defend the Saga Gorge (Map15). The Twenty-second Schützen was held up during the night at the Podcela Bridge so the Fiftieth could redeploy on the line at M. Guarda-Prvi Hum-M. Stol (Map 13). It seemed that the welcome mat was spread out for the Krauss Group advancing from Plezzo along the V. Uccea (Map 23). Until midnight the Saga was still in the hands of the Fiftieth Division, as Cavaciocchi's (in) famous order had not arrived.

The II Army headquarters had received the bad news concerning the IV Corps but as yet had not digested the total disaster concerning the XXVII and VII Corps. The OIR noted in its report of the day's events that the II Army was worried, as was the Comando Supremo, but neither had a clear idea of the disaster in the making. As yet *le voile est déchiré* had not happened. At the Battle of Leipzig Napoleon had uttered this phrase, meaning, the enemy's intentions are known (literally the veil has been lifted). The Comando Supremo's task was to the protect the headwaters of the Judrio River, while the II Army was more preoccupied with its left wing (Map 20). At 1000, the II Army had sent a summary of events to the Comando Supremo whose only answer was not to be wasteful with ammunition. When Montuori notified Capello that the Saga Gorge had been abandoned he received the order "At all costs troops which retreat from the Saga area must garrison Montemaggiore and the slopes of the Stol where they are to fight to the death." He also sent a staff officer, Major Pompeo Campello to find Badoglio and get information on the situation of the XXVII Corps. Badoglio was also notified that he would receive the I Bersaglieri Brigade (which with the V, constituted the Forty-seventh Bersaglieri Division) which was on its way from Val Judrio to Kambresko.

These troops were to reinforce the already-withdrawing *Puglie* deployed on the Globocak. With this information, the Comando Supremo enlarged the Zona Carnia (XII Corps) sector toward the south to give a united command to the defense of the V. Uccea (Maps 13,23). Breaking through here would allow the attackers a direct penetration to the middle Tagliamento, endangering troops from the Zona Carnia to the Adriatic as well as the reserves. Arriving at 1940 at the Cividale rail station coming from the Vicentian Alps, the *Alpini* V. Leogra Battalion was to be immediately deployed in the Stol sector and P. di Montemaggiore. These weary men were to stop an advance without knowing the terrain or linkups. The scale of the disaster was slowly dawning on the Italian generals.

Thinking that the enemy could not advance quickly through the mountains, reserves thought to be adequate were deployed south of Cividale (See chapter XIV). News arrived at the Comando Supremo indicating that there was a large breach in the Italian line in the shape of a fan with the IV and XXVII Corps going in opposite directions and the VII Corps in the center with little contact with the enemy.

Italian VII Corps

At 1805 Capello with no idea of the real situation ordered the VII Corps to attack the enemy advancing along the valley floor. This was simply a generic order and worthless, since he was not cognizant of the real situation. Later, he was criticized in the OIR which noted that this order specified neither a task, nor an objective.[72]

By the end of today, Stein's men were on the west bank of the Isonzo and at the foot of the Kolovrat, while the I Corps was at Saga west of Caporetto.

Comando Supremo

Cadorna now realized that a breakthrough in the left wing sector of the II Army would be disastrous for Italy. Another reserve division was detached to the II Army. Two divisions (Sixteenth and Twenty-first Infantry Divisions), were taken from the III Army and sent to the sectors of Nimis and Bergogna, north of Udine. Two divisions from the First Army were to be deployed in the Udine-Tarcento sectors to support the II Army (Map 35).[73] He feared that Conrad would now attack in the Trentino (Map 14A).

2100. In Milano at the Olympia Theatre, the headline read, "The Song of the Swan" a comedy by Duval and Roux. The first two rows of seats were reserved for the honored officers of the II and III Armies. The Duke of Aosta had given them this night off because they had distinguished themselves at the front. However, it was all a fallacy as none of these officers had seen action. They were simply the few well-liked privileged and favored officers who had been given a night on the town. These men were called *imboscati* by the troops.[74] Due to the pending offensive, troops in the front line trenches had not been allowed to go home even for the death of a parent.[75] Events like this had long been the norm for the *imboscati* and were being noted by the illiterate infantrymen who never could get a furlough or any consideration despite the terrible battlefront conditions.[76] Like many things Italian a song evolved describing the *imboscati.*

Giornale in mano, la sigaretta
Mentre noi all'assalto alla baionetta
Come le mosche ci tocca a morir
(They have a)
Newspaper in hand smoking a cigarette
While we go on a bayonet charge
It is our fate to die like flies

At 1430 the War Diary of the Comando Supremo included a notation about the IV Corps sector. The XXIV Corps (III Army), was preparing a counterattack for some terrain lost, while the XXVII Corps reported heavy bombardment and loss of communications.[77] In the afternoon Cadorna visited II Army Headquarters. Reserves had been called up. The Sixteenth and Twenty-first Infantry Divisions were deployed south of Tarcento (Map 35).[78] The Sixtieth Infantry Division and the VII *Gruppo Alpini* were sent to Breginj to block the route leading from Caporetto to Tarcento and the upper Tagliamento (Maps 29, 35).[79] A regiment of field artillery with more than twenty eight batteries of medium caliber guns were transferred from the II Army to the III Army.[80] The *Ionio, Messina* and *Avellino* (Thirteenth and Twenty-third Infantry Divisions), were sent to a sector south of Cividale where the new headquarters of the II Army would be.[81] Realizing the full extent of enemy moves, some officers of the Comando Supremo finally realized that both the II and III Armies were in danger. Confusion reigned in Udine. About 1600 there was an accidental meeting of some officers. Col. Melchiade Gabba, secretary to Cadorna stated that he knew nothing of what was happening. Cadorna told his historian, Col. A. Gatti, that it was impossible for the enemy to break through three defensive lines.[82] Badoglio told Cadorna that opposite his troops, there had been no great enemy preparations.[83] Gatti the Comando Supremo historian, was told by others who had gone out to inspect the battle areas that the defenses were far from perfect, but little could be learned about the advancing enemy.

Finally, Col. Riccardo Calcagno of the Situation Office arrived reporting that nine German divisions had been identified, and felt that if there were no enemy attack in the Trentino, the offensive would be in the middle of the battle front.

1800. Col. Gatti discussed the battle with Cadorna in the "Plastic Room." This was a scaled model extended on a table showing the hills, valleys, etc. Talking about the Tolmino Basin, Cadorna noted how it would be impossible to take Cemponi (Map 20). However, the Austro-Germans, using new tactics not seen on the Italian Front did not frontally attack the fortresses, they simply isolated them, and proceeded in northwest and southwest directions. *As yet the Comando Supremo had no idea concerning either the characteristics of the attack nor its objectives.* Italian artillery had controlled all the roads of Volce, Kozarsce and the Isonzo. Gatti suggested that the troops should be informed that the Germans were with the Habsburgs, because the former fought differently. The Germans tried to knock out enemy artillery at any cost and first thought of strategic necessities, then the tactical.[84] This was the first recorded thought that anyone at the Comando Supremo gave as to how the battle would play out. After supper, Col. Gatti went to a movie. When he returned to the Comando Supremo about 2200, he noted many officers in animated conversation. They had come from the front asking questions which the General Staff officers could not answer. The phrase, "tactics destroy strategy," meaning that the German tactics had destroyed the Italian strategy was heard over and over. The Comando Supremo had no experience nor any knowledge of how to deal with maneuver warfare. There had been no news from the Forty-third and Fiftieth Infantry Divisions. Perhaps, 20,000 men had been lost as prisoners. The Germans had crashed through while the Italians were already planning to retreat beyond the Tagliamento River. Were the Germans crazy? Did they not know of the tremendous Italian defenses? These words were heard over and over during the evening. There were three superbly fortified lines of defense. Were the hundreds of thousands of Italian dead over the past two years all for nought?. There was talk of an Italian Sedan.[85] As the OIR noted, at 2300 Cadorna telegraphed Capello ordering the left wing link to up with the right wing of the XII Corps (Zona Carnia Command) at Montemaggiore (Map 23). Tassoni had a great deficiency in men and supplies. A partial wording of the telegram read as follows:

"The left wing of the army should use Montemaggiore as a hinge where it shall fuse with units of the right wing of the XII Corps. The plan had been discussed with Capello.[86]

Successive lines of resistance are: the mountains, Maggiore, Stol, Matajur,

Kolovrat, Jeza, (*Map 13)*

Maggiore-Lupia-Matajur-Globocak-

Maggiore-Carnizza-Korada (northwest of Plava) *See Maps 4,12, for orientation.*

Each line was to be held as long as possible. As Cadorna went on, "It was especially important to resist on the Stol" (*Map 23*).

Final lines of resistance were individually listed from Montemaggiore to Globocak, and the Korada. Reiterated was the importance of the Stol.[87] These orders did not correspond to reality. Where were the troops to defend these areas to come from? There were no reserves in these sectors. Withdrawing troops had to simultaneously halt the enemy advance, establish defensive positions and link up with the newly arrived troops while the advancing enemy did not want to give the Italians any respite. Below pushed his men. The III Army was to retreat and deploy from the Bainsizza-Gorizia sector to the line Isonzo-Gorizia Bridgehead. Cadorna still did not know what the enemy plans were. He had written to the French and British Allies telling them that the offensive would develop from Plezzo to the Adriatic with the preponderance of forces from Plezzo to Tolmino.[88] With these communications he showed that he was aware of all enemy troop movements right down to the name of the commander of the enemy offensive and where the enemy would attack. Unfortunately, as already noted, he could not deploy his divisions in time to meet the enemy onslaught nor could allied artillery be returned in time. Since he no longer went on the offensive, the allies had requested that it be returned. As noted realizing that there would be a great enemy offensive, Cadorna notified Rome.[89]

Zona Carnia Command

Tucked between the Italian II and IV Armies, this command (Lt. Gen. Giulio Tassoni) reported directly to the Comando Supremo. Its main task was to hold the front between the II Army and itself which was the weak-recognized link. Known as the roof of the Isonzo, it was supposed to cover any movements of troops between the Piave and Isonzo Rivers. Two months prior to the Austro-German assault defensive lines ran from M. Peralba to Passo Monte Croce Carnico to Monte Cavallo, then to Pontebba, across Val Fella to approach but not include the Rombon (Maps 29, 35 for orientation). To the north was the Austrian-Hungarian X Army opposed by the XII Corps (Twenty-sixth and Thirty-sixth Infantry Divisions). Cadorna had predicted the possibility of a retreat of the Fiftieth Infantry Division (IV Corps), down Val Uccea, and had ordered Tassoni to prepare a withdrawal plan. Since the X Army had not moved, the *Edelweiss* and the *Jäger* Divisions proceeded west and northwest down Val Venzone, Valle di Resia and Valle Raccolana posing a threat to the Italian above-named divisions (Maps 23, 27, 29).

Home Front Events

In Rome, there was an intensive debate in the Parliament. The Socialists requested investigation as to who was financing the interventionist press. Lt. Gen. Gaetano Giardino, the War Minister, took the floor and noted that he had received communications from the war zone that an enemy offensive was imminent. "You have read in the papers that there is talk about an enemy offensive with German participation. It has been ascertained that they are in the Tyrol and probably also on the Isonzo. In the past few days the body of a Prussian soldier has been fished out of the Isonzo. The enemy is aware of our preparations and wishes to drive his sword through our plans and blow our alliance. Let the enemy come, we do not fear him." A warm applause followed (except from the socialists). The *Corriere della Sera* wrote that the delirium of the applause was equal to that of the days of May 1915. Two hours later, Giardino went to his offices in Via XX Settembre. He was greeted by bureaucrats who also gave him warm applause. The first act he did was to read a telegram from the front which noted that there had been a large breakthrough with the occupation of the Saga Gorge and the loss of a great deal of equipment and thousands of prisoners. He realized that Italy was in danger. For some time in political circles in Rome there had been rumors of the military crisis. The first thing that the French Ambassador told the Italian Colonial Minister, Ferdinando Martini was that he hoped that the Foreign Ministry would not have any changes, as the Allies only trusted Sonnino.

By the end of the day, the Italian II Army had been routed, thirty thousand prisoners had been taken, and the Italian III Army was in danger.[90] There were now two breaches in the Italian line. One was between the Zona Carnia and the left wing of the Italian II Army, the other between the IV and XXVII Corps. A few days later, Giardino resigned as War Minister and left for the front to fight in the biggest battle Italy ever had. The Socialists, who were not in the government, had actively opposed the war. Now apparently with a guilty conscience, they seemed to have a change of heart. As Giardino was leaving, radical Socialist Deputy Oddino Morgari whispered to him, "General, Save Italy." Previously Morgari had severely criticized the war, the army's behavior and social conditions in Italy. Now he realized that his words were seriously affecting the war effort. Socialists now would become good Italian patriots, like their brothers in other European nations. Late in the day, the Italian government begged London for help.[91] As noted above, Cadorna had previously written noting he could hold out for five weeks, so London was not unduly alarmed.

Following is a summary of the events of the first day of the battle.

Pertinent Events

I. The rapid advance along valley floors by Imperial and German troops aided by fog and rain made all military tactic texts on the subject obsolete. This maneuver was a dagger to the heart of Italian defenses. In addition in some sectors Habsburg trenches were on mountain slopes above Italian trenches lower down making a concentrated advance easier. Italian orders passively reacted to the Austro-German movements. There was no active Italian movement to counteract the assault.

II. During the first phase of the attackers' shelling, their massed troops were not bothered by any Italian shelling which had been ordered to start firing in the *second phase* of the Austro-German shelling which did not fire on Italian trenches but on warehouses and command centers far to the rear thus destroying communications and assembly points. Italian artillery fired uselessly on vacated Austro-German infantry assembly points while the enemy was advancing through the fog toward the unsuspecting Italian lines.

III. By changing his headquarters five times in one day, Badoglio made it difficult for dispatch couriers to reach him with information so he could make informed decisions. It was his duty to stay in touch with the corps headquarters. He also did not carry out the orders of Cadorna to withdraw artillery on the Bainsizza to across the Isonzo. His actions and results are fully discussed on page 380.

IV. II Army reserves were sufficient but inadequately placed. There were no plans for an in-depth defense of a salient, *ergo* the breach would have to be closed by Comando Supremo reserves (few and far away).

V. Along the line M. Plezia-Doblar were deployed two brigades belonging to two different corps. There could be no synchronized movements with these conditions. This was similar to the Battle of Leyte Gulf, with different commanders for troops in the same locale (To be fair, at Leyte, it involved army and naval personnel) At noon VII Corps had ordered the *Elba* to deploy along the line Passo Zagradan-Pusno, while at 1400, the XXVII Corps ordered the *Puglie* to deploy along the line Pusno-Srednje-Auska (Map 20).

VI. By noon, the reserve function of the VII Corps was over. It had had no enemy contact except the firefight for the Sella di Luico (Golobi) by the IV Bersaglieri. Its only reserve now was the *Firenze.*

VII. Both the Comando Supremo and the troops had no experience in handling the maneuver warfare moves of the attackers. To do this one had to make educated guesses where the enemy would be in one week and defend accordingly. Being completely wrong would lead to disaster.

In all this chaos and disaster on the Italian side, there was a bright spot. The II *Armée Isonzo* on the southern point of the Italian deployment, with its Sixtieth and Thirty-fifth Infantry Divisions attacked the Twenty-second, Sixty-fourth and Sixty-fifth Infantry Divisions of the Italian XXIV Corps, being severely mauled by the retreating Italians who took 500 prisoners.[92]

Specific Situations

After the Silesians took Caporetto, the *Salerno* deployed onto the Matajur. It has been said that it was asked to attack the Silesians in their left flank but the order could only come from its divisional commander. It would have been difficult descending the Matajur (5000 feet) attack and possibly be caught in a cross fire if it had to retreat. Describing units can be confusing.[93]

Chapter One Endnotes

Day One, The Disaster Began

1 OULK: *Das Kriegsjarhr 1917*, Vol. VI, op. cit., p. 525.

2 USSME: Relazione Ufficiale, Vol. IV, Tomo 3° bis, *Le Operazioni del 1917 (Gli Avvenimenti dall'Ottobre al Dicembre) Narrazione*, ILTE, Torino, 1954, p. 224

3 Kriegsarchiv, Vienna, Bibliothek, *Bericht ad A.O.K.*, OP Nr. 58400 (n.p., 1917)

4 Field Marshal Alfred von Schlieffen, Chief of the Prussian General Staff, architect of famous Schlieffen Plan for the invasion of France during the First World War.

5 OULK, Vol. VI, op. cit.,-p. 525

6 Stuhlmann, Friedrich, *Die Artillerie des Alpenkorps in der Durchbruchschlacht von Tolmein am 24 Oktober 1917* in *Wehr und Waffen*, H 1, 2, 1935, pp. 38-39

7 Krafft, Konrad von Dellmensingen, Vol I, *Der Durchbruch am Isonzo*, 2 volumes, Oldenburg, Stallings, 1926; Vol. I *Die Schlachte von Tolmein und Flitsch*, Vol. II, *Die Verfolgung über den Tagliamento bis zum Piave*; Vol. I, p. 48

8 Luigi Cadorna, *Lettere Famigliari*, Milano, Mondadori 1967, p. 227

9 Cesare DeSimone : *L'Isonzo Mormorava*, Mursia, Milano, 1995, p. 20

10 Ibid, p. 20

11 Sonnino Microfilm, reel 47, British War Cabinet Minutes, reel 47, 6-7 Nov. 1917, University of Michigan, Ann Arbour, MI.

12 Angelo Gatti, *Caporetto. Dal diario di guerra*, Bologna, Il Mulino 1964, p. 25.

13 *Relazione della Commissione d'Inchiesta su Caporetto, Dal Isonzo al Piave*, Rome, 1919, 2 volumes, Vol. II, *Cenni Schematici degli Avvenimenti*, p. 279. From now on this work shall be abbreviated as RICC

14 Ibid, Vol. II, p. 279

15 USSME: Relazione Ufficiale, Vol. IV, Tomo 3° bis, op. cit., p. 240

16 OULK, op. cit., Vol. VI, p. 524

17 Hermanny-Miksch, *Die Durcbruchsschiacht bei Flitsch im Oktober 1917*, Hall in Tyrol, 1924, p. 40

18 Krafft, op. cit., Vol. I, p. 46

19 Idem, p. 84

[20] DeSimone, op. cit., p. 44.

[21] Storia Illustrata, Mondadori, April 1970, p. 4, *Alpini tra i ghiacci dell'Adamello.*

[22] Heyendorff, Major d.R. Walther, *Der Gaswerferangriff bei Flitsch am 24. Oktober 1917, Militarwissenschaftliche Mitteilungen,* n.v., n.d. (1934), p. 316.

[23] Fritz Weber, *Le Tappe della disfatta,* Milano, Corticelli, 1935, p. 126

[24] Alessandro Sforza, *Badoglio a Caporetto, L'Astrolabio,* Dec. 25, 1964, p. 33

[25] USSME: Relazione Ufficiale, Vol. IV, Tomo 3°, *Gli Avvenimenti Dall'Ottobre Al Dicembre, Documenti.,* 23 Ottobre, 1917, Doc. No. 61, IV Corps Commander Protocol No. 6183, *Difesa della Conca di Plezzo,* p. 115

[26] USSME: Relazione Ufficiale, Vol. IV, Tomo 3° bis, Doc., Comando 43a Divisione *Predisposizione contro offensive nemica,* Doc. 96, Protocol 5116, October 18, 1917, p. 235

[27] Alfred Krauss, *Das Wunder vom Karfrait,* Lehman, Munich, 1926, p. 65

[28] *Il Giorno,* Dec. 17, 1961. Account of Oct. 24, 1917 by Vittorio Pallú.

[29] USSME: Relazione Ufficiale: Vol. IV, Tomo 3° bis, Doc. op. cit., 22 October, 1917, Doc. No. 77, Protocol No. 6128, IV. Corps Command, *Sistemazione Difensiva a Monte Plezia* p. 177

[30] Leo Benedetti, *Virgilio's Caporetto Odyssey,* www.worldwar1.com/itafront/virgilio. August 10, 2001.

[31] Below War Diary, Entry of 24-10-17

[32] Krafft von Dellmensingen, Vol. I, op. cit. p. 91

[33] L. Capello, *Note di Guerra,* Milano, 1920. Vol. II, p. 386 Quotation attributed to Lt. Col. Giorgio Boccacci, Chief of Staff, Italian II Army.

[34] Artieri, G., *Il Diario di Vittorio Emanuele III, Epoca,* Jan 14-March 3, 1968. (excerpts from the king's diary), third installment, p. 66

[35] Enrico Caviglia, *La Dodicesima Battaglia, (Caporetto),* Milano, Mondadori, 1933 p. 271.

[36] Krafft, Vol. I op. cit., p. 53, & 58.

[37] Future German Field Marshall in the Second World War, known as the Desert Fox for his stealth and surprise tactics in France and North Africa.

[38] Krafft, op. cit., Vol. I, p. 54-55.

[39] Both men would eventually attain the rank of Field Marshal in the German Army and would be awarded the Knight's Cross with Oak Leaves, Swords and diamonds.

40 Series of articles in *Frankfurter Zeitung* Dec. 6-10, 1917.

41 R. Bencivenga, *La Sorpresa Strategica di Caporetto,* Gaspari Editore Udine, p. 58

42 A. Gatti, op. cit., p. 424.

43 USSME: Relazione Ufficiale, Vol. IV, Tome 3°, op. cit. p. 299

44 Emilio Faldella, *La Grande Guerra* 2 vol. Milano, Longanesi, 1965; Volume II, *Da Caporetto al Piave,* p. 140

45 USSME: Relazione Ufficiale, Vol. IV, Tomo 3°, op. cit., p. 308

46 Ibid, p. 238, 299

47 PRO: WO 106 805 Report of French Gen. Fayolle on "The Situation of the Italian Army," Dec. 26, 1917.

48 Krafft, op. cit., Vol. I, p. 59

49 USSME: Relazione Ufficiale, Vol. IV, Tomo 3°, op. cit., p. 301, 333; Faldella op. cit., Vol. II p. 141

50 USSME: Relazione Ufficiale, Vol. IV, Tomo 3° bis, Doc., Commander VII Corps, No. 74, Protocol No. 11067, October 22, 1917, *Composizione e compiti* del VII Corpo d'Armata p. 138

51 E. Caviglia, op. cit., p. 111

52 G. Sironi, *I Vinti di Caporetto,* Gallarate 1921.

53 Any white bread?

54 USSME: Relazione Ufficiale, Vol. IV, Tomo 3° bis, Doc., Comando VII Corpo d'Armata, *Ordini per lo schieramento della 3a e della 62a Divisione,* Doc. No. 114, Protocol No. 11249-11250, October 24, 1917, p. 282

55 *Aspirante Ufficiale* : By the fall of 1917, Italy was running out of non-commissioned and field officers. To alleviate the latter graduates of a *liceo* were put through a a rapid training course then placed in the trench with the noted rank. Should they perform suitably, they would be promoted to *Sottotenente.* The rank was comparable to the rank of Standard Bearer in the Habsburg Army. (*Enciclopedia Militare Italiana,* p. 770)

56 "You can do nothing, all has been smashed. We have already taken Cividale." Actually Cividale fell on October 27.

57 Felice Troiani, *La Coda di Minosse,* Milano 1964

58 USSME: War Diary, IV Bersaglieri Brigade, Oct. 1917 to Nov. 1918. Repertorio B-1 Racc. 131D 180d.

59 USSME: Relazione Ufficiale: Vol. IV, Tomo 3°, bis, Doc. No. 116, Comando

Supremo, Protocol No. 130969, October 24, 1917, *Trasferimento unità dalla 1a Armata alla zona della 2a Armata* p. 284

60 Mario Schettini, *La Prima Guerra Mondiale, Storia e Letteratura*, Firenze, Sansoni 1965, p. 577-577.

61 USSME: Relazione Ufficiale, Vol. IV, Tomo 3° bis, Doc. op. cit., Doc. No. 101, *La Difesa dello Jeza (24 Ottobre 1917), nel racconto di un aspirante ufficiale (Stefano Barucchi)*, p. 264

62 Ibid, p. 307

63 USSME: Relazione Ufficiale, Vol. IV, Tomo 3° bis, p. 307

64 USSME: Relazione Ufficiale, Vol. IV, Tomo 3° bis, Doc., Comando 22a Divisione *Novità alle ore 14,* Doc. No. 113, Protocol No. 11, 24 October 1917, p. 281

65 OULK, Vol. IV, op. cit., p. 494; Cramon, op. cit., p. 193

66 USSME: Relazione Ufficiale, Vol. IV Tomo 3° bis op. cit., p. 306, 267f

67 Ibid, Vol. IV Tome 3, p. 308

68 USMME: Relazione Ufficiale, Vol. IV, Tomo 3° bis, Doc., Comando 65a Divisione *Communicazione sulla sitauzione inviagte al Comando XXVII Corpo d'Armata* October 24, 1917, Doc. 103, p. 267

69 USSME; Carlo Geloso, *La 65a Divisione,(15 luglio-31 ottobre)* 1928, p. 159

70 USSME: Relazione Ufficiale, Vol. IV, Tomo, 3° bis, op. cit., p. 307

71 Cesare DeSimone, op. cit., p. 30

72 USSME: Relazione Ufficiale, Volume IV, Tomo 3° bis, op. cit., p. 325, Order No. N 6245

73 L. Cadorna, *Altre Pagine Sulla Grande Guerra,* Milano, Mondadori, 1925, pp. 177-180; In this book, Cadorna seems to have written an *Apologia* for his conduct in the Caporetto debacle.

74 Cesare De Simone, *L'Isonzo Mormorava,* Mursia, Milano 1995 p. 40.

75 Report given to Cesare De Simone (author of *L'Isonzo Mormorava)* by Loris Innocenti, at Figline Val d'Arno (Florence) Aug. 12, 1965

76 *Imboscati* were shirkers of the national duty to serve in the armed forces (literally hiding in the woods). Men belonging to the privileged class often received cushy positions in the military far from harm's way, and received medals for bravery though they had never seen action.

77 USSME: Relazione Ufficiale, Volume IV, Tomo 3° bis, op. cit., p. 286

78 Idem, p. 119

79 L. Capello, *Caporetto, Perchè*, Torino, 1967, p. 233

80 *RICC:* Vol. II p. 294.

81 USSME: Relazione Ufficiale, Vol. IV Tomo 3° bis, op. cit., p. 361

82 Angelo Gatti, *Caporetto. Dal diario di guerra,* Il Mulino, Bologna, *1964* p. 258

83 Gianni Pieropan, *Storia della Grande Guerra sul Fronte Italiano,* Mursia, Milano 1988, p. 432

84 Strategic and tactical were phrases often used in the Great War. To define each, one could use the German Michael Offensive in the spring of 1918. The Germans burst through the Allied lines, (a tactical victory), but failed in their aim to reach the channel ports, a strategic failure.

85 Gatti, op. cit., p. 261

86 Caviglia, Enrico, op. cit., p. 166.

87 USSME: Relazione Ufficiale, Protocol No. 4964, Vol. IV Tomo 3° bis, op. cit., p. 330

88 Translated letter from Cadorna to Robertson, Oct. 24, 1917, Robertson Papers, 8/3/33, Protocol 4942; Idem, covering letter from Brig. Gen. Delmé-Radcliffe, Chief of British Military Mission, Oct. 24, 1917, No. 1448, all in Robertson Papers, King's College, London.

89 USSME: Relazione Ufficiale, Vol. IV, Tomo 3° bis, Doc., Comando Supremo, *Communicazione al Governo,* Doc. 51, October 23,1917, Protocol No. 4929, p. 86

90 Alfred Krauss, *Das Wunder von Karfreit* (Munich, 1926) p. 65.

91 OBARI, op. cit., p. 58

92 USSME: Relazione Ufficiale, Vol. IV Tomo 3° bis, op. cit., p. 102

93 After contacting experts on the Habsburg Army Mr. Erwin Sieche has notified the author that often times Kaiserjäger, Feldjäger and Kaiserschützen were labeled Jäger in the literature so one had to read carefully.

CHAPTER II

THE SECOND DAY

October 25, 1917

By the early a.m. a tremendous breach had developed in Italian defenses. The Italians had already lost both banks of the Isonzo above Tolmino and would lose the Stol today.[1] *II Army reserves deployed in the wrong places were unable to stem the enemy advance which was so rapid it gave no time for the defenders to organize any resistance. Capello proposed a retreat to the Tagliamento River which Cadorna accepted then changed his mind wanting simply to disengage from the enemy. There was complete paralysis in the Italian command structure. Italian troops fought without spirit hoping the nightmare would to go away by itself. Stein's and Krauss's troops linked up. Koschak's troops (Armée Isonzo) pushed down the Isonzo Valley below Auzza driving the Italians who were leaving the Bainsizza southward. The Italian Cabinet fell with Vittorio Emanuele Orlando becoming the new Prime Minister.*

War is the Realm of Uncertainty

Karl von Clausewitz

THE WEATHER NOW changed from fog and rain to a splendid sunny day. To emphasize that he was in command of the whole offensive Charles visited the headquarters of the XIV Army. Vienna now wished to halt all operations being satisfied as to how far the troops had progressed. Krafft and Below wanted a victory with annihilation, not a simple victory. They had put a great effort into the offensive both in men and equipment. Around their neck, platoon leaders carried a booklet of topographical maps as well as small electric lights to read them in the dark. Italian military down to the simple soldier, feeling there had been a betrayal were asking how this could have happened. The *fanti* knew that it was not their fault, that the reason for the developing disaster was elsewhere. Pointing four fingers of his right hand at the author, one veteran of the battle related how Italian cannons were all lined up ready to fire at the enemy but did not. Unaware of Badoglio's orders, he felt there had been a betrayal.

Events at the Italian II Army Headquarters

At 0800, Capello was vomiting, having abdominal cramps, and albumen and blood in the urine.[2] He was advised by the medical officer, Col. Morino to be admitted to the hospital. The II Army commander tried to keep the seriousness of his medical problems from all save his Chief of Staff. Later in the a.m. meeting him in the hallway of II Army headquarters, Staff Officer Lt. Ardengo Soffici asked him how he felt, receiving the response, "Very well thank you, it is my left wing that is ill."[3] That evening he was admitted to a military hospital. Italian II Army headquarters was now not at Cormôns which had adequate communication with the Comando Supremo, but at Cividale, where cables to Udine had been cut by advancing Germans.

In the afternoon the XXX Corps notified the II Army that it would not be able to deploy two divisions, still marching enroute, until October 27, while the other two coming from the Trentino would not be ready until October 28, and the final three deployed on the Carso with the III Army were still there. With this information, as Capello later noted, "the mood became somber and surreal. All faith in the army, in oneself or in the fate of the *Patria* were being lost.[4] He now realized that there was only one decision to make, a withdrawal to the Torre Creek (sometimes a river), then the Tagliamento River causing Cividale, Udine and the eastern Friuli to be abandoned (Map 35). This had been Italian Army strategy since 1909 when the first defensive fortifications were built on the Tagliamento. Later with the two bridgeheads of Codroipo and Latisana, it also assumed a base for an offensive.[5] Leaving Cividale by 1500 the II Army commander was at Udine for his last meeting with Cadorna notifying him that the last mobilized reserves from the Trentino were superfluous as the II Army had not used up all its present reserves (See Critique chapter XIV) The key was getting the reserves *in time to where they were needed.* Returning to Cividale, Capello ordered a withdrawal to the line Monte Maggiore-M. Cavallo-M. Korada, pausing at the Torre Creek along which would be deployed fresh divisions and then proceed to the Tagliamento (Maps 23,35). Different from previous experiences of the *fanti* here, there was no front, nor any enemy trenches. The *fanti* would be on the receiving end, while in the past they had undertaken the *attacco frontale* on enemy trenches being the only maneuver that they had been taught. Everyone was afraid of a Conrad offensive in the Trentino (Map 14 A)

As dawn arrived the defenders of the Rombon and M. Cuklja attempted to avoid encirclement by starting a painful retreat westward along the desolate snow-covered Altipiano del Canin. Their objective was Sella Prevala and V. Raccolana. Pursuing them was the CCXVI Brigade (*Edelweiss*), while the CCXVII Brigade proceeded along the left side of the V. Uccea attempting to climb to Resiutta along a non-existent road finally arriving at M. Guarda situated on the summit opposite the head of the V. Resia (Maps 13, 23). Periodically, over the last eighty years, the remains of those brave men from both sides of the trench have been found when the icy mountains feel like giving them up.

Krauss Group (I Corps)

Objectives were now outlined for today:

> German Jäger Division would maintain readiness
> to attack on the slopes of the Polovnik.

Twenty-second Schützen would assault the Stol then proceed beyond, always linked with theTwelfth Silesian
Fifty-fifth Infantry Division would proceed toward Caporetto
Edelweiss would push forward as noted above, while one of its brigades (217) would follow the Twenty-second Schützen

At 0800, the Twenty-second Schützen having crossed the Podcela Bridge, marched rapidly toward the Saga Strait. Leaving their knapsacks behind at 0500 they started to climb the Stol, meeting little resistance (Map 23). A few days prior the king and Cadorna had visited this fortress declaring it to be impregnable. Taking each defensive line in turn, led by Capt. Charwat of the 6 Company by midnight, the III/1 Kaiserchützen reached the 5000 feet summit. There had been no walkways connecting the trenches but each defensive point was protected by another. Charwat was lucky in that his men found an opening in the barbed wire and poured through. The fate of M. Stol and the rear Breginj basin was sealed, while the danger to P. di Montemaggiore and the Passo Tanamea started to increase (Maps 13, 23).[6] Krafft later wrote, "The Italians had no reason whatever to abandon the Stol especially on its northern part."[7]

Observers of the Imperial Fifty-fifth Infantry Division noted that Italians deployed on the Polovnik were withdrawing attempting to find salvation on the Isonzo (Maps 14,16,17). Troops crossed the river via the Idersko bridge then proceeded to Caporetto and Staroselo. Most of the attacking troops spent the night on the left bank at Ladra. Marching behind the Imperial Fifty-fifth Infantry Division was the German Jäger Division. Troops which were at Podcela, crossed the river on a newly arrived pontoon bridge, reached Saga, proceeding on the right side of the river to the hamlet of Ternovo, finding warehouses full of food and wine (Maps 15, 23). As usual, Cadorna wrote a letter to his son, Raffaele, an Italian army officer, wherein he stated that his troops did not fight.[8] How could he come to this conclusion? What about the hundreds of thousands of dead in the past twenty nine months? This really gives witness to how far away he was mentally concerning his troops. Caviglia wrote that Cadorna was wrong in accusing the soldiers of cowardice. The blame for the disaster laid squarely on the shoulders of the command structure.[9] How could the illiterate *fanti* be blamed for the enemy's success? For over two years in frontal infantry attacks, they had done their duty assaulting machine guns.

Italian IV Corps

This unit lost nearly the whole Forty-sixth and Forty-third Divisions as well as all its artillery. Remaining were the remnants: the Fiftieth Infantry Division, the newly arrived 282° and some units from the mauled Thirty-fourth Infantry Division. By midnight, Arrighi still had not received the (in)famous order to abandon the Saga sent by Montuori. During the night there was a retreat to positions on M. Stol and M. Guarda to protect the head of the V. Resia (Map 23). Division command was installed on M. Stol. Arrighi felt that M. Stol should be defended, and access to the V. Uccea be blocked. In a classic "mailed fist" thrust, the enemy attacked the Sol, not with small units, but *with the whole Twenty second Schützen Division.*[10] Unable to stop the enemy, Arrighi decided to again withdraw based on information he had received at 1520 from the IV Corps. Protecting the withdrawal toward Platischis were units of the *Genova* of the Forty-sixth Infantry Division (Map 23).

Problematic now for the Comando Supremo was the unsealable breach between the Friulian Plain and the Carnia, stretching from the Globocak to M. Cergnala (Map 14). Arriving at the front was the XXX Corps, too tired to accomplish anything, along with the *Potenza* with which it was hoped to start forming anew the Thirty-fourth Infantry Division.[11] Troops arrived tired, disoriented, lacking machine guns, munitions and manpower. Battalions down to 300 men were asked to close the breach between M. Stol and M.

Matajur (Map 19). Remaining in the IV Corps was only the Fiftieth Infantry Division deployed (Map 23):

1. Headquarters at Za Mielem (northern slopes of M. Stol)
2. *Alpini* troops *Ceva* between M. Guarda and Za Mielem
3. 280° plus one battalion of the *Friuli* blocking Val. Uccea

The remnants of the *Friuli* minus the I/88° and the *Alpini* Monte Argentara, deployed at Za Mielem.

The Thirty-fourth Infantry Division had its headquarters at Boriana, as did the *Potenza.* Its few troops were deployed as follows:

271° on the upper and middle Stol.
272° barricading from Potoke-S. Volario.
273° barricading Robic, the old border town.[12] (Map 19).

Other remnants of the XXXII and XXVIII Bersaglieri Battalions retreated to the Stol. The Comando Supremo had no troops to close the breach in V. Uccea, but did give the II Army the Sixty-third Infantry Division (*Vicenza,* three regiments), plus the *Massa Carrara,* all of which formed the XXVIII Corps. To close the breach in the Val Uccea, the Comando Supremo appealed to the Zona Carnia Command for help, knowing it could not. With the defender's confusion as well as lack of reserves the attackers overcame resistance between M. Mia and M. Canin resulting in opening the way toward a *Strategic Success.* The Austro-Germans were advancing too rapidly. Decisions made were relayed to defensive positions already occupied by the advancing enemy. Montuori now ordered Lt. Gen. Pier Luigi Sagramoso to set up a defense at the Torre Creek with the Thirteenth, Sixteenth, Twenty-first, Twenty-third, Thirtieth, and Sixtieth Infantry Divisions which were reserves (Maps 35, 40).[13] Plans had been made to block the valleys, but the attackers were coming along the tops.

Clearly describing the chaos and destruction of the IV Corps is its War Diary. At 1140, Cavaciocchi receiving news that the position of Prvi Hum was lost, deciding to retreat to Platischis and Nimis (Map 23). Instead orders from Montuori obligated him to remain in Breginj. At 1300, informed that the enemy was descending from the Stol onto Breginj, he departed, but realizing it was a false alarm returned. Later Arrighi realized he could not hold the Stol, and withdrew. When Boccacci, Chief of Staff of the IV Corps called the Fiftieth Infantry Division headquarters, a voice answered in German. Cavaciocchi now ordered the Thirty-fourth Division to defend Breginj, linking up with the Fiftieth on the left, assuring its retreat. Yesterday, the Thirty-fourth had no troops but now had been assigned three regiments (the 271°,272° and 273°), of the reserve *Potenza*, deploying them from the upper ridge of the Stol to the Natisone River Valley floor (Map 23). These depleted units were to block access to Breginj and garrison a four mile front (Map 23).[14] P. di Montemaggiore and M. Cavallo were to be defended by the arriving *Alpini* battalions as well as units of the Fiftieth and Thirty-fourth Divisions (Map 23). An officer of the Thirty-sixth Infantry Division (Zona Carnia, XII Corps), arrived, reporting that the Stol held only enemy troops.[15] At 1620 the IV Corps telephoned the II Army that it had no troops to defend the areas assigned to it. It was supposed to garrison from Montemaggiore to M. Mia (Map 13). The Thirty-fourth Infantry Division garrisoned the saddle between M. Joanaz and M. Carnizza in the *linea ad oltranza* sector against enemy incursions.[16] While walking along the road toward Nimis, Cavaciocchi met Major General Asclepio Gandolfi (Thirty-first Infantry Division) driving along who notified him that he was assuming command of the IV Corps (Map 23).[17] So much for communication from the Comando Supremo. By 1200 the Austro-Germans had gone through the Saga, broken through the Val Uccea and aimed for the Val Resia (Map 23). Troops of Thirty-fourth Infantry Division with the Fiftieth Infantry Division on their right, deployed between M. Matajur and M. Mia and were obligated to retreat to the Breginj basin. *In a strategic sense the attackers had already won a victory.* The objectives of the A.O.K. had been achieved, while those of Krafft and Below were more ambitious. Below realized that Cadorna was heading for a disaster.[18] Once beyond the Saga Strait he would be in the Val Uccea from which the upper Tagliamento River was easily accessible. Proceeding southward along its west bank he would be behind the Italian troops and a new threat to the *Zona Carnia* (Maps 15,23).

Zona Carnia Command

Cadorna ordered the Sixty-third Infantry Divisions (III Army reserve) plus six *Alpini* and five bicycle battalions to reinforce its right wing.

Stein Group

Since October 22, Below had given this group the following orders:

> Twelfth Silesian would proceed along the valley floor especially the north side with its task to facilitate the advance of the Austro-Hungarian Fiftieth Infantry Division. Selisce had to be captured. The Silesians were to occupy Idersko west of Kamno, then proceed and occupy the Matajur together with the Alpenkorps (*Map 16*).
>
> Austro-Hungarian Fiftieth Infantry Division would occupy the line between Vrsno and Krn, then occupy the terrain between the right border of the attack sector of corps and Idersko, then proceed together with the Twelfth Silesian toward the northwest slope of the Matajur as well as M. Mia (*M. Mia*).

To accomplish this rapidly, it was ordered that knapsacks were lightened for the front line troops so they would not be tired when they arrived at the Matajur.

The III Mountain Brigade (Austro-Hungarian Fiftieth Infantry Division) eliminated all resistance on M. Nero and Kozljak while at M. Plece the *Alpini* M. Albergian Battalion still resisted. Arriving at Robic the XV Brigade started to climb the slopes of M. Mia to conquer that stronghold of the middle V. Natisone (Maps 13, 19). To its left, it linked up with the Alpenkorps which had the task of occupying M. Matajur. One column proceeded to Breginj to link up with the Twenty-second Schützen descending from the Stol (Map 23) In the afternoon units of the 63° proceeded from Robic to Stupizza inflicting heavy losses on a cavalry unit which attempted to block them (Map 23). Other Silesian units arrived at the hamlet of Golobi, where the Italians counterattacked suffering heavy losses. At 1600 white rockets were fired off to the left, denoting the arrival of the AlpenKorps at Sella di Luico, to the rear of the defending Italians. By 1800 Luico was in German hands (Map 14). During the morning, units of the AlpenKorps were mobilizing at Passo Zagradan, while the 1st Jäger, was still busy on Costa Duole and by nightfall had reached the Podklabuc. As Krafft later wrote, "The Italians were deployed on the crest of the Kolovrat, just in front of M. Kuk di Luico knowing that should this fall, the whole defensive system would crumble." Advancing toward the Kolovrat crest were three battalions of the *Infanterie Leibregiment* (Bavarian Guards) with the Würrtemberg Mountain Battalion (WMB) on their right. Realizing that the assault would be long and difficult Lt. Rommel of the WMB offered to climb the undefended steep north side. The main Italian position ran along the highest part of the mountain from this ridge to the several hundred feet higher ridge of the Matajur (Map 14). Setting out in darkness with two rifle companies and one machine gun company he overpowered Italian sentries and proceeded along the slopes parallel to the Italian positions above. Picking an assault point he climbed to his left taking many prisoners but lost his surprise. Up on the Kolovrat ridge the Italians were massing for a counterattack. He placed one light machine gun far off to the left on lower ground and waited for the counterattack. When it came this fired into the Italian flanks while his troops counterattacked capturing a whole battalion. He soon was on M. Kuk then descended toward Luico signaling his presence toward to units led by Major Eischorn which were held up at Golobi (Map 18). He was soon far out in front of the Guards who were proceeding along the Italian military road west of the Kolovrat and Kuk arriving at Sella di Luico, descending onto onto Polava and Cepletischis (Map 18). This blocked an Italian brigade proceeding to Luico which was being pursued by units of the Twelfth Silesian and was looking for refuge on the Matajur which the Rommel Detachment would soon assault. Rommel was now two miles behind Italian lines. With these infiltration tactics as he would in the Second World War he had created a narrow corridor deep into Italian lines resulting in collapse of enemy morale as well as inability to receive supplies. Rommel had learned well the lessons taught by Krafft.

Defending the Kolovrat was the *Arno* whose commander wrote that the enemy's attack was completely a surprise. Years later, Capello wrote that Maj. Gen. Negri di Lamporo stated that his brigade was surprised, but the previous day Golobi and M. Piatto were lost. How could these nearby positions be lost and not known to him.?[19]

Italian VII Corps

By 1300 the Sixty-second Infantry Division realized that it could not link up with the IV Corps. It had left the Trentino to arrive on the Kolovrat and Matajur the night of October 24, not knowing the terrain nor that the Silesians was in the neighborhood. Bongiovanni reported to Montuori that should the enemy break through at Sella di Luico, the road to Cividale and Savogna would be open. Thirty minutes later, the commander of the left wing of the II Army reported that the last line of resistance (*linea di resistenza ad oltranza*), for the VII Corps was line M. Matajur-M. Kuk (*linea dell'armata)* plus, the Luico-Kolovrat-M. Podklabuc-M. Planino line with the defensive line of Rucchin. No one knew that the Podklabuc was in enemy hands making *this whole defense worthless.* On October 26, Capello made the line Korada-Castelmonte-M. Purgessimo-M. Mladesena, which was the last defense before Cividale would fall (Map 22). All Italian plans now started to unravel.

At 0800, Capello telegraphed Montuori and commanders of the IV, VII and XXVII Corps the following message. "It is now certain that enemy units which have entered our lines, are weak enemy forces. Officers and men should come to the realization of this and the just evaluation not only to resist but to throw them back. All must subscribe to this concept."[20] The OIR described this as passionate and vehement with Capello still having illusions. It noted that much of the euphoria was due to the conduct of corps commanders who would order counterattacks, giving the impression of possible success when there was none. The "weak units" had destroyed the *Napoli*, *Elba*, *Arno* and kicked the *Firenze* off the Podklabuc as it thought it was climbing M. Piatto. The IV Bersaglieri Brigade deployed at Luico fought and lost it to the Germans, retook it in the a.m to lose it later in the day. At 1100 in a meeting at Cividale with Cadorna, Capello felt that now there had to be a general pull back, and expressed this via a personal letter hand-delivered to Cadorna at 1330. In it he recognized that the enemy had broken through in the sectors of the IV and XXVII Corps and the Bainsizza sector was becoming untenable. "If some units have fought, others have not." He felt that a retreat to the Tagliamento was indicated. Here Capello seemed to want to indicate in writing that an enormous disaster was in the making, and wished to remedy it as soon as possible. Febrile from a recurring case of chronic nephritis, in the afternoon he left for the military hospital at Verona.[21] Before leaving for the hospital, he signed the execution warrants of eight men belonging to the 57° (*Abruzzi),* whom the *Carabinieri* had surprised making disheartening phrases to their comrades in the trenches.[22] Cadorna agreed to the Tagliamento option and asked him to write an evaluation of the status of his army. Thus we saw a complete about face by Capello concerning the battle in just a few hours. Caviglia later wrote, "He was sickly, but did not wish to leave his post and ceded it to Montuori only when the fever was above 38 C° (100.4 F). The Comando Supremo should not have allowed this. On October 24, even with the fever, he directed operations, but on that day his physical condition underwent such a collapse that he had to leave his command. It was a great misfortune for him because afterwards, he was subject to unjust accusations. It would have been better for him if he had died at his post. With the letter, there started to be the beginning of a movement to place the complete fault of all errors committed in the battle squarely on the shoulders of the II Army commander. With this, an injustice was committed which still weighs on the Italian conscience."[23] Before going on sick leave, Capello telephoned Gabba at Comando Supremo headquarters, where he was told that the breach was too large to repair. As requested, he sent Cadorna a precise summary of the status of the Italian II Army.

"I confirm in writing what I have already told you. Having crashed through the IV Corps defenses, the enemy has spread out to the left bank of the Isonzo and crossed the river at Caporetto. It is now crossing at Kred and advancing on the Stol *(Map 23)*. The enemy also has attacked the left bank of the river, has taken the Jeza and is pushing against Luico. Other enemy units having left Tolmino are proceeding toward Ronzina and pressuring the defenses of the XXIV and II Corps. The situation is grave. The left wing of the II Army has been ruptured, with the middle pierced in many sectors. The troops on the Bainsizza must withdraw, they cannot stay there. If many units have fought well and done their duty, others have not, or have resisted in a very small way. In this situation, I feel that it is my duty to explain to Your Excellency the question, if with the situation as it is, would it not be better in the national interest, not to waste divisions in attempting to re-establish a situation already hopeless, but to keep them with equipment to dominate future events. This is the only decision to be taken at this time, even though it is a painful one. A withdrawal should be started with a good screening rear guard. Withdraw to where? To the Torre or to the Tagliamento? This painful decision is the one to take at this time. Logistical decisions must be made immediately to start this move."[24] By the time Capello entered his auto to go to the military hospital, the Kolovrat had been lost, the Fiftieth Infantry Division was evacuating the Stol, while the Silesian had entered the Val Natisone (Map 35). Had Cadorna given the orders to withdraw to the Tagliamento River as he first indicated, hundreds of thousands of Italian troops would have escaped the trap. Instead he vacillated. One must remember about past Italian politico-military history. In 1898 as the army proposed to withdraw in time of war to certain defensible postions there had been a great hue and outcry.[25] Non-military men could not understand that abandoning the *suolo sacro* could make tactical sense. This had always been used in warfare, and even was being used by Vienna's forces which retired to the so-called Military Borders. Capello gave verbal orders to the XXIV Corps to withdraw. Montuori issued orders that his army have two different wings, with the left commanded by Gen. Etna consisting of the remnants of IV, VII, XXVII Corps as well as the reserve XXVIII Corps (Map 29). The latter unit was under the command of Lt. Gen. Alessandro Saporiti with its Twenty-fifth and Fifty-third Divisions between the IV and VII Corps. The right wing was commanded by Lt. Gen. Giacinto Ferrero with the II, VI, and XXIV Corps. Krafft wrote that the Italians had thrown in their reserves against the XIV Army peace meal, with no concrete plan in its northern sector.[26] The redeployment would be in two phases, with a pause on the Torre Creek, using the XXX Corps with its four divisions of eight brigades (Maj. Gen. Pier Luigi Sagramoso) as a rear-guard. Cadorna had agreed in principle to this plan, except in the speed factor. He felt that the retreat should be slower holding up the enemy and saving the artillery. At 0800 Cadorna met with Aosta to elaborate orders which were later written down. He also assigned the Twentieth and Sixty-third Infantry Divisions to the left wing of the II Army. A summary of the orders follows:

> Take the medium and large non-mobile artillery
> to Treviso as quickly as possible.

Take the medium and large mobile artillery west of the *Vallone* keeping in mind its future possible redeployment to the Piave (*Map 5).*
For now leave east of the *Vallone* the few field artillery pieces indispensable for defense *(Maps 5,12).*
With two reserve divisions garrison the line of the *Vallone* (*Southeast of Tolmino*) so as to protect the retreat should it be ordered (*Map 5)*
Should it become necessary take all the steps to effect a redeployment to west of the Tagliamento and to now assign the access roads of the bridges of S. Giorgio di Nogara-Latisana and Delizia *(Map 29).*

The OIR noted that Luico was lost at 1800 by the IV Bersaglieri Brigade which then set up defenses in the mid-V. Rieca near Cepletischis, extending its left wing to M. Craguenza to link up with the *Salerno* on M. Matajur but was unable to link up on its right with the *Firenze* (Map 22). The Third Infantry Division deployed:

Arno from M. Kuk di Luico to M. Piatto (Map 17).
Napoli with three surviving battalions around the Passo Zagradan and on the slopes of the Podklabuc
Firenze with four battalions reinforced the *Napoli* on the defensive line of the right border of the head of the V. Judrio.
Elba deployed on the crests between the basins of Cosizza and Judrio having as a hinge in its rear, the large M. Kum (Map 17).

The *Napoli* and *Firenze* had vainly counterattacked on the Podklabuc. The *Arno* (subsequently accused of cowardice and almost completely captured), was attacked on one flank by the Alpenkorps advancing on the roadway Zagradan-Luico, and on the other flank by the WMB (Maps 17,18).). Forced to withdraw it uncovered a flank of the IV Bersaglieri Brigade at Luico. As they withdrew toward Cepletischis a flank of the *Salerno* deployed on the Matajur was left unprotected (Map 17).[27] The survivors of the *Arno, Napoli, Firenze* plus survivors of the Nineteenth Infantry Division assembled on the spurs between Rieca and Cosizza under the command of the Third Infantry Division (Map 19). The *Elba* was deployed between M. Kum and the hamlet of Rucchin.

By noon, what would later be described as a "military strike" started to occur. Men were taking off their uniforms, donning civilian clothes and started to walk home toward Sicily or Bari as the case might be.[28] As reserve troops marched toward the front they were greeted with the cries of *Crumiri* by the newly dressed civilians.[29]

Berrer Group

At dawn, the 3° Jäger (Two Hundredth Infantry Division), moved from the Jeza along the Italian military road toward Podklabuc, reaching M. Natpricciar at noon, where it captured ten 210 mm. howitzers (Maps 19, 20). By noon it arrived at Cappella Slieme where it linked up with the 4° Jäger. Halting further advancement was the garrison on M. La Cima which fired on the roadway. Entrusted to eliminate it was the XI/4° Jäger which was accomplished by 1800. Having removed these obstacles, both Jäger units proceeded toward the villages below Drenchia, Trinco, Lase, Prapotnizza and Clabuzzaro (Map 16). From Ciginj (Cighino), the 5° Jäger climbed toward the Jeza via Jesenkak, while behind it the Twenty-sixth Division proceeded to reinforce the Two Hundredth Infantry Division (Maps 19, 20).

Austro-German Scotti Group

Early in the morning the Austro-Hungarian First Infantry Division attacked the defensive line Globocak-Cicer-Vrh-Subjuk and broke through by 1100 (Map 20). By eve, the right bank of the Isonzo between Doblar and Ajba was under their control as well as Ronzina (Map 12 for geography) Similar events happened to the V. Judrio (left side) between Ostry Kras and Kambresko. The Fifth Brandenburg Infantry Division climbing from Ciginj onto Varda Vrh met no resistance. These men plus the VIII Grenadiers aimed for M. Kum (Map 17). The Fifty-Second Infantry Division maneuvered along the slopes of the Colle Glava arriving to the south of M. Kum to support the coming assault by the VIII Grenadiers while the XII Grenadiers were bivouacked at Pusno, to the rear. By evening the XIV Army realized that the Italian defenses were crumbling, but Globocak still had not been taken.

Italian XXVII Corps

From Clabuzzaro Villani (Nineteenth Infantry Division), withdrew to Lombai accompanied by many stragglers. On the way he met many unarmed Italian troops chanting "the war is finished, we are civilians now." So complete had been this division's destruction that the staff of the Comando Supremo felt it had been swallowed by the earth as there had been no report from it. The destroyed *Alpini* Val d'Adige Battalion had only fifty survivors. Survivors included the *Puglie* (1500 rifles), the intact I and V Bersaglieri Brigades, (Lt. Gen. Giuseppe Boriani of which much will be written concerning the First Battle of the Asiago Plateau) and the survivors of the *X Gruppo Alpini.* At 0620 the commander of the latter unit had notified XXVII Corps that he had noted a 280 mm. howitzer emplaced on the road to Kambresko awaiting Badoglio's orders, as well as noting that units of the *Vicenza* were defending the retreat of the heavy artillery from Doblar. Badoglio answered with the following message: "Phonogram No. 1946 Answer to communication of 0620, stop. As soon as you are sure that the *Treviso* occupies the whole Subjuk, you shall place yourself in reserve, stop. Keep in touch with this command at Liga stop." The brigade occupied Cicer Vrh while the enemy had stopped on the line Krad Vrh-Cukli Vrh (Map 20). The Subjuk was the south ridge of the Globocak on the other side of the river. In his book Krafft, noted that the Italians still had no clear concept of the offensive, and therefore launched their reserves too far to the north in a fragmentary way. The Austro-German plan was to quickly get to the heights on the margin of the Friulian plain before the Italians could mount a steep resistance.

0645 Badoglio notified II Army headquarters that the whole Globocak up to Srednje was in Italian hands and he had established communications with M. Kum and Srednje (Map 20). The XXVII ordered the *Treviso* to occupy the spur Cicer Vrh-Subjuk descending from Globocak onto Ronzina in the Isonzo Valley. The I Bersaglieri Brigade deployed on the Globocak, while the V was told to establish the line of Colle Glava-Pusno and therefore on the line Srednje-Globocak-Cicer Vrh (Map 20). As the OIR narrated, "There was a continual and methodical shelling of Italian rear and front line positions by the enemy while the XXVII Corps attempted to reinforce its positions." Despite severe attacks by the 52° Brandenburg, Hill No. 678 garrisoned by the 12° Bersaglieri held on.

1915 After the loss of the crest of Globocak-Cicer-Vrh held by the 21° Bersaglieri and the71° (*Puglie)*, Badoglio ordered that troops start to redeploy onto the Korada starting at 2330 in order to block the entrance of the Judrio into the plains (Map 12, and Map 35 for reference). With the loss of the Globocak, there was a danger of the Italian II and III Armies being completely surrounded. Troops across the Isonzo and particularly those on the Bainsizza were in serious danger. *By now, except for its staff, the XXVII Corps ceased to exist.* Its three divisions on the left bank of the Isonzo had been detached to the XXIV Corps, with the remnants of the Nineteenth Infantry Division attached to the VII Corps.

Italian XXIV Corps (Lt. Gen. Enrico Caviglia)

This unit had not been exposed to the Austro-German avalanche but now had to retreat to the *linea D* which was the *linea di resistenza ad oltranza.* Aware of the battle situation from communications from Badoglio and Capello its commander spent the evening napping by the telephone. This instrument would bring the loss or salvation of 20,000 men in a bulge in the Italian lines across the Isonzo. Fate had put them in his hands. Becoming aware of the situation of the XXVII Corps divisions (Sixty-fifth, Sixty-fourth, and Twenty-second Infantry), which had been cut off and seemingly forgotten by Capello, he finally obtained permission to withdraw with them (along with his Forty-ninth, Sixty-eighth and Tenth Infantry Divisions) for a total of sixty-four battalions with artillery.[30] Boroevic's troops were finally on the move. Units of the Austro-Hungarian I Corps led by GdI Koschak were pushing down the Isonzo forcing Italian troops withdrawing from the Bainsizza southward even outflanking those deployed on the Globocak (for geography please see Map 12, Vol. I, Map 17 this volume). While troops deployed on the Altipiano della Bainsizza were retreating in an orderly fashion on the line Veliki-Vrh-Na Gradu-Oscedrik-Jelenik, those belonging to the XXVII Corps were still at their original posts across the Isonzo beyond the Avscek Creek (Map 12). At 1500, Caviglia received the order to withdraw to the right bank, while the II Corps was retreating to the Vodice. There was still hope to hold the line Globocak-Liga-Korada-Plava-Palieva and not move the VI Corps deployed around Gorizia. At dawn the remnants of the three divisions previously in the XXVII Corps, slowly redeployed onto the valley of Krestenica southwest of Anhovo in the Vrh basin behind the Oscedrik (Maps 4,12).[31] The *Roma* (Sixty-fifth Infantry Division) was given the task of deploying on the line Auzza-NaGradu to protect these movements (Map 12).[32] The Forty-ninth Infantry Division deployed onto the Vrh basin, leaving the Auzza-Loga road free. Caviglia ordered Maj. Gen. Vigliani (Forty-ninth Infantry Division) to relay to other commanders that the withdrawal should start at 0200. Arriving at Sixty-fourth Infantry Division headquarters at midnight, he met with Gen. Coffaro the commander, who told him that the redeployment would not take place until 0600. Fearing enemy wire taps of telephone lines, the orders had been relayed via dispatch couriers. In sending written orders, Coffaro *erroneously stated that the Roma had surrendered. Actually it had suffered heavy losses.* This erroneous information was routinely sent to II Army headquarters by Caviglia resulting that instead of being honored, the *Roma* was labeled as cowardly. With the *Roma* providing the rear guard, three regiments which formed the *Belluno* reached the Auzza rail tunnel, thus gaining the right side of the Isonzo to arrive at the entrance of the Krestinica Valley (Map 12). In later years Caviglia acknowledged his error in forwarding erroneous information.[33] Pushed by politicians and probably the king, the Caporetto Inquiry Commission did not dig deep into the subject, probably to prevent inquiries into the actions of the XXVII Corps commanded by the king's favorite general. Slowly it started to dawn on the Comando Supremo that serious problems were developing. At the northern end of the front, the *Edelweiss* had reached the Uccea Creek from which as noted they could easily go via the Passo Tanamea to the Torre Creek, Tarcento; then via Val Resia-Val Fella to the upper reaches of the Tagliamento River (Maps 23, 35). Easily crossing the river in the upper sectors, they could then proceed southward along the west bank to fall on the rear and north (left flank) of the Italian defenders along the river (Maps 27,29,35). Accomplishing this, the Zona Carnia troops would be in danger as well as the southern sector of the Italian II Army. The Italian armies needed time to stop, catch their breath and establish defenses. Rivers such as the Tagliamento and Piave were ideal for this purpose. With the heavy rains in the mountains, streams that had been creeks now were raging rivers. To put things in proper perspective, Austro-German forces had reached the west bank of the Isonzo, gone along the valley to Caporetto, through the Saga Strait while Italian forces were still on the Bainsizza east of the river (Maps 4,12,23).

By 1430, the II Army ordered the redeployment of the XXIV Corps onto the right bank of the Isonzo, in two phases, thus abandoning the Altipiano della Bainsizza. The first phase was finished by 1500 but with the enemy incursions into the Vrh Basin and Ronzina, the planned deployment between Globocak and the Isonzo was nullified.

The only task left to the XXIV Corps was to withdraw along the line at M. Korada-Liga (V. Judrio) in the dark, crossing the Isonzo at Loga, Anhovo and Canale, then destroy the bridges (Map 12). Caviglia installed his headquarters at Debenje one mile north east of M. Korada behind the crest between the Judrio and the Isonzo. At midnight, the VIII Corps and the command of Gorizia was transferred to the III Army.

1630

The Comando Supremo sent the Zona Carnia Command a telegram noting that should the II and III Armies have to retreat to the Tagliamento, the XII Corps would have to retreat to the Carnic PreAlp line, linking up with the II Army at P. di Montemaggiore while the contact with the IV Army would be at Casera Razzo (Maps 23, 28). Tassoni was ordered to be ready for any eventuality in the sector, but not distribute the orders. On Sept. 1, Cadorna had issued directives: "The Zona Carnia, due to its position constitutes the linkage between the IV and the II Army. Above all, it constitutes the security for movements of troops between the Piave and Isonzo, south of the Carnic PreAlps" (Map 2). Naturally, ditto for the movements from the Isonzo to the Piave.[34] As Montuori transferred his command post to Udine, at 2030 Col. Ugo Cavallero, the Comando Supremo's Operations Chief arrived there posing the question, "Was the retreat to the Tagliamento necessary?"[35] Querying his corps commanders he received answers by 0005 on October 26. The *modus operandi* of the Italian military hierarchy was to take no responsibility. By querying his corps commanders, he spread the blame, if any. They in turn, answered, "We shall resist," knowing that an answer other than that would lead to immediate dismissal. Receiving the results of the poll Cadorna issued orders to hold at the Torre Creek.[36] The orders to subordinates had the preamble "With previous authorization of the Comando Supremo," to determine the holding line at P. di Montemaggiore-M. Iauer-M. Joanaz-M. Mladesena-M. Purgessimo-Castelmonte-M. Korada-Paljevo-Kuk-Vodice-M. Santo-Sella di Dol-Salcano-Gorizia (this was an elaborate defense setup which covered a great deal of ground and never used, Maps 4. 12. 23. 35). This order cancelled the preparations already under way to retreat to the Tagliamento, and deployed troops as indicated. It had taken two years of bloody fighting to take the conquered terrain, and in a few hours all had changed. Cadorna felt he could hold if he held the line from Punta di Montemaggiore to the Korada. Later, he wrote that this was why he rescinded the order to retreat to the Tagliamento.

By the end of the day, fifteen Italian and four Austro-Hungarian planes had been downed. The German Air Service suffered four casualties.[37] Thousands of prisoners, plus a great deal of war booty had been captured. To assist in the breakout into the plains, Berendt placed large howitzers at Caporetto to fire on Cividale twelve miles away, as well as on S. Lucia to fire on the Korada to the southwest, also twelve miles away. Giving an idea of Italian morale, Krauss reported 1500 Italian prisoners streaming back to his rear line without a guard.[38] The *I Armée Isonzo* still had not moved, while the *II Armée Isonzo* had just started with its I Corps. To avoid traffic jams, towards evening, Below ordered Krauss to halt the Jäger Division and send it in the direction of the Passo Tanamea (Map 23). From there it could proceed to either Gemona, Tarcento or Venzone. Airplanes were used as reconnaissance as well to support ground troops. There was now talk in Austro-Hungarian headquarters of halting the offensive, but Below and his staff just laughed.[39]

1947

Cadorna sent his (in) famous telegram to War Minister Giardino "Enemy offensive has resumed on the line Saga-Stol-Luico and on the Altipiano di Lom. Successful enemy attack at Luico and Auzza. Enormous losses in missing and cannons. About ten regiments have surrendered without fighting. I see the outline of a disaster against which I shall fight to the last. I have arranged to resist as much as possible in the mountains and on the Carso and have arranged, without issuing orders, for the retreat to the Tagliamento. I ask you to inform the government, asking that the whole bulletin not be made public." Upon receiving this Giardino resigned, and left for the battlefront. By evening, long columns of refugees, and soldiers were retreating soutwestward. Riding along with them in his auto accompanied by Porro and Cadorna was the worried king. The trio on their way to a war council at Bergogna but could not get through due to road congestion. When seeing soldiers without rifles Cadorna would exclaim, "Why doesn't someone execute them?" Porro would just shrug his shoulders.[40] This again showed how distant he was from direct involvement with the troops. Why did he not leave his auto and take a direct hand in the withdrawal? Obviously his help was needed. The Comando Supremo sent the reserve XXX Corps to the scene, one division to Torreano, the other to Nimis (Maps 13, 23,). Soldiers among the crowds of refugees were throwing their rifles away, removing their military insignia and exclaiming, "Long live Russia, the war is over, we are all civilians now." The *fanti* were anxious to get home to help with the harvest as the government was giving no help to families at home. Some of the (un) lucky men were wounded, missing an arm or leg, but how could they work the fields in that condition? Slowly the peasant mind took hold. It is the author's contention that Caporetto was partly a result of the *terrible home and battlefront conditions* as well as the poor training and ineptitude of the officer class. The *fanti* had shown that they knew how to die. Otherwise, why did the infantry *two weeks later* engage, hold and die fighting the Austro-Germans on the Grappa and Asiago Plateau by which time the *fanti* had been promised different conditions on the battlefield and at home. One must take nothing away from the new tactics of the Germans, as well as their daring skill and courage but propaganda at the front was having its effect on men who did not know that the nation of Italy existed. Even Lenin had had his part in the propaganda war in Italy.[41] As one writer wrote, "The attack! The attack of this war is one of the most terrible things that a human mind can think of, so terrible that since yesterday I dream of nothing else but only to remove it from the head of my son."[42] Daily the *fanti* had been asked to perform multiple assaults on enemy positions. Similar orders on the Western Front had led to the French Army mutiny in April 1917 (See vol. I, chapter XXXII, Decimation). In Rome, at the Parliament, the Foreign Minister was analyzing the Pontifical Note for the members. The Parliament had heard the Hon. Francesco Saverio Nitti state that a Marxist revolution was not technically possible. Some members then thought of the novel, *I Promessi Sposi* by Alessandro Manzoni in which Don Ferrante noted that Bubonic Plague was not a substance and therefore did not exist. He died of the plague. And in fact, if in the Friuli, one was at the beginning of an agony, in Rome, the death knell was already ringing. The king was thinking of abdicating to avoid the humiliation of surrender.[43]

Comando Supremo

Early in the morning as was his usual wont, Cadorna wrote letters to his family members. He was now minimally aware of the problem, but not of the impending disaster. To his son he wrote, "How can one maneuver when one cannot count on anyone. How can the disaster be repaired? If things go wrong in this dear country, they will curse me."[44] To his daughter Carla he wrote, "I am serene . . . . Often one goes toward his destiny which is in the hands of God. . . . There has been no attack on the Carso."[45] In the p.m. he wrote again to his son Raffaele he wrote, "The troops do not fight. I have ordered a retreat to the Tagliamento. My conscience is clear." Between the two letters, Cadorna realized that a catastrophe was in the making.[46]

0700

With Gabba his Operations Chief Cadorna studied the defense of M. Korada garrisoned by the XXIV Corps which protected the rear of the III Army. Gabba felt that assisted by the VII Corps the Korada could be held. Feeling that there was now a military strike Cadorna did not share that opinion and ordered a withdrawal to the right side of the Isonzo.

By 0830, Cadorna met with Aosta, Lt. Gen. Giuseppe Vaccari the Chief of Staff of the III Army and Col. Montasini giving them orders to prepare to retreat beyond the Piave.[47] As he exited the meeting the Generalissimo met Gatti. Placing his hand on the shoulder he declared "The army is tired, it has been polluted by enemy propaganda. The troops do not fight, shameful; I have troops on the Bainsizza which are in danger."[48] The colonel noted that this was the most important talk which he had ever had in his life. Saga and Caporetto had been lost, entire divisions were incommunicado, all due to the rapid enemy advance.

Home Front Events

Italian Home Front morale was still good. In Palermo Countess Annetta Tasca outfitted a hospital for the wounded, while in Milano the Vallardi (publishing) family lent a large villa to the government for recuperation of the war-wounded. The Edoardo Bianchi Co. donated an armored car to the army.

Pertinent Events on October 25

1. In the strategic sphere, the most important event was the low morale of the troops, as well as deficiency in armaments. Without good morale, equipment and training one does not fight. At Caporetto illiterate, ill-trained and ill-led troops could not handle the maneuver warfare not knowing what a 90° turn was, often not knowing a left from a right turn.
2. For over two years, the Italian Army mind-set was on offense not defense. Its only maneuver was the *attacco frontale.* It could not handle enemy tactics.
3. Badoglio disobeyed orders to keep the majority of his forces on the right bank of the Isonzo and did not deploy the *Napoli* on the Foni Strait floor, but rather high up to observe. Using the Volzana trap theory he witheld permission for his artillery to fire. When he gave it, he had neither guns nor communications.
4. There were two open breaches. The first between the Zona Carnia and the II Army, second between the IV Corps and VII Corps. The first produced the huge breach

between M. Cergnala and the Globocak (Map 14), while the second resulted in the Twelfth Silesian *strolling* along the banks of the Isonzo River with the IV Corps deployed along the mountain range going northwest of Tolmino and the VII Corps on the Kolovrat (Map 14).

5. Reserves were not fresh troops operating as a unit. Upon receiving orders to march to the battle sectors, they would arrive tired, demoralized and deprived of artillery and basic trench tools. The only reserve in the II Army was the *Sassari,* while the Comando Supremo had two divisions plus some cyclists (See Chapter XIV).
6. The attackers controlled the northern slopes of the Kolovrat-Jeza-Globocak range, while Italian troops were still on the Bainsizza.
7. By nightfall, the XIV Army dominated the Isonzo triangle plus the chain of mountains which controlled the plains from the Saga Gorge to the Upper Tagliamento.
8. Cadorna was still afraid of a Conrad offensive in the Trentino (Map 14 A)

Government Events in Rome

During one of the worst disasters in Italian history, the Boselli government fell by a vote of 314 to 96, all caused by a parliamentary battle between neutralists and interventionists. The new cabinet was headed by Vittorio Emanuele Orlando a Sicilian.

Chapter II Endnotes

The Disaster's Second Day

1 OULK, *Das Kriegsjahr 1917,* Vol. VI, p. 536

2 *RICC:,* Volume II op. cit., p. 294

3 M. Silvestri, op. cit., p. 445, quotation attributed to A. Soffici, in his book, *La Ritirata del Friuli,* Firenze, 1960

4 See L. Capello, *Note di Guerra,* Milano, 1920.

5 AUSSME: *Archivio dello Stato Maggiore dell'esercito* (Henceforth known as AUSSME) *Ordine del riservatissimo n. 26 ; Appunti relative ai criter secondo i quali sarà preordinata la mobilitazione N.E. a datare dal Marzo 1911 ed a datare dal Marzo 1912*

6 Krafft Vol. I, op. cit., p. 101 & p. 107.

7 Krafft, Vol II, op. cit., Appendix, the author noted that the Stol was also assaulted by the Slzalay Battalion (Hermanny-Miksch, op. cit. p. 31). If the Stol was easily taken as Krafft noted, this was either untrue, or with the "mailed fist theory" of blitzkrieg adding to a superabundanceof troops.

8 L. Cadorna, *Lettere Famigliare,* op. cit., entry dated, *24-10-17.*

9 Caviglia, Enrico, op. cit., p. 257

10 Kraft, Vol. I, op. cit., p. 90, 101, 107; Hermanny Miksch, op. cit. p. 31

11 Bencivenga, op. cit., p. 86

12 Bencivenga op. cit., p. 83

13 USSME: Relazione Ufficiale, Vol. IV, Tomo 3° bis, op.cit., p. 411

14 USSME: Relazione Ufficiale, Vol. II Ter, *Le Forze Belligeranti del 1915, (Carte e Schizze)*, p. 336-337

15 Ibid, p. 340

16 Ibid, p. 341

17 Ibid, p. 341.

18 Krafft: Vol. I, op. cit., p. 133

19 Luigi Capello, *Caporetto Perché?,*Torino, Einaudi, 1967, p. 179

20 See Luigi Capello, *Note di Guerra,* 2 Vol. Milano, 1920.

21 *RICC:* Vol. II op. cit., p. 294

22 Rino Alessi, *Dall'Isonzo al Piave,* Milano, Mondadori, 1966, p. 141

23 See Enrico Caviglia, *La Dodicesima Battaglia,* Milano, 1933

24 AUSSME: Communication Capello to Cadorna, Oct. 25, 1917

25 AUSSME: *Verbali delle sedute della Commissione speciale nominata col dispaccio 21 Novembre 1898-N. 7492,* p. 46, (session of Dec. 23, 1898), Carteggio Commissioni di difesa, b. 1

26 Krafft, Vol. I, op. cit., p. 113

27 USSME:War Diary, IV Bersaglieri Brigade, October 1917-Nov. 1918; Collection B-1, Folder 139S 1719e,

28 *RICC:* op. cit., p. 484-486

29 The Italian word *Crumiri* means "Scab" or Strike-breaker

30 M. Silvestri, op. cit., p. 439.

31 USSME: Relazione Ufficiale, Vol. II, Tomo 3° op. cit., p. 404

32 USSME: C. Geloso, *La 65a divisione dal Carso al Piave,* Roma, 1928, pp.114-115

33 Caviglia, Enrico, op. cit., p. 278

34 Roberto Bencivenga, *La Sorpresa Strategica di Caporetto,* Gaspare Editore, Udine 1997, p. 95

35 Ugo Cavallero later became Chief of the General Staff.

36 USSME, Relazione Ufficiale, Vol. IV, Tomo 3°, op. cit., p. 363.

37 Norman Franks, Frank Bailey, *Casualties of the German Air Service 1914-1920,* Rick Duiven, Grub Street, London, 1999, p. 234.

38 Alfred Krauss, *Das Wunder von Karfreit,* Lehmann, Munich, 1926, p. 42-3.

39 Below diary: entry of October 25, 1917

40 Cesare DeSimone, *L'Isonzo Mormorava,* Mursia, Milano, 1995, p. 57.

41 Lenin, *Sul movimento operaio italiano,* Rome, Rinascita, 1952. This book contained a reprint of an article dated July 26, 1915, "The destruction of one's own government in Imperialistic wars."

42 L. Gasparotto, *Rapsodie,* Milano, 1924.

43 CAB 24/31/2594 (Nov. 6, 1917); Malagodi, *Conversazioni* op. cit., II p. 390; Giovanni Artieri, *Il re, i soldati, e il generale che vinse,* Rocca S. Casciano, 1951, p. 96

44 L. Cadorna, *Lettere Famigliare,* op. cit., p. 228

45 Ibidem, p. 229-230

46 Ibidem, p. 230.

47 Emilio Faldella, *La Grande Guerra,* Milano, Longanesi, 1965, Two Volumes; Volume II, *Da Caporetto al Piave,* p. 225.

48 A. Gatti, op. cit., p. 263-64.

CHAPTER III

DAY THREE AS THE AUSTRO-GERMAN JUGGERNAUT CONTINUED TO ADVANCE October 26, 1917

Italian defenses had been pierced in several places but the most damage occurred in the center. Upon hearing that Montemaggiore was in enemy hands, Cadorna gave orders to retreat to the Tagliamento River. There were no troops available to seal the wide open breaches. Warfare had taken on a new character. No longer was the infantry to charge and occupy enemy positions. Tactics now were for small units to penetrate deep into enemy rear causing chaos while other troops would attack the enemy frontally confusing the defenders. Certain points would be subjected to massive bombardment followed by an overwhelming infantry assault. The demoralized, illiterate Italian infantry were not trained to oppose these tactics nor could they adapt resulting in their surrendering in droves. Cadorna did all to favor the withdrawal of the intact III Army and did little to help the withdrawal of the survivors of the severely mauled II Army whose Thirty-fourth, Forty-third, Forty-sixth, Nineteenth, Fiftieth, Sixty-fifth, Sixty-fourth and Twenty-Second Infantry Divisions had ceased to exist. Unguarded Italian prisoners streamed toward the Austro-German rear reflecting an enormous drop in Italian morale. The II Armée Isonzo reached the Italian third defense line on the Bainsizza, while the Berrer and Scotti Groups approached the Korada. Krauss occupied Monte Maggiore while Stein approached Cividale.

"Lay him low, lay him low,
In the clover or the snow!
What cares he ! he cannot know;
Lay him low!
George Henry Boker, "Dirge for a Soldier"

TODAY WAS A sunny day with good visibility. Hour by hour, the Italian defenses were crumbling. Not being trained in maneuver warfare Italian commanders from the low to the highest were paralyzed in their thinking, rarely reacting to events. Refugees and soldiers all in a human swarm were fleeing to the rear clogging the roads. Officers related how they would meet stragglers who related that the war was over. Refugees narrated how *Carlino* governed in Udine, while unarmed soldiers marched home singing *Addio Mia Bella Addio, Ho fatto la pace* (Goodbye my lovely goodbye, I have made peace).[1] Concerning the line Montemaggiore-Salcano, Cadorna told the II and III Armies, "One must conquer or die,"[2] He accused the infantry of cowardice, an accusation denied by many of his subordinate officers.[3]

0200

At first light, the Italian Rombon units started their retreat westward across the mountains to escape the net that the Austro-Hungarians had drawn around the Rombon. Many died. In the *Dronero* out of 1,500 fifty survived.

Krauss Group

Below issued orders, "The XIV Army should advance quickly with a strong right wing onto Resiutta and Venzone so as to cut off the enemy troops that are facing the Tenth (Krobatin) Army.

The mass of the army should attack as quickly as possible on the line of Gemona-Tarcento-Cividale to the rail line on the Tagliamento-Cornino-Maiano-Udine *(Map 29).* The Thirteenth Schützen Division should go from the reserves to the Stein Group and the Fiftieth to the Krauss Group."[4] The rapidly advancing Twelfth Silesian Division had invaded the combat sector of the I Corps but with the euphoria of the moment, who cared? In his writings Krauss, like Krafft glorified the military capabilities of German-speaking men but also criticized himself in that he should have had armored cars and cavalry available to exploit the breaches his troops caused.

In a polar atmosphere, the CCXVI Brigade (*Edelweiss*), was trying to go from the crest of M. Canin to M. Cergnala, while the CCXVII was occupying the heights north of V. Uccea (Maps 13,19, 23). After taking M. Guarda, the IV/ 14° entered the V. Resia and reached Stolvizza. Maj. Gen. Von Wieden divided his forces into three columns. The first (German Jäger) would proceed across the Sella Carnizza, toward Resiutta. To its right, the second aimed for Chiusaforte in V. Fella, attacking the defenders in their rear as the third, after crossing the Passo di Tanamea, descended onto Venzone across the V. Venzonassa (Map 23). By afternoon the black and yellow banners of the *Edelweiss* were noted on the northern slopes of the Valle Uccea. About noon, units of the Twenty-second Schützen descending from M. Stol, entered Breginj. The I/3° KaiserJäger went from the crest of M. Stol toward P. di Montemaggiore which it occupied at 1700 (Map 23). Simultaneously, the XLIII Brigade reached the headwaters of the Natisone and Cornappo Rivers the latter being a creek in normal weather (Map 23). After a brief pause, Mueller ordered the advance toward the villages of Platischis and Montemaggiore. From there the troops would advance along the crest between M. Pridolna and M. Cavallo overlooking the Taipana Basin (Map 23). The XLIII Brigade occupied Platischis and the Natisone-Cornappo watershed. M. Jauer was still occupied by Italians.

Two infantry divisions, the Fifty-fifth and the Fiftieth moved forward, the former going from Idersko to the upper V. Natisone reaching Sedlo in the evening, while the latter, occupied M. Mia, as its XV Brigade reached M. Lubia. Toward evening, another unit occupied the undefended M. Joanz. Slowly Italian defenses between the Natisone River and the Torre Creek were dissolving.

The remainder of the *Edelweiss* was to occupy the entire dorsum of the Rombon up to to plains, thus causing the defense of the Zona Carnia to collapse. Feeling that there were not enough troops to accomplish this, Krauss requested that the Twenty-ninth Infantry Division which he had commanded with great success in Serbia be assigned to him. The response of the A.O.K. was "There are other plans for it." It was assigned to the *Armée Isonzo* and never fired a shot in the whole campaign.[5] From the XIV Army he finally did receive the German Jäger Division which was to reach the Val Uccea today to be placed under the command of Maj. Gen. von Wieden. In the end Krauss described this German division to be useless and only a traffic hazard.

Zona Carnia Command

Tassoni now realized that he would be involved in the battle. His XII Corps, had been inserted between the II and IV Armies. Two defensive lines in V. Resia, garrisoned by units of the Sixty-third Infantry Division and the *VIII Gruppo Alpini* which was about to arrive, were planned. Also to be defended were the access paths to V. Venzonassa and the Passo Tanamea (Map 23). Attempts to link up with the troops on P. di Montemaggiore (*Alpini* V. Arrosica, M. Clapier Battalions and two battalions of the 36°) were unsuccessful.

The Montemaggiore defense had been batted back and forth like a ping pong ball. On October 24, it was under the jurisdiction of the II Army, next day it was transferred to the Zona Carnia Command and on the day after that it again returned to the II Army.[6] No command was issued to seal the breach, not by the Comando Supremo which had the *VIII Gruppo Alpini* enroute from the Trentino (I Army), not by the II Army which had recently been assigned the *VII Gruppo Alpini* also coming from the Trentino, not by the Zona Carnia Command whose recently assigned Fiftieth Division descended from the Stol onto the plains.[7] At 1430, Cadorna notifed Tassoni that he wished M. Sflincis the extreme strong point west of Resiutta, in the lower V. Fella (second line of defense) to resist to the end; Forte di M. Festa should get ready to do likewise (Maps 2, 35).

Italian IV Corps

During the night, the *VII Gruppo Alpini (*Bicocca and V. Leogra Battalions) reached P. di Montemaggiore but linkup attempts either with the survivors of the Fiftieth Infantry Division at Breginj, or Zona Carnia units were unsuccessful (Maps 23). Col. Brig. Luigi Sapienza, commander of the *II Raggruppamento Alpini*, realized that the enemy had occupied the hamlet of Montemaggiore (one mile away). At 1720, fearing encirclement, he ordered a redeployment of the two *Alpini* battalions to the line of Monteaperta-SS. Trinitá, thereby leaving the head of the V. Cornappo undefended (Map 23). He did anticipate redeploying them onto M. Bernadia, the last stronghold above Nimis and Tarcento. This clarified the statement that the I/3° Kaiserjäger entered the sector without firing a shot. Since September 10, an Austro-Hungarian company (four officers and 145 men) had been training under Lt. Schäfer to occupy Montemaggiore but it saw no combat today.[8] Cadorna had given the order to occupy Ponte di Montemaggiore because losing it would give the attackers a way to get into the plains below and put the III Army in danger.

There has been much ado about the loss of Montemaggiore. Information later developed revealing that its guns had been removed and there were no troops on the summit until the *Alpini* battalions arrived in the evening. Some authors have declared the withdrawal to be "deplorable and unjustified."[9] When the commander of the north sector, Gen. Mozzoni received the news from Sapienza, he could only approve it as the moves had already been started. He simply asked that M. Bernadia be considered as the *difesa ad oltranza.* (defense to the end). Studying the situation years later, one can see that the loss of P. di Montemaggiore, was an incentive to withdraw to the Tagliamento. At 2320 Cadorna issued orders that Sapienza attempt to re-occupy the summit which failed. The move of the I/3°Kaiserjäger caused one million Italian troops and 500,000 refugees to withdraw (p. 98). On the Italian side of the trench there was lack of communications, tiredness and hunger resulting in low morale at all levels, with headquarters requesting impossible things to do. One such situation was the center group (Fiftieth Infantry Division, Lt. Gen. Arrighi), of 1300 men, almost out of ammunition, which was ordered to garrison the crest of M. Cavallo (Map 23). As darkness arrived the *Bisagno* (210°) deployed one battalion on the summit of M. Cavallo resulting in no real defenses due to the Italian retreat from P. di Montemaggiore. The other troops were in reserve in V. Lagna. The group on the right (Basso) was to deploy on M. Joanaz which it reached at 1500; but the II/277° pushed back from M. Joanaz redeployed onto the Sella di Canebola, where it was joined by a battalion from the *Siena* (Maps 13).

The *Vicenza* deployed on the crests of M. Joanaz-M. Craguenza-M. Mladesena with the 277° and 279° while the 278° was in reserve at Torreano (Map 22). Having lost M. Joanaz to units of the enemy Fiftieth Infantry Division, they were also attacked by units of the same division coming from Stupizza and Loch which were able to advance unopposed once its Bosnians had taken M. Lubia and M. Mia. By nightfall, the attackers had crossed the crest descending into Canalutto in the upper V. Chiaro thus going around M. Mladesena. The Twenty-fifth Infantry Division, (other unit of the XXVIII Corps), had ceded the *Ferrara* and *Girgenti* to the VII and XXVII Corps respectively. Remaining to block the enemy advance into the Natisone River Valley was the *Ionio* which deployed one regiment on each bank. The *Avellino* divided its battalions between the *Vicenza* and *Ionio.* Krafft later wrote that after the the taking of M. Mia by the Fiftieth Imperial

Division, he had suggested the sending the 63° (Twelfth Silesian) to M. Joanaz, where it later met the Bosnians who were already on the peak. At 1600, units of the German 23° proceeded from Luico toward the Matajur. They had already been preceded there by Rommel's men so they descended onto the Natisone River between Pulfero and Brischis where the headquarters of the Twelfth Silesian was located (Map 22). The latter had already ordered units toward Azzida to open the way for the AlpenKorps coming from the left (Map 22).

By the evening of October 25, in the VII Corps only the six battalions of the *Salerno* remained intact. A few hours prior, these troops were in the relative tranquility of Bassano del Grappa, then transported via rail to Cividale, trucked to Savogna arriving on the evening of October 23. Due to heavy traffic, the trucks were abandoned with the troops proceeding on foot to the Matajur which they reached the evening of the next day. All supplies were lacking, including trenching tools, barbed wire, munitions, etc. Since the roadway up the mountain had not been completed, heavy equipment and large caliber artillery were left behind to be captured by advancing Germans. Its new commander Col. Donato Antonicelli (formerly of the 89°), received orders to withdraw. The orders read to withdraw the morning of October 27. The Courier Officer swore that the orders should have read the morning of October 26 but Antonicelli would not move unless the written orders were changed forcing the lieutenant to return to obtain precise instructions, by which time the brigade was surrounded. Losses were 3,800 prisoners, 1,400 dead and wounded with 1,000 escaping to fight again. As their former commander Brig. Gen. Ottavio Zoppi noted, "To expect that a soldier, surprised and surrounded before fighting, use his bravery to change a situation already inexorably jeopardized, is folly.[10] In forty-eight hours, the VII Corps no longer existed. Long forgotten were the troops on M. Nero (30,000) who lacking all, food, water and munitions finally surrendered in the afternoon.

At 0400 the German 23° proceeded from Luico, and climbed toward the Matajur which (as we shall see) was already in friendly hands, then descending to the Natisone between Brischis and Pulfero, linking up with the command center of the Twelfth Silesian which had pushed its troops to open the way for the Alpenkorps who had come from the left arriving in the morning attempting to scale the Matajur's eastern slope but meeting stiff resistance. Attached to this elite group was the Würrtemberg *Gebirgsbattailon.* Noting the enormous number of prisoners taken by Rommel and thinking that the Matajur was in friendly hands Sproesser had ordered him to withdraw an order which the future Desert Fox ignored. Feeling that Sproesser did not know all the facts he attacked the Matajur and took many more thousand prisoners including the *Salerno's* second battalion. He was mentioned in the Alpenkorps Order of the Day.[11] His unit had been in constant combat for fifty-six hours taking 4,000 prisoners, thirty cannon and many machine guns. There has been a great debate as to who took the Matajur. Originally it was thought that Lt. Schneiber with four companies of the Silesian 63° which Krafft and Capello wrote. The official Silesian report noted that Schneiber had arrived one hundred meters from the summit. Lt. Schneiber proceeded to wear the *Pour le Mérite* until he was killed in France in 1918. As Rommel was dictating his report of the capture of the Matajur summit, a sergeant accompanied by four men from the Silesian 23° arrived. Now to solve the problem. It seemed that the 63 was none other than the regimental number of the infantry to which the 4 company (Lt. Schneiber belonged). Easily noted is how the numbers are linked. One can see the 4 company of the 63° and 4 *Infanteriesten* of the 23°, all belonging to the Twelfth Silesian Division. In the A.O.K. bulletin, the number 4 (4 men) was increased to 4 companies. The *Kriegstagebuch* (War Diary) of October 26 noted that there was a four man patrol with a correction of 63 written over the 23. Different people had written the report. The WMB *Gefechtsbericht* (Battle Report), noted that four men of the 63° reached the summit one hour after Rommel had already arrived there. Krafft had not given him credit for the feat. After the war Sproesser put up such a fuss that in later editions, Krafft gave credit to Rommel for first occupying the Matajur. Proceeding toward the Natisone, the Alpenkorps went along the V. Rieca, reaching S. Pietro as darkness approached.

Berrer Group

Following the Alpenkorps was the Two-Hundredth Infantry Division along the military road from Podklabuc to Luico, then to Ravne, after which it it proceeded southwest toward the Natisone (Maps 16, 17, 18). Aware of the Italian collapse, the tired Austro-German troops did not halt. By evening some units (4° Jäger), took M. S. Martino without firing a shot. Other units reached Azzida encountering resistance (Map 22). The Twenty-sixth reached the hamlet of Cravero.

Italian VII Corps

On its left was the Sixty-second Division, plus some 800 survivors of the *Salerno.* Survivors of the IV Bersaglieri Brigade, redeployed to M. Purgessimo which was held by the *Ferrara* (Map 22). The remnants of the Third Infantry Division, which also included survivors of the Nineteenth Infantry Division, withdrew toward Castelmonte where they were reinforced by the *Milano.*

XXVII Corps

Having lost the Jeza, Villani was withdrawing toward Cividale. Stopping at a small village called S. Leonardo, he halted to have a meeting with his staff. Here he was joined by the fifty survivors of the *Alpini* Val d'Adige Battalion. Suddenly he excused himself leaving the room. From another room a shot was heard, after which he was found seated at a desk with a self-inflicted head wound. A note was addressed to his chief of staff.

Caro De Medici,
Lascio a Lei di proseguire il terribile compito. Io non ne posso piú.
Generale Villani

Dear De Medici,
I leave you the task of continuing. I can stand it no longer.
General Villani

Hastily buried, his body was not found until thirteen years later.

Scotti Group

Its first objective was the conquest of M. Kum and the widening of the breach in the Globocak (Map 20). At 0500 minus artillery the VIII Grenadiers assaulted the mountain finally occupying the summit by 1100. With the arrival of other units, the whole *Elba* was captured (eighty officers and 3500 men). After a brief rest, the Grenadiers descended onto Tribil di Sotto, while at Tribil di Sopra bivouacked the Fifty-second Infantry and the 12° Grenadiers (Map 20). By nightfall the II *Armée Isonzo* which had finally gone on the move occupied the Korada with its Fifty-seventh and First Imperial Infantry Divisions.

The Italian XXVII Corps issued orders at 0900 regarding the line of defense which it was to occupy in the Judrio Valley. It was about two km. (1.2 mile) from the hamlet of Cosson to M. Korada with the left flank descending into the valley floor. The OIR narrated that there were eleven battalions plus six in reserve besides the survivors of the X *Gruppo Alpini.* There were also remnants of the *Puglie* and those of the I and V Bersaglieri Brigades. Artillery pieces on Kambresko were abandoned, as there was no more ammunition for them.[12] Toward the afternoon, the *Taranto* arrived as well as the Thirteenth Infantry Division (Maj. Gen. Rubin de Cervin), which consisted of the *Girgenti, Belluno and Treviso.* As Caviglia narrated, on October 26, all his divisions plus those from the XXVII assigned to him redeployed behind the Korada. Ferrero commanding the right wing of the Italian II Army arrived in the afternoon just as the withdrawing Tenth Infantry Division arrived from the Bainsizza. The defense line of the XXIV Corps was now at M. Korada-M. Planina-Plava-Paljevo, astride the Isonzo (Map 4). The heavily mauled divisions were sent west of the Torre Creek while the Thirtieth Infantry Division garrisoned the defense line (Map 35). Beyond the river was the II and VI Corps. The latter two placed one brigade per each division on the right side of the Isonzo and kept the defensive line, Vodice-M. Santo-Sella di Dol-Veliki-Gorizia (Map 4). There had been little contact between the opposing armies as the attackers wished to arrive at Cividale, while the defenders wished to withdraw toward the Torre Creek. Attacking troops smelled a great victory with a poet in a Jäger battalion writing a few verses which summarized all their feelings.

> "Still we see the villages in a flaming light
> and Death laughs, mocking and cold,
> in our victory-proud faces.[13]

At the XIV Austro-German headquarters at Kranj, aerial reconnaissance reports noted tremendous confusion of Italians at Cividale, both civilians and military. Below pushed his men to go forward as long as their legs were able. He told them that they must advance so as not to give the Italians a chance to recover. In fact, it seemed that the Italians were retreating from Gorizia which made it seem that there was a disaster in the making.

Events at Austro German XIV Army Headquarters

At noon, Archduke Eugene offered Below the opportunity to establish the southern operative margin of the XIV Army, but that afternoon the A.O.K. ordered that the pursuit sector of the *II Armée Isonzo* should extend to the line M. Podlkabuc-Azzida-Cividale (Map 13). With this act, the Scotti and Berrer Groups would be compressed in favor of the Habsburg Army. The new orders allocated vacant areas of pursuit to Boroevic's troops which were still far behind. This was the cause of the first violent argument between the two allies, as well as the reason why the total annihilation of the Italian Army did not occur. Krafft proposed that the *Edelweiss* and the German Jäger Divisions be transferred to the Tenth Austro-Hungarian Army as soon as they arrived at Resiutta. Everyone was waiting for Conrad to go on the offensive in the Trentino (Map 14 A). Realizing that the Anglo-French would send divisions to assist the Italian Army, Krafft wanted a Battle of Annihilation now before help could arrive in the plains. Cadorna planned to use two rivers as defensive bulwarks.

Beginning Dissent Between the Victorious Allies

There were ten roads for sixteen Austro-German divisions. Krafft felt that there were too many troops for the roads along the whole front. Below protested to Eugene that the new pursuit sectors would seriously compromise the Scotti and Berrer Groups which were advancing swiftly. The *II Armée Isonzo* was far behind and seemingly would never catch up.

Events at the Comando Supremo

Feeling better while in the hospital, at 0660 Capello had an officer send a telegram to Cadorna that he was feeling fine and ready to return to duty. He received a negative reply. The Generalissimo noted that a change in commanders would be harmful to the II Army which was having poor communications. Orders and troops would arrive at a location where everything had dramatically changed. For example, four assault units were transferred to the XXVII Corps with these orders to Lt. Col. Giuseppe Bassi: "The assault units should immediately proceed toward Senico, a hamlet on the left of the V. Judrio, somewhat more than two km. (*approximately one mile*) to the southwest of the fortification established there by the XXVII Corps, where they should be placed at the disposal of Gen. Badoglio who will use them as he sees fit, to defend the Korada or to fend off an attack from the Korada itself, stop: If the II Assault Detachment deployed at Cosson has not joined up with the others, it should do so immediately, stop." As the OIR noted, "One is dealing with a simple reinforcement without a precise aim for which the units were trained and without a clear vision of the usefulness which they could have more opportune than that which Gen. Badoglio 'would use them as he sees fit.'" Orders were not being given in clear concise language. At 0130 via the French Military Mission, Cadorna informed Foch of the gravity of the situation.[14] Brig. Gen. Delmé Radcliffe, Chief of the British Military Mission, also notified London of the seriousness of the situation. History seems to repeat itself. There were similar situations with U.S. troops in Somalia and in Kosovo being used to perform tasks for which they had not been trained for similar to the illiterate Italian troops being asked to perform maneuver warfare. Montuori was constantly being questioned by the Comando Supremo. His response was that he was awaiting to consult with Gen. Etna who was commanding his left wing (P. di Montemaggiore). Moments later, Cadorna informed him that this position had been lost to counterattack (Map 23). Later, when Montuori questioned Etna, the latter confirmed that loss as well as M. Cavallo. Montuori notified the Comando Supremo that there were counterattacks in progress to retake P. di Montemaggiore, but later reported that it had been lost.[15] This was the hinge between the Zona Carnia Command and the left wing of the II Army. He also stated that he was linking up on the left with the Zona Carnia Command and on the right with M. Joanaz. *This simply showed that he did not know that either move was impossible.* At 1620, the IV Army was informed that the retreat would go to the Tagliamento and that all artillery which could be moved, should go to the right bank of the river via Pederobba-Asolo-Montebelluna. Retreating in this manner, the troops would have to proceed through the Brenta, Cismon, Cordevole and Piave River Valleys, all the while under attack by the Austro-German XIV and Austro-Hungarian X Armies (Map 35). Toward evening,

Cadorna issued his "*Directives for the Redeployment on the Tagliamento line*" to his subordinate commanders, acknowledging that the defenses would not hold.[16] Cadorna also issued specific orders making individual commanders responsible for maintaining discipline using the most severe measures.[17] This thirty-six-hour delay in the withdrawal resulted in sad consequences for the troops in the field, making the number of Italian prisoners rise to astronomical numbers.[18] In his Memoirs, the Generalissimo admitted that the optimism he had in the morning dissipated by the evening. He also announced the formation of a Special Operations Group, or *Corpo Speciale* deployed astride the Tagliamento composed of two divisions commanded by Lt. Gen. Antonio DiGiorgio recalled from Rome via telegram.[19] He was a deputy in the Parliament and had been summoned the second day of the enemy offensive and given four brigades,[20] the *Lombardia, Barletta, Bologna* and *Lario.* These units had all been mauled in the Carso offensives, and were resting at Palmanova (Map 35). They were commanded by one general senior to DiGiorgio (Maj. Gen. Lorenzo Barco), and another who was technically his superior (Lt. Gen. Ugo Sani). Meeting with Cadorna, he was told that his troops were already marching toward Pinzano where he should join them (Maps 27,29). He had neither artillery, nor staff, nor food, nor telephones nor transportation slowly accumulating what was needed from discarded equipment left about. At Pinzano there were neither trenches nor machine gun emplacements. He was soon to lose the *Bologna* in the defense of M. Ragogna, and the *Lombardia* a few days later, but his unit was enlarged by retreating efficient Italian units. These were the survivors of the *Siena,* the 9° Bersaglieri, the *VII Gruppo Alpini* (which had to abandon Montemaggiore) and the Sixteenth Infantry Division, *(Siracusa* and *Rovigo).* Going for his usual walk today in the company of Rev. Giovanni Semeria the Generalissimo again declared that the troops did not fight.[21] What about the hundreds of thousands that had died? Toward midnight, the news that P. di Montemaggiore had been abandoned arrived at the Comando Supremo.[22] Now all defensive hope was lost. Orders were also given that DiGiorgio's troops should hold the bridges at Pinzano and Trasaghis (Map 27). The collapse of the left wing shielded troops in the mid-Tagliamento Valley, and offered many surprises along the way. In addition to the military crisis there was now a political crisis. As Colonial Minister Ferdinando Martini noted, "Not that the nation would accept an Orlando government, but the Parliament wants it, by now it can impose it, and the nation will tolerate it as long as Sonnino remains. And then, what can the nation do?" Toward evening, the Italian Military Attaché in Paris telegraphed Cadorna, that since no particular requests for help had been received, Foch would simply follow events from afar. The king left Rome for Udine to be near the front. On the III Army front the Seventeenth Infantry Division of the *Armée Isonzo* occupied Dosso Faiti (Map 5).

Chapter III Endnotes

Day Three As The Austro German Juggernaut Continued to Advance

1 *RICC*: Vol. I, pp. 438-484

2 *RICC:: Le Cause e le responsibilità*, Vol. II, p. 110

3 Caviglia, Enrico , op. cit., p. 257

4 Below diary, entry of *Oct. 27, 1917.*

5 Krauss, op. cit., Vol. I p. 75

6 R. Bencivenga, *La Sorpresa Strategica di Caporetto,* Gaspare Editore, Udine, 1997 p. 99

7 Idem, p. 100

8 Viktor Schemfil, *Das k.u.k. 3. Der Tiroler Kaiserjäger im Weltkrieg 1914-1918,* Bregenz, I.R. Teutsch, 1926, p. 467; Gianni Pieropan, cited work, p. 456

9 E. Faldella, Vol. Vol. II, op.cit., p. 240-41

10 Ottavio Zoppi, *Resto Del Carlino,*(Bologna), Jan. 27, 1933; E. Caviglia, *La Dodicesima Battaglia (Caporetto)* 1933, Milano, Mondadori, p.295

11 David Fraser, *Knight's Cross, A Life of Field Marshall Erwin Rommel,* 1993, Harper Collins, N.Y., p. 68-69.

12 Italy had purchased Krupp guns. Ammunition for these was only delivered until May 1915, after which Germany stopped deliveries. Italy had declared war on Austria-Hungary, but not on Germany until August 1916

13 Jacob Baxa, *Alpen in Feuer. Mit den Karntner Achterjagern an der italienischen Front* (Klagenfurt: Artur Kollitach, n.d.), p. 23

14 *Les Armée Française dans la Grande Guerre,* Ministère de la Guerre, Etat Major de l'Armèe. Service Historique, Paris, tome VI, Volume II, p. 114, henceforth known as FAR; DDI Series V, 1914-1918, Vol. IX, Sept. 1-Dec. 31-1917, Rome Poligrafo di Stato, 1983, doc. 310

15 USSME: Relazione Ufficiale, Vol. IV, Tomo 3°, op. cit., p. 377,382.

16 USSME: Ibid, p. 304, Protocol No. 4999

17 USSME, Relazione Ufficiale, Protocol No. 4988, Volume IV, Tomo 3°, op. cit., Doc, p. 289

18 Piero Pieri, *La Prima Guerra Mondiale, 1914-1918 (Problems of Military History)* Torino, Geroni, 1947, p. 299-300.

19 USSME: Relazione Ufficiale, Vol. IV, Tomo 3° bis Doc., Protocol No. 5010, Comando Supremo, *Costituzione Corpo Armata Speciale (C.A.S.) e altri disposizioni,* October 26, 1917, Document No. 124, p. 293, October 26, 1917

20 USSME: Relazione Ufficiale, Vol. IV, Tomo 3°, op. cit., p. 230; Troops were obtained from the II Army, the Thirty-third and Twentieth Infantry Divisions; *Relazione,* op. cit., Volume IV, Tomo 3°, p. 305

21 The priest was the chaplain at the Comando Supremo. He belonged to the Regular Clerics of St. Paul, commonly known as the Barnabites after their church in Milano which is St. Barnabas (Catholic Encyclopedia p. 302). It seemed that after Gorizia Semeria noted that he facilitated a rapprochement between Cadorna the observant Catholic and Cappello the atheist and Freemason but this is difficult to establish.

22 Ibid, p. 382.

CHAPTER IV

THE DISASTER'S FOURTH DAY
October 27, 1917

Cadorna gave the order to retreat to the Tagliamento and transferred his headquarters to Treviso while his assistants, the colonels Gabba, Calcagno, Pintor, Cavallero, Gazzera, Gatti, and Aymonino, as well as Porro went to Padua.[1] *The Italian Army was now like a ship in a storm without a captain, with the Comando Supremo out of contact with all subordinate commanders.*

"But hark! the far bugles their warnings unite;
War is a virtue, weakness a sin;
There's a lurking and loping around us tonight;
Load again, rifleman, keep your hand in!"

Anonymous

THROUGHOUT THE BATTLE zone it rained heavily but the heaviest blow for the Germans was received at Bad Kreuznach. While Germans were fighting and dying for Austria-Hungary's aims, Vienna was attempting to negotiate a separate peace. Learning of this, the German military became very upset (See chapter XV). Heavy rains caused streams to become rivers with fast-flowing currents prohibiting the construction of pontoon bridges at Tolmino across the Isonzo, and made telephone traffic erratic.

Realizing that the breaches were beyond repair at 0230 Cadorna issued orders to the effect that the Zona Carnia (now

XII Corps) troops should immediately be withdrawn to a position in the Carnic PreAlps, with a strong defense at M. Sflincis and linked up with the IV Army at Casera Razzo (Maps 28, 40). All supplies and munitions not immediately needed in the withdrawal were to be destroyed. At 0250 and 0350 the II and III Armies respectively received orders regarding the withdrawal.[2] Pertinent sections of the orders shall be quoted.

"The present directives, reserved only for the army corps commanders, shall discuss the most unfortunate hypothesis which I feel is most probable, that is, that no effort, can stop the piercing of the front. Should this occur, it would be necessary to withdraw the II and III Armies to the Tagliamento, and the XII Corps to the line of the PreAlps. Predispositions should be made for this, taking care that all orders shall be ready to be issued should the necessity arise. First, the heavy artillery and bulky pieces should be moved. The other equipment should be moved according to the following schedule. The withdrawal should take place in the following sequence: (*Maps 29,35*)

I. Withdrawals shall take place under a strong rear guard.
II. The first stopping point for the II and III Armies shall be the Torre (*Creek*) (*Map 35*). The XII Corps should keep its right wing linked up with the left wing of the II Army.[3]
III. The III Army shall withdraw together with the II Army, making sure that its northern flank is covered *(by the right wing of the II Army)*.
IV. At the Torre, the II Army shall hold the front upstream from the Delizia (Codroipo) bridges to where it comes in contact with the Zona Carnia (*now known as XII Corps*) troops halfway to the Trasaghis Strait whose defense is entrusted to the XII Corps. All terrain between Pinzano and Trasaghis shall be strictly guarded to stop any enemy penetration. The III Army shall be responsible for the front from the Delizia bridges to the sea.
V. In the redeployment, the locations of the new commands shall be as follows:

I Comando Supremo: Padua.
II Army Command: Pordenone (Maps 29,35)
III Army Command: Motta di Livenza (*Map 29*).

VI. The Intendence General shall give orders to withdraw the factories of the respective armies in harmony with the orders issued."[4]

The withdrawal orders allotted the following bridges:

A. Third Army—(*Map 29*)

Latisana: stone bridge and railway bridge;
Madrisio: (five miles north of Latisana), a permanent floating bridge.
Codroipo: a permanent footbridge, railway bridge, and a stone bridge called Delizia.

B. Second Army: (*Map 29*)

Bonzicco: a trestle bridge (partly carried away by flood on October Twenty-seven)
Pinzano: stone bridge and permanent foot bridge to the north.
Cornino: railway bridge.

With this crazy allotment, the right wing of the Italian II Army would have to make a flank march across the enemy's front to reach the Pinzano-Cornino bridges.[5] At 0230, orders were sent to the XII Corps that it should withdraw to the line of the Carnic Prealps (Maps 2, 40) west of Trasaghis and link up with the IV Army at Casera Razzo (Map 28). At 0330 orders went out to the II Army.

"The II Army shall start its withdrawal today. To save the army, it is necessary to defend to the last, the line at Lusevera-Poujac-M. Cladis-LeZaffine-M. Joanaz-Madlesena-Purgessimo-

Castelmonte-Korada-Sabotino (Map 22). The garrison on the Sabotino and Korada (VI, VIII Corps) would remain until the last possible moment. To gain time, a tenacious defense shall be done on the line Kuk-Vodice-M. Santo (Map 12). The Twentieth Infantry Division previously proceeding toward Nimis instead is to proceed toward Codroipo."[6] The central hinge was to have been M. Joanaz *already in enemy hands (Map 13).*

Following the Caporetto assault plan the *I Isonzo Armée* (GO Wurm), attacked the III Army (XI and XIII Corps) deployed between Castagnevizza and Fajti Hrib (Map 5 for orientation). Receiving orders at 0250, the III Army troops were still beyond *Vallone* on the Carso (Map 2). To get a good idea of the distance the reader should consult Map 14A noting Monfalcone along the coast and realizing that the Carso is just to the east of it. They started to withdraw in the evening and by 1030 of the next day, all its men were on the right bank of the Isonzo. Wurm's troops had been nailed to their positions for years, and were unable to swiftly pursue the withdrawing troops. The left wing and the central core of the II Army started its withdrawal to the Torre (Map 35). The right wing would withdraw on the line Buttrio-Manzano-Podgora. The reader is reminded that with these orders the VIII Corps (II Army), had been transferred to the III Army with the task of protecting its northern flank.[7] Cadorna now was willing to sacrifice what he called the broken II Army, to save the intact III Army. Three corps of the II Army, the XXIV, II, and the VI Corps were ordered to pivot backward from Gorizia having their left at Cividale (Maps, 29, 35). These men were uselessly sacrificed to save the III Army. In the center of the II Army now was the VII Corps formerly in reserve along with the *Corpo Speciale*, both of which withdrew to the Torre Creek. Feeling secure there, they were surprised by advancing German units which drove a wedge between the two wings of the Italian II Army. The rear guard of the III Army was made up of the Fourth Infantry Division, while to the north-east was the VIII Corps with the First Cavalry Division and the 2° Gruppo Bersagliere Ciclisti. This was the time to withdraw the three mentioned corps.

However, the order for their withdrawal was not given until October 29. The VIII Corps had previously been the right wing of the II Army.

Defense of the Grappa was transferred from the I to the IV Army.[8] Cadorna had been unhappy with the rate of progress of defense work made by the I Army. While Cadorna was moving his headquarters and thus incommunicado the enemy broke through the Italian rear-guard and proceeded toward Cividale (Map 29).

At 0545 the IV Army was told to redeploy on the so-called Yellow Line linking up on the left with the I Army at C. Caldiera.[9] The orders read, "With the present situation, Your Excellency will take over the construction of the defense works of the I Army on the Grappa, now to be garrisoned by the Fourth Army. You shall immediately organize its defenses, should we need to retreat there and deploy artillery so as to be easily removed, as prescribed by yesterday's Order No. 4998." *(Order sent on October 26).*[10] Immediately DiRobilant issued orders for the retreat of men, guns and material.[11] Cadorna was already planning to retreat to the Piave.[12] It is not known in what hour Cadorna sent the following message to the War Minister, but it was sent today. "Following further acts which the enemy has done to the left wing of the II Army in the zone of M. Cavallo-Montemaggiore there is a possibility of complete encirclement of the defenses in the Julian Front (*Map 23*). In view of this and the low morale of the troops, in an attempt to save the Army, I have planned to have the II and III Armies retreat to the right bank of the Tagliamento. Movements are starting today. Headquarters are being moved to Treviso. I request that Your Excellency inform the Royal Government of that which I have above stated." Pecori-Giraldi (I Army) was also informed.

By now Italian military desertions were of two types.[13] In all they talked as if they had performed a good deed.[14] The public did not know of poor food, repeated useless infantry attacks, decimation, lack of furlough, long stays in the front line trenches etc. This was a protest not only against the war, but against the

Italian government which was so distant from troops in the trenches as well as their families at home not responding to their needs. Fewer executions were carried out as now Italy needed the manpower. There was now the *Sacra Italianissima* Guerra. After Caporetto, when the infantry was granted furloughs, upon arriving home they saw that Rome had done nothing to alleviate the sufferings of their families. To work the fields were only old men, women and children. If there was no harvest, there was no food and the families starved.

Another case of Italian organized confusion would be that of poor Lt. Gen. Pier Luigi Sagramoso. On October 25 he had been ordered to set up defenses with six divisions at the Torre Creek (Map 35). Unfortunately, in classic Italian fashion, three divisions had already been transferred to the IV Corps while on the next day the other three were transferred to the XXVII, XXVIII and XXIV Corps respectively. He found himself troop-less. Since the Roman times of Gaius Marius (157-86 B.C.) units had been detached to fight elsewhere. He changed this not allowing cohorts (480 men) from different legions to be mixed. It seems that the Italian Army on the Isonzo still had not learned this valuable lesson. Montuori (new II Army commander), ordered him to consult with corps commanders on the situation at hand. As the *Relazione Ufficiale* noted, this was a far cry from the original order. Even after being criticized by the allied military for constantly transferring troops about, the Comando Supremo persisted in doing this.

At 0815, Cadorna informed the respective II and III Armies that they should establish bridgeheads on the Tagliamento according to where they would cross. The II Army would cross at Pinzano and the III Army was to use the bridge at Codroipo (Map 29). DiGiorgio's Group would be responsible for the Pinzano bridge near the Cornino. There would be no resistance until the Piave River.[15]

Col. Angelo Gatti, the historian of the Comando Supremo, described the scene at Udine. "The city was in panic, in flight, and was a horrible spectacle. There were lost, undisciplined, unarmed soldiers who had descended from the mountains onto the Friulian plain spreading fear throughout the city." It seemed like biblical exodus, with both military and civilian refugees fleeing. Among foreign observers of the spectacle was Hugh Dalton, future Chancellor of the Exchequer, serving with a British Artillery unit in Italy, as well as George M. Trevelyan a British conscientious objector serving in the British Ambulance Corps in Italy. He noted thousands of fleeing peasants with no one directing traffic. Similar observations were made in the OBARI. Periodically one heard the explosion of an ammunition dump, while the night was illuminated by burning buildings and fuel. Looking at a map, one could easily ascertain that the Austro-Germans, having already gone through the Passo di Tanamea (over 2500 feet), into the Val Resia, were closer to the Tagliamento than the right wing of the II Italian Army and the whole III Army (Maps 23,29, 35). The king wrote in English in his diary "What caused it all?.[16]

Civilian authorities also fled. Usually the only authority figure left in the village was the parish priest.[17] This was the classic Italian *Si salvi chi può* (Let those who can save themselves). Similar events happened on Sept. 8, 1943, when Italy surrendered to the Allies, during which all important functionaries disappeared.

Krauss Group and X Army.[18]

Due to Italian resistance and a snow storm, the joint actions of the CCXVI Brigade from Sella Prevela and the LIX Brigade (X Army), from V. Rio del Lago were unsuccessful in taking Sella Nevea and descending into V. Raccolana. In the freezing cold, weapons froze solid. Units of the German Jäger and *Edelweiss* under the command of Major Gen. Von Wieden formed three columns. The right column took Prato di Resia, while the left column pushed through Passo Tanamea and occupied Forcella Musi at the head of V. Venzonassa (Map 23). The center column descended Val Raccolana into Val Fella as the defenders withdrew to M. Musi. The Twenty-second Schützen occupied M. Jauer with the Fiftieth Division taking M. Carnizza and M. Nagrad. All troops now rested as the Italians withdrew to both banks of the Tagliamento.[19] Krauss announced to his men that the Italian plains were just beyond.

Stein Group

To eliminate resistance in the Natisone Valley would be the task of the Berrer Group, while to its west would be the responsibility of the Stein Group (Maps 13,15). The Alpenkorps and the Silesians occupied M. Craguenza, and M. Mladesena (Map 22). Assisting them was one half of the Württemberg Battalion, which along with the 63° descended onto Faedis from Canebola along with the 23° which deployed its troops before Cividale while the 63° bypassed it going northwestward. The remainder of the Württemberg Battalion joined up with the right wing of the Twenty-sixth Division in the Natisone Valley advancing on Cividale from two directions crushing that city's defenders deployed on M. Purgessimo in a vise (Maps 13, 22). Arriving at the roadway to Faedis, it joined up with the rest of the battalion.

Proceeding from S. Pietro to the right bank of the Natisone River, the Alpenkorps was unable to ford it due to shelling by Italian artillery (Map 22). Only one company was successful as its fording area was in a dead angle of Italian artillery. It immediately started to climb the steep eastern slopes of M. Mladesena, arriving at the summit by 1000 where it was joined by the X Jäger coming up from the northern slopes (Map 22). As the Stein Group was proceeding northwest the Berrer Group on its left was aiming for Udine. Later, the former's troops were ordered to align on the line Maiano-Udine. From Stupizza, the One-Hundred-Seventeenth Division approached Cividale, while the Thirteenth Schützen marched between Caporetto and Robic (Maps 13 and 23).

Berrer Group

At dawn, the 4°Jäger (Two Hundredth Division), attacked Azzida but were temporarily halted from proceeding toward Cividale by defenders on M. Purgessimo (Map 22). Assaulted from the northwest, the mountain was occupied by units of the Twenty-sixth Infantry Division. Units of the Two-Hundredth Infantry Division proceeded to Udine while the Twenty-sixth Division entered Cividale. Hofacker pushed his men who had marched fifteen miles over a foot-path taking them to the left of Udine arriving at its outskirts at midnight.

Scotti Group

After heavy fighting units of the VIII Grenadiers (German Fifth Infantry Division) took M. Spigh (Map 22). Commanders were now asking themselves why were the Italians abandoning all these strongholds. By 1830, the *I Armée Isonzo* arrived at Castelmonte on its way to Cividale (Maps 13, 22).

Events at XIV Army Headquarters

At 0900, Kraft discussed a possible Habsburg offensive in the Trentino area with Waldstätten (Map 14A). He offered troops and artillery to the Conrad Group but received no serious affirmative response. Three divisions of the *I Armée Isonzo* which were east of the Isonzo were requested to remain there to avoid a traffic jam. Munition transport would take precedence. Meanwhile, XIV Army intercepts of Italian radio communications gave them good information about the the defenders' intentions.

At 1900, feeling that the *Isonzo Armées* would never arrive in time to halt the Italians from crossing. Eugene gave permission to the XIV Army to proceed toward the bridges of Codroipo. Had this have been carried out earlier, the Italian II and III armies would have been annihilated. Below issued orders to the effect:

"Bridges on the Tagliamento at Ragogna, Dignano, and Codroipo should be taken, before they are destroyed. Following are the assigned areas of pursuit:

> Krauss: to the left to Colloredo south of S. Daniele-Sacile *(Map 35).*
> Stein: to the left up to Plaino-Silvella-Gradisca.
> Berrer: to the left up to Chiavcis-San Marco-Coderno-Arzenutto
> Scotti: to the left up to the railway at Udine-Codroipo-Casarsa."[20]

Further Dissension Between the Attacking Armies

When Below learned that Boroevic would soon send six divisions across the Isonzo near Plava, he realized that the roads would be flooded with troops making munition supply flow difficult (Map 4, Vol. I). At 2200 the XIV Army issued orders that the southern boundary of its pursuit sector was Udine-Codroipo (Maps 29, 35). This was the seed of future conflict between allies.

By evening, Tassoni ordered the withdrawal of troops from the V. Raccolana, V. Dogna, and V. Fella. His men were deployed as follows:

> Twenty-sixth Division from M. Peralba to M. Permula (Map 29) Thirty-sixth from M. Zemulla to M. Canin and the Sixty-third from the mouth of the V. Resia to Forcella Musi (Map 13), which however, was already in enemy hands.

At 2200 Cadorna notified Tassoni that the enemy was aiming for the bridge at Trasaghis having rolled up the right flank of the II Army which was redeploying onto the Torre. Efforts should be made to halt them there. The Sixty-third Division deployed between Trasaghis and Braulins forming a bridgehead. The retreating Italian II Army divided its troops into three sectors. The left wing (Gen.

Etna) with the IV Corps (Sixteenth and Twenty-first Infantry Divisions), the center consisting of the VII, XXVII, XXVIII Corps, commanded by Gen. Petitti di Roreto and as noted the right wing by Gen. Ferrero consisting of the II,XXIV, and VI Corps (Map 29). As noted the VIII Corps had been detached to the III Army to protect its northern flank as it withdrew from the Carso. The *Corpo Speciale* was along the Tagliamento River up to Trasaghis being responsible for the bridgeheads at Cornino and Pinzano (Map 29). All looked good on paper, but there was no communication among the units. Individual and group acts of heroism and cowardice continued throughout the withdrawal. The task of the II Army's right wing was to save itself as well as the Italian III Army. Hearing of the loss of Cividale, at 1540 Montuori ordered his commanders that starting immediately, they should deploy from the source of the Torre Creek, follow it to Pradamano, continue along the heights north of the railway Butrio-Cormôns-Lucinico thus covering the left flank of the III Army. All was to be completed by the next day. His command was immediately transferred to Codroipo. The whole deployment would be in the form of a socket facing Udine, whose inferior base lined up with other fortifications to the east and whose northern apex, represented by M. Korada, linked up with the II Corps still deployed beyond the Isonzo (Map 12).

Within this salient stood the XXIV Corps where, in the morning Caviglia received orders to retreat to the Tagliamento. Explaining the situation to his subordinates, the general noted that the Austro-Germans were at Cividale, proceeding to Udine while the XXIV Corps was still east of the Isonzo. It was farther away from the Codroipo bridge than the enemy (Map 35). Escape had to be across the bridges at Latisana and Madrisio. British guns with the III Army made for Latisana on the Tagliamento. In the initial phase, the XXIV Corps was on the left bank of the Isonzo while its *Venezia* was astride of it. After the II and VI Corps crossed the river the brigade blew the bridges at Plava and deployed on the right bank of the Isonzo. Caviglia narrated that when the 83° and 84° assembled at Verhovlje, he embraced their commander Lt. Gen. Reghini, as a typical Italian would do.[21] The last unit to leave the Korada was the *Livorno,* which was protecting the flank of the I and V Bersaglieri Brigades. The latter had lost contact with their XXVII Corps and became part of the XXIV Corps. Abandoning the Sabotino, the II Corps linked up with the XXIV between M. Quarin and Capriva. At dusk, the VI moved to the line at Capriva-Calvario-Lucinico to link up southward with the VII Corps of the III Army (Map 4, Vol. I for geography).

Having received the order to retreat at 0250, the III Army started to make plans. Aosta divided his army into five retreating corps. Protected by a screen, the troops east of the *Vallone* were to start to withdraw at 2100 (Map 5). After telephone conversations with Montuori, Aosta changed it to 1800. The protective screen commanded by Lt. General Giuseppe Paolini with his Fourth Infantry Division would be in place until the III Army had passed the heights of Medea. The troops were to aim for the Tagliamento bridges at Madrisio, Latisana and Codroipo (Map 29). By dawn of October 28, the troops on the Gorizian Carso were to start withdrawing. About 2200 the whole VIII Corps was on the right side of the Isonzo, between the Versa Creek and the heights of Medea; the XI Corps reached S. Vito al Torre-Romans; the XIII Corps crossed the *Vallone*, then the Isonzo aiming for Aiello; the XXIII reached Turriaco and proceeded to S. Giorgio di Nogara. To move last was the reserve XXV Corps deployed at Mortegliano. As the OIR noted, all went well, except for the XI Corps whose *Torino* and *Ancona* counterattacked and suffered heavy losses. Following through on Cadorna's disciplinary order of October 26, Aosta issued his own Order No. 10013, noting that artillery and machine guns would fire on troops who would desert to the enemy.[22] Noting the withdrawal, Wurm ordered an attack and easily occupied Gorizia after minimal resistance by the Italian VIII Corps.

Chapter IV Endnotes

The Disaster's Fourth Day

1 USSME: Relazione Ufficiale, Volume IV, Tomo 3°, p. 413

2 USSME: Relazione Ufficiale, Volume IV, Tomo 3° bis, Doc. Comando Supremo *Ordine di ripiegamento alla 3a Armata,* Doc. No. 126, Protocol 5012, October 27, 1917, p. 295; Idem, Comando Supremo, *Ordine di ripiegamento alla 2a Armata e direttive per difesa ad oltranza,* Document No. 127, Protocol No. 5014, October 27, 1917, p. 296

3 USSME: Relazione Ufficiale, Vol. IV, Tomo 3° bis, Doc., II Armata to commanders :*Direttive per la sosta al Torre,* Doc. No. 140, Protocol No. 280/G., 28 October 1917, p. 319

4 R. Bencivenga, *La Sorpresa Strategica di Caporetto,* op. cit., p. 100

5 USSME: Relazione Ufficiale, Vol. IV Tomo 3° bis Doc., Commando III Armata, *Disposizione per la utilizzazione dei ponti* Doc. No. 143, Protocol No. 13/R 29 October 1917, p. 324; The document bears the date of October 29, but apparently orders went out sooner (October 27)

6 USSME: Relazione UfficialeVol. IV, Tomo 3°, op. cit., p. 387

7 USSME: Relazione Ufficiale, *Vol. IV, Tomo 3°* bis, Doc.,Comando Supremo, *Passaggio dell'VIII Corpo d'Armata alle dipendenze della 3a Armata,* Doc. No. 120, Protocol No. 4977 25 October, 1917, p. 288

8 USSME: *Relazione Ufficiale,* Vol. IV, Tomo 3° bis, Doc., Comando Supremo, *Ordini alla1a Armata per cessione lavori Grappa alla 4a Armata,* Doc. No. 129, Protocol 5031, October 27, 1917, p. 298

9 USSME: Relazione Ufficiale, Vol. IV, 3° bis, Doc. Comando Supremo, *Ordine di ripiegamento alla 4a Armata,* Doc. 128, Protocol No. 5015, October 27, 1917, p. 296

10 Ibid, p. 359

11 Ibid, p. 350, DiRobilant's order was No. 11298.

12 USSME: Relazione Ufficiale, Vol. IV, Tomo 3, op. cit., p. 458

13 The first type of desertion was the soldier who put down his rifle, joined his comrades in roaming the Friulian countryside, stating that the war was over. These men preached that the conflict was a tool of the capitalists to kill the peasants. The illiterate peasant infantry related military duty to their peasant duty. When unhappy with work conditions at home, they simply

put down their tools and crossed their arms. These men were picked up by the *Carabinieri* to be sent to camps in the Val Padana where another army was being formed.

The second group were those that by any means traveled home to help the family with the harvest. Using a primitive navigation system illiterate men noted that in the a.m. the sun would be on their left while in the evening it would be on their right, as they progressed homeward down the peninsula. At home they were picked up by the local *Carabinieri,* manacled, and sent to the first line trenches at the front. Deserters now were not executed, as Italy now needed manpower. This was a catch-22 situation. Unless an example was made executing deserters, the men would keep abandoning their post. However, the army now needed men and those sentenced to death for disciplinary infractions were often induced to join the *Arditi,* where they would probably be killed in action.

14 Letter sent by the soldier Cesare Savoldi to *Avanti* on Feb. 14, 1918. It was not published due to post-Caporetto severe censorship, but saved in the archives of the editor of the paper, Giacinto Menotti Serrati. The Serrati Fund is located at the Gramsci Institute in Rome. (this letter is in envelope 37/3)

15 Aldo Cabiati, *La Battaglia dell'Ottobre, 1917,* Milano, Corbaccio, 1934, p. 175-176

16 Giovanni Artieri, *Cronaca del regno d'Italia,* Milan, 1977, II, 129-30

17 L. Gasparotto, *Rapsodie (Diario di un fante),* Treves, Milano, 1925, fifth edit. p.170

18 OULK, Vol. VI, *Das Kriegsjahr 1917,* p. 550

19 USSME: Relazione Ufficiale, Vol. IV Tomo 3° op. cit., p. 393

20 Below's War Diary, Entry, October 27, 1917

21 See E. Caviglia, *La Dodicesima Battaglia,* Milano, Mondadori, 1933

22 USSME: Relazione Ufficiale, Vol. IV, Tomo 3°, op. cit., p. 317

CHAPTER V

THE ITALIAN ARMY'S FIFTH DAY OF AGONY October 28, 1917

In the blitz assault of the Austro-Germans there was no front and no trenches confusing Italian rear guard troops who gave way. German troops arrived at Udine threatening three army corps with encirclement. Recognizing this, Montuori asked Cadorna to allow the II Army to use the Codroipo Bridge which was denied. Italian political parties who had opposed the war now feared that their behavior had harmed the nation, while each economic class in the nation had different aspirations. Cadorna asked the British and French General Staffs for help.

Then let memory bring thee
Strains I used to sing thee,
O, then remember me!
Thomas Moore "Irish Melodies"

TORRENTIAL RAINS FILLED the small streams resulting in an overflow of the banks.

Krauss Group

Krauss was pleased with the progress of his men and felt that praise was in order. Today in his Order of the Day he praised them, especially the Schützen. Telephone lines went from his headquarters to the front lines as well as to the XIV Army headquarters wherever they were. Placed alongside the roads, they were often cut by military convoys but quickly repaired by technicians on bicycles patrolling the cables.

The Wieden Group kept up pressure on Italian troops in the V. Resia sector (Map 23) as did the Twenty-second Schützen surrounding many Italian units on M. Cavallo and forcing them to surrender. Following it in reserve marched the Fifty-fifth Infantry Division which proceeded toward Borjana and Kred (Map 13). To the left of the Schützen marched the Fiftieth Infantry Division arriving at Robidisce.

Orders for the I Corps now were:

> Fiftieth Infantry Division by October 29 would reach the Tagliamento River bridge at Pinzano *(Map 40)*
> Fifty-fifth Infantry Division by the same date would occupy the rail bridge across the Tagliamento north of Roncis and Tarcento *(Map 35)*
> Twenty-second Schützen by the same date would reach Gemona *(Map 35)*

The *Edelweiss* and German Jäger had made little progress, while the Twenty-second Schützen Division surprised the garrison at Forte di La Bernadia above Tarcento (Maps 29, 35). The XLIII Brigade, waited on the left bank of the Torre. The IIC Brigade forded the river and approached Tarcento from the north (Map 35). Behind the Twenty-second was the Fifty-fifth Austro-Hungarian Division, while the Fiftieth Division marched through the rain and reached Attimis and S. Gervasio.

In the spirit of what today would be called *blitzkrieg*, Krauss wanted to keep his headquarters forward. Informed that it was impossible to go forward due to the overflowing streams, he found a gangway which no one knew about and crossed the Slatnik Creek (Map 15). From there he arrived at Cezsoca, then proceeded to Serpenizza where he found some of his staff already there completely soaked due to lack of shelter. Orders were issued that the bridge over the Tagliamento south of Tarcento be repaired so artillery could move forward.

Stein Group

The Twelfth Silesian reached the Torre Creek at Savorgnano but could not cross. Luckier were the II Bavarian Guards Battalion (Alpenkorps), who crossed at Salt before the bridge was blown. Other units arrived so a bridgehead was formed including the hamlet of Godia. Headquarters were transferred from Idersko to Vernasso, near Cividale (Maps 22, 29, 35). As evening approached, the Two-Hundredth and the Twenty-sixth Infantry Divisions closed ranks before entering Udine. Leading the Two-Hundredth Infantry Division were the XVIII and the XX/III/5° Jäger. During the night, units arrived at the left bank of the Torre meeting fierce resistance by survivors of the *Salerno* deployed on the opposite bank. After an intense fire-fight at 0400 the XVIII Battalion led by Capt. Gustav Stoffleth crossed and occupied the hamlet of Beivars northeast of Udine. It then proceeded southward along the raging Torre River repulsing an Italian cavalry attack as well as another at Musig, entering Udine from the north at at 1530. In addition to the two aforementioned breaches a third breach had developed between the two wings of the II Army with the right wing being on the line Gorizia (excluded) to Buttrio (five miles southeast of Udine), while the left wing's southern flank was swung back to Fagagna, eight miles above the Torre Creek with the northern flank in much confusion (Maps 35,40).[1]

Immediately, roads coming from the east were blocked so Italians coming from the Torre sector would be captured. When units of the 3° Jäger and the XXIII arrived, Stoffleth's troops rested. The main road from Udine via Codroipo to the river was now open.

Entering Cividale the Twenty-sixth Infantry Division was followed by the VI/4° Jäger (Two Hundredth Infantry Division). The Jäger proceeded to Udine while the division veered off to the left. En route the battalion encountered Von Berrer in his auto informing him that this was the most forward German position. Convinced that the Twenty-sixth had already entered Udine, Berrer continued forward. Traveling by auto with his aide, he arrived at S. Gottardo, a suburb of Udine, where he was shot and killed by retreating Italian troops.[2] He was the classic example of the *blitzkrieg* commander, always in the forefront, ready to make immediate necessary decisions.

Leutnant Marschall Heberhardt von Hofacker, commander of the Twenty-sixth Infantry Division assumed command of the Berrer Group while Maj. Gen. Duke Ulrich von Württemberg assumed command of the Twenty-sixth. The latter crossed the same afternoon at S. Gottardo and Remanzacco on partially destroyed bridges, entering Udine to be greeted by the Two Hundredth Division. Crossing the raging Torre Creek (today a river) was Capt. Redl with his IV/4° Bosnians. The vanguard of the Scotti Group ((Fifth Infantry Division), with its XII Grenadiers also entered Udine during the night. The VIII Grenadier was left at Orzano, while the Fifty-second was left at Remanzacco. Via radio, Scotti proposed to the XIV Army that on the morrow his Austro-Hungarian First Division delayed by destroyed bridges and rapid river flow advance south of the railway, to Udine-Codroipo. Instead it was entrusted with the military governance of Udine.

XIV Army headquarters now went from Kranj to Cividale (Map 35). The A.O.K. transferred the Twenty-first Schützen and the One Hundred-Sixth Landsturm Divisions to Conrad's Army Group Tyrol which was preparing for a big push. Troops arrived in seventy rail convoys of fifty cars each. Radio intercepts had made Conrad aware that the Italians would be retreating to the Piave. Of the reserve divisions, the Thirteenth Schützen arrived at Caporetto, the Fourth Austro-Hungarian Infantry reached Volzana while the Thirty-third Austro-Hungarian Infantry arrived at Camina-Vollaria (Map 14).

With a static warfare mind-set the *Armées Isonzo* was slow in its pursuit reaching north of Cormôns.[3] The *I Isonzo Armée* met resistance at Podgora, while part of its VII Corps crossed the Isonzo at the confluence of the Isonzo-Vipacco Rivers (Maps 4, 5 for geography). The XXIII arrived at Monfalcone (Maps 5,14A). The OAR reported that Arz still had not accepted pursuit beyond the Tagliamento while the OIR described the deployment in the Zona Carnia of a bridgehead near the mouth of the V. Resia (Map 23).

The Italian II Army deployed on the line of the Torre, from M. Stuba to Pradamano except the salient at Udine, a result of retreating at Salt and Beivar.[4] The retreat toward the Tagliamento bridges at Cornino, Pinzano and Dignano continued.[5] The III Army also was on the line of the Torre Creek protected by the right wing of the II Army (Maps 29, 35).

By evening, Cadorna had two choices. The first would have the three corps in the right wing of the II Army join the III Army, and proceed in it to Codroipo (Map 29). The other was to have efficient units avoid the Codroipo Bridge using it only for refugees and soldiers who were trying to rejoin their units. The bridges at Madrisio and Latisana would be used by the organized units, who would cross efficiently and with a massive rear guard. The Codroipo bridges were unable to handle large units so the VIII, XXIV, II and VI Corps finally crossed on the Madrisio and Latisana bridges (Map 29). Authors have noted that the Comando Supremo should have known this and taken appropriate measures.[6] A German War Bulletin noted that pushed by their officers, successes were obtained in this battle which seldom happened in this war.[7] The main reason were the excellent non-commissioned officers in the forefront.

From Paris, Foch telegraphed the Comando Supremo, *Le Gouvernement Français vous fait savoir que, si vous avez besoin de nos troupes, nous sommes prêtes à marcher.*[8] Like many of his contemporaries Foch was a man who appreciated cold steel. Having little knowledge of maneuver warfare, he was a man of the frontal infantry attack.[9] Gen. de Gondrecourt French Army liaison to the Comando Supremo communicated to Cadorna that French troops were immediately leaving for Italy via railway. The first contingent would be the XXXI Corps (two divisions), then two other divisions with artillery. French War Minister Paul Painlevé also contacted Cadorna with offers of assistance.[10]

Without consulting the military Lloyd George ordered two divisions to be sent to Italy overruling Lt. Gen. William Robertson Chief of the Imperial General Staff. The Prime Minister knew that with Russia, Serbia and Romania out of the war should Italy also be defeated the Central Powers could then deploy almost five million battle-hardened troops on the Western Front before the Americans arrived.[11] Should the Germans take the channel ports, where would the Americans land? He is also alleged to have stated that war was too important to leave to generals. Instead this was a phrase first uttered by Talleyrand and quoted to Lloyd George by Minister Aristide Briand of France during the conflict.[12] Haig was ordered to send a "good man" to command the British troops in Italy.[13] Cadorna had sent a memorandum to Brig. Gen. Charles Delmé-Radcliffe, requesting British troops which was received on October 27. Radcliffe, promptly telegraphed the Imperial General Staff in London receiving the response that reports of the impending disaster were exaggerated. He was ordered to steady the Italians and not make them panic, but promise no troops.[14] In retrospect, we see that the correct military decision was taken by a non-military person, the British Prime Minister, who overruled Robertson. The Welshman also realized that by helping Italy, she would become dependent on Britain, and thus diplomatically more pliable.[15] Telegrams now went out from London to British headquarters in France ordering troops to be sent to Italy and to the British Military Mission in Italy, that troops were on the way.[16] Sent was the XIV Corps (Lt. Gen. the Earl of Cavan), with the Twenty-third (Maj. Gen. Sir. J. M. Babington), and Forty-first (Maj. Gen. S.T. B. Lawford), Divisions. French troops sent were the Tenth Army (Gen. Duchêne), with the Forty-sixth, Forty-seventh, Sixty fourth, and Sixty-fifth Infantry Divisions. French and British artillery on the way back from Italy to France was now returned to the Italian Front and deployed to cover the bridges on the Tagliamento. Telegrams passed between Robertson (who did not want to send any troops), and Foch who responded "It is incontestable that General Cadorna has all that is necessary in material, troops and lines of resistance to stop the enemy, if he knows how to use them; but events, not the dictates of reason, dominate the situation."[17]

While the Italian military front was crumbling, Cadorna was expounding on the paintings of Gubbio of Assisi to his guests, the Generals Gaetano Giardino, ex-War Minister and Munitions Minister Alfredo Dell'Olio.[18] Invited to the Isonzo cauldron now were American troops. A Declaration of War by Washington against Vienna was also requested.[19]

Cadorna requested the Anglo-French troops to be immediately deployed in the line to relieve the tired Italian troops which was rejected by the respective governments. The allies were preoccupied with Italian lack of reserves as well as the real possibility that Italian troops would yield and expose the Anglo-French flanks. Anglo-French troops deployed to the rear as a reserve. What impressed the Anglo-French was the tremendous number of men heading home without their rifles. Being officers in armies with long national experience and tradition, they could not understand what was happening to the illiterate army which had no sense of national identity. Robertson felt that the Austro-Germans could not advance rapidly due to the fact that they had only one railhead, Tolmino, to supply them. Lt. Gen. Sir Herbert Plumer plucked from the Western Front decided to deploy his British units where the mountains met the Piave flatlands. If these units held Italy was safe.[20]

The OIR noted that the situation at 1300 was much less dangerous than the (in)famous bulletin issued by the Comando Supremo. This had stated, "Lack of resistance by units of the II Army which cowardly retreated without fighting or shamefully surrendered to the enemy has allowed Austro-German forces to break through our lines on the Julian front. Valiant efforts of other troops has not stopped the enemy advance onto the sacred soil of our Patria. Our lines are retreating according to a pre-established plan. Abandoned warehouses in the villages have been destroyed. The valor demonstrated by our soldiers in many memorable battles, fought and won during two and one half years of war gives faith to the Comando Supremo that again this time, the army to whom has been entrusted the honor and salvation of the Patria, shall fulfill its exact duty." As usual, the bulletin was sent to the foreign press and the Minister of War in Rome. Another bulletin was sent about which named the units involved, but this was probably by agents of the Central Powers. When the bulletin reached Rome, the politicians there naturally reacted with horror, and modified its text to read "The violence of the attack and the lack of resistance of several units of the II Army has allowed . . . . ." It gave the nation the impression that its soldiers did not fight, but many of them did fight, with valor and honor, especially against the Germans. Cadorna's bulletin was castrated per request of the Interior Ministry and the king.[21] The Comando Supremo had already telegraphed the text to the Swiss News Agency in Basle. As a result, from all over, questions were being brought to Sonnino regarding the disaster described in the bulletin of October 28.[22]

With the events and finger pointing, the dissent between the politicians and military came into the open. It seemed that the main focus of blame was on those who were on the front lines laying their lives on the line but politicians were not entirely blameless. On receiving the bad news, the Honorable Dugoni, member of the Socialist Party, announced that the Socialists, due to the seriousness of the moment, would no longer oppose the government in its actions (admitting it had), to win the war. A group of parliamentary deputies, *Unione Parlementare,* eighty five in number, met daily, not to help the government, but to check on the outcome of the ministerial crisis. The man who was to communicate with the Comando Supremo, the Honorable Leonida Bissolati, was so overcome by the events, that he contemplated suicide. In Italian political circles, everything showed a lack of cohesion to fight the war.

The middle class, which initially thought that the disaster was due to troop cowardice now realized that the huge mass of humanity fleeing the Austro-German troops identified with the proletariat and could be a future threat to itself. The lower classes whose sons were dying hoped for peace. They now felt bitter toward those whom they felt were responsible. Finally, the man in the trench who was doing his duty, going again and again on the attack, felt the disaster was not his fault. Pointing four fingers of his right hand at the author, a veteran of Caporetto noted, "Our cannons were arrayed like this, but did not fire. There had been a betrayal." Naturally, the veteran did not know of Badoglio's orders to the artillery not to fire until ordered. The public could easily see through the lies of government propaganda. All these factors would influence events in the post war period.

There were now three breaches in the Italian Army defenses. Strolling along the Isonzo the Twelfth Silesian had caused one, the second was between the Zona Carnia Command and the left wing of the II Army while the third was between two wings of the Italian II Army. Under normal circumstances advancing troops would have poured through these sectors. Instead the terrible weather, tiredness, temptation of food and wine (troops had to live off the land, were given little food), bridge destruction all contributed to the halting of the Austro-German juggernaut.

The Comando Supremo had been faced with a situation with which its staff could not cope. Appropriate orders were not issued, nor was there a mechanism to see if they were obeyed, nor was the refugee and military traffic controlled all of which led to chaos and a tremendous lowering of troop morale.

Chapter V Endnotes

The Agony's Fifth Day

1 Accounts concerning the II Army speak of the right, center, and left wings. The latter was made up of the remnants of the XXVII and IV Corps The center and right kept together as a unit, and shall be collectively referred to as the right wing.

2 Many ideas have been brought forward regarding the killing of Berrer. It seems that the following is the most authoritative. Capt. Francesco Prina commanded the troops who committed the act. He reported that many who had been given credit were in impossible positions to take aim. Only his unit was in the vicinity. Although a member of the *Carabinieri* was given credit for the episode, the War Diary of that unit made no mention of the incident. Prina declared it was an anonymous member of his unit the III Battalion of Cyclist Bersaglieri who performed the act; *Storia Illustrata,* Mondadori, Milano, August, 1967, *Colloqui coi Lettori,* p. 15.

3 OULK, Vol. VI, *Das Kriegsjahr 1917,*op. cit., p. 554

4 **USSME: Relazione Ufficiale,** ***Le Operazioni del 1917,(Gli Avenimenti dall'Ottobre al Dicembre)/Documenti, Vol. IV, Tomo 3° bis*****, Comando Seconda Armata, 28 Ottobre, 1917,** *Direttive per la sosta al Torre,* Protocol No. 280/G, p. 319

5 USSME: Relazione Ufficiale, Vol. IV, Tomo 3° bis, op. cit., Comando Ala Sinistra Seconda Armata, 28 Ottobre, 1917, *Ripiegamento sulla destra del Tagliamento,* Protocol No. 2943, p. 322

6 R. Bencivenga, op. cit., p. 109

7 RICC, Vol. I, p. 274. Quoted was a German War Bulletin.

8 *Les Armée Françaises dans la Grande Guerre,* Ministre de la défense, Paris, tome VI, Vol. I, Annexe 22

9 Aston, G, *Biography of Foch,* 1929, London, p. 122. Classic of generals of the era was this collection of phrases not acknowledging new weapons of war: *Mon centre céde, ma droite recule, situation excellent. J'attaque!* My center is giving way, my right is in retreat ; situation excellent. I shall attack.

10 S. Cilibrizzi, *Storia Parliamentare Politica e Diplomatica d'Italia,* Milano Tosi, 1925 Vol. VII, p. 123.

11 OBARI : op. cit., p. 58.

12 The Oxford Dictionary of Quotations, Second Edition London, 1955, p. 525; These words have been also attributed to Clemenceau; As noted it is often difficult to attribute quotations to one person. Talleyrand served in French government positions from Louis XVI through to the Bourbon monarchy.

13 Military Operations, Italy, 1915-1919, The Battery Press,' Nashville, Tenn. (U.S.A.) or Imperial War Museum, London, 1949, J. E. Edmonds, H.R. Davies, p. 59; Lt. Gen. Sir Douglas Haig was the commander of British Forces on the Western Front

14 PRO WO 106770 :Telegram No. 44030, C.I.G.S. to Brig. Gen. Delmé Radcliffe, British Military Mission, Italy, Oct. 27, 1917.

15 L. Albertini, *Venti Anni di Vita Politica,* Bologna, Zanichelli, 1950-53, Vol. 2, III: 37-38.

16 PRO: Telegram No. 4067, from C.I.G.S. to C.in C. France, Oct. 27, 1917, 2020. PRO WO 106770: Telegram No. 44069, from C.I.G.S. to Brig. Gen. Delmé Radcliffe, Octobe 27, 1917, 1900; USSME: Relazione Ufficiale, Vol. IV, Tomo 3° bis, Doc., Missione Militare Britannica, *Preavviso invio truppe britanniche in Italia,* October 28, 1917, Doc. 217, p. 442; Idem, Addetto Militare Italiano a Parigi, *Notizie circa invio truppe francese in Italia,* Doc. 216, Protocol 259, October 27, 1917,p. 441

17 *Les Armées Françaises dans la Grande Guerre,* Tome VI, Vol. I, Annexes 1, 1927, p. 62, *Ministêre de la guerre, êtat major de l'Armêe Service Historique*

18 A. Gatti, op. cit., p. 274.

19 *Foreign Relations of the United States,* 1917, Supp. 2, Page to Lansing, November 10,1917; Library of Congress, Wash. D.C.

20 PRO: CAB/45/84, Writing the *Official British History : Military Operations Italy 1915-1919 ;* In 1943-46 to write his text, Brig. Gen. J. Edmonds queried several British participants of the campaign, among them Lord Cavan eventual commander of British forces as well as Lt. Gen. Maurice Wingfield and his brother-in law, Lord Templeton, who was on Lt. Gen. Chichester'staff at Seventh Infantry Division; Cavan noted that he had lost his war diary in 1922, and had a fuzzy memory. All these hand-written reports to Edmonds are in the PRO.

21 Scaroni, Silvio, *Con Vittorio Emanuele* Mondadori, Milano, 1934, p. 134.

22 L. Aldrovandi Marescotti, *Guerra diplomatica. Ricordi e frammenti di diario 1914-19.* Milano, Mondadori, 1937. p. 477

CHAPTER VI

THE AGONY'S SIXTH DAY
October 29, 1917

The Stein and Hofacker Groups had penetrated like a wedge into the flesh of the Italian deployment.[1] *The Germans were now ready to use the "Vernichtungsstrategie" or strategy of annihilation, as preached by Clausewitz.*[2] *An exemplary product of German officer training, Lt. Gen. Hofacker realized that occupying the bridges at Latisana would trap the Italian III Army and give the Austro-Germans a victory that all generals dream about. Such was not to be due to the obstinancy of Boroevic. Signs of dissension appeared between the victorious Central Powers armies.*

But you're only a boy, young fellow M'lad
And you're not obliged to go
I'm seventeen and a quarter, Dad
And ever so strong, you know.

Anonymous

ON THE HOME front, Italians awoke, walked to their news stand, greeting the vendor with the words "give me a penny's worth of lies." In the morning, they were surprised to find the text of the Comando Supremo's bulletin of Oct. 28. The readers did not know that this was a complete pack of lies with earlier editions having been seized by Orlando's orders and a milder text substituted.

Krauss Group

By nightfall, units of the *Edelweiss* and German Jäger Divisions occupied Resiutta and stopped at the hamlet of Venzone. The Twenty-second Schützen crossed the Torre Creek via a new gangway and occupied Tarcento and Gemona (Maps 29, 35). By 1230 Col. *Freiherr* von Passetti (26° Schützen) reported that a company of his men had already entered Tarcento crossing via an emergency gangway with other units following. His surname showed the vastness and complexity of the Habsburg Empire. The whole XIV Army was racing toward the Tagliamento.[3] The Fiftieth Division proceeded toward the bridges at Pinzano, while the Fifty-fifth went to the railroad bridge at Cornino. The men of the I Corps were tired, soaked and hungry but their spirits were high. They knew that what they were accomplishing in these days was something special.

Stein Group

Preceded by a squadron of Uhlans (lancers) the Twelfth Silesian met little resistance arrived at Cascina Campeis. The AlpenKorps formed a commando unit to occupy the bridges at Bonzicco but transport was lacking, so the unit stopped at Fagagna (Map 40). Units of the German Two Hundredth Infantry Division reached the Bonzicco bridge only to find fifty yards of it carried away by the flood. To the rear marched the One Hundred-Seventeenth Infantry Division and Thirteenth Schützen. At 0645, Hofacker ordered the 4°Jäger (Two Hundredth Infantry Division) to occupy the Dignano and Codroipo bridges before they were destroyed. By 2100, the Tagliamento still could not be crossed. The garrison at Dignano resisted strenuously, but eventually succumbed. The 121° (Twenty-sixth Infantry Division), leaving Udine, reached Mereto di Tomba and the Tagliamento between Turrida and Riva. Cividale now was like a magnet attracting advancing troops and thousands of prisoners (Map 40). Since Hofacker was unsuccessful in linking up with the XIV Army, he directed the Twenty-sixth Division to proceed toward the Latisana bridges via Pozzuolo with the Fifth Infantry Division (Scotti Group) on it's left (Map 40). The Two Hundredth Infantry Division would compress the Italian position around Codroipo (Maps 29,40)). Losing contact with the Scotti Group the Fifth Division had linked up with Hofacker, while the First Austro-Hungarian Division was far behind. Shortly after 0600, an orderly officer sent by Lt. Col. Heymann Chief of Staff of the Hofacker Group arrived at Udine delivering Below's orders to proceed forward, not stopping until the Tagliamento bridges were taken. Immediately, the XII Grenadiers (Fifth Infantry Divison), left for Campoformido. These troops had a difficult march. The road showed an unimaginable view of the Italian collapse. There were arms, vehicles and baggage littered all over. The entire roadway of Udine-Codroipo, sixty feet wide, was blocked by an enormous number of parked military vehicles and artillery of all calibers, with horses still tied to their vehicles. A single pedestrian would have a hard time walking through. One author reported 350,000 soldiers and 400,000 civilians in the mass of humanity.[4] Fleeing peasants remained with their carts afraid and sad, painting a picture of an uncontrolled and incredible flight. Most of the deserters fleeing southward were halted at the Po River Bridges but some made it to Naples, Bari and Sicily.[5] *Carabinieri* tried to set up check points, but were overwhelmed by the military and civilian flood which flowed toward their stations. Traffic control was impossible in the sea of retreating people. Officers sought to maintain discipline with the soldiers they knew, but realized they had no authority with those they did not. Some men kept their rifles, some discarded them. Cries of "The war is over" were constantly heard. There had been no food for the troops for over one week. Be it in a retreat or rapid advance, supplies never arrived because troops were never where they were supposed to be.

At 0011 the offensive-minded Grenadiers reached Campoformido, halting with the fear of remaining isolated, as there was still combat to the southeast. Due to the slowness of the Austro-Hungarian First Infantry Division, the Fifth Infantry Division had formed a wedge toward the west, whose southern border was not covered. Nevertheless, both Wedel and Hofacker were convinced that it was important to quickly continue to the Tagliamento. At 1500 they resumed the advance and reached Basagliapenta, where they were met by three squadrons of Italian cavalry led by their commander accompanied by a monk in a grey habit riding at his side. Not caring about death, they charged the German troops and were cut down by machine guns. Hofacker met Krafft (who had just arrived from Kranj) at Udine giving him his intention to proceed southwestward to take the bridges at Latisana (Map 29, 35). This proposed maneuver has been lost to historians enveloped in the tragedy of Caporetto. If his proposal was carried out, there would have been a victory with annihilation, knocking Italy out of the war. Hofacker, newly promoted to corps commander, should be commended for his overall vision of how the battle was developing. His men were proceeding due west. Proceeding parallel and to his south was the *II Armée Isonzo.* Proceeding westward toward the Latisana and Madrisio bridges parallel and south of the Austro-German troops, closer to the Adriatic was the Italian III Army pursued by the *I Armée Isonzo.* Armed with legal agreements with the O.K.L. The Serb threatened to arrest and place in his army any German soldier crossing his lines. Krafft knew that in performing his maneuver Hofacker would cross the areas of pursuit of the *Armées Isonzo,* but felt that they were far in the rear and could never reach the retreating Italians. Not wanting to lose the opportunity for an annihilation victory he asked Hofacker to make all the preparations, but it was necessary to await the return of Below for final approval. Hofacker went back to his headquarters, certain that he had convinced Krafft about what he wished to do issuing the following orders at 2100 for the morrow.

> The Two Hundred Infantry Division was to occupy the bridges at Dignano and Codroipo (*Maps 29, 35)*

The Fifth Division was to remain at Codroipo and subsequently follow the right wing of the Twenty-sixth Division.

The Twenty-sixth and Fifth Infantry Division followed by the Austro-Hungarian First Infantry Division were to proceed in a southwest direction with the First to follow the Fifth.

A big decision was to be made concerning crossing the Tagliamento River. The A.O.K. had agreed to proceed only as far as the river, while the XIV Army had not received permission from Bad Kreuznach to go beyond.[6] Below and Krafft realized that if they proceeded beyond the river, there would be a great opportunity to annihilate the whole enemy II and III Armies knocking Italy out of the war. They wanted not a simple victory, but an annihilation victory. The keys were the bridges at Latisana where there were foot and railway bridges. If these were taken, the Italian III Army could not cross and would be trapped. To its rear and north would be the *Armée Isonzo* while to the south was the Adriatic Sea. *If they crossed it would mean many battles in the future.* There had been no news from the *II Armée Isonzo* for some time. It had arrived with its Twenty-seventh Infantry Division at Buttrio, the Twenty-eighth at Pradamano, the Sixtieth and Thirty-fifth further to the south, with the XXIV Corps at Cormôns. It was decided that Hofacker's Group would take the Latisana bridges by October 30. Thinking that Boroevic's men were far to the rear Krafft and Below issued these orders at 2200 thus nullifying Hofacker's orders:

I. The Tagliamento must be crossed without waiting for orders.

II. The left wing of the army must aim for Latisana without awaiting orders to advance. This task is entrusted to the Scotti Group with the First, Fifth, and One Hundred-seventeenth Infantry Divisions.

III. The Hofacker Group (Twenty-sixth and Two-Hundredth Divisions) should proceed to Codroipo, then proceed further north with the intention of pursuing as well as passing the enemy on the right. Its left wing should arrive at S. Vito al Tagliamento *(Map 40)*

IV. The Krauss and Stein Groups should proceed westward beyond the Tagliamento. Their right wing should follow the foothills of the mountains.[7]

By day's end the Torre Creek had been crossed by four divisions of the XIV Army. Orderly officers now were sent with orders to the different commands. About midnight an officer of Hofacker's staff arrived at XIV Army command to note that all was in preparation for deployment in the a.m. according to the "agreement with Krafft." However, arriving at XIV Army Headquarters, the poor officer was informed of different plans outlined as just noted, and was upset and confused. It seemed that the preparations had gone beyond such, and were taken as tantamount to movement orders.

The A.O.K. headquarters was very much to the rear while the X Army's was at Tarvisio, the *II Armée Isonzo* at Logatec, the *I Armée Isonzo was* at Sesana, both far to the rear (Map 29 for Tarvisio). Boroevic was at Postumia while Archduke Eugene with his SouthWest Command headquarters was at Maribor still attempting to make up his mind about crossing the river. Not being used to maneuver warfare Boroevic's men advanced very slowly. The *Armées Isonzo* had not received the orders which Below had issued regarding the area of pursuit of the *II Armée Isonzo.*

Continuing Dissension Between the Victors

There was now dissension between the victors about future strategy. The Germans wanted to pursue beyond the Tagliamento River while the A.O.K. was happy to push the Italians beyond the national borders and advance no further. Eugene's orders had given the *Armées Isonzo* the pursuit sector from the Adriatic to north of the Codroipo bridges (actually the line Pozzo-Udine), causing a conflict with the XIV Army (Map 35). The *II Armée Isonzo* continued to advance moving into an area of pursuit occupied by the XIV Army. The Austro-Hungarian First and Fifth Infantry Divisions met stiff Italian resistance. To keep up the pressure on the Italians, Below wanted to cross the Tagliamento never thinking that Boroevic would catch up.

Further problems arose in another sector. In the Krauss Group Sector, Maj. Gen. von Wieden now commanding the *Gruppe Wieden* made up of the German Jäger Division and units of the Edelweiss arrived in Val Fella. This was important due to rail connections to Villach in Austria as well as Gemona and Udine (Maps 2,29,35). However, all these railways were dominated by the Italian-held M. Festa. Krauss ordered Wieden to capture M. Festa. The plan was to cross the river at Tolmezzo, then attack M. Festa. However, he soon found that the Austro-Hungarian Ninety-fourth Infantry Division (X Army) had the same idea. Aware of this, Krauss ordered the Jäger Division to veer away and proceed to Gemona. The outcome was that only on November 7 was M. Festa taken by the German Jäger Division.[8] Visiting homes in Tarcento, Krauss was very upset at the looting that the fleeing Italians had done. He was unable to proceed toward Cividale via the roadway that started near M. Stol and went to Platischis because the Italians had dynamited the road. He had to proceed along the Natisone River Valley (Map 23).

The Koschak Group (*Armée Isonzo*) reached Percoto-Soleschiano-Corno di Rosazzo. The XXIV and XIV Corps entered Cormôns. The VII reached Sagrado in time to save the bridges while the XXIII crossed the Isonzo on a gangway at Pieris.

At another level, Ludendorff asked the A.O.K. to send five German divisions back to the Western Front, a request which was denied as these divisions were in the forefront of the attack. Arz telegraphed Hindenburg that it would be best to let the operations continue until the Piave.[9] Of critical use now would have been cavalry units to pursue the Italians but the Alpenkorps and German Jäger Division had none of these units. No one has ever explained why cavalry units of other divisions were not used in pursuit. The author feels that the Austro-Germans had no idea that the offensive would be so successful and hence were not prepared to fully exploit the breach. Unable to achieve surprise in capturing the bridges over the Tagliamento, Hofacker ordered that the attempt be abandoned.

The Allies to the Rescue

Having received the bad news the British and French War Cabinets decided to send their military leaders to the Italian Front. Foch arrived at Treviso during the evening with Robertson arriving the next day. The Italian III Army covered by the VIII Corps and First Cavalry Division crossed the Tagliamento at Pinzano as did the British guns which were now used to bolster the temporary defense of the river.

At 0100, Montuori received orders from the Comando Supremo transferring the XII Corps and the *Corpo Speciale* (Special Group) to the left wing of the II Army.[10] Arriving via rail to the west bank of the river the *corpo* was to defend the bridges at Cornino and Pinzano. Its *Bologna* was deployed on the hills of M. Ragogna as a bridgehead on the left (east) bank of the Tagliamento (Maps 27, 29). Finding it impossible to cross the river at Rivis and S. Odorico via gangways troops of the left wing of the II Army (Gen. Etna) were ordered to the bridges at Trasaghis and the rail bridge at Cornino. The right wing (Gen. Ferrero) was ordered to the bridges of Dignano. The center (Gen. Petiti di Roreto) was proceeding to bridges at Pinzano. Meanwhile the bridge at Dignano was damaged so those troops had to proceed to Codroipo, crossing after the north wing of the III Army. One can imagine the crowd and confusion of peasants with their goods, retreating soldiers, some armed, some not as well as equipment some discarded, some not. During the night the Sixtieth Infantry Division (Italian IV Corps) crossed the Trasaghis bridge, then destroyed it. Surviving men of the Fiftieth Infantry Division and the VII Corps crossed at Cornino. The survivors of the XXVIII and XXVII Corps attempted to put up some resistance on the left bank of the Tagliamento. The latter corps was reduced to the Thirteenth Division which had the task to protect the bridge at Dignano. Covered by the Second Cavalry Division the left wing of the II Army reached the river at Pinzano and Cornino. These horsemen with a group of Bersaglieri were defending the line at Fagagna-Plasencis-S. Marco and were obligated to retreat to Cascanetto. Notified of this, Badoglio deployed the Thirteenth Division on the line Arcano-Rive d'Arcano linking up to the north with the troops at M. Ragogna, thus establishing a bridgehead to protect S. Daniele and the bridge at Pinzano (Maps 27,29,35).

The corps of the right wing of the Italian II Army had the task of protecting itself as well as the north wing of the III Army and the bridges at Codroipo. These men were now in a difficult situation. The roads from Palmanova and Udine converged on the bottle neck of Codroipo (Map 40). Moving down these roads was a mass of artillery and transport of the retreating troops. Soon the heavy equipment was abandoned forming a huge obstacle to any quick-flow of traffic. All the while enemy planes strafed and bombed the troops causing panic in the unaccustomed troops. Caviglia with his staff left Villanova and arrived at Pozzuolo at 0400. The streets were deserted with no lights in the houses as people afraid of advancing as well as retreating troops. Here as elsewhere the roads going out of town were crowded with wagons, guns, trucks, soldiers, civilians with children, animals and equipment of all kinds.[11] The military disaster had transformed the beautiful Friulian region full of vigor and life into a squalid area. Panic now reigned in the homes of the citizens. The area had belonged to Austria-Hungary with many of the surnames being German. At 2300 a defensive line was established by the XXIV Corps between Basagliapenta and Lestizza, while the VI Corps arrived at Mortegliano and Talmassons after heavy combat at Podgora. This protective action of the right wing of the II Army, enabled the untouched III Army to redeploy to the river and cross on the rebuilt bridge at Madrisio (Map 40). Precise orders were issued.[12] Most of the XIII Corps crossed during the night. Keeping the linkup with the IV Army at Casera Razza, the Italians crossed the Tagliamento at Ampezzo marching along its right bank to the Cornino bridge (Maps 27, 29). Situated there was an extension of the bridgehead of S. Daniele-M. Ragogna which proceeded to the right bank at Rivis (Map 29). At Palmanova there was another bridgehead with its apex facing east (Maps 35,40). This would give the II and III retreating Italian armies an axis on which to withdraw to the west. In the evening, the Comando Supremo issued new orders to the II and III Armies as well as to the Intendent General (Lt. Gen. Vittorio Zaccone) entitled, "Directives for the retreat to the Piave" which are summarized below.[13]

> The line Carnic PreAlps-Tagliamento should be held by the II Army (now including the XII Corps) and the III Army, as long as possible (*Map 40*).
>
> The II Army should pay special attention to its left wing from Casera Razzo to M. Ragogna, as any infiltration through the line at Maniago-Cornino would compromise the resistance at the Tagliamento (*Maps 27,28,29*).
>
> There is a danger that the salient in the Vicentine PreAlps may be threatened so the III Army must send two divisions to Brescia and an army group to Bassano-Thiene, to be taken from the first divisions who had arrived at the Tagliamento.
>
> Working with the II Army, the Intendence General shall transport stragglers to the Bacchiglione-Brenta sector (Maps 14A,29,35).
>
> The redeployment onto the right bank of the Piave when ordered shall take place step-wise starting from the left with the following deployment: (*Map 40*)

I, IX, XII, XVIII Corps which were transferred
from the I to the IV Army
Four French divisions from M. Grappa to
Ponte di Priula (excluded)
III Army (three corps) from Ponte di Priula
(included) to the sea

Cadorna thus acknowledged the presence of Allied troops in the theatre, but there was no mention being made of the redeployment of the II Army to the Piave. He also notified the British and French that more troops would be needed. Finally, there was danger in the Vicentine (Belluno) PreAlps (Map 40). The A.O.K. fixed November 10 as the date for the Eleventh Army (Conrad Group) to go on the offensive with the objective of the interdiction of the Brenta Canal (Maps 14 A, 24, 31). It had assigned the Twenty-first Schützen and One-Hundred Sixth Landstürm Divisions to Conrad, with the Fifty-second to arrive later.

Little information concerning the impending disaster had reached the Italian IV Army headquarters. Soon there was a question whether the withdrawal should be to the Tagliamento or Piave Rivers. Col. Pintor (Operations Chief of the Comando Supremo) later related that Cadorna always wanted to go to the Tagliamento while DiRobilant in a communication to his subordinate commanders declared that "the Comando Supremo would rest at the Tagliamento, then proceed to the Piave."[14] Finally, Order No. 11389 was issued noting that the troops would withdraw to the Tagliamento and perhaps later to the Piave. They would garrison the front Grappa-Ponte di Priula (Map 42).[15] The Italian IV Army commander reluctance has been addressed by other Italian commanders who studied the problem.[16] Per Cadorna's request he was to study local defenses and wished to set up fortifications in advance lines not abandoning favorable positions an opinion which led him in conflict with the chief of staff. To him is due the glory of the resistance on the Grappa not to Giardino who came along much later and received all the honors. He was very secretive and is one of the heroes of the war who did not receive acclaim.

The author has visited the battle sector using a small-tracked *trenino* to travel about some areas of the battle sectors up to almost 10,000 feet. It was a beautiful sight to climb to the mountain tops in a train but frightening to think of troops fighting at that altitude. The Fourth Army did not wish to move to an unknown sector but sectors are not chosen.[17] Battle sectors are usually not chosen. It was to retreat from the Yellow Line (Ospedaletto in V. Sugana-M.Agaro-Mt. Pavione-Piz di Sagron-M. Tamer-M. Civetta-M. Fernazza-M.Penna-M. Ritte-M. Antelao-Marmarole-Cima Gogna-M. Tudaio-Casera Razzo) to the Piave and M. Grappa. These fortifications were twenty miles behind the front and had been deprived of guns which had been sent to other fronts.

Cadorna had written to Foch and Robertson giving an explanation as to why the Eleventh Battle had not been continued. However, he did not state the bad condition of his armies. The pending disaster here would have grave repercussions with the Allies. The Italian General Staff asked the British Military Mission in Italy for small contingents of French and British troops to encourage the nation and the troops.[18]

Brig. Gen. Charles Delmé Radcliffe, Chief of the British Military Mission to Italy, notified Cadorna that two divisions were on their way from the Western Front being the troops which Lloyd George had insisted be sent. No one knew whether the Piave Front would hold. If it did not, the only alternative was to sue for peace.[19] Italy had no troops left to defend the boot. DeGondrecourt notified Cadorna that on October 28 French infantry had started its railway journey to the Italian Front. It was composed of the XXXI French Army Corps (two divisions) plus two other divisions, twenty six batteries of heavy artillery and eighteen mountain artillery batteries. Italian morale which had been steadily declining for two years, had now hit rock bottom. Seeing oncoming German troops, many officers had fled the scene. Aware of this, the illiterate Italian peasant *fanto* stole civilian clothes, discarded his rifle, and with the words, "The war is over," started his journey home. Later he was amazed to see Anglo-French troops. The peasant mind slowly processed the thought that foreigners were here fighting in his trenches. Perhaps he should stay and fight. What were these foreigners fighting for? The concept of Italian nationhood was taking shape in the trenches.

Chapter VI Endnotes

The Agony's Sixth Day

1 Krafft, op. cit.,: Entry of Oct. 29.

2 Gordon A. Craig, *The Politics of the Prussian Army,* 1956, Oxford University Press p. 63.

3 OULK Vol. VI, p. 562.

4 Luigi Cadorna, *Altre Pagine sulla Grande Guerra,* Mondadori, Milano, 1925, p. 202

5 Personal Communication

6 Bad Kreuznach was the site of the German Army Supreme Headquarters (O.K.L.)

7 Below's War Diary, Entry of Oct 29, 1917.

8 A. Krauss, op. cit., p. 88

9 OBARI, op. cit., p. 66

10 In the military language of the period, Group was the same as Corps; USSME: Relazione Ufficiale, Vol. IV, Tomo 3° bis, Doc. op. cit., Comando II Armata Doc. No. 144, 29 October 1917, p. 0100, *Passaggio XII Corpo alle dipendenze II Armata,* p. 326

11 Enrico, Caviglia, op. cit., p. 204

12 USSME:Relazione Ufficiale, Volume IV, Tomo 3° bis, Doc., op. cit., Comando III Armata, *Disposizioni per la utilizzazione dei ponti,* Doc. 143, Protocol 13/R, October 29, 1917, p. 324

13 USSME: Relazione Ufficiale, Vol. IV, Tomo 3° bis, Doc. Comando Supremo, *Direttive per eventuale ripiegamento,* Doc. 149, Protocol 5137, October 30, 1917, p. 332

14 AUSSME: rep. b1, vol. 18e: Diario Storico della 4a Armata, Allegati, all. n. 34, Protocol 11389 of 19-11-17 ; Col. Pintor's letter to Caviglia is in the

Museo del Risorgimento in Milano, Archivio della Guerra, fondo Caviglia reg. 27254 cartella 159, busta 3

15 Ibid, p. 350

16 Nuova Antologia, 1931, No. 1413, pp. 307-314 Enrico Caviglia, *La ritirata della 4a armata,*

17 USSME:Relazione Ufficiale, Volume IV, Tomo 3°, op. cit., p. 458

18 House of Lords Library, F44/3/27, No. 503

19 RICC: Vol. II, 548; Cadorna, *Lettere Familiare,* p 238; PRO CAB 24/31/2503 (Nov. 3, 1917, Delmé quoting Cadorna; Orlando, *Memorie,* op. cit., p. 296, 503-4

CHAPTER VII

DISSENSION BETWEEN THE VICTORIOUS ALLIES

October 30, 1917

Harsh disagreements developed between the victorious allies allowing the Italian III Army to escape. Foch met with Cadorna at Treviso.

Slav and Teuton, I count them all
My friends and brother souls,
With all the peoples, great and small,
That wheel between the poles.

Alfred Lord Tennyson,
"Epilogue to the Charge of
the Heavy Brigade"

HEAVY RAINS PERSISTED all day resulting in an overflowing and raging Tagliamento halting all attempts by the *Edelweiss* and German Jäger Divisions to ford the river (Map 29,35). The X Army occupied Moggio Udinese. The Fiftieth Infantry and Twenty-second Schützen Divisions were on the left bank of the river occupying the disarmed fortifications of Osoppo, Ospedaletto, and Tricesimo. Reports showed that the rapid advance was taking a toll on the advancing troops. Passetti (Kaiserschützen) reported that his regiment was exhausted lacking food, munitions and exposed to the elements. The Fifty-fifth Division reached Tarcento (Capt. Redl, IV/4° Bosnian), then occupied the railroad bridge at Cornino. Passing Maiano near Farla, the unit engaged in heavy combat aided on its left by the 63° (Twelfth Silesian). The bridge had two spans resting on the island of Clapat in the middle of the river both under constant machine gun and artillery fire.

By 1300, Lequis ordered two battalions of the 23° to advance toward Rive d'Arcano, Giavons, and Villanova, attacking S. Daniele from the west and south. Subject also to an attack from the east by the 62°, its fate was sealed (Maps 29,35). By nightfall, the left bank of the river at Pinzano and Spilimbergo was in German hands, while to the south, the Alpenkorps proceeded in two columns toward the bridge at Bonzicco (Map 29). The gangway at Spilimbergo had been destroyed but Italian troops were noted to be still withdrawing via the intact bridge at Pinzano (Map 40). The commander of the II/1° Jäger climbed the bell tower at Dignano and noted that there was a one hundred twenty foot piece missing on the western extremity of the Bonzicco Bridge (Maps 29, 40). This would have been a good place to cross, but the commander of the I Jäger ordered his troops to return to Dignano and Bonzicco crossing there avoiding the pursuit area of the Twelfth Division.

Receiving the new orders Hofacker was upset thinking that he was being criticized. Later he found out the truth about some of the top officers of the A.O.K. who really did not care if the battle was won but only wished to impose harsh conditions on Germans. The Fifth Infantry Division could not communicate with Scotti so it became part of Hofacker's unit as he ordered the Twenty-sixth and Two Hundredth Infantry Divisions to move out. The vanguard of the II/121° reached the Delizia bridges (Codroipo) while the XI/4° arrived at a nearby rail bridge. With advancing Germans and withdrawing Italians on the bridge explosive charges on it were detonated killing all. In the afternoon at Campodiformo Wiedel (*Edelweiss*) met the C.O. of the Habsburg Twenty-eighth Infantry Division who showed him written orders from the II Corps which was advancing in the right wing of the *II Armée Isonzo.* To accomplish his orders (proceed north of Codroipo), he would have to cross German lines. What happened? Now started the biggest political problem on the Austro-German side of the battle. As previously noted, Below thought that the *Armée Isonzo* was far behind. Before he left for Udine, an Austro-Hungarian officer (II Corps), arrived at headquarters reporting that his unit was approaching the railway at Udine-Palmanova (Map 35). By late evening, its Twenty-eighth Division had reached Pradamano, while the Fifty-seventh had reached Buttrio (Map 40). He realized that there would be traffic problems. There were other Austro-Hungarian divisions immediately to the south (Thirty-fifth and Sixtieth Divisions). South of Cormôns was the XXIV Corps. As the river water levels receded clearing the Udine-Palmanova railway the II Corps was able to cross the Torre Creek. Gen. Kaiser (C.O. II Corps) became aware that the Austro-Hungarian First Infantry Division (Scotti Group), was marching in a direction going southwest diagonally across the path of his corps. The officer noted that the pursuit sector of the II Corps had as its northern sector the line Udine-S. Odorico. The XIV Army commander was surprised and apprehensive about this news. A letter was sent to the Austro-Hungarian II Corps commander asking him to order his men to accompany XIV Army troops in a southwest direction toward Latisana (Maps 29,35). He noted that if successful they would trap the entire Italian III Army. Without a bridge to cross the Tagliamento Aosta's men would be in a sack. To its rear was the *I Armée Isonzo* to the south was the Adriatic, to the west would be Hofacker's men while Boroevic's other *Armée Isonzo* was to the north. With the huge number of troops and lack of boats evacuation by sea was not an option. Feeling that Habsburg troops would go along Below changed orders so that the First and One-Hundred-Seventeenth Infantry Divisions would proceed in their pursuit sectors, while the Fifth Infantry Division which was far ahead would veer southwestward. The Twenty-sixth Division proceeded to Codroipo occupying the town. The Fifth Division advanced in two columns. The column to the right (Lt. Col. Amman von Borowsky) made up of the XII Grenadiers while that on the left, Col. von Jena led the VIII Grenadiers. The first reached Rivolto and Bertiolo, while the second arrived at Flambro. The Fifth Division was now assigned to the Hofacker Group, while the One-Hundred-Seventeenth aimed southward toward Pozzuolo (Map 40).

Below's plans did not come to fruition. It seemed that Boroevic was still upset that he had not been given command of the XIV Army insisting on the enforcement of the legal agreements. Far from the front, on a map, he drew the areas of pursuit assigned to his armies. Assigned to the *II Armée Isonzo* was a strip north of the line at Orzano-Udine-S.Odorico-Pozzo, which was exactly the line of Gen. Kaiser. The demarcation line of the *I Armée Isonzo* was furnished by the line at Cormons-Medeazza-S. Maria la Longa-Mortegliano-S. Vidotto. Consequently, between the two armies (XIV and *Isonzo*) there was a potential for a big traffic jam. Even the OAR acknowledged that if the original plans of Hofacker were carried out, the Italian armies on the left (east) bank of the Tagliamento would be annihilated. It criticized Boroevic for establishing areas of pursuit from his headquarters faraway in Postumia without consulting Below. If the Fifth Infantry Division had arrived at Rivignano there would have been more problems. The slow-moving Habsburg troops allowed the Italian III Army to escape while Udine was drowning in Italian prisoners who were guarded by units of the Thirteenth Schützen. The Austro-Hungarian First Infantry Division broke through the fortification at Sammardenchia and proceeded westward as Boroevic had insisted. By midnight all Italian troops had crossed the bridges over the Tagliamento, so the question of pursuit was academic. *The annihilation victory desired by Below and Krafft was denied them by their own allies.*

The Italian IV Army issued Message No. 11387 noting to the Comando Supremo that some realignment had been made on its right flank to keep the juncture with the Zona Carnia Command at Casera Razzo (Maps 28, 35).[1] At Codroipo there was great food booty for which the two commanders, Hofacker and Ernst von Below (Otto's cousin), received the *Pour le Mérite* from the Kaiser. In a great switch, soldiers who usually received packages from the home front were able to send food packages of fifty-lbs. per month home to their families who were starving due to the British naval blockade. Within three months, bread rations would be reduced to 200 grams per day to the troops.[2] Bread lines were starting to be noted in many cities of the Central Powers. Due to The Serb's non-cooperation Below now had to issue new orders: (Maps 27, 29, 35,40)

> Krauss was to take the crossings at Cornino-Gemona (Map 35)
> Stein was to take the crossing at Dignano aiming for Pordenone (Map 35)
> Hofacker (Fifth Division included),was to attack Varmo east of the river, but also take the bridges west of Codroipo and aim for Motta di Livenza (Map 29,35)

Scotti with the German One-Hundred-Seventeenth Infantry and the First Austro-Hungarian Divisions would push the enemy beyond Mortegliano to attack Latisana. Krafft reported 60,000 Italian prisoners were taken from the VIII, IX Corps of the III Army which were marching toward Codroipo together with the remnants of the II, VI, XXIV and XXV Corps. Many of these units deviated toward Madrisio and Latisana to avoid capture.

Events on the Italian Side of the Trench

Cadorna now issued orders for the withdrawal of the northern wing of the II Army along the Carnic PreAlps, always linked to the right wing of the IV Army.[3] Keeping the Passo Mauria in Italian control was the responsibility of the left wing of the II Army which also was to guard the Alemagna Road (Maps 28,29)[4] Likewise the IV Army would secure the Ponte Nelle Alpi until the II Army had crossed the meridian of Vittorio Veneto none of which went according to plan.

The divisions of the Italian XII Corps (Twenty-sixth, Thirty-sixth and Sixty-third Infantry Divisions), deployed in the Carnic-Prealp areas (Map 40). At the end of the day, the *Siracusa* and *Genova* remained on the left bank of the Tagliamento as well as on the small island of Clapat, defending the rail bridge at Cornino. The *Bologna* was on M. Ragogna protecting the bridge at Pinzano. Maj. Gen. Rubin di Cervin the commander of the Thirteenth Infantry Division (it had been attached to the XXVII Corps) committed suicide after being accused by Badoglio of retreating too quickly during combat on the Isonzo and Torre Rivers. In an attempt to block the Austro-German advance in the direction of Udine-Codroipo, Maj. Gen. Giacinto Ferrero ordered the XXIV, VI, and II Corps to attack the enemy in the left flank and establish a bridgehead at Codroipo. The Seventh and Forty-eighth Infantry Divisions counterattacked at Pozzuolo and Mortegliano then withdrawing from Pozzuolo formed three columns all under the command of Lt. Gen. Agostino Ravelli. The right column proceeded from Pozzuolo to Campoformido with the *Bergamo.* Near Carpeneto, when it came in contact with the enemy One-Hundred-Seventeenth Division it redeployed to Pozzuolo where the II Cavalry (Maj. Gen. Ermo Di Capodilista) was deployed (Map 40). It was to be held to cover the Italian withdrawal through Codroipo. As Habsburg First and Sixtieth Inf. Divisions arrived machine guns placed on roof tops slowed their advance. To further slow the enemy at about 1300 the IV Squadrons (*Novara*) and later of the *Genova* charged the enemy resulting in almost 100% casualties known as the "Balaklava of the Italian cavalry." By 1900 the attackers held the town while by nightfall combat had spread to Mortegliano garrisoned by the 21° Bersaglieri and by units of the *Ravenna.* The 240° (*Pesaro)* was east of the hamlet. All were overcome and captured. These small firefights slowed the attackers, allowing the Italian III Army to be saved. Montuori now felt that the major danger to the III Army and the left wing of the II, no longer came from the east, but from the north west, the bridges at Codroipo where Hofacker's Twenty-Sixth Infantry Division appeared in the early afternoon

(Maps 29,35). Those assigned to the defense of these bridges, about 4,000 men of no particular unit, held until 1100. The bridges were blown up twelve hours prematurely trapping many Italian troops. Twelve thousand men on the east bank of the river were captured as well as much war booty. The War Diary of the II Army, noted that the Delizia bridges (stone bridges at Codroipo) were prematurely destroyed leaving much war equipment and supplies as well as men to the enemy.[6]

Having arrived the evening before, Foch was at the Comando Supremo by 0700 noting chaos as well as the fears of Cadorna regarding the morale of his troops. Initially the Frenchman agreed with everything the Italian stated about a possible enemy attack in the Trentino (Map 14A).[7] Later there developed an ugly confrontation with the visitor constantly asking questions as to whether certain procedures had been carried out (they had been). He wanted a reserve strike force to be available to seal the possible enemy breakthroughs either across the Piave or through the mountains.[8] The Italian was somewhat miffed that the newly arrived troops would not be under his command.[9] He agreed to deploy troops from the Adige to the Mella Rivers to halt any enemy incursion from the Giudicarie Mountains. There was much discussion as to where the next line of defense should be the Piave or Adige Rivers. Cadorna felt that the stand should be on the Piave as to withdraw further would cause the army to melt.[10] In any case he ordered the inundation of the Adige River sector. (Map 35). Foch seemed to have favored the Piave.[11] Both Robertson and Foch were in agreement that twenty Anglo-French divisions were not needed. It was felt that the Italian Army could hold at the Piave. At Cadorna's request two French divisions were sent to the Bolzano sector and two would remain in the Verona sector (Map 14A).[12]

Events on the Home Front

Malagodi had a long conversation with Luigi Albertini (editor of the *Corriere della Sera)* who had just returned from a meeting with Cadorna in Treviso where he reported that the troops did not fight especially the *Roma, Foggia,* and *Reggio.* All through history reports of battlefield events have been forwarded erroneously to the harm of the units involved (chapter II). The *Reggio* was not deployed on the Isonzo and the reports on the *Roma* had been erroneous.

During this one of the most difficult times in Italian history, Rome was without a government from October 25 to October 30. The new Prime Minister of Italy was Vittorio Emanuele Orlando, a Sicilian. In the past, he had pushed for peace, but in his new position, this was unthinkable. The new War Minister was Lt. Gen. Vittorio Alfieri. At 2030, the new Prime Minister telegraphed Cadorna, that in assuming his new post, he wanted to assure him that the government and the people were behind them in this hour of crisis. "Not for one moment has their faith in the army and its commander been shaken." One hour later, another telegram, "Reconfirming the faith and admiration that I have always had toward Your Excellency, overcoming large difficulties, with the strength of soul and the great of mind." He concluded with these words, "My full faith and that of my government regarding the miracle that undoubtedly Your Excellency will perform." Cadorna responded on the next day, noting that he had done his duty, and added, "I feel the necessity to have the closest collaboration and solidarity with the government. For this, your words are the best promises." Orlando had used the beautiful language of politics and diplomacy while planning for Cadorna's replacement.

Chapter VII Endnotes

Dissension between the Victorious Allies

1 USSME: Relazione Ufficiale Volume IV, Tomo 3°, op. cit., 1967 p. 460

2 Kriegsarchiv, Vienna: Stöger Steiner, *Memoire über die Möglichkeit des Durchhalten im Winter, 1917/1918,* KA MKSM 1917 69-2/7

3 USSME: Relazione Ufficiale, Vol. IV., Tomo 3° bis, Documenti, 1967, op.

cit., Comando Settore Sinistra, 2a Armata, 30, Ottobre, 1917, *Ripartizione della fronte. Dispozione varie,* Doc. No. 145, Protocol No. 30, p. 327

4 USSME: *Idem,* Comando Supremo, *Ordine per lo Sbarramento direttrice Fella-Mauria,* October 29, 1917, Document No. 146, Protocol 5114, p. 329

5 Giacomo Viola *La Battaglia di Pozzuolo del Friuli,* Gaspare Editore Udine 1998, p. 80.

6 AUSSME: War Diary of the Italian II Army, entry dated Oct. 30, 1917

7 OULK: Vol. VI, p. 493-494; The A.O.K. had considered an attack through the Trentino but lacked sufficient number of mountain troops (twelve divisions) and nearby railheads

8 Les Armées Françaises dans la Grande Guerre, op. cit., (VI, 1), 97

9 USSME: Relazione Ufficiale, Vol. IV, Tomo 3° Roma, 1967, op. cit., p. 422

10 USSME: Relazione Ufficiale, Vol. IV, Tomo 3° bis, Doc., op. cit., Comando Supremo, 30-Ottobre 1917, *Direttive per eventuale ripiegamento sul Piave,* Doc. No. 149, Protocol No. 5137, p. 332

11 FAR, tome VI, Volume I, p. 95

12 USSME: Relazione Ufficiale, Vol. IV Tomo 3° bis, Documenti, op. cit., Comando Supremo, 30 Ottobre 1917, *Dislocazione truppe francese,* Document No. 245, Protocol No. 5160, page no. 498

The author is indebted to Col. Marco Centritto of the Italian Army for clarifying events concerning the actions of the Italian cavalry at Pozzuolo del Friuli on 10-31`-17.

CHAPTER VIII

THE LOST BATTLE OF ANNIHILATION

October 31, 1917

On this sunny day due to the overflowing and raging river advancing troops could not cross. Below's problems with the Armée Isonzo persisted. Boroevic's obstinancy allowed the Italian III Army to escape the trap.

Each of the heroes around us has fought for his
land and line,
But thou has fought for a stranger, in hate of a
wrong not thine.

Elizabeth Barrett Browning,
"A Court Lady"

Krauss Group

BY EARLY A.M. most of the Italian Army had crossed the Tagliamento. At 0200 Von Wieden received new orders. The German Jäger Division was to proceed toward Ospedaletto and Gemona (Maps 29, 35). The *Edelweiss* was to proceed toward Artegna. Unable to cross the river, the Twenty-second Schützen was held up at Osoppo. A battalion of the German Jäger Division was sent to Amaro to attempt to cross the Tagliamento and to take Forte di M. Festa while Italian troops remained on the right bank. Joined by the III Brigade (Fiftieth Infantry Division), the

Fifty-fifth Division stopped at the bridge at Cornino (Maps 27,29,35). Arriving at the river banks Capt. Redl (with a Bosnian battalion) noted the island of Clapat in the middle of the river with one span going to each bank. The bridge was constructed of a metal lattice-work resting on stone pillars. Around some of the pillars were noticed explosives which due to the rapid German advance had not been detonated. Fuses had already been installed. All was quiet on the island occupied by Italian infantry companies plus fifteen machine guns. Fooled by the noted lack of enemy activity a group led Capt. Von Tisljac assaulted the island suffering heavy losses including his death. During the night Austro-Hungarian engineering troops succeeded in removing the fuses on the near spans. Careful plans were now made to assault the island. Two unsuccessful attempts were made with heavy losses. To the south, the XV Brigade (Fiftieth Infantry Division), with the Twelfth Silesian, failed in their attack on M. Ragogna (Map 27). Stein emphasized that it was important to take M. Ragogna to halt the Italian destruction of the Cornino and Pinzano bridges. Even with the addition of the Thirteenth Schützen Division the assaults failed. Air reconnaissance had noted a small bridge over pile-driven logs between Cornino and Pinzano, as well as Pontaiba. The water level in the river had decreased by eighty cm. (thirty two inches), but it still was not fordable. Attempting to swim across many troops drowned in the swift current. The Alpenkorps deployed near Bonzicco failed in attempting to cross while the Hofacker Group was still trying to cross at Delizia (Map 40). The Two-Hundredth Infantry-Division started its march southward reaching Gorizzo and Gradiscutta. The Fifth Infantry Division (von Wedel) was to cross at Madrisio and proceed to Rivolta and Bertiolo isolating Italian troops south of Codroipo instead crossing was impossible due to a full moon and incessant Italian shelling.

The One-Hundred-Seventeenth and First Austro-Hungarian Divisions had no difficulty in advancing, but the German Two-Hundredth and Fifth Divisions started to have traffic difficulties as the Austro-Hungarian divisions approached from the east. At

1100, Col. Podhaisky, Chief of Staff of the II Imperial Corps arrived at the Austro-German XIV Army headquarters at Udine. He reported that his unit had received multiple orders from Boroevic to proceed westward while German troops previously proceeding on a parallel to its north were now proceeding southwestward crossing his lines. A few minutes later, Major von Jansa, liaison from the A.O.K. to Krobatin's X Army reported that the Italians were dismantling their radio stations in the Trentino all the way to Cortina d'Ampezzo (Map 35). This could only mean that the Italians intended to withdraw to the Piave, so the resistance on the Tagliamento was only to cover the retreat. Below was in Cividale for Berrer's funeral, so Krafft gave the order for the II Corps to halt in its tracks subsequently approved by Below. At 1700 Kaiser arrived at Udine reporting that he had not carried out Krafft's orders. This had been an attempt to stop a traffic jam as German troops had been going in a southwest direction, through the westward marching Habsburg troops. He also noted that according to stipulations signed by both armies, Habsburg troops had precedence in the right of way when advancing to the battle sectors. Force was to be used against the Germans if needed. If German troops were found in their area of pursuit, they were to be made subject to the Austro-Hungarian command. Below told him that the Habsburg troops moved too slow. He was unable to reach Eugene or Boroevic to obtain authorization as both were incommunicado while moving their headquarters. Not wanting to place his troops under the command of others, Below simply wanted the *II Armée Isonzo* to stop in its tracks until the next day. Krafft and Below knew that if Boroevic continued his slow march, all that the XIV Army would have was a victory while they were aiming for an annihilation of the entire Italian Army. The *Armées Isonzo* were letting them get away.

Coalition warfare is never simple. In this instance there was a military commander subordinate to an allied superior. Below had the right of access to the O.K.L. Often during the Second World War Soviet, British and American officers constantly quarreled among themselves regarding matters of policy and procedure, provoking disagreements and accusations. However there was always the objective of defeating the Nazis. At Caporetto, such was the animosity between German and Austro-Hungarian officers that it seemed some Habsburg generals did not care whether the Italians were defeated or not.

Since the right wing of the XIV Army could not advance Below ordered the Hofacker Group to attempt to cross at Codroipo, placing the Fifth Division on its right flank. The One-Hundred-Seventeenth Division returned to the Stein Group deploying near Pantianicco. The Scotti Group and its headquarters with the Austro-Hungarian First Infantry Division would withdraw to Udine becoming the second line. This was the first pause in the attack since October 24. Kaiser did not heed the advice of his brother Habsburg general Goiginger, to have his troops march next to the German troops when the traffic jams arose. His Sixtieth Infantry Division arrived simultaneously with the German Fifth Infantry Division, at the Madrisio bridge. Being the senior general in the Koschak Group (*II Armée Isonzo*) and unable to communicate with them he had his division cross alongside the German troops. By nightfall, the Fifth Division was at the Varmo ford, the One-Hundred Seventeenth at Rivignano, while Goiginger's men were mixed in with the Germans at Bertiolo; the Austro-Hungarian Thirty-fifth Infantry Division at Arcis (seven miles from Latisana), the First Austro-Hungarian Infantry Division (II Imperial Corps), at Pozzuolo, nine km. (approx. five miles), southwest of Udine (Maps 29,35 and Map 40 for geography). More bad news arrived when Below was informed that the Austro-Hungarian X Army (FML Krobatin), had made no forward progress to capture the railway that went to the Tagliamento.[1] There were now four corps on its banks unable to advance just waiting for the flow rate and water level to decrease. Below was also worried that he had no bridging equipment to cross the Tagliamento or Piave Rivers.

The southward advance with three divisions had lost its impetus resulting in retreating Italian troops using the Madrisio and Latisana bridges to save large units. Today the *I Armée Isonzo* occupied Latisana (Map 29). Strong units tried to capture the Italians on the western bank, but reached the bridges when the enemy had already disappeared. At 1800, when telephone communications were available with the Archduke Below discussed the traffic problem concerning the *II Armée Isonzo.* He requested that it not advance until tomorrow. As usual no answer was immediately forthcoming. Attempting to avoid any episodes of his troops coming under the orders of allied commanders, Below issued the following orders:

1. The Hofacker Group should attempt to cross at Cornino with the German Fifth Infantry Division on its right (Map 35)
2. The One-Hundred-Seventeenth Infantry Division should march northward to link up with the Stein Group.
3. The Austro-Hungarian First Infantry Division shall disengage northeast of Udine and rest.
4. The Scotti Group should proceed to Udine and become the second line.
5. The Austro-Hungarian Fourth Division should remain near Cividale.

All this resulted in the first halt in the offensive. No movements would be made until the Tagliamento was crossed.

Krauss reported only casualties of two of his divisions for the period of October 24 to October 31. The *Edelweiss* suffered officers dead, eight, with 210 men killed, while wounded were officers twenty-three and men 740. Most of these losses were in the *Gruppe Rombon* where the casualties were officers six and men 155 lost, of which nine were frozen to death indicating the terrible battle conditions, with wounded being fourteen officers and 500 men. In the same period, the Twenty-second Schützen suffered four officers and seventy-nine men killed. Wounded were eighteen officers and 485 men. Thus we see that the four battalions of the *Gruppe Rombon* suffered more casualties than the eleven battalions of the Schützen Division up to reaching the Tagliamento showing that mountain combat is often bloody.

On the Italian side of the battle bulletins were issued (but who could read them) that anyone who had discarded his rifle would be subject to immediate execution. It was difficult for the illiterate infantry to understand that this was a severe military infraction. In their minds they had fixed the idea that the war was over, and they were going home to help with the harvest, no longer needing a rifle. Cadorna, feeling that a temporary halt on the Tagliamento would give troops time to rest ordered all artillery to be sent to the Piave.[2] This pause gave Below's men time to catch up. The danger from the Austro-Germans now came from the Carnic-PreAlps as the decreasing river levels gave them many places to ford the river (Map 40). At 0100 Montuori ordered that the XII Corps now be detached to the left wing of the II Army as was DiGiorgio's *Corpo Speciale*. Knowing this, Cadorna made plans to contain the enemy advance. The Comando Supremo issued new orders to the II and III Armies which are summarized below.[3]

1. "The withdrawal shall be stepwise starting with the left wing with a strong rear-guard in successive stages to: *(Maps 29, 33, 40).*

   Cellina-Casarsa-Tagliamento-Livenza *Rivers)* plus the Monticano (*River)*, where the troops shall rest until further orders. Cavalry units shall also assist in the rear-guard action.
2. The II Army shall be responsible for traffic control.
3. The III Army shall be responsible for the rear-guard action which shall include units of the II Army and cavalry now assembling at Aviano *(Maps 27, 29,35).*

   The northern wing must be very strong.

4. The orders to the XII Corps stated in part, "The withdrawal of the troops east of the line Tramonti (*excluding it*), should proceed along the foothills of Travesio-Paludea-Maniago and guard the outlets of Paludea and Travesio until the *Corpo Speciale* had passed. Forces on the left (*east)* bank of the Tagliamento to west of the Tramonti line shall proceed westward toward the Passo Mauria" (*Map 28*). The orders further stated "Forces on the west bank of the Tagliamento and to the left of the Tramonti line about noon shall send one column westward through the Forcella di Palla Barzana and another further to the north via the Forcella Clautana *(Map 28)*. The two columns shall link up in the Passo S. Osvaldo—Barcis remaining there until the IV Army has crossed the parallel of Longarone *(Map 40)*. The Clautana column shall descend onto Longarone via Erto and Casso and shall place itself in the rear of the IV Army while the other column shall meet them in the plains."

After these steps the XII Corps issued orders which are summarized below:

1. Units of the Twenty-sixth Infantry Division deployed on the left bank of the Tagliamento River should withdraw to the Passo Mauria, linking up with the I Corps at Casera Razzo and cover the flanks of the IV Army (*Maps 28, 29*). Those on the right side of the Tagliamento would withdraw along the Val Meduna and detach a battalion to guard the mule path at Forcella Clautana (*Maps 17, 28*).
2. Units of the Thirty-sixth Infantry Division should withdraw stepwise along the Arzino Valley while the Sixty-third would withdraw along the same valley to deploy astride the roads Arduin to Clauzetto and Colle di Pontaiba-Celante-Paludea (*Map 28*). Linkups would be as follows:

A. The two columns of the Twenty-sixth Infantry Division should keep linked via the passes on the summits of M. Cavallo-M. Cridola (*Map 28*).
B. Linkups between the Twenty-sixth and Thirty-sixth Infantry Divisions would take place along the dorsums between Val Arzino and Val Meduna
C. The Sixty-third Infantry Division should linkup with the *Corpo Speciale.*

Basically, the withdrawal should have first taken place by the divisions of the XII Corps. One body was supposed to aim for the Passo Mauria and cover the Cadore Basin. The others would aim for the outlets of the Arzino and Meduna Valleys into the plains and protect the northwest movements of the *Corpo Speciale* on its northern flank. Later, the XII Corps was to proceed along the foothills toward the Cellina River (*Map 27*). One body of the troops was to seal the breach between the right wing of the IV Army and the left wing of the II Army, aiming for Forcella Clautana.

Etna ordered the left wing of the XII Corps (Twenty-sixth Infantry Division), to keep linked up with the right wing of the IV Army along the peaks of the Carnic Prealps at the line of M. Cridola-M.Duranno-Col Nudo-M. Cavallo, descending from the Altipiano del Cansiglio to Vittorio and then S. Pietro di Feletto to Nervesa (Map 40). This was possible only on paper since do this, the Twenty-sixth Division would have to be divided into two columns, which was impossible. At noon, Montuori noted that most of the troops which crossed the Tagliamento had crossed on the bridge at Pinzano. Other units made plans to withdraw.[4]

At 1930 Aosta informed his subordinate commanders that most of the III Army troops had passed to the right of the Tagliamento while remaining on the left bank were most of the troops of the II Army. "The crisis of the retreat is over," he declared. However, it must be noted that the III Army had lost half of its artillery, and had given 130 of its 150 trailers to the II Army on October 24. The 193 heavy and medium caliber artillery mouths, together with 149 mouths from dependent corps. were immediately sent to the Piave. The units of the right wing of the II Army were now retreating because of the attacks coming from the line at Carpeneto-Pozzuolo-Mortegliano and also to get away from the Habsburg Sixtieth and German Fifth Infantry Divisions. Caviglia crossed the Tagliamento at Latisana at 0200 noting the bridge to be empty. Wondering out loud, he thought, "How come the III Army is crossing the congested Delizia bridges, while here the bridge is empty." He concluded "Montuori had a great subordinate in Lt. Gen. Giacinto Ferrero to whom is owed the salvation of the right wing of the III Army."[5]

During the day the Italian Sixtieth Infantry Division (IV Corps) withdrew across the Trasaghis bridge which was then destroyed. The survivors of the Fiftieth crossed on the Cornino bridge as did the VII Corps. The XXVII and XXVIII Corps remained on the left bank of the river attempting to halt the enemy. The Thirteenth Infantry Division whose commander had committed suicide established a bridgehead at Dignano attempting to hold the bridge.

Having arrived the previous evening at 0700 Foch arrived at the Comando Supremo. Robertson would arrive the next day. Gatti described the latter, "A typical heavy English peasant with heavy eyebrows who spoke little French, and brought his own whiskey to the dinner table. He was very attentive, immobile, and listened without batting an eyelash."[6] He had risen from the ranks to become Chief of the Imperial General Staff. He later telegraphed Paris that there would be an attempt to hold at the Tagliamento River, but a withdrawal to the Piave would probably be necessary.[7] Much thought was given to withdraw to the Adige River (Maps 29, 35).[8] There was much discussion about the possibility of invasion by Conrad from the Trentino. Cadorna wanted the French to deploy on the Montello or Piave, a request which was denied by the allies. At this time, no one was sure of how Italian troops would behave in combat. After a victory (or loss), there are always recriminations or boasting by different commanders concerning their participation in the battle. The French Military Mission to Italy's account declared that there would be an attempt to halt the enemy on the Tagliamento and possibly make it a a permanent halt.[9] After many hours of conferences Cadorna sent Rome a summary of the agreement signed by the three Chiefs of Staff. The document noted that only the II Army had been defeated while the III was still intact and withdrawing to the Tagliamento and beyond. Troops from the allies to reinforce Italy's armies were on the way. It also delineated the fact that Italian troops and commanders must man the defense line on the Tagliamento and possibly later the Piave. Nothing in the deployment of the Italian Army was changed. One must agree with the decision of the Allies not to be involved in the battle on the rivers. Italy has gone through a period of time attempting to deprecate the assistance given by the allies at this time. Italian troops were demoralized and ready to throw in the towel. Initially Foch reported to Paris that French troops definitely would not be deployed on the Piave later changing his mind.[10,11] Anglo-French troops were in the right place at the right time to stem the Austro-German advancing tide. After all these meetings, the Allied generals told the new Prime Minister, that Caporetto was due to the shortcomings of Cadorna and his senior staff, requesting that all should be removed.[12] Robertson noted a lack of grip of the situation at the Comando Supremo.[13] This was true, but with his experience of serving in an army with a long history as well as fighting overseas he could not fathom the difficulties that the Italian Army had with inexpert officers, and illiterate troops. Many in Britain thought that there were only a few German troops on the Italian Front.[14]

At 1330, already knowing the thoughts of his allies, Cadorna dictated a telegram to IV Army, stating that it should guard its eastern flanks from attacks coming from the Carnic PreAlps and the Venetian plain (Map 40). As the telegram read, "Following accords with our allies, this front is assigned to this army, from the Vidor bridge to, and excepting, the Ponte Priula."[15] Therefore the I Corps (IV Army), coming from Cadore and Comelico would have to be deployed from Vidor and the Priula Bridges to replace the no longer available French divisions (Maps 38, 42 for geography). DiRobilant responded that according to Montuori, there was no need for alarm. There was also a great fear of the developing breach between the IV Army and the left wing of the II Army.[16] At 1730, Cadorna telegraphed that the eastern bank of the river should be defended at all costs even after all troops had passed over the bridges. He issued orders to the effect that the bridges were to remain intact up to the last minute leading to the hasty and incomplete destruction of the Cornino Bridge. At 2100 he insisted that men and heavy guns be brought to the Piave as quickly as possible as the situation was bad.[17]

During the night a telegram arrived at the headquarters of the XIV Army from the O.K.L stating, "The arrival of units of the XIV Army at Latisana could be decisive." One could only imagine the rancor of the two commanders when they received this message.

Chapter VIII Endnotes

The Lost Battle of Annihilation

1 Below Diary entry, Oct. 31. 1917

2 Cadorna, *Altre Pagine Sulla Grande Guerra,* op. cit., p. 204

3 USSME: Relazione Ufficiale, Vol. IV, Tomo 3°, bis, Doc., Comando Supremo, *Eventuale ripiegamento sulla linea del Piave,* Doc, No. 152, October 31, 1917, Protocol No. 5195, p. 336; Idem, Doc. No. 153, Comando 3a Armata, *Difesa del Tagliamento,* Protocol No. 105, p. 338

4 USSME: Relazione Ufficiale, Vol. IV, Tomo 3° bis, Doc., op. cit.,Comando Truppe Altipiani *Disposizione per lun eventuale ripiegamento,* Doc. 223, Protocol 57821, October 31, 1917, p. 452

5 E. Caviglia, op. cit., p. 221-223.

6 A. Gatti, *Caporetto, Diario,* 4th Edition, Bologna, p. 286.

7 FAR, tome 6, Volume I, p. 95

8 Cadorna, op. cit. p. 263

9 FAR, Annex No. 41, Foch to Prime Minister, 30-10-1917, p. 79

10 Idem, Annexe No. 44, signed by Foch and Robertson, 31-10-1917, p. 81; USSME: Relazione Ufficiale, Vol. IV, Tomo 3°, op. cit., p. 618

11 Ferdinand Foch, *Mémoires* Vol. II, p. 37

12 PRO: FO, 438/10/243(Nov. 3, 1917, Rodd); *Maréchal* Ferdinand Foch, *Memoires* à *servir* à *l'histoire de la guerre*, Pflan, Paris, 1931, II, XXXVII.

13 OBARI op. cit., p. 73

14 DDI, Series V, Vol. IX, op. cit., doc. 345; Imperiali to Sonnino, 1-11-1917, p. 241

15 USSME: Relazione Ufficiale, Vol. IV, Tomo 3° bis, Doc, op. cit., Comando 2a Armata, *Situazione mezzogiorno 31 ottobre*, Doc. No. 164, Protocol No. 6458 October 31, 1917 p. 335

16 USSME: Relazione Ufficiale, Vol. IV, Tomo 3° bis, Doc., Comando Settore Sinistra *Contatto con la 4a armata,* Document No. 154, Protocol No. 47, October 31, 1917, p. 340; *OULK:* Vol. VI, op. cit., p. 626

17 USSME: Relazione Ufficiale, Vol. IV, Tomo 3°, op. cit., p. 462

CHAPTER IX

THE ITALIAN III ARMY ESCAPED THE TRAP

November 1, 1917

Problems persisted between the victorious commanders. Boroevic insisted on sticking to the prescribed westward direction of pursuit instead of going southwestward. Efforts of the Bologna *(brigade cut off from escape) to hold up the Austro-Germans were recognized by Below.*

The soldiers who buried the dead away
Disturbed not the clasp of that last embrace,
But laid them to sleep til the judgement day,
Heart to heart, and face to face.

Sarah T. Bolton,
"Left on the Battlefield"

THE SUN WAS splendidly shining as the level of the Tagliamento was decreasing. Hindenburg officially announced to the Kaiser the great German victory in Italy. He requested all bells in Germany be rung, with cannons to fire salvos in all the territory of the Reich and Alsace-Lorraine. The Reichstag sent congratulations to the Kaiser and Hindenburg.

Facing the Austro-Germans was now the problem of crossing the Tagliamento River (Maps 29,35). Several attempts had failed. Below now decided to turn the Italian line from the north via

Tolmezzo giving the order that the river must be crossed tonight with Longarone on the Piave as the objective (Maps 29,35).

Krauss Group

Demolition charges on the Cornino bridge set off at 0430 by retreating Italian troops did not damage to the eastern span (fuses had been removed by quick-advancing Austro-German engineers) while the center of the western span was destroyed. Reconnaissance patrols noted that Italian troops had evacuated the island. The Pinzano bridge was destroyed at 1125 sacrificing the *Bologna*. One of the Codroipo bridges remained intact even though the Germans thought it was not. Camped at Cornino were the Habsburg Fiftieth and Fifty-fifth Infantry Divisions (Maps 27,29). The island of Clapat was the center piece of the crossing but only its eastern span remained serviceable with a whole battalion employed in restoring it.

As it arrived at Gemona, the German Jäger Division now constituted the north flank of the Krauss Group (Map 35). Approaching Venzone darkness halted the Twenty-second Schützen and *Edelweiss* whose artillery wound up in the Natisone Valley due to the destruction of the Azzida Bridge (Map 13). At 1430, Krauss arrived bringing the news that units of the Twelfth Silesian and Fiftieth Divisions had occupied M. Ragogna insuring ease in crossing of the river (Maps 27, 40 for geography). The defenders still fought, but with little hope, as the bridge that was to be their salvation had been destroyed (see above). Afraid that enemy shelling would destroy the demolition wires Lt. Gen. Ugo Sani, commander of the sector had given the order to demolish the bridge.[1] The Comando Supremo prepared for a retreat to the Piave with detailed routes for each unit and bridges of the river to cross.

On the last page of his excellent text, Krauss rightly reported that his men should feel proud and could justly state that "I was there at Caporetto." Their sons, nephews and grandsons could also state that their father, uncle or grandfather as the case might be was there. Theirs was a great accomplishment and characterized a new type of warfare revolutionizing warfare which up to then was simply the *attacco frontale.*

As the bridge was blown the men of the *Bologna* (40°) realized that their link to home had been broken but nevertheless did not surrender. Krauss realized that it was vital that M. Ragogna be occupied and brought in fresh troops as combat spread to the small hamlet of S. Pietro di Ragogna. Finally out of munitions the Italians surrendered with a small column of Italian prisoners being led into the large Piazza S. Daniele, where they were halted by an Italian-speaking German officer. Turning to Lt. Vescovi, who was the highest ranking soldier present and whose pistol had not been taken from him, he explained that Gen. von Below wished to honor the survivors of the *Bologna.* Now took place one of the most singular episodes of the Great War, confirming that between protagonists of one of the deadliest slaughters in history, sentiments of respect toward a beaten adversary existed. There occurred a sincere expression of authentic values, which in later years, would be lost as conflicts turned toward the ideological arena. The German officer said, "I shall be at your side." To a signal from the German officer-guide,.with orders from Vescovi, the Italian prisoners neatly marched past. The piazza was full of soldiers. As the Italians marched past, German troops presented arms. The prisoners then assembled in front of the bell tower. Below, flanked by Stein and Krafft, stepped forward, saluted the Italians and gave a brief speech, slowly so it could be translated into Italian for the prisoners. "It is my duty as a soldier to recognize and concede the honor of arms to those who with such great valor knew how to redeem the honor of their army and honor their flag and their *Patria* with a great sacrifice."[2] As the sun went down over the horizon, Vescovi presented his side arm to the accompanying German officer. This is all verified by a snapshot which shows, the three generals with the prisoners.[3] The commander of the *Bologna,* Col. Brig. Carlo Rocca was praised by Below for his valorous defense.

Stein Group

The One-Hundred-Seventeenth Infantry Division newly assigned to the group arrived at Flaibano. The Thirteenth Schûtzen deployed at S. Daniele, while the Alpenkorps continued its preparations to cross at Bonzicco (Map 40). In one week, the Stein Group had taken 80,000 prisoners, 700 cannons, an enormous number of machine guns and tremendous amounts of war material.

Hofacker Group

At Codroipo the 121° (Twenty-sixth Infantry Division) failed to cross while the Two Hundredth Infantry Division failed to cross at the Delizia bridges. Under Hofacker's personal supervision the Fifth Austro-Hungarian Infantry Division (which had been transferred to him) also failed in its crossing attempt of the Madrisio ford. In the previous week, this group had taken 99,000 prisoners, (1,000 officers and two generals), 690 cannons, 700 vehicles, 2,400 horses, 3,200 carts plus two field hospitals. The Pinzano bridge and Pontaiba gangway were severely damaged. All crossing failures were due to the swift current of the river which varied from eighteen to thirty feet per second.

Difficulties with Kaiser continued. The *Armée Isonzo* transferred its headquarters from Logatec to Cormons, trying to put the Hofacker Group under its command. Krafft noted that in such situations, the Southwest Command would intervene very late and in such a manner that caused more conflicts between the allies. To avoid further arguments, Below, sent Major Willisen, the Operations Chief of the XIV Army, to Cormons, which resulted in an agreement with Col. Gen. Heinrich von Henriquez of the *II Armée Isonzo* as follows:

1. Units of the XIV Army which had not crossed the Tagliamento remained under Below's command.
2. These same units should have precedence in crossing, and once done, should be deployed in the pursuit sectors assigned. Thereafter the *II Armée Isonzo* would proceed to the river having its sector left free by the advancing XIV Army. There was now peace between allies, but for how long.?

Scotti Group

Designated by Below as the army reserve it deployed between Cividale and Udine consisting of the Austro-Hungarian First, Fourth, and Thirty-third Infantry Divisions.

Armées Isonzo

The OAR noted that the *I Armée Isonzo* deployed its XXIII Corps between Latisana, S. Giorgio di Nogara and Cervignano, while the Italian IV Corps was still beyond the Isonzo (Maps 29, 35). The *II Armée Isonzo* deployed near Codroipo with the OAR making slight mention made of the difficulty with the Hofacker Group. Its XVI Corps arrived at Flambro, Passariano and Gonars. The Forty-fourth Schützen as the vanguard of the still rear-end VII Corps was at Madrisio. Boroevic had specifically ordered the Sixtieth Infantry Division (FML Goiginger) not to deviate southwest to the bridges at Latisana. This order allowed the Italian III Army to escape via the bridges at Latisana.

Via radio intercepts, the XIV Army came to know that the Italians would try to hold at the river. However, as noted, this would soon change. Intelligence reported that 100,000 French soldiers were on the way. Meanwhile, Below wanted to know if the A.O.K. would be attacking from the Trentino, as he had suggested on October 27 (Map 14A). Realizing that there would soon be Anglo-French troops in the sector, Ludendorff advised the A.O.K. to make a massive thrust advancing to the Livenza River then unleash the decisive attack (Map 35). He also requested the return of the German divisions which was denied by the A.O.K., which stated that it needed them for the final push. By now the whole eastern bank of the Tagliamento was occupied by the Austro-Germans.

Austro-Hungarian communiqués noted that 180,000 prisoners and 1,500 guns had been taken. To this would be added the approximately 300,000 stragglers throughout the countryside who had been separated from their units and were now attempting to rejoin the army.[4]

The French Forty-sixth and Forty-seventh Infantry Divisions arrived and were deployed between Verona and Brescia as agreed (Map 14A). The citizens of the latter city were terrified as the statue of "Winged Victory" had been removed from the municipal museum.[5] After all the meetings, Foch and Orlando left for Rome. The Italian IV Army reported to the Comando Supremo that it continued to garrison the Yellow Line, and was arranging for the rapid withdrawal of its troops.[6] Gatti noted in his diary, that a stand must be made at the Tagliamento, because the army would not be able to hold together if it had to retreat to the Piave. Returning to Treviso Gatti met that evening with an anxious Cadorna as DiRobilant's troops had still not begun their withdrawal as ordered at 0545 on October 27. The Chief of Staff later wrote that October 29 and 30 were the most anxious days for him.[7] Anglo-French officers arriving at the Comando Supremo noted utter chaos. Cadorna had insisted that all paper work go through him and his Operations Chief, formerly Col. Roberto Bencivenga, now Col. Melchiade Gabba. In times like these, the flow of paper did not go smoothly. Therefore questions were not answered, troops were not correctly deployed, supplies were not sent. One also noted constant changing of Italian plans and inability to adapt or counter the Austro-German moves.

Italian Army Deployments now were:[8]

Italian Second Army

Left Sector:

A. XII Corps with the Twenty-sixth, Thirty-sixth and Sixty-third Infantry Divisions
B. backed up by the *Corpo Speciale* with the Twentieth and Thirty-third Infantry Divisions
C. IV Corps with the Twenty-first, Thirty-fourth, Fiftieth, Sixtieth, Sixteenth, and Forty-third Infantry Divisions

Central Sector:

A. VII Corps with the *Lario* under the direct orders of the Comando Supremo
B. Third and Sixty-second Infantry Divisions
C. XXVIII Corps with the Twenty-third, Twenty-fifth Infantry Divisions
D. XXVII Corps with the Thirteenth and Sixty-seventh Infantry Divisions

Right Sector:

A. II Corps with the Eighth and Forty-fourth Infantry Divisions
B. VI Corps with the Twenty-fourth and Fifty-sixth Infantry Divisions
C. XXIV Corps with the Tenth, Forty-ninth, Thirtieth, Twenty-second, Sixty-fourth and Fifty-fifth, Sixty-eighth Infantry Divisions as well as the Bersaglieri Division

Italian Third Army (deployed from left to right)

Left Sector:

A. VIII Corps with the Seventh and Forty-eighth Infantry Divisions

B. XIII Corps with the Fifty-fourth and Fourteenth Infantry Divisions

Center Sector

Fifty-ninth Infantry Division with the *Porto Maurizio*, *Modena* and units of the *Regia Finanza.*
Twenty-eighth Infantry Division with the *Arezzo* and *Catania* Right Sector:

A. XI Corps with the Thirty-first and Forty-fifth Infantry Divisions
B. XXIII Corps with the Twenty-eighth, Fifty-eighth and Sixty-first Infantry Divisions

Reserves of the III Army

XXV Corps with the Fourth Infantry Division.

Italian equipment losses had been enormous and are fully listed on p. 232. In addition twenty-two airfields were also lost two beyond the Tagliamento necessitating improvising airfields beyond the Piave.[9] Italian troop morale was now taking a significant turn. Italy was down but not out.

Chapter IX Endnotes

The Italian III Army Escaped the Trap

1 USSME: Relazione Ufficiale, Vol. IV, Tomo 3°, op.cit., p. 445

2 War Diary of Below: entry of Nov. 1, 1917.

3 Snapshots are in the Below Family Collection.

4 USSME: An enemy communiqué is quoted to give the prisoner figures. Relazione Ufficiale Vol. IV, Tomo 3°, op. cit., p. 440. The number of stragglers were mentioned in the same volume, p. 415.

5 Luigi Aldrovandi, *I Convegni di Rapallo e Peschiera, 6-7-8, Novembre, 1918.*

Frammenti del diario, Nuova Antologia, Vol. 1508, Jan. 16, 1935, p. 214

6 USSME: Relazione Ufficiale, Volume IV, Tomo 3°, op. cit., p. 462

7 Luigi Cadorna, *La Guerra alla fronte italiana,* Milano, 1919.

8 USSME: Relazione Ufficiale, Volume IV, Tome 3° bis, Doc. op. cit., *Le Operazione del 1917, Gli Avvenimenti dall'Ottobre al Dicembre/Documenti;* there is no page no.

9 Paolo Ferrari, *La Grande Guerra Aerea, 1915-1918.* October 1998. Gino Rossato, Valdagno, p. 38

CHAPTER X

WITHDRAWING ACROSS THE TAGLIAMENTO AND PIAVE RIVERS NOVEMBER, 1917

As the Italian withdrawal continued, Cadorna's plans to have the IV Army redeploy behind the Piave were delayed by DiRobilant. Efforts to save the Zona Carnia Command failed as its divisions were enveloped by the enemy. The Austro-Germans crossed near the origin of the Tagliamento River far to the north, proceeding south on its west bank. French troops arrived in the battle sector. Cadorna sent a letter to the Italian Cabinet wherein he indirectly mentioned the possibility of an armistice, forcing the cabinet to replace him. The I and IV Armies (including the XII Corps) were brought closer, allowing the battle front of the II Army to be reduced.

Wheel me into the sunshine
Wheel me into the shadow
There must be leaves on the woodbine
Is the king-cup crowned in the mead?

Sidney Dobell
"Home Wounded"

November 2

THE TAGLIAMENTO RIVER starts just about Tolmezzo flowing in a west-east direction joined after four miles by the Fella (Creek) River (Maps 29, 35). Past Tolmezzo in an ninety degree turn, it proceeds southward to the Adriatic.

At Pinzano it breaks into the plains where it started to be bordered by banks that are twenty feet in height giving excellent cover for machine gun nests. Italian armies were deployed on the right (west), bank of that portion of the river. Plans had been made in 1909 to use the river as a defensive as well as the springboard for a counteroffensive. On the northernmost tip of the defensive front were deployed the Twenty-sixth and Thirty-sixth Italian Infantry Divisions (formerly with the Zona Carnia Command, now with the II Army) reinforced by the Sixty-third Infantry Division of the III Army (Map 29). From the III Army reserve were deployed going southward the Twentieth and Thirty-third Infantry Divisions now the *Corpo Speciale* of Lt. Gen. Antonio DiGiorgio. Closer to the Adriatic Sea were deployed the II Army's VII, XXVII and XXVIII Corps of which the XXVIII Corps was brought up from its reserve. By now these battle-weary units had changed composition. The VII Corps was made up of the Third Infantry Division plus a brigade of the Sixty-second Infantry Division. The XXVII Corps consisted of the Thirteenth and Sixty-seventh Infantry Divisions. To the right of these troops was deployed the III Army with its VIII, XI, XIII and XXIII Corps. East of the river were one million Italian troops. In war games prior to the war, it had proved a natural defense, and easy to reach, instead now the rapid retreat had stretched the Italian supply system.

While four corps waited, Austro-German engineers worked feverishly under a sunny sky to repair bridges over the Tagliamento River as its level rose. Troops were proceeding forward as fast as their legs would carry them, being ordered by Below not to give time to the Italians to regroup. Five divisions had been withdrawn into reserve under the command of Scotti. Below's strategy now was to fix the north-south line of Longarone-Vittorio Veneto-Tezze as the next objective always keeping the right wing strong (Map 40). Eugene now ordered a general concentric advance:

> Tenth Army: march southwestward with its left on the line Longarone-Belluno-Feltre toward the Asiago plateau *(Map 40)*
> Two *Isonzo Armées:* proceed westward with their northern flank on the line Codroipo-Sacile-Conegliano *(Map 35)*
> Conrad with ten divisions was to attack on the Asiago Plateau on November 10.

With the swift current at the Cornino bridge site, Maj. Gen. Prince von Schwarzenberg almost drowned in a crossing attempt. The Cornino bridges had been only partially destroyed because explosives being transported to the bridge were hit by an enemy artillery shell. With enemy troops arriving, there was no time to set another charge. Heavy shelling had destroyed the II/234° which was guarding the bridge at Cornino. It had been deployed from Sompcornino to the entrance of the Pontaiba gangway.

In a personal reconnaissance Krauss noted that the island of Clapat in the middle of the river, had a partially destroyed span going from the island to the opposite bank a distance of one-half mile. The gangway at Pontaiba was also partially destroyed. At 1600 protective machine gun fire and shelling kept Italian troops on the opposite bank hunkered down while troops used ladders to connect the pillars. A company of sappers and engineers managed to repair the bridge. At 1830 the previous evening, preceded by grenade-throwing assault troops the aforementioned IV/4° Bosnians commanded by Capt. Redl crossed to the other side.[1] By 2200 they were at Cornino, then proceeded toward Forgaria and Flagogna.[2] In the hamlet of Farla combat was house to house and hand-to hand. Finally the attacking Bosnians overcame the defenders. By the end of the day Krauss reported that the Bosnians had taken twenty Italian officers, 1,500 men with much other equipment. Also crossing was the 16 company (Lt. Stein). With heavy fog the two units became separated. Suddenly at 0200 a voice accompanied by hoof beats called out through the fog "Capt. Redl." It was the trumpet-master of the 16 company riding a captured Italian horse. Soon more reinforcements arrived with Lt. Col. von Bizzarro arriving at 1630 (Another Italian name fighting under the Habsburg banner). Both De Rizzoli (Capt. in the *Corpo Speciale*) and Caviglia noted that a small group of infantry with good up-close artillery coordination could have easily prohibited the crossing at Clapat.[3] With this crossing, Italian troops in the middle Tagliamento as well as the two divisions to the north.were in danger. These Italian divisions which could have attacked the enemy in its flank were now themselves cut off by Krauss' Corps. Breaking through here compromised the XII Corps whose line of withdrawal from the upper Tagliamento, lay through Paludea which was three miles northwest of Pinzano (Maps 27,28, 40). The II Army's rapid withdrawal left the Alemagna Road (along which the IV Army was withdrawing), unprotected. This was the road that went along the Piave Valley up to Tai di Cadore from which it proceeds eastward toward Cortina d'Ampezzo until Villach where it joined with the roadway of the Val Pusteria (Maps 35, Vol. I, 2).[4] The Twelfth Silesian, Fiftieth and Alpenkorps Divisions failed in multiple crossing attempts. The One Hundred-Seventeenth Infantry Division replaced the Alpenkorps on the river edge as the Bavarians were ordered to proceed to Treppo and Farla. During the day, five Austro-Hungarian divisions arrived at Codroipo. Fearing problems with Vienna's troops, the German Twenty-sixth Infantry Division received permission to withdraw. The Two-hundredth was sent to Fagagna while the Fifth proceeded to Udine (Map 40). With these two crossings, a large breach was opened in the Italian line between Gajo and S. Rocco.

Bosnian Moslem troops with characteristic fez and supply horse.

Italian armored train with artillery.
The navy had these on railways along the coast
to halt enemy naval bombardments.

Habsburg Infantry sloshing through the rain in Oct. 1917

Alpini climbing toward the trenches during the winter of 1917-1918.

An Austro-Hungarian telephone switchboard simulating a large deployment of troops in the Trentino region during the Caporetto offensive.

Using Codroipo (which had three bridges rail, stone, and foot) as the dividing point, to the north were the Italian XXVII and VII Corps which had borne the brunt of the attack, as well as the *Corpo Speciale*, the survivors of the IV Corps and the XXVIII Corps (Map 29). In the Tagliamento curve were deployed the Twenty-sixth, Thirty-sixth, and Sixty-third Infantry Divisions. South of Codroipo was the Italian III Army with the VI, VIII, XI, XIII, and XXIII Corps with deployments all the way to the Adriatic.

By 0300 of the next day, protected by shelling from the guns of the Krauss Group, the whole XXXVIII Brigade of the Austro-Hungarian Fifty-fifth Division had crossed to the other bank. At noon, Cadorna, issued the "Directives for the Pause at the Tagliamento." as it seemed the enemy pressure had decreased.[5] Even though stopping at the Tagliamento, he made plans to retreat to the Piave, and bring all personnel and equipment across it.[6] Fifty machine gun companies were allotted to the III Army to defend the crossing, but they soon were forced to withdraw due to long range enemy artillery fire.

Below received a telegram from Kaiser Wilhelm II, thanking him personally and "In the name of the Fatherland for his incomparable gifts, whereby under his guidance, the Fatherland had been able to touch with its hands our faithless ex-allies, who shall feel the ire of the Germans." On November 2 Lt. Gen. Earl of Cavan and staff left London for Italy to command the British XIV Corps. Arriving there he noted the usual multiple defects in Italian military operations. There was no contact between Italian artillery and infantry, exposing the infantry to useless losses plus bad orders, faulty deployments all criticisms of the Italian Army which would be constant and never-ending. These valid criticisms were also in reports issued by allied commanders. If the Piave held, the whole front would hold. The critical time would be between November 15 and 22, i.e. until the British troops arrived and were deployed.[7]

Over 300,000 Italian troops in the Trentino, were to assist in safeguarding the withdrawal. These troops were the Zona Carnia Command (now integrated into the II Army as the XII Corps) and the IV Army.[8] The Carnia divisions were to safeguard the left wing of the the *Corpo Speciale.*[9] In his diary today, Gatti noted that the Italian government still did not realize that the withdrawal to the Piave signified the loss of the Cadore (Map 29).

Events in the Zona Carnia Command (XII Corps)

Commanded by Lt. Gen. Giulio Tassoni, it seemed destined to be far away from the travails of Caporetto. This all changed when the enemy occupied Pinzano on November 3 blocking the Tagliamento River Valley route for supplies (Maps 27,29). The command was now given to withdraw (The initial moves are noted in the chapter VIII). The XII Corps (also known as Zona Carnia Command) was to proceed down the Piave Valley past

Longarone and Belluno.[10] The latter city was not to be abandoned until the II Army had passed the meridian of Vittorio Veneto (Map 40).

At 1100, the Italian Twenty-sixth Infantry Division (Maj. Gen. Giuseppe Battistoni), was ordered to proceed in one column via the Passo della Mauria, with another along the V. Meduno; the Thirty-sixth Infantry Division (Major Gen. Alfredo Taranto),would go via the Arzino Valley while the Sixty-third would follow Forca Armentaria (Maps 27,28, 29,40). With the enemy crossing at Cornino, the two divisions which were to protect the left flank of the *Corpo Speciale* were now in a trap themselves, and it was up to the *Corpo* to protect their withdrawal (Map 27). Tassoni issued Order No. 214 for an eventual retreat.[11] The Twenty-sixth Infantry Division deployed on the left bank of the Tagliamento would leave by the Passo Mauria (Maps 28,29). The four battalions on the right side of the Tagliamento (Col. Denise) would withdraw down the Meduna Valley to Chievolis, then through the mountains to the Piave River Valley.[12] The Thirty-sixth Infantry Division was to withdraw along the Arzino Valley, while the Sixty-third Infantry Division would first go to Alesso, then proceed via a mountain path to the Arzino Valley following the Thirty-sixth Infantry Division (Maps 27, 40).[13] As Gatti later wrote "the IV Army commander, Maj. Gen. di Robilant did not know or understand the situation and waited too long to move from Cadore."[14] However, in the general's defense it must be noted that he had been studying the possibility of setting up a fortress defense in the Cadore.

Meanwhile Foch was making the rounds in Rome attempting to replace Cadorna. Bissolati, sometimes minister, sometimes not, had returned from the front reporting to Orlando that the Comando Supremo presented a gloomy and confused situation.[15] In Rome there were multiple discussions concerning a separate peace. Leader of the "no surrender" faction was Sonnino who together with Orlando decided to dismiss the general.[16]

Events on the Home Front

Malagodi again met with Albertini who related that the Comando Supremo felt that there had been some type of betrayal similar to what almost occurred at Carzano (see Vol. I).[17] Officers had reported that troops had discarded their rifles. Troops belonging to the *Friuli, Roma, Alessandria* or *Caltanisetta* while on home leave removed the identification tabs on their collars. Noting them, women would call them cowards and traitors or members of the "Take Flight Brigade." These men were erroneously accused due to wrong reports being forwarded. Subsequently, those who did forward these reports, among them Caviglia, apologized. Rumors flew throughout Italy of betrayal, that Cadorna was being court-martialed, of the rail station in Padua being transformed into a place of execution of officers, and that Capello had been executed.

November 3

Repair work on the bridges at Cornino and Pontaiba continued at a feverish pace. Finding it impossible to cross upstream, the German Jäger Division crossed at Cornino, following the Fifty-fifth Division (Maps 27, 29, 40).[18] The latter crossed all night holding up the Pappritz regiment made up of the I Jäger (reserve) and the II Jäger, reinforced by the I Jäger Guard. They all finally crossed the next morning. Temporarily transferred to the X Army, the *Edelweiss* proceeded toward Tolmezzo where it was joined by the CCXVI Brigade. The XXVI Brigade crossed the Tagliamento arriving between Pinzano and Flagogna (Map 40). At 0800, the Twelfth Silesian forded the river at Valeriano, overcame resistance and made a bridgehead on the right bank of the river awaiting a counterattack which never occurred (Map 27). The actions of the Silesians and Fifty-fifth Infantry Division, would have a devastating impact on the Italian XII Corps. Proceeding forward, the Austro-Germans opened a breach of about twelve km. (approx seven miles) in the left wing of the Italian II Army. North of the breach were the divisions of the XII Corps plus the *Lombardia* isolated from the *Corpo Speciale* (Map 27). After losing seven battalions at M. Ragogna, no reserves were left to throw into the breach. The only alternative was to retreat, attempting to break contact with the enemy but the Austro-Germans kept at their heels. Deployed east of the Meduna River, the XII Corps (Sixty-third and Thirty-sixth Infantry Divisions, plus the *Lombardia),* could not expect to proceed along the Arzino River Valley to the plains, as the Austro-Germans had already occupied Paludea which was the junction point of the mountains and plains (Maps 28,40). Tassoni proposed that the troops proceed westward through the mountains.[19] Italian II Army Headquarters insisted that XII Corps should open its own breach to escape. It was to proceed along the Arzino Valley attacking the enemy in the left flank as it proceeded toward the Meduna River, but events did not play out in that manner. The Italians reached the outlet to the plains, finding the enemy already there. The best account of this sorry episode is by Murari.[20] The Italian Twenty-sixth Infantry Division (eleven battalions), was transferred to the I Corps with units assigned to defend the Passo Mauria.[21] The Twenty-second Schützen following the *Edelweiss* from Venzone was ordered to leave the X Army and follow the Fifty-fifth Division, returning to Gemona to stay the night. The XXXVIII Brigade (Fifty-fifth Division) occupied M. Santo, northwest of Manazzons, slowly enlarging the bridgehead. Stein ordered the III/23° to go south to ease the crossing of the Alpenkorps which were pinned down by enemy shelling. By evening, the German divisions had abandoned the area assigned to the *II Armée Isonzo* which deployed the II Corps between S. Odorico and Rivis, the Koschak Group from there to Pozzo and finally the XXIV Corps behind the Delizia Bridge (the stone bridge at Codroipo). Just as the news of crossing the river at Cornino reached the German commander Eugene arrived at his headquarters. The German commander wanted to proceed to the Adige River while the Archduke stated he would be happy with the Piave for the moment (Maps 35, 40). Both Krafft and

Below insisted that an offensive be started in the Trentino to ease pressure on their troops (Map 14A). They wished to reach the western shores of the Piave at Belluno, proceed south, causing the Italians lines between the Astico and Brenta Rivers to collapse (Maps 14A, 35, 40). Conrad's troops would force the Italians to retreat behind the Adige River (Map 35). Krafft noted that by reaching the Adige with the fortresses of Verona on the right, and Venice on the left, Austria-Hungary would have earned an unshakeable position regarding Italy. It could use its forces to destroy the latter or use them on other fronts. Eugene's attack now had three points. Krobatin's Tenth Army would proceed southwestward with its left on the line Longarone-Belluno-Feltre (Maps 14A, 29,35,40). Boroevic's armies would proceed westward in two sections with their northern flank on the line of the railway Codroipo-Sacile-Conegliano (Map 40). Meanwhile Ludendorff told the A.O.K. of his intention to remove the German divisions after crossing the Piave, unless the Anglo-French sent the eight-ten divisions to the Isonzo as had been rumored.[22] Below wanted the Krauss Group to climb Val Cellina reach Longarone and occupy the Alpago (Map 28). In later years Krauss wrote that it would have been better for him to have proceeded along the mountain foothills, reach Vittorio, Fadalto and finally Belluno to save a few days (Maps 29, 40). On November 10, Conrad (with six divisions) was to attack in the Trentino proceeding southward from the Tyrol to the northern Asiago plateau.[23] Cadorna's thirty-six hour delay in ordering the retreat to the Piave caused the loss of the units at M. Ragogna, *(Bologna)* and the two excellent divisions of the Italian XII Corps deployed in the Zona Carnia sector.

Appointed Inspector General of the Retreat was Major Gen. Andrea Graziani, a severe disciplinarian and former commander of the Thirty-fourth and Forty-fourth Infantry Divisions. With flying squads of *Carabinieri* he toured the front dispensing immediate and crude justice. A classic case was at Noventa di Padua. As he reviewed troops, one soldier still had a cigar in his mouth. In front of many civilians he caned the soldier, then ordered his escort to execute him. In an a newspaper article, he defended his action as necessary to impose discipline on a disintegrating army.[24] The army felt that this was the only way to instill discipline in an illiterate infantry.

The Saga of the Italian IV Army

The Caporetto Inquiry Commission reported that during the evening of November 2 the Austro-Hungarian Fifty-fifth Infantry Division crossed the Tagliamento on the railroad bridge at Cornino and quickly occupied S. Rocco on the west bank. It proceeded toward Forgaria and the bridge across the Arzino at Flagogna. As noted the Silesians forded the river at 0800 at Valeriano causing an unsealable breach in Italian defenses (Map 27). The only option open was to withdraw to the Livenza River (Maps 27,35,40). Tassoni wanted to proceed westward into the mountains instead was ordered to attack the enemy which failed.[25] Poor commander he was receiving orders from the Comando Supremo, the II Army and the left wing of the II Army. The II Army headquarters felt that DiGiorgio's *Corpo Speciale,* should do all the protecting, but it turned out that it needed the protection, as the Sixteenth, Thirteenth, and Twentieth Infantry Divisions, some in the *Corpo,* some not, were destroyed protecting it. DiGiorgio withdrew westward to the Meduna Creek, the next defensive line. The Italian IV Army was to have linked up with the XII Corps at Casera Razzo (Map 28). It had been ordered many times since October 27, to align itself on the Yellow Line going east to west: Col Trondo-M.Col-M. Agudo-Cresta della Marmarole-case Bestioni-M. Antelao-M. Pelmo-M. Fernazza-M. Civetta.

When the Austro-Germans crossed the Tagliamento, the Italian IV Army had to move.

DiRobilant had been in very comfortable quarters and did not want to move. He had been ordered by Cadorna to study the feasibility of a *ridotto cadorino* where his men would halt the enemy using favorable defense positions.[26] He has been severely criticized for the delay in moving his army, but apparently he was making a study of the local terrain. With the rapid enemy advance it was difficult for him to know exactly what was going on. Few if any of his staff could handle the paper work involved in counteracting the enemy advance. His XVIII Corps was ordered to proceed to Feltre, while the IX Corps would go to Belluno (Maps 29, 35). Farthest away was the I Corps in Cadore, which would have to proceed along valley floors exposed to the enemy. Cadorna related in his Memoirs, that the retreat to the Tagliamento was to give the troops a breather before the retreat to the Piave but it also gave a chance to the Austro-Germans to catch up. As De Rizzoli narrated, "Receiving the news at 2200 that the enemy had crossed the river at Cornino, Lt. Gen. Lorenzo Barco, commander of the Twentieth Infantry Division ordered the *Lombardia* (73° and 74°), to counterattack the enemy troops which were now on the right bank of the river."[27] All efforts were unsuccessful.[28] The attackers penetrated across the Arzino Creek to Paludea where they were stopped by some Bersaglieri Cyclists and a mountain battery sent by DiGiorgio (Maps 28,40). At 1120, Etna notified Tassoni of the dangerous situation between Pinzano and Cornino bridges as the troops of the *Corpo Speciale* retreated to the Sequals Hills (Map 27). As a result the Thirty-sixth and Sixty-third Infantry Divisions plus the right wing of the Twenty-sixth Infantry Division were ordered to redeploy at Travesio and Meduna where the mountains break into the plains attacking the enemy's right flank.[29] Plans for withdrawal beyond the Piave had been in effect since the stewardship of Lt. Gen. Enrico Cosenz.[30] This would involve using the fortress of Venice as the right wing of the retreating army and the towns of Bassano and Citadella as the left wing fortresses.[31] Plans had later been drawn up for a withdrawal from the Adige if needed (Map 35). Orders for the withdrawal from the Tagliamento to the Piave River were drawn up.[32]

The Italian withdrawal would be in a great arch along the line Grappa-Piave (Maps 35,40) using the Piave River as the main line of defense.[33] To the northwest where it wrapped around the

Montello and M. Grappa the defenses were formidable as they had been fortified at the time of the *Strafexpedition* in 1916. As the river proceeded northwest beyond these two bastions it became one mile wide while at the Montello it was only 1000 ft. wide. At Nervesa on the eastern end of the Montello, it was about 3000 feet wide. Defenses were established with the Italian III Army deploying from the eastern end of the Montello to the Adriatic, while the IV Army would defend from Nervesa westward.

On October 30 Cadorna had ordered that the XII Corps and the right wing of the IV Army should linkup as they withdrew along the line at Casera Razzo-M. Piove-M. Cridola-M. Duranno-Col-Nudo-M. Cavallo-Vittorio-S.Pietro di Felette-Nervesa. Initially they would withdraw along the Carnic PreAlps (Map 40). The IV Army was to cover the outlet of Ponte nelle Alpi until all troops had left the mountains (Map 28). Di Robilant moved his quarters to Barcis (Map 28). Summoned to the Comando Supremo he was briefed and personally ordered to bring his troops onto the Grappa and Montello issuing orders at 2330 to move his troops.[34] Gatti described him as having long white hair, with a beard, looking much like an ancient Piedmontese noble. *The IV Army moved seven days after orders were issued by Cadorna.* In this episode it is difficult to evaluate the situation. As noted some authors state that he had been ordered to evaluate a possible defense, being the reason why he did not move. In any case he was the hero of the First Battle of the Grappa. The *Campania* (XVIII Corps) was sent from V. Sugana to the Montello, while the part of the Twenty-sixth Division proceeding to Passo della Mauria-V. Piave was put under orders of the Italian IV Army. The I Corps was to go down the Piave River Valley, the Eighteenth Infantry Division down the Val Cordevole to the Piave River Valley, both arriving at a fifteen-mile stretch of the Piave, below Pederobba (where the river emerges from the mountains) and Nervesa (Maps 29, 35, and 38 for geography of Pederobba). Since the I Corps moved slowly, on November 6, the II Corps (II Army), was detached to the Italian IV Army to garrison the sector temporarily.[35] Morale was so low in the Italian Army, that the Comando Supremo would not even consider a counterattack. Large hydroelectric plants in the Cadore region and Meduna and Cellina River Valleys were now abandoned.

Years later Cadorna wrote a letter to Krafft which that author placed in his text explaining his reasons for withdrawing to the Piave.[36]

I. Due to the rout of the II Army, he had only four corps (III Army) to defend the almost-always easily fordable Tagliamento River front of seventy-five km. (*forty-five miles*) between the Adriatic and M. Covria.
II. He feared an attack by Conrad in the Trentino which if successful would have trapped the whole Italian Army deployed on the Venetian plains *(Map 14A)*.
III. He needed time to withdraw a long distance giving him time to organize and hold up the enemy up in the mountains.
IV. He felt that only the Piave River would fulfill these requirements and as time has shown, in this case he was right.

Cadorna wrote a long letter to Rome which he gave to Gatti to personally deliver to Vittorio Emanuele Orlando, the new Prime Minister, who also kept the Interior Cabinet post.[37] "I must finally confirm what I have telegraphed to Your Excellency this evening. That is to say, that if I am successful in bringing the II and III Armies in good order to the Piave, it is my intention there to play my last card, awaiting a decisive battle. Should I retreat under difficult conditions to the lower Adige and Mincio, with the participation of the I Army, this would cause me to lose all my artillery and cancel all that remains of an army in being, causing me to renounce the last attempt to save the honor of the army." The letter continued "I have wished to explain the situation, painful as it is, and worthy of consideration outside of military motives. The government may consider taking steps outside of my competence and duties." With those sentences indicating a separate peace, there would be no keeping him in his position.[38] His fate was sealed. The Treaty of London forbade a unilateral peace agreement by Italy. Having already decided to resist the cabinet interpreted his letter as recommending an armistice. Other countries such as Belgium and Serbia had been conquered but there was no peace treaty. The Cabinet had already decided to resist. The telegram resulted in Cadorna's dismissal. After receiving this letter and reading between the lines, Orlando ordered the new War Minister, Lt. Gen. Vittorio Alfieri, to go to the Comando Supremo and make plans to replace Cadorna. Alfieri disliked Cadorna who had called him "a fat man" in public. As Orlando later noted concerning the telegram Cadorna had sent, "The telegram in its first part simply reproduced the pessimistic opinions of Cadorna, namely that it's impossible to hold the Tagliamento, difficult to hold at the Piave and probably will need to retreat to the Mincio."[39] No one could imagine that one year later there would be an armistice with the roles reversed.

November 4

The *Edelweiss* failed attempting to cross the Tagliamento south of Tolmezzo (Maps 27, 29, 40). Bissolati noted in his diary that at the Comando Supremo there was absolute paralysis. Learning that Paludea had been lost by the II Army at 1035, the Comando Supremo telegraphed the II, III Army commanders to start withdrawal to the Piave and informing the IV Army of the move.[40] Also complicating matters was that it was receiving information via the *Consulta* which had received it from the King of Spain, that the Austro-Germans would attack in the Trentino.[41]

Krauss Group (Maps 27,28)

The Fifty-fifth Imperial Division crossed at Cornino and after heavy resistance arrived at Oltrerugo and Travesio. The German Jäger Division sent the Pappritz regiment and the Guard Jäger

Battalion across, but as the Schützen battalion was crossing, the gangway collapsed, causing a delay in crossing until the next day. As soon as the Pappritz regiment arrived at the right side of the Tagliamento, it started on the road to Peonis, where it was halted by Italian units. The Fiftieth Division proceeded behind the Twelfth Silesian crossing at Pontaiba, but during the day, only the artillery crossed. During the night, units of the Silesians reached the line at Istrago-Spilimbergo, where there were various encounters with Italian armored cars (Maps 29, 35). On the right bank, the advance parties of the Fifty-fifth arrived near Sequals. Meanwhile the AlpenKorps and the Thirteenth Schützen Division waited their turn to cross the river. XIV Army headquarters was informed of the retreat of the IV Italian Army. The pontoon bridges could not support the weight of Boroevic's trucks while there was no cavalry for pursuit. This resulted in the *Isonzo Armées* halting at the Tagliamento. Late in the evening Archduke Eugene finally gave Below the order to chase the Italians without stopping, not giving them a chance to entrench themselves at the Piave. The minimum objective would be the Brenta River with the near objective being Belluno (Map 40). The same orders noted that Conrad would be attacking southward on November 10 with five divisions from the Altopiano dei Setti Communi, while the X Army would be advancing on Pieve di Cadore-Longarone-Belluno-Feltre to gain possession of the southern belt of the Altopiani dei Setti Communi. Below felt that the XIV Army would arrive at Longarone before November 10 and therefore asked the Archduke for authorization to attack the right bank of the Piave (Map 40). The SouthWest Front ordered the XIV Army to proceed toward the banks of the Piave loop northeast of Belluno-Vittorio-Conegliano. The Tenth Army would proceed along the roads of Forcella Clautana and upstream from Longarone (Map 14A). Krafft and Below wanted to separate the Italian IV Army and XII Corps from the rest of the Italian troops, then link up with Conrad's troops on the Altopiano dei Sette Communi. Both Krafft and Below (known as K-B), thought that the best route to Belluno would be from near Meduno to the Piave Valley below Longarone then down the river to Belluno (Maps 35,40). The XIV Army would have the left bank while the X Army coming from the mountains to the north would have the right bank. During a visit by Emperor Charles, K-B obtained permission to attack Longarone on the right bank. There now occurred a disagreement betwen K-B and Krauss on how best to proceed to Belluno from Meduno. Advances would involve moving in roadless mountains (up to 7000 ft.) with heavy equipment. Guessing correctly that mule paths would suffice for elite mountain troops, K-B noted that the shortest route was via Chievolis and Cimolais to Longarone. Instead Krauss decided to take the more circuitous route not through the mountains but along the main roads taking more time even though there was a narrow steep valley between Vittorio Veneto and Belluno (Map 40). On November 5 he ordered the Fifty-fifth Infantry Division to proceed along the main road via Vittorio Veneto, while the Fiftieth Division would take another main road farther away from the foot of the mountains. Below was very upset with Krauss concerning the slowness of his troops. In his diary entry of November 6, he noted that Krauss had not performed his tasks, as his most advanced units wound up in front of Stein's Corps. To avoid a traffic jam, he assigned his most advanced troops to Stein. Those still in the mountains would remain with Krauss, while those much to the rear (Twenty-second Schützen) would proceed to Longarone. The Württemberg Mountain Battalion was assigned to the German Jäger Division marching with it toward Longarone. During the day, the II Imperial Corps (*II Armée Isonzo*) occupied a small bridgehead on the Tagliamento from S. Odorico to Rivis; the Koschak Group extended from there to Goricizza. The Italian XXIV Corps had deployed between the bridges of Delizia and S. Vidotto. The *I Armée Isonzo* had its XVI Corps from Varmo to Madrisio and the XXIII at Latisana, while its headquarters transferred to Cervignano. Only that evening did elements of the Italian XXIV Corps succeed in crossing south of the railroad bridge at Delizia. Boroevic transferred his headquarters from

Postumia to Pradamano. Some cohesion was returning to the Italian forces.

In the early morning hours the Imperial Fifty-fifth Infantry Division went on the offensive in the Castelnuovo sector as well as between Celante and Paludea, the objective being the road to Clauzetto, where the Cosa Creek breaks out from the Carnic Prealps (Maps 28,40). Reaching it, caused an imminent threat to Toppo and Meduno, right behind the left wing of the *Corpo Speciale.* At Spilimbergo the Italian Second Cavalry Second Cavalry Division was ordered to proceed to Toppo, while the *Siena* was at Madonna di Zucco halfway between Usago and Lestans. It had been joined by some Bersaglieri cyclists, and survivors of the *Alpini* Bicocca and V. Leogra Battalions, who altogether attacked the southern flank of the enemy, stabilizing the situation (Map 27). In the operation they liberated the whole command of the Italian Twentieth Division which had been taken prisoner.

In the evening, DiGiorgio complied with orders from the II Army to withdraw from the Meduna to the Cellina River putting into enemy hands the outlets of the Cosa and Meduna Rivers.[42] At 1035 Cadorna telegraphed orders to the II and III Armies to retreat to the Piave starting the next night with a copy to the IV Italian Army. Cadorna's plan was to use successive rivers as the Cellina, the Livenza and the Monticano to hold up the enemy before attempting to make a stand at the Tagliamento (Maps 28, 40).). The IV Army was deployed as noted, linking up with the I Army at Ponte della Priula (Map 38 for geography). The III Army was deployed from there to the Adriatic. The two most efficient divisions of the II Army were to be deployed near Castelfranco (Map 42 for geography). The XII Corps was to be deployed around Montebelluna. The remaining II Army troops would be deployed between the Bacchiglione and Brenta Rivers (Map 35). The IV Army was again notified not to leave the Ponte nelle Alpi Gorge undefended until the II Army troops had passed the meridian of Vittorio Veneto (Map 28). The IV had withdrawn slowly due to the artillery mouths it was taking to the Grappa equipment which would prove critical to the mountain's defense. Cadorna was worried about the Thirty-sixth and Sixty-third Infantry Divisions. With a telegram issued at 1820, he ordered the troops to rest for two days on the Livenza, and one day on the Monticano Rivers (Map 40). He personally transferred to the elegant Dolfin Boldri Palace in Padua where sitting on a beautifully upholstered chair of red satin, Cadorna received his officers who had to explain how they lost contact with their troops or why they had to retreat. So far the situation was that the III Army with the right wing of the II Army had hardly fought while from Codroipo northward the IV, XXIV, XXVII and VII Corps (II Army) had borne the brunt of the combat. Going northward toward Cornino was the *Corpo Speciale,* followed by the IV Corps survivors and finally the XII Corps which held the river where it angled westward.

The Continued Saga of the Zona Carnia Command (XII Corps)

Montuori notified the Cadorna that every effort was being made to recapture the sector where the Twentieth and Thirty-third Divisions had been overwhelmed which was where the Cosa Creek broke out at Paludea (Maps 27, 28). Tassoni ordered units of the two divisions deployed in the upper V. Meduna to withdraw westward along the line at Barcis-Cimolais-Longarone (Map 28). Still dreaming, he ordered them to attack the advancing Austro-Germans in the right flank.[43] Commanding the operation would be Lt. Gen. Francesco Rocca (Sixty-third Infantry Division), who also commanded the Thirty-sixth Division, both deployed in the Arzino Valley. The *Benevento (*Thirty-sixth Infantry Division), would be moving down the Meduna Valley. The Austro-Germans kept up the pressure with the Tenth Army coming from the north and with the XIV Army coming from the east. The objective of the two groups was to block off mountain exits in the sector delineated by Meduno-Forgaria-

Tolmezzo and Ampezzo (Maps 28,29). At 2000 Di Robilant issued the following orders:[44]

By November 7 the XVIII Corps was to be on the Grappa covering the unprotected flanks due to the rapid withdrawal of the nearby IX Corps which was supposed to be in new positions on the right bank of the Piave. Finally the I Corps was to garrison Ponte nelle Alpi and subsequently proceed to the Piave via fifty trucks (Map 28). Its mission was to halt as long as possible the enemy from proceeding to Vittorio Veneto (Maps 28,40).

Toward evening the II Army had already started its withdrawal to the Tagliamento, the deployment of the troops in the upper Cadore and upper Tagliamento were as follows:

> I Corps was still in the Boite and Ansieri Valleys (Map 35). Linked up with it was the Marelli Group (Twenty-sixth Infantry Division, XII Corps) which had reached the Passo della Mauria there to protect the eastern flank of the corps (Map 28)
>
> Twenty-sixth Infantry Division (Minus the Marelli Group) was in Val Meduna, garrisoning the outlet into the plains (Maps 27,40)
>
> XII Corps remainder, (Thirty-sixth and Sixty-third Infantry Divisions) plus the *Lombardia* was in the Arzino Valley attempting to break out into the plains (Map 27)

Austro-German troops having crossed the Meduna, proceeded toward Maniago with their flank protected by the II Cavalry Corps. They drove like a wedge between the-above-named troops and the *Corpo Speciale* which had been trying to help them as they descended the Arzino Valley (Maps 27, 28). DiGiorgio's troops had now withdrawn to the Cellina River with the VII Corps to their right (Map 27).

Not realizing that Cadorna's letter no longer interested anyone, Gatti was surprised when upon arriving in Rome, he was informed that Orlando would not see him until the next day. He was however invited on the train to Rapallo and told to meet with Orlando at 0800 the following a.m. when all important Italian leaders were going to meet others in the alliance. Rumor had it that the new military leader would be the Duke of Aosta, with the vice chiefs being Generals Diaz and Giardino. After much bickering, the Italian Cabinet decided that two things should be offered to the nation. The reader will note that this was at the beginning of the twentieth century when only two percent of the Italian population mattered. Convincing them would make effective policy. What a difference one hundred years later when there are fifty political parties each with its own agenda. The first item offered was to change the Commander in Chief of the Army, with the second being an assurance from the alliance that help would be forthcoming in the quantities needed. Cadorna's letter seemed to suggest making peace. Bissolati noted in his diary, "Terrible news from the Tagliamento. In addition, the Information Office, which had been so optimistic in September-October now reports ten to fifteen German divisions in the Trentino. Actually, there was only one moving through there, with little artillery which was never employed."

November 5

Krauss Group

Even though tired the *Edelweiss* along with the LIX Brigade (X Army),were ordered to go from Tolmezzo in a fan-like move onto Tramonti di Sopra, to cut off the retreating Italian XII Corps. When Krauss found out that the German Jäger Division was attacking on the line at Avasinis-M. Cour, he directed most of his troops westward toward Gerchia and Chievolis. The Württemberg Mountain Battalion was to be the outrider proceeding toward Longarone across Chievolis-Forcella Clatuana-Claut and Cimolais (Map 28)[45] For several days the WMB failed in attacks in the *Forcella* which was defended by two Italian infantry companies which withdrew by November 8. The Pappritz suffered heavy casualties attacking Col di Forca and Avasinis. A column was formed of the two remaining regiments. These troops were halted by a road block and had to go via the road from Anduins to Clauzetto. The vanguard was a Jäger Battalion which was severely mauled by the retreating Italians who were attempting to escape via the Cosa Gorge. The Germans lost their commander and one hundred men. The Fiftieth and Fifty-fifth Divisions proceeded toward Montereale Cellina and took the bridges at Sequals as well as the hamlet of Colle. Some battalions went to the Meduna assuring possession of the bridges west of Arba. Both divisions blocked off the exits of the Arzino and Meduna Valleys. Crossing at Tolmezzo, the Austro-Hungarian Ninty-fourth Infantry Division proceeded southward in the Arzino Valley, as the *Edelweiss* (now in the Tenth Army) came northward in the Meduna Valley (Maps 27,40). The Italian divisions were now in a vise. Finally, the Twenty-second crossed the Tagliamento, with Krauss establishing his headquarters at Travesio (Map 28).

Italian II Army

Italian generals were now giving orders as if they were dreaming. Orders went out to units that no longer existed to occupy positions already in enemy hands. Not knowing the situation, Montuori ordered Etna to assure the retreat of the XII Corps. It was felt that there was a need for a screen. Armored cars, cavalry and Bersaglieri on bicycles were assembled under the command of Lt. Gen. Count of Torino (Third Cavalry Division.).[46] Etna in turn informed Tassoni of the pending attempt, but was ordered to cancel everything as there were no longer communications with the Thirty-sixth and Sixty-third Infantry Divisions. The Zona Carnia Command was thus abandoned. All Italian troop movements were unsuccessful, leading to encirclement by Jäger troops. The only future reference to these units was in the Caporetto Inquiry Commission.[47] The

I Corps (IV Army), was assembling at Pieve di Cadore (Maps 28,29,40).

Stein Group

Headquarters was established at Spilimbergo. During the morning, the Italians evacuated Bonzicco leaving the bridges which the One-Hundred-Seventeenth Infantry Division crossed during the evening (Map 40). Forte di M. Festa still was blocking Austro-German advances into V. Fella (Maps 35,40). In the afternoon, Krauss met with Emperor Charles, and GO Arz outlining his plan to them having discussed it the previous day with Eugene. All were in agreement except that the Archduke wished any troops reaching the west shore of the Piave to be placed in the X Army. Krauss reiterated that he wished to make his right wing strong, and advance on Longarone. That evening all units of the *Armées Isonzo* crossed the Tagliamento. The *I Armée* crossed and reached the line of Bagnarola-Sesto al Reghena-Fossalta di Portogruaro-Concordia Sagittaria-Giussago, while the *II Armée* reached the line at Azzano Decimo-Taido-S. Vito al Tagliamento (Map 40). Without firing a shot Austro-Hungarian troops occupied Cortina d'Ampezzo (Map 35). All positions from Colbricon to Peralba had been abandoned (Map 29). At dawn the *Corpo Speciale* composed of the Thirty-third and Sixteenth Divisions plus the survivors of the Twentieth Infantry Division, was between S. Leonardo, Sedrano and S. Focia proceeding to Aviano (Maps 29,35).

Italian III Army

During the evening, the III Army protected by a cavalry screen, retreated westward. At 1300, Aosta issued orders for the deployment on the right (west) bank of the Piave:

> VIII Corps (Maj. Gen. Grazioli), from Ponte della Priula to Salettuol, with its Forty-eighth and

Fifty-eighth Divisions from Nervesa to Palazzina (Map 42 for geography)
XI Corps (Maj. Gen. Giuseppe Pennella) with the Thirty-first and Forty-fifth Infantry Divisions from Salettuol to S. Bartolomeo (Map 33)
XIII Corps (Maj. Gen. Ugo Sani), from S. Bartolomeo to Zenson with the Fifty-fourth Division and the *Acqui* and 3° Bersaglieri; from Zenson to the Adriatic (Map 40)
XXIII Corps (Lt. Gen. Armando Diaz), with the Sixty-first and Twenty-eighth Divisions deployed from Zenson to the Adriatic (Map 40)

Reserves consisted of the Fourth and Fourteenth Infantry Divisions composed of two assault units and six brigades commanded by Paolini. At 2000 a bulletin stated that the retreat was going well as the XIII and XXIII Corps maintained a rearguard action on the east bank of the Livenza River. Bissolati's Diary reported that Cadorna had renewed faith in his soldiers.

The Italian IV Army's Saga (Continued)

Worried by the slowness of the troops of the IV Army, Cadorna set up a group (four battalions) commanded by his former Operations Chief, Col. Roberto Bencivenga, who had been just released from prison. After a violent argument with Cadorna, the exact nature which is not known today, he had been in solitary confinement for six months. Apparently the Generalissimo appreciated his talents because now in times of need he was given a command. These men were to proceed from from Seren to the remote Val Stizzon (Map 24).[48] The summits of of Col Caprile Asolone-Pertica-Prassolan-Col d'Orso-Tomba had been occupied by the Italians (Map 24).

The I Corps was still assembling at Pieve di Cadore, getting ready for its withdrawal (Maps 28, 29). As its eastern flank was unprotected, two battalions were taken from protective actions at Forcella Clautana and Barcis to form a screen. The IV Army also had to protect the eastward section of Alemagna Road.

At 0800 Gatti was given an audience with Prime Minister Vittorio Emanuele Orlando in his railway car on the way to the conference at Rapallo. Before any discussion could take place, the train arrived at Rapallo postponing any discussion. The Italians were installed on the third floor of the Casino Hotel, while the British were on the first and the French on the second. To be discussed at this conference were three items: the replacement of the Italian commander, how many Anglo-French troops were needed and where they would be deployed.[49]

During the day, meetings were held with Lt. Gen. Porro (Vice Chief of the Italian General Staff) who represented Cadorna at the conference. He made a very poor impression on the Anglo-French delegates with his poor knowledge of the facts and exaggerating the number of German divisions to over twenty.[50] The British Prime Minister later wrote, "Porro made the poorest impression on everyone at the conference."[51] Poor Porro! For years the Allies had been criticizing him.[52] They were now convinced that the army was sound, but poorly led, a condition which remained through the Second World War. Orlando informed the Allies that only the king could replace Cadorna, so a meeting with him was requested and scheduled at Peschiera which took place on November 8.

Cadorna's problem was that he had an outdated military mentality and was opposed by the great combination of Krafft and Below using new tactics unknown on the Italian Front. Like many of his British and French contemporaries he would not acknowledge the efficacy of the machine-gun nor that of quick-firing artillery in repelling the *attacco frontale.* He also was a strict disciplinarian and unpopular with the troops. As one contemporary Italian diplomat noted, "Cadorna was a seventeenth century general who understood war as nothing more than a gigantic siege operation, where the soldier was kept at his post by the whip. His lack of ideas was concealed behind a gruff silence, which was interpreted by Italians as strength, but the millions of soldiers at the front knew the truth, paying with their blood to learn it. A sterling example was when he ordered mass executions of his own men, many of whom were shot although they had been at home on leave the day their alleged crime had been committed."[53] How things have changed! No longer do generals walk on water with nothing to learn. In a dinner one evening in Rome, an Italian general told the author that he often went to classes to learn about things he knew nothing about. Gatti met that evening with Sonnino and Orlando. Orlando's Memoirs have no mention of a meeting except to state that a letter from Cadorna had been delivered. He lobbied to keep the present Generalissimo but the politicians gave him no definite answer. It seemed that the Anglo-French Allies had requested the dismissal of Cadorna, which if done would assist the Italians in obtaining more supplies as food, coal and artillery which they desperately needed. Later, Orlando wrote in his *Memorie* that the letter was interpreted as a suggestion for a separate peace. In Cadorna's position, this was a death knell for him in this situation.[54]

Foch felt that only the II Army had been defeated, there were still three others all going toward the Piave, which would have a shorter defensive line. There were over 700,000 men who if given good orders and supervision should be able to accomplish the task. Both he and Robertson felt that the Comando Supremo should adopt a defensive plan and stick to it. Allied forces would only complement the Italian Army which had to do most of the fighting.[55] That evening Cadorna wrote to his wife that the Piave would be the last defensive line because if the Austro-Germans broke through, no longer would there be an army.[56]

November 6

Krauss Group and Tenth Army

The left wing of the X Army with the *Edelweiss* and German Jäger Divisions continued advancing in the Carnic PreAlps.

Advancing rapidly, they were trying to encircle the retreating XII Italian Corps. The Fiftieth and Fifty-fifth Divisions had no difficulty in crossing the Cellina River (Maps 28,40). The Twenty-second Schützen arrived at Meduno, where Krauss ordered it to advance on Longarone and Belluno crossing the mountains which separated them from the Piave. The Württemberg Mountain Battalion was detached to the Twenty-second Schützen Division and allocated to the XIII Brigade. Maj. Gen. Müller then ordered that brigade (Maj. Gen. Eduard von Merten) with the WMB in the vanguard to proceed toward Longarone without stopping. They were to go along the line Chievolis-Forcella Clautana-Cimolais (Map 28). Proceeding northward, past Chievolis, they encountered and took 1,200 Italian troops prisoner, part of the Danise column. By nightfall from there the Austro-Germans returned to Chievolis. The IIC Kaiserschützen Brigade (Col. Brig. Adolph von Holodow Slonika) aimed for Ponte nelle Alpi and Belluno across the line at Maniago-Andreis-Barcis-V. Caltea-Pian Cavallo-Casera Palantina e Farra d'Alpago (Maps 27,28,40). K-B were anxiously awaiting the exit of the Fiftieth and Fifty-fifth Infantry Divisions from the mountains after which they were to proceed to Longarone.

Italian II Army

The reader will remember that II Army orders were to stop at the Cellina River (Maps 27,37, 40). However, after the Austro-Germans crossed the Tagliamento, this was no longer possible. Italian troops withdrew to the Livenza River, opening the Alemagna Road from Feltre northward.

Italian IV Army

The I Corps (Lt. Gen. Settimio Piacentini), was still at Pieve di Cadore (Maps 28, 29,35 40). Withdrawal would be in steps with a rear guard to protect the passes coming from the east. The first echelon was to withdraw by truck and railway today. The second would withdraw on November 7, while the third would move the next day. Troops from the *Fortezza Cadore-Maé* would be responsible for the screening, and would remain on the Yellow Line until November 10, starting to withdraw the next day. It was part of the *linea ad oltranza* about thirty km. (eighteen miles), behind the front lines. The line's northern end was the *Fortezza Cadore-Maé* which was a group of forts near Pieve di Cadore commanding the road from the Piave to Cadore.[57] The whole fortification system was a false defense. It was completely devoid of guns which had been sent elsewhere. The difficulty now was that with the Austro-German pressure forcing the II Army to withdraw to the Monticano River, the Belluno basin was unprotected (Map 40). Cadorna still wished to rescue the Thirty-sixth and Sixty-third Infantry Divisions, but was dissuaded by subordinates. Rocca's men encountered the German Jäger Division in the Arzino Valley as the latter was coming up from the plains below (Maps 27,29). After a furious battle many trapped Italian troops surrendered.[58] By November 9, Rocca absolved the men from their military oaths, told them to break up into small groups and take off to the mountains. He himself was taken prisoner on December 18 at the mouth of the Tagliamento. He was stealing a boat with the intention of reaching the Piave. As the *Benevento* proceeded along the Meduno Valley, it was caught at Tramonti between the Ninety-fourth Division attacking its rear, and the *Edelweiss* coming across from the Arzino Valley (Maps 27, 28). By November 7 the fighting had stopped with 5,000 men captured. Col. Danise had been ordered to set up a rearguard in the Meduna Valley at Redona to protect their withdrawal over the Clautana Pass from any attacks coming from the south.[59] Proceeding along the valley, these troops ran into the Twenty-second Schützen coming up the valley while the units of the X Army were coming down the valley, trapping them (Map 27). Figures vary as to how many prisoners were taken, but they were about 10,000. Most of the Twenty-sixth Infantry Division withdrew over the Passo Mauria (Maps 28,29). The topography of this sector has been changed due to the construction of hydroelectric plants creating Lake Selva and Lake Tramonti. In driving through the area, the author was impressed by the steep mountains rudimentary roads and wondered how one ever arrived then fought battles in the area.

Stein Group

The Twelfth Silesian followed by the Thirteenth Schützen reached the bridges on the Livenza River at Faschetti, Sacile and Cavolano, finding them all destroyed. The Alpenkorps remained on the left side of the Tagliamento.

Hofacker Group

The One-hundred-seventeenth Division entered Pordenone and sent advance patrols to the Livenza River while the restoration of the bridge at Bonzicco allowed the passage of artillery and trucks as well as the Twenty-sixth Division.

Italian IV Army

Headquarters was transferred from Belluno to Castelfranco Veneto (Map 42 for geography). By now the whole thrust of the XIV Army was to place the whole Italian defensive line V. Sugana-M. Grappa into confusion and disorder accomplishing both (Map 43 for geography).

The Comando Supremo now became aware of the danger arising with the movement of Austro-German troops from the Carnic PreAlps to the Piave along the base of the mountainous system sending the army the II and the reconstituted XXIV Corps which arrived on the right bank of the Piave between Volpago and Nervesa as well as the XII which now existed only on paper. Three *Alpini* battalions of the I Corps arrived to protect the Fener Bridge (Map 24). By 2230, DiRobilant assured the Comando Supremo that a bridgehead had been established at Vidor using Bersaglieri Cyclists and the IV Assault Detachment deployed at

Pieve di Soligo (Map 42 for geography). Toward evening the I Corps reached the Tai di Cadore Basin, deployed in the fortified sector Cadore-Maè. IX Corps deployed the Seventeenth Division between S. Nazario in V. Brenta-Fonzaso-Sedico and the Eighteenth having some units at Pederobba and some walking toward the area between Quero and Mas (Maps 24,43). Of note were the actions of the *Comando Truppe Operante Grappa* subordinate to the XVIII Corps and commanded by Col. Brig. Roberto Bencivenga who issued the following bulletin: (Map 24)

> "In order to have a common knowledge of the tasks expected of each unit under my order, I am stating, that with the *Alpini* M. Matajur, Feltre and Aosta Battalions, as well as the newly conscripted II Bersaglieri, I have been given the task of establishing an embryonic occupation of the strongholds of the line, M. Grappa from the slopes west of M. Tomba to the bottom of V. Brenta in the Rivalta sector."[60]

The Bersaglieri unit was to link up with the XX Corps (I Army) at Rivalta; the Aosta was deployed along the M. Asolone, Col Caprile and Col della Berretta line; the M. Matajur along the M. Prassolan, Col dei Prai, and M. Pèrtica; the Feltre from Col dell'Orso, to Solaroli, to M. Fontanasecca to M. Pallon where it would link up with the IX Corps. Three batteries of field artillery would be deployed between M. Pallon and M. Pèrtica. The main task of these units was to guard the approaches to the Grappa from the north. All terrain was to be contested, with no retreat unless authorized by the commandant. The orders further read, "So that this set of orders can have a perfect execution, it is absolutely essential to take care not to exhaust the troops in useless labors, and to take care of the morale of the troops, letting them know the very important task and the tremendous responsibility we have." Finally, he noted that his headquarters was situated in the barrack of the infirmary on M. Grappa. In this document, we see a clear indication of what job Italians were to do on M. Grappa, *but also a new policy of explaining to the troops what was expected of them, something that until then had sorely been lacking in the Italian Army.* Krafft, in his position would likewise explain to his lowliest private in the same method what was expected of them. With the capture of several German officers, the plans of Krauss became known and the Italians defended accordingly. By 1540, the Comando Supremo established the defense line on the hilly system from Vittorio Veneto to Conegliano to cover the Piave as it flowed in front of the Montello (Maps 38, 40). Montuori placed his command at Conegliano and ordered all bridges to be destroyed (Map 35). However the enemy had already crossed the Livenza River at its source and had already established a bridgehead on the right(west) bank.

Aosta notified his III Army that there would be no more retreat, as the honor of the army and the salvation of the nation was at stake. His army had been involved in little combat and was full of fight. Bell towers near the river were destroyed so as to deny the advancing Austro-Germans any observation posts. All means of crossing the river were destroyed such as span bridges, pontoon bridges, as well as the rail bridge at S. Donà.

Politico-Diplomatic Moves (Cont'd)

Britain had called for the Rapallo meeting. Representing the British were Generals Jan Smuts, William Robertson and Henry Wilson plus Prime Minister Lloyd George; for France, Generals Weygand, Pétain, Foch, de Gondrecourt, with President Paul Painlevé and Henry Franklin-Bouillon; for Italy, the usuals including Orlando, Sonnino, plus War Minister Vittorio Alfieri. So worried were the Allies that Pétain had put forward a proposal to divide the Italian Front between two Allied generals.[62] Porro represented the Comando Supremo reiterating that the Italians would hold at the Piave and carried a message from the Comando Supremo requesting troops and artillery.[63] Sonnino reported that the class of '99 had been called up, but would not be placed in the front line trenches. Porro noted that the III Army had 100 battalions on the Piave, the IV Army had 127 battalions between the Brenta and the Piave Rivers, with 118 battalions of the I Army between the Brenta River and Lago di Garda. Finally the III Corps had 39 battalions from the Garda to the Stelvio.

The conference now entered a period of bitter recriminations. Robertson and the British Prime Minister noted that in a previous meeting in London during August the Italian delegate (Lt. Gen. Albericco Albricci) had peremptorily declared that after October 15 there could be no offensive in the Trentino or Carso[64] (See Vol. I, chapter XXX, Eleventh Battle). Knowing that the enemy offensive had started on October 24, Porro could offer no satisfactory response. Lloyd George further declared that there would be nothing forthcoming from the allies with the present command structure, to which Orlando replied that this would be changed as soon as the King gave his approval. Although not a military expert, the British Prime Minister had deep insight into strategy and tactics. Noting the stagnation of the trench warfare on the Western Front, he had proposed an allied attack on the Isonzo which had been refused by all parties concerned. Robertson constantly made note that Italy had no need of foreign troops. With a British mind set, thinking of his troops he was right. However, being considered were the illiterate peasant infantry which could not do any maneuver except the *attacco frontale.* They were not well-trained like British troops had low morale and needed some stimulus to continue to fight. Not having any national identity, they had no idea what Italy was. Perhaps seeing foreign troops fighting on their soil, would give them that mental push. Lt. Gen. Sir Herbert Plumer, the future British commander in Italy was instructed not to put his troops in a compromising position. As had been noted to the allies, "The military and moral situation required a new man for the tasks at hand."[65] Plumer got along very well with the new Italian commander Armando Diaz. At one point in an attempt to bolster Italian morale he invited him to inspect British defenses.[66] Diaz told Plumer that the Italian Army would fight "even if it had to retreat to Sicily."[67] With great surprise, the Anglo-French noted the different races present in the Italian Army from the short swarthy Sicilian to the tall blond blue-eyed troops from the Piedmont and Lombardy.

Orlando later wrote that the Rapallo Conference was like the Garden of Gethsemane, a place of blood, sweat, but I would like to see it again as a place where I had suffered much."[68] He was made to understand that the allies would put no troops under the command of the present Comando Supremo.[69] The Allies had no faith in the command structure nor in the fighting value of the Italians. In all his political life, Orlando had never been under such pressure. Lloyd George as great a politician as there ever was, stated that the allies should have their offensives and defensives better coordinated, suggesting the establishment of a Superior War Council at Versailles. It would be composed of the prime minister plus a member of the cabinet as well as a military person each from the British, French and Italian Staffs. Finally, he would have the generals subservient to the politicians, which he had desired for a long time.[70] Foch was nominated by the French, but soon after gave it up to become Generalissimo of all forces in the alliance. Members representing their respective nations would be Generals Weygand and Wilson. Foch stated that he felt that the Italians could hold at the Piave with its natural barrier, provided the area was fortified with barbed wire and the defenders had enough munitions.

German aviation noted Italian troops fleeing the northern sector of the front toward Belluno, Feltre and the Piave. The withdrawing Italians would have to flee through the narrow valleys of the Piave and that of the Brenta River farther to the west (Map 40).

November 7

The Ninety-fourth Imperial Division (Tenth Army) occupied the Passo della Mauria facing central Cadore, forcing the Italians (I Corps) to retreat to Lorenzago in the Piave Valley (Maps 28,

29).[71] The tired *Edelweiss* (now with the Tenth Army) and the LIX Brigade (Gen. Theodor von Hordt) were placed in the rear of the Twenty-second Schützen advancing toward Claut-Longarone. At Barcis, the Kaiserschûtzen (Col. Brig. von Sloninka), fought and destroyed two *Alpini* battalions (Map 28). The gross Austro-German movements showed Krobatin's X Army marching southwestward with its left on the line Longarone-Belluno-Feltre. Boroevic's *Armées Isonzo* were to proceed westward with their northern flank on the line Codroipo-Sacile-Conegliano (Map 40).

North of the source of the Livenza River, Italian units were overcome resulting in the abandonment of the Livenza defense line as enemy troops proceeded south on the river's west bank to assault the left flank of Italian troops deployed there (Map 40).[72] Krauss and von Stein immediately arrived to coordinate the advance on Vittorio Veneto (Map 40). The German Jäger Division proceeded in the plains, while the Twelfth Silesian Division was in furious combat at Sacile. At 1400 the AlpenKorps started to cross the river on a repaired bridge at Pinzano. The One Hundred Seventeenth infantry Division marched toward the Livenza River, while the Twenty-sixth Division was deployed at Pordenone east of Sacile. Both units had trouble with the area of pursuit of the II Imperial Corps. The latter were always getting in the way of the Hofacker Group. News started to reach the Austro-Germans that Anglo-French troops were in the vicinity.

Differences of opinion now started among the attacking commanders. Krauss wished to advance along the valleys. He was reminded of the order to reach Longarone and Belluno preceding the X Army which was to push toward Feltre, in support of the rest of the army which was attacking the left bank of the Piave (Map 40). The Krauss Group now consisted of the Twenty-second Schützen and German Jåger Divisions plus the Alpenkorps. On its left flank would be the Scotti Group composed of the Fifty-fifth and Fiftieth Divisions plus the First Imperial Division. With all this manpower advancing on Feltre, plus the X Army, Below requested Eugene to order Conrad to place on the left wing of the XIV Army any troops he could from the Dolomite Front.

While the XVIII and IX Corps (IV Italian Army) continued their withdrawal without any pressure, the loss of Passo della Mauria was announced, with only about 100 men escaping the net. The *Alpini* Tolmezzo Battalion was captured. The attackers occupied the Tai Basin and broke through the first fortifications, forcing Piacentini to set up strong defenses in the mid-Piave Valley between Rivalgo and Perarolo. These garrisons were to assist units coming from the Carnia. Having been notified that Sacile was lost, Piacentini sent the II/23° to Farra d'Alpago to obstruct any Austro-German advance from Fadalto toward Ponte nelle Alpi (Map 29). Among the units which flowed in small groups from the Carnic PreAlps were the survivors of the *Alpini* V. Leogra, M. Clapier and V. Arroscio Battalions had started at P. Montemaggiore. The rear guard of the III Army was still between the Livenza and Monticano Rivers while most of the troops had crossed the Piave.

By 2100 the attackers had crossed the Livenza at its source as well as below Sacile. Conegliano was abandoned. Houses, shops and wine cellars were vandalized throughout by the Italians as well as by the Austro-Germans. De Rizzoli wrote that there were many refugees on the left (east) bank of the Piave as well as troops who had strayed from their units, all causing chaos throughout.[73] Austro-German units were short of foodstuffs, so they stopped to eat and drink, much to the consternation of their leaders. Wine was literally flowing in the streets for hours. One must remember that these troops had to live off the land. Now a curious situation developed. Austro-Hungarian troops were allowed to send home monthly a fifty pound package of foodstuffs. The British blockade had caused severe food shortages at home reversing the flow of aid packages which now went from the War Front to the Home Front.

Problems persisted between the victors. Faced with a problem Below usually sent a staff officer to Munich to telephone the O. K. L. which would promptly contact the A.O.K. resulting in a prompt favorable resolution. Below now decided on another ploy. He asked Major Jansa, Eugene's liaison to the XIV Army, to have a confidential conversation with him. Below wanted to assault Longarone without having troops released to the X Army. He was afraid that if the troops were intermingled in the Grappa sector it would result in a request for a single command there, depriving him of a command. Good generals are also good politicians.

The Continuing Saga of the Italian IV Army (Maps 29,35,40)

Soon Bencivenga's troops were in place on the northern summits of the Grappa. The I Corps continued its withdrawal down the Piave River Valley with its rear guard doing effective work, past Lorenzago, and the road from Passo Mauria with the Ninety-fourth Infantry at its heels.[74] Approaching from the east was the Twenty-second Schützen while the Austro-Hungarian Tenth Army was proceeding from the north. With the Italian II Army withdrawing to the Monticano River, Belluno was now unprotected.[75]

Events at the Comando Supremo

Gatti returned to the Comando Supremo headquarters where he had discussions with high military officials about the decision taken at the Rapallo Conference, i.e. the dismissal of Cadorna. Who was supposed to notify him? Porro felt it should be the King Orlando, Sonnino and Alfieri left for Padua where on the morrow the latter would pick Lt. Gen. Armando Diaz whose appointment had already been agreed to by His Majesty.[76] Orlando and Sonnino left for Peschiera on Lago di Garda (Map 43 for geography).

Headquarters were now in Padua in the Dolfin-Boldú Palace. At 1930, a tragic dinner was served. Porro told Cadorna that he had been given a new post as Italian emissary to the Supreme

War Council in Paris. Cadorna realized that he was being dismissed, and refused the new post.[77] He made note that the House of Savoy had a history of being ungrateful.[78] As noted, the new Chief of Staff was to be Diaz with two Vice-Chiefs Badoglio and Giardino. The King always told everyone that he had personally selected Diaz.[79] After the battle of the Sabotino, Badoglio had a meteoric rise. His columns advancing on M. Sabotino had been watched by His Majesty who remarked, "They seem to be Roman legionnaires," as the *grigioverde* columns advanced toward machine gun nests. Badoglio was now the king's favorite general and was rapidly promoted. During the meal, Diaz was nowhere to be found.

November 8

Heavy rains persisted. Daily heavy rains were making the many streams and rivers swell over their banks. Creeks now became raging rivers swollen by waters flowing down from the mountains. There was also a rain of decorations from both emperors. From the Habsburg Emperor Below received the Grand Cross of the Order of Leopold, (but felt that he deserved a higher decoration for directing the last victory of the empire). Krobatin was promoted to *Feld Marschall* while Boroevic received the *Pour le Mérite* from the Kaiser.

At 0730 the King arrived at the headquarters of the Comando Supremo. During the meeting with Cadorna, the latter stated, "Majesty, Gen. Porro states that either by the wishes of the Allies, or the Prime Minister, or the Ministers, I am being dismissed. Please do not tell me that I have been offered the job in the Interallied Council. This is a pretext. I shall never accept the position offered to me." The King replied, "You are right." After a brief meeting he said to Cadorna "General only the mountains stay still, we shall meet again." As he left, the King paused at the doorway taking a long look at him while other staff members felt that Cadorna's era was over. At noon

Col. Alfredo Rota arrived with three letters. The first regarded the dismissal of Cadorna, without stating the exact date, the other concerned the appointments of Diaz, Giardino and Badoglio.

The Italian news agency *Stefani* disseminated this news, placing Cadorna in the position of a *fait accompli*. Gatti who was very friendly to Cadorna noted that Rota who wore the Cross of Savoia, had never seen a trench.[80] When Cadorna received the letter, he stated out loud, "They want to dismiss me. I want them to state, that I am no longer useful. Only then can I be sure of myself and to be that which I am."[81] Giardino stated he would accept the position, because he had a responsibility. However, there was no sign of Diaz. Some officers thought that should he not accept, perhaps Aosta would be the new commander. Perhaps, Cadorna would remain, with Porro, Giardino and Diaz at his side. Later, Gen. Pecori-Giraldi arrived making note that he was against the nomination of Diaz. Aosta arrived, stating that he would not be nominated due to the danger to the Savoy throne (the Aosta and Savoy families had been rivals for years). The Aosta branch had started off with Amedeo, Duke of Aosta, son of Vittorio Emanuele II. The duke was king of Spain for eighteen months surviving two assassination attempts before abdicating and returning to Italy. His son was Emanuele Filiberto, Duke of Aosta and commander of the Third Army. Bissolati had pushed for Aosta.[82] When apprised of the promotion, Diaz noted, "You have given me the order to fight with a broken sword."[83]

As many accidental happenings occur in these situations it is a curious story as to how Badoglio was appointed. Apparently, Orlando, Sonnino, Bissolati and newspaper reporter Ugo Ojetta were in a railway car at Rapallo. After dinner, there was a discussion concerning to whom to appoint as Vice-Chief. The reporter brought up the name of Badoglio, whom no one knew. Ojetta recounted Badoglio's exploits on the Sabotino, the Vodice, and the Kuk. He was not aware of the problems with the XXVII Corps early in the battle. The Prime Minister agreed with the recommendation telegraphing Rome to change the text of the news bulletin, adding Badoglio, whose first name no one knew.[84] Thus in a quirk of fate, Badoglio who would be prominent in the fate of his nation for the next thirty years, (including Sept. 1943), was brought to prominence by a reporter. It has been reported that while his divisions were in grave trouble during October, 1917, he was at Udine to lobby for the Vice Chief's job.[85] Other authors later recounted how at Caporetto Badoglio had fled leaving three divisions without orders, causing the loss of 40,000 men abandoned by him across the Isonzo on Oct. 24, 1917.[86] Bissolati, (the self appointed Minister to the Comando Supremo) who was now Minister of War Pensions) wrote a letter that he would like to meet Diaz. Arriving at 2100 Diaz met with Cadorna in his office for over 90 minutes after which an indignant Cadorna exited the room. He had been shown a letter which Alfieri had sent Diaz giving him immediate command of the armies. The copy given to Cadorna showed no date of the changing of commands.

Simultaneously the famous meeting at Peschiera on Lago di Garda took place with Prime Minister Lloyd George of Great Britain, accompanied by the Generals Smuts, Wilson and Robertson (Map 43 for geography). France was represented by President Painlevé and Foch ; Italy was represented by Orlando, Sonnino, Leonida Bissolati plus the king. French newspapers were already filled with accounts of small numbers of Austro-German troops attacking larger Italian units which withdrew. Added to this erroneous account was the text of Cadorna's telegram which noted many units had surrendered without fighting.[87]

The king, conversant in French and English presented a three hour-talk in English for Lloyd George in a small classroom that was a battalion headquarters. With English nannies, it could be said that Italian was his second language. Orlando did not speak English. Political questions were presented by Lloyd George while Wilson asked the military ones. The king acknowledged that his ministers were wrong in turning down the offer of allied help the previous January and that his generals had been at fault the past month.[88] Thirty thousand officers had been lost.[89] If the enemy crossed the Piave, the king explained, it would result in the loss of Venice, the only naval base on the Adriatic. Bari and Taranto were too far to be effective. To hold at the Piave, the Italian positions on the Montello and Grappa must be held. It seemed that the Anglo-French as well as the Italians were in agreement that the enemy assault would be between the Asiago Plateau and the upper Piave.[90] Lloyd George requested a change in command of the army, but this already had been done. The King did not agree to the autonomy of the Anglo-French forces in the sector and invited the generals Foch and Wilson to visit Gen. Diaz about this. The only written account of this meeting was by Gen. Jan Smuts.[91] The conference decided that it was necessary to hold at the river, not only for Italy, but also for the Allies keeping Italy in the war, thus tying down Central Powers troops. During the Rapallo Conference Lloyd George had promised two more divisions.[92] Later he told Italian Ambassador to London Imperiali that he felt that the Italians would not hold on the Piave.[93] Many military authorities including Falls, have questioned why there was such a change of behavior in the troops from the Plezzo-Tolmino sectors to the Grappa. One witness felt it was due to the army made up of militias which broke apart at the first contact with the enemy.[94] However one must also take into account the change in morale from Plezzo to the Grappa. Men on M. Grappa as opposed to those on the Isonzo were respectful, deferential and obedient with a high morale.[95] Convinced that they were fighting for their families their behavior took on a different aspect.

L'ho trovato io! (I found him). This was how the king described the new commander. His surname bore evidence of the Spanish domination of his Neapolitan birthplace. He was a quiet unassuming man who often addressing subordinates in Neapolitan dialect with words like *Guaglion!* which means "boy," but as a term of endearment. That same day, Cadorna dictated a letter to the troops. "With terrible pain for the supreme salvation of the army and the nation, we have had to abandon a margin of the sacred soil of the *Patria*, bathed by the glorified blood of the most pure heroism of the Italian soldiers.

But this is not the time for tears. It is the hour of duty, sacrifice, of action. Nothing is lost if the spirit of the retaking is ready, if the will does not bend.

Already once before on the Trentino Front, Italy was saved by heroic defenders who held high its name before the world and the enemy.

Let those with a good conscience be aware of the grave and glorious task entrusted to this army.

Let every commander, soldier know what his duty his, to fight, to win, without retreating one step.

We have decided with no deviation, on the newly reached positions, from the Stelvio to the Piave, the life and honor of Italy shall be defended. Let each combatant know what the cry and the command that comes from the conscience of the Italian people: Death, but no retreat."

Results of the New Chief of Staff

With the desertions, mutinies, and a new Chief of Staff, the government now started to change conditions for the common soldier. The daily ration of meat was increased from 250 grams per day to 350, pasta from 100 grams to 150, coffee from 15gm. to 20 gm. and sugar from 10 gm. to 30 gm (there are 456 grams in a pound). Daily wine distribution was increased to 25 centilitres (approximately one quarter of a quart). In addition, the daily pay was increased to ninety *centesimi.* Daily newspapers for the men in the trenches would be started (but who could read?). Cinemas in the front lines were instituted, and finally, subsidies to families who were in dire straits. Conferences were instituted between the military hierarchy and the lowly private to find out what the latter really needed to fight better. Again this was something strange and new. Before, the lowly conscript was *told what he needed to fight better.* With *Circolare* No. 170 issued on May 4, 1918, by the Commando Supremo, money was available for the impoverished families of the soldiers and officers. Monies were sent directly to the families in need by the corps commanders.

Returning again to the illiterate theme, when the families went to the local post offices to collect the money, they were told it had not arrived.[96] In many cases postal employees were lending out the money at usurious rates, so there was no money for the starving families. Here was another bad effect of the rampant illiteracy in the nation. The families had no one to turn to. To complain to the government one needed to fill out an expensive *Carta Bollata* (a special government paper purchased at government licensed stores) which the politicians had devised to isolate themselves from the people. The illiterate peasant was trapped. Being illiterate and poor, to obtain the monies due them, a government complaint form had to be filled out. They could neither afford to purchase it nor were they able to fill it out. The government started to debate a law on how best to give land to the landless peasant (*fanti*). It was thought that this would put an end to emigration and was one of the many promises not kept.[97] Few realized that emigration was a relief valve for the tax strikes caused by the massive poverty as well as an important factor in the balance of payments. Finally an insurance policy was made available to the soldiers with the approval of the Treasury Ministry with the creation of the *Opera Nazionale dei Combattenti*. The government wanted to give the peasant infantry no more excuses to go on a military strike.

The new Chief of the Italian Army General Staff had a different method of operation. He was a skilled organizer and would use the Intelligence Services of Col. Odoardo Marchetti, as much as possible (as opposed to his predecessor). Delegating much authority he made all feel that they belonged on the same team. His Operations Chief was Col. Ugo Cavallero, future Chief of the General Staff and Marshall of Italy. He had good relations with Badoglio using him as a right arm and even prohibiting him from testifying at the Caporetto Inquiry Commission which would have damaged the Vice-Chief's career. Twice a week Diaz would dine with the king and three times monthly with Orlando.

On his staff was a young major, Giovanni Gronchi, future President of Italy during the years 1955-62. However as in all walks of life there was jealousy in that many felt superior to the new Generalissimo when years later disparaging remarks were made concerning him.[98]

The Italians retreated from *Fortezza Cadore-Mae,* which was soon occupied by the Habsburg X Army.[99] At daybreak the Württemberg Battalion occupied the village of Forcella Clautana while the *Sturmkompagnie* of the 3° Kaiserjäger took the *forcella* (Map 28). By the afternoon, it reached Cimolais, while the XLIII Brigade (Maj. Gen. Eduard von Merten) following it, rested at Claut (Map 28). A regiment of the X Army descended along the Settimana Valley, arrived near Claut. After resting at Barcis, the southern column of the Twenty-second Schützen Division climbed the Caltea Valley arriving at Pian Cavallo in early afternoon in a heavy rain. Notwithstanding this, they kept climbing crossed the southern crest of M. Cavallo then descend into the vast district of the Alpago (Map 28). Reaching Hill 1650, they were halted by fog and a snow storm.

The Alpenkorps had been assigned to the the Scotti Group. Krauss ordered the Fifty-fifth Infantry Division to proceed to Belluno and detached a regiment at the bend of the Piave, between Polpet and Ponte nelle Alpi, to block the Italians who were retreating from Cadore. Converging on Vittorio (Veneto) was the Fiftieth Infantry Division (Scotti), the Twelfth Silesian, and the Fifty-fifth Infantry (Maps 35,40). By now, the thermometer registered minus 12° Centigrade in the mountains (10° F). The Hofacker Group and the *II Isonzo Armée* arrived almost simultaneously at the Monticano River, while the *I Armée Isonzo* occupied Fossalta and Chiarano southeast of Oderzo (Maps 28, 29, 40,43).

In France Haig (Brit.commander) selected the Seventh Infantry Division (Major Gen. T.H. Shoubridge) and the Forty-eighth Infantry Division (Maj. Gen. R. Fanshawe) as the second group to go to Italy accompanied by the Fourteenth Wing of the Royal Flying Corps. Simultaneously, Pétain selected the

French Twenty-third and Twenty-fourth Infantry Divisions to send to Italy under Gen. Nourrisson. Foch wanted the Anglo-French troops under the command of French Gen. Fayolle, a good tactical move, but politically unpalatable to the British. Plumer, the new British commander had already been given a letter confirming on him complete independence.[100] The king now issued his well-known pronouncement, "Citizens, Soldiers, Be One Army."

Italian Army Events

Troops of the IV Army were still in Longarone while the left wing of the II Army was still withdrawing at Conegliano (Maps 14A, 29, 35, 40). By November 9 when enemy troops broke through Passo S. Osvaldo, Italian troops had no chance of flight. At the Piave, the retreating Italians were now having a problem. The I Corps plus units of the Italian Twenty-sixth Division were being compressed by attacks from the Austro-Hungarian Tenth Army which had arrived at Pieve di Cadore (Maps 28,40). On their left was the Krauss Group which had as its last obstacle the Passo di S. Osvaldo garrisoned by a rifle company (Map 28). The IV Italian Army Command was now worried about the XII Corps which had been ordered to proceed to Longarone across the Vajont Gorge, with the existing rifle company at Passo S. Osvaldo as rear guard (Map 28). Evidently, the command was not in tune with reality. As noted above, Krauss wanted his units to reach Belluno by November 9 placing a regiment at the bend of the Piave near Polpet-Ponte nelle Alpi to cut off the retreating Italians along the Piave Valley. Specialized attack units were sent to take the bridges at Ponte nelle Alpi and Belluno (Maps 28, 35, 40). Long range artillery was brought forward to shell the railway at Longarone-Belluno. The German Jäger arrived this day in the area of S. Lucia-Aviano-Marsure (Maps 29,35). The Twelfth Silesian and Fiftieth Imperial Divisions encountered heavy resistance at Vittorio (Veneto). Units of X the Army arrived at Pieve di Cadore pursuing the Italian I Corps which on its left was threatened by the Krauss Group.

At 0250 the Comando Supremo ordered the II Army to make its large units and artillery ease down the right bank of the Piave, giving some resistance in the line when needed. In the evening Montuori notified the Comando Supremo that most of the troops of the central (Carlo Petitti di Roreto) had gone to the far bank of the Piave, while the pressure was increasing on the near bank. DiGiorgio was ordered to place a protective veil on the to slow the enemy advance. His troops were to redeploy across Ponte di Priula (Map 38 for geography). The same day, the last operative order of the II Army was given ordering DiGiorgio (copies sent to Generals Etna and Sagramoso) to have all troops cross the Piave at the Ponte di Priula bridges by November 9 (Map 38 for geography). *Arditi* Battalions would be directed to the bridgehead at Vidor (Maps 38,42 for geography). Meanwhile the VIII Corps (Lt. Gen. Francesco Grazioli), made contact at the Montello with the Italian IV Army, while the Italian III Army slowly arrived at the right bank of the Piave. Providing a rear guard and suffering heavy losses were the the *Granatieri di Sardegna.*

With a military disaster in the offing, Allied politicians and generals ran to Italy. Pressure was put on the government to change military leadership which was done by announcing to the world the formation of a Supreme War Council with members of all nations involved. The Italian delegate was Cadorna, who at first refused. However, he was convinced "to do it for the *Patria.*"

November 09

At six p.m. Maj. Gen. Sir Herbert Plumer relinquished command of the British Second Army in France and started his voyage to Italy where he would command the British contingent. In meetings with Haig as well as with the French he had been instructed not to endanger his troops as the Anglo-French still had no faith in the fighting qualities of the Italian Army.[101] Aiming to avoid enemy troops at Passo di S. Osvaldo, units of the 3° Schützen were ordered to proceed along the Ferron Valley then attack the Passo defenders in their rear (Map 28). Preceding them along the dangerous ice was a company of the Würrtemberg Battalion which had lost its commander, Capt. Gössler. As the Italian garrison of the Passo retreated, it eased the advance of a battalion of the 26° Schützen toward the hamlet of Casso (Map 28). Units led by von Merten arrived at Erto where they thought they would rest, but such was not to be. Cyclist units of the Würrtemberg Battalion (using captured Italian bikes), had not been able to halt the Italians from blowing up the viaduct over a deep gorge east of Casso. On the next bridge (over the Vajont Gorge) a small audacious group ran to the explosives halting the demolition as rapid waters ran through 450 feet below. Units of the 2nd *Gebirgskompagnie* commanded by *Unteroffizier* Brückner arrived just in time to extinguish the fuse. Hopefully, decorations were awarded for this daring feat in the face of a pending explosion. Only by that bridge could the gorge be crossed. The cyclists proceeded toward Longarone, noting the destroyed rail and roadway bridges over the Piave with the town beyond. Major Theodor Sproesser (WMB commander) called them the *Radverein* or cyclist club. German infiltration tactics were being acknowledged as efficacious even by the troops.[102] Deciding to take the initiative, Müller used the tired XLIII Schützen Brigade to cross the river and attack the Italians. Meanwhile, some Styrian machine gun companies had crossed to the right side of the river, got lost in the dark and were taken prisoner by Italian troops while other units of the WMB blocked the road to Belluno.

For years, Rommel has been incorrectly given credit for capturing Longarone *alone*, Slowly the real story came out. In addition to the War Diary of the WMB, there have been three accounts of the episode all credible, some with eyewitnesses. Troops of the Austro-German X Army (Ninety-fourth Infantry-Division) waded the river north of Longarone in water up to their knees reaching Codissago on the left bank opening fire on the town. Two officers, Lt. Anders and Second Lt. Walter Bräuer, who spoke perfect Italian, proceeded southward alone on bicycles toward Longarone. An article by Alexander Hubner noted that arriving in town surrounded by Italian troops, they were directed toward the commander to whom they explained that they had machine guns on the heights overlooking the town inviting him to surrender.[103] Simultaneously, as darkness fell, using a submerged gangway south of the hamlet, Lt. Erwin Rommel with his company plus another of the 26° Schützen, crossed the river, occupying the road that led to Belluno and entered Longarone while the surrender was being negotiated by the two officers in the main square.

Another account was by Major General Karl Korzer who quoted Hubner, but also a letter from an eyewitness plus reports by the Belluno War Press Office (*Kriegspressequartier*).[104] As the WMB moved northward toward Longarone, it was met by Italian troops waving white handkerchiefs. As soon as they arrived close to the Germans, they opened fire, taking Lt. Schöffel (1st company) prisoner.[105] Krafft originally incorrectly reported that Rommel captured the garrison at Longarone all alone.[106] Consequently all historians up to Desmond Young reported this as noted. Later the episode was reported differently. As one author reported it in later texts, Maj. Gen. Korzer, Col. Gellinek and FML Lawroski (Aust. Hungarian Ninety-forth Infantry Division) met in a sector "north of Longarone." Second Lt. Anders of the *Tiroler Landsturm* accompanied only by another officer, alone bicycled into the town. They were greeted by troops who stated that they would send them quickly to Sicily (as war prisoners).[107] Meanwhile, Sproesser proceeding northward along the river banks had sent in an Italian prisoner of war with the offer to surrender (to be considered with enemy troops coming southward). The aforementioned German officer taken prisoner also urged the Italians into surrendering. So it was in a complex operation, in the early hours of November10 over 10,000 men with 100 machine guns surrendered. Included in this mass of troops were the previously mentioned Styrians who were now freed. For his great success, young Rommel was awarded the *Pour le Mérite.* With the inclement weather the 10,000 prisoners as well as the Austro-German troops scrounged for lodging and food in the village. Invading troops had been allotted no food but were told to live off the land. Now they had to find food and lodging for the prisoners as well which was a problem for the villagers. This whole disaster was directly due to the delay of the withdrawal of the IV Army which as noted was due to the fact that it was taking along much-needed artillery for the Grappa's defense. Krafft later wrote that the most important thing happening was that the road to Belluno was now open which was a heavy blow to the defenders. An amusing anecdote was the unplanned meeting between an Italian *fanto* who had worked in Germany and his German job's foreman serving in the enemy army.[108] Seen in the valley road to Ospitale was a great deal of Italian equipment on the move which was the tail end of the unlucky Italian Twenty-sixth Infantry Division (I Corps).

The southern column of the Schützen spent a terrible night on the slopes of M. Cavallo then descended onto Tambre d'Alpago (Map 28). The Fifty-fifth Division tried to force the gorge of Fadalto but was unsuccessful (Map 29). All the bridges over the Piave were blown, as the Austro-Germans crossed at Cornino and Pinzano. However, these troops were too few to hinder the Italian troop withdrawal to the Piave, and blowing all the bridges after crossing over.[109] By now four-fifths of the Italian Army had melted. The invading Austro-Germans had occupied the provinces of Udine, Belluno as well as parts of the provinces of Treviso, Vicenza and Venezia, containing a population of 1,151, 503 in 14,000 square km. (approximately 5,000 sq. miles).

Stein, Scotti & Hofacker Groups

The Fiftieth Division reached Follina and Cison di Valmarino. The Twelfth Silesian reached S. Pietro di Feletto and Pieve di Sogno wanting to cross the same night. The Hundred-seventeenth advanced in two columns, with the right one stopping at the rail station of Susegna, while the left one reached Tezze. Retreating Italians destroyed the Priulia railway and roadway bridges.

Boroevic's Army Group

Headquarters was installed at St. Vito al Tagliamento, with the arrival at the Piave of its XXIV Corps between Ponte di Piave and Cimadolmo (Maps 33,40). The VII Corps arrived at Salgaredo and the XXIII between St. Donà and Grisolera (Maps 33). Archduke Eugene transferred his headquarters from Marburg to Udine.

Continuing Italian Troop Withdrawals

Confusion still reigned in Italian ranks. Some tried to reach Belluno moving between M. Serva and the Schiara Group, while others unsuccessfully attempted to open a route between the roadway and railway. The latter units were the *Alpini* M. Nero, Assietta and Fenestrella Battalions, as well as the XXXVIII Bersaglieri, all under the command of Lt. Gen. Enrico Nasi. Attempts were made to cross the mountains between V. Maè and V. Cordevole proceeding toward Sedico. By evening, the whole IV Army had redeployed as ordered while confusion still reigned in the II Army. Montuori had been wounded by artillery fire and unable to give orders increasing the chaos. *Arditi* now guarded the Priula bridges (Maps 38,42 for geography). Remaining were the XXVII Corps at Vedelago, with the Twenty-third and Sixty-seventh Infantry Divisions, the XIV Corps (Gen. Pier Luigi Sagramoso) at Camisano; the IV at Piazzola sul Brenta; the XXX Corps and the *Corpo Speciale* at Abano, the VII Corps at Mestrino and a cavalry corps between Noale and Scroze. Petiti di Roreto assumed command of the XXIII Corps replacing Diaz while Ferrero was placed at the disposal of the War Minister. Italian troop stragglers now numbered over 300,000. They were sent to Emilia to form the V Army which would become the *Massa di manovra.* Last to cross the Piave were the *Arditi* who repulsed multiple German assaults as the XIV Army troops advanced stepping over the cadavers of the defenders. To the south the III Army was crossing. Its units were deployed as follows:[110]

Nervesa to Palazzina the VIII Corps (Gen. Francesco Saverio Grazioli), with the Forty-eighth and Fifty-eighth Divisions (Map 33 for orientation)
Palazzina to Candelú, the XI Corps (Lt. Gen. Giuseppe Pennella),with the Thirty-first and Forty-fifth Divisions
Candelú to Zenson, the XIII Corps (Lt. Gen. Ugo Sani) with the Fifty-fourth and Fourteenth Divisions
Zenson to the Adriatic, the XXIII Corps with the Twenty-eighth and Sixty-first Infantry Divisions

Reserves were the Fourth Division (Lt. Gen. Giuseppe Paolini), with three brigades and two assault battalions and the Fourth Cavalry Division. According to the OIR, the breakthrough on the Isonzo and withdrawal to M. Grappa and the Piave River, had cost the Italians 10,000 dead, 30,000 wounded, about 300,000 prisoners plus 350,000 deserters walking home. Equipment losses were enormous including 3,000 machine guns, 3,152 pieces of artillery, 1,732 bombards, 2,000 machine pistols, over 300,000 rifles, twenty two airports, and a tremendous amount of war material. The army was reduced to 700,000 able bodied men of which 400,000 were the III Corps and the First Army deployed between the Passo Stelvio and the Brenta River; the other 300,000 were the III and IV Armies defending the line from the river to the Adriatic.[111] Differing from Soninno's statements at Rapallo the class of 1899 had been called to arms and placed in combat situations as of November 15. British Army reports declared that the Italian Army had established itself on the Piave without any outside help.[112]

For reasons unknown to all, Italian troops were now fighting with a different morale. Many authors have tried to explain this but failed. Paraphrasing the little-noticed and key phrase "For your wives, sweethearts etc." the smart politicians had not appealed to the men's patriotism but asked that they fight to protect their *families* which worked. With the shortening of the front, and the increased production of war materials, the soldiers were now getting the materials they so urgently required which perhaps helped in boosting morale. The new commander, had a more humane sense and did not uselessly throw men against machine guns as his predecessor did. Italian politicians now realized that the *fanti* would have to be treated better or another military strike as at Caporetto would happen. Allied leaders related to the King (theoretically Supreme War Leader), that the troops were good, while the former chief of staff and senior generals left much to be desired.[112A] With the first meeting with the Generals Badoglio and Giardino, Diaz ended it with the words, "To each of us three, luck has been with us, it shall not abandon us." And as Giardino wrote in his diary, "And luck still smiled on us." On the morning of November 9 Diaz notifed all commands, "I assume the position of Chief of the General Staff of the Army and count on everyone's faith and self denial." A few minutes later he met with the Allied Generals Foch, Wilson and Weygand, all of whom were asking questions about which he knew nothing having just been appointed to his post.[113] The former army chief had refused to see them, but had arranged for the defenses at the Piave. Summary executions, even of high rank officers continued. As Cadorna later wrote, "On the Piave River, was in play the salvation and the honor of the *Patria.* All purveyors of false rumors should be searched out and punished. These purveyors either with words or behavior. destroyed the morale of the troops and decreased the will to resist to the end." Both Ludendorff and Hindenburg later wrote that the best result of Caporetto was the dismissal of Cadorna. Krafft wrote that the Italian nation should be thankful to Cadorna for planning the retreat to the Piave, rather than the Adige, which was what Foch had wanted.

The new front measured 400 km. (240 miles) long, eliminating mountainous frontage from the Brenta River to the middle Isonzo which had taken up a great deal of men and materials. The next great question was where to place the line of defense. Chosen was the line Adriatic Sea along the Piave to the elbow it makes going round the Montello then turning northwestward to M. Grappa to meet the I Army deployed on the Brenta River (Map 35). Both the Montello and the Grappa were heavily fortified. The Italian I Army (Lt. Gen. Pecori-Giraldi), was deployed as follows:[114]

> Passo Stelvio to the Lago di Garda was garrisoned by the III Corps with the Fifth and Sixth Infantry Divisions (Map 1, Vol. I).
> Garda to the Brenta River—XXIX Corps from the Garda to the Vallarsa Valley (Map 35)
> Vallarsa to Val Pòsina—V Corps (Map 3, Vol. I) X Corps from Val Pòsina to the Astico River
> Altopiano dei Sette Communi (Asiago Plateau) were deployed: Comando Truppe Altopiano (Maps 11,31 for geography)
>
> XXVI Corps (Lt. Gen. Augusto Fabbri) with the Eleventh and Twelfth Infantry Division deployed on M. Cengio (Map 31)
> XXII Corps (Lt. Gen. Antonio Gatti) from the Ghelpach Gorge to Gallio with the Fifty-seventh and Second Infantry Divisions
> XX Corps (Lt. Gen. Giuseppe Francesco Ferrari) from Gallio to C. Caldiera

In all the I Army of Pecori-Giraldi was composed of 320,000 men in 122 battalions, with 1,380 artillery mouths.

Badoglio arrived at the Comando Supremo the next day and was informed of his new position. Was he just being coy and playing the politician? After supper, at 20,45 as his auto approached the front door, Cadorna shook the hand of everyone present. He thanked Minister Bissolati for the faith he had in him, and turning to Diaz, stated, "I wish you luck, which goes beyond you personally, but to the whole army and the nation." Among the accounts of Cadorna's leadership one should read that of Bencivenga who had been his Operations Chief. He wrote what would soon be noted as an unbiased opinion of Cadorna's stewardship:

> "The story of Caporetto has been sufficient to call for the crucifixion of Gen. Cadorna. And yet, he gave to Italy the most brilliant example of a surprise, namely Gorizia. Still, not only he among all the warriors of the war was taken by surprise.
>
> We would be wrong to make our wounds larger with our fingernails. We go looking for the most hidden reasons to explain the reason for the failure. We place in doubt the valor and the discipline of our soldiers. We look in our victories over a period of three years of war, for the cause of the defeat. We curse that which is the best virtue of a warrior, namely confidence in one's self. We all trample to find a cause for that which has happened without thinking that it was all summarized in one word, *Surprise.*"

November 10

Jansa must have had a good effect on the Archduke. Orders were issued for the Krauss Group to be responsible to assault the Grappa. The Tenth Army would remain where it was, while the *Edelweiss* which was down to 2000 soldiers would be returned to the XIV Army. With these orders the XIV Army and Conrad's Group would be together on the Altopiano dei Sette Communi. Conrad had assembled five infantry divisions, the Nineteenth, Fifty-second, Sixth, Twenty-first Infantry plus the One Hundred

Sixth Landsturm Division. Commander of the Assault Group was Gen. Krautwold Ritter von Annau. The *Feld Marschall* felt that attacking on the Altopiano dei Sette Communi would weaken Diaz's defenses on the Piave. The *Edelweiss* arrived at Longarone via the Passo Clautana as the Fifty-fifth Infantry Division had gone over M. Faverghera, north of Fadalto arriving opposite Belluno (Map 29). Of the sixty-five Italian divisions on October 24, only thirty-eight were in combat readiness but had lost their artillery. Pursuing them were the Austro-German with 4500 artillery mouths. The most dangerous sector was from the Astico River to the Adriatic Sea (Map 35). Deployed in this sector were:

> Between the Astico and the Brenta Rivers was the Italian I Army with six divisions (Map 35)
> From the Brenta to and including the Montello was the IV Army with seven divisions (Map 40)
> From Nervesa to the sea were deployed the III Army divisions (Maps 29, 40)
> Behind the III Army troops were four divisions of the II Army
> Opposing them were:
> Nervesa to the Adriatic were the *Armées Isonzo* with twenty divisions (Map 40)
> Nervesa to the Brenta was XIV Army deployed with fourteen divisions
> Brenta to the Astico Rivers was the Army Group Tyrol (Conrad) with seven divisions (Map 35)
> On M. Grappa, the XIV Army had four divisions (Krauss Group with one German and three Habsburg divisions (Maps 24,35,40)

In classic blitzkrieg fashion thirty Austro-German divisions would go over the top opposed by eleven Italian in the mountains plus a similar number on the river. Conrad's two best divisions had been detached to the XIV Army on the Grappa. He was awaiting two divisions to arrive from the Isonzo and was assigned the XX Corps which had been opposing the Italian IV Army. This corps was composed of older men, who could not handle the maneuvers needed in mountain fighting. Finally the Habsburg Tenth Army detached two divisions to Krauss for the attack on the Grappa. Ludendorff ordered German artillery to be returned to the Western Front for the battle going on in Flanders. This action coupled with the low strength of the Imperial divisions gave no chance to the Austro-German forces to cross the river in their condition. The *I Armée Isonzo* had eight divisions on the Piave none at full strength and some at half-strength.[115] The effectives of the *II Armée Isonzo* has not been exactly reported, but one can do the arithmetic by subtracting from the total *Armées* divisions quoted above.

Continuing the Italian IV Army's Saga

Proceeding eastward. the XIII Brigade (Twenty-second Schutzen) with the WMB had reached Longarone at 1200. The Italians were now hemmed in from the north by the Tenth Army, to the south by the XIII Brigade and to the east by units of the Twenty-second Schützen. Some Italian troops fled to the mountains to the west but the bulk surrendered as the XIII Brigade continued southward toward Belluno. The other brigade of the Twenty-second Schützen (IIC Brigade) had proceeded through the cold mountains descending onto Tambre above the road from Vittorio Veneto to Belluno. Withdrawing Italian troops proceeded rapidly toward Belluno, but were captured by the Austro-Hungarian Fifty-fifth Infantry Divsion proceeding northward from Fadalto (Map 29). About 10,000 Italian soldiers were captured resulting in the road to Belluno now open. The whole loss had been attributed to the procrastination of Di Robilant's withdrawal orders. Cadorna had been very upset with his procrastination stating out loud, that if the IV Army was not saved, he would have DiRobilant shot.[116] Most of the IX and XVIII Corps plus their guns were now deployed on the Grappa. They were deployed as follows:[117]

Grappa Sector: XVIII Corps between the Brenta (excluding it) and M. Tomba but excluding it (Map 24)

M. Spinoncia : Fifty-sixth Infantry Division (Lt. Gen. E. Pittaluga)

M. Asolone: Fifty-first Infantry Division (Lt. Gen. Francesco Tamagni

From M. Tomba to Vidor on the Piave: IX Corps, Seventeenth, Twenty-third and Twenty-fourth Infantry Divisions plus the *Como*

From the Montello to Vidor-Ponte Priula (I Corps) (Map 42 for geography)

Artillery: Col. Baumgartner (who was Italian notwithstanding his last name)

As noted above a roadway had been constructed to bring supplies to the summit of the Grappa, while in the Val Sugana, facing northward there were reinforced concrete artillery positions with new trenches.

In the war's aftermath, the Caporetto Inquiry Commission accepted the prisoner figures without comment.[118] However, as in all inquiry commissions, errors were made. No credit was given to the pressure brought by the 26° Schützen.[119]

When the Austro-Germans halted the campaign would now have three theatres: the Piave, the large rock massive known as M. Grappa, and the Altopiano dei Setti Communi (Map 35). Below heard rumors of the arrival of Anglo-French troops in his sector and wanted to cross the river before they could deploy. By today the French XXXI Corps composed of the Sixty-fifth and

Sixty-fourth Infantry Division as well as the Forty-seventh and Forty-sixth Infantry Division had arrived in Italy. The French XII Corps composed of the Twenty-third and Twenty-fourth Infantry Division would all arrive by November 22. The Twelfth Silesian and the German Thirteenth Schützen tried to capture the bridge at Vidor but were repulsed by *Arditi* and *Alpini* (Maps 38, 42 for geography). Supplies were starting to lack. From the railhead at St. Lucia di Tolmino to the combat area was from 100 to 140 miles over bad roads and terrible bridges (Maps 35, 40). Often such a trip would take over a week. The railway from Tarvisio-Gemona-Udine had limited damages, but was starting to be used. The railway at Gorizia-Udine-Codroipo, once put into use would be reserved for the armies of Boroevic.

Speed was now of the essence for the Central Powers. Winter was approaching, the allies had troops on their way to the Piave, where the Italians were furiously working at making strong defenses. The victorious monarchs did not seem to be in a hurry as Charles accompanied by Arz visited Trieste from November 5 to November 18, while Wilhelm and the King of Bulgaria visited the front wasting the time of officers who should have been planning further advances.

In another thought from afar, Ludendorff had wanted to attack in the Trentino (Maps 14A, 35). Troops trained in mountain warfare, the One Hundredth Ninety-fifth Infantry Division and the AlpenKorps would be sent from the Trentino toward Verona. As previously noted this double thrust was not activated due to lack of troops and time to activate the assault. Conrad's attack in the Trentino (west of the Piave River), scheduled for November 10 had bogged down due to the weather and breakdown of supplies (Maps 14A, 35).

Nov. 11

Eugene issued orders that the XIV Army and the *Armées Isonzo* should cross the Piave and proceed southwest while the Krauss Group would advance between that river and the Brenta (Maps

35,40). They deployed from M. Tomatico to the Quero Gorge opposite forward Italian defense lines not fully garrisoned (Map 24). Diaz asked that these troops hold for ten to twelve days, the weather would take care of the rest. In all on the Grappa there were forty-seven battalions, twelve heavy artillery batteries, and forty mountain artillery batteries.

With all this there was not much hope in the British camp that the Italians would hold. Lt. Gen. Sir Henry Wilson reported to the Imperial General Staff that should the Piave not hold, the next defensive line would be at the Adige (Map 35).[120] He would become Chief of the Imperial General Staff in 1918 when Robertson resigned. Aware that the Anglo-French commanders were acting independent of Lloyd George, Orlando telegraphed Bissolati who was liaison to the Comando Supremo. His mission was to come to an agreement with the allies as to where to deploy their troops.[121] The French Government was so worried that Painlevé ordered Foch to remain in Italy until the situation was stabilized.[122]

Nov. 14

In coordination with attacks on the Grappa, the Stein Group vainly tried to cross the river with its Thirteenth Schutzen and Twelfth Silesian but was repulsed. The promised pontoon bridges which Vienna was to bring from Romania never did arrive. Large and medium caliber artillery had been sent back to the Western Front in Flanders. The XIV Army Artillery Chief, Gen. Richard von Berendt, ordered the artillery of the Stein and Scotti Groups to go closer to the river bank, orienting them to support the Krauss Group.

On November 22 after a conference, it was agreed that Anglo-French troops would enter the line to the right of the Italian IV Army in the sectors known as Monte Tomba and the Montello (Maps 24,35).[123] On November 29 Ludendorff, after discussions with Below, proposed to the A. O.K. to halt the offensive. The latter concurred, but requested that the battlefront between the

Piave and Brenta, be brought on the line between Bassano and the Montello (Map 35). Krafft felt that crossing the Piave, had more risks than any advantage derived. Col. Gatti, less of a military *persona* than the above beautifully summarized why the Italians had stopped withdrawing and the enemy had ceased advancing, "tiredness."[124]

The Italian Parliament convened with the news that Italy was no longer a conqueror but fighting for its very existence. Defeatist propaganda had to be silent for the moment. The Socialists declared that they had not supported nor sabotaged the war effort. Orators stated that now was not the time for finger-pointing which would come later. There was only a one day session, which closed after many patriotic speeches.

The *Armées Isonzo* had a different situation. On November 12, units of the Forty-fourth Schutzen Division in a surprise attack near Zenson reached the right (west) bank (Map 33). Only a violent counterattack by the *Catania* stopped any more damage but could not push the invader back across the river, while the next a.m. the *Pinerolo* (XIII Corps) also failed in its counterattack. Plumer reported by telegram that he thought that two more divisions would be needed. Should the Italians hold at the Piave, there was hope for the Anglo-French to hold the line. He arrived in Mantua to take command of the British forces from Lord Cavan who reverted to command of the XIV Corps. On November 13 the Imperial Twenty-eighth Division (II Corps) attacked from Cimadolmo to Grave di Papadopoli forcing the Italians to retreat onto the right side of the river at Saletttuol (Map 33). The bridge was destroyed. The Austro-Hungarian XXIII Corps coincidentally opposed by the similarly numbered Italian XXIII Corps, attempted to cross the river. It sent the Tenth Infantry Division to cross via a ferry at Musile and Intestadura opposite S. Donà but was repulsed by 139° (*Bari*) which took one hundred prisoners (Map 33). The 139° (Col. Gioacchino Nastasi had been involved in digging the approaches to the Sabotino months earlier. At Grisòlera near the sea, a violent attack forced the 140° to withdraw to the line *Piave Vecchio* maintaining a bridgehead at Caposile (Map 34). Two battalions of the *Granatieri di Sardegna* detached from the Fourth Division were sent to the XXIII Corps and thrown into action. Water pumps in the swampy area between *Piave Nuovo* and *Piave Vecchio* were destroyed flooding the area which remained so until the conflict's end.

At Villa Manin di Passariano, near Pordenone, Kaiser Wilhelm II awarded Below the Order of the Black Eagle the maximum Prussian military award. With his troops returning to Western Front he was worried about the ability of Habsburg forces to continue the campaign on their own. Being in the mountains, he felt that the Italians could attack the rear of the Austro-Hungarian forces, cutting them off in a manner similar to what had already happened to the Italians at Caporetto.[125]

After multiple daily scouting missions the air commander of the XIV Army issued a report that the Italians had no intention of going on the offensive.[126] Diaz was presented with an assessment of what remained of the *Regia Aeronautica's* remaining airfields.[127]

After multiple conferences Foch reported to Paris the possibility of three scenarios.

I. The Italian Army would not halt the enemy on the Piave, retreating to the mountains (Pasubio, Bacchiglione, Euganei and Berici) while the allies would counter-attack (Map 35).
II. The Italian Army would withdraw to the Po-Mincio Rivers further to the west, allowing the Anglo-French to use only twelve divisions.
III. The Italian Army would halt the enemy at the Piave River, obligating the allies to provide eighteen (from sixteen) divisions. Here there would be an advantage in that with this terrain there would be a possibility of counterattack and not be obligated to remain on the defensive.[128]

By the end of the year, the British Twenty-third Division had suffered 121 casualties while the Forty-first Division had 141.

Chapter X Endnotes

Withdrawing Across the Tagliamento and Piave Rivers

1 Werner Schachinger, *Die Bosniaken kommen ! Elitetruppe in der k.u.k. Armee, 1879-1918*, Graz, Stocker, 1989, p. 197.

2 Redl, Emil, Militarwissenschaftlichen und technischen Mitteilungen, *Crossing the Tagliamento at Cornino with the IV Battalion of the 4° Bosnian*, May-June, 1923, Vienna; OULK, Vol. VI, p. 593-605

3 Tullio DeRizzoli, *Il Corpo d'armata speciale,(DiGiorgio)* Torino, Lattes, 1922, p.112; Enrico Caviglia, *La Dodicesima Battalia, (Caporetto)*, Milano, 1933, p. 231.

4 Maurizio Ruffo, *L'Italia nella Triplice Alleanza*, USSME, Roma, 1998, p. 146, footnote.

5 USSME: Relazione Ufficiale, Vol. IV, Tomo 3°, op. cit., *Gli avvenimenti dall'ottobre al dicembre (Narrazione)*, Roma, 1967, p. 413-458

6 USSME: Relazione Ufficiale, Vol. IV, Tomo 3° bis, Documenti, op. cit., Comando Supremo 4 Novembre 1917, *Direttive per l'occupazione della linea del Piave*, Protocol No.5293, p. 387; Comando Supremo, 3 Novembre 1917, *Imbastitura prima occupazione della linea del Piave*, Protocol No. 5280, p. 389

7 OBARI, op. cit., p. 90

8 USSME: Relazione Ufficiale: Vol. IV Tomo 3° bis, op. cit., Comando 2a Armata, *Passaggio XII Corpo alle Dipendenze 2a Armata*, Doc. op. cit., No. 144, 29 October 1917, p. 326

9 USSME: Relazione Ufficiale, Vol. IV Tomo 3° bis, Doc., op. cit., Comando Supremo, *Ordine di ripiegamento alla Zona Carnia*, Doc. No. 125, Protocol No. 5011, 27 October 1917, p. 294

10 USSME: Relazione Ufficiale, Vol. IV, Tomo 3° bis, Doc., Comando 4a Armata *Ripiegamento del XII Corpo d'Armata*, Doc. No. 184, Protocol No. 11792, November 8, 1917, p. 386

11 USSME : Relazione Ufficiale, Volume IV, Tomo 3° bis, Doc. op. cit., p.346

[12] Ibid, Volume IV, Tomo 3°, op. cit., p. 477

[13] USSME: Relazione Ufficiale, Vol. IV, Tomo 3° bis, Documenti, op. cit., Comando Settore Sinistra, 5 Novembre, 1917, *Tentativo di disimpegnare le Divisione 36a e 63a,* Protocol No. 237, p. 395; Comando XII Corps, *Prescrizioni circa l'azione delle Divisione 36a e 63a,* Protocol No. 14, p. 394; Comando XII Corps, *Istruzioni speciale alle Divisioni 36a e 63a,* Protocol No. 218, Novembre 3, 1917, page 393; OULK*:* Vol. VI, op. cit., p. 621

[14] Angelo Gatti, *Caporetto,* op. cit., p. 134

[15] Vittorio Emanuele Orlando, *Memorie* (1915-1919), *Milano Rizzoli, 1960, p. 238-240*

[16] Ibid, pp. 504-505

[17] See Olindo Malagodi, *Conversazione della Guerra 1914-1918,* edited by Brunello Vigezzi, Milano-Napoli, 1960

[18] OULK*:* Vol. VI, op. cit., p. 593

[19] USSME: Relazione Ufficiale, Volume IV, Tomo 3°, op.cit., p. 349

[20] Sebastiano Murari, *Un episodio di guerra nelle Prealpi Carniche,* Milano, Mondadori, 1935, p. 327.

[21] USSME : Relazione Ufficiale, Volume IV, Tomo 3°, op. cit., p. 467

[22] OULK*:* Vol. IV, op. cit., p. 614

[23] Krafft, op. cit., Vol II, p. 213.

[24] *Resto del Carlino,* August 6, 1919, Bologna, p. 1.

[25] USSME: Relazione Ufficiale, Volume IV, Tomo 3°, op. cit., p. 455

[26] Enrico Caviglia, *La Ritirata della 4a Armata, Nuova Antologia,* 1931, n. 1413, p. 307-317

[27] Tullio DeRizzoli, op. cit., Torino, 1933, pp.199

[28] USSME: Relazione Ufficiale, Vol. IV, Tomo 3° op. cit.,p.463

[29] USSME: Relazione Ufficiale, Vol. IV, Tomo 3° bis, Doc., op. cit., Comando Settore Sinistra, *Ordine di ripegamento delle Divisioni 63a e 36a,* Doc. 159, Protocol 226, November 3, 1917, p. 348

[30] First Italian Army Chief of Staff who served from 1882-1893.

[31] AUSSME: Chief of Staff Enrico Cosenz, *Studio circa la difensiva e l'offensiva Nord-Est,* F4, 11

[32] USSME: Relazione Ufficiale, Vol. IV, Tomo 3°, bis, Doc., Comando Truppe Mobili *Direttive per il ripiegamento dal Tagliamento al Piave,* Doc. No. 211, Protocol No. 5783, November 3, 1917, p. 425

[33] USSME: Relazione Ufficiale, Volume IV, Tomo 3° bis, Documenti, op. cit.,Comando II Armata, 3 Novembre 1917, *Situazione per penetrazione nemica a Cornino* Protocol No. 5, page 344; Comando II Armata, 3 Novembre 1917, *Dispozioni all'ala sinistra per fronteggiare situazione a Cornino,* Protocol No. 5, p. 345

[34] USSME : Relazione Ufficiale, Volume IV, Tomo 3° op. cit., p. 463

[35] USSME: Relazione Ufficiale, Volume IV, Tomo 3° bis, Doc., op. cit., Comando I Corps 3 Novembre 1917, *Ordine per la Marcia in Ritirata,* Protocol No. 1949, p. 362

[36] The letter, dated Sept. 30, 1926 is in Krafft's book, *Durchbruch am Isonzo*

[37] Enrico Caviglia, *Le Tre Battaglie del Piave,* Milano, 1935, pp. 214-218; Within the same pages is the full text of the letter sent by Cadorna to the Prime Minister.

[38] Luigi Cadorna, *La Guerra alla fronte italiana,* Two Vol., Milano, 1923, p. 215-216. ;L. Segato, *L'Italia nella guerra mondiale,* 2nd edition, 4 volumes, Milano, 1934. p. 271-73; E. Caviglia, *Le Tre Battaglie del Piave,* Milano, 1935, p. 215-218, contains the full text of Cadorna's letter.

[39] See *Memorie,* Vittorio Emanuele Orlando, Milano 1960

[40] Luigi Cadorna, *Altre Pagine sulla Grande Guerra,* Milano, 1925, pp. 235-237

[41] DDI, Series V, Volume XI, doc. 364, Sonnino to Cadorna, 4-11-1917, p. 252

[42] USSME: Relazione Ufficiale, Vol. IV, Tomo 3°, op. cit., p. 430-458

[43] Idem, p. 455

[44] USSME: Relazione Ufficiale, Vol. IV, Tomo 3° bis, Documenti, op. cit., Comando 4a Armata, 6 Novembre 1917, *Occupazione della linea del Piave,* Protocol No. 11697, p. 374; Comando 4a Armata, 6 Novembre 1917, *Direttive per occupazione Piave da Nervesa a Vidor,* Protocol No. 11712, p. 375

[45] *Forcella* means narrow Alpine pass

[46] USSME: Relazione Ufficiale, Vol. IV, Tomo 3° bis, Doc., op. cit., Comando Settore Sinistra *Tentativo di disimpegnare le Divisioni 36a e 63a,* November 5, 1917, Doc. 192, Protocol 237, p. 395

[47] RICC, Volume II, p. 170

[48] USSME: Relazione Ufficiale, Volume IV, Tomo 3°, op.cit., p. 468

[49] Sonnino Microfilm, reel 47, University of Michigan, Ann Arbour, MI.

50 PRO: CAB, 23/4/163 (Nov. 9, 1917, (War Cabinet minutes); Wilson Papers (diary for 8 Nov.,1917); L. Aldrovandi Marescotti, *Guerra Diplomatica. Ricordi e frammenti del diario 1914-19.*, Milano, Mondadori 1937, p. 150

51 Lloyd D. George. *War Memoirs,* Two Volumes, London 1938 p. 1396

52 C. à Court Repington, *The First World War 1914-1918,* Vol. II, p. 33, Constable, London, 1920, p. 33

53 Carlo Sforza, *L'Italia dal 1914 al 1944 quale io la vidi,* Rome 1945, pp. 45-46. Count Sforza was the brother of Capt. Alessandro Sforza, liaison from the Comando Supremo to the XXVII Corps.

54 RICC, op. cit., Volume II, p. 548.

55 OBARI, op. cit., p. 72

56 L. Cadorna, *Lettere famigliare* op. cit., p. 238

57 USSME: Relazione Ufficiale, Volume IV, Tomo 3°, op.cit., p. 458.

58 Ibid, page 455-56.

59 Ibid., p. 477; Volume IV, Tomo 3°, Doc., op. cit., p. 346

60 AUSSME : War Diary, "Aosta ", Nov. 6, 1917.

61 Sonnino microfilm, reel 57, University of Michigan, Ann Arbour, Michigan.

62 OBARI, op. cit., p. 79. The proposal never got off the ground.

63 USSME: Relazione Ufficiale, Vol. IV Tomo 3° bis, Documenti, op. cit., Comando Supremo, 5 novembre 1917, *Argumenti per il gen. Porro da prospettare agli alleati nel Convegno di Rapallo,* Protocol No. 5323, p. 500 Comando Supremo, 6 novembre 1917, same topic, Protocol No. 5366 p. 501

64 Luigi Aldrovandi, *I Convegni di Rapallo e Peschiera : 6-7-8 Novembre, Frammenti del Diario,* Nuova Antologia, Jan. 1, 1935, p. 101

65 G. Volpe, *Ottobre 1917, Dal Isonzo al Piave,* Milano, Mondadori, 1930, p. 64; Appendix I

66 PRO: CAB 45/84, Wingfield to Edmonds, July 4, 1943

67 Ibid.

68 See V.E. Orlando, *Memorie, 1915-1919.* Milano, 1960

69 USSME: Relazione Ufficiale, Vol. IV, Tomo 3° bis, Documenti, op. cit., Presid. Cons. Minis., *Convegno di Rapallo,* Document No. 246, Protocol No. F.T.12/G, p. 499

70 PRO : FO Cab 28/2, Nov. 6 & 7 1917; Sonnino *Diario*, 1916-1922, Nov. 6,1917; Lloyd George Papers, House of Lords Library, F/120/2/24, Report on Rapallo.

71 USSME: Relazione Ufficiale, Volume IV, Tomo 3°, op.cit., p. 471

72 OULK: Vol. VI, p. 616

73 Tullio DeRizzoli, *Il Corpo d'armata Speciale (DiGiorgio)*, Preface by Lt. Gen. Luigi Segato, Torino, 1933, pp. 21-199. In the same book is a chapter by Carlo Borntraeger, *Dal Tagliamento al Piave. L'artiglieria del Corpo d'armata Speciale DiGiorgio,* Milano-Roma, Dante Alighieri, 1934, p. 29

74 USSME: Relazione Ufficiale, Volume IV Tomo 3° op. cit., p. 473

75 **USSME: Relazione Ufficiale, Vol. IV, Tomo 3°** bis, Documenti, Comando 2a Armata, 6 Novembre 1917, *Successive resistenze sino alla linea Monticano,* Protocol No. 6646, p. 396

76 Angelo Gatti, *La Parte dell'Italia,* Milano, 1926, p. 162; Leonida Bissolati, *Diario Di Guerra*, Torino, Einaudi, 1935, p. 93-99; Luigi Aldrovandi Marescotti, *Guerra Diplomatica. Ricordi e frammenti di diario 1914-19,* Milano, Mondadori, 1937p. 132.

77 Angelo Gatti, *Caporetto, Dal diario della guerra,* Bologna, Il Mulino, 1964, p.337

78 Angelo Gatti, *Un italiano a Versailles,* Milano, 1958. p. 312-3

79 Silvio Scaroni *Con Vittorio Emanuele* Mondadori, Milano p. 139

80 Angelo Gatti, *Diario, p. 338.*

81 Ibidem, p. 332-333.

82 A. Gatti, *Diario* op. cit., p. 451

83 Giorgio DeVecchi di Val Cismon, *Armando Diaz*, Storia Militare, Nov. 1968, p. 25

84 A. Gatti, op. cit. p. 453-454.

85 Carlo DeBiase, *Badoglio, Duca di Caporetto*, Milano, Ed. del Borghese, 1965 Testimony given by Parliamentary Deputy, Edoardo Rotigliano p. 18.

86 E. Caviglia, op. cit. p. 4-5

87 DDI, Series V, Volume IX, doc. 365, Italian Ambassador to Paris, Salvago Raggi to Sonnino, 4-11-1917, p. 252

88 Sonnino Microfilm, reel 47, (8 Nov. 1917 British War Cabinet Paper I.C.32), Univ. of Michigan, Ann Arbour, Michigan; Smuts Papers, 682/44 (24 Nov., 1917), Cambridge University Library

89 Ibid.

90 DDI, Series V, Vol. IX, doc. 391, Minutes of the Peschiera conference, 9-11-1917, p. 272.

91 *Nuova Antologia,* Luigi Aldrovandi, Jan. 1, 1935, p. 235.

92 OBARI op. cit., p. 80

93 A.S.M.E., D.D.I., Imperiali to Sonnino, November 17, 1917, Doc. 460, p.314

94 Antonino Di Giorgio, *Ricordi della Grande Guerra,* Fondazione Whitaker, 1978, p. 155-156; Cyril Falls, *Caporetto, 1917,* London, Wedenfeld and Nicosin.

95 Gatti, *Caporetto,* op.cit., p. 374 quoting Col. Gazzera's report to the General Staff. The troops on the Grappa were also reported as indifferent, but when one volunteers to die, one is not indifferent to the cause.

96 Personal Communication.

97 Alessandro Luzio, *Il Comando Supremo con Armando Diaz,* Vercelli, 1920, p. 7

98 E. Caviglia, *Diario Aprile 1925-Marzo 1945,* Rome, Casini, 1952, p. 34. The author wrote "He never understood why Italy had won on the Piave and Vittorio Veneto and died without knowing how."

99 USSME: Relazione Ufficiale, Vol. IV, Tomo 3° bis, Doc., op. cit., Comando I C.A. 6 Novembre, 1917,*Ripiegamento della Fortezza Cadore-Maè*, Protocol 10933, p. 376

100 OBARI op. cit., p. 99

101 Ibid, ppg.424-425; see Appendix I this vol. for text

102 HStASt, M 130 Bü 5. WGB, *Gefechtsbericht über die Zeit vom 24-31-.10.17*

103 Hubner, Alexander, *Die zwölfe Schlacht am Isonzo und die Isonzokrieg,* Verlag Karl Harbauer, Vienna and Leipzig, 1918; Hubner was a major in the Austro-Hungarian Army and on the scene.

104 Korzer, Karl, *Vom Pusterial ins Piavetal,* Militärwissenschaftliche und technische Mitteilungen H. 5/6, 1930

105 HStASt., M411, Bü 247 *Kriegstagebuch des Geburgs Batls 11.10.17-26.2.1918.*

106 Krafft von Dellmensingen K., *Der Durchbruch am Isonzo,* Vol. I, p. 197

107 Schwarte, Max, *Der Grosse Krieg 1914-1918,* V Bd., *Der Österreichisch-ungarische Krieg,* various editors, 1922, p. 444.

108 Schittenhelm, Helmut, *Im toten Winkel,* Verlag Kohlhammer, Stuttgart, 1935, p.71. From the huge no. of Italian prisoners, one suddenly exclaimed

to German Cpl. Gottlob Graze, in his Swabian dialect, *Gottlob, Gottlob, wie kommscht Du do her?* (How come you are here?) They had been comrades working in a construction crew in Germany.

109 USSME: Relazione Ufficiale, Vol. IV, Tomo 3°, Narrazione op. cit., p. 511; OULK p. 622

110 USSME: Relazione Ufficiale, Vol. IV, Tome 3° bis, Documenti, op. cit., Comando 3a Armata 5 Novembre 1917, *Ordine di Battaglia per lo Schieramento sulla destra del Piave,* Protocol No. 278, p. 409

111 USSME: Relazione Ufficiale, Vol. IV, Tome 3°, op.cit.p.460

112 Official British Army Report, Military Operations in France and Belgium 1917, Imperial War Museum, London, 1948, p. 274.

112A Imperial War Museum, London: Delmé-Radcliffe papers, June 28, 1918, Gen. Wilson; At time of this writing, these papers had been donated by the family and were being catalogued; Robertson Papers:, 1/34/40 (December 4, 1917, Gen. Plumer)

113 C.E. Callwell, *Field Marshal Sir Henry Wilson* Vol. II, London, 1927. II, p. 24

114 USSME: Relazione Ufficiale, Vol. IV, Tomo 3° bis, Documenti, op. cit., Comando 1a Armata, *Situazione della forza della 1a Armata,* 8 novembre 1917, Protocol No. 65676, p. 466

115 Kriegsarchiv, Vienna, *Manuskripte, Weltkrieg, 1918, Series* "J," *Italy, No. 18,* Anton von Pitreich, *Die K.u.k. Piavefront,* Part I, pp. 11-14

116 T. Marchetti, *Ventotti Anni nel Servizio Informazioni Militare,* Trento, 1960, p.274.

117 USSME: Relazione Ufficiale, Vol. IV, Tomo 3° bis, Documenti, op. cit., Comando XVIII C.A., 6 Novembre 1917, *Occupazione linea della Grappa,* Protocol No. 3, p. 381

118 RICC: op. cit. Volume I, p. 370; Volume II, p. 177ff.

119 Ibid, vol. I. p. 370

120 OBARI, op.cit. p. 94

121 DDI, Series V, Volume IX, doc. 403,404, Orlando to the king's aide di camp, Gen. Cittadini, pp. 278-279; Martini's Diary, entry of 3-11-17, noted that the allies did not wish to be involved in a situation similar to that in Russia losing artillery mouths which then would fire on them on the Western Front, p. 1031

122 *Les Armée Françaises,* Annexe 67, "War Minister to Chief of the General Staff," 11-11-1917, p. 119

123 OBARI, op. cit., p. 101

124 E. Ludendorff, *Meine Kriegserinnerungen,* 1919, Berlin, Mittler & Sohn, p. 72; The First QuarterMaster wrote that he met with Krafft in the beginning of December; The XIV Army Chief of Staff *Durchbruch am Isonzo,* op. cit., noted this to be December 14, p. 344; OULK Vol. IV, op. cit., p. 677; Cramon op. cit., p. 199-200, declared that the A.O.K. wanted the Germans to remove their troops, but this is really not to be believed, as simultaneously the O.K.L. was asking the A.O.K. for troops to send to the Western Front.

125 Below Diary, op. cit., diary entry, Nov. 21, 1917

126 Bundesarchiv-Militärarchiv, PH 5 II/362, Kommandeur der Flieger 14, Bildaufklärung vom November zum Dezember bis Dezember 1917, 11-30-17

127 USSME: Relazione Ufficiale, Vol. IV Tomo 3° bis, Doc., *Situazione dell'Aeronautica nel mese di Ottobre 1917,* Doc. 213, p. 431

128 FAR tome VI, op. cit., Annexe 79, *Rapport,* 16-11-1917, p. 135

CHAPTER XI

THE FIRST BATTLE ON THE ALTOPIANO DEI SETTE COMMUNI (ASIAGO PLATEAU)

November 1917

The Italian Army accumulated men and material on the west side of the Piave. Troops from the Zona Carnia Command and the II Army were now standing fast as opposed to the troops on the Isonzo River a few days prior. In the III Army, morale was high, because as yet they had neither fought nor been defeated. Should the Austro-Germans break through either on the altipiano, the Grappa, or cross the Piave, Italy would be out of the war as there were no more troops to stop the enemy onslaught. Enemy troops would proceed to Milano, Venezia and even Rome. Fighting here was maneuver warfare in the classic sense which neither Italian staff officers nor troops in the field could handle. Habsburg forces on the altipiano fought in relatively small units which one could easily identify and note their long history. Italian units had no such history as the Italian Army had been in being less than fifty years. Suddenly for unexplained reasons the Italian troops morale changed. Alpini and fanti fought on the altipiano and M. Grappa. Combat was in the rain, snow, fog and cold, often without food and shelter always lacking proper clothing, but the peasant infantry and Alpini had only one cry "Di qui non si passa," loosely translated as "They shall not pass." In the high altitude and bitter cold, combatants on both sides froze to death. Many of the Italian troops had never seen snow nor experienced the bitter cold but they stopped the Austro-German juggernaut. The men were now fighting for something they were aware of (their families) rather than some concept called Italy which being illiterate they could not understand.

With their troops in the line as of November 29, the allies were preoccupied about the retreat of the alpini, Italy's best troops. In the Melette sector the defenders yielded resulting in the enemy arriving at the border of the Val Brenta. Detailed graphic maps of various interrelated sectors are provided.

"They're over like demons, mid bullets and gas,
And the line it holds, we fight to the last.
The smoke it clears, the battle is won-
But for many a boy, the war is done . . .
Walter J. Baldwin, "I Wonder"

PROCEEDING FROM THE Adriatic Sea westward Italian defense sectors included three different topographical areas, the Piave River, M. Grappa and the Altopiano dei Sette Communi also known as the Asiago Plateau. As the Piave curved to the southeast it was overlooked by a small hill called the Montello which was east of the Grappa (Maps 29,35). Defending artillery on its summit could halt any Habsburg crossing of the river. Damp winds coming off the Adriatic often provide thick mist or torrential rain.

Topography The plateau is twelve miles long in a north-south direction and is five miles wide with the central basin having an altitude of 3,300 feet. The terrain is limestone making trenches hard to dig. On the undulating plateau were small villages bordered on the east by the Val Brenta and west by the deep Val d' Astico. It was named for seven municipalities, Asiago, Energo, Conco, Roana, Foza, Gallio and Lusiana. North of Asiago lay heavily wooded areas followed by M. Ortigara (6,300 feet) and M. Mosciagh (5,000 feet), after which there is a deep drop into the Val Sugana running east to west containing the upper portions of the Brenta River (Vol. I, Map 3). Proceeding southward from M. Ortigara it is flat, then rises slowly in a steep slope up to a heavily wooded area at 4,500 ft. being 1,500 ft. above the altipiano with the woods sloping gently toward the plains. This was where the *Strafexpedition* had petered out. In its northwest sector the rolling pasture land is bisected by the Ghelpac Creek Gorge where there are also two deep valleys, the Val Frenzela and Val d'Assa. In a historical note when Dante saw the Val d'Assa he was so fear-struck that he described it as the "Mouth of Hell" in the *Divina Commedia*. To the east are undulating foothills which gradually rose so that from four miles away, one had a clear view of the scene west of the Piave. The whole sector was devoid of water and roadways, but had some mule paths. A narrow gauge railway brought supplies to the southern foothills from whence cable cars lifted them up to the plateau. Dogs and mules were also used to pull sleds or carts according to the weather. Water being scarce Italian engineers had built a system to bring water from the Astico River up 2,500 ft. to distribution points on the altipiano.

With the Italian troops abandoning the Cadore and Carnia sectors the new defensive line of the IV Army would be the Grappa-Asolone-Col Moschin (Map 24). On October 29 Cadorna met with Pecori-Giraldi (I Army) and Di Robilant (IV Army), explaining the situation as it stood. The XX Corps (Lt. Gen. Ferrari), was ordered to change its deployment from westward to the north with the hinge on M. Nos, cross the core of the Melette and the Brenta Canal and link up to the east with the IV Army on the Grappa (Maps 11, 24,25). The Comando Supremo had withdrawn troops southward to the level of the northern borders of the Asiago basin. Troops were deployed as follows:

Passo Stelvio to the west shore of Lago di Garda was the III Corps (Maps 1,2)

Garda's eastern shore to the Brenta River, I Army (Maps 1,29)

Garda eastward to the Vallarsa Valley with the XXIX Corps

Vallarsa Valley to Val Pòsina, the V Corps (Map 3)
Val Posina to the Astico River, X Corps (Maps,3,35).

On the Altopiano dei Sette Communi (C.T.A.) troops were deployed:

XX Corps (Lt. Gen. Giuseppe Francesco Ferrari), Gallio westward to C. Caldiera (Maps11,31).

All-*Alpini* Fifty-Second Division (Raggruppamenti *Alpini* I, IV) from M. Badenecche to Val Brenta, along the right margin of the Val Gadena (Map 31).
Twenty-ninth Infantry Division-(*Regina,* III *Gruppo Alpini)* deployed along the line M. Badenecche-M. Tondarecar-M. Castelgomberto M. Fior-Torrione-Bocchetta Slapeur-Meletta Ristecco-Casara Meletta Davanti-Monte Zomo (Map 25)

XXII Corps (Lt. Gen. Antonio Gatti) from Ghelpach Gorge to Gallio (Map 31)

Second Infantry Division (*Toscana,* XVI Assault Unit, 5° Bersaglieri) from M. Zomo-Val Frenzela-Malga Slapeur-M. Sisemol (Maps 25,26)
Fifty-seventh Infantry Divisions (*Pisa, Toscana*) went from Sisemol-Bertigo-Pennar-Meltar-to S. Sisto linking up with the XXVI Corps (Map 31)

XXVI Corps (Lt. Gen. Augusto Fabbri) in the M. Cengio sector with the Eleventh and Twelfth Infantry Divisions (Map 31).

In all there were 320,000 men consisting of 122 battalions and 1,380 artillery pieces. The reader is reminded of the order sent at 0545 on October 27 to Lt. Gen. Pecori Giraldi (First Army) concerning the new deployments after the loss of P. di

Montemaggiore, which transferred to the Italian IV Army the defensive construction on the Grappa (See Chapter IV).[1] Also to be noted is that embattled M. Ortigara (Vol. I, chapter XI) is on the northern border of the Altopiano dei Sette Communi (Asiago Plateau) so the battles are intricately related. The aim was to halt the enemy from proceeding into the plains below. Realizing this, on October 31, Major Gen. Ricci Armani (C.T.A. commander) sent out a memorandum entitled "Regulations for an eventual retreat." Why the sudden pessimism? The XX Corps would be involved in the defense of the Mellete di Gallio and Foza as well as the defense of the Brenta River Valley (Map 25). It deployed on the right bank while the XVIII Corps (IV Army), would deploy on the left. The core of defenses on the altipiano would be the Melette where in June 1916 four battalions of *Alpini* and two of the *Sassari* had halted the Habsburg offense. Only light artillery would be deployed here while the heavy pieces would be emplaced on the southern fascia of the altopiano where the orders were to fight to the last. Using these mouths would be the XXII and XXVI Corps which would employ them in actions on Brenta Canal and consequently the Grappa (Map 24). M. Castelgomberto and M. Fior were made impregnable while M. Tondarecar and M. Badenecche to the east left much to be desired in their defenses. These garrisons could only be supplied via the steep Val Vecchia road, otherwise they were isolated (Map 25).

On November 4 the IV Army announced that its XVIII Corps would start withdrawing from the V. Sugana during the next night and the I Army (XX Corps) would do likewise, making a hinge of its Twenty-ninth Infantry Division on its left (Map 3) The *Alpini* Monte Baldo and Vestone Battalions were deployed in Val Brenta linking up with the XVIII Corps deployed to the east on M. Grappa. These *Alpini* had the task to halt any enemy infiltration into Val Brenta. The *Alpini* division was deployed on the Melette di Foza, blocking the gorge at V. Gadena-Canal di Brenta (Maps 25, 31). Should the Habsburgs occupy the Melette place artillery on the eastern border of the altipiano they could shell the rear of

Italian troops deployed along the Brenta Canal in the Grappa sector. They could also proceed down the Brenta to Bassano and on to the Vicentian Plain (Map 31).

With troops complaining about leaving comfortable quarters, two corps (XX and XVIII), slowly withdrew from November 5 to November 9 under a protective shield of *Arditi*. We can only think of what condition their morale was. Leaving good quarters, notified of many defeats, now withdrawing to where? The Comando Supremo subsequently changed orders again, but these were rejected by the I Army (too confusing and too late). As the OAR noted, these were the same battlefields of the *Strafexpedition* of 1916 known to both sides of the trench. Conrad, who knew the area well, asked for more troops to mount a serious offensive before the Anglo-French troops arrived which was refused. Correctly noting that there was an exuberance of divisions after Caporetto, he felt that with two divisions proceeding from the Valsugana Valley (Map 43 for geography) southward he could break through. On October 28, arriving from the Trentino to reinforce Army Group Tyrol were the One-Hundred-Sixth Landsturm and the Twenty-first Schützen. A plan was devised a plan by which he would aim for Valstagna via Val Vecchia and Val Frenzela (Map 31). Instead on November 9 he was ordered to attack on November 12 from Asiago in a southerly direction. Feeling more troops were needed and aware that the imperial train was passing through the Trentino, Conrad arranged for an audience and after a short talk with the emperor received one cavalry division, plus twelve infantry battalions. His troops were deployed:

III Corps deployed between the Astico River Gorge and M. Zebio:

Sixth Infantry Division-(Major Gen. Josef Ritter von Schilhawsky) would attack in the Ferragh-M. Ongara sector (Maps 25,26 with No. 25 illustrating the sector north of 26)

Fifty-second Infantry Division (GdI Heinrich Goiginger) this division had the task of holding down the Italian XXVI Corps.

The assault group was the III Corps known as the *Eiserne* (Iron) *Korps* commanded by GdI Josef Krautwold with Col. Karg as Chief of Staff. Strong like iron when asked to hold a position it did. Asked to assault and occupy a position it was always succesful. There was a total of forty-one battalions plus 361 artillery pieces. In reserve at Lavarone was the Hundred-sixth Landsturm Division while near Trento was the Nineteenth Infantry Division as a corps reserve, all totaling nineteen battalions (Map 3). Between M. Zebio and the northern border of the altopiano thirteen battalions of the *Gruppe Kletter* (GdI Kletter) were deployed (Map 11 for geography). Seventy trains of fifty cars each were used to bring all men and supplies into position. The plan was to break through near Gallio and reach the heights west of Valstagna to stop any Italian supplies proceeding along the Val Brenta through which passed a roadway and railway (Map 31). Among the assaulting troops were the *Bergführer-Sturmkompagnien* officers and men drawn from the Kaiserjäger, Kaiserschützen and the Tyrolean Standschützen. These were upper-mountain fighting troops (over 10,000 feet), who had undergone assault training at Levico followed by maneuvers near the Adamello Glacier. The former chief of the general staff was convinced (correctly so) that the Italian Army had no means to halt Austro-Hungarian attacks from the Stelvio eastward. (Maps 1,2,3).

November 9

Italian troops noted increased enemy patrol activity starting the First Battle of the Melette. During the evening, units of the Austro-Hungarian III Corps had occupied M. Catz and Cimon di Fiara. The *Gruppe* found M. Baldo and M. Fiara deserted (Map 31). The attackers arrived at the hamlet of Gallio where after a furious battle, they overcame the defenders proceeded forward surrounding it and overcame three companies of the

Italian 77° (Maps 26,31). Major Gen. Michele Salazar, commander of the Italian Second Infantry Division personally took command. Losing the hamlet at this time would have guaranteed a premature loss of the overlooking M. Òngara which would have impeded the withdrawal of many Italian troops. Italian troops now fought completely different from the manner of two weeks ago on the Isonzo. They knew that death rode the wind but they stayed, fought and died. No longer would they retreat. The enemy was at the door of their house. They wanted to slam the door in his face. Afraid of harm to their families is the only way to explain this sudden turnaround in Italian troops morale. They caused such great losses to Conrad's forces that eventually the offensive was suspended.

November 10

In the early dark hours Kaiserjäger units (three battalions of the I Brigade, Sixth Infantry Division, commanded by Major Gen. Otto Ellison von Nidelef), attacked and occupied Gallio, M. Ferragh, crossing the Ghelpach Gorge.[2] At 0600 a newly conscripted unit of the Fifth Bersaglieri composed of 150 rifles proceeded toward Gallio, deployed to block the road to V. Frenzela and counterattacked, later being assisted by the XVI Assault Unit (Map 26). Combat in the dark and cold was house to house forcing the Austro-Hungarians to retreat from the scene. Cadavers were strewn all over the streets of the village. Two battalions of the *Pisa* counterattacked occupying the summit of M. Ferragh. The OAR noted that Habsburg troops had to protect themselves from an attack from the east before proceeding toward Bertigo.[3] The new defense line was now at Ferragh Gallio-M. Ongara (Maps 31, 26)

November 11

Units of the 17° *Kronprinz* attacked toward Contrada Costa di Gallio and Casara La Tesa, finally reaching the summit of M.

Ongara.[4] At 1700 the first and second battalion of the 27° *König der Belgier* attacked Italian positions on M. Ongara while the *Kronprinz* units would circle around to the south of the mountain.[5] Conrad's troops now realized that opposing them were not the disorganized and low morale troops of the previous month, but men who fought tenaciously to the bitter end.[6] Twice the attackers reached the summit only to be pushed off and back to the line of departure by furious counterattacks by the 5° Bersaglieri, *Alpini* Verona Battalion, units of the 77° assisted by artillery of the Second and Twenty-ninth Infantry Divisions. All of the Verona's officers were killed, but the opened breach due to the seizure of the summit was sealed. The *Alpini* knew that they would die on these mountains but felt it was their duty to hold the position which had been denied to the enemy the previous year when they had halted the enemy's advance. Faced with strong Italian resistance the Eleventh Army decided to cancel the assault on Bertigo scheduled for the next day as there was a possibility of counterattacks against the III Corps from the Valstagna direction.

The possibility of Conrad's attack had been discussed by Italian and British army circles. Even Col. Gatti got into the act being called a *disfattista* (defeatist) for his efforts.[7] There was a pervasive fear by all that the Austro-Germans would attack in the Trentino much as they had done the previous year. After he was replaced, Cadorna still subscribed to this theory in a letter to his son.[8]

November 12

In the late afternoon, the Austro-Hungarians started heavy shelling of Italian positions on the northwest slopes of M. Sisemol and M. Òngara, with infantry attacking the Ferragh sector (Map 31). The Twenty-first Schützen attacked at Ferragh while the *Gruppe Kletter* attacked the Melette (Map 25). As darkness arrived Kaiserjäger units preceded by assault units infiltrated west of M. Ongara. Defending were the *Alpini* Sette Communi, Verona and Bassano Battalions. Due to the fierce fighting and heavy losses, men on both sides were given cognac to raise their spirits and give them courage and decrease their inhibition reflexes. Drunken humans do things they would not do when sober. Combat was hand-to-hand with both sides using knives, clubs and daggers. When the Italian garrison on M. Òngara was overcome survivors withdrew along the Val di Campomulo. Under a black sky from the cold slopes emanated cries of the wounded and men near-death throughout the night.

November 13

At 0630, Gen. Gatti notifed Ricci Armani, that he would not be able to send the garrison on M. Òngara reinforcements (four Battalions of the *Ligure)* as even in daylight there was scarse probability of success. He established the final line of defense on a line at M. Sisemol-Malga, Stenfle-M. Zomo, thereby surrounding from above the beginning of the Frenzela Valley (Maps 25,26). Only the decreasing firing heard from M. Òngara would tell the surrounding troops that the Italians had been overcome. The OAR noted that the III Corps had occupied Gallio and M Òngara, but did not capture many retreating troops due to Italian resistance. The Comando Supremo reported 2,000 dead, wounded and missing. The A.O.K. reported 300 prisoners. No longer were there the mass surrenders as in the prior three weeks. Italian troops were now deployed as follows:

M. Zomo-I/158° (*Liguria)* (Maps 25, 31)
M. Zomo to the Gallio-Foza roadway—II/77° (*Toscana)*
The roadway to the end of Val Frenzela—III/57° (*Liguria*)
Val Frenzela to and excluding Sisemol-XXXVI/5° (Map 26)
Sisemol Redoubt—*Mantova*

Ready reserves:
- Ronco di Carbone—XIV/5° Bersaglieri
- Contrada Dalla Bona—I, II/77°, (*Toscana*)
- Near Case Gianesini-I, II/ 157° (*Toscana*), 5° Auxiliary Bersaglieri
- Case Gianesini—An assault battalion
- Covola-Sisemol Trenches: *Alpini* Bassano Battalion

Encouraged by the capture of M. Òngara (the left defensive pillar of Val Frenzela), Conrad now attacked on other fronts.[9] In the afternoon Styrians of the 27° as well as Kaiserjäger proceeded north of M. Òngara, descended into Val di Campomulo to assault the slopes of the Melette di Gallio and M. Zomo from an oblique angle (Map 25). Gallio was occupied by the men of the *Kronprinz* while the *Gruppe Kletter* attacked the whole Melette and to the south the Twenty-first Schützen occupied Ferragh (Maps 25, 26 with No. 25 illustrating the sector north of Map No. 26)

Eleventh Army headquarters felt that by not resisting on the Melette, the Italians had picked as the principal position of their new defensive line, the knot of M. Cengio, the southern border of the Asiago basin and the rocky gorge of the V. Frenzela (Map 31). Assisted by the III Corps and the CX Landsturm Brigade the *Gruppe* was ordered to occupy the Melette immediately. That same afternoon a heavy clash took place near Ferragh with victorious Habsburg troops threatening the hamlets of Bertigo and Turcio (Maps 26,31). Attacks on the western slopes of M. Sisemol were blocked by the newly arrived *Liguria*. Neither bad weather nor darkness halted combat as at 2130 during a snow storm, units of the *Gruppe* proceeded from the lower V. Campomulo to the upper dorsum of the Melette di Gallio aiming for the Casara Meletta Davanti saddle where they overcame units of the *Regina* (9°, 10°). From there, they descended into the basin of Malga Slapeur trying to attack M. Castelgomberto and infiltrating south toward the head of the Miela Valley (Map 25). The 75° assaulted the north sector of the Melette Davanti, infiltrated to the defender's rear (Italian 9°), but due to heavy losses had to withdraw (Map 25).[10]

Conrad now requested that the A.O.K. send him reinforcements declaring that the principal attack should be on the altipiano. Simply put, he wanted control of the whole mountain offensive which did not happen. The emperor's entourage at the A.O.K. would not give any power to the dismissed chief of staff, while the Germans felt he was too independent and could not be controlled. The response of the A.O.K. was simple declaring that the Krauss Group would ease the passage of Habsburg troops across the Piave and therefore would still belong to the Austro-German XIV Army whose offensive was to be restarted on the following day. The old marshal may have been right. At the time Italy had neither the artillery nor the available reserves to stop any enemy offensive on the altipiano. A massive offensive would have spelled disaster for the Italians.

November 14

In the morning, units of the *Alpini* Pasubio and M. Baldo Battalions arrived on the Melette to reinforce the exhausted *Regina,* while others went to Malga Lora to garrison the north slopes of M. Fior (Maps 25,31). Toward noon, attacking troops massed at Meletta Davanti prior to an assault on M. Castelgomberto. The defenders held until evening when units of the 172° Landsturm and the 35° occupied the Torrione of M. Fior which was a spur northwest of M. Fior (Map 25). Occupying it gave the attackers a closer position to M. Castelgomberto. Poor visibility negated using artillery, resulting in combat being again hand-to-hand. At 1340 the XX Corps was notified that the Austro-Hungarians were breaking through. A few minutes later, Ricci Armani notified all his commanders, that the Comando Supremo had ordered the node of the Melette and the barricades at the Canal di Brenta west of the Grappa to be held at all costs (Maps 25, 24). Traveling in trucks units of the *Alpini* Stelvio Battalion were immediately sent to the Malga Lora Basin, situated on the eastern slope of the Melette di Foza between M.

Castelgomberto and M. Fior. In the evening, Conrad gave up attacking from Asiago in a southeast direction, to concentrate his energies toward V. Frenzela and the southwest corner of the altipiano. Orders were issued to attack the Melette di Foza and M. Zomo thereby arriving in the rear of the defenders (Map 25).

November 15

The weather was cold with a bitter wind. Clinging to the slopes at dawn units of the III/27° *König der Belgier* and the 35° attacked Meletta Davanti.[11] Defending was the *Regina* which was infiltrated to its rear causing it to withdraw. Counterattacks by the *Alpini* Battalion M. Baldo and others of the 9° pushed the attackers back but these were not to be denied. Preceded by five hours of shelling, Habsburg troops proceeded along V. Miela which was the junction point of the Italian Second Infantry Division (deployed from the Zomo to Meletta di Gallio) and the Twenty-ninth Infantry Division deployed from Val Miela to Badenecche (Map 25). After repeated attacks, the Italians retreated to V. Miela, thereby leaving M. Fior and M. Castelgomberto unprotected. One attacking battalion tried to surround M. Tondarecar at the northwest extremity of the Melette, but was repulsed with heavy losses (Maps 25,31) The left wing of the *Gruppe Kletter* now consisted in the Eighteenth Infantry Division some of whose units departed from Energo while others climbed the mule path of M. Pèrtica which linked the Valsugana to the Grappa sector (Maps, 24,31).

One author who was an eyewitness really summarized the combat noting that the attackers would arrive in close order and used cadavers to step over the intact barbed wire. An artillery captain from Naples crawled to his position declaring in his native dialect, *Mbé pa' 'a primma vota che vedo chisti alpini, me pàreno guaglioni in gamba!*[12]

November 16

As the combatants awoke, wind, snow and cold greeted the combatants clinging to the slopes of the mountains on the altipiano. During the evening, remnants of the Ninth Infantry Division (*Regina*) were replaced by the 129° (*Perugia)* which had just arrived from M. Pasubio via trucks (a rare mode of transportation in the mountains). Arriving at the beginning of Val Miela they started to climb and deploy. Also arriving from the Pasubio was the *Alpini* M. Cervino Battalion which linked up with the Second Infantry Division across the rocky V. Miela, making contact with a battalion of the *Liguria* deployed on the steep, rocky, southern slopes of the Melette Davanti. The new defensive line in this sector ran from M. Zomo-Casara Melette Davanti-barricaded the Val Miela, climbed M. Fior-Castelgomberto-Tondarecar-Badenecche reaching V. Gadena and Val Brenta, the latter position separating the altipiano from M. Grappa (maps 24,25)

After the Italian withdrawal in Val Miela and the loss of Meletta Davanti, the A.O.K. thought that the Comando Supremo would order a general retreat. An assault on the whole front was ordered. Multiple bloody attacks on M. Zomo by the Kaiserjäger were repulsed by the 77° as well as the2/157° and 6/157° forcing the attackers to withdraw to the slopes facing the outlet of V. Campomulo (Map 25). The OAR summarized it all. "At 2100, the 2° Kaiserjäger occupied M. Zomo after a violent engagement, which however, due to fierce enemy counterattacks had to be again evacuated." Originally, the Italians thought that this was a worthless piece of real estate, but later realized that it controlled the area where the V. Campomulo ran into the the Val dei Ronchi as well as the roadway Gallio-Foza, functioning as a hinge for Italian defenses between Val Frenzela and M. Sisemol to the southwest and the Melette to the northwest (Maps 25,26). This explained why Conrad assaulted these positions with his elite regiments the Kaiserjäger, the *Kronprinz* and the *König der Belgier*. Preceded by heavy shelling, at 1900 Vienna's troops again went on the attack against M. Zomo and in Val dei Ronchi. Units of the 77° (*Toscana)* repulsed them with a bayonet charge but the Tiroler Kaiserjäger were not to be denied. Favored by a heavy fog again they went on the attack and were again repulsed.

Acrid smoke enveloped by heavy fog filled the air on M. Zomo on whose slopes were cadavers and wounded which fearing enemy snipers no one would care for.

November 17

Notwithstanding heavy losses the 1° and 2° Kaiserjäger again attacked M. Zomo arriving at the first barbed wire fences but were thrown back by the *Alpini* Monte Cervino Battalion and the *Liguria.*[13] Conrad must have learned a bitter lesson, for after attacking for eight days with his best troops, his successes were minimal resulting in a suspension of the assaults. The *König der Belgier* was now reduced to 100 rifles. Major General Giuseppe Boriani, the new commander of the Italian Twenty-ninth Infantry Division ordered a new attack on Casar Melette Davanti by the II and III/129° which failed. Combat was at high altitudes, in the cold, without food or water with Conrad insisting on attacking even before bring up his artillery resulting to heavy losses.

November 18

Depleted Habsburg units were reinforced by men from nearby units. At dawn, the *Alpini* Stelvio, Saccarello and Pasubio Battalions in a bayonet counterattack occupied the northwest spur of M. Fior known as Torrione di M. Fior (Map 25). New attacks were now planned by Conrad on the Melette in the presence of the new emperor, Charles, who only asked that human lives be not unnecessarily wasted.

November 19

Headquarters of the Habsburg Eleventh Army issued orders to the *Gruppe Kletter* for an attack on the Melette to take place on November 22. The Hundred-sixth Landsturm Division would occupy M. Castelgomberto and M. Fior, while the Eighteenth Infantry Division would attack the rear positions of M. Tondecar and M. Badenecche. Simultaneously, the III Corps would occupy the hills east of Gallio, then proceed toward M. Bertiaga. Involved were thirty-three battalions and 345 artillery mouths.

An interesting episode (and there were many) was that of the priest and altar boy who simultaneously arrived at the small Church of the Madonna della Salute. One did not speak Italian while the other did not speak German, so they conversed in a then-common language, Latin which the boy who was in his second year of Gymnasium was familiar with. While saying Mass, the priest was shedding tears as he looked out the window toward M. Zomo obviously upset about the terrible events that had recently occured there. *Tempore belli, Mons Zomo sicut vulcanus erat* (In time of war M. Zomo was like a volcano). Only later by looking at his shoes under the cassock did the boy realize that the priest was the chaplain for the 1° Tiroler Kaiserjäger.

November 22

Bearing Charles the imperial train reached Trento from which he proceeded eastward to Campomulo, climbed the mule path to Fiaretta, finally reaching the observatory on M. Fiara (Map 31). Hoping to close the Melette campaign Conrad had deployed:

Four battalions of the Eighteenth infantry Division to surround and assault M. Tondarecar and M. Badenecche forcing the garrisons to surrender (Map 25)

Two battalions of the One Hundred-sixth Landsturm Division to occupy M. Castelgomberto and M. Fior.

Twenty four of the thirty battalions of the *Gruppe Kletter*

Three battalions of the Sixth Infantry Division (including Kaiserjäger units) In a semi-circular to the rear of these troops were deployed 345 artillery mouths.

Defending were eleven battalions, with six of the *Perugia* plus the *Alpini* Stelvio, M. Cervino, Saccarello, Pasubio, and M. Baldo Battalions.

Preceeded by furious bombardments, including gas, unsuccessful assaults were again attempted on the Melette, M. Castelgomberto, and M. Tondarecar with heavy loss of life. Enemy troops had infiltrated into Val Miela attempting to separate the Cervino troops from the II/129°. Instead of the usual rifle or machine guns, combat today was hand-to-hand with many losses. The Italian Twenty-ninth Infantry Division repulsed five enemy attacks sealing breaches as they developed. Conrad wished to persist in the attacks, but was ordered by the A.O.K. (probably at the insistence of the emperor) to halt the attacks.[14] By November 26 there was a relative quiet on the Setti Comuni sector. On November 25 fighting in the first line trench, Col. Brig. Euclide Turba, commander of the *Perugia,* fell in action. Posthumously for his deeds he received the *Medaglia d'Oro al Valore Militare.*

November 23

The All-*Alpini* Fifty-Second Division (Maj. Gen. Como Dagna) blocked the Brenta Valley near the hamlet of Colicello with its Tirano Battalion. Three *Alpini* battalions were deployed on the southern slopes of M Badenecche along the V. Gadena to the entrance into the Brenta (Map 25). Seeing the enemy advance along the mountainous border which dominated both sides made Dagna abandon the barricades at S. Marino and withdrew to Grottella to avoid being encircled. At the time, he did not know of the loss of Col Bonato on the Grappa. With the enemy making a surprise attack on the left side of the valley destroying the garrison at S. Marino in his rear, he was given no time to withdraw. A counterattack failed so the garrison survivors had to withdraw between the outlet of V. Gàdena to the west and that of the Grotella to the east. The Conrad Group War Diary noted, forty-seven officer deaths, 262 wounded and seventeen missing. Troop deaths were 831, wounded were 6,352, and missing were 582.

Hospitalized were 239 officers, and 6,723 troops for a total of 15,000 casualties. The Habsburg Sixth Infantry Division had to be withdrawn being reduced to 6,400 rifles from 8,400. Italian losses were also heavy. In the only personally-directed action Conrad had lost over 15,000 men. The OAR confirmed that by now the decisive moment for the Conrad Group had passed. Controlling the Melette would only have a local effect. As Arz had noted the major task of the Tyrol Group now was to tie down enemy troops which could be used elsewhere. Archduke Eugene had ordered a suspension to the offense on November 29, but Conrad insisted on continuing the offensive receiving permission to attack on December 3 without reinforcements. The One-Hundred-Sixth Landsturm Division (*Gruppe Kletter*) was rotated to the rear but other troops were not available. Kletter now had twenty-nine battalions with the adjacent III Corps having forty-one. The assault plan had two phases. The first was to occupy M. Zomo and M. Badenecche so as to compress the central nucleus of the Melette which would be occupied on the following days (Map 25).

Opposing would be:

> Italian Second Infantry Division (XXII Corps) deployed from Malga Stenfle to M. Sisemol (Map 26)[15]
>
> 5° Bersaglieri and the *Liguria* (Col. Brig. Umberto Zamaboni) at M. Zomo (Map 25)
>
> Reserve was the IV Bersaglieri Brigade (Maj. Gen. Piola Caselli) with the 14° and 20°, *Toscana* and the IX and XIX Assault Detachments.
>
> The Twenty-ninth Infantry Division (XX Corps) deployed on the southern slopes of the Meletta di Gallio with the XIX and XXXVI Bersaglieri Brigades in V. Miela with the 129° (Map 25)
>
> On M. Fior were deployed the *Alpini* Pasubio, M. Cervino and Saccarello Battalions, while

units of the Marmolada, Cuneo, and V.Dora were at M. Castelgomberto.

The IV Bersaglieri was between M. Tondarecar and M. Badenecche, reinforced in its wings by two battalions of the VI Bersaglieri.

Reserves were units of the *Perugia* and two battalions of the XII Bersaglieri.

All-*Alpini* Fifty-second Division was deployed on the floor of the Brenta Valley to the right of the Twenty-ninth Infantry Division

In all there were 48 battalions. Pecori Giraldi noted that the Twenty-ninth Infantry Division had a reported strength of 26,000 men, but actually had 14,000 effective rifles, 200 machine guns with 110 machine gun pistols and 48 artillery mouths of small caliber.

November 24-December 3

Conrad was notified on November 28 that on the following day Below and Boroevic's troops would attempt to cross the Piave while he was to attack on the altipiano. Austro-German artillery situated in Val Galmarara opened up on Italian positions late on December 3 (Map 11). Early in the morning using yprite and explosives Conrad attacked. Fog made shelling difficult as all communications were reduced to dispatch couriers who had difficulty walking the paths in the fog-bound mountains. At 0900 attacking infantry proceeded toward the Melette di Gallio-M. Zomo to the west, and M. Tondarecar-M. Badenecche to the east. There were furious hand to hand battles on M. Zomo and the Melette. as the *Liguria* repulsed four enemy attacks on M. Zomo with bayonet assaults. Later Conrad massed troops on the right bank of the Val Miela to attack Italian troops near Casara Meletta Davanti defended by units of the *Perugia* which surrendered after being surrounded. With the serious threat on the Melette di Gallio Boriani sent the I and III/130° to assist the

the Bersaglieri. By 1200 Austro-Hungarian units descended through the breaches into V. Miela, threatening the positions of the 129° on the south west precipices of M. Fior (Map 25).

On M. Tondarecar the situation was the same. Units of the III Kaiserschützen and the XXII Feldjäger (Austro-Hungarian Eighteenth Infantry Division) occupied the saddle between the Tondarecar and M. Badenecche infiltrated and surrounded both sides and overcame the defenders (Map 25)[16]. This Feldjäger unit was 100% German-speaking and was recruited in Prague. Over 3,000 prisoners were taken on M. Tonderecar. Immediately the attackers descended onto M. Miela, surprising and capturing the I Bersaglieri Brigade, and occupied the beginning of the V. Vecchia. From all these positions, the attackers spread to other areas, including behind M. Fior destroying the III Group of the 35° Field Artillery. Losing M. Badenecche forced the *Alpini* Vicenza Battalion deployed on the right, which together with the *Alpini* Bassano and Sette Communi Battalions formed the IX *Gruppo Alpini* to withdraw to the rocky border of V. Gàdena (Map 25).[17] At 1930, Boriani recommended that the XX Corps should deploy to the line at Buso di V. Frenzela-Contrade Costalta e Pubel-Carpene di-Sasso Rosso (Map 25). Habsburg forces now controlled the Melette while the Italians controlled the summits of M. Castelgomberto but had lost M. Fior and M. Badenecche.

At 2105, the Italian First Army notified C.T.A. that the Melette must be retaken and kept at any cost. The Eighty-fifth Infantry Division arrived in trucks at Stoccaredo on the right side of the V. Frenzela (Map 26). All the efforts were for naught except for the tremendous loss of life on both sides. The Twenty-ninth Infantry Division was now ordered to prepare for a counteroffensive receiving the 10°. It already had two battalions of the 77° plus the 85° of the XXII Corps. Headquarters also assigned it the 9° and a battalion from the *Mantova* plus assistance of the Second Infantry Division.

Kletter received Eleventh Army approval to attempt to eliminate all the enemy forces between Val. Gàdena and V. Frenzela (Map 25). He received the XXXVII Brigade to reinforce the depleted One-Hundred-Sixth *Landsturm* Division. Later the XCVI Infantry Brigade and the LIX and XXIX Mountain Brigade were assigned to the Conrad Group as well as twelve battalions of the Landsturm with four being sent to M. Grappa to reinforce the Ninety-Fourth Infantry Division as well as the *Edelweiss.* Habsburg commanders were elated with the results of the first day which had surpassed all expectations. They felt that by December 5 the gorge of Val Frenzela would be reached making it easy to proceed beyond.

As darkness approached the defenders were exhausted, cold, lacked food, shelter, blankets and water with munitions almost down to zero. Melted snow was the only source to quench the men's thirst. Counterattacks were unsuccessful. At 0740 Boriani notified XX Corps headquarters of the reality of the situation but to his surprise at 0815 received orders for a counterattack. The defensive line was very fragile and could yield in the center. If this happened it would threaten the right wing of the All-*Alpini* Fifty-second Division and the left wing of the Second Division. Before dawn, the XXIII/12° Bersaglieri occupied M. Miela, staying there until 1000 when it had to withdraw. Enemy artillery destroyed the command center of the Italian Twenty-ninth Infantry Division which threatened by encirclement was withdrawing to Stoccareddo (on the right of the V. Frenzela). On its extreme left on the slopes of the Meletta di Gallio stood the survivors of the XXXVI/12° Bersaglieri with the regimental headquarters. Having received no orders to withdraw, they ran out of ammunition and were taken prisoner. A similar fate befell the 130°. After a furious clash, the XXIII Bersaglieri and IX Assault Detachment at Casar Montagna Nuova, descended the steep slopes arriving on the line of Foza-Pubel-S. Francesco, remaining there until nightfall (Map 25). To the right, *Alpini* units were in a furious fight with the enemy who were descending from M. Badenecche onto Foza which was in flames. With the onset of darkness, they withdrew to Sasso Rosso and S. Francesco, blocking the V. Vecchia and the roadway to Valstagna which they garrisoned (Maps 25, 31). The survivors retreated toward Buso in V. Frenzela where they would climb the opposite side toward Stoccareddo (Maps 26, 31). Others walked toward Valstagna where they met Lt. Gen. Andrea Graziani (he of the Pasubio and Inspector General of the Caporetto debacle), who had been recently put in charge of the fortifications in the Brenta Canal (Map 31). Unaware of the previous day's events, Graziani climbed the roadway to V. Vecchia noting two tunnels. In one tunnel he found the 10° which had just arrived via trucks, and was to be used for the inevitable counterattack. Assembling the 10°,the dispersed *Alpini* and Bersaglieri he formed three defensive lines along the Brenta Canal to halt an enemy attack on Valstagna. The Twenty-ninth Infantry Division had lost among dead, wounded and missing, 539 officers and 14,263 troops. On December 1, it reported that of the 800 officers and 23,000 men of the division, 252 officers and 9, 144 men had arrived two days prior.[18] Having lost the Melette di Foza, the garrison on M. Zomo had to be evacuated. The *Liguria* performed a slow and orderly withdrawal holding off the Austro-Hungarian Fifty-Second Infantry Division. Withdrawing in the dark from M. Zomo the I and II/158° met Graziani's men. Also withdrawing was the IV/84° along the roadway of V. Vecchia arriving at the other tunnel where there were troops waiting for the enemy coming from Valstagna.

The OAR noted 16,000 prisoners taken, with 200 machine guns, and 90 cannons. Schiarini noted the loss of about 19,000 men of the XX and XXII Corps with 3,000 men not accounted for. This must mean they were dead, resulting in the Italian Twenty-ninth Infantry Division being down to 2,000 survivors.[19] Following this success the Eleventh Army planned to occupy M. Sisemol which remained unprotected on three sides after the fall of M. Zomo. Its troops would simultaneously climb the right bank of V. Frenzela proceeding to the occupation of M. Valbella and Col del Rosso. Realizing that there were unforeseen Italian defenses and tenacity, on December 2 the A.O.K. called off the attack, but Conrad insisted on trying once again.

Entering the line on December 1 was the British Forty-first Division to relieve the Italian First Infantry Division. It deployed opposite the Austro-Hungarian Thirteenth Schützen and the German One-Hundred Seventeenth Infantry Division. The British Twenty-third Division relieved the Italian Seventieth Infantry Division. The French Sixty-fifth and Forty-seventh Divisions deployed to the left of the fore-mentioned British units, with the British Seventh Division in reserve. Unlike their Italian ally the Anglo-French did not deploy most of their troops in the forefront to be massacred by enemy artillery. Simple things as synchronization of watches were unknown to the Italian officers. Lacking official interpreters Italians who had emigrated to the U.S.A. where they had learned English filled in as unofficial interpreters.[20]

December 4

At 0400 five hundred Austro-Hungarian artillery mouths opened up on Italian XX Corps positions on the Zomo, Tondarecar and Badenecche summits knocking out communications. Assaulting the Zomo defended by the *Liguria* was the I/2° and III/3° Kaiserjäger. Fighting was hand to hand using knives, rifle butts and clubs with the attackers finally being repulsed by a bayonet charge but many assaults were to follow. In a platoon of Kaiserjäger five out of forty-five survived.

The *Perugia* defended the Casara Meletta Davanti sector against enemy troops which had assembled in the Val Miela (Map 25). Preceded by assault troops, units of the One-Hundred-Sixth *Landsturm* Division attacked and after fierce combat forced the Italians to withdraw.

On the Tondarecar and Badenecche summits Italian defenses were weak and showed it (Map 25). Enemy troops climbed the northern slopes of M. Badenecche while others proceeded toward Castelgomberto. Initially they were thrown off, but persisted in attacking so that by noon on M. Tondarecar (Hill 1639), all combat ceased with the XLIII Battalion of the IV Bersaglieri surrounded and captured (Map 25). Also occupied was M. Badenecche resulting in a large breach opening leading into Val Vecchia. From both mountains, Habsburg troops descended in a southwestward direction, crossed the Val Vecchia and proceeded toward M. Spil and M. Fior. Others proceeded south along the Val Miela arriving at Buso, turned west assaulting the rear of the Italian 129° (Map 25). Troops on M. Fior and M. Castelgomberto (*IV Raggruppamento Alpino*) realized they would be encircled. Troops of the *Alpini* Val Dora, and Cervino Battalions who had been on the Torrione were ordered to M. Fior. The M. Cervino was made up of men of the class of 1899. Enroute they encountered Kaiserschützen and Hessen units resulting in a firefight which ended with the battalion having only seven survivors, three officers and four troop.[21] A similar fate befell units of the *Alpini* Pasubio and Cuneo battalions which were overcome by the CLXXXI Brigade of the Hundred-sixth Landsturm Division. The sector between M. Zomo and the Melette Davanti was garrisoned by the XIX/6° Bersaglieri. After being subjected to horrific shelling they were attacked by the XXXVII Brigade of the Landsturm Division all led by an assault unit. After a furious fight the Bersaglieri withdrew flanked on the left by the XIX/6° which had seen little action. Only the decimated Italian garrison of M. Castelgomberto (*Alpini* Marmolada and Cuneo Battalions) had not yet yielded. The situation was grave. The Italian line had been pierced in several places resulting in Habsburg troops going into the Val Miela threatening the defenses of the 129° there. Boriani now proposed to the XX Corps to withdraw along the line V. Frenzela-Pubel-Sasso Rosso (Maps 26,31).

Italian troop deployments now were:

M. Zomo: I and III/158° *Liguria* as right wing of the Second Infantry Division

The southern slopes of the Melette di Gallio (survivors of the XIX/6° Bersaglieri) plus survivors of the 130° deployed up to Casar Melette These positions also were garrisoned by the Twenty-ninth Infantry Division (Map 25)

Astride Val Miela up to M. Fior: I, III/129° *Perugia* with two battalions in reserve and two Bersaglieri battalions near the Gallio-

Foza roadway bridge crossing the Val Miela.

The southern slope of M. Spil with about one hundred men commanded by Lt. Col. LoCurcio who had to withdraw.
M. Fior-Val Segantini: Six *Alpini* battalions of the *IV Raggruppamento Alpini* (Col. Rho)
M. Fior: *Alpini* Cervino, Pasubio and Torrione Battalions
M. Castelgomberto (two summits)—*Alpini* Cuneo and Marmolada Battalions surrounded by the One Hundred-Sixth Landsturm Division and the Austro-Hungarian Eighteenth Infantry Division
Malga Lora-Saccarello and Val Dora in reserve
Costalta: (not on map) was the 130° of the *Perugia*
Badenecche-Val Gadena-Sasso Rosso: extending Boriani's defense line were the *Alpini* Vicenza, Monte Berico and Sette Communi Battalions of the All-*Alpini* Fifty Second Division.

On M. Castelgomberto were survivors of the *Alpini* Cuneo and Marmolada Battalions who were soon surrounded by the One-Hundred-Sixth Landsturm Division and the Austro-Hungarian Eighteenth Infantry Division.

As one eyewitness wrote, "As darkness approached, it was cold and windy. Will the reinforcements arrive? In the meantime, without food, or blankets, lacking shelter, munitions and water tenaciously we cling to the mountain awaiting the enemy advance."[22] It seems that the descriptions were always the same.

Conrad now assembled 500 artillery mouths of which six were 305 mm. to shell the Melette. Firing would be in a concentric pattern to the rear, front and flanks giving the impression that Italians (who had 160 artillery mouths) were shelling their own.

Eugene had ordered a suspension to the offensive, but Conrad insisted and obtained permission to persist in the assault on the Melette. The attack would proceed from the northwest toward the M. Zomo-Meletta Davanti, while from the northeast the attack would be on M. Tondarecar-Badenecche. Attacking M. Zomo was the I/2° and III/3° Kaiserjäger which were repulsed after many assaults by the I and III/158°. The III/3° Kaiserjäger suffered 50% casualties while the I/2° lost four officers and 185 troops. Lt. Col. Tassilo von Cordier of the 1° Kaiserjäger had the most precise report of the combat in its War Diary. He noted that of 45 men in one platoon, only four remained unhurt. There were thirty dead and fourteen wounded. At one point an Italian flame thrower's flame slowly glimmered forward in a quivering motion and burned alive a whole platoon man by man. Combat was either with grenades at an arm-throwing distance or a close quarters with bayonets. *Alpini* officers would lead their men in an assault, as if they wanted to be the first to die.

Halted on M. Zomo and the Melette Davanti, Conrad decided to attack toward—M. Tondarecar and M. Badenecche (Map 25). Defenders there had neither caves, nor trenches, nor permanent defenses and finally no good place nearby where reserves could deploy. At 0800 he assaulted enemy positions with the 3° Kaiserjäger, the 14° Hessen, the 81° and the 22 Feldjäger Battalion as a tremendous fire-fight ensued.[23] The defending XIII/6° repulsed attacks on the saddle between the summits.[24] On M. Tondarecar the XIII Battalion of the 4° Bersaglieri held off the attackers but then was encircled and captured. Units of the *Alpini* Marmolada Battalion moved forward to assist, but after a furious fire-fight were surrounded and captured on the summit of M. Tondarecar. By noon all combat on the Tondarecar had ceased.

On M. Badenecche after furious enemy shelling only forty of the XXXVII/4° Bersaglieri survived. They quickly abandoned the summit descending the southern slopes to link up with the *Alpini* Vicenza Battalion. A counterattack by the *Alpini* M. Berico and Bassano Battalions pushed the enemy off the summit of M. Badenecche, but another enemy assault forced them to withdraw.

The Habsburg advance toward Foza was temporarily halted (Maps 25, 31). The attackers now moved to isolate M. Badenecche by overcoming the defenses of one of its spurs, Hill 1441, thus eliminating the Tondarecar and Badenecche defenses. Opening this great breach, they proceeded quickly toward Val Vecchia taking the whole command structure of the I Bersaglieri Brigade prisoner, then proceeded via a mule path toward the beginning of Val Vecchia then toward Malga Lora not stopping there (Map 25).

From the upper slopes of M. Tondarecar, Lt. Alois Windisch of the X/14° Hessen noted that nearby M. Miela had a small Italian garrison.[25] Obtaining permission to proceed and reinforced by a machine gun company, his men quickly descended M. Tondarecar, crossed the Val Vecchia and clinging to the steep eastern slopes of the mountain reached the northwest part of the flat summit from which they descended southwestward toward M. Spil (Map 25). On the way they were joined by units of the Fifty-second Infantry Division coming from Melette Davanti. Both units arrived at Busa del Sorlaro where they attacked the rear of the Italian 129° deployment (in the Val Miela), surrounded and captured them. By now the whole Val Miela up to M. Spil was in Austro-Hungarian hands (Map 25). Meanwhile other Kaiserschützen troops proceeded to advance along the southern part of M. Miela, arriving at M. Spil to assist the X/14° Hessen.[26]

Simultaneously troops of the II/3° Kaiserschützen descended M. Badenecche crossed the Val Vecchia to climb the southwest slope of M. Miela. Along the way they encountered pieces of the Italian 35° Field Artillery near today's Casara Melette di Foza. Turning the cannons around, the Italians fired over open sights, but the attackers kept coming. Destroying the pieces, the artillery men withdrew to the southern slopes of M. Spil.

Looking carefully at a map, today one realizes that a circle was forming around the IV Raggruppamento *Alpini* which was deployed from M. Fior to M. Castelgomberto. As a result the *Alpini* Cervino Battalion was ordered to withdraw from Torrione di Fior and to deploy on M. Fior together with a company of the Val Dora (Map 25). The *Alpini* of the Dora had been deployed at Malga Lora and now faced the advancing Hessen and Kaiserschützen. The *Alpini* Monte Pasubio Battalion which was ordered to M. Castelgomberto to assist the Cuneo held its own but eventually was surrounded by the CLXXXI Brigade of the One Hundred-sixth *Landsturm* Division which was coming from Torrione di Fior.[27] After the breakthrough between M. Badenecche and M. Tondarecar, the reserve *Alpini* Saccarrello and Val Dora Battalions (two companies each) were attacked by enemy troops, surrounded and captured.

As nightfall arrived the whole front of the Italian Twenty-ninth Infantry Division was had been pierced in many places. Troops were now deployed: (Map 25)

Melette di Gallio—remnants of the XIX/6° and XXXVI/12° Bersaglieri remnants of the 130° linked up with the 129° in Val Miela

Monte Spil (southern slopes)—remnants of 35° Field Artillery

Monte Miela (southern slopes)—XXIII/12° Bersaglieri and II/130°[25]; IX Assault Unit on southern side of Val Vecchia linked up with *Alpini* and the IX Assault Unit

M. Castelgomberto—*Alpini* Cuneo Battalion on the western summit *Alpini* Marmolada Battalion on the eastern summit, both surrounded by the CLXXXI Brigade (One Hundred Sixth Landsturm) and the I Mountain Brigade of the Eighteenth Infantry Division

From the southern slopes of M. Badenecche to Sasso Rosso (Map 25) *Alpini* M. Berico, Bassano, Stelvio, Vicenza, Sette Communi, and M. Baldo Battalions.

Breaking through here would allow the enemy to attack M. Grappa from the western, north and northwest directions. There was hand-to-hand fighting throughout. The enemy had been halted but for how long? As usual *Alpini* deployed on the slopes lacking the five items mentioned above.

December 5

Headquarters on both sides of the trench had no clear idea of what had happened. News of the breakthrough by the Hessen, and by the II/3° Kaiserschützen toward M. Miela then M. Spil and M. Fior was unknown to commands on both sides (Map 25). Lacking information neither could make any decisions. Quizzed on his intentions by the A.O.K., Conrad responded that he would gain the southern border of the altopiano then descend onto Bassano as soon as three fresh divisions arrived. When this was denied, he gave the task to the Eleventh Army. As the OAR noted, "The unexpected success should have been greatly increased if the way was opened to the southern margin of the altipiano. If the Army Group had provided two or three fresh division . . . ."

At Casa Stona, headquarters of the Italian Twenty-ninth Infantry Division there was no news of any link-ups with flanking troops (Map 25). Boriani decided to send three of his officers to obtain information from troops in the line. They never returned. Enemy troops now proceeded along the Val Vecchia and Val Miela with enemy shelling arriving at Boriani's headquarters at Casa Stona forcing him to move it to Sasso Rosso. His division was now reduced to 2,000 effectives. Unaware of the lost positions the Italian I Army issued orders to hold the Melette and stabilize the situation in the Val Miela.

Receiving the 10° and 85° via truck (they disembarked at Stoccaredo on the right side of V. Frenzela) he was ordered to counterattack (Map 26, 31). The enemy was not to be allowed to proceed along the Val Vecchia. The Seventh Infantry Division was to arrive at Lusiana to garrison the line Osteria del Puffele and the Col D'Astiago. Later the Twenty-third Infantry Division would arrive as Lt. Gen. Edoardo Ravazza (XXV Corps) arrived at headquarters of the Comando Truppe Altopiano (C.T.A.) to synchronize the deployment of these reinforcements which never arrived. Knowing the attack was doomed and declaring that "orders are orders," he ordered the 10° to depart from the slopes of M. Badenecche to assault M. Tondarecar and M. Fior. The XXIII/12° Bersaglieri occupied M. Miela up to 1000 when it was forced to withdraw by enemy shelling which also destroyed the Twenty-ninth Infantry Division Headquarters. Reinforcements from the Second Infantry Division were to include the 9° and the *Mantova.* They never arrived. Weather conditions made a counterattack out of the question.

After a fierce fire-fight the Italians were forced to withdraw toward Sasso. Killed in action was Lt. Col. Ugo Bassi commander of the 113° (*Toscana).* By the end of the day, the Italian Twenty-ninth Infantry Division was destroyed.[28] Boriani was forced to withdraw which was done in an orderly fashion to the line of Buso di Gallio-Sasso Rosso as follows (Map 25)

> The remnants of the 77° (*Toscana)* withdrew to the bridge over Val Miela
> Col. Lo Curcio's men withdrew to Stoccaredo (Map 26)
> The remants of the II/130°, XXIII/12° Bersaglieri and the IX Assault Unit to Foza, Pubel, and Croce di S. Francesco
> The remnants of the 129° to Buso di Gallio

Receiving no orders to withdraw the XXXVI/12° Bersaglieri on the south slopes of the Meletta di Gallio was surrounded and captured. As darkness arrived the I and the II/158° were surrounded by the Austro-Hungarian Fifty-second Infantry Division and forced to surrender. Strong enemy forces were descending from the Melette. A similar fate befell the 130° while the IX Assault Unit and the XXIII Bersaglieri descended the steep slopes of the Foza-Pubel line. Surrounded and taken prisoner on M. Castelgomberto were units of the *Alpini* Cuneo and survivors of the Marmolada Battalion.

Alpini taken prisoner often shed tears of rage. Many of them had been through heavy battles at Ortigara, the Valsugana with splendid results, but now this. So impressed were the Austro-Hungarians by the valour of the *Alpini* Marmolada Battalion, (Major Boffa) that the emperor allowed its commanding officer to keep his sword even in the prisoner of war camp. Habsburg attention went now to M. Zomo where aware of the problems with the Melette the garrison commander was thinking of withdrawing. It was isolated and assaulted from three directions. Four times the defending *Liguria* counterattacked and four times they were repulsed. Observers on the Sisemol noted hand to hand combat which ended as the survivors surrendered (Map 26). Conrad had noted in his Order of the Day that M. Zomo was assaulted by the *whole* Fifty-second Infantry Division.

Early in the morning orders were issued to the *Liguria* evacuate. Conrad's troops would give them no respite. Surrounding the *Liguria* they halted all Italian attempts to break the ring. Today on M. Zomo a marble placque commemorates the *Liguria's* heroism. Why did the *fanti* not fight in a similar fashion six weeks prior at Caporetto? This is a question that shall always be debated. The longer the debate, the less the orators know. Gas had been successfully used in the assault showing that Italian masks did not work. In 1918 British masks would be issued to Italian troops.

December 6

Victorious on the Melette and M. Zomo, Habsburg troops spread out from Val Vecchia, Val Miela and Val di Campomulo (Map 25). The next objective was the Sisemol-Stenfle defenses which now were subjected to shelling from three sides. Habsburg troops were arriving perilously close to the plains to the south.

As in June 1916, the battle's report returned to the vast tortoise like shell of M. Sisemol, with steep wooded slopes while the northern woody slope started near the head of the Val Frenzela. The circular redoubt in the shape had barbed wire and machine guns defenses and was called the *Anello di Sisemol* garrisoned by the newly reconstituted IV Bersaglieri Brigade (after the tragedy of Caporetto) commanded by Col. Brig. Pio Caselli. Defensive deployments were as follows: (Map 26,31)

> 5° Bersaglieri-from the southern slopes of M. Valbella across the Stenfle and Ronco Carbone to Roncalto Perk (Map 26)
> 14° Bersaglieri-from Roncalto Perk to the Sisemol summit (*Anello di Sisemol*) to Bertigo (Map 31)
> 20° Bersaglieri-from Bertigo to the east and north east slopes of the Sisemol
> LXI/14°—deployed on the slopes between the summit and the roadway Gallio-Turcio, north of the hamlet of Bertigo.

The assault began at 0845 with aerial strafing, followed by shelling and infantry assaults on the northern slopes. Attacking from the north was the Austro-Hungarian Fifty-second Infantry Division, while from the west advanced the Twenty-second Schützen Division with the IV/1° Kaiserschützen. With overwhelming manpower and huge guns, after bloody hand-to hand combat the attackers occupied the Sisemol. North of Stenfle only a few trenches were taken while the assault on Buso failed.

By 1600, the summit was captured with the Italians in full retreat. Since shelling had destroyed all communications, pigeons were used for communications between the Bersaglieri and the XXII Corps. A counterattack was considered using the 5° Bersaglieri still on M. Valbella and Malga Stenfle, but finally the XXII Corps decided to withdraw to the line Pennar-Capitello Pennar-M. Tondo-C. Eckar-M. Valbella-Portecche-Zàibena-Stoccareddo-Col d'Echele just about to the right border of the V. Frenzela (Map 26). Vienna's troops now approached Bertigo. The three regiments of the IV Bersaglieri Brigade had suffered 50% casualties on the *Anello di Sisemol* causing the Bersaglieri to withdraw. Losses amounted to 86 officers and 3,000 troops among dead wounded and missing of which 69 officers and 2,450 troops belonged to the three regiments of

Bersaglieri. The OAR stated, "The Eleventh Army therefore suspended operations there, to prepare for new attacks on Col del Rosso." Pecori Giraldi transferred the 217° and the assault battalion of the X Corps to Ricci Armani. The troops arrived at Magnaboschi on December 7 with the intention to attack the enemy in the right flank should they advance (Map 31). This would be the scene of bloody fighting the following June.

The OAR noted 2,000 prisoners were taken on the Sisemol by November 21 the Schützen (III Corps) and by the Fifty-second Infantry Division (*Gruppe Kletter*). In the attack on the Sisemol, four battalions of Kaiserschützen in the attack were deployed. As Conrad later noted, "On the Sisemol, the combat was extraordinarily violent with hand to hand fighting." The victors now remained quiet licking their wounds not attempting to proceed forward for some time.

With the loss of the Melette di Foza, the Comando Supremo moved its reserve XXV Corps (Seventh and Twenty-third Infantry Divisions) to Sandrigo. As soon as the loss of the Sisemol was known, the XXX Corps was sent to Sandrigo replacing the XXV detached to the I Army. Troops on both sides suffered frozen feet which often required amputation of toes or the whole foot. Some troops on the extreme left (Meletta di Gallio) did not receive the orders and were captured. As the OIR reported combat went on all night in the cold with the machine guns freezing up and troops lacking everything necessary to survive.

With the Sisemol being evacuated, the new Italian defense line was M. Valbella-Col del Rosso-Le Portecche-Zaibena to the right border of the V. Frenzela (Map 26). Thus ended the Second Battle of the Melette.

There were now many recriminations in the Italian military upper echelons concerning the position losses (Melette and Sisemol). Major General Pompilio Schiarini, the historian of the Italian I Army noted that after the loss of M. Ongara, Pecori-Giraldi was tormented about what to do. Should he fortify the Melette or retreat to the right side of V. Frenzela? Doing the latter, he could shorten the front and not withhold any help to the Grappa garrison. However, one must also take into account the political situation. Be it the king, the government or the army all sounded one phrase "No retreat." With this phrase there were severe losses suffered on the Melette which did not have to happen if a purely military decision was made. This was similar to the useless slaughter at Verdun on the Western Front where the same mentality pervaded the French military hierarchy. This would happen several times during the war.

On December 8 Generals Fayolle and Plumer met with Diaz to give him their planned deployment. From the sea proceeding westward would be the Italian III Army, British and French divisions, then Italian divisions in the mountains. The Anglo-French did not have any winter mountain equipment or clothing, so they really would not be much help there. On December 1 two other British divisions arrived to be deployed near Vicenza. Plumer advised his commanders that the Italians had the main responsibility for the defense. Should the enemy break through the mountains Anglo-French troops would attempt to halt them from breaking into the plains below.

December 21

The Krauss Group (XIV Army) was transferred to the Conrad Group so there would be one command in the mountains as the Eleventh Army prepared to attack.

On the Italian side, there were febrile efforts to reinforce the line at M. Valbella-Col del Rosso-Col d'Echele which had the same topography as M. Sisemol (Map 31). The defenses were assigned to the XXII Corps with the Fifty-seventh Infantry Division (Major Gen. Arcangelo Scotti) made up of the *Pisa* and *Mantova* plus the 5° Bersaglieri deployed from M. Kaberlaba to and excluding C. Eckar. From there to the eastern extremity of the altopiano was the second Infantry Division (Maj. Gen. Arturo Nigra) with the *Livorno* and *Verona* which after heavy fighting on the Isonzo along with the *Toscana* had been made over.

December 22

Conrad started to shell M. Valbella-le Portecche and Buso di V. Frenzela. He had 550 artillery mouths of which 100 were medium and ten were heavy caliber. Attacking would be the internal wings of the III Corps and *Gruppe Kletter* which would proceed forward with the following units:

Sixth Infantry Division
  XII Brigade (17°, 27°)
  Vidossich Brigade (I/51°, I/102°, I/27°, X/59°)
  XX Feldjäger and the 22 company of High Mountain Combat
Eighteenth Infantry Division
  IX Mountain Brigade (3° Kaiserschützen, IV/87°, IV/84°, IV/12°) CLXXXI Brigade
Five reserve battalions

There was now ten inches of snow, with a temperature of minus 10° Centigrade (10° Fahrenheit).

December 23

Austro-Hungarian infantry went on the attack at 0930. By 1100, clinging to the slopes from V. Frenzela to Portecche, they crashed through the lines between M. Valbella and Col del Rosso, defended by the Italian 33° and 86° (Map 26). Climbing the northern slopes of the Col del Rosso after arriving at the summit they proceeded toward M. Melago to attack the rear of the *Verona* deployments. Simultaneously, the right wing climbed from Malga Melaghetto to M. Valbella forcing the 33° to withdraw toward Costalungo. A large breach thus opened in the gutter called Buso del Termine between C. Eckar to the west and M. Melago to the east garrisoned by a company of the 77° (Maps 26,31). Sent to assist the *Verona* deployed in the Col del Rosso, was the 78° (Map 26).

Austro-German effort was mainly at the southeast border of the altipiano against the Second Infantry Division. After going through it, they arrived at the gap of Passo Stretto south of the Osteria del Puffele. With the heavy shelling and bad weather there were deserters from both sides. The weather varied from fog to rain to snow, depending on the altitude of the battle, i.e. the mountains, or the valley floor with temperatures hovering at zero or below.

Having lost the central part of the defense, the Italians now lined up from M. Tondo along the Costalunga, to C. Eckar, the entrance to V. Melago, the south slopes of M. Melago whose peak had been lost and Col d'Echele abandoning the hamlets of Stoccaredo and Zaibena. By nightfall the situation was serious. The 33° (*Livorno)* was practically annihilated, while the 34° had to retreat from Busa del Termine, thereby leaving undefended the V. Melago Gorge. Although surrounded, survivors of the *Toscana* and *Verona* kept fighting until their ammunition ran out. Into the cauldron, were thrown piece meal parts of the XVI Assault Detachment, the 5° Bersaglieri, and the 9° divided between C. Eckar and M. Melago. From the Vicentian Plain, the rejuvenated *Sassari* and *Perugia* and the IV Bersaglieri Brigade started to march toward the altipiano. Also marching to assist was the 217° and the XXIV Assault Unit which arrived at Granezza. The OAR noted that the line of the Italian Second Infantry Division had been pierced. To stablize the situation, the defenders ordered a counterattack to be started at 0200 of December 24 which was supposed to be done mainly by the 5° Bersaglieri. As the latter's XIV Battalion linked up to the left with the defenses of Busa del Termine, the XLIV and XXXIV Battalions aided by the III/9° attacked M. Melago during the night (Map 26). They reoccupied Hill 1231 at 0700 reaching the summit, where they took back artillery pieces and machine guns which they had left there the day before. Proceeding quickly, the troops marched toward Col del Rosso, while from C. Eckar another column composed of three infantry battalions descended on Busa del Termine to give them flanking support. Toward noon, the Italian line had gained some breathing space, extending from Costalunga to the line at

Busa del Termine-southern slopes of Col del Rosso-M. Melago-Case Caporai-Col d'Echele and Case Grulli, where they linked up with the fortification below V. Frenzela held by the All-*Alpini* Fifty-second Division. Attempts to take Col Del Rosso were repulsed with heavy losses. In the afternoon, units of the *Pisa* occupied M. Valbella, but then had withdraw. Again the Italians attacked Col del Rosso using the 78°, 9° and assault units, all doomed to failure.

By 2320, the Italian situation was serious. The XXII Corps sent the 151° (*Sassari*) to the junction of V. Melago into the V. Chiama, thereby halting any enemy advance. The Bersaglieri and 78° were to be taken from the line with the *Sassari* to be used in the attack.

December 25

Today was known as "Bloody Christmas," as a violent battle between two Christian nations continued with no quarter given. The invocation of "Peace on earth to men of good will," was heard around the world but not on the Asiago Plateau where combat continued with a great fury. During the evening, a battalion of the 77° aided by another of the 129° was busy engaging the attackers at Costalunga and M. Valbella without good results. With heavy Austro-Hungarian resistance, Italian counterattacks by the 151° plus units of the 5° Bersaglieri on the Col del Ross proceeded slowly. Meanwhile, near Case Caporai situated near the saddle that separates Col del Rosso and Col d'Echele Austro-Hungarian units broke through the Italian defenses and surrounded Col d'Echele (Map 26). Of the defending battalion which was almost annihilated by heavy caliber shelling (78°) only about 40 men were able to escape through enemy lines. Later, units of the 9° vainly tried to retake Col d'Echele while the 151° was unsuccessful in assaulting Col del Rosso. With darkness the survivors, retreated beyond the lower V. Chiama to the Col dei Nosellari, thereby abandoning the hamlet of Sasso (Map 26). They crossed C. Cischietto and M. Melago to Busa del Termine and then to Costalunga and C. Eckar. With this operation the First Battle of the Asiago Plateau was concluded. The enemy had arrived on the southeast border of the altopiano in sight of Bassano and the Vicentian Plain but could not crash through. Both sides had fought with tenacity and were exhausted.

Schiarini noted that the losses in particular of the Second Infantry Division on December 23, through to December 25 were difficult to evaluate.[29] There had been twenty dead officers, eighty-five wounded, with 865 men killed and 2,187 wounded. There were over 8000 troop missing due to the quick maneuvers, and retreats in the valleys and mountains. Freezing cold contributed to this high number. Many froze to death. The I and II/78° reported about 1100 men dead and missing; the two battalions of the 5° Bersaglieri had 300 dead and missing; the XXIV Assault Unit, lost eight officers and 180 men in dead and missing. In all Italian casualties were 30,000 men.[30]

With these actions on the Asiago Plateau and the Grappa, it was shown that the *fanti* and *Alpini* knew how to fight and knew how to die. Unlike the *fanti* on the Isonzo weeks before who yielded for whatever reason these men halted the enemy from breaking into the plains below. To this day it is unclear as to why the sudden change in morale and fighting spirit. Frightened by the horrific cost, the A.O.K. had second thoughts about persisting on the Altopiano dei Sette Communi and stopped offensive actions. The *fanti* had done their duty by halting the enemy's attempt to break into the plains below.

Chapter XI Endnotes

The First Battle of the Altopiano dei Sette Communi (Asiago Plateau)

1 USSME: Relazione Ufficiale, Vol. IV 3° bis, Doc., No. 129, Protocol No. 5031, 27 October 1917, Comando Supremo, *Ordine alla Prima Armata per cessione lavori Grappa all 4a Armata*, p. 298

2 OULK: Vol. VI, *Das KriegsJahr 1917*, p. 646

3 Ibid, p. 646

4 Mountain fighting was with smaller units affording the possibility of researching the them. The *k.u.k. Infanterieregiment Rupprecht Kronprinz von Bayern No. 43* was formed in 1814. Its honorary colonel (*Inhaber*) was Crown Prince Rupprecht, heir to the Bavarian throne. Its recruiting post was in Karánsebes. It was composed of 5% Magyars, 80% Romanians, and 15% German. Its command post was at Fehértemplom.

5 The *k.u.k. Infanterieregiment Albert I, König der Belgier No. 27),* was formed in 1682. Its honorary colonel (*Inhaber)* since 1910 was King Albert I of Belgium.

6 OULK*:* Vol. VI, op. cit., p. 650

7 A. Gatti, *Caporetto,* op. cit., entries of October 28, 1917, p. 275; October 31, 1917, p. 284 entries of November 3, 1917, p 302, 303, 305, 306; November 5, p. 310. The word means seeing a disaster in everything and propagating this notion.

8 L. Cadorna, *Lettere famigliare,* op. cit. 242

9 OULK*:* Vol. VI, p. 706

10 The *k.u.k. Infanterieregiment Nr. 75* was formed on February 1, 1860. Its position of *Inhaber(* honorary colonel) was vacant. It was made up of 90% Czech and 10% Germans and was headquartered in Salzburg. Its recruitment center was Neuhaus.

11 The *k.u.k. Infanterieregiment Freiherr von Sterneck Nr. 35* was formed in 1683. Its *Inhaber* since 1890 was the Superintendent of the Artillery Arsenal Moritz Baron von Sterneck. It was composed of 65% Czech, and 35% German with its recruiting center in Pilsen as was its headquarters.

12 Paolo Monelli, *Scarpe al Sole,* Milano, Mondadori, 1965, Preface to Fourth Edition, "Well, this is the first time that I have seen these *Alpini,* but it seems that they are able fellows."

13 The Kaiserjäger originated with the Fenner-Jägerkorps established in 1813, becoming the Tiroler-Jägerregiment Kaiser Franz recruiting its troops from the Tyrol and Vorarlberg. In 1895 four regiments were established Tiroler Kaiserjäger) which were among the elite units in the army. For all four regiments the *Inhaber* was Emperor Francis Joseph. The 1° and 2° were recruited in the sector of Innsbruck, with the command center at Trento for the 1° and 2° at Bolzano. All regiments were composed of sixty percent

German-speaking with forty percent Italian-speaking. The 3° had its command center at Rovereto being recruited in the Trento province. Finally the 4° was recruited in Hall in the Tyrol with its command center at Trento.

14 **OULK: Vol. VI, op. cit., p. 679**

15 USSME: Relazione Ufficiale, Vol. IV, Tomo 3°, bis., Doc., op. cit., Comando XXII, C.A., *Concorso della 2a divisione al contrattaco della 29a per la riconquista delle Melette,* Document No. 240, Protocol 6696, December 4, 1917, p. 492

16 Ernst Wisshaupt, *Der Tiroler Kaiserjäger im Weltkrieg 1914-1918;* It was composed of all German-speaking men. Amon Franz Göth, 1936, Vol. II, p. 368.

17 *Battaglione Alpini "Vicenza"*, Franco Brunello, Gino Rossato Editore, Valdagno, 1986, p. 66

18 Boccardo,B.,*Melette 1916-1917,*Gino Rossato Editore, Valdagno,1992, p. 224

19 AUSSME : *Difesa della regione Melette,* E1, collection 17; This was a report to the Comando Supremo, dated Dec. 14. 1917, No. 74192. It is not signed but probably was sent by Italian First Army Headquarters.

20 Post First World War there was a Federation of Italian World War Veterans (*Associazione Nazionale Combattenti in U.S.A.*) in the U.S.A. consisting in the hundreds of thousands who had returned to the mother country per request of their families. Also participating were Italian soldiers who had migrated to the U.S.A. after the Great War. With the advent of the Second World War, the association in the U.S.A. dissolved.

21 These two regiments were among the elite of the Austro-Hungarian Army. The Kaiserjäger have been described above. Originally 100% German-speaking by the war's outbreak they had forty percent Italian-speaking troops. The *k.u.k. Infanterieregiment Ernst Ludwig Grossherzog von Hessen und bei Rhein Nr. 14* was founded in 1733 having as its *Inhaber* since 1893, Ernest Louis Granduke of Hesse. Its four battalions made up part of the Third Infantry Division (*Edelweiss*) all of whose men came from Linz which was where they were recruited.

22 Paolo Monelli, *Scarpe al Sole,* Milano Mondadori, 1965. Capt. Monelli fought in the *Alpini* Cuneo Battalion in the battle.

23 The Feldjäger were battalions of light infantry. They had to be expert with a rifle prior to joining the military and in excellent physical shape. The

mentioned *k.u.k. Feldjägerbattaillon Nr. 22* was such a battalion. It was composed of 100% of German-speaking men with its recruitment center in Prague. The *k.u.k. Infanterieregiment Freiherr von Waldstätten Nr. 81* was formed on February 1, 1860. Since 1887, its *Inhaber* was GdI Baron Johann von Waldstätten. Its recruitement center was Iglau, with its composition made up of 15% German-speaking and 85% Czech-speaking. Originally there were twenty six such battalions later increased by seven. In addition there was one Bosnian Feldjäger battalion.

24 Between two mountains there usually was an elevated flat-hilled summit called a saddle connecting the mountains.

25 M. Miela at 5400 feet has a flat summit in the upper Val Vecchia near the mountains M. Badenecche and Tondarercar. Its northwest slope overlooks Malga Lora, while to the southeast its steep slopes arrive at Foza (Map 25). Westward it moves toward a saddle which then links it up to the slopes of M. Spil (5500 ft.)

26 The Kaiserschützen (originally called Kaiserjäger) were men recruited in the Tyrol section of the empire. In 1870, the *Landesverteidigungsgesetz Tirols* created the famous defensive units. Initially they were called Landesschützen, or Territorial Sharpshooters. These were sharpshooting mountain-fighting Tyrolese German-speaking men but 40% were Italian speaking. On January 16, 1917, due to their valor they were given the name Kaiserschützenregimenter by Emperor Charles. The respective seats of the three regiments were Trento, Bolzano and S. Candido

27 Torrione di Fior is not on the map but is a spur northwest of M. Fior

28 OULK, Vol. VI, op. cit., p. 683, reported the destruction of the Italian Twenty-ninth Infantry Division

29 USSME: See Pompilio Schiarini, *La Battaglia d'Arresto sul Altopiano d'Asiago,* Rome, 1934

30 USSME: Relazione Ufficiale, Vol. IV, Tome 3°, op. cit., p. 593.

CHAPTER XII

THE FIRST BATTLE OF THE GRAPPA 1917

Suddenly for unknown reasons, Italian troop morale soared and combativeness increased. For the Austro-Germans, the last obstacle before the plains was either the Grappa-Altopiano range or the Piave River. Defenses on the Grappa had been strengthened after a visit by Cadorna a few weeks prior to the Caporetto offensive. Against overwhelming odds the peasant infantry held. Lacking winter clothing the fanti who had never seen snow, nor experienced such cold temperatures halted the enemy attempts to crash through to the plains below. Songs and movies have commemorated the bitter battles on the Altopiano dei Sette Communi, the Grappa and the Piave. The linchpin of the Italian defense was the Grappa. Proceeding westward from the Adriatic was the Piave itself a formidable obstacle followed by the Montello, the Grappa and the Asiago Plateau also known as the Altopiano dei Sette Communi. Crashing through here would allow the enemy to assault the rear of Italian forces deployed along the Piave (Maps 29,35). These epic battles have long been celebrated by the Italian nation as the turning point of the Caporetto campaign. By the end of December the summits of Col della Berretta, Asolone, Valderòa and Spinoncia were in enemy hands to be used as future springboards for assaults on Italian positions in the coming spring. At the entrance to the Hofburg in Vienna stands a large marble placque commemorating all the important battles of the Habsburg armies. M. Asolone is the last one listed. With Italian resistance increasing, Habsburg forces coined the phrase, "Victors but dead."

The Valiant Never Taste of Death But Once
William Shakespeare "Julius Caesar"

M. GRAPPA RISES AS a rocky structure one mile high between the Piave and Brenta Rivers. Controlling it, the Italians blocked Austro-German access to the Venetian plain to the Southwest (Maps 35,40). Linking the Piave and the altopiano fronts it connects the Venetian PreAlp foothills (to the west) to the Bellunese PreAlpine foothills). Breaking through its stony structures to the plains below would spell disaster for the Italian defenders. To the north, its border was the inferior branch of the Cismon and that of the Sonna Valleys with the latter running into the Piave Valley to the east (Map 24). Surrounded by many other rocky structures, the whole perimeter was about one hundred kilometers (sixty miles). For six weeks its rocky branches were defended by the Italian IV Army (forty-seven combat and four engineering battalions) and assaulted by the XIV Army. From the Venetian plain it abruptly arises with a complex architecture. The principal peak known as *Cima Grappa* (M. Grappa), and its massive spurs contain deep valleys oriented in a north-south direction and collectively are called *Nave di Grappa.* From the latter originate several huge spurs, separated by valleys with the spurs having an altitude of many thousands of feet. From the *Cima* one could easily observe and fire westward toward the Brenta River (five miles), and eastward toward the Piave River (seven miles). Its slopes are deprived of grass or vegetation having only some conifer trees.

On a west-east axis, is the spine of the system beginning with the spur of M. Meatte-C. della Mandria-M. Pallon, which faces east descending and ending on Fener with the straight crest at M. Tomba-Monfenera (Map 24). Westward it extends linearly from M. Rivon to M. Asolone, then extends northward to Col della

Berretta, and finally then resumes its original course to Col Caprile. From there it projects southward along the hills of Colli Alti that defines the deep gorge of Canal di Brenta, and sinks its roots north of Bassano, while on the opposite slope collapses on the rocky V. di S. Felicita. From the Canal di Brenta to the altipiano there was only one alpine foot pass at Rocce Anzini (Map 24).

From the *Nave* a solid spur descends westward onto M. Pèrtica from which it goes northward up to M. Cismon, crossing the declining heights of Col Buratto, M. Prassolan, M. Fredina, M. Cismon, Col di Baio, and M. Roncone. From Col di Berretta and Col Burratto, two spurs descend onto the hamlet of Cismon in Canal di Brenta, determining and restricting the gorges in the upper areas of V. Cesilla and in the lower, that of V. Goccia. Again describing the *Nave* we follow another great spur proceeding in a north east direction with the Col dell'Orso, the Solaroli, M. Fontanasecca, M. Peúrna, and the depression of Forcella Bassa. Beyond this, always in the same direction, arises the final spur of M. Tomatico, which dominates the Feltre basin to the north. To the east a small system blocks the Piave Valley, while to the west, the Tegorzo Valley, joins it near Fener, with M. Tese, M. Cornella, slowly descending and ending at Quero.

Not to be forgotten is the spur which starts on the principal axis at C. di Mandria, descending slowly to the north, then to the east, with M. Spinoncia and P. Zoc embracing the Alano Basin, which in turn was easily controlled by the system to the south made up of M. Pallon, M. Tomba, and Monfenera. If one wishes to describe it in a different manner, one would note the high mountains (5,000 feet) and deep valleys to the north, with ridges running north-south. These ridges end at M. Roncone (3600 feet) and M. Tomatico (4,800 feet). Deep gorges running north-south contained the Piave River to the east and the Brenta River to the west of the massif forming boundaries (Map 24). Accurately describing the structures will assist the reader to understand the dramatic battle that occurred on its slopes.

Today driving toward Trento one passes through Bassano del Grappa noticing the large statue of Lt. General Gaetano Giardino (C.O. Italian IV Army) facing the Grappa. He had a statue constructed as the Savior of the Grappa. Commanding that army in 1918 he wrote excellent accounts of combat there in that year. After his death on December 21, 1935, per his request, he and his wife, Margaret John Rusconi were buried there. On their tomb are inscribed the words, *Gloria a Voi O Soldati del Grappa,* (Glory to you O Soldiers of the Grappa).

Instead the real hero of the Grappa, was Lt. Gen. Nicolis DiRobilant who commanded the IV Army in the terrible months of November-December, 1917. This general was very secretive, did not promote himself and thus was left by the wayside in the dust bins of history. Garrisoned by the Italian I Army since September 1916, on October 27, 1917, the task of defending it was given to the IV Army.[1] In May 1916, Cadorna had realized that the Grappa could be a defensive bulwark. In November of that year work was begun on fortifications facing west to defend against an attack from the Trentino. With the formation of the Italian VI Army on December 1, 1916, defensive measures were amplified, especially to link up with the defense of Cadore, the already mentioned "Yellow Line." This army was dissolved to be replaced by the I Army, but defense workings to the west continued. Visiting the sector a short time prior to Caporetto, Cadorna insisted on the construction of a redoubt (*ridotto centrale*) on the summit from which would come the last resistance. Artillery had been placed facing east but now was also facing north. When the need arose in October, 1917 the defenders found emplaced artillery as well as trenches dug in Valstagna, Val Brenta and on the western slopes of the mountain (Maps 24, 31). The *ridotto centrale* was in position with machine guns and artillery. Since the Grappa lacked water, cisterns had been dug with a mechanical pump at Madonnina which pumped the liquid via tubes to many of the positions. Roads were installed going to the summit from

Romano Alto, Crespano and M. Pèrtica all totalling twelve miles. First and foremost was the Cadorna Road which at a certain point would have a branch go westward (nine feet wide), with an incline of 7° toward Col Bonato and Col della Berretta (Maps 24, 37). These would allow the quick transference of troops to where needed during a defensive battle. Another road had been constructed from the crest to M. Pèrtica. Also installed was a cable car system from Santuario del Covolo to the summit, another from S. Nazario in V. Brenta, climbing to the Colli Alti specifically to Col Raniero.[2] In all there were seventy machine-gun positions. Artillery positions on the Grappa summit amounted to twenty-three batteries. There were six mouths of 105 mm., ten of 75 mm. and seven of 65 mm. Some mouths were emplaced within caves on the slopes descending toward Croce dei Lebi.

Cadorna had again inspected the Grappa on October 7, 1917, accompanied by members of his staff and Col. Antonio Del Fabbro, Chief of Engineers at the location. There was only a steep cartway from Santuario del Còvolo to Val della Madonna. Three layers of fortifications were constructed in Val Brenta: The first, between S. Marino and Rivalta ; the second at Carpané-Valstagna, and the third descending from Col Moschio near the hamlet of Merlo.

Del Fabbro was ordered to make the summit impregnable from any direction. In case of a disaster it would be defended from there.[3] On November 5, the Comando Supremo placed all the artillery in the Ponte della Priula-M. Grappa sector under the orders of the IV Army (Map 42). The first three field batteries which arrived were emplaced between M. Pèrtica and M. Pallon, all of which were crucial in this battle. German troops would attack in the eastern sector, while the Austro-Hungarians would attack the western sector. Neither were aware of the new improvements. Withdrawing troops proceeded along the funnel-shaped valley system leading to the Grappa which acted as a cork.

Toward the end of the Nineteenth Century, the Club *Alpini* Italiano (Bassano), had erected a small refuge on the Grappa's summit, while in 1901 a chapel had been erected and consecrated. To honor those who stopped the Austro-German advance, a huge monument and ossuary has been constructed. There are 2,283 known dead buried plus 8,049 whose names are not known, for a total of 10, 332. There is also an Austro-Hungarian monument which contains the remains of 295 identified men, and 10, 296 unknown soldiers. Most of the defending infantry had never seen snow, nor experienced such cold, but they steadfastly held the line in a manner which no adequate words can describe. Krauss had as his objective M. Grappa with his troops deployed:(Maps 29, 33, 35, 40,42)

Edelweiss near Arsiè with the 14°, 59°, the III Kaiserjäger, with a battalion of the IV Kaiserjäger at Fonzaso

The Twenty-second Schützen near Arten, with the 98 Kaiserschützen marching toward Feltre to be a reserve.

The German Jäger Division near Belluno

The Fifty-fifth Infantry Division across the Piave River

The III Corps (Bavarian) was to cross between Ponte della Priula and Vas.

November 5

With the withdrawal of the XII Corps (Zona Carnia Command) the front decreased by about two hundred km (120 mi.) of trenches. Charles congratulated Krauss on his victories, reminding him that he had had the best troops in the army.[4] On November 7, the Italian IX Corps arrived at the Quero Gorge which was filled with war refugees, making any movement difficult (Map 24). Hoping for bad weather Diaz telegraphed the defending troops that the aim was to prevent Habsburg and

German troops to link up. Plans were made for a defense system to the west, but these ideas were nullified by concomitant enemy shelling from the altopiano to the west synchronized with attacks on the Grappa (Map 24).

As the Austro-Germans crossed the Tagliamento, posters appeared in the Veneto, the area about to be invaded ordering the populace to remain calm. As in September 1943, the leading civilian authorities had already fled. By November 3, the *Regie Poste* had already ordered that any postal money orders destined for the eastern Veneto or the Cadore would be stopped at Vicenza.

Preceded by the music of the *Khevenuller Regimentsmarsch,* the military march of the 7° Carinthian, the Austro-Hungarian Fifty-fifth Infantry Division entered Feltre on November 7.

November 9

Rome had guaranteed the safety of allied troops but the *Consulta* had not kept the Comando Supremo in the loop. Would Italian troops fight? When asked to deploy their troops, allied generals demurred, referring all questions to the Italian Foreign Ministry. Orlando had told Diaz that the allies were afraid of Italian troops running away and putting their troops in jeopardy.[5]

Diaz met for the first time with Foch and Wilson. After looking at maps of the defense sector they insisted that M. Tomatico and M. Roncone, very far forward be garrisoned. These positions would be easily infiltrated and were difficult to supply. DiRobilant vehemently opposed this but Diaz ordered it done with the prefix, "It shall be noted to be an error in one week's time and we shall pay for it." The positions were garrisoned with volunteers.[6] This was a classic case of generals with inadequate information in far away headquarters making decisions affecting the lives of those on site. Foch and Diaz agreed that the Italian defenses would be set with three main pillars, the Grappa, M. Asolone, and M. Tomba.[7]

Italian infantry killed after an enemy assault.

A German machine gun co. in action during the Caporetto assault.

M. Pertica showing its naked slopes resulting from shelling by both sides.

Telegramm

Ankunftsnummer Aufgabenummer Gattung Wortzahl

Aufgegeben in ss gr h qu 10/12= Uhr Min. vorm. nachm.

Angekommen in Stuttgart am 191 Uhr Min. vorm. nachm.

= an des koenigs von wuerttemberg majestaet stuttgart

:telegramm seiner majestaet des kaisers und koenigs --

= ich habe den koeniglich wuerttembergischen offizieren , major sproesser und oberleutnant rommel vom wuerttembergischen gebirgs · bataillon auf vorschlag des oberbefehlshabers der 14. armee in anerkennung ihrer glaenzenden leistungen in den schwierigen vorhutkaempfen gegen den italienischen feind und bei eroberung des monte matajur den orden pour le merite verliehen , es macht mir freude , dich hiervon in kenntnis setzen zu koennen = wilhelm .+

36 B VI 2a

Text of telegram from Kaiser Wilhelm announcing that Lt. Rommel was Awarded the *Pour le Mérite*, *Courtesy of Hauptstaatsarchiv, Stuttgart*

Lt. Rommel on Dec. 13, 1917 posing with his newly awarded medal. A few hours later he was in heavy action. *Courtesy Hauptstaatarchiv, Stuttgart*

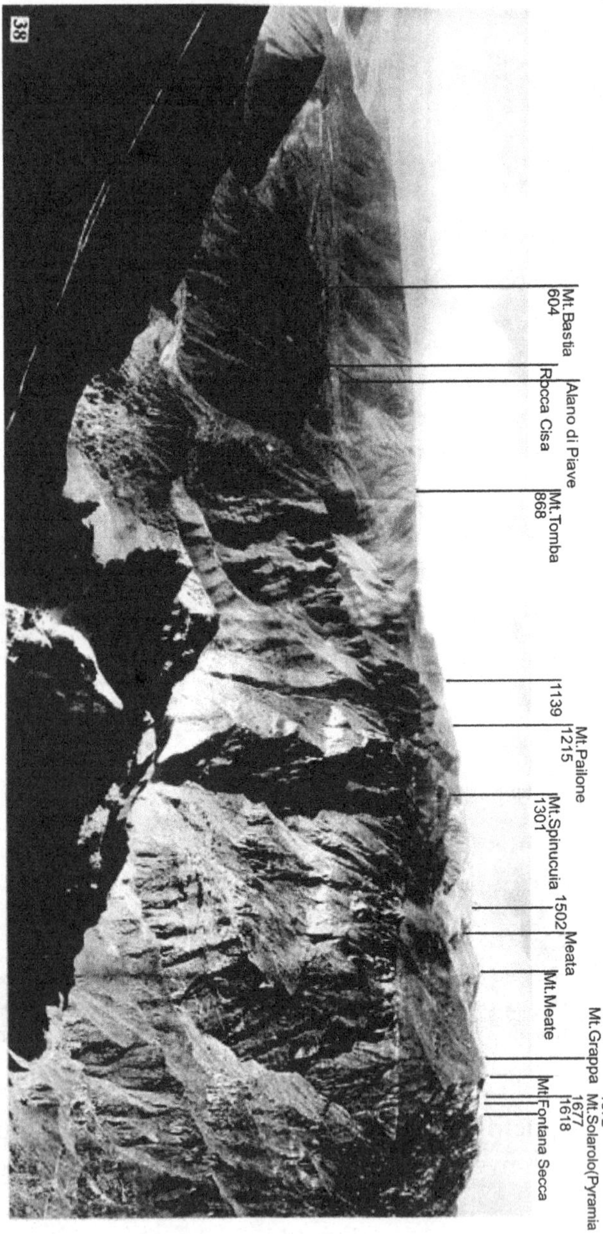

A panorama of the eastern section of the Grappa taken by a Habsburg officer in 1918 *Courtesy Wolfgang Dolezal*
Heights are in meters

Men of the WMB arrayed on the Vajont Gorge Bridge after its capture *Courtesy Wolf-Albrecht Kainz*

The snow-covered M. Valderoa (*Sternkuppe* to the Germans) *Courtesy Marco Rech*

Schutzen of the WMB. Notice the left side of the cap carries a white decoration awarded by the *Edelweiss* for fighting in their division *Courtesy Wolf-Albrecht Kainz*

November 10

Italian IV Army units withdrawing along both banks of the Piave were strafed by Austro-German planes causing panic which would increase on both sides of the trench as this new weapon of war came onto the scene. By morning the Austro-Germans were at the foot of the Grappa as well as on the eastern shores of the Piave from Grisolera westward to Quero where it opens into the plains (Map 24; Map 34 for geography) At dawn the XVIII Corps ordered Col. Abele Piva to form a rear guard for the retreating Fifteenth, Fifty-first and Fifty-sixth Infantry Divisions.[8] He was assigned the *Alpini* M. Rosa, M. Arvenis, M. Pavione, V. Brenta, and Cividale Battalions as well as two battalions of the 6°. His mission was:

A. Allow the XVIII Corps to arrive onto the Grappa and garrison the advanced outposts of the Tomatico and Roncone (Map 24)
B. Allow the stragglers from the I, XII and IX Corps gathered at Belluno to enter the Brenta Valley, thus avoiding capture (Map 35)

Interestingly enough, his orders were open-ended, reading that he should resist as long as possible, then he was on his own as he could count on no reinforcements. Italian strategy on the Grappa was:

1. Have troops in a solid line from the altopiano to the Piave (Map 40).
2. Assist with flanking fire the defense of the Altopiano dei Setti Communi (Asiago Plateau) from which Italian shelling would help Grappa defenders (Maps, 24,40).
3. Hold up enemy advance between the Brenta and Piave Rivers as long as possible. Weather would take care of the rest. All these defenses were intertwined (Maps 35,40). Any local collapse would lead to a general collapse.

November 12

All the bridges over the Piave had been blown but Krauss became aware of a stone-bottomed sector of the river. Working in the icy river water up to their chests his sappers emplaced trusses for a bridge on this strong base to cross and arrive at Feltre by the next day.

November 13

Below's attention was now riveted on M. Tomba. Occupying this bastion would give free access through the Piave Valley to the east (Map 24). Early in the a.m. the XLIII Brigade (Twenty-second Schützen Division) and the Fifty-fifth Infantry Division entered Feltre. Feeling that Italian defenses on the northern spurs of the Grappa were only advance scouts, Krauss immediately ordered the occupation of the villages of Arten, Carposo, and Rasai (Map 24). Simultaneously, a battalion of the 2° Bosnians and an assault battalion of the German Jäger Division moved along the right bank of the Piave, arrived at Sanzen. In Val Brenta units of the Austro-Hungarian First Mountain Brigade entered Primolano after having occupied the mountains on the right side of the Val Cismon (Maps 3,Vol. I, this Vol, Map 24). The I Corps commander felt that once the Grappa was taken, his men could break into the Venetian and Lombardy plain.[9] *Nach Milan* had become a password. Krauss divided his troops into two contingents. The first under the command of Maj. Gen. von Wieden, composed of the *Edelweiss* and the XLIII Schützen Brigade, was to proceed toward Bassano across the valleys of Cismon and Brenta while a secondary force would proceed from the village of Cismon to occupy M. Asolone (Map 24). The second, commanded by Maj. Gen. Prince Schwarzenberg, composed of the Fifty-fifth Infantry and the German Jäger Divisions, was to break through along the right bank of the Piave aiming for Pederobba (Map 38 for geography). Between these two, the 3° Schutzen (Twenty second Schützen Division) was to climb the Grappa in a north-south direction along the axis of M. Roncone-M. Pèrtica-M. Grappa-Crespano (Map 24). It was felt that the shock of the two groups would overcome the Italian defenders. By proceeding along the Brenta and Piave River Valleys, the *Cima Grappa* and *Nave Grappa* would be isolated. The attack would gravitate along the valley floors which is why there were few troops on the mountain (3° Schützen). Since the assault had neither surprise nor artillery fire, Krauss's staff was against the plan. The valleys were narrow, steep and easily defended with Italian artillery firing from the opposite side. Müller presented his objections noting that Wieden's Group was to perform the task assigned to the 3° Schützen. He strenuously insisted that the three regiments of the 98 Brigade of Kaiserschützen be employed. These specially trained High Mountain fighting troops were never used remaining at Rasai (Map 24).

By evening the XVIII Corps (Lt. Gen. Alberto Tettoni), was deployed between the left bank of the Brenta River and M. Tomatico. In the advance positions at Col di Baio was the *Alpini* V. Tagliamento Battalion. Between V. Stizzon and M. Peúrna was the LXXII Bersaglieri Battalion as well as a company of the *Alpini* M. Arvenis Battalion. Diaz now had thirty three divisions deployed compared to fifty nine prior to October 24. Garrisons on the Grappa (Map 24) were divided as follows:

XVIII Corps (Gen. Tettoni) deployed from the Brenta River (excluded) to M. Tomba (excluded)

Fifty-first Infantry Division (Lt. Gen. Tamagni) deployed to the west in the M. Asolone sector with *Aosta* (5° and 6°) *Alpini* M. Matajur Battalion, LX Bersaglieri eight field artillery batteries and an engineering battalion

Fifteenth Infantry Division (Lt. Gen. Quaglia) on the Grappa's center with the 149° (*Trapani*) and the *Alpini* V. Natisone, V. Tagliamento Battalions, the LXXII Bersaglieri, with artillery and engineers.

Fifty-sixth Infantry Division (Maj. Gen. Pittaluga) in the Spinoncia sector with the 144° (*Trapani*), *Alpini* V. Cismon, M. Arvenis, V. Camonica Battalions

Corps reserves were the *Alpini* V. Brenta, M. Rosa, M. Pavione and Cividale Battalions

IX Corps (Lt. Gen. Ruggiero Laderchi) deployed from M. Tomba to Vidor

Seventeenth Infantry Division with the *Basilicata* (91° and 92°)

Como (23°, 24°) two battalions of the 60°, *Alpini* M. Granero, Val Pellice Battalions. There were fifteen artillery batteries.

Eighteenth Infantry Division plus the *Udine* Mountain Group

I Corps deployed from Vidor-Montello-Ponte Priula (Map 42)

In all there were forty-seven battalions plus four engineering battalions. Units of the *Chasseurs des Alpes* arrived along with many British planes.

November 14

With the thoughts of Caporetto fresh in their minds the Austro-German forces started their assault. The XLIII Schützen Brigade proceeded from Seren to Roncon (3° Schützen), and toward the Peúrna (26° Schützen plus the 59° Rainier). The assault on the *Nave* was assigned to lateral units.

Assaulting the Grappa were four divisions of the Austro-Hungarian I Corps. To the west the *Edelweiss* with the Twenty-second Schützen would assault M. Cismon, then proceed toward Bassano. To the east, the Fifty-fifth Infantry Division with the German Jäger Division in reserve would proceed along the Piave River Valley toward Pederobba (west of Nervesa), with a battalion of the 7° and another of the 2°Bosnian (Col. Mihailic) (Maps 24, 40). To occupy this town it was necessary to occupy M. Tomba which overlooked it (Map 43). Krafft noted that the Italians now fought fiercely as opposed to the previous weeks.[10] They were no longer retreating troops, but holding-fast-troops who had decided to stand, fight and die. He described how Italian prisoners would often glare at their captors. The epic of the Grappa has intrigued writers for many years. Commanded by Col. Zedwitz, the XXXVIII Brigade went forward with five battalions on the right of the Piave, while the remaining six battalions of the XXVI Brigade proceeded to Carpen as a reserve. Meanwhile the IIC Schützen Brigade (Twenty-second Schützen Division) went to Porcen and Rasai ready to be used to assist to assist in the breakthrough in the Brenta Canal. Müller and Wieden feeling the summits must be occupied decided to use the troops of the *Gruppe Merten* to assault the two defense pillars, the Roncone and Peúrna. Zedwitz insisted that M. Cornella be occupied before the assault on Quero would begin.

At 0630 the assault on M. Tomatico began. Defending was Lt. Col. Gabriele Nasci with the *Alpini* M. Arvenis and

V. Cismon Battalions as well as the 5 Battery of Mountain Artillery emplaced on M. Santo. Lacking barbed wire, after a few attacks, the *Alpini* had to retreat to avoid being encircled. Italian patrols reported that contact with the Italian 23° deployed on the spur of M. Tese, M. Cornella-Quero was lost (Map 24). Fearing encirclement, during the night, the Fifty-sixth Infantry Division ordered a withrawal from the Tomatico and Peúrna toward the Grappa summit. Only M. Roncone remained in Italian hands. The 23° had been ordered by the Italian IV Army to withdraw on the previous day. However it never received such orders and was forced to retreat to M. Cornella defended by the *Como*. The Cornella was being assaulted by the enemy XXVI Brigade while the Italian 24° blocked the Quero Gorge roadway. Krauss was unimpressed with the results. Leaving his CCXVI Brigade (*Edelweiss*) at Fonzaso Wieden would not allow his men to proceed along the lower V. Cismon while the Italians still held strong defensive positions. Italian lines had not been pierced.

November 15

In the severe cold, men on both sides of the trench froze to death in the cold. The attack front was from Quero to M. Roncone which was garrisoned by the *Alpini* V. Tagliamento Battalion defending against the 3° Schützen while M. Peúrna was defended by the *Alpini* M. Arvenis Battalion. Krafft ordered Krauss to head southward from Feltre to take the Grappa (Map 29). The I Corps commander was convinced that the clash would be on the line of Enego-M. Pèrtica,-M. Grappa-M. Pallon-M.Tomba-Pederobba (Maps 24,40). Habsburg patrols reported new fortifications in place, with stiff resistance southwest of Feltre where the Italians had garrisoned the northern spurs of the Grappa, including the spurs of M. Tomatico and M. Cornella giving them control of the right bank of the Piave.

Showing his opposition to the Krauss's plan Wieden sent the whole XLIII Schützen Brigade from the Sella di Arten toward the northern spur of M. Grappa while the 3° Schützen would proceed toward the Roncone. To the left toward M. Peúrna would proceed the 26° Schützen with a battalion of the 59°. Krafft described Italian sharpshooters deployed on all rocky hills being very bothersome. At M. Tomatico Mihailic's men occupied C. Sassumà at the extreme south west point of the battle sector enabling them to descend onto the Forcella Bassa, thus helping the efforts of the 26° Schützen at M. Peúrna. Some of Mihailic's men proceeded toward M. Santo and M. Tomatico where they ran into the *Alpini* V. Cismon Battalion whose men were from the Grappa region.[11] As these men left their homes proceeding toward the combat zone they were surrounded by their families lamenting the fact that perhaps their men would die in action that day. Wives, children and older members of the family lamented as only a Latin family can. Finally, with one last good-by they turned to go home, always giving a glance to their loved one going toward harm's way. The author feels that this was one of the main reasons for the Italian sold defense on the Grappa. The troops were afraid of what would happen to their families.

Feeling that it was futile to attack along the valley floors, the three attacking generals, Wieden, Müller and Schwarzenberg, had a violent argument with Krauss. As noted Wieden had decided to contradict the orders of his superior, with an energetic attack on M. Grappa assaulting it through M. Roncone and M. Pértica (Map 24). Entrusted with this task was the *Gruppe Merten* consisting of the 3° Schützen, the II/59° plus as much artillery as could be spared from the Twenty-second Schützen.

A concentric attack on the *Nave Grappa* was now planned. The 1/4° Kaiserjäger would assault the Col dei Prai climbing the V. del Corlo, then converging on M. Pértica (Map 24). The other battalions of the 59° would cross the Cismon Valley and proceed toward M. Asolone and Col della Berretta. Once accomplished, the attackers would deploy along the line of Col dei Prai-Colicello in Val Brenta. The CCXVII Brigade would then break through in the valley floor proceeding toward Valstagna (on the Asiago Plateau, see Map 31), assisted by the IX Mountain Brigade of the Conrad Group (Map 9 for geography). By proceeding along the Brenta and Piave River Valley floors which bordered the Grappa, the A.O.K. hoped to encircle the *Nave*. A better plan would have been to attack the Grappa summit followed by an advance downward into Italian valley defenses. Instead of following orders Krauss' subordinates dissipated his forces using neither a massive attack toward the summit nor one proceeding along the valley floors.

Preceded by shelling, the Fifty-fifth Division occupied the already evacuated M. Tomatico and M. Santo (See further in this chapter). Units of the Austro-Hungarian 216 Infantry Brigade climbed the valleys that arrived at M. Cismon attacked and broke through the line M. Fredina-Col Baio defended by LX Bersaglieri and *Alpini* Matajur Battalions. The *Alpini* withdrew to the Prassolan, while the Bersaglieri found refuge in Col dei Prai resulting in the *Alpini* Val Tagliamento Battalion on the Roncon being isolated. The *Alpini* M. Arvenis Battalion withdrew to M. Fontanasecca while the Val Cismon descended into V. Tegorzo, then crossed the V. Calcino and climbed the Grappa. Using darkness as a cover, with a bayonet charge the *Alpini* broke through enemy lines arriving at the Grappa summit via the Seren Valley. Others deployed in the Val Stizzon were forced to withdraw to Col dell'Orso along with LXIII Bersaglieri. On the opposite slope of V. Tegorzo the defenders resisted on the spur of Rocca Cisa situated on the extremity of the crest separating V. Cinespa from V. Calcino resulting in the attackers being unable to reach the Quero Gorge from the northwest. The 26° Schützen quickly occupied the evacuated M. Peúrna and proceeded toward M. Fontanasecca.

The first assault of the *Gruppe Merten* had immediate good results. The 3° Schützen with the II/59° successfully assaulted M. Roncone, causing a retreat of the *Alpini* V. Tagliamento Battalion. Other Austro-German units had climbed directly from V. Cismon, arriving at the crest between Col di Baio and M. Fredina, proceeding southward to Col Zaloppa forcing the Italians to retreat toward the defensive line line of M. Prassolan and Col dei Prai. The War Diary of the surrounded V. Tagliamento noted that there were many dead and wounded on M. Roncone, with the survivors retreating to M. Prassolan, the Forcelleto, and finally on to M. Grappa where there were only two companies of 120 men each.[12] A similar fate befell the *Alpini* V. Natisone Battalion and LXII Bersaglieri which were attacked at V. Stizzon as they attempted to block the attackers on M. Roncone from spreading. The *Alpini* M. Matajur and the LX Bersaglieri Brigade were to redeploy from Col Zaloppa onto the Prassolan, whose garrison had been reinforced by the II/149°. However, the latter *was not true.* Only the very weakened third battalion of the 76° was deployed there exposing the right wing of the IV Corps. The War Diary of the IV Corps showed the enormous problems which happened in the two days preceding the battle. Units of the Salzburg 59° occupied the hamlet of Cismon, but could not proceed along the Brenta due to the Italian shelling. As the CCXVII Brigade (Wieden), arrived, artillery support to proceed to Valstagna was requested. Conrad was having difficulty in getting his offensive started due to bad equipment and lack of troops.[13] By nightfall the Italian line was Col dei Prai-Prà Solan-Val Stizzon-Solaroli-Fontanasecca-Rocca Cisa-Cornella (Map 24). In darkness the German One-Hundred-Seventeenth Infantry Division crossed the Piave at Ponte di Piave but was completely halted by the defenders who took 600 prisoners (Map 38 for geography). It was a small victory, but desperately needed by the Comando Supremo to lift morale. At day's end of the enemy's objectives, much to Krafft's amazement the river bank lines had not been pierced.

View of War Monument on the Grappa with the ossuary and *Casa dell'Armata* in left background and *Rifugio Bassano* on the right.

A painting of King Vittorio Emanuele III explaining the situation to British Prime Minister Lloyd George as well as French representatives on November 7, 1917 at Peschiera
Courtesy Museo del Risorgimento, Milano

Getting rid of body lice during combat on the Grappa

The two kaisers during a field reconnaissance

Fleeing refugees, a result of the Austro-German invasion

GdI Verdross inspecting troops. Branches of oak and pine on the helmet signified that they would soon enter combat.

A solitary Italian sentry on duty on the Piave
during the winter of 1917-1918

Kaiser Wilhem II giving Below a medal in Italy in
November 1917

IN NOME DI S. M. VITTORIO EMANUELE III
PER GRAZIA DI DIO E PER VOLONTÀ DELLA NAZIONE
RE D'ITALIA

IL TRIBUNALE DI GUERRA
DEL V. CORPO D'ARMATA
CON FUNZIONI DI TRIBUNALE STRAORDINARIO
ha pronunciato la seguente

SENTENZA

NELLA CAUSA CONTRO:

1. PRESSI Luigi di Bortolo, nato il 25 agosto 1889 a Monteforte d'Alpone, soldato.
2. PIASTRA Giuseppe di Cesare nato nell'ottobre 1882 a Fivizzano (Massa Carrara), soldato.
3. VOLPIANA Domenico di Cesare nato il 12 aprile 1896 a Crespadoro, soldato.
4. FURIANI Antonio di Vincenzo nato nel 1882 a Anagni, soldato.
5. POSENATO Bortolo di Battista nato il 24 ottobre 1894 a Monteforte d'Alpone, soldato.

Tutti della Compagnia Speciale Alpini del Battaglione Val Toce. Detenuti.

ACCUSATI

di diserzione in presenza del nemico (art. 137 C. P. Es.) - perchè trovandosi col loro reparto a Ponte delle Prigioni, località in presenza del nemico, se ne allontanavano senza ordine od autorizzazione, il PRESSI, il VOLPIANA e il POSENATO, nella notte dal 29 al 30 gennaio 1918 e il PIASTRA e il FURIANI il giorno 30 detto, rendendosi latitanti. Il PIASTRA veniva arrestato il 1° febbraio 1918, verso le ore 13 in Recoaro; il POSENATO e il PRESSI si costituivano ai CC. RR. di Monteforte d'Alpone il 3 febbraio 1918; il VOLPIANA e il FURIANI rientravano al corpo dopo oltre 24 ore di assenza. Con recidiva specifica per il VOLPIANA.

In esito all'odierno pubblico dibattimento, tenuto alla presenza della truppa riunita sotto le armi, seguite le forme di legge per il procedimento dei Tribunali Straordinari, letti gli atti, sentiti il P. M. e gli accusati che coi loro difensori hanno avuto per primi ed ultimi la parola;

DICHIARA

i soldati PIASTRA Giuseppe, POSENATO Bortolo, PRESSI Luigi, FURIANI Antonio, VOLPIANA Domenico colpevoli di diserzione in presenza del nemico; Letti ed applicati gli art. 137, 570 del Codice Penale per l'Esercito

CONDANNA

i soldati PIASTRA Giuseppe, POSENATO Bortolo, PRESSI Luigi e FURIANI Antonio, col beneficio delle circostanze attenuanti (art. 58 C. P. Es.) alla

PENA DELL'ERGASTOLO

previa degradazione; e il soldato VOLPIANA Domenico alla

PENA DI MORTE

previa degradazione. Tutti alle conseguenze di legge.

Ordina la pubblicazione della sentenza nei modi di legge.

Raossi, sei febbraio millenovecentodiciotto.

All'originale seguono le firme.

La presente sentenza è stata eseguita lo stesso giorno 6 febbraio 1918.

Per estratto conforme
IL SEGRETARIO

50

Poster reporting death sentences for desertion carried out the same day as the trial

Habsburg Infantry serving in a trench dug through the snow

The execution of an Italian soldier who had discarded his rifle at Caporetto (*Courtesy of the Museo del Risorgimento, Milano)*

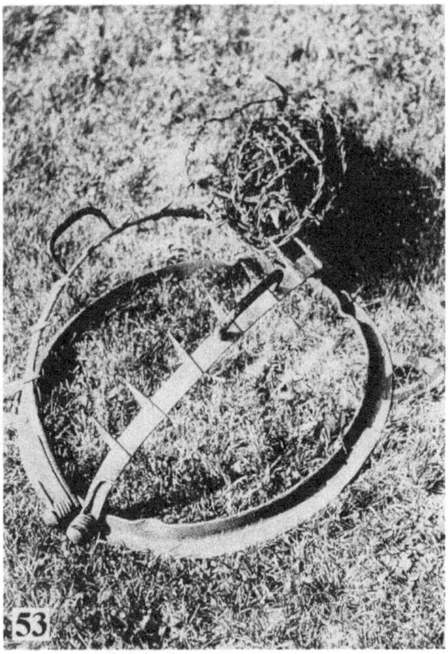

A Habsburg foot trap placed under the snow around troop positions to injure approaching Italian infantry
Courtesy Luca Girotto

Capt. Luigi Rizzo with his crew after he sank the *Wien* on Dec. 9, 1917

A Habsburg Skoda 420 howitzer. Each shell weighed one ton and traveled nine miles. *Courtesy Luca Girotto*

The brothers Karl (16) and Leopold (17) Koller of the volunteer Schützen Regiment from upper Austria. Karl was seriously wounded while Leopold was killed in hand-to hand combat *Courtesy Luca Girotto*

Dead Austro-Hungarian soldier with a lethal head wound. A companion placed some of his skull contents into his mess-tin *Courtesy Luca Girotto*

Engelbert Dolfuss future Austrian Chancellor as a second Lt. in the 2° Landesschützen on the Italian Front

View of the Melette di Gallio to the left, the Val Miela in the center with the rocky spurs of the Montagna Nuova followed by M. Spil to the right

Barracks of Italian-speaking citizens of the Austro-Hungarian Empire at Branau am Inn. They had been transported there from their homes in the Trentino.

November 16

Combat continued without a pause. Aware of events on the preceding day, Krauss ordered that the breakthrough happen along the Piave between M. Tomba and the river (Map 24). The I Corps commander wanted the assault during the night with troops proceeding from Quero toward M. Tomba. In the dark Italian artillery on M. Pallon would not be able to fire on advancing enemy troops so that as daylight arrived the objective would have already been occupied. By the time the Fifty-fifth Infantry Division reached the Alano Basin, the arriving Jäger Division was to have conquered the spur of the M. Tomba-Monfenera, assisted by artillery deployed on the left of the Piave. Below assigned the Austro-Hungarian Ninety-Fourth Infantry Division (Gen. Lawrowski) to leave Belluno in two days to assist the Krauss Group.

Arriving at his tactical headquarters (S. Maria), Krauss was astounded that his orders had not been carried. So it was not only the Italian generals that did not obey, Habsburg generals did likewise. Schwarzenberg notified him that an attack along the valley floor would be impossible due to the Italian artillery. As noted Zedwitz wanted M. Cornella an Italian stronghold to be taken first. The I Corps commander immediately ordered the assault battalion of the Jäger Division to assault the gorge as soon as darkness fell. This division was made up of very young men who had been rejected for the first call to arms, but its training was equal to other divisions. Schwarzenberg was ordered to suspend the attacks on M. Cornella and have the XXVII Brigade follow the assault. When he objected stating that his troops were very tired Krauss responded that the troops would have much time to rest when they broke into the plains. Having issued orders, Krauss returned to Feltre.

Many of the officers of the Krauss Group objected to the attack as ordered. Instead they ordered a simultaneous attack on the Quero and M. Cornella. By 1300 the next day, Quero was taken, and by midnight, M. Cornella was taken by the 2° Bosnian, after which they proceeded to the Alano Basin on whose southern border rose the last obstacle, the heavily wooded spur of M. Tomba-Monfenera. Rocca Cisa was also taken along with most of the *Como*. Attacking here they realized that these were no longer the times of Caporetto. There was no surprise. To this date no one knows how or why the combative spirit of the defenders rose to the task. Italian artillery ensconced on M. Pallon, Fontanasecca, Spinoncia poured enfilade fire on the attackers forcing them to withdraw with heavy losses.

Starting at dawn, Austro-German artillery started its shelling of positions of Col dei Prai-M. Prassolan garrisoned by the *Alpini* M. Matajur Battalion with the LX Bersaglieri and some infantry units (I/149°). Other infantry units were in reserve between Osteria del Forcellato and M. Pèrtica. Commanding all these defensive forces was Lt. Col Pietro Gilberti who was wounded and taken prisoner.

Meanwhile, the 3° Schützen Artillery lengthened its range, aiming at positions on Col dei Prai-M. Prassolan. At 0900, the I/3° Schützen (Capt. Andics), reached its objective (Prassolan), isolating the three companies of the Italian 149° some of which successfully broke out but 800 *Alpini* were taken prisoner.[14] The victors had reassessed their new position on the Prassolan while the I/3° Schützen commanded by Lt. Franz Lorenzoni proceeded toward Col Buratto, then toward the unoccupied summit of the Pèrtica. On its opposite slopes the Italians were digging trenches with their bayonets.

At 1000, Col. Heinrich von Tenner commander of the (3° Schützen) arrived and immediately ordered a continuation of the attack resulting in the full occupation of Col Buratto at 1400 despite meeting fierce resistance. Halting to rest and await reinforcements, a twist of fate occurred which changed the outcome of the battle. The War Diary of the Krauss Group sadly noted that the IIC Kaiserschützen Brigade was available but not used. Krafft later wrote, "No criticism should be addressed toward the brave Schützen (I Battalion) for having interrupted their action. The decision of their commandant (Capt. Andics), was correct.

In addition, it was doubtful that an assault in this condition would have been successful." The defenders (I/149°) had so strongly resisted that an advance across M. Pèrtica was denied. Advancing troops did not have their flanks protected, and were subjected to shelling from Italian positions on Col dell'Orso.

Having lost M. Prassolan, Major Gen. Clemente Assum (responsible for the Grappa summit) realized that the situation was desperate. Remaining were only the I/149° as the *Alpini* V. Tagliamento, V. Natisone and Matajur Battalions and the II/149° had been annihilated. The LX Bersaglieri were exhausted, the III/149° and the LXII Bersaglieri were at Solaroli. Assum was now gripped by fear, as he had no reserves left. In the approaching darkness, the *Alpini* M. Rosa Battalion (Major Umberto Benedetti) arrived which was immediately deployed between M. Pèrtica and Croce dei Lebi along with the survivors of the V. Tagliamento and the Matajur giving the I/149° a chance to rest.

Clinging to the slopes, the 59° Salzburg proceeded from Cismon to the V. Goccia, up to Col Bonato, pulling along two mountain batteries, soon to be aimed at M. Asolone and Col della Berretta. Along the Brenta Canal, assault units of the *Edelweiss* were held up at Colicello by Italian shelling.

Marching from Feltre to Quero, the German Jäger Division encountered great difficulties resulting in its commander changing the attack date on M. Tomba to November 18 much to the consternation of Krauss. He felt surprise was still the biggest weapon. The attack was still going to be on M. Tomba-Monfenera with the newly arrived XXVI Brigade and Württemberg Mountain Battalion attacking V. Calcino and V. Cinespa arriving at M. Spinoncia and M. Fontanasecca. The rest of the Fifty-fifth Infantry Division would be deployed at Alano and Campo. Thus it seemed that the attack on the eastern sector would gravitate toward the Piave. Assum, meanwhile received reinforcements to fill out the II/149° placing them between the I/149° and the *Alpini* V. Natisone Battalion.

Late in the afternoon both sides battled ferociously for control of the Pèrtica the western pillar of the Grappa summit defenses. Both sides shelled it depending on which side occupied the summit. The Italians held. Farther west, the *Edelweiss* occupied the hamlet of Magnola getting closer, ever closer to Col della Berretta. On M. Tomba foreseeing an enemy assault Tettoni sent the 264° (*Gaeta*) and the 144° (*Trapani*). The 263° of the *Gaeta* was in reserve with some units replacing the *Como.*

November 17

Due to its central position vital to both sides today would be the beginning of M. Pèrtica's tragic odyssey. It would be constantly shelled by both sides so that its slopes would become devoid of anything living, animal or human. Assum deployed the *Trapani's* (I/149°) together with a machine gun company on the Pèrtica.(Map 24). The *Alpini* M. Rosa Battalion was deployed from the Pèrtica to Cà Tasson. From the Croce dei Lebi to the Solaroli were deployed the 13° Bersaglieri (LIX, LXII Battalions) together with the III/149°. Defense of the Solaroli-Croce dei Lebi was now given to the Fifty-Sixth Infantry Division which included *Alpini* deployed between Spinoncia and Fontanasecca. M. Tomba was reinforced by the *Gaeta* with its 264° and the *Trapani* 144°. In second line defenses was the 263° reinforced by the survivors of the *Como.*

In his diary Rommel noted "No longer do we have the happy walks of the past days."[15]

Several of the 149° officers were captured. A court martial was convened per request of a Bersaglieri officer with the officers sentenced *in absentia.* After the war the sentence was overturned.

November 18

At dawn men of the German Jäger Division attacked M. Tomba-Monfenera. One regiment proceeded along the roadway intending to attack Fener from the east. Initially chestnut trees protected the attackers but Italian artillery on M. Pallon gave excellent flanking fire for the defenders soon denuding the slopes.

Italian machine gun fire from positions within caves on the base of Monfenera together with *fanti* of the *Basilicata* (91° & 92°) stopped them. Another regiment arrived on the summit but was stopped by the hastily assembled Italian 60°. The third enemy regiment (XXVI Brigade (Fifty-fifth Infantry Division) arrived on the M. Tomba summit but was pushed off due to Italian shells falling on its right and rear.

Disappointed by the failures, Below decided to mount a direct attack on the Grappa Massif, entrusting the task of attacking the spur of Monfenera-Tomba to Maj. Gen. Ludwig Tutscheck with the German Jäger and Alpenkorps.

Except for the WMB the Krauss Group was now comprised only of Austro-Hungarian troops (*Edelweiss*, Fifty-fifth and Ninety-fourth Infantry and the Twenty-second Schützen Divisions). They would be divided into two groups. The Ninety-fourth had been detached from the X Army. The first group, (Maj. Gen. von Wieden) with the CCXVI Brigade (*Edelweiss*), the 3° Schützen (Twenty-second Schützen) and the XXV Brigade (Ninety-fourth Infantry Division), would attack between the Brenta River and Col dell'Orso. Müller would command the second group which would occupy Fontanasecca-Spinoncia, Pallon, and the ridge to M. Tomba. It consisted of units of the WMB (recently transferred to the Twenty-second Schützen), the IIC Brigade and the 26° Schützen. The two groups were to link up on Col dell'Orso. The sector from M. Tomba to the Piave was taken over by the Scotti Group, consisting now of the German Jäger Division and the Alpenkorps brought up from the reserve. The Italian IV Army now strengthened its defenses.

> The Grappa received the *Massa Carrara* (251° and 252°)
>
> The Tomba-Monfenera received the *Re* (1° and 2°) and *Calabria* (59° and 60°)
>
> The Tomba received the XXVII Corps which together with the IX Corps deployed on the rear slope of the Tomba.

On the Spinoncia were the *Alpini* Val Camonica, Feltre Battalions with the Val Maira on the rocks of Porte Salton, with the M. Arvenis Battalion further to the rear. Italian artillery was deployed from M. Spinoncia to Porte di Salton. The 13° Bersaglieri, III/149° were deployed from the Solaroli to Cason dei Lebi. By the end of the day, Italian forces were exhausted,

The Württemberg Mountain Battalion (known as WMB), arrived at Alano and Uson. It was to cross the Grappa and descend onto Bassano. Leaving Alano the WMB proceeded and occupied Rocca Cisa firing no shots.

November 19

Starting in the afternoon, M. Pèrtica was subjected to a methodical bombardment while infantry attacks unleashed at 2200 were repulsed. Attacks and counterattacks continued for several days wearing out both sides of the trench. With no reserves Assum was fearful of the outcome. His only remaining troops were the exhausted I and II/149°, plus units of the *Alpini* M. Rosa Battalion, which had held out for five terrible days. To reinforce them he sent his last troops two companies of the 252°. The WMB's attempts to take M. Spinoncia were unsuccessful.

November 20

Multiple wave attacks on the Pèrtica continued, but the defenders of the summit held. Troops of the German Jäger Division reached a point south of Fener. By the next day all attacks on the Solaroli, Col dell'Orso and the Tomba-Monfenera sectors had failed. In his diary, Below noted some alarming items. Horses were starving due to lack of fodder because Charles was too weak to force Hungary and Bohemia to furnish foodstuffs for the front. Munitions were starting to lack because the *II Armée Isonzo* subalterns would not let German columns proceed below Pordenone territory which was in the Habsburg pursuit zone (Map 35). Throughout history, coalition warfare has been difficult. It is hard to imagine allies arguing about the road an ammunition column should take during a battle which could influence the outcome of the war (as it did).

On the Italian side, the IV Army was constantly asking for reinforcements but the Comando Supremo had none to give. All it gave were remnants of the XXVII and VI Corps to be sent to the Tomba-Monfenera sector, the latter corps having been declared to be in bad shape.

November 21

Grey was the color of the hills, the snow, the fog as well as the cannonades. Everything was grey. Below now decided to eliminate the Grappa as a defensive factor. He was very upset at the loss of German lives to satisfy Habsburg interests.[16] The Kaiserschützen proceeded along the line V. Calcino attacking and occupying M. Fontanasecca severely mauling the *Alpini* V. Camonica Battalion. On the Grappa in the Spinoncia and Fontanasecca sectors Italian troops were deployed as follows: (Map 24)

> *III Raggruppamento Alpini (Gruppi Alpini Benussi* and *Nasci)* with the Feltre, Val Cismon, Val Camonica, Val Maira, Arvenis, supported by five mountain batteries.
>
> LXII and LIX Bersaglieri and III/149°.

The WMB failed in its attempt to take M. des Tas and M. Spinoncia. Counterattacks by the VII Assault Detachment to retake Fontanasecca were unsuccessful.

Assaults on the Pèrtica continued. Gen. Ferrari (XX Corps on the Asiago Plateau) sent the *Alpini* Morbegno, Val d'Adige, and Tirano Battalions to deploy between the Val Brenta and Col Moschin (Map 24). Another unit arriving was the 252°.

Defenses on M. Tomba were weakening. Mule-carried artillery was sent there along with the XXVII Corps (Lt. Gen. A.

DiGiorgio) all to defend the line Tomba-Pizzo-Pallon. Cold weather and permanent snow was fast approaching. The A.O.K. decided that the best thing was to establish winter quarters on the plains but first had to crash through the mountains.

November 22

Austro-German attacking troops were now deployed in tactical units

Tutschek Tactical Group: Alpenkorps and German Jäger Division deployed between M. Spinoncia and M. Monfenera

Wedel Tactical Group: German Fifth, Two Hundredth Infantry Divisions Austro-Hungarian Ninety-fourth Infantry Division deployed on the Solaroli

Wieden Tactical Group: *Edelweiss* and the Twenty-second Schützen deployed between the Val Brenta and M. Pèrtica

Reserves would consist in the Krauss Group (Austro-Hungarian Sixtieth, Fiftieth, Fifty-fifth (Bosnian) Infantry Divisions deployed in the Feltre sector with the German One Hundredth-ninety-fifth and Austro-Hungarian Fourth Infantry Divisions in Val Brenta

The complete deployment did not take place until December 5.

The Italian IV Army now consisted of:[17]

XXVII Corps (Lt. Gen. Antonino DiGiorgio) deployed to the left between M. Asolone and the Grappa with its Fifteenth and Fifty-first Infantry Division with the Twenty-third Infantry Division as a reserve

XVIII Corps (Lt. Gen. Adolfo Tettoni with the Fifty-sixth and Twenty-fourth Infantry divisions which garrisoned the sector from Spinonica to Solaroli

IX Corps (Lt. Gen. Ruggeri Laderchi) on the extreme right of the deployment with its Seventeenth Infantry Division on M. Tomba and the Eighteenth as a reserve.

VI Corps (Lt. Gen. Stefano Lombardi) with its Sixty-sixth and Sixty-seventh Infantry Divisions deployed as a corps reserve deployed behind the IX Corps. This deployment would be completed by November 26.

Having silently accumulated artillery mouths, 0525 the Austro-Germans unleashed a furious barrage silencing the Italian guns on M. Pallon. Five minutes later using flamethrowers, a battalion of the German Jäger Division successfully attacked occupying Monfenera by 0800, while by 1250, the II/Jäger had occupied M. Tomba. Suffering heavy casualties in assisting the Jäger was the 1/ 4° Bosnian and the 26° Schützen, with the whole operation resulting in the usual counterattacks (*Re* and *Calabria*), that only retook the western tip of the summit. Involved in this were two battalions of the 92° with the *Calabria* being almost annihilated. As a precautionary measure, the Italian IV Army sent the Sixty-seventh Infantry Division to garrison the southern spur of the Tomba which descended onto Cavasa. As darkness arrived, the Tomba-Monfenera sector was transferred to Alpenkorps which had just arrived. The whole sector of the *Nave* and M. Tomba was permanently covered with snow.

Entering the spotlight now was the Pèrtica which was shelled during the night and attacked by the 3° Schützen (Graz). Favored by fog, one battalion proceeded from Osteria del Forcelletto overcoming the 134 Company of the *Alpini* M. Rosa Battalion under the right summit opening a breach in Italian defenses. Pouring through it, they found themselves in the rear of the defending I/149° and II/ 149° which after a firefight retreated to the slopes between M. Pèrtica and the Grappa. Austro-Germans were now in possession of the

Pèrtica summit. Informed of this serious situation, the Italian Fifteenth Infantry Division detached the III/263° (*Gaeta)* to Assum who ordered an artillery barrage on the positions followed by a counterattack which by noon was crowned with success. The Pèrtica summit was again in Italian hands. Meanwhile the *Messina* (93° and 94°) part of the Fifteenth Inf. Div. (along with the *Massa Carrara)* commanded by Col. Brig. Adolfo Gazagne arrived on the Grappa. In the afternoon, preceded by a violent artillery barrage, the Austro-Hungarians attacked and again occupied M. Pèrtica for a short time. Preceded by heavy shelling from the overhanging Grappa Italian troops including the II/ 93° successfully counterattacked as dead, dying and wounded wearing the Italian *grigioverde* or Habsburg field grey dotted the mountain slope which furnished a bed of snow. Wounded were not cared for due to constant intermittent shelling by both sides. Col della Berretta west of the Grappa.

November 23

Combat on the M. Tomba and Monfenera sectors seemed to calm down, but combat persisted on M. Pèrtica. Used were machine guns, mine launchers and flamethrowers, but the most feared and efficient weapon system was the artillery on the Grappa. Holding the summit was almost impossible. Artillery which surrounded it starting a constant shelling prior to an attack. A new defensive line was planned for the slopes of Pèrtica-Grappa. Benedetti commanded the defenses wanting to counterattack but could not due to constant enemy pressure. The 14° Linz attacked in the Val Brenta, while units of the Kaiserjäger assaulted Col della Berretta.

November 24

Attention on M. Pèrtica persisted. The linkups, with the positions of Col dell'Orso across the head of the V. Stizzon, were defended by the exhausted survivors of the *Alpini* M. Rosa,

V. Natisone and V. Tagliamento Battalions which were replaced by the the 93° (*Messina*). Command of the Grappa sector was transferred from Assum to Gazagne. The I and II/149° survivors were described as "human larvae."[18] They were exhausted, hungry, thirsty and dirty. A similar description could have been made of the survivors of the *Alpini* battalions. Fighting now among the troops were the young draftees born in 1899 impressing Assum who wrote an account of the Grappa's defense. The Austro-Germans now kept up their attacks on V. Calcino toward M. Spinoncia, the Solaroli and the Col dell'Orso with little success.

Using poison gas the Alpenkorps assaulted the Tomba but were repulsed and lost many men as prisoners. Rommel temporarily assumed command of the Württemberg Mountain Battalion replacing Major Theodor Sproesser. Years later he denoted the delusions of these attacks, as well as the inadequacies of the Austro-Hungarian command structure while the good soldier Š*jevk* kept attacking when ordered.

November 25

Assisted by the newly arrived Ninety-fourth Infantry Division the Twenty-second Schützen assaulted the western slope of M. Casonet as well as Col dell/Orso-Solaroli. The first defense line was lost in the a.m. but an Italian counterattack in the p.m. regained it. The southern slope of M. Valderòa was lost.

Charles had a summit meeting at Feltre with Arz and the corps commanders. Krauss still believing that the Italians could be defeated, had a violent argument with Charles who was afraid of both the inclement weather and lack of supplies. The emperor belonged to the Peace Party as opposed to Conrad and Krobatin who belonged to the War Party. Krauss advocated attacking in the Adige Valley, as well as the Lago di Garda further to the west (Maps 35,43). Boroevic's forces would also have to attack on the Piave so the enemy could not concentrate its forces. However the I Corps commander was fighting Habsburg aristocracy serving in the military many of which he had openly criticized. His plans were not accepted. German commanders who had already decided to withdraw their troops watched this show with amusement.

The XIV Army realized that its attack on the Grappa had been a failure. It only occupied a piece of the summit ridge of M. Tomba whose supply route was under direct artillery fire from M. Pallon. The Rommel Detachment had been asked by Sproesser to break through to the Grappa. He was to descend into the Val Stizzon, then attack the Solaroli from the north, isolating the Valderòa.[19] German troops described the taking of the Valderòa as *besonders schwierig* (very difficult).

November 26

Under a heavy snow storm preceded by shelling which started at dawn the *Edelweiss* attacked the Italian Fifty-first Infantry Division sector. At 1400, shelling was concentrated on Col della Berretta and M. Asolone using 305 mm. howitzers deployed near Cismon. Defending from Col Caprile to M. Asolone was the *Aosta* (Col. Brig. Roberto Bencivenga) assisted by the *Alpini* V. Brenta Battalion, the III/94°, plus the LX Bersaglieri with the 263° in reserve. Toward evening Bencivenga released his last reserves, the III/94° forcing the attackers to withdraw to the departure line. The *Edelweiss* which now had only 2000 effective rifles had been stopped by the Sicilians of the *Aosta*.

The assault had been led by the *crème de la crème* of Austro-Hungarian infantry. There was the 14° and 59° as well as the 1°, 2°, and 3° Kaiserjäger. Should the left wing of the Grappa defense crumble, the *ridotto centrale* of the Grappa would be enveloped. The Col della Berretta was lost, but later retaken.[20] The Rommel Detachment (now the full WMB) got lost in the mountains and much to the consternation of the Austro-Hungarian Ninety-fourth Infantry Division entered its assigned combat zone. The latter unit was afraid that now Rommel would partake in the glory of taking the Solaroli. Complaints were so many, that Sproesser insisted to his superiors, that his unit be immediately pulled out of its present position.[21] The next night troops of the *Alpini* Moncenisio Battalion attempted to retake the dorsum of Monfenera but were repulsed by the crossfire of enemy machine guns a failure which resulted in an argument within the staff of the IV Army. By now the Grappa was covered with snow, fog, wind and freezing temperatures making daily conditions very difficult. Temperatures hovered about minus ten to twenty degrees Centigrade (Ten to minus five degrees Fahrenheit).

In the Zenson sector enemy troops that had crossed the river were now withdrawn to the eastern shore (Map 33 for geography).

To the east British troops proceeded to the Montello. Troops of the Italian I Corps were relieved as follows:

> First Infantry Division by the British Forty-first Infantry Division
> Seventieth Infantry Division by the British Twenty-third Infantry Division

November 27

In today's diary entry, Below was upset because he had found out that the *II Armée Isonzo* had been without ammunition since the second day of the offensive on the Tagliamento. An Italian counterattack there would have crashed through. With the suspension of the offense, the O. H. L. (later O.K. L.) felt there was no reason to keep its troops in that sector. It took the One Hundred-Ninety-Fifth Infantry Division out of the line to send to France followed by the Twelfth Silesian on December 3. The Twenty-Sixth Infantry Division was replaced by the German One Hundred-Seventeenth Infantry Division and the Austro-Hungarian Infantry Division of *Lt. Marschall* Ludwig Goiginger. Austro-German munitions supply problems developed on the Grappa. Mountain Divisions (Alpenkorps, the Two-Hundredth Infantry Division and the Fifth Infantry Division) were pulled out of the line while the Austro-Hungarian Fourth Infantry Division replacing the *Edelweiss.*

The Krauss Group now had the following objectives: (Map 24)

> Fourth Infantry Division: Col della Berretta and M. Asolone;
> Ninety-fourth Infantry Division: M. Coston and M. Grappa;
> Wedel Group (German Fifth and Two-Hundredth Infantry Divisions) Col dell'Orso, Solaroli, M. Spinoncia and later, M. Pallon and M. Boccaòr. At his disposal Von Wedel had the Austro-Hungarian Fifty-fifth Infantry Division in reserve north east of Feltre, as well as the *Edelweiss* and Twenty-second Schützen being refitted plus the the K. u. k. Sixtieth Infantry Division.

A two week pause in attacks gave the Italians time to bolster their defenses. Since December 8, Below had noted that French troops (Lt. Gen. Maistre), had entered the defensive positions on Tomba-Monfenera. Mistakenly the A.O.K. announced that the Anglo-French had sixteen divisions in Italy with thirteen divisions in the Brenta sector.[22] Only by November 23 did the Austro-Germans receive accurate information on Anglo-French troop deployments.[23]

November 29

Eugene ordered a suspension of the offensive to get better organized for an attack on the Grappa. Charles ordered the offensive to be halted without letting the Italians know.[24] Krauss kept insisting on attacking on the Adige-Lago di Garda sector while Conrad went on the offensive on the altipiano and Boroevic crossed the Piave (Maps 29,35). Below and

Krafft felt that large successes were no longer possible.[25] There had been seven counterattacks on the Asolone and three on the Pèrtica, which showed that the morale of the Italians had radically changed.[26]

December 2

By now courage and daring had fully returned to the Italian psyche. Starving, lacking proper clothing, enduring frostbite, eyelids covered with ice, they held. One can only think about the *fanti* who had never seen snow, now facing the elements as well as a determined enemy. Weather would become a deciding factor. The Italians hoped it would hold the enemy, while the attackers hoped they would soon crash through the Grappa to spend the winter on the plains below. Should the *fanti* not hold the enemy would be pouring into the Italian heartland of Milano, Venezia, Florence, Rome, with no one to stop them. Somehow for reasons unknown to themselves, as well as to the enemy, the Italian morale had changed. The cry now was *Di qui non si passa*, loosely tranlated meaning "They shall not pass." These were the same troops which two weeks prior British officers had declared would never put up a fight again.[27] How wrong they were!

Troops started to be moved on both sides. Three British divisions deployed on the Montello while three French divisions replaced the IX Corps on M. Tomba while the Germans withdrew four divisions sending them to the Western Front. With the movement of troops and severe weather on the Grappa, there now developed a period of relative calm.

December 4

Having accumulated artillery, Conrad attacked and occupied the Melette.[28] The A.O.K. now asked the O.K.L. to leave two mountain warfare divisions in this sector for the final push on the Grappa, which lasted from December 11 to December 19. It became bitterly cold with temperatures hovering about the zero mark. The K.u.k. Thirty-fifth Infantry Division replaced the German Two Hundredth Infantry Division on the Piave, which had replaced the Silesian Division. It remained as a reserve until the middle of the month when it was sent to the Western Front.

December 6

The Twenty-first Schützen Division assaulted the Sisemol on the Asiago Plateau taking 2000 prisoners (Map 26). Notified of this, the Comando Supremo feared another Caporetto. The new Italian defense line now went between the village of Valstagna and the Val Frenzela which descends from the altipiano onto the Val Brenta (Map 31).

On December 7, Plumer met with Fayolle to discuss Allied troop deployments to halt any enemy incursion through the mountains.[29] A plan for the troops deployment was submitted to Diaz the next day which was approved. The grouping was for tactical not for administrative purposes.

Right Group: (Aosta): Italian III Army
Center Group: (Lt. Gen. Sir Herbert Plumer) deployed on the Piave up to Pederobba (Map 40)

French XXXI Corps (French Forty Seventh Infantry and Sixty-fifth Division with one Italian brigade).
British XIV Corps (British Twenty-third and Forty-first Divisions) with the British Seventh Division in reserve, plus one Italian corps.
Artillery: mountain guns 48, field guns 368, heavy guns 294

Left Group (Lt. Gen. Denis Auguste Duchêne)

French XII Corps (French Twenty-third, Twenty-fourth, and Forty sixth Divisions.
British XI Corps (British Forty-eighth and French Sixty-fourth Divisions)
Reserves: British Fifth Division and one Italian corps.
Artillery: mountain guns 36, field guns 428, heavy guns 230[30]

Should the defensive line yield, a new one was to be prepared from Pederobba going southwest behind the Grappa defenses just clear of the foot of the mountains toward Bassano east of which it would join the Left Group line (Map 40).[31] Four miles behind the Pederobba-Bassano line another was to be dug (Map 43 for geography). The Left Group here would extend the Pederobba-Bassano defenses westward to the Astico River behind the Asiago defenses (Map 35).

December 9

Vienna's troops now started to prepare their *Dauerstellung* (position from which an offensive could be mounted). In upper V. Calcino, units of the German Fifth Infantry Division occupied M. Spinoncia overcoming fierce resistance of the Italian 38°. To the right, the German Two-Hundredth Infantry Division crossed V. Cinespa from M. Fontanasecca aiming for the Solaroli and Col dell'Orso with the objective to converge on M. Grappa. Fog caused failure in a simultaneous assault by both the divisions. Below noted in his diary that this was due to the fragile nerves of a regimental commander. Shelling had inflicted severe damages and casualties to the defenses and garrison on the Solaroli. The 136° was deployed from Solaroli to Col dell'Orso. The *Alpini* M. Arvenis Battalion garrisoned the extreme northeast sector of the Solaroli. West of the Grappa, along the line of Asolone-Col Caprile and Col della Berretta, an attack by the Fourth Imperial Division overcame the 57° with the *Alpini* M. Matajur Battalion on the Col Caprile being surrounded.[32] To the rescue came the *Abruzzi* and *Massa Carrara* as well as the *Alpini* M. Clapier Battalion. The breach was sealed except on Col della Berretta and Col Caprile. Krafft now admitted that Italian morale had drastically changed for the better. According to the OBARI Diaz now was very pessimistic informing Plumer that he planned to withdraw toward Rome where the peninsula was narrower and easier to defend. The German Fifth Infantry Division proceeded toward M. Fontanasecca while the Two Hundredth would soon be involved in more combat.

December 10

A sultry hot wind called the sirocco blew up from the Sahara over the Grappa. Snow and ice would melt during the day, then freeze during the night resulting in ice formations causing movements to be extremely difficult. The *Abruzzi* now replaced the *Aosta* in the line (Caprile, Berretta and Asolone).

December 11

The Col della Berretta was occupied by the K. u. k. Fourth Infantry Division, M. Spinoncia by the German Fifth Infantry Division. Failures were assaults by the German Two-Hundredth Infantry Division on Val Stizzon, while multiple Italian counterattacks failed. Flame throwers silenced machine guns.

December 12

DiGiorgio ordered a counterattack which he assigned to the newly reformed *Alpini* V. Natisone, V. Tagliamento, and M. Rosa Battalions. These troops occupied Hill No. 1476 along the dorsum M. Asolone-Col della Berretta, but not the highest elevations of the latter Hills 1458 and 1424. On the Asolone, units of the 49 *Sturmkompagnie* of *Sturmbataillon 4* (49°, Fourth Division), occupied the summit known as Spiedon (4328 feet). The *Edelweiss,* right wing of the Krauss Group was replaced by the Austro-Hungarian Fourth Infantry Division.

December 13

Returned to the line after only a few hours rest was the *Aosta,* while the *Basilicata* (which had fought on M. Tomba) also returned to the line. The *Modena* replaced the *Massa Carrara* deploying next to the *Alpini* Tolmezzo, Pinerolo and Susa Battalions with all garrisoning the sector downstream between Osteria del Lepre and Col Caprile.

Preceded by heavy shelling, the German Two-Hundredth Infantry Division assaulted the Solaroli dorsum. Approaching via the gutter that separates the spurs of M. Fontanel to the north and M. Valderòa to the south the Germans overcame the *Alpini* V. Cenischia Battalion which had only 120 survivors resulting in the *Alpini* Feltre Battalion position having a naked flank which was later reinforced. M. Fontanel was the only terrain lost. M. Asolone and Col dell Berretta were kept under constant Austro-Hungarian shelling.[33] Austro-German troops occupied the Pyramid Summit (a lesser summit of Hill 1385) which on a certain angle resembled a pyramid. Persistent efforts to take Hill 1385 were unsuccessful. Due to bad weather and combat weariness, the Krauss Group was withdrawn. Its sector was garrisoned by the Austro-Hungarian Fourth Infantry Division (western M. Grappa), the German Two-Hundredth Infantry Division (Fontanasecca-Pèrtica), the German Fifth Division (Fontanasecca), and M. Tomba by the Alpenkorps.

December 14

German attacks on the Valderòa were successfully repulsed by the 38° (*Ravenna*) and the newly arrived 45° which had replaced *Alpini* on the position. Without preparatory shelling the I/8° (*Cuneo),* successfully performed a surprise attack on M. Pèrtica occupied the summit and proceeded to the right toward Osteria del Forcellato and to the left toward Cima Casara.

All this disoriented the Austro-Germans. Shelling the Asolone-Col della Berretta, they steadfastly attacked. Defending were the *Alpini* Susa, Pinerolo, Tolmezzo, and Clapier Battalions which had to redeploy onto Rocce-Anzini-Cà d'Anna-Osteria del Lepre-Hill 1275-Hill 1471-between Col della Berretta and the Asolone. The 49 *Sturmkompagnie* of the Fourth Infantry Division occupied Col Caprile. Attacking officers were so impressed by the strong defenses that when Italian officers were captured here, they were invited to tea and biscuits by the victors.[34] Toward evening, *Lt. Marschall* Ludwig Goiginger assumed command of the right wing of the Krauss Group (Fourth, Ninety-Fourth & Fifty-fifth Infantry Divisions) and was given the task of occupying the Asolone.

Diaz finally realized what Below's plans was namely to surround the *Nave*, then assault it from the west.

On M. Valderòa German troops occupied the summit but units of the 38°, the *Alpini* Feltre and Val Cismon, pushed them off. Large caliber guns shelled the Col Caprile-Asolone-Cà d'Anna sector as the 14° Linz occupied Col Caprile. During the assault four *Alpini* battalions enroute to Col della Berretta for a counterattack were surprised and destroyed.

December 15

Below now decided to again assault M. Asolone and M. Coston with the attack group commanded by Goiginger. Should this be successful, the supply route to the Grappa would be cut off. Assembling artillery pieces here was difficult. The attack on Cà d'Anna was unsuccessful. Eugene ordered an attack on M. Asolone. Further influencing warfare on the Grappa was the news that Russia had surrendered to the Central Powers.

December 16

Italian units (Fifty-ninth Infantry Division) departing from Ca' d'Anna assisted by units of the *Basilicata* assaulted the Col Caprile. Simultaneously, units of the *Modena* (III/42°) and the *Alpini* Courmayeur Battalion assaulted the Col della Berretta along the Asolone dorsum. Heavy counterattacks pushed the Italians further back than their original departure point of Ca' d'Anna to the line at Col Moschin-Col Fenilon resulting in more Italian counterattacks to arrive at the original defensive line showing the see-saw movements of the battle.

In the Val Brenta the Habsburg 49° broke through the defenses of the *Modena* (41°) and *Aosta* (III/5°). The untrained Italians gave way after a big fight but reinforcements sealed the breach.

December 17

Below's diary noted, "We are now in full winter, with the beasts of burden having difficulty climbing due to the ice, and the men have nothing to make a fire with." With rain, cold and snow, the German Two-Hundredth Infantry Division covered by MG 08 and assisted by the WMB assaulted M. Valderòa (known to the enemy as the *Sternkuppe*), the Solaroli and Col dell'Orso, defended by the *Campania* and *Ravenna* reinforced by the *Reggio* and *Como*. Again combat was in a seesaw mode. The War Diary of the *Alpini* Val Cismon Battalion summarized it all, "We resist, the assault is halted." Now it is our turn to counterattack. The terrain is covered with cadavers. For many days up to December 21, repetitive attacks take place, which are minuscule compared to combat on December 17."[35] The battalion performed well and its casualties noted this, from November 14 to December 21 with five officers dead, twenty seven missing and wounded, and 137 soldiers dead with 568 wounded and missing. Today, the XIV Army stated it was suspending the offensive. As Below wrote, "Making a mess after a good operation is typical of the Austro-Hungarians." Assaults on the Solaroli failed as one German author wrote of the attackers "Here your proud waves are smashed."[36] In the assault the WMB reported thirty eight casualties plus twenty one men who had frostbite.

December 18

At dawn, preceded by heavy shelling Goiginger's troops went on the attack from Rocce Anzini to M. Asolone putting a conclusive phase on the battle for the Grappa as the 7° Carinthian suffering 600 casualties occupied the Asolone summit but failed in assaulting Ca'd'Anna which was securely held by the Italian 240° and 42°. Defending Italian troops now dug trenches on the slopes with the enemy 7° Carinthian a few yards above them on the crest. The *Basilicata* and *Modena* were almost wiped out, so that if the enemy counterattacked, they would easily have taken the position, but Habsburg forces were also in poor shape so nothing happened. The Italian deployment went in a semi-circle from Ca'd'Anna to V.S.Lorenzo from the western slopes to south of M. Asolone, arriving on the right slope of Casara Santino in the upper V. Damoro. From here the lines went to the summit of Asolone-Col delle Farine (Hill No. 1490). M. Asolone was finally taken while the Solaroli remained in Italian hands. The Asolone was about 2.5 miles from the Grappa summit and about 1000 feet below it. There were multiple unsuccessful Italian counterattacks resulting in heavy casualties. From the Asolone, part of the main access road to the Grappa was under German control. The last German offensive action was an assault just below M. Casonet which was firmly repulsed by the 135° (*Campania*). A decision now had to be made by the Italians whether to attempt to hold or withdraw. It was to hold.

Disturbed by the non-compliance of his subordinates, Krauss announced that he was going on furlough. As noted soon due to constant clashes with the A.O.K. and emperor on strategy, he was transferred to the Ukraine, a non-combat zone while his talents would be sorely missed in the June 1918 offensive crossing of the Piave by Vienna's troops. It was a well-known fact that the emperor was not a military genius although the sycophants who surrounded him made him feel he was. In addition German as well as Habsburg officers found that the leadership of Arz left much to be desired. FML Alois Klepsch-Kloth von Roden liaison of the A.O.K. to the O.H.L described the chief of staff as a man who was a good corps commander but unable to run the whole army.[37]

December 20

In his diary, Below noted that German cavalry had to chase Austrian deserters roving the country-side. The Alpenkorps left its position on the spur of M. Tomba-Monfenera to be replaced by the Austro-Hungarian Fiftieth Infantry Division. This position would be held for a future spring (1918) offensive. Plumer sent two staff officers to evaluate the loss of the Asolone.[38] They found poorly constructed defenses, troops and reserves poorly deployed with men dying nightly from exposure. Italian troop deployments had at least 70 percent too many in the front line where all machine guns were; the reserve brigades were down in the valleys miles away.[39] There were no communication trenches while front trenches were not deep enough. All this was reminiscent of the *Strafexpedition.* After today, there were no longer any Austro-German offensives while Italian advances were now measured in yards.

Below now realized that with stiffening Italian resistance there would be no dramatic breakthrough, thus there would be no strategic reason to continue the offensive.

December 21

The Supreme War Council in Versailles declared that no more guns should be sent from the Western Front to Italy.[40] Under a heavy snow fall the *Porta Maurizio* failed in its attack on the Asolone. The snow covered bodies of both sides, as Lundendorff ordered his troops back to France.

December 23

Conrad made his final push on the Asiago Plateau occupying Valbella, Col del Rosso and Col d'Echele, but could not break through the Italian defenses. Fayolle informed Foch that the Italians would be able to hold. Like the classic Christmas, there was a heavy snow fall on the day before the holiday. Aware that he had lost 25,000 men on the Grappa and the Melette (Altopiano dei Sette Communi, chapter XI) Cadorna wrote his son that should this continue, the cost would be terrible.[41] In the two Battles of the Grappa, Austro-Hungarian dead were 50,000.[42]

December 25

The Italian XXVII Corps was withdrawn to the plains and replaced by the IX Corps between Col Moschin and the slopes of Asolone (Map 24). The VI Corps remained in the Col delle Farine sector, and the spur north of the *Nave* del Grappa; the same for the XVIII Corps between M. Casonet at the limits of M. Tomba. The French Forty-seventh Infantry Division (Lt. Gen. Dilleman) known as *Chausseurs des Alpes* planned an assault on M. Tomba. It would take place on the end of the month with 197 medium and small caliber artillery mouths, mostly French, sixty eight heavy caliber mouths from the French XXXI Corps plus pieces from the XIV British and XVIII Italian Corps. In all there would be 450 artillery mouths. Defending would be the Austro-Hungarian Fiftieth Infantry Division with ten battalions of the III and XV Mountain Brigades, with three field artillery regiments.

From December 28 to December 29, French artillery shelled M. Tomba-Monfenera sending patrols with instructions to find out what they faced. Moving out in three columns at 1605, the *Chasseurs des Alpes* went on the attack. Italian air reconnaissance photos were made available to French commanders, as well as giving covering fire to the advancing troops.[43] The left wing (LXX Battalion) occupied Hills No. 876 and 879 on M. Tomba; in the center, the CXV Battalion reached and passed the eastern summit; on the right the LI Battalion reoccupied Monfenera in less than one half hour. French losses were fifty four dead, with 205 wounded. In the Italian units there were four dead and ten missing. The Austro-Hungarian Fiftieth Infantry Division lost over 500 dead counted by the French, with forty seven officers, 1,564 soldiers taken as prisoners, as well as cannons and machine guns. Having still not departed, the German Jäger Division was also involved in the battle. It had suffered over one thousand casualties with some battalions down to 200 men. Below ordered a retreat from the line of M. Spinoncia to the southern border of the Quero with advance patrols on the Ornic Creek.

Historians and military strategists have ignored this feat of the *Chausseurs.* There was now no longer any danger of an assault from M. Tomba toward Bassano or Asolo. Should this have occurred the upper Piave and the Montello would have been isolated and Italian defenses would have been attacked in their rear (Maps 35, 40).

The Supreme War Council via Joint Note No. 6 solemnly reported that the Italian Army had shown very considerable powers of resistance, and should be able to hold the line Piave-Grappa-Asiago.

December 26

In a humorous note, British sentries on the Montello were alarmed when enemy troops fired off many rockets. However, it was only Hungarian troops celebrating the feast of St. Stephen the patron saint of Hungary.

With the XIV Army returning to France, the A.O.K. divided up responsibilities in the Conrad Group, with the Eleventh Army receiving two divisions and the Sixth Army also two. Ideally, it would have been better to have one army group with headquarters at Belluno.

December 30

Below received a coded telegram from the O.K.L. ordering him transferred to the Western Front. In his text, Krafft described a meeting with Krauss and Below he had on Nov. 11. The latter stated that he was completely unaware of the construction of military roads on the Grappa, without which the defense would have been impossible. The information that Krauss had given them was over one year old and was incomplete. The XIV Army was unaware of Cadorna's improvements to the *Nave*. Below finally became aware that the enemy was in a fighting mood when the Italians fought tenaciously in the northern Grappa (to gain time to build fortifications) and was notified that the enemy XXVIII Corps (three divisions) was marching toward the battle. There was no success here as there had been on the Isonzo due to the lack of surprise and artillery as well as the change in Italian troop morale. A question was always raised "Attack in the valley or on the peaks?" The answer was "Attack in the valleys and on the peaks." Krauss felt that the best way to break into the plains was to go along the roadways that flanked the Piave and Brenta Rivers later writing that had his orders been carried out, his troops would have arrived at the plains.[44]

Krafft later wrote, "Thus was halted, a short distance from its objective, an offensive rich in hope, and M. Grappa became the sacred mountain of the Italians, who rightfully can be proud to have victoriously defended it against the best Austro-German troops." The battle was fought in the mountains, almost in complete isolation, with all types of supplies lacking except courage on both sides.

The Grappa Battles entered into the Italian psyche with the usual songs as well as some movies. Some words of one especially patriotic song are related.

Monte Grappa tu sei la mia Patria,
sei la stella che addita il cammino,
sei la gloria, il volere, il destino,
che all'Italia ci fa ritornar!

M. Grappa you are my Patria,
you are the star that shows us the way,
you are the glory, the will, the destiny,
which shall make us return home to Italy!

At the end of the battle, on December 18, the commanders of the XVIII and IX Corps, Generals Tettoni and Laderchi respectively, were dismissed. Caviglia wrote, "These two corps on the Grappa wrote several of the most beautiful defensive pages in our war." No one knows why these officers were dismissed. However, it should be remembered that a great number of officers were dismissed during the war. During Cadorna's twenty-nine month stewardship there had been 217 generals, 225 colonels, and 335 other officers dismissed. During the twelve month period of Diaz, there were 176 officers dismissed. By this time the officer corps were younger and started to have more battle experience.

A common complaint of the British troops were inadequate quarters a result of deficient Comando Supremo staff work. Italian officers were unaccustomed to allotting roads and billeting areas so even British officer (who had to sleep fully clothed) accommodations were less than satisfactory.

Jan. 2, 1918

As Maj. Sproesser (WMB), went home on furlough, his main recommendation to his men was to avoid any conflict with Austro-Hungarian troops as serious punishments would result.[45] It seemed that many commanders of the forces of the Central Powers on the Italian Front shared a fear of a conflict between soldiers of the same-language, but different national armies.

Jan 14, 1918

Three Italian columns (mostly troops of the Sixty-Sixth Infantry Division), assaulted M. Asolone. The right column (*Massa Carrara),* was to climb Val Cesilla, the center (22°, *Cremona)* with the left (*Bari,* 139°) proceeding toward Hills 1440 and 1486 west of the Asolone. The offensive was halted by the inability of the *Massa Carrara* to advance together as well as by an enemy counterattack. The 22° occupied Hill 1520 of the

Asolone which was the first success since Caporetto. Several days later it was lost but the morale-boosting effect was there.

Chapter XII Endnotes

The First Battle of the Grappa

1 USSME: Relazione Ufficiale, Vol. IV, Tomo 3° bis, Doc., op. cit., Comando Supremo, *Ordini alla 1a Armata per cessione lavori Grappa alla 4a Armata,* Doc. 129, October 27,1917, Protocol No. 5031, p. 298

2 USSME: Relazione Ufficiale, Volume IV, Tome 3°, op. cit., p. 676.

3 Museo del Risorgimento, Milano, archivio generale, Cadorna, Luigi, plico 1 reg. 48874, *Memoria sui lavori difensivi eseguiti sul Grappa prima di Caporetto,* signed by Gen. Antonio Del Fabbro. There is no date, but it was between March and June 1922. Cadorna was given a copy to read and wrote comments in the margins.

4 Krauss, A. *Die Ursachen unserer Niederlage*, Munich, Lehmann, 1923, p. 238

5 Kraft, op. cit., p. 612

6 USSME: Relazione Ufficiale, Vol. IV, Tomo 3° bis, Doc., op. cit., Comando 4a Armata, *Occupazione del Tomatico e del Roncone,*10-11 November 1917, Documents 232,2333, Protocols 11976, 15075, pp. 472,474

7 AUSSME: War Diary of the Italian Fourth Army, Vol. 18e, rep. b1, enclosures

8 USSME: Relazione Ufficiale, Vol. IV, Tomo 3° bis, Doc., op. cit., Comando XVIII Corpo d'Armata, *Ordini per il ripiegamento delle Divisioni 15a, 51a, 56a,* Document 172, Protocol 2279,November 3, 1917, p. 368

9 OULK, Volume VI, *Das Kriegsjahr 1917,*op. cit., p. 661.

10 Krafft, Vol. II, op. cit., p. 213

11 OULK, Vol. VI, op. cit., p. 661

12 AUSSME, Rome. War Diary of V. Tagliamento defending the Grappa, Nov. 14 to Nov. 28, 1917

13 OULK, Volume VI, op. cit., p. 666

14 Below's diary, entry of Nov. 15, 1917; The OULK notes that this happened on November 16, 1917.

15 Erwin Rommel, *Infanterie greift an,* Ludwig, Boggenreiter Verlag, Potsdam, 1941

16 Below's Diary, entry of 11-21-17

17 USSME: Relazione Ufficiale, Vol. IV Tomo 3° bis, Doc., op. cit.,Comando 4a Armata *Ripartizione dei tratti di fronte assegnati ai Commandi sulla linea del Grappa,* Doc. 238, Protocol No. 12927, November 22, 1917, p. 487; Idem, Comando 4a Armata, *Dislocazione dei comandi e formazione della 4a Armata alla sera del 22 novembre, 1917,* Document No. 237, November 22, 1917, p. 485

18 Clemente Assum, *La Prima Difesa del Grappa,* Torino, Gobetti, 1924

19 Erwin Rommel, *Infanterie greift an,* op. cit.,p. 396.

20 OULK: Vol. VI, op. cit., p. 688

21 Sproesser, Theodor, *Die Geschichte der Würrtemberg Gebirgbsschützen* Chr. Belser AG, Verlagbuchhandlung, Stuttgart, 1933, p. 326

22 Krafft, Vol II op. cit., p. 212.

23 Max Ronge, *Kriegs und Industrie Espionage, Zwölf Jahre Kund Schaftsdienst,* Zurich, Vienna, 1930, p. 315.

24 OULK : Vol. VI, op. cit., p. 676

25 M. Schwarte, *Der grosse Krieg 1914-1918,* Five volumes, Leipzeig, 1922., Vol. V p. 450

26 Ibid, p. 451.

27 OBARI, op. cit. p. 100

28 Ibid, p. 688

29 OBARI, op. cit., p. 110

30 OBARI op. cit., p. 110; Duchêne was rotated back to the Western Front to command the French Sixth Army, and on Dec. 17, was succeeded by Lt. Gen. Maistre.

31 OBARI, op. cit., p. 117

32 OULK*:* Vol. VI, op. cit., p. 688

33 Ibid, p.693

34 Heinz von Lichen, Alessandro Massignani, Marcello Maltauro, Enrico Acerbi, *L'Invasione del Grappa,* Gino Rossato Editore, Valdagno, 1993, p.310

35 USSME :Roma, War Diary, *Alpini* Battalion, V. Cismon Dec. 17 to Dec 21, 1918.

36 Rango, Ralf von, *Das Jäger Nr. 3,* Buchdruckeerie und Verlagsanstalt, Anton Dreselly, Munich, 1929, p. 330

37 Peter Brourcek, *Chef des Generalstabes und Oberstter Kriegsheer. Aus den Erinnerungen des Feldmarschalleutnants Alois Klepsch-Kloth von Roden, k.u.k.*

Delegierten im Deutschen Grossen Hauptquartier 1915/1918. Mitteilungen des Österreichischen Staatsarchiv, Bd. 27, 1974, pp. 395; 385-401

38 OBARI, op. cit., p. 116

39 Idem

40 The Official History of the Great War, Military Operations France and Belgium, Vol. I Imperial War Museum, London, pp. 57-59, Joint Note No. 3; the report noted that Marshal Cadorna was a member. This was in error. Cadorna was finally made a Marshal of Italy by Mussolini in 1924.

41 L. Cadorna, *Lettere famigliare,* op. cit., p. 250

42 Heinz von Lichem et al. *L'Invasione del Grappa,* op. cit., Gino Rossato Editore, Valdagno, 1993, p. 145

43 *La Grande Guerra Aerea 1915-1918*, Edited by Paolo Ferrari, Gino Rossati Editore Valdagno,1994, p. 40

44 OULK, Volume VI, op. cit., p. 695.

45 Sproesser, T., *Die Geschichte,* op. cit., p. 344

CHAPTER XIII

THE FIRST BATTLE OF THE PIAVE, November, 1917

About one quarter of Italian troops reached the western bank of the Piave. Pursuing them were fifty divisions and 4,500 cannons. The dangerous sector was from the Astico River to the Adriatic (Map 35). The Italians had to hold here or lose their country. Boroevic's troops crossed the Piave at the Zenson loop but had to eventually withdraw.

Freeze, freeze thou bitter sky,
thou dost bite so nigh
As benefits forgot:
Thy sting is not so sharp
As friend remembered not.
Wm. Shakespeare "As You Like It"

THE PIAVE RIVER with its meandering, large river bed and many islands, signals the change from the mountains to the plains, as it marches to the Adriatic Sea. Starting at M. Peralba in the Trentino, it marches always in a southern direction surrounded by lagoons just before emptying into the sea (Maps 29,35). In the eastern foothills of the Grappa and the western extremity of the Bellunese PreAlps, the river breaks into the plains at the Quero Gorge, and progressively widens its river bed, flowing toward Vidor, with an ample curve from the southeast (Maps 24,40). Two bends followed along an axis to the southeast as its flow was slowed by the tortoise-shape of the Montello where it rose 1,100 feet. From there it proceeded on its northern bank to the *Quartier de Piave*, with the flattening strip of Sernaglia and the splendid region between Valdobbiadene, Soligo and Refrontolo Creeks, which flowed slowly toward Conegliano (Map 40). Here the river was over two miles wide containing many channels. In many areas of the river there were *grave* which were shingle (stone), beds which had acquired a vegetation coat forming an island which upon enlarging a name. One (Grave di Papadopoli), had belonged to a Venetian family of Greek extraction and had tactical significance during the war. At the eastern extremity of the Montello with Nervesa to the south and Falzè to the north, the Piave ran in a southeastern direction always with high embankments (Maps 32,40). It continued its flow southward and finally emptied into the area north of the Venetian lagoon as well as the lagoon. Eighty years have passed with the seaward side of the river no longer appearing as it did in 1917. The swamps have been drained eliminating the malaria problem while the delta is now a luxury area of bathing for Europe's elite. In the fall of 1917, its width varied greatly. At the Montello it was about two hundred-seventy-five yards wide, while a few miles to the north it was one mile wide. To the south at the island of Grave di Papadopoli it was two miles wide. There were now three theatres of operation the Piave, the massive rock formation known as the Grappa and the Altopiano dei Sette Communi (Asiago Plateau). Italian troops were deployed with six divisions between the Astico and Brenta Rivers (Map 35).[1] There were seven divisions (IV Army), from the Brenta to and including the Montello, eight divisions (III Army) from Nervesa to the Adriatic (Map 40).

Italian IV Army troops were deployed in the mountains in the upper course of the Tagliamento in an east-west direction. To withdraw they had to go down the Piave Valley past Longarone and Belluno (Map 40). DiRobilant had neglected to start his withdrawal on October 27, but on page 377 is noted why he delayed. In reserve were four divisions of the II Army. The Austro-Germans had: (Map 40)

> Adriatic to the Brenta River; Boroevic with twenty divisions
> XIV Army with fourteen divisions
> Astico River to the Brenta: Conrad seven divisions

Against the Grappa, the XIV Army had four divisions while on the Piave, it had fourteen divisions. In all there were thirty Austro-German divisions along the Piave, against eleven Italian, with eleven divisions in the mountains opposing a like number of Italians divisions.

Defending Italian troops now had fire in their belly. In fighting on the Isonzo (today Soca) River they had been beyond the national borders. Now the enemy was at the Italian borders. The peasant infantry had been indoctrinated that this was the Italian border, the door to their home. They wanted to slam the door in the enemy's face and they did. To better understand the battle the river shall be divided into geographic sectors.

The Upper Piave

The Austro-Germans were preoccupied with the news that many Anglo-French Divisions were on their way to the Piave. Intelligence had reported the arrival of twenty Anglo-French divisions totaling 360,000 men and 400 guns.[2] If the river could not be crossed in a frontal assault, a maneuver similar to the crossing of the Tagliamento would have to occur. The mountains to the northwest would have to be crossed before attacking the rear of Italian troops deployed on the river. On November 10, the Twelfth Silesians tried to take the bridgehead at Vidor, but were repulsed by *Alpini* and *Arditi* troops who blew the bridge (Map 40).

The attackers were now outrunning their supplies.[3] The rail head was at S. Lucia di Tolmino, after which supplies were sent by truck to the battle area (Maps 14,35, 40). The railway from Gorizia to Udine and Codroipo was for Boroevic's armies (Map 35). Another rail line from Tarvisio to Udine was slowly being reactivated (Map 40). As Clausewitz had written "The friction of war" took place with all plans of the attackers being upset.[4] Below's forces had advanced over one hundred miles. Supplies arrived after taking one week through the terrible mountain roads. It would take fifteen days for enough supplies (11,000 tons) to arrive at the Piave for a three-day offensive.[5] Only 750 tons could be accumulated. There were not enough men to break through in addition to which Conrad's attack would not meet with success (Map 14 A).[6] Consideration was given to using the railroad which ran to Vittorio (Veneto), but this would not be ready until December. The roadway to the north in the Valsugana was also considered but it would be full of Conrad's troops. Finally, the railway along Val Belluna was briefly considered but discarded as all the bridges along it had been blown. Instead, convinced to advance, on November 11 Eugene gave the order to cross the river and advance to the southwest. The Krauss Group would remain with the XIV Army, advancing between the Brenta and Piave Rivers (Map 40). On November 14, Stein Group forces (Twelfth Silesian and Thirteenth Schützen Divisions) failed in two crossing attempts at Vidor (Map 40). The river narrowed here and was crossed by a stone bridge which had been partially destroyed by the Italians. Krafft later wrote that the lack of heavy artillery, which had been sent back to France, and the lack of pontoon bridges which were to have been brought by the A.O.K. from Romania, led to unsuccessful attempts.[7] Actually, the *I Isonzo Armée* was proceeding carrying pontoon bridges. Informed of this Boroevic immediately ordered them to be left behind as munitions were more valuable to carry. Both he and Below felt that only a strong organized attack would yield a successful crossing. Berendt ordered the artillery of the Scotti Group to be brought closer to the river, to support the Krauss Group. It was now time to regroup and await developments in Conrad's Group in the mountains which was to attack on November 10 but was delayed due to heavy fog and snow enveloping the Grappa.[8],[9] The weather became the Comando Supremo's new ally forcing the Conrad Group back to Asiago.[10] Meanwhile the men of the Krauss Group were down to fifty cartridges per man, while the artillery had thirty shells per mouth.[11]

November 9

As noted previously Diaz, Foch and Wilson met for the first time. After negotiations the French assigned Duchêne to Brescia west of Lago di Garda (Maps 29, 43 for geography). The Italian III Corps and two French divisions at Brescia were placed under his command. Another French division was at Vicenza with the other at Garda. British troops were deployed near Mantua, while other French units were near the Bacchiglione River to the rear of the Piave (Map 35). Next day the Austro-Hungarian Twenty-eighth Infantry Division occupied Grave di Papadopoli Island in the Piave (Maps 33,40).

The Lower Piave

November 12

Units of the Forty-fourth Schützen Division reached the right bank of the Piave, and occupied the curve which the river takes at Zenson (Maps 33, 40). The *Catania* was successful in containing the occupied position. Repeated attacks by the *Pinerolo* were unsuccessful in ousting the attackers.[12] The three divisions of the Italian IV Corps (Fifteenth, Fifty-first and Fifty-sixth Infantry Divisions) finally reached their destination on the Grappa.[13] In walking to their assigned positions, M. Tomatico (5,000 feet), M. Peurna (4,200 feet),and M. Roncone (3,600 feet), they had encountered no interference from Krobatin's X Army (Map 24).[14] Aosta had already elaborated orders for troops of the II Army to use bridges over the Piave.[15]

November 13

Preceded by heavy shelling, the Twenty-eighth Infantry (Austro-Hungarian II Corps) attacked from Cimadolmo toward Grave di Papadopoli (Map 38 for geography). After destroying the bridge, the Italians retreated to the right bank at Salettuol.[16] The Austro-Hungarian XXIII Corps with its Tenth Infantry Division attempted to cross via barges at Musilie and Intestadura but were repulsed by units of the Italian 139° which took many prisoners (Map 33). Commanding the defenders was Col. Gioacchino Nastasi, who had been in command of the fortifications on the Sabotino. At Grisolera near the sea, an attack forced the Italian 140° to withdraw to the line of *Piave Vecchio* with a bridgehead at Caposile (Map 33).[17] The Italians now had their backs to the edge of the Venetian lagoon which was garrisoned by sailors of the Venetian garrison known as the *Piazza Marittima*. Four battalions of the San Marco Naval Regiment guarded the mouth of the Piave.

Into the battle line were now placed two battalions of the *Granatieri di Sardegna* detached from the Fourth Infantry Division and assigned to the Italian XXIII Corps. All enemy attacks were repulsed. As a result of the destruction of the pumps the swampy terrain between *Piave Nuovo* (new) and the *Piave Vecchio* (old) was flooded (Map 33). It remained so until June 1918.

Brig. Gen. Charles Delmé-Radcliffe, Chief of the British Military Mission in Italy dispatched a note to the Lt. Gen. Sir William Robertson (Chief of the Imperial General Staff), noting that the Austrians had crossed at Zenson on the previous day, and had not been thrown back. Both the king and Diaz were apprehensive.[18] Eventually they were thrown back.[19]

November 14

German heavy guns had been rotated back to the French Front. Both Kaisers enjoyed the pleasure of a victory with Wilhelm visiting the Italian Front and Charles inspecting troops in Trieste.

Robertson sent a note to the War Cabinet warning against depleting Britain's manpower to assist Italy. He felt that with Russia out of the war, Germany would throw all her divisions against the Anglo-French forces on the Western Front alluding to the shaky French situation (army mutinies) and stretching the British forces too thin.

Finally, he did not feel that the Italian Army was capable of rising and fighting again recommending that Britain cut her losses.[20]

Next day in the Piave Delta sector, the *Honvéd* Forty-first Infantry Division crossed the river and occupied Cava Zuccherina (today called Jesolo) which was fifteen miles from the Venice Lagoon.

November 16

At Salletuol Austro-Hungarian attempts to reach the west bank of the Piave met with failure leaving 300 prisoners (Map 33).[21] Preceded by heavy shelling, the Twenty-fourth Infantry Division (XXIVCorps) assaulted Candelú while the Sixty-fourth Infantry Division attacked at Ponte di Piave (Map 33). Simultaneously farther west there was to be a massive crossing of the Piave, by the Hofacker and Stein Groups with Treviso as the objective (Map 40). The Austro-Germans crossed the river at Casa Folina near Candelú but were repulsed by units of the *Lecce* (266°) later crossing at Fagarè spreading out, attempting to attack S. Bartolomeo from the west (Map 33). Maj. Santo Ceccherini organized a counterattack with the 18° Bersaglieri and a battalion of the 153° (*Novara*). The Italian III Army added the 268° (*Caserta*). Launching an attack, the Italians re-occupied the right bank and took five hundred prisoners.

Referring to this battle Gioacchino Volpe wrote, "Side by side, fighting here were found the old veterans from the Carso, who had undertaken an orderly redeployment, survivors of beaten units, who had asked for a rifle, and new recruits of the class of '99, who via trucks had just arrived bedecked with flowers, with the songs and speeches still in their ears. They all attacked together and died bravely when needed. This day at Fagarè plus the victory at Ponte di Piave were much-needed victories to lift the morale of the troops (Map 38 for geography). There was hope, faith, and a strong will, diffusing throughout the troops, with the words 'They shall not pass, they shall not pass, were stated over and over."[22]

Also involved was the Italian Navy. In February, Admiral Thaon de Revel had taken over the navy from the Duke of Abruzzi (the Aosta Duke's brother). The A.O.K. had placed several large ships along the coast to shell Italian troops deployed on the river. In the swampy waters of the Venice Lagoon the *Balaton* and *Novara* were shelled by Italian artillery on mobile platforms in the waters forcing them to withdraw. Later, using torpedoes, Italian MAS attacked the Austrian battleships *Wien* and *Budapest* in the Adriatic where they were supporting the crossing of Imperial troops forcing them to leave the scene. A few days later the *Wien* was sunk while at anchorage in the port of Trieste by Commander Luigi Rizzo aboard his MAS.

Prior to leaving on the November 24 Plumer and Foch authorized Diaz to deploy their troops on the Piave and Montello if needed.

November 29

Eugene accepted the halting of the offensive hoping to bring the battle line from between the Brenta and Piave to the line between the Montello and Bassano (Maps 35,40). As Krafft later wrote, "Going further would offer risks which were more than the results, and therefore, with the recommendation of Below, the offensive was suspended." Combat activity died down on the river which flowed along the Montello's northern border then went southeast to the flatlands. Along the banks were steep cliffs. Facing the British XIV Corps were the German One-Hundred-Seventh Infantry and the Habsburg Thirteenth Schützen Divisions. On December 3 the French Sixty-fifth and Forty-seventh Infantry Divisions entered the line to the left of the British. Strange as it may seem, there was a lack of interpreters which was filled by Italian soldiers who had emigrated to the U.S.A. and returned home to fight per request of their family.[24] On December the Comando Supremo made a sad assessment of its aviation situation.[25]

The Anglo-French troops allowed Italian troops to rest and also allowed the Comando Supremo to assemble a reserve unit to be used as needed. This would be the XXV, I, XXVIII and XXX Corps while the reconstructed VI and XXVII Corps were assigned to the IV Army. A significant gesture by Plumer which showed that he was a better diplomat than general (he has been called the best British general on the Western Front), was to request that Diaz his inspect troops. This was a great morale booster for Italian troops which were still in shock after the debacle. However, it was difficult to make Italian staff officers understand that orders must be obeyed, even those which one does not like. Fearing enemy troops coming through the mountain passes, Allied troops considered defending them, but then realized that with winter coming, they did not have the correct mountain gear. Plumer told Diaz that even if the Italians withdrew, his troops would remain on the Piave to fight. On December 14, he reported to Robertson that he was "distinctly hopeful."

The Comando Supremo now started to assemble stragglers, newly enlisted, recently wounded discharged from hospitals in a vast camp about seventy miles behind the lines at Mantua and Modena all collectively called the Italian V Army.

December 5

The French XXXI Corps replaced the Italian IX Corps deploying the Forty-seventh Infantry Division, *Chasseurs des Alpes* and the Sixty-fifth Infantry Division near Monfenera and the

Sixty-fourth Infantry Division in reserve (Map 24). The British XIV Corps replaced the Italian I Corps, deploying the Seventh, Twenty-third and Forty-first Infantry Divisions on the Montello between Ciano and Nervesa along with British and Italian artillery on the Montello which was like a little mound with cartways (not roadways) going in a north-south direction (Maps 32, 35, 40).[26] At this point the river was about one-half mile wide with dense vegetation on its banks. Over 300,000 men had been lost as prisoners so far in the Italian Army.[27]

The *II Armée Isonzo* occupied the island of Papadopoli but did not reach the far bank (Maps 33, 40). After the Piave, the next defensive line corresponded to the Mincio-Adige Rivers (Maps 29, 35).[28] Should a withdrawal beyond the Piave be necessary defenses east of Verona would be abandoned as had been planned since the days of Italian Army Chief of the General Staff Enrico Cosenz.[29] To the west (Lago di Garda sector), *Alpini* units permanently stationed there would have to hold the line. With its concave shape, the Adige lent itself to a counterattack at the appropriate moment. Now there was a procession of foreign diplomats going to Rome to find out about the spirit of the Rome government. All were deluged with charts, maps, and talks and it was hoped that all would understand that Italy would fight on. Meanwhile in the front lines, the calls were emanating for the exhausted troops to be replaced. There was a tremendous disagreement between the military (who had not been informed of diplomatic moves) and the government which had guaranteed the safety of allied troops on the Italian Front.

A long discussion took place in the highest military and political circles regarding the line of last resistance. Prime Minister Orlando was for the line at the Mincio-Adige Rivers while Cadorna liked the Piave (Map 35 for Adige River). The troops were exhausted and needed rest. The Anglo-French arrivals would be welcomed if they could be allowed to go into combat. On On November 15 Foch telegraphed Paris that the Italian Army had good defensive positions and that the morale of the Italian soldier had been lifted.

By now Allied troops were now arriving in large numbers and were deployed as follows:

FRENCH FORCES
TENTH ARMY

Sent was the staff of the Tenth Army and the staff of the XXXI Corps with the Forty-sixth, Forty-seventh, Sixty-fourth and Sixty-fifth Divisions as well as groups of French heavy artillery still in Italy but on the way back to France.[30] Eighty percent were rotated back to France in a few weeks.

Commander: General Duchêne
Chief of Staff: Col. Brion
Artillery: Heavy, Field and Mountain to be attached to XII and XXXI Corps

Deployed at Verona

Forty-sixth (*Chasseur*, General Levi) and
Forty-seventh (*Chasseur*, General Dilleman) Divisions

XXXI Corps (General Rozée d'Infreville)

Brescia : Sixty-fourth Infantry Division (General Colin), west of Lago di Garda (Map 14A)
Lago di Garda to Chiese: Sixty-fifth Infantry Division (General Blondin)

XII Corps (General Nourrisson) would arrive later comprising:

Twenty-third Infantry Division (General Bonfait)
Twenty-fourth Infantry Division (General Odry)

British divisions were deployed near Mantua.[31] They were:

BRITISH FORCES IN ITALY

Commander: Lt. Gen. Sir Herbert Plumer

XI Corps

Consisted of auxiliary troops, Signal, Supplies, Corps School etc. Arrived December 1, 1917, returned to France March 13, 1918

XIV Corps:

Arrived in Italy November 5, 1917, became G.H.Q. Italy on April 18, 1918

Fifth Infantry Division:

Arrived in Italy November 27, 1917
Left for Western Front April 1-9, 1918

Seventh Infantry Division: (Major Gen. T.H. Shoubridge)

Arrived in Italy, November 17, 1917
Demobilized in Italy 1919

Twenty-third Infantry Division : (Major Gen. Sir J.M. Babington)

Arrived in Italy, November 6-16, 1917
Demobilized in Italy, March 1919

Forty-first Infantry Division : (Major Gen. Sir S.T. B. Lawford)

Arrived in Italy, November 16, 1917
Returned to Western Front, March 1, 1918

Forty-eighth Infantry Division : (Major Gen. R. Fanshawe)

Arrived in Italy November 22, 1917
Demobilized in Italy, March 31, 1919

December 9, 1917

With a sudden attack, the Austro-Germans occupied the bridgehead at Capo Sile, but lost it to units of *Arditi* and the *Arezzo* (Map 33).[32] As previously noted the *Pinerolo* had been unsuccessful in eliminating the enemy bridgehead at Zenson. Later, due to intense artillery fire, it was evacuated so that by January 1, 1918, the whole of the right bank of the Piave was in Italian hands. The A.O.K. now realized what the Twelfth Battle was all about.[33]

Chapter XIII Endnotes

The First Battle of the Piave

1 USSME: Relazione Ufficiale, Vol. IV Tomo 3° bis, Doc., op. cit., Comando 4a Armata, *Sbarramento provenienze dal Brenta,* Doc. 235, Protocol 12476/1, Nov. 16, 1917, p. 483

2 Kriegsarchiv, Vienna, *Manuskripte,* Weltkrieg, 1918, Series "J", Italy, No. 18, Brigadier General Anton von Pitreich, *Die k.u.k. Piavefront,* Part I, p. 11-14.

3 Cramon, op. cit. p. 130

4 Clausewitz, Karl von, *Vom Krieg* (On War) eds. Michael Howard and Petere Paret (Princeton University Press, 1984)

5 Krafft, op. cit., Vol. II, p. 237

6 Alfred Krauss: *Das Wunder von Karfreit* (Munich 1926) p. 202-203

7 Arz, *Geschichte des Grossen Kriegs,* op. cit. p. 182

8 Krafft, op. cit., Vol. II, p. 199

9 Ibid, p. 203

10 Ibid, p. 203

11 Ibid, p. 206-07

12 Ibid, p. 577

13 USSME: Relazione Ufficiale, Vol. IV, Tomo 3° bis, Doc., Comando XVIII C.A. *Disposizione per ripiegamento delle Divisioni 15a, 51a, 56a,* Doc. No. 172, Protocol No. 2279, November 3, 1917, p. 370

14 Ibid, p. 559-560

15 USSME: Relazione Ufficiale, Vol. IV, Tomo 3°, bis, Doc., op. cit., Comando 3a Armata, *Uso dei Ponti sul Piave pel passaggio della 2a Armata,* Doc. No. 210, Protocol No. 10104, November 8, 1917, p. 423

16 Ibid, p. 577

17 Ibid, p. 577

18 PRO: WO 106/797 : Telegram Delmé-Radcliffe to Chief of the Imperial General Staff, No. 669.

19 OULK Vol. VI, p. 611

20 PRO: WO 106/796, Robertson to the War Cabinet, Nov. 14, 1917, (0.1/131/376)

21 Ibid, p. 578.

22 See Gioachino Volpe *Ottobre 1917, Dall'Isonzo al Piave,* Milano 1930

23 OULK: Vol. VI, p. 676

24 OBARI, op.cit., p. 106

25 USSME: Relazione Ufficiale, Vol. IV, Tomo 3°, bis, Doc., op. cit., *Situazione e dislocazione delle forze aeronautiche a fine dicembre 1917,* Doc., No. 244, p. 497

26 USSME: Relazione Ufficiale, Vol. IV, Tomo 3° bis, Doc., Comando Supremo, *Direttive per lo schieramento delle artiglierie sul Montello,* Doc. No. 173, Protocol No. 5321, November 4, 1917, p. 371

27 USSME: Relazione Ufficiale, Volume IV, Tomo 3° bis, op. cit., p. 521; This must be an error as the figure was much more approaching 600,000 which will be noted.

28 USSME: Relazione Ufficiale, Vol. IV Tomo 3° bis, Doc., op. cit., Comando Supremo, *Direttive per il ripiegamento sulla linea Mincio-Po,* Doc. 214, Protocol 5565, November 12, 1917, p. 433

29 USSME: *Relazione della Commissione per lo studio della sistemazione a defesa nel teatro della guerra nord-est,* 26,27, Novembre 1880

30 OBARI, op. cit., p. 59

31 OBARI, op. cit., Appendix I, p. 388-89

32 OULK*:* Vol. VI, p. 667

33 OULK: VII, p. 557

CHAPTER XIV

A CRITIQUE OF THE EVENTS IN OCTOBER-NOVEMBER 1917 ON THE ISONZO FRONT

Warfare in the fall of 1917 on the Isonzo was of a type unknown to the Italian Army which had only been trained in the frontal infantry attack. Using new tactics, the Austro-Germans infiltrated Italian lines creating havoc in the rear confusing the peasant infantry. Italian generals could not quickly react to enemy advances, resulting in defenses crumbling throughout while morale hit rock bottom. Depending on the side of the trench blame for poor results could easily be spread from Cadorna to Boroevic to Charles as well as to Ludendorff.

Military history, accompanied by sound criticism,
Is indeed the true school of war.

Antoine Henri Jomini

RECENTLY A MULTITUDE of books have been published in Italian in the past few years concerning what happened at Caporetto. One would wonder why they had not been published before, the obvious answer being that in a nation of thirty six million with a huge illiteracy rate who would read the book? When a book was published, the printing runs were low, so it quickly went out of print. With the advent of Fascism and its quest of army support, any criticism of the generals would lead to severe punishment as some authors found out.[1]

A whole new type of warfare called *blitzkrieg* (as British newspapers would call it during the Second World War) led to a devastating defeat and an almost battle of annihilation that October 1917 on the Isonzo. Fortunately the Austro-Hungarians had limited objectives but should the plan of the local German commanders have succeeded it would have led to a battle of annihilation. Using deception, speed, boldness and aggressiveness the Austro-Germans kept the Comando Supremo confused as to their intentions. At Caporetto officers were taught by Krafft that movement brought victory an idea to which Guderian subscribed twenty years later.[2] Subsequently the German Army adopted the credo that "only movement brings victory."[3] Caporetto illustrated the fact that no longer could a commander simply look at the battlefield and decide how to deploy his troops from his comfortable rear echelon position. He should be near the forefront of his troops ready to make the immediate necessary decisions. He would need intelligence either from agents or aviation. He would have to guesstimate where the enemy would strike next and prepare accordingly. Cadorna did none of these. Rommel learned these precepts at Caporetto and illustrated them magnificently in France and North Africa in the Second World War. Reports of the Caporetto campaign in the English language have been Anglocentric resulting in little meaningful writings in this language. An excellent report was done by Krafft, so much so that it was incorporated into the Official German Army Report. Fearing retribution Italian authors did not complete any writings during the Fascist period. Later authors have written fragemented reports. The Royal Caporetto Inquiry Commission attempted to find those at fault on the Isonzo, but instead blamed no one and produced a cover-up as shall be discussed. The author feels that there was plenty of blame to spread around from Cadorna to the troops to Ludendorff to the Krauss Group. Warfare was in two completely distinct theatres of operation, the mountains and the plains. A breakthrough on either would imperil troops in the other sector. The first was hampered by lack of roads, elevated altitude and bitter cold. In the second lack of railways and poor roads impeded any significant advance as supplies could not be brought forward. Strange as it may seem *fanti* fighting alongside *Alpini* at high altitudes were not issued the essential mountain clothing until 1918. During non-winter months intense heat and malaria affected those fighting down on the plains.

At the time, Italy was worse than a Third World country. Its army had experience only in chasing bandits in Calabria or Sicily and Bedouin tribesmen in Libya. There early in 1915 the army had suffered a severe defeat at the hands of the Arabs[4] which almost led to the dismissal of Cadorna avoided only because of the imminence of war. The embarrassment and humiliation was considered equal to Adua the severe Italian military defeat in Ethiopia. The Comando Supremo was surprised by the enemy's moves that October on the Isonzo and unable to react or accurately predict the enemy's moves. Fortunately the A.O.K. as well as Ludendorff had a limited objective otherwise the Italian army would have been annihilated. Italian industry was almost non-existent. The dialect-speaking only *fanti* did not have any barbed wire cutting tools. As Nasser found out years later, you cannot take an illiterate Bedouin off a camel and place him at the controls of a tank or jet fighter. First you have to teach him how to read and write. Only by the Tenth Battle of the Isonzo did the corps commander start to check to see if the barbed wire fence was cut prior to the infantry assault. Italian officers thought that soldiers were like supernatural warriors who due to loyalty to their commanders would be killed without feeling pain. Lidell Hart summed it up by noting that the endless frontal attacks against machine guns had a crippling effect on troop morale.[5] Large and medium caliber artillery mouths were lacking, a deficiency which was made up by the lives of the *fanti.* Linking this feature to massive firepower brought enormous successes in the Second World War. Up to 1914 generals had calculated one man one bullet. Now with the "force multiplier" of machine guns and quick-firing artillery, this was no longer the case. Heavy fire-power could be brought to bear in one sector with devastating effect.

However the concept of massive overwhelming local fire power was not a new one. One century prior Napoleon had assembled many cannons opposite a certain spot which would be shelled creating a breach in the enemy's defenses through which his infantry would pour through. Further back in history during the Thirteenth Century the Teutonic Knights would go on the attack in a wedge-shaped formation called a "pig's snout." Five mounted lancers would ride at the apex of a triangle followed by seven in the second line, nine in the third line etc. always in increasing numbers. Infantry was deployed to the rear of the wedge ready to push through the breach created. The principle of tremendous firepower was not a new one but the Germans added a few wrinkles to confuse the enemy in October, 1917 and would do so again against Anglo-French forces in France in May, 1940.

Literally minutes before the enemy offensive, Italian troops were being shifted around giving them no time to acquaint themselves with the terrain or with flanking friendly troops. Advised not to continue this, the Comando Supremo kept doing it anyway.[6] Confusion existed even in the artillery inventory. In a nation that had invented double-entry bookkeeping, a unit's inventory would state that it had a certain number of artillery mouths assigned, but actually had half that. Ludendorff agreed to lend German troops and artillery but limited the time frame to use them as well as how far Below could advance. The Italian Army lacked national identity. Most of the troops were illiterate, not even knowing what Italy was. Millions had emigrated from the Italian boot to the Americas. If they did not present themselves for duty in the far-flung Italian Consulates the family home would have a poster affixed declaring that a deserter lived there. Hundreds of thousands of men returned to serve as thousands died for a nation they did not know existed and a king who looked like them. If a man lived in a dirt floored hovel, with no plumbing, electric or other conveniences, what could one expect from him? Like any executive or general, the Generalissimo should have checked to see if his orders were carried out. Authors have written that Cadorna would check whether his orders were carried out, but this author emphatically disagrees with this statement.[7] He was an aristocratic martinet who enforced severe disciplinary measures only on the lower rank troops while ignoring discipline infractions of his generals. Two of these, Badoglio and Capello blatantly disregarded his orders leading to the debacle, but with no serious consequences to themselves. DiRobilant delayed in withdrawing his forces toward the Grappa, but apparently was working on a plan to fortify the Cadore region. Men of his rank were simply dismissed. The RICC reported 307 colonels and generals dismissed while in the first ten months of 1917, ten corps commanders were replaced. Once the Generalissimo's mind-set was made up one could not change it. Playing with his model of the battlefield located in his office, he never had contact with his troops thinking only of establishing winter quarters and rejecting all intelligence as useless. A tornado was approaching him and he had not the slightest notion of its arrival. The Comando Supremo was not aware (nor did it care) of troop tiredness and low morale all leading to huge desertions, nor how the severe disciplinary measures contributed to these factors. Italian Intelligence and enemy deserters had fully informed him of the offensive, but he still would not believe it. Russian Intelligence informed him of the withdrawal of Habsburg troops from their front to his. German troops had been noted on his front. No provisions were made for a defense in depth as the Germans had done (their famous *Segenstoss auf den Tiefe)*, whereby entire divisions were to be used to counterattack. Reserves were not accurately placed. The Comando Supremo was paralyzed by the enemy's quick movements and could not react fast enough. Errors of May 1916 (lack of linkup between the Val Sugana and the altipiani (Map 3), in the Trentino were repeated on the Isonzo in Oct., 1917 (lack of linkup between the Zona Carnia and the II Army). Wishing to do everything himself and fearing being criticized by knowledgeable subordinates, he used his Vice Chief of Staff and Operations Chief as bureaucratic paper shufflers. Ideally, there should have been an Army Group Command in the Trentino sector but Cadorna was very jealous and would not give anyone authority. When the Generalissimo finally realized what the enemy was up to it was too late to move any troops.

He could have simply ordered persistent air reconnaissance of the sectors involved which would have allowed him to *déchirer le voile* of the enemy, but he did not believe in the air arm. He resembled the proverbial farming grandfather in the twentieth century who would have nothing to do with telephones, autos, television, airplanes or radio, and stuck with his horse and buggy, ignoring all the modern inventions. There was only one assault mode the *attacco frontale* usually with the bayonet, which had been eclipsed at Gettysburg fifty years prior. His army had one foot in Waterloo-style warfare with the other exposed to quick-firing artillery, machine guns and airplanes, but not really appreciating their value. Generals of his era "knew everything" while those of today go to school constantly to learn what can help them be better officers. The debacle was a tale of Italian units being attacked during their march to the battlefield positions or as soon as they arrived, exhausted, uncoordinated, scattered, lacking trenching tools and artillery support. It also was a tale of disheartened troops feeling the war was over, surrendering *en masse* to the Austro-Germans. In any army it is the Second Lt. and Non-Com who made sure that the army performs its assigned tasks. In correspondence with Capello, Cadorna had referred to the lack of Non-Coms (Vol. I, chapter XXXIII). Soon after the outbreak of the war the Comando Supremo instituted the rank of *Aspirante Ufficiale*. The quality of Non-Coms was often criticized.

Retreating he simply wrote off the smashed II Army, giving all support to the intact III Army. At the Comando Supremo there was indecision, chaos, lack of energy, no communications, anxiety, but above all paralysis of the will. A combat leadership must have aggressive vision, mastery of strategy and the ability to extract the maximum in fighting qualities from both men and equipment. Italian staff officers were unable to handle maneuver warfare in any aspect. The thirty-six hour delay in ordering the withdrawal to the Tagliamento River insured the rout of the Italian troops. In peacetime maneuvers, the river had been shown easy to defend. There were no defensive plans in depth, whereby a reserve was ready to seal the breach in any locale. On the Bainsizza Plateau, were four divisions belonging to two different army corps, a recipe for disaster in any battle. Of paramount importance during the pre-October 24 period was the fact that from October 1 to October 19 Cadorna was on furlough at Vicenza where he was writing his Memoirs, while Capello was in the hospital for certain periods. Who was minding the store? Neither Gabba nor Porro could handle the paper work which was manifestly shown when the Comando Supremo moved to Treviso. No staff member remained in Udine, where there were good communication facilities but all went with Cadorna. Where would orders originate? With all this, the Generalissimo later wrote that if Italian artillery had started shelling when he ordered it to, the outcome would have been different.[8] His final comment before he left for Paris as Italian delegate to the Supreme War Council was that the Italian infantry had gone on strike. He had not noted that after a few days, the advancing Austro-Germans realizing that there was no Italian defensive strategy threw caution to the winds and proceeded forward as fast as possible. The delay in withdrawal to the Piave caused several bad results. Insisting that the Tagliamento River bridges not be destroyed after troops withdrew, the Comando Supremo placed the *Bologna* in danger. Panicked local commanders blew the bridges across which it was to withdraw. As the left wing of the II Army withdrew, it uncovered the escape route of the Thirty-sixth and Sixty-third Divisions, causing them to be cut off and captured.

In all honesty one must admit that in the final analysis it was Cadorna's planned defenses on the Grappa which he had ordered just a few days prior to the Caporetto offensive that saved Italy. Krafft acknowledged this in his text admitting that his forces were surprised about the new defenses without which his troops would have advanced onto the Italian plains.

Capello was slowly building a reputation for victories, but to the troops he was a butcher pushing them forward into machine gun nests. Blatantly disregarding orders he deployed his troops in a counteroffensive mode. His planned attack was to be from the Bainsizza Plateau north-westward against the enemy's left flank in the Vrh Valley, placing his second three-line corps northwest of Gorizia near the Isonzo, around Plava-M. Kuk and south of Caporetto.

Personally ordered by Cadorna to stay on the defensive, on the eve of the enemy attack, he had his men change to a definite defensive mode. Going from a counteroffensive mode to a defensive only hours before the enemy assault would confuse the best of troops. Disobeying an order in any army is a court-martial offense but Capello went ahead anyway. Caviglia later wrote that it was wrong to allow him to go on sick leave, as it would have been better that he died at his post. He acknowledged that Capello unjustly bore much of the blame for Caporetto. On September 18 Capello had been ordered to move troops further north from the Bainsizza in defensive positions. Both commanders prepared defenses for an assault coming from the Tolmino bridgehead proceeding along the line at Matajur-Kuk-Piatto-Na Gradu-Jeza Globocak (Map 14). However, the Austro-Germans attacked *north of the bridgehead* crossed the Isonzo arriving at the bottom of a ridge going from the Piatto to the Matajur where there were neither troops nor defenses. The Comando Supremo knew that the assault would be north of Tolmino (See Chapter I). Capello was a strict disciplinarian. His headquarters was based on "fear, threats, oppression being hated by the majority of his officers and men."[9] During his service in Libya he was given the name butcher while the military cemetery at Derna was nicknamed "Villa Capello." Between the two generals, Capello was the more intelligent. Often he would present an idea receiving no rebuttal from the Generalissimo feeling that he had made his point. The latter would think about it for a few days then change what the II Army commander felt had been agreed to.[10] Acknowledging that his huge gargantuan-size army was too big to handle, he belatedly placed Montuori in charge of the left wing.[11] Knowing about the breakthrough, Capello did not make sure that his staff issued appropriate orders or made sure that retreating traffic was controlled. As Lidell Hart relates, Capello became the Gough of the Italian Army alluding to the British General Gough whom Lidell-Hart accused of poor direction and staff work at Passchendaele.[12]

On October 27, Di Robilant was ordered to move his IV Army behind the Piave. He was comfortably ensconced in his headquarters, having little knowledge of the Austro-German attack, and refused to move. Finally, when summoned to headquarters of the Comando Supremo where the situation was explained to him, he issued the necessary orders. Previously he had been ordered to make a survey concerning *un ridotto cadorino,* seeing if he could halt enemy advances into his sector. His delay in moving them resulted in the destruction of three Italian divisions.

Zona Carnia Command

This sector was the roof of the Isonzo-Piave sector. As the II Army withdrew to the Piave, it left these troops isolated as its line of deployment went no further than the Punta di Montemaggiore causing a breach to develop between the II Army and the Zona Carnia deployment (Rombon to Montemaggiore) (Map 23). The Zona's troops withdrew to the the Carnic Alps, then the Carnic PreAlps. Due to its strategic importance this breach should have been sealed by the Comando Supremo (Map 40).). In pre-war maneuvers, this had been practiced many times, but when the real show arrived, there were no reserves. The three corps commanders of the Italian II Army were like corks on stormy waters being battered about while the IV Army commander wanted to stay away from the storm altogether.

IV Corps Commander and Events

Lt. Gen. Alberto Cavaciocchi was appointed corps commander in July, 1917. His corps dissolved so quickly that in certain allied quarters, along with his divisional commanders, he was accused of treason.[13] His defense sector went from the Rombon to the Gabrje sector on the Isonzo (Map 16). Looking up at the enemy trenches its troops garrisoned defenses on the slopes of the Slieme, Mrzli and Vodil. In a conference ten days before the enemy offensive he declared that there was a possibility of an enemy breakout from Tolmino proceeding toward the Kolovrat and Jeza then attacking the rear of the IV and XXVII

Corps. He noted that the IV Corps was responsible for the defense of the sector from Hlevnik to the Isonzo. Here at the river bed its right wing was to link up with the XXVII Corps which never happened. Two infantry and two Bersaglieri companies were to garrison that sector.[14] A prime example of the reckless shifting about of troops would be the Thirty-fourth Infantry Division (Lt. Gen. L. Basso), constituted in October, 1917, with the *Napoli* and 2° and 9° Bersaglieri. After two days, they were all transferred away while he was assigned to the IV Corps where the Thirty-fourth was reconstituted again with the *Foggia* (280°, 281°, and 283°) plus the 2° and 9° Bersaglieri°.[15] Words written on paper do not tell all. Orders written on October 23 stated that the 280° was at the disposal of the Fiftieth Infantry Division, while the Bersaglieri regiments were to be deployed near the Forty-third and Forty-sixth Infantry Divisions. When these orders were issued, Basso had only two regiments when he arrived at Kred. Next day he had none. The 281° went to the Forty-third Infantry Division while the 282°, went to the Forty-sixth Infantry Division.[16] Later he felt that the northern tip of his front should be strengthened by having the Fiftieth Infantry Division withdraw to a better defendable sector similar to the so-called Military Border to which Habsburg troops withdrew to in time of war. The *Comandante Interinale* (temporary commander) of the II Army (Lt. Gen. Montuori) agreed, but required Cadorna's approval as well. This never happened as the enemy soon started its offensive. On October 23 the Thirty-fourth Infantry Division arrived in the IV Corps sector. Cavaciocchi assigned it the 2° and 9° Bersaglieri. Early on October 24 the *Potenza* arrived near Breginj with its orders reading that it was still under the direct control of the II Army. Thus a brigade arrived in the IV Corps sector, which it could not use. While the attackers made little progress on the Rombon, they did break through at M. Jeza. So far there was nothing catastrophic. This breach was of tactical importance and should have been dealt with by the II Army *which had no readily available reserves to seal the breach.* Thus we see that neither the Comando Supremo nor the II Army could adequately deal with the problem of reserves (See elsewhere in this chapter).

The northern bank of the Isonzo was under its jurisdiction. As noted its right wing it was to link up with the XXVII Corps. It had been warned about an Austro-German breakthrough attempt from the Tolmino bridgehead along the Isonzo Valley and should have planned accordingly. Ideally its troops should have descended from M. Nero, but could not, because they were under attack from the south by troops that proceeded *undisturbed* on the right bank of the river (Map 14). Should they have descended the road-less Matajur, cross the river, and go to the aid of troops deployed along the line M. Nero-Saga, they could have come under enemy cross fire. It would have been risky climbing back up the mountain with enemy artillery firing at them. The only real reserve was the *Firenze* en route to Passo Zagradan. *There were no reserves to seal this second breach between the IV and XXVII Corps.*

In classic *blitzkrieg* fashion it received a massive thrust. As noted with its Fiftieth Infantry Division it defended the sector of Plezzo-Saga Strait (Map 15). With its Forty-third and Nineteenth Infantry Divisions the XXVII Corps was defending the sector M. Nero to Doblar, where *five enemy divisions* attacked (Map 14). When subjected to this type of assault the defending army must keep few troops in the front line trenches, keep a large mobile reserve and *have commanders ready to act.* None of these requirements were met because even its counterattack on the Jeza was too late. Austro-German troops proceeded from the Val Uccea to the Tagliamento River, then marched southward along its western banks nullifying any attempt to seal the breach in the center of the front. While in the prisoner of war camp at Rastatt, Farisoglio (Forty-third Infantry Division) wrote a memorandum concerning what happened. He noted that on the morning of October 24 he had sent the 9° Bersaglieri (Col. Arturo Radaelli) toward the Isonzo intending to hold up the Silesians and gain time. Instead Cavaciocchi halted these units and sent them to M. Nero where they never arrived.

Reserves in this sector often turned out to be tired disoriented troops (Map 23). They were:

1. *Saga Strait:* One regiment of the *Foggia* and the *Alpini* Monvisio and Argentera Battalions.
2. *Caporetto*: remnants of the *Foggia* (six battalions) to block the Isonzo Valley
3. *Behind the Nineteenth Infantry Divison* was the *Puglie* on the right bank of the Isonzo.

The XXVII Corps Commander and Events

In charge of a successful assault on the Sabotino Badoglio had been noticed and rapidly promoted by Capello (VI Corps) By August 23, 1917 he was a Lt. Gen. commanding the XXVII Corps deployed opposite the heights of S. Maria and S. Lucia di Tolmino. Badoglio must have been born under a lucky star. While his prepared defenses were being destroyed by the advancing Austro-Germans, he was promoted as his mistakes were buried. He rose to the highest military and political leadership in Italy. At Caporetto he was guilty of four errors. The first was keeping four divisions on the Bainsizza instead of opposite Tolmino to contain the already known Austro-German breakout from the bridgehead. Second, he knew the artillery shelling schedule of the enemy, yet took no steps about it, sticking with the Volzana trap mentality and was fooled. *There never was a Volzana trap because the hunter could not close the cage.* His artillery chief Col. A. Cannoniere requested orders to open fire, but was refused. When the order finally did come there were no longer any artillery mouths in Italian hands. Third, on the first day, he changed his headquarters five times often being incommunicado. There was a reason for this. Using a new communication medium called the radio as the enemy listened he communicated with the Comando Supremo *en clair* describing the damage that enemy shelling had done to his headquarters. Thus he allowed enemy guns to *establish the position of his tactical headquarters and destroy it.* As Berendt the XIV Army artillery chief noted in 1924, "Rarely has artillery during a battle received encouraging news on the effect of its shelling right from the target."[17] Enemy 150 mm. guns followed him about destroying each of his headquarters being unwittingly directed by the corps commander. Having been involved in the Battle of Tannenburg on the Eastern Front, Below must have been amused because there the Russians used the radio in a similar fashion enabling the Germans to achieve a massive victory. The fourth, and to the author's mind, the most serious criticism was the use of the *Napoli.* It was supposed to block the Foni Pass which would close the road from Tolmino to Caporetto. On the right bank he was to have had twenty six battalions (along six miles), while on the left there were supposed to be twenty-two (along two miles). Instead Badoglio felt that the Nineteenth Infantry Division had to hold fast *alone* while other troops would counterattack toward the Lom and Santa Lucia. On October 22 he received a telegram that he would receive the *Napoli* (six battalions, p. 382) to garrison the line Plezia-Foni-Isonzo. Obviously this meant the river bank, while the IV Corps would defend the river bed and the left side of the Isonzo. With one battalion of the *Napoli* deployed high up on the hill overlooking the Foni Strait the Silesian Infantry was allowed to *stroll* toward Caporetto in the breach between the IV and XXVII Corps across four Italian defensive lines on the first day and get to the rear of the Italian IV Corps.[18] The defense commanders did not have the vision to seal it. No meetings ever took place between the two corps concerning the river defense. There was no linkup between the IV and XXVII Corps while Villani was ordered to abandon Volzana and deploy on Costa Raunza and Val Kamenca resulting in the right wing of the IV Corps waving in the wind (Maps 16,17). With no linkups the artillery mouths on the Kolovrat and Costa Raunza went unprotected. No longer was there a continual defense to contain the Tolmino bridgehead. With the ½ mile breach in the right bank defenses, the Germans had an open road to Caporetto.

Breaking through the Italian positions at Slieme and Mrzli the Austro-Hungarian XV Mountain Brigade proceeded south to attack the rear positions of the two companies of the *Alessandria* defending Dolje. In the first line a machine gun company had been removed the night before leaving a vacuum in the defenses.[19] Lacking here was a commander with a vision who would realize what was happening and seal the breach between the IV and XXVII Corps through which the Silesians *walked* through undisturbed.

The Caporetto Commission took testimony from a captain and colonel of the 155° who declared that the machine gun company had received orders to deploy elsewhere. Orders signed by an officer of the 207° had mysteriously disappeared. Preoccupied with the headwaters of the Judrio, Badoglio left the right bank unguarded even over riding the complaint of the Nineteenth Infantry Division's Chief of Staff easily eliminating the second defensive line (Map 21). On Sept. 30 Capello had told Badoglio and Cavaciocchi that the enemy would break out from Tolmino aiming for Passo Zagradan and the Jeza. The Italian third defensive line at Idersko had two companies of the 282° who had just arrived and were not linked up with the VII Corps.[20] At Caporetto there was only one battalion of the 282°. The attackers went around them and attacked from the mountains. The Italian fourth defensive line was at Staroselo garrisoned by survivors of the third line plus a machine gun company. The Silesians simply surrounded and took the town.

On specific orders from the King and Orlando both of whom had picked him for Vice Chief of Staff, the Caporetto Inquiry Commission made no criticism of Badoglio.[21] In fact, thirteen pages were removed from the report as they were highly critical of Badoglio.[22] Under Orlando's secret instructions Senator Giuseppe Paratore approached the Hon. Orazio Raimondo, a member of the commission to remove the critical pages. Machinations of Italian politics even reached into the Inquiry Commission! Even Capello took Badoglio to task regarding this situation.[23] Of the *Napoli's* six battalions, one went to M. Plezia (to "watch" the Foni Strait), two went to Passo Zagradan, three went to the origin of the Judrio (Map 17).[24] In the fog the Plezia battalion was captured, leaving an open door through Foni toward Caporetto. On the first day of the offensive, as the *Napoli* became unhinged, none of these positions were successfully defended. The reader is reminded that the IV Corps was responsible for the riverbed and the left bank of the river, while the XXVII Corps was responsible for the right bank.

Defended by the Nineteenth Infantry Division and the *X Gruppo Alpini*, the Jeza commanded a great view of the Isonzo and Judrio Rivers, as well as Tolmino, Canale and Caporetto (Map 14). Machine guns could have covered some non-garrisoned sectors. Using newly developed tactics the attackers with four divisions infiltrated behind Italian troops and took it in twenty-four hours.

On the first day of the enemy offensive as the *Foggia* was deployed near Caporetto, it was ordered to send one regiment to Saga, then to Selisce proceeding along the left bank allowing the Silesians to easily *stroll* along the right bank capturing Italian artillery pieces deployed east of Idersko as noted. The other regiment was to deploy at Volnik near M. Nero. As the Alpenkorps penetrated along the Costa Raunza and Val Kanmenca, it unhinged the VII Corps attacking it from the rear (Kolovrat and Matajur), as well as from the Jeza (Map 16). Badoglio planned to counterattack in the direction of Srednje-Ostry Kras which never happened because the XXVII Corps staff could not handle the paper work concerning the quick enemy penetrations (Map 20). Described on page 382 are events in the XXVII Corps' third defensive line which went from Foni to M. Plezia to Costa Raunza to Val Kamenca, climbing Costa Duole arriving at the Jeza across mountain tops to the Isonzo River upstream from Doblar (Maps 16,17). Behind this was another defensive line proceeding from Passo Zagradan across the dorsum of the Kolovrat to Podlabuc, the Jeza, Globocak and finally M. Korada, just southeast of Cividale. Deployed along the line M. Plezia-Doblar near the Jeza were two brigades belonging to two different army corps (*Puglie* of the XXVII, and *Elba* of the Third

Infantry Division, VII Corps). The only use for these units was to counterattack which never happened as with two different commands it would be difficult to synchronize an assault. With the premature destruction of the bridges across the Isonzo all troops north of the river were captured (IV Corps). One Italian division could have held up the enemy advance until reinforcements arrived but where would they come from? Badoglio survived these events to become Italy's military leader for twenty years as well as its political leader in the agony of September, 1943.

VII Corps Commander and Events

A week before the enemy offensive, Major General Luigi Bongiovanni was appointed commander of the VII Corps. In classic Comando Supremo fashion all troops were taken from him, but Capello then assigned him the Third and Thirty-fourth Infantry Divisions, the *Napoli,* and the 2° and 9° Bersaglieri. Poor Bersaglieri! They were like ping pong balls being batted about. The tasks of the VII Corps are specifically discussed (Vol. I, Chapter XXXII). It was to *garrison* the second line from the Kolovrat to the Matajur, link up with the IV and XXVII Corps, be ready to <u>counterattack</u> also acting as a reserve. With all these tasks it would be difficult to classify it as a reserve, it was more like a garrison <u>anchored</u> to its post. Being a garrison, it could not counterattack, except with Capello's personal permission. Deployed in the Passo Zagradan sector its troops could not link up with the other two corps of the II Army (Map 17). To do this, troops would have to be deployed on the dorsum of the Matajur. The rest of the troops would be deployed in the upper Isonzo and along the line at Caporetto-Idersko-Luico-M. S. Martino. Reserves would have to be on the slopes of the Matajur. In the end almost none of the VII Corps was actively engaged in combat and in the end it served no useful purpose. The Bersaglieri were assigned to the IV Corps, to be replaced by the Third Infantry Division which had not yet arrived. This was a defect of the Comando Supremo which not even constructive criticism by the Anglo-French was able to correct.[25] The Thirty-fourth Infantry Division was transferred out to be replaced by the Sixty-second Infantry Division which was yet to arrive. One wonders how could any commander impart orders, or make defensive plans with such a traffic in troops coming and going? An example of the deployment was the Third Division (*Arno* and *Elba*) on its right flank. The *Arno* faced north with most troops deployed around Drenchia with some patrols on the Kolovrat (Map 17). The *Elba* with its troop deployed around Lombai with patrols in the mountains, and the *Firenze* (Corps reserve) in Val Cosizza. These brigades were to assist the Nineteenth Infantry Division (XXVII Corps) if needed. Who would give such an order? Capello, Bongiovanni or whomever? One is reminded that at 1200 on the first day the VII Corps was ordered to garrison the Kolovrat-Matajur. *With this order the reserve function of the VII Corps was over.* Toward noon Bongiovanni received vague news that the Germans had advanced along the Isonzo up to Selisce. He now received and deployed the Sixty-second Infantry Division from M. Matajur to M. Kuk di Luico and the Third Infantry Division from M. Kuk to Passo Zagradan and Pusno (Map 17). Part of the arriving Sixty-second Infantry Division was the *Salerno* which was deployed on the Matajur. Some authors have noted that it could have descended the Matajur (5000 feet) and attack the advancing enemy. Should it have been necessary to retreat back up the mountain, it would have been caught in a cross fire. Three-quarters of the VII Corps was deployed facing north, while one quarter (*Elba*) was in the Passo Zagradan facing east (Map 14). The reserve *Firenze* was still in Val Cosizza, far away from the needy XXVII Corps or the defense of the Jeza (Map 17). Knowing that the Jeza would come under attack the Comando Supremo had two brigades nearby for eventual assistance. *However these units were not in the XXVII Corps, but the VII Corps, rendering a rescue almost impossible.* Episodes like this are repeated throughout military history. With a multiplicity of tasks, the VII Corps accomplished none. Newly arrived on location and deployed parallel to the enemy's penetration, Bongiovanni's men were attacked in their front and rear and easily overcome when the onslaught arrived. At 1700 the VII Corps ordered the *Elba* (deployed at the Passo Zagradan) with the *Napoli* (was XXVII Corps, now attached to the VII Corps), to attack in direction of Bucovna Jeza and M. Plezia. These two units, along with the *Firenze* were to be the *massa di manovra,* but arrived too late on location at dawn of October 25. Bongiovanni's subordinate commanders had not disclosed the urgency of the crisis. When the IV Corps ordered the Sixty-second Infantry Division to attack the enemy in the left flank, it was too late.[26] Even if Capello had ordered the VII to seal the breach, with no roads, it could reach neither the IV nor the XXVII Corps nor could it link up with the internal wings of the two which came close at Gabrje because its deployment was perpendicular to the other two. The best way would have been to deploy forces in the Upper Isonzo River, others in the Val Cosizza, with heavy forces on the slopes of the Matajur (Map 17). All this would have added up to deployment along the line, Caporetto-Idersko-Luico-M. S. Martino. Erroneously the VII Corps commander reported that the *Arno* did not fight obligating its surviving men on furlough to cover their unit identification. At the Caporetto Inquiry Commission, Bongiovanni admitted that all the commanders (including himself) were at fault. Eventually, he commanded an air unit in the Veneto and went on to command the *Regia Aeronautica.*

The Episode of the Saga Strait

As Habsburg troops crashed through the three Italian defense lines at Plezzo, there remained only one obstacle before they could flow into the plains westward, the Saga Strait. Much to Krafft's relief the Italians prematurely evacuated it. He felt that even a machine gun company could have held up his men for a day or so. It seemed that erroneous news had reached the Italian Fiftieth Infantry Division that the enemy had broken through on the right of the Saga.[27] Even the RICC entered the discussion with its comment.[28]

Krauss Group (Austro-German XIV Army)

On November 2 troops crossed the Tagliamento at Cornino (Maps 27,29,40). Should they have proceeded along the foothills arriving at the Piave, crossing at its source and proceeded southward along its banks, serious consequences would have befallen Cadorna's IV Army. The Italians would not have had time to deploy on the Grappa while troops in the middle and lower Isonzo and Carnia would have been isolated. Annihilation would have been achieved. For the Italians there was nowhere to go. Instead the troops became embroiled in the Carnic PreAlps capturing only three Italian divisions and the rear guard of the Italian IV Army at Longarone (Map 40).

On November 16, Krauss ordered an assault by the German Jäger and K.u.k. Fifty-fifth Infantry Divisions on M. Tomba. His subordinates changed his orders resulting in a failed assault for the day. He later wrote that if his orders had been carried out his I Corps (right wing of the XIV Army) would have arrived on the plains below. His troops were the key to Below's strategy. They had defeated Serbia, Russia and Romania and were guided by the best tactician in the Habsburg Army. The assault would have to be a solid stroke at the Italian defenses and advance rapidly not giving any time to the Italians to reorganize their defenses.

Writing about a more general topic Krauss listed all the causes for the failure of the Caporetto campaign to bring about a definitive result.[29] He was one of the few Habsburg generals who presented an honest summary of events after the conflict even with self-criticism. Troops proceeding rapidly in the plains could have easily blocked the Italian withdrawal into the mountains with disastrous consequences for the defenders. Instead he had to send elite troops into the mountains to assault Italian enemy positions at great cost. He also felt that too much responsibility was given to the mountain forces while Boroevic's forces as well as most of the XIV Army lay idle on the Piave due to lack of pontoon bridges. Attacking in the mountains was costly in men and supplies and could only be done by small units. The *I Isonzo Armée* had taken bridging equipment along to enable troops to cross the Piave, but was ordered by The Serb to leave it behind, resulting in neither troops nor artillery being able to cross. Wanting to do everything orderly and efficiently Krauss was accused of being a *Teutonphile*.

Returning to the theme of mountain warfare he noted that there one had to construct roads and establish overhead cableways. On the Italian Front combat up to the debacle was described by Krauss as slow suicide. Requesting German help the A.O.K. attacked resulting in enormous gains which were not used either politically or militarily. Had the Italian Army been annihilated all of the empire's people would have enthusiastically supported the monarchy. Instead Vienna had no will to proceed beyond its Military Borders. Krauss's brother a corps commander on the Eastern Front discussed the situation on the Isonzo with his superior Gen. Berhnardi. Both felt that the Italian III Army could easily be trapped. However, as the I Corps commander related one needed the will to do this, which was lacking. For years Austro-Hungarian combat on the Isonzo was only in a defensive mode. The concept of maneuver warfare was unknown to the A.O. K. He also acknowledged that it was a large error for Boroevic not to have allowed German troops to deviate southwestward which would have trapped the III Army as well as the King. Conrad had insisted on attacking on the altopiano which led to a disaster which everyone forsaw. Toward the end of the war as Charles took over the conduct of the war troops felt that A.O.K. stood for *Alles-Ohne-Kopf* (all without a head) referring to useless maneuvers.

The Withdrawal Across the Tagliamento and Piave Rivers

Cadorna delayed in giving the order to withdraw. Italian prewar exercises retreating to the Tagliamento like the Schlieffen plan, had no contact with reality. In August, 1914, the Germans had three million men on the move on the Western Front, while in the fall of 1917, there were one million men retreating to the Piave. Numbers like these were never considered by Schlieffen. Munitions and other supplies were a constant problem, as units never were where they were supposed to be. There were, nor could there be any set-plans for the withdrawal, as planners never conceived the enormous number of men involved. Advancing Austro-Germans gave the Italians no time to perform the "scorched earth" acts which worked so well on other fronts. Delay in ordering the withdrawal to the Piave River caused enormous harm to the Italians, as did postponing the retreat from the Isonzo to the Tagliamento River. Italian troops arrived at the Tagliamento on October 30 but no order was given to withdraw to the Piave until November 4 at 1000. By then, enemy troops had crossed the river at the M. Ragogna bridgehead and were proceeding south along the west bank of the Tagliamento aiming to attack the rear of Italian troops deployed on the river. Cadorna waxed and waned from pessimism to optimism, never having a concrete persistent thought. On October 29, he telegraphed the II, III Armies that the right bank of the river should be held at all costs, and not to be evacuated unless under his specific orders.[30] On October 30 after receiving depressing news he telegraphed the IV Army that the situation on the Tagliamento was grave, ordering it to abandon everything except artillery and proceed to the right bank of the Piave. He felt that the II Army had dissolved and would have III Army units perform rear guard action as the I Corps withdrew. This was followed by another telegram on October 31, "Continue to resist at all costs on the left (east) bank of the river and also deploy on the right (west) bank. In any case, I am again confirming that intact bridges should not be demolished unless there is grave danger." Thus we note much optimism which is again noted on November 2 with another telegram. "The withdrawal of the II, III Armies to the Tagliamento has been completed. Enemy pressure seems to have abated, after the first initial jump forward, as the Austro-Germans now have problems with supplies and distances. We therefore must prolong our stay on the Tagliamento as long as possible as noted in my directives . . . . if conditions warrant, it should be transformed into a *permanent stay.*" A few hours after receiving this telegram, the enemy crossed the river at Cornino (Maps 27,29). Still Cadorna was not preoccupied only giving the order to withdraw two days later. As if there had not been enough of them, this would cause two serious additional disasters. The first disaster was the loss of the *Bologna* at the M. Ragogna bridgehead. Together with a battalion of the *Barletta,* it was guarding the bridgehead. By 0900, on October 31, the defending commander requested permission to cross the Cornino bridge, which was denied. Demolition charges had been hastily and incorrectly emplaced, so only part of the bridge was demolished allowing the attackers to cross November 2. The only hope of the *Bologna* was blown with no hope of salvation (Map 27). Charges could have been emplaced on October 30 , giving enough time for them to be set off and all to cross. *Zona Carnia Command (XII Corps)*

Zona Carnia Command (XII Corps)

The second disaster was in this sector. As the II Army withdrew to the Tagliamento the Zona Carnia troops were isolated. Withdrawing to the Carnic Alps then the Pre-Alps, on their way to the Piave, they were to be protected by reserves of the Comando Supremo which would be deployed from the Rombon (north of Plezzo) to the Venzone Strait (Map 40). Cadorna had decided that three divisions would be needed for safeguarding them, but there were none to be had. The Zona Carnia garrison was now in a vise, with the Austro-Hungarian X Army (Krobatin) coming from the northeast, and the *Edelweiss* and German Jäger Divisions (Krauss Group) proceeding westward and northwestward toward them via the Saga Strait, the Val Venzone, the Valle di Resia and Val Raccolana

(Map 27). The Italian divisions should have quickly withdrawn through the mountains toward Longarone. Instead they were ordered to attack in a north-south direction in a failed attempt to open their way into the plains after which they attempted to go westward toward Longarone, but were surrounded. By November 7, when the Livenza River line had been abandoned the *Alemagna Road* to Longarone and Cadore was left unprotected. Cadorna was lucky that Krauss did not proceed from Vittorio Veneto toward Ponte nelle Alpi and Longarone (Map 28). The Italian IV Army's eastern flank was uncovered from November 5 to November 11 due to DiRobilant's delay in withdrawing. Austro-German troops crossing at Cornino had opened an unsealable breach between the Italian Thirty-sixth, Sixty-third Infantry Divisions and friendly troops on the Friulian Plain isolating the two divisions (Map 27). *As a result the Italian II Army deployed on the west bank of the Tagliamento had to hurriedly withdraw to the Piave and leave the above mentioned divisions to their fate.* Enemy troops were also proceeding southward along the west bank of the Tagliamento threatening the left (north) flank and rear (west) of defending Italian troops. In an attempt to rest the troops, Cadorna had ordered troops to rest on the Tagliamento, giving a chance to the non-resting advancing Austro-Germans to catch up. The place to rest should have been in the terrain between the two rivers, making it an obstacle course, much as the Germans had done in the Second World War, in their withdrawal to the Rhine.

Troop and Italian Society Behavior

There was no will on the Italian boot to conduct a war. People were interested in surviving, to find something to eat that night rather than the romantic ideals of the *Risorgimento.* Throughout the war a spirit of defeatism had spread from society to the army. This resulted in thousands of deserters, some to the enemy, some to the Italian *hinterland.* Cadorna realized that the propaganda was destroying the morale of the army and asked the government to put a stop to it. What was not realized was that a major cause of poor morale emanated from the army itself. The infantry was ill-trained, there was no synchronization with artillery, assault troops were envied due to privileges accorded them *(However, no one wanted to take their place)* while officers had little understanding of the troops and their conditions. There were many well-connected men who were placed in cushy jobs in the military far from harm's way which did not escape the attention of the *fanti.* Furloughs were almost non-existent, men were left for many months in the filthy trenches suffering enormous casualties. The troops were tired, had been subjected to repeated useless assaults resulting in horrific losses. After time the first line troops felt that the nation was not even aware that they were there. All these factors led to poor-morale and nourished the defeatism which pervaded many sectors of Italian society. Good morale is a necessary component of combat power. At the time the *fanti* had none. Surprise was also a factor in the Battle of the Bulge twenty-seven years later as German panzers were over-running American infantry. However, there the men had been relatively well-treated, were literate, had a sense of nationhood and knew their duty holding at Bastogne. At Caporetto the illiterate infantry had been ill-treated and ruled by a bunch of men who did not even acknowledge that they existed for any purpose except to die in some useless battle which the *fanti* eventually realized.

In his excellent text on the Battle of Caporetto, Krafft noted that on the first day, many Italian soldiers were coming down from the mountains waving white handkerchiefs and yelling *Eviva Germania* as they walked unguarded toward Tolmino (the rear of Austro-German lines). Panicked by the new enemy tactics which they could not fathom, the men took off their uniforms, donned civilian clothes, threw away their rifles, and started to walk toward Sicily, Calabria, Bari, or wherever their homes might be. They had fought valiantly for twenty seven months *causing* the *Battle of Caporetto* to be fought. It is certain that some units did desert over to the enemy *en masse,* but to this day it is not certain which ones. Often a unit would be accused of cowardice, a statement later to be found in error. A classic example is the description of the surrendering *en masse* of the 87° at Caporetto.[31] Noting the enormous number of casualties, and not aware of the German gas shelling, an author simply deduced an erroneous conclusion and published false information. Some troops awaited the order for a counterattack which never came as the officers had run off. Some troops were exclaiming "Either go home or as prisoners of war, but to hell with the war."[32] The Caporetto Inquiry Commission reported that the military strike started about noon of the third day.[33] Reserve units walking to the battlefront were greeted with calls of "Scab" by men who had taken off their uniforms and were walking home. Drunken troops, panic and arson pervaded the Friulian plain that October. After several years of poor treatment they had had enough fighting for a nation they did not know existed whose citizens spoke a language they did not understand. There was still no concept of nationhood among the troops.

Left-leaning writers have written about Caporetto being the start of the class struggle which was in its embryonic stage but then aborted (during the Fascist period).[34] Some felt that the August, 1917 events in Torino gave birth to the military strike in October. It was felt that an insurrection took place by the people who were trying to achieve their aims and better their economic conditions with Caporetto being a reflection of the October Bolshevik Revolution.[35] Palmiro Togliatti, future chief of the Italian Communist Party wrote that the Socialists were at fault because they did not take control of the revolution in the trenches, creating an "October revolution" and a "Brest-Litovsk" peace.[36] He felt that Caporetto was a catharsis of all of Italy's social ills. In 1915 Lenin had written an article subsequently translated into Italian that the revolutionary class had to hope for the defeat of its very government.[37] After Bainsizza (Eleventh Battle), the Italian peasant infantry's morale had plummeted to an all-time low as the men yearned to be home to help with the harvest not to fight in a far-distant place. With each successive offensive, they had been promised that this was the last offensive. Finally, like having difficulties with the *padroni* they simply crossed their arms and refused to fight. The infantry remained in the trench until seriously wounded or killed with furloughs seldom being given.

At one point the government realized that men in the trenches sent home on a thirty day furlough could help with the family's harvest. In another classic bungling job, the paper work took so long to process that the harvest was over by the time it was approved. In the Province of Rome there were 20,000 furlough applications, 2000 were approved for a by-now useless furlough for the harvest. Cadorna tried to place all the blame on the front-line troops, but how could those uneducated peasants be responsible for the whole disaster?[38] As in all massive withdrawals, there were episodes of individual heroism and cowardice. Interviewing artillery veterans of the battle, the author was told that after noting enemy infantry advancing toward them, their officers fled by auto, without saying a word to the men. Krafft noted that some gunners fought the German infantry with pistols before being overcome. It is the author's contention that after Caporetto there was an attempt by the government which often was Left-Leaning (except in the Fascist period) to improve the conditions of its citizens which persists to this day. This will be fully discussed in the final chapter in Volume III of this work.

In politics, two prominent Socialists, Filippo Turati and Claudio Treves, wrote an article published in *Critica Sociale* (Nov. 1, 1917), noting the return of the party to the Italian *Patria.* Who could believe them, after all the propaganda that had been disseminated? The upper and middle classes were afraid of the *revolt* of the peasants who had never participated in the Italian state. A quasi-military dictatorship to save the nation was established but the authorities soon noted that there was no revolution, no leader only an illusion so gradually the military controls of the population were relaxed. The reader will note that the author constantly refers to the illiterate peasant infantry. In many interviews over the past fifty years, he has realized that they lived in a world unlike any he has known. When one considers that they could not read signs, written instructions, letters from loved ones, newspapers and did not even know what Italy was, it does not surprise one that at a certain point, they threw in the sponge. Their horizons were limited to the family. Yet lacking a clearly defined reason a few weeks later on the Grappa, they fought like wounded tigers as acknowledged by Krafft. Troops which had been retreating for days exhausted, hungry, thirsty and bewildered suddenly answered the call to duty and halted the invaders. For them there was only one thing that counted the *family* which the politicians had skillfully woven in their appeal to duty. From November 10 to December 25, 1917 the unfortunate days of that October on the Isonzo were redeemed by thirty one *Medaglie d'Oro al Valore Militare* issued by the Italian Army to men of all ranks and branches. In his writings Cadorna often noted that the illiterate *fanti* were easily swayed. Almost a century later and ten thousand miles away an illiterate mother in India had refused to complete her daughter's anti-polio vaccination resulting in the child contracting polio. Her defense echoed Cadorna's writings many years prior. "We are illiterate, not very intelligent and easily swayed."[39]

Why the Surprise?

As the Caporetto Inquiry Commission noted, the Central Powers closed the Swiss borders on September 14, so no one could enter and notice their troop movements. Troops were transferred from the Trentino to the Isonzo, while the Twelfth Silesian left Alsace on September 23, to go to Vienna, to pick up some mountain gear. Where would it go? Certainly not the Eastern Front where the war was almost over. Many Austro-Hungarian divisions had left the Eastern Front to go to the Isonzo. Russian Intelligence had been notifying Cadorna about this but he still did not believe the information. His Information Office (Intelligence) accommodated him by reporting on September 28, that no enemy offensive action was imminent except perhaps some diversionary action. In his Wellington-era mind set, this was not the time to start a major offensive, it was the time to establish winter quarters with Germany only lending a few battalions for a limited offensive, and perhaps an attack in the spring. He later stated that the information was too piece-meal and not consistent. The information had been furnished, the question was would it be believed? What about the news brought by Lt. Maxim who even brought the shelling schedules or that sent by Col. Brancaccio, Italian Military Attaché in Paris. By October 17, troops were reported in the Idria Valley with units of elite Carinthian Infantry in the Plezzo Basin. One could only surmise an attack and soon.[40] Finally, on October 24, Cadorna had written to Robertson *specifying the attack front (Plezzo to Tolmino)* as noted in Vol. I, p. 508. So in the end it really was not a surprise in the classic sense, but a *Strategic Surprise.* It was impossible to move the divisions in time through the roadless mountains to where they were needed.

Why Did the Artillery Not Fire?

Some authors felt that it was not to waste ammunition.[41] Artillery crews were ordered to wait until they heard machine guns open up verifying that the enemy was attacking.[42] However the main reason was that the XXVII Corps' commander had assumed control over all artillery in a vital sector. Guns were to fire only on his personal orders.[43] There was no formal link between the infantry and artillery.[44] If the machine guns were firing, it was too late for artillery barrages as the enemy had already left their trenches. The best time to combat an infantry assault was *before* the enemy infantry left the trench, or at the latest, at its established assembly points. By the time he gave the order to fire, all artillery mouths had been captured by enemy infantry and mountain troops. Cadorna had ordered artillery to be redeployed to the rear. Instead it was bunched up in two groups, one west of Tolmino, the other southwest, easy pickings for the advancing troops.[45]

Italian II Army Reserves

In discussing reserves one should establish definitions. Reserves should be well-rested troops, mobile, well-armed, motivated and ready for battle. They should have been deployed near a truck park or rail depot. This was the situation of the reserve Italian V Army in the *Strafexpedition.* No such Italian troops existed at Caporetto. Reserves there were tired, poorly equipped men recently rotated to the rear, prematurely sent back to the front knowing neither their officers, nor the terrain to be defended nor did they have any contact with friendly flanking troops or with their artillery. II Army reserves were the XXVIII, XIV Corps plus the *Milano* and *Sesia.* It deployed the 353 battalions of which seventy two (noted above) were reserves which must be emplaced where probably needed and easily available. For instance, even a partial breakthrough on the Bainsizza would endanger the Zona Carnia and the Julian Front. Of these seventy-two battalions, twelve were in the Gorizia Basin, twenty-four in the Isonzo Valley between Canale and Plava (near the Bainsizza), with twelve astride the Judrio at Canale, and twenty-four at Cormôns (Map 36). As can be noted, none of these were easily available to the left (north) wing of the Italian Army deployment. For *tactical reasons,* the Comando Supremo decreased its forces that should have helped it in a *strategic sense.* Italian reserves would be used to lengthen the Rombon Front to the Venzone Strait, or to redeploy from the Carnic Alps to the PreCarnic Alps (Maps 2, 40). In vogue during the Great War were the terms strategic and tactical. The Comando Supremo reserves were to be used in a strategic sense but sometimes were used in a tactical sense.[46] *At noon on October 24, when the VII Corps was ordered to garrison the Matajur (5,000 feet), its reserve function was over.* Only the *Firenze* now remained as a reserve unit. As it was marching toward Ruchin it received orders to approach Passo Zagradan to constitute the *massa di manovra.* Assigned to the II Army as a reserve force was the XXX Corps (Sixteenth and Twenty-first Infantry Divisions) deployed south of Palmanova which could not get to the front in time (Map 35). Since no reserves could arrive to seal the breaches, there was no choice but to retreat to the Tagliamento.

The first defensive line of the II Army was at Rombon-M. Nero-M. Jeza-Isonzo, which linked up with the Zona Carnia on the Rombon (Map 14). By withdrawing to the Tagliamento, the II Army could not deploy beyond Montemaggiore, thus creating a breach between the Zona Carnia Command and the left wing of the II Army isolating the Carnia troops (Map 23).

Comando Supremo Reserves:[47]

On the eve of the battle, the Comando Supremo had 114 battalions of which ninety-nine were on the Julian Front. Using the *Strafexpedition* as a point of reference, one noted that 200 enemy battalions attacked an almost similar number of Italian troops, reinforced by another 100 battalions, with a *Strategic Reserve* of five corps (130 battalions) on the Venetian plain. During that battle Cadorna personally visited the Reserve V Army to explain its function.

The Caporetto reserves were assembled in two groups. One was four divisions (two corps) near Palmanova, while the second was three divisions deployed along the line at Cormôns-Cividale (Map 35,36,40). None of these were able to seal the breach on the first day. Not those near Gorizia, nor troops in the lower Isonzo, nor those near Cormôns. There were enough reserves but they were not *well-distributed* to meet the oncoming onslaught. Deploying some in the north, they could have attacked the advancing enemy in a north-south direction. Instead they were deployed too far south near the front lines and not able to seal the Zona Carnia breach. To reach the desired sector going north reserves would have to pass through Italian troops in active combat. Even knowing the enemy's plans in advance the Comando Supremo did nothing to alter the deployment of its reserves. Cadorna declared that on October 3 he had drafted orders to place six divisions in the angle of the Tagliamento near Gemona (the exact place where needed), but the order was not issued.[48]

The various possibilities which could arise had to be examined by the Comando Supremo. The first was the possibility of retreat which would have to be to the Tagliamento River. However, this could not be accomplished in one step. An intermediate stop would have been the Torre Creek (or raging river) (Map 35). To think of covering Udine in the retreat, using the Torre as a defensive river, and hold the front of forty-miles, nine divisions would be needed.[49] The large centers of Udine, Palmanova and Cervignano would have to be defended, needing nine divisions (Map 35).

Withdrawal to the Tagliamento would need three strongly defended bridgeheads: the first at Cornino-Pinzano, the others at Codroipo and Latisana, each with three divisions to insure no enemy infiltration (Maps 29, 40). The total number of reserve divisions now needed approached twenty. *Withdrawing to the Torre Creek, the northernmost point of the II Army line could only reach Montemaggiore, opening a breach as noted in the linkup with the Zona Carnia Command.* The new defensive line was now Rombon-M. Nero-Isonzo (Map 14). There was also an expected (but not concluded) linkup Zona Carnia to Rombon. This would have to be sealed by Comando Supremo reserves which should have deployed to the north near truck depots or a rail head.

Capello and Cadorna would later note that reserves were deployed around Cividale because from there they could be sent to the Jeza and the Kolovrat. However, Intelligence also had reported enemy activity *near the Plezzo basin.* How could troops arrive there from Cividale in time? A possible breakthrough in the south (III Army) also had to be considered. Should this have occurred on the Carso, the II Italian Army should have been ready to attack the Austro-Germans in the right flank, in a north-south direction proceeding toward the Adriatic. The Comando Supremo had only two divisions and twelve battalions of cyclists in reserve. To close the breach to the north, the Comando Supremo ordered a division of the VIII Corps to proceed northward. Crossing troops of the II Army in active combat, it would not be emplaced and battle-ready until October 30 resulting in the loss of the Matajur. Meanwhile opposed by no reserves, the enemy advanced through the breach. The Great War found Allied generals unprepared to use large numbers of reserves *or with plans of how to move them quickly to the needed sector.* The October, 1917 lesson on the Isonzo was not learned by the French either, who on the following March at Amiens had a similar experience. In a fatal move, Italian commanders had insisted on placing the bulk of their troops in the first lines. As these troops suffered the shock of the enemy attack, fears and anxieties spread to the rear lines. Like their Western Front counterparts Italian generals insisted on not losing a yard of terrain.

As the enemy advanced into the Val Uccea, the Comando Supremo had no available reserves to halt them (Maps 13, 23). Nor were there any reserves to seal the breach between the IV and VII Corps. Thus the attackers easily occupied the sector betwen M. Mia and M. Canin as the closest reserves were at Cividale and Palmanova, there being no central reserve (Map 13). By nightfall, the only reserve of the Comando Supremo was the *Sassari.*

TABLE I

Deployments of the Italian Army Reserve during the days of October 24 and 25

October 24
Reserves of the Comando Supremo:
(Adapted from the Royal Italian Caporetto Inquiry Commission)

Units		*Deployment on 10-23-17*	*Destination 10-24-17*
Twelve Cyclist Battal		Trentino	Unknown.
VII Gruppo Alpini		traveling from 1st Army	Montemmaggiore
53rd Inf. Div. *(Vicenza)*		Cividale	Stupizza Strait
13th Div.	*Ionio*	S. Andrat	disp. of II Army
	Massa Carrara	Cividale	Stupizza Strait
	Teramo	Bigliana	disp. of II Army
60th Div.	*Taranto*	Cormons	idem
	Ferrara	Ipplis	idem.
XX Corps	20th Inf. Div.	Palmanova	unknown
	63rd Inf. Div	Idem	unknown
XXX Corps	16th Inf. Div.	Trivignano	disp. of II Army
	21st Inf. Div.	Rivignano	idem
II Army Reserves			
25th Inf.	*Palermo*	left bank of Isonzo	unknown
	Livorno	idem	idem
30th Inf.	*Treviso*	Anhovo	at disp. XXIV Corps
	Girgenti	idem	unknown.
23rd Inf.	*Messina*	Medana	unknown
	Sassari	Manzinello	idem
	Venezia	Medana	idem
	Avellino	same	same
47th Inf.	1st Bers. Br.	Podresca	Globocak
Div.	5th Bers. Br.	Maria Zell	same
	Milano	near Gorizia	unknown
	Seisa	same	VIII Corps

October 25

		Deployed the eve of Oct. 24	*Destination on Oct. 25*
20th Inf. Div.		*Palmanova*	unknown
33rd Inf. Div.50		Cervignano	unknown
63rd Inf. Div.		Palmanova	unknown
VIII Alp. Grp.		On the way from the I Army	Zona Carnia
12 cycl. batt.		Trento sector	unknown
II Army Reserves.			
13th Inf. Div.	*Teramo*	Venco	unknown
	Sassari	Manzano	unknown
23rd Inf. Div.	*Messina*	Ipplis	XXVIII Corps
	Avellino	Galliano	XXVIII Corps
30th Inf.	*Livorno*	Verholje	XXIV Corps
60th Inf. Div.	*Taranto*	Oleis	XXVII Corps
	Milano	*Prepotto*	VII Corps
21st Inf. Div.		Rivignano, Talmassons	IV Corps
16th Inf. Div.		Trevignano	left wing II Army

Defensive Scheme of the Comando Supremo

The last line of resistance was the right bank of the Isonzo and its natural prolungation, the *Vallone* (Maps 4,5,12 for geography). On the left bank, the Vodice, Kuk and the fortifications in Gorizia all linked up to the right bank, with twenty three divisions from the Rombon to the Adriatic. In situations such as which developed at Caporetto, the defender had to be ready to quickly act in any direction, while the attacker knew exactly which way he was going to move. In October 1917, the Comando Supremo seemed paralyzed. On the northern part of the salient, (Rombon-M. Nero), the Austro-Germans had little luck in penetrating. There were tactical successes (Plezzo) but the defensive lines held. On the western end of the salient ((M. Nero-Doblar), there was a deep penetration in the Isonzo corridor with penetrations of the Habsburg Fiftieth Infantry Division between the Slieme and Mrzli and the German Twelfth Infantry Division along the banks of the Isonzo. The defect in Italian defenses was that *there were no available reserves to seal the breach.*

From Tolmino, Austro-German troops proceeded in two directions. The first was along the dorsum of the Kolovrat, the second proceeding between the Isonzo and Judrio Rivers toward the Globocak (Map 14). To paralyze this offensive, the Italian XXVII Corps would have had to attack from the Globocak toward the Jeza, along with troops of the VII Corps (*Firenze* & *Napoli*). At 1700, the VII Corps ordered a counterattack in the direction of M. Plezia and Bucova Jeza. *With troops from two different corps on the same location it was impossible to simultaneously go on the attack which never happened.* By evening, the Comando Supremo did not have the available reserves. Those of the II Army did not come into play, clearly demonstrating that the reserves were poorly deployed.

The Caporetto Inquiry Commission

On January 12, 1918 via Royal Decree No. 35, the Caporetto Commission of Inquiry was instituted. One January 17, 1918, Cadorna at Versailles received a telegram from Orlando notifying him that he would be called before the commission regarding the facts of Caporetto. Composing the commission were Lt. Gen. Carlo Caneva as Chairman, Vice Admiral Senator Canevaro, Lt. Gen. Ottavio Ragni, an attorney with the surname of Tommassi as Military Judge Advocate, Senator Prof. Bensa and from the Parliament the Hon. Prof. Stoppato and the Hon. Orazio Raimondi. The commission secretary was Fulvio Zugaro. On May 17, after Vice Admiral Canevaro's resignation, Admiral de Orestis succeeded him. On May 21, Ragni passed away.

The main theme of the inquiry was to avoid implicating Badoglio or Orlando of malfeasance. At the end it was Cadorna and the command structure who were rendered guilty. Badoglio was called to testify but not "at the disposal of the commission as were Capello and Cadorna." Defending himself he criticized Cadorna's deployment of reserves which really upset the generalissimo who had promoted him from Lt. Col. The commission held 241 sessions, consulting 2,310 documents and listened to 1,012 witnesses from all levels of the military. A report was published.[51] Some pertinent facts noted are that starting on Friday, October 26, it was evident that soldiers were throwing away their arms, taking off their identification patches and stealing civilian clothes. Thousands reached their homes in southern Italy.[52] As they marched through the Veneto they declared *La guerra è finita, abbiamo un accordo con gli Austriaci* (The war is over, we have made an agreement with the Austrians). This was a protest against the subhuman conditions at the front, as well as against the Italian Government which was uncaring and unresponsive to the needs of their families. Another pertinent fact was the removal of thirteen pages of the War Diary of the XXVII Corps (reported elsewhere in this chapter), which were critical of Badoglio at Caporetto. Subsequently Caviglia's account was also censured by the wishes of the king and the new Prime Minister of Italy, Benito Mussolini.[53] Cadorna's conduct was also severely criticized for sending troops on frontal infantry attacks with no probability of success nor of weakening any of the enemy's defenses.[54]

Two volumes were published, the first entitled *Cenno Schematico degli Avvenimenti* containing a scheme of events, while the second entitled *Le Cause e le responsiblità degli Avvenimenti*, describing the causes and names those responsible. Interestingly enough, only the second was distributed to parliament.

A proposal to amplify the investigation into the political arena which could have put some politicians into the proverbial hot seat was denied. On September 14, 1919 the commission folded its tent with the words "No one is without fault. We must forget them in turn and forget them in the vision of the greatness of the results which followed."

It noted that errors in the disaster were all human while everyone knew that horses and mules made no errors. Finally it appealed to history to judge those guilty. In the past writers from the OBARI to others have written that there were no real reports on the military and technical events of the conflict.[55]

Almost a century has passed with time to analyze the commissions findings and conclusions. How objective could these be when the ex-Interior Minister was now Prime Minister while an ex-War Minister and a commander of an army corps whose front had been broken through were now Vice-Chiefs of the General Staff. These men controlled the commission similar to the fox guarding the hen house. A web of intrigue was spun from the politicians to the military, certainly not a glorious chapter in Italy's history. The government had been afraid that in criticizing the military too much the war opposition would use the inquest as a means to stop the war. Italy had lost 300,000 rifles, 3,000 machine guns, 1,732 mortars and 3,152 artillery mouths.[56]

Events on October 24

Perhaps using his crystal ball at 2200 Cadorna issued orders to the II and III Armies to have the Tagliamento River defensive line in good working order. Other orders issued that evening did not correspond to reality. There was a great difference between what Cadorna wished and what would happen. The Comando Supremo knew that it had no reserves to seal the breach opening between the Zona Carnia and the left wing of the II Army at Montemaggiore (Map 23). In addition no orders were given for the withdrawal to the Tagliamento nor for the evacuation of the Bainsizza or the Gorizia Basin. His orders still stated that the left wing of the II Army should be linked with the Zona Carnia at Montemaggiore halting any enemy incursion from the Val Uccea. What troops would accomplish this? Not the Zona Carnia command which lacked troops. Not the Fiftieth Infantry Division tired and worn out deployed on the Stol being unable to reach the breach as a mule path ordered to be emplaced in June, 1917 had not been constructed (Map 23). There was no way the Generalissimo's orders would be implemented.

Events on October 25

Two breaches had developed. The first was between the IV and XXVII Corps (Twelfth Silesian) while the second was on the left wing of the II Army which was to linkup with the Zona Carnia blocking Austro-German troops which had proceeded along the Val Uccea into the Val Resia (Maps 13,40). As the enemy advanced along the Kolovrat, Italian defenses fell like dominoes. The *Arno* (on M. Kuk di Luico) was attacked in its rear and on its right. Illiterate troops could not perform (and did not understand) a turn to the right of 90° resulting in almost all being captured. As the *Arno* defenses fell, the IV Bersaglieri deployed at Luico was endangered and had to retreat. This endangered the flank of the *Salerno* on the Matajur. Again there were no reserves to seal the naked flanks. When the Austro-Germans occupied the northern bastions of the Globocak and Jeza on the Kolovrat the road to Cividale was open. All II Army troops east of this meridian were endangered especially the Italian troops on the Bainsizza. The Generalissimo had agreed with Capello's recommendation to withdraw to the Tagliamento, but then hesitated thirty-six hours, causing these many thousand troops to be trapped. These men could have been used to fight another day. In withdrawing his troops to the Tagliamento, Cadorna made a tactical error. His orders of September 1 read that the Zona Carnia Command was a link between the II and IV Armies and would cover any movement of troops from the Piave to the Isonzo and naturally, any withdrawal. The Carnia was the roof of the Friuli Plain covering troops which maneuvered from the Cadore to the Julian Alps (Map 40). Withdrawal of the II Army left the Zona Carnia Command unprotected.

When Montuori was asked by Cadorna if it was necessary to retreat to the Tagliamento, he showed himself to be wise in the way of Italian generals by spreading responsibility. He ran a poll among the generals involved, asking them if they could resist on the *linea del'armata.* This was the so-called defensive army line which the British had called out of date.[57] Of course all responded positively else they would be immediately dismissed. Receiving the optimistic report in a futile gesture he threw the few available reserves piecemeal into the cauldron. The left wing of the II Army had 102 battalions deployed over fifty miles of front but being terrible mountain terrain was actually triple that distance. Attacking Austro-Germans were using tactics unknown to the Italian commanders. The Comando Supremo only reacted to enemy moves, and did not take any initiatives. *As the II Army withdrew, its left wing could not deploy further northward than the Globocak-Montemaggiore sector, creating an unsealable breach from M. Cergnala to that sector leaving the Zona Carnia unprotected* (Map 14). *On this day Cadorna should have evacuated the Bainsizza, and Italian positions on the Vallone in the Carso (Map 5).* Sealing this breach was a function of the Comando Supremo reserves which never happened. Austro-German troops proceeded from Val Resia to the Tagliamento crossing it on November 2 at Cornino then proceeding southward along its west bank. It had taken twenty-seven months of bloody combat to occupy these territories. Enemy troops were almost at Cividale while Italian troops were still on the Bainsizza which is due north of Gorizia (Maps 12, 35).

Events on October 26

As Cadorna wrote in his *Memorie,* this morning he was still optimistic about sealing the breach to the north and that between the Korada and the Carso (Maps 29, 35), as long as the orders of the previous day to the II Army were carried out. Later he noted, that his hopes of halting the enemy were not fulfilled. In a report on Italian Army conditions, the Allied Military Command in Italy noted that the Comando Supremo constantly shifted military units and defense sectors about.[58] This was the case of Montemaggiore, which was under the jurisdiction of the II Army on October 24, the Carnia Command the next day, and again the II Army on October 26. None of these units had enough disposable troops to defend it. As the Italians abandoned Montemaggiore, the Austro-Germans arrived up to Azzida and penetrated into Val Resia (Maps 22, 13). Krafft noted that by today Austro-German forces had occupied the Stol, M. Mia, and the entrance of the Natisone

River Valley. He also criticized the Comando Supremo for sending in reserves piecemeal.

Cadorna decided to take some troops from the III Army (VIII Corps, Map 29), which were neither rested nor coordinated. Being in the northern wing of the III Army it would arrive too late at its destination point to do any good. They would have had to proceed northward across the III Army and active combat II Army which would have created chaos. *The reserves of the Comando Supremo absolutely did not decide any sector of the battle.*

Events on October 27

Austro-German successes today were entirely due to actions by non-coms. Early in the a.m., as orders were issued for the withdrawal to the Tagliamento, accompanied by his staff officers Cadorna changed his headquarters giving the impression of abandoning his men who looked to him for guidance. His first obligation was to his men but his only comment was "they do not fight." As the III Army withdrew from the *Vallone* it was ordered to cross at the Codroipo bridge while the II Army was to withdraw to the Torre Creek (River) and eventually cross the Tagliamento at the Pinzano Bridge (Maps 27, 29, 35). Since most Italian artillery had been lost, defensive perimeters had been established at the bridges by the *Corpo Speciale* using ten machine gun companies obtained from the III Army. As soon as the Austro-Germans started to shell Italian positions, the outranged machine guns withdrew.

A reality check would have shown that the Ragogna bridgehead did not exist prior to the war with trenches being entirely inadequate. To protect the III Army, the II Army was ordered to use the II, VI, and XXIV Corps. Being left in place until October 29, these units were destroyed. Comfortably ensconced in Treviso, the Comando Supremo could not make an informed decision on the status of the three corps, nor could it verify the validity of the reports.

Events on October 28

The whole III Army had crossed by 1030 which was the time to have the aforementioned right wing of the II Army (three corps) withdraw. Instead they were left there until the next day. At 2035, the II Army requested of the Comando Supremo, that the three aforementioned corps be allowed to use the bridge at Codroipo, a request which was denied, mentioning the intact III Army (Map 40). The flooding river had swept away the trestle bridge at Bonzicco. Cadorna assigned the Pinzano bridge to the three corps composing the right wing of the II Army. But how could they leave Udine proceed northwest with enemy troops on their flanks? There was more than enough room at the Madrisio and Latisana bridges defended by the *Corpo Speciale* for the III Army as well as the three aforementioned corps of the II Army. The *Corpo* had just arrived from Palmanova with neither artillery nor communication equipment (Map 36). The rest of the troops would defend at Valerio (Maps 27, 29). Prior to the war there had been emplaced a twelve mile defense perimeter at Codroipo. During the war, the guns were removed, but with infantry, it could still have been a defense perimeter for a short time. Instead filled with refugees and the III Army still far away it could not be defended. As previously noted there were only two solutions now which had to be implemented by the Comando Supremo. The first would be using the Codroipo bridges only for organized efficient units with the second being detaching the three aforementioned corps from the II Army and attach them to the III Army which was withdrawing across the Madrisio and Latisana bridges.

Events on October 29

With the enemy already at Udine, the three unlucky corps of the II Army deployed south of the city started their withdrawal northwestward. As they proceeded Austro-German troops leaving that city fell on their flanks. Forced to proceed toward the Pinzano bridges, they became isolated and were destroyed.

Events on October 30

The Italian VIII Corps ordered the Fifty-ninth Infantry Division to form a protective bridgehead at Codroipo to help the three corps coming from southeast of Udine. Austro-German troops chasing remnants of the II Army arriving north of the bridgehead were unable to cross the river, turned southward along the left (east bank) of the Tagliamento and fell on the north and east flank of this division. Infiltrating it they attacked from the south, north and east. Unable to handle this type of attack the Italian troops panicked, blew the Codroipo bridges and fled to the west (right) bank. The XII Corps would be responsible to hold Passo Mauria (Map 28, 35). The rear guards of the IV Army were to hold the Ponte nelle Alpi position until the II Army has passed the meridian of Vittorio (Veneto) (Map 28). These orders were beautiful on paper but did not respond to reality as Austro-German troops had orders "not to rest but keep moving at all costs to give the Italians no chance to reform their defenses."[59]

Events on October 31

By the early a.m. all Italian troops had crossed the river at the Pinzano and Cornino bridges except those on M. Ragogna. Logically, one would then order the destruction of the bridges. However, the Comando Supremo, far from the scene of action insisted that the *Corpo Speciale* remain on the left (east) bank of the river, and *not to destroy the bridges unless they were in grave danger.* What greater danger could there be than approaching enemy troops? These words sealed the fate of the troops on the left bank and led to the incomplete destruction of the Cornino bridge allowing the Austro-Germans to repair the bridges and cross the Tagliamento.

On the other side of the trench Boroevic refused Hofacker's troops permission to cross his lines to capture the bridge at Latisana. The Serbian *Feld Marschall* was insulted that he had not been appointed commander of the XIV Army and would do everything to make things difficult for Below. This would eventually lead to the Lost Battle of Annihilation at Caporetto.

Events in November 1917

Delay in the withdrawal of the IV Army (supposedly to save its artillery), could have led to a catastrophe. From the November 5 to November 10 its eastern flank was unprotected by the II Army. This could have led to very serious consequences. Heavy concentrations of enemy troops could have fallen on the IV Army before its I Corps had reached the Belluno Basin. Instead the A.O.K. with its petty politics came to the rescue of the terrible predicament of the Italian Army dividing the command of the sector in two (Carnia and Friulian Plain (Map 40). During the disagreements the Italian troops escaped. When Italian troops arrived at the Tagliamento on October 30 Cadorna hesitated until November 4 before ordering the withdrawal to the Piave. He had the false hopes that the enemy could be contained in the mountains as well as permanently stopped on the Tagliamento. In fact on November 2 he telegraphed the II and III Armies declaring that enemy pressure had come to an end. A few hours later the enemy crossed the river at Cornino.

The Problems With the Bridges and the Episode of the Codroipo Bridge.

The Codroipo Bridge had been assigned to the III Army which on October 28 was far from the Tagliamento as stragglers for disbanded units rushed toward it (Map 40). Having no bridgehead defenses the army attempted to assign the VIII Corps to be the rear guard, but it had already been assigned to cover its northern wing. Other units of the corps and II Army arrived at the village of Codroipo which was now encircled from three sides. Fearing complete encirclement the Italian troops broke out toward the south and the Madrisio bridge.

If Cadorna were aware of the situation at Codroipo, he would have certainly changed the orders. However the Generalissimo was not in contact with field commanders. Such were the events that only the Comando Supremo could have solved the problem. It could have formed an independent corps of the forgotten II, VI and XXIV Corps and proceeded there. With this maneuver, the III Army would have been limited to the bridges at Madrisio and Latisana. Another solution would have been to take the aforementioned three corps from the II Army ordering them toward the Codroipo bridge as an independent unit attached to the III Army. There were no reserves available for the Codroipo and Ragogna bridges. A severe mix-up occurred because the Codroipo bridges had been used by both the Italian II and III Armies. Moving the II Army units to Codroipo resulted in a catastrophe for the Italians. Stragglers should have been able to approach the nearest bridge, cross the Tagliamento and then be reorganized into effective units to fight again.

Strangely, Cadorna, faced with an enemy offensive in 1916, assembled the Fifth Army ready to oppose any Conrad break through. Now why did he not do the same.? In warfare, the aim is not to hold on to every inch of terrain, but to destroy the enemy's forces. As Bencivenga noted, he could have assembled units of the II Army in the moraine amphitheatre of S. Daniele, while the III Army could have withdrawn to the lower Tagliamento.[60] Links between the two units would be via mobile troops. The middle of the river would have been the focus of attention. Enemy troops would probably aim for that sector and thus have the II and III Armies fall on their flanks. Such was not to be, as enemy surprises continued until the Piave, with daily individual acts of bravery and cowardice. By the evening of October 25, the XIV Army controlled the Isonzo triangle as well the chain of mountains which dominated the plains from the Saga Gorge to the upper Tagliamento.

At the same time, not being able to help the left wing of the II Army, Cadorna gave the order to retreat. This was later rescinded and issued again the evening of October 26. The III Army retreated in an orderly fashion with about 300,000 men to the Piave while the 230,000 of the IV Army from Cadore to the Grappa along with many stragglers. Most of the 90,000 men of the Zona Carnia Command were taken prisoner because of the late order to withdraw.

Another important point was the separation of infantry and artillery in the Italian Army. The artillery was deployed and static, while the infantry was deployed, fought, was rotated and *had no contact with the artillery.* Both British and German generals were amazed at this fact. German artillery moved with the infantry wherever it went.

A final word about the German Army First Quartermaster. Ludendorff allowed the Strategic Reserve to go to the Italian Front but withdrew its artillery after two weeks. Major Georg Wetzell chief of the General Staff Operations Section had proposed to him that a larger force be sent to Italy which was rejected.[61] Knowing his keen politico-military mind why did he not accept this plan? Knocking Italy out of the war meant being able to transfer millions of battle-hardened Austro-German troops to the Western Front which could easily overcome the manpower-starved Anglo-French forces making any Allied offensive plans impractical.

After so many words, the reasons for the Disaster may be summarized as follows:

1. The Italian Army troops were ill-fed, ill-led, ill-trained, ill-equipped and illiterate with the command structure unable to react to the XIV Army's quick deep penetration.
2. The German Army's excellent training, leadership, morale and use of new tactics which cannot be praised enough.
3. Needed were commanders who had aggressive vision, mastery of tactics and strategy and the ability to exact the maximum in fighting qualities from both men and equipment qualities sorely lacking in the Italian Army.
4. The Cadorna-Capello disagreements regarding tactics confused troops.
5. The lack of troop deployment in the Foni Strait.
6. The lack of linkups among the IV, VII and XXVII Corps.

7. The premature evacuation of the Saga Strait.
8. Badoglio's four miscues and most of all
9. Inadequately placed reserves.

Chapter XIV Endnotes

Critique of Events of October-November, 1917 on the Isonzo

1 During the Fascist regime, Gianni Baj-Macario was sent to a remote border town for a year for criticizing Lt. Gen. Pecori-Giraldi.

2 Guderian, Heinz, *Panzer Leader,* DaCapo Press, New York 1996, p. 40

3 *Militär Wissenschaftliche Rundschau,* 1937, Vol. III, p. 326, Issued by the German Army General Staff.

4 Martini, F., *Diario 1914-1918,* 285, 452-453, 462; Angelo Boca, *Gli italiani in Libia 1860-1922,* Bari, 1986, 294-295, 305

5 Lidell-Hart, Basil H., *The Real War 1914-1918,* Little Brown & Co., 1964, p. 362

6 PRO : WO 106/805, Lt. Gen. Fayolle, Report of Allied Military Commission on Italian Army: Dec. 26, 1917

7 Lord Northcliffe, op. cit., p. 12-13

8 Carlo Emilio Gadda, *Giornale di Guerra e di Prigioneria,* Torino, Einaudi

9 *RICC: Dal Isonzo al Piave* op. cit.,-Vol. II *Le Cause e le Responsibiltà*, Rome p. 279

10 A. Gatti, *Caporetto,* op. cit., p. 12-13.

11 USSME: Relazione Ufficiale, Volume IV, Tomo 3° bis, Doc., op. cit.,*Le Operazione del 1917 in Ottobre-Dicembre/ Narrazione,* Torino, 1954, p. 236

12 Gough commanded the British V Army which was directly attacked by the German XVI Army in the "Michael Offensive" of March 1918. According to S.L. A. Marshall, Gough was aware that the tactics of Riga and Caporetto would be used against him; S.L.A. Marshall, *World War I,* American Heritage Press, 1971, p. 344.

13 DDI, Series V, Volume IX, Doc. 346; Imperiali to Sonnino, 1-11-1917, p. 242

14 USSME: Relazione Ufficiale, Vol. IV, Tome 3° bis, Doc., op. cit.,p. 99

15 Ibid p. 116

16 Ibid, p. 296.

17 Richard von Berendt, *Die Artillerie in der 12 Isonzo-Schlacht* in: Allegmeine Schweizerische Militärzeitung, H. 12, 1935, pp. 795-796

18 RICC: Vol. II, op. cit., pp. 129-133; L. Capello, *Note di Guerra,* op. cit.,Vol. II, p. 324.

19 RICC : Vol. II, op. cit., p. 127.

20 Ibidem p. 135; L. Capello *Note di Guerra* Vol. II p. 341.

21 RICC: *Dal Isonzo al Piave* Vol. II, *Le Cause e le Responsibilità,* op. cit., Rome, p., 1010.

22 RICC: Volume I, *Cenno schematico degli avvenimenti,* op. cit., p. 373; Nuova Antologia, August, 1960 pp. 447-468, Raffaele Cadorna *"Le Memorie di Vittorio Emanuele Orlando,"* ; the supplement to this article explains Badoglio's behavior at Caporetto; Nuova Antologia, idem, Rodolfo Mosca, *La Svolta di Caporetto,* p. 478 explains the words of Senator Paratore.

23 L. Capello, *Per La Verita',* Milano, Treves, 1920, p. 292.

24 L. Capello, *Note di Guerra,* Vol. II, p. 324; RICC, Vol. II pp. 129-133.

25 OBARI, op. cit., p. 144

26 USSME: Relazione Ufficiale, Vol. IV, Tomo 3, op. cit., p. 313.

27 RICC: op. cit., Vol. I, op. cit., pp. 110, 119; idem, Vol. II, op. cit., pp. 108-110

28 RICC: op. cit., p. 103-110

29 Alfred Krauss, *Die Ursachen unserer Niderlage,* Munich, Lehmanns, 1926

30 USSME: Telegraph File, Comando Supremo to II, III, IV Armies, Oct. 29, 30, 31, 1917.

31 Enrico Barone, *La Storia Militare della Nostra Guerra fino a Caporetto,* Bari, 1919

32 Letter sent by Cesare Savoldi to *Avanti,* February 14, 1918. Due to tight censure after Caporetto, it was not published, but kept in the personal archives of the editor of *Avanti,* Giacinto Menotti Serrati. The Serrati Foundation is c/o the Gramsci Institute in Rome, with the letter being in envelope 37/3.

33 RICC: Vol. I, op. cit., p. 484-486.

34 Kurt Suckert (later known as Curzio Malaparte), *Viva Caporetto ! La Rivolta dei Santi Maledetti,* Milano, Mondadori, 1981, p. 60-61

35 R. Grieco, *Stato Operaio,*1927, No. 9-10, p. 990-991, *Le Ripercussioni della Rivoluzione Russa in Russia*

36 Palmiro Togliatti, *Ordine Nuovo,* October 18, 1919, quoted in "Dopo Caporetto" by Giuseppe Prezzolini who subsequently emigrated to the U.S.A. and became Director of the *Casa Italiana* of Columbia University in New York City.

37 Vladimir Ilich Ulyanov (Lenin), *La Disfatta del Proprio Governo Nelle Guerre Imperialiste,* July 26, 1915; This was subsequently quoted in "Sul Movimento Operaio Italiano, Rome, Edizione Rinascita, 1952.

38 USSME: Relazione Ufficiale, Vol. III, Tomo 1, *Le Operazione del 1916, Gli Avvenimenti Invernali Gennaio-Aprile/Narrazione* p. 170

39 New York Times, January 03, 2003, p. 1

40 USSME: Relazione Ufficiale, Vol. IV, Tomo 3° bis, Doc., op. cit., Comando Supremo, *Situazione delle forze nemiche secondo le informazioni pervenute a tutto il 6 Ottobre 1917,* Doc. 9, Protocol 801, October 2, 1917, p. 14

41 RICC: L. Capello, op. cit., Vol. II, p. 208 ; L. Capello, *Per La Verita'* op. cit., p. 143.

42 *Relazione del comando d'artiglieria del XXVII Corpo d'Armata* in L. Capello, *Per La Verita',* Milano, 1920, pp. 277 & 280.

43 USSME: *Relazione Ufficiale,* Vol. IV, Tomo 3° bis, Doc., op. cit.,Comando Artiglieria XXVII Corps, *Disposizione circa schieramento artiglieria,* Doc. 66, Protocol 5277, October 11, 1917, p. 127

44 OBARI, op. cit., p. 144

45 Major Walther Meyendorff, *Cadorna-Capello: Die italienische Führung vor der Schlacht bei Karfreit.* Offprint from *Militärwissenschaftliche Mitteilungen,* 1933, pp. 856-57; it also discusses the bunching up of artillery.

46 To differentiate between a tactical and strategic victory, an excellent example would be the Michael offensive on the Western Front. The Germans broke through the enemy lines achieving a tactical victory, but did not reach the Channel ports, which would have given them a strategic victory denying the allies supplies coming from the U. S.A.

47 USSME: Relazione Ufficiale, Vol. IV, Tomo 3° bis, Doc., Comando Supremo, *Assegnazione Riserve,* Document No. 119, Protocol 4970, October 25, 1917, p. 287

48 L. Cadorna, *Altre Pagine Sulla Grande Guerra,* Milano, Mondadori, 1925, p. 132. The Generalissimo wrote this book as a defense of his actions.

49 Roberto Bencivenga, *La Sorpresa Strategica di Caporetto,* Gaspari Editore, Udine 1997. p. 67

50 The Thirty-third Infantry Division was made up of units of the Twentieth and Sixty-third Infantry Divisions.

51 RICC: *Dall'Isonzo al Piave,* Rome, 1919

52 Ibid, pp. 484-486

53 Melograni, P., *Storia della Guerra,* p. 420-3; Pier Pieri and George Rochat, *Pietro Badoglio,* Torino, 1974, p. 319-26; E. Caviglia, *Diario,* St. Antony's Documents 249/067661 (5 May 1932, Mussolini)

54 RICC: p. 58-59

55 The Official British Army Report, Italy laments this fact while the Italian reporter Ugo Ojetti writing in the *Corriere della Sera,* July 11, 1919 also lamented the fact of the lack of information. He noted that the official report of the 1866 war was finally released in 1908. The author feels that no one in the *Ufficio Storico* would report on Caporetto initially for fear of offending higher-ups and later for fear of Fascist retribution.

56 Krauss, *Das Wonder von Karfreit,* op. cit., p. 66

57 OBARI, op. cit., p. 46-47

58 Idem, p. 108

59 Below's Diary Entry, dated, Oct. 30, 1917

60 R. Bencivenga, op. cit., p. 111

61 National Archives, Washington, D.C., Von Seeckt Papers, File M-132, Roll 20, Item 90; Wetzell had written to Seeckt (who had been kept out of the O.K.L. by the professional jealousy of Ludendorff) that if he were helping to make decisions more troops would have been sent to Italy.

CHAPTER XV

POST-CAPORETTO MILITARY AND OTHER EVENTS 1917-1918

By the end of 1917, Vienna had won a massive victory but nonetheless started to negotiate with the allies about a separate peace. President Wilson and Lloyd George were convinced that the allies could not win. Negotiations took place throughout neutral nations in Europe. The United States had declared war on Germany on April 6, 1917, but still had not entered the military or diplomatic equation. For the A.O.K. now there only remained one last offensive push which hopefully would bring better terms at the peace table.

The old order changeth, yielding place to the new,
And God fulfills Himself in many ways.
Alfred Lord Tennyson, Death of Arthur

BY THE END of 1917 the Great German General Staff was making military as well as diplomatic and politcal decisions in Germany and having a dominant role in the war effort of the Central Powers. Ruling from Riga on the Baltic to Palestine, it moved men about like chess-board pieces. Local military decisions were left to commanders on the spot, but the big strings were pulled by the O.K.L. Wilson lectured Europeans on human rights which has been noted as the dawn of American diplomatic power which has persisted to the Twenty-first Century. Previously, President Theodore Roosevelt had been the arbiter of the Russo-Japanese peace treaty with representatives of the belligerent nations meeting with him in Portsmouth, New Hampshire in 1905, but his actions did not yet reflect America's burgeoning diplomatic power.[1] His role was not due to America's might but as a result of a Japanese request that he mediate the dispute.

Foch left Italy on November 23, sure that the Piave Front would hold. On December 15, the Central Powers signed an armistice with the Russian Bolshevik Government. Germany would now have the time to get organized and make the final push on the Western and Italian Fronts. In classic forward-looking German Army fashion, at a meeting of the German Crown Privy Council, Hindenburg had insisted on the annexation by Germany of a belt of Polish territory extending as far as Warsaw. He noted that this was "for maneuvering of my left wing in the next war."[2]

Developments in the Italian Army

George M. Trevelyan, a conscientious objector who became a British Red Cross driver on the Italian Front wrote a summary concerning the troops. He reported that the only men who had *Risorgimento* ideals were the upper and middle classes while the *contadino* (peasant), from the south who placed the welfare of his family above all else was very unhappy as he would have to do all the fighting.[3] Officers had little contact with the *fanti* fearing that one would kill them.[4] Italian morale which had been very low at Caporetto, a few weeks later soared for unknown reasons. Writers have not been able to explain why morale and military performance went from the low of the last decade of October to a strong-willed, devil-may-care, defend-to-the-death-attitude defending the Grappa the first days of November. Perhaps it was because now they were faced with in invader and were told that their homes and women would be taken from them. Low morale had been due to poor conditions and treatment which led to the so-called "military strike" as described by Cadorna and the RICC. Suffice it to say that after

Caporetto, in their fighting on the Grappa, even Krafft, the architect of Caporetto agreed that the morale of Italian prisoners had changed.

By mid-November, two new Italian armies were being formed about seventy miles to the rear of the front. In large encampments beyond Mantua were assembled soldiers of the class of 1899 (170,000), plus stragglers from Caporetto (Map 14A). Many men from this group would later fight on the Grappa. Eventually these troops would constitute the newly formed V Army. These troops plus those of the class of 1900 increased the Italian Army troop count by 800,000. The only good organized units were the I Army (400,000) while the III and IV Armies totaled 350,000 but had had little enemy contact. The reserve 260,000 man class of 1900 was to have no contact with the enemy for the moment. The II Army (VI, XXV, XXVIII, and XXX Corps) was a disorganized mass of men which was being reorganized between Verona and Vicenza. In December 1917, the VI, and XXV Corps were sent to the Grappa. The II, XII, and XIV Corps reduced to mere skeletons would now be molded into the new V Army while the IV, VII, and XXIV Corps were not reconstituted. Using British and French equipment an artillery training camp was installed near Bologna.

Assault troops (men specially trained and equipped in assault tactics) in division size were formed. From January 30 to February 2, 1918, there was another meeting at Versailles. Representing Italy were Ministers Orlando, Sonnino and Alfieri as well as the ever present Col. Gatti, the Comando Supremo's historian. Foch declared that the allies would go on the defensive from the English Channel to Venice until American help arrived. Diaz was happy with this decision as now he had time to reorganize his forces, giving them better food, clothes, and furlough, all to boost morale. Newspapers were introduced to the men in the trenches, but who could read them? The government finally got the message to properly equip the troops on the Grappa. Italian aircraft production now had arrived at 1,740 planes and 1,230 motors for the year 1917.[5]

Lastly the tactics would change. No longer would there prolonged ineffectual artillery barrages followed by costly frontal infantry attacks against machine guns but firepower (as at Mukden) rather than manpower would be the deciding factor using machine guns and mortars with supporting strong points. The principle of force-multiplier taught by Giulio Douhet, an Italian staff officer was finally appreciated. A machine gun was worth many hundreds of men with the bullets it threw against the enemy, a doctrine which had not been accepted by British, French or Italian generals. Douhet would go on to write about aerial bombing and would be called the "Father of Strategic Bombing." As for defenses they would have to be in depth together with a new technique, the counterattack borrowed from their respected Austro-German enemies. Allied staff officers noted that Italian staff officers were energetic but had no organizing capacity nor could they adapt themselves to maneuver warfare resulting in units not kept intact (as Diaz lamented) and troops being kept in the front line trenches indefinitely with no relief. There was no defense in depth with troops being left in the front line trenches with no reserves. Finally there was no liaison between artillery and infantry plus no good knowledge of how to carry out a counterattack which was often done late rendering it ineffectual.

On December 10, 1917, Rome issued a decree (published on December 17) that there would be an insurance policy for the troops, effective Janaury 1, 1918. Speaking to Parliament on December 22, 1917, Orlando summarized the government policy in one word, "Resist." That day, the vote was 345 to 50 in favor of the government.[6] Giolitti was asked to make his thoughts known, but demurred.

Sonnino stated that there should be only two things happening. First was the change in military leadership; second was the Allies' promise to furnish what was needed to achieve victory.

After reaching Versailles, Cadorna requested that Gatti join him. The Italian Army historian wanted to continue his work in investigating what happened at Caporetto. Badoglio refused to answer any questions put to him while Diaz finally told the colonel to stop his investigations, as it would concern documents which were still secret.

America entered the Diplomatic (and Military) Equation

On Jan. 8, 1918, in an address to Congress Wilson announced his well-known Fourteen Points[7] which were well-received by Habsburg ethnics but not by European diplomats. The principles were not new. They had previously appeared in an address by Lloyd George of Great Britain.[8] Subsequent to this address, Wilson made other important addresses in the next few weeks (especially concerning self-determination).[9] On February 11, 1918, again in an address to Congress, he cited another principle, "The court of mankind had decided that there shall be no annexation, no contributions, no punitive damages."[10] On July 4, at Mount Vernon, he listed as among the first, "The destruction of every arbitrary power anywhere that can separately, secretly and of its single choice disturb the peace of the world; or if it can not be presently destroyed, at the least its reduction to virtual impotence."[11] Germany had already requested peace on the basis of the Fourteen Points (and subsequent addresses). Hearing these words European diplomats felt emboldened to impose terms in conflict with the Fourteen Points. Wilson was preaching self-determination, an unheard principle in Europe causing European diplomats who had always used the balance of power concept to raise their eyebrows. He noted that it was for the different nationalities, not for him, to see what concessions they wanted from the Austro-Hungarian government.

Since the Congress of Vienna in 1815, territories had been assigned to noble rulers without the input of the residents which seems odd in today's big push toward democracy in nations. This was followed by the Congress of Berlin and the Treaty of London all following the same principles. The American President was preaching morality to a group of European diplomats who did not even know how to spell the word. However, if one thinks honestly about the problem European diplomats were correct in predicting periodic wars among the small Balkan nations which were unwilling to subordinate their ambitions in the interest of peace. They would never subvert their tiny interests for the common good.

Changes in the Allied Supreme Command

The Supreme Interallied Council met at Versailles on February 8, 1918, with the aim of establishing a general reserve with a contribution of each nation. Italy was to furnish seven divisions, France thirteen, and Britain fourteen. Petain bargained Foch down to eight, while the British stated that they could not furnish any. Finally, after much bickering, the matter was referred to the Supreme War Council to meet in London on March 14. Again, there nothing was resolved. Foch later declared, "Only a disaster could correct the error made in London in March 1918." On March 21, on the Western Front, the Germans started an offensive which destroyed the British Fifth Army (Lt. Gen. Herbert Gough), opening a breach between allied armies. Noting that the enemy was aiming for Amiens, Foch realized that Paris was in danger, as were the Channel ports. He immediately notified Clemenceau that another supreme military body was needed as the above-mentioned bodies had performed badly in the past few weeks. Coincidentally, Haig, the British commander in France had telegraphed Gen. Henry Wilson who had succeeded Robertson as Chief of the Imperial General Staff requesting that he come to France to nominate a Supreme Military Leader. This has been current information but like the taste of a soup as new ingredients are added history keeps changing as new facts are uncovered.[12] Recent introduced evidence reveals that Haig had never sent the oft-mentioned telegram. Next day Wilson arrived at Boulogne. A meeting of leaders was scheduled on March 26, in the town of Doullens. Present would be President Raymond

Poincarè of France, Lord Alfred Milner, as representative of the British Prime Minister, Premier Georges Clemenceau of France and Gen. Petain. After much discussion, Foch was nominated to head the allied military effort on the Western Front. He immediately requested the French Tenth Army be withdrawn from Italy. This explained why the four French divisions and subsequently the two British divisions were withdrawn.[13] Foch stated that he wanted additional powers, noting he could not run the war with the existing powers. He wanted the Supreme Allied Command of all allied troops and bases from the English Channel to the Aegean Sea. In another meeting on April 3 he was given the power to do the strategic planning, while the tactical planning would be done by the national chiefs of staff. Regarding the Italian Front, Orlando and Sonnino obtained a compromise. Since the king was the army's nominal commander he could not supersede him. The front would be under his nominal command but the army would be under local control unless outside help was requested.

Events on other Home Fronts

Russia

By 1917 the Russian Army had collapsed. It had lost 2,500,000 dead with 3,850,000 wounded and 2,400,000 prisoners. In February 1917, units started to mutiny. On March 15, 1917, the Czar abdicated to be followed by a number of provisional governments. Finally the Bolshevik faction of the Russian Social Democratic Party took over the government. Led by Lenin, Russia sued for peace so the Bolsheviks could reinforce their control over Russia. On March 3, 1918, the peace treaty was signed at Brest-Litovsk ceding Germany a huge piece of Russian territory which today includes the Ukraine Republic, Poland as well as Baltic territories.[14] Germany was to have a huge agriculture and mining area but the treaty was annulled on Nov. 11, 1918.

Imperial Germany

By 1917 there were mutinies and riots on the Home Front. The O.K.L. still wanted to pursue the war. Lloyd George reported to the Commons that German worker output had decreased thirty-three percent due to the British blockade on German importation of foodstuffs.[15]

France

After the army mutinies of 1917, the army paused in its offensive ardour (Vol. I, p. 448). A new general Phillipe Petain, was more humane than his predecessor. The nation was also realizing the importance of total war. In a speech to the French Chamber of Deputies, on January 2, 1917, Minister Aristide Briand noted, "Censure should not be applied only to military and diplomatic information. Instructions have been given so that campaigns in favor of a peace which we are not in favor of shall not be tolerated."[16] It should be noted that information about the Russian Revolution was heavily censored in Paris and London.

Great Britain

People were suffering from food shortages due to the submarine menace. Fresh colonial troops were arriving as well as supplies and munitions from the U.S.A. Britain and France were now anxiously awaiting the arrival of fresh American divisions. In London prior to the Christmas Recess, Lloyd George declared to the House of Commons that the aim of the Allies was the destruction of Prussian military power and a free government in Germany not to obtain some German colonies in Africa.[17] He went on to lament the inadequate rail facilities in Italy, making troop transport tedious and lengthy, and had had the foresight to appoint a British Military Mission in December 1916, to study the transportation facilities for just such an eventuality.

When the need arose the following October the British at least had a plan.

Italy

Food shortages were also starting to be felt. Prior to the war, Italy was almost self sufficient in grain production. In 1913, it produced 5.8 million tons of wheat and 2.7 million tons of corn, with imports totaling 1.2 million tons. As men and quadripeds were taken from the farm for the war effort, grain production dramatically dropped. By 1917, the total cereal production was 5.9 million tons with a shortfall of 3.8 million tons.[18] After Caporetto as refugees poured into the boot there was a dramatic increase in food needs. Orlando appealed to Lloyd George noting that he would need almost 700,000 tons of coal per month as well as wheat. The British Prime Minister fulfilled the request.[19] Italy had sent 100,000 men to work as military laborers in France in return for coal. When the Germans captured the coal fields Italy was left with no coal but 100,000 laborers in France. Fewer trains were running, and central heating in public and private buildings had ceased. By November, 1918, 800,000 tons of coal had been shipped to Italy from Britain by sea.[20] As archives are made available to historians, this man, not an Italian, is becoming more important in the salvation of Italy. The Catholic Church also found itself in a curious position. The Savoys had taken all its temporal possessions with King Vittorio Emanuele II being excommunicated in 1870. It was in close contact with the Holy Roman Empire (Austria-Hungary), with many in the Vatican supporting it. The prominent Cardinal Maffi now talked to Italians of a "Noble appeal for union and sacrifice."[21] In the whole nation the masses felt that they had suffered humiliation (at the hands of the army) as well as danger of invasion whereby their women would be violated by the hated "hereditary enemy." A supreme effort was now made to better organize the war effort. The nation was now insisting that the invader be thrown out of Italian territories. Italy was down but not out. The reader will have to understand that this meant the two percent of the population that really meant anything in the Italian political landscape of the time. It did not mean the peasant class which wanted peace at any cost.

After October 1917, there was finally a betterment of relationships between the politicians and social classes especially the middle classes which now were starting to increase rapidly. Teachers, doctors, government employees all felt a surge of patriotism as opposed to the illiterate peasants who were still pining for peace and did not know Italy existed. The upper classes felt that it was troops in the advanced units sympathizing with the masses, which allowed the enemy to penetrate Italian lines. The masses felt that it was the military hierarchy who allowed the enemy to advance. Some wanted to have Cadorna tried by a military tribunal. On July 12, 1917, in a speech to the Parliament, Socialist Deputy Claudio Treves declared, "Gentlemen of my government and of the governments of all Europe, hear the voices that rise from the trenches which have torn the breast of Mother Earth. She dictates the ultimatum of life or death: Next winter no longer to be spent in the trenches."[22]

In the parliament Cadorna who had already been dismissed was severely criticized in secret sessions. He was noted to never have had any meetings with his subordinates regarding his orders or future strategy and exercising a reign of terror. Socialist Deputy Santulli moved to have Cadorna, Porro and other members of the past three cabinets arrested and tried by the Italian Supreme Court. Orlando reacted vigorously to this with the phrase "Our sons are fighting to defend the nation. Let us hope that they will never learn that which has been stated in this chamber." The Giolitti faction remained silent. The maneuvers in parliament were likened to a "witches cauldron of intrigue and conspiracy," and "distasteful and sordid."[23] British Ambassador Rodd prophetically noted that there were many schemers but a strong man was needed. How right he was! Less than five years later the strong man would appear in the person of Benito Mussolini.

Deputy Modigliani stated that the allies must be induced to make peace or Italy would sue for peace, otherwise there would soon be a revolution. Following the October Revolution all Socialists world-wide awaited the Socialist takeover of the world. The allied position at this time was very difficult. American help had not arrived, Russia had been defeated, France and Great Britain were drained both of men and money. The neutralists started to make their move. They formed the *Fascio di Difesa Nazionale* which in the Lower House enrolled 158 and in the Senate 92. National sentiment however, was changing. The hundreds of thousands who had fled or deserted within the national borders now started to present themselves to army posts in Emilia and Romagna. Peasants in the countryside had been giving them the cold shoulder. Why should their husband, son, or brother die at the front while this young man was alive but not doing his duty?

On December 19 the Italian Parliament session was opened to the public presenting the Italian discord in which everyone and everybody was accused of military and government errors. Opposing were the Socialists with the Giolitti faction voting with the government.

Changes and Events in the Habsburg Army and Society

During the Brest-Litovsk discussions appeared the first big diplomatic discordant note between the Central Powers. Germany was hard and tough, while Charles had instructed his emissaries to go easy on Russia. On February 8, the Ukraine proclaimed itself independent with a peace treaty being signed on the next day. It negotiated with Vienna the famous "bread for peace" whereby in exchange for being awarded some Polish territory, it would send to Vienna, one million tons of cereals by August 1. However, with the chaotic situation in the new republic, no wheat was forthcoming resulting in another fairy tale. On March 7, a peace treaty was signed with Romania whereby it gave up a strip of land on the Hungarian frontier to Hungary as well as Dobrugia. Romania was also promised eventual authority over Bessarabia.

At home, Charles also had to deal with the Hungarian crisis especially the *Ausgleich* that was to be negotiated every ten years. After ascending the throne that April Charles had replaced War Minister Krobatin with GdI Rudolf Stöger-Steiner. He also replaced Conrad with Arz while GeneralOberst Samuel Baron Hazai former Hungarian Minister of Defense became chief of the replacement branch reporting directly to the emperor. This whole group became known as the "second A.O.K." In August Stöger-Steiner had sent Charles a memorandum noting that the empire was in dire straits. Everything was now lacking in the empire. Food, clothing, and workers were in short supply. Replacements in the army could be provided up to May, 1918 while arms and munitions were adequate except for machine gun production which had been cut from three thousand per month to fifteen hundred. He noted that while military production was increasing, the factory workers were demoralized due to poor food in quantity and quality.[24] There had been disorders throughout the empire but the important ones were in Hungary. In May 1917 Tisza had been dismissed as premier to be replaced by the ineffectual Prince Moritz Esterházy who resigned after two months. He was replaced by Alexander Werkele to whom he promised in principle a separate Hungarian army after the war but the minister kept pressing for a separate army to be constituted immediately.[25] Charles convoked a Crown Council resulting in the decision that this would be possible after the war.[26] In November GdI Alexander Baron Szurmay, the Hungarian Defense Minister demanded that the army completely separate into Austrian and Hungarian entities. The following January army commanders assembled at Baden opposed the separation of the armies. Nonetheless secret negotiations continued.[27] With the disorders at home, GdI Prince Alois Schönburg-Hartenstein was appointed as commander of the Home Front troops.[28] Eventually seven combat divisions had to be sent by the A.O. K. to quell civil riots on the Home Front while three *Honvéd* divisions were sent to Hungary to scour the countryside for food which the nation needed both on the Home and Battle Fronts. There were now widespread strikes and work stoppages forcing Charles to order the army to respond which it did with operations "Mogul" and "Revolver" sending several divisions from the battle front to the home front to control any emergency. Hungary which was always a thorn in Vienna's side became even more of a problem.

Charles was Emperor, Supreme Warlord and commander of the army but it is doubtful if he could fill only one of these positions let alone all three. The food crisis was temporarily and partially resolved at Caporetto when troops sent food packages home. Charles also ended (against the opposition of Arz) all executions of military in the field.[29] In a failed effort to obtain support of Czech units he also pardoned Czech political prisoners who promptly returned home to continue their political activities. The emperor was very resentful that his nation's very existence now depended on Germany. In November the A.O.K. finally noted that all ranks suffered from lack of food and clothing.[30] As in Italy, women were now entering the work force both in the home and non-combat roles in the battle sectors. The replacement situation began to tighten up again as Hazai was told to investigate the use of female auxiliaries and to comb the rear areas for replacements. There was a great never-ending cycle of crises. Food was starting to lack because the farmers were at the front. Munitions started to lack because industrial workers were at the front, while raw materials for the manufacture of munitions could not arrive at Central Powers ports due to the British blockade. Rations for the industrial workers were increased while those to men at the front were decreased. Soldiers at the front were malnourished and consequently susceptible to many diseases. In January 1918 bread rations were reduced to 165 grams per day on the Home Front. By the end of the year the A.O.K. had used all the foods taken at Caporetto and food supplies were in dire straits.[31] In Dec. 1917, men at the front were to be issued 16.45 ounces of *Mehl* (farina), per diem and 3.5 ounces of meat per week. Troops often received less than one-quarter of the farina and meat.[32] Most fearful of all was malaria which was rampant on both sides of the trench in the Piave Delta. Boroevic reported over 600 men a day taken ill with malaria with no quinine to give them.[33] With less food for the remaining workers, and less raw materials, munitions manufacture decreased resulting in less shells and bullets for the front. With the bad conditions in the army many in rear echelon units were deserting. It must be emphasized that the fighting units at the front still had good morale notwithstanding the poor conditions. They did not want to be beaten by the hated Italians.

Austria-Hungary weary of the war, suffering starvation, lacking many basic essential items was going through severe social agitation which became more volatile when the returning prisoners of war came back from Russia. The government was afraid of these men fearing that they had been indoctrinated with Bolshevism. Few rejoined the army, most deserted amounting to 250,000 men.

After Caporetto the A.O.K. faced an Eastern Front of 325 miles with thirty two infantry and twelve cavalry divisions while in Italy there were thirty-seven Habsburg and eight German divisions along a 290-mile front. However, the Bolsheviks had already agreed to sign a peace treaty which would take place at Brest-Litovsk in March 1918. Troops from the Eastern Front would now be sent to the Italian Front. In Serbia there were only 15,000 troops as an army of occupation. By the end of 1917 in the Dual Monarchy 8,420,000 men had been called to military duty, of which 4,010,000 men had been lost to the army with 789,000 dead, 500,000 invalids and 1,600,000 prisoners. These were terrible figures for Charles and the A.O.K. to read and realize that the barrel of manpower was running dry. Regiments were fighting at half strength. The SouthWest Command of Archduke Eugene was abolished. By the winter of 1917-18, Vienna had two Army Groups deployed on the Italian Front commanded by two *Feld Marschalls* Conrad and Boroevic the latter having been recently promoted to *Feld Marschall.* The first was the Tyrol Army Group deployed from the Passo Stelvio to V. Astico with the X Army Group (FM von Krobatin, Maps 1, 43). From there to the Quero Gorge in the Grappa was the Eleventh Army (GO Count von Scheuchenastuel). The second was Boroevic's Group which was the XIV Army minus German troops rotated back to France on January 3. This consisted of the Sixth Army on the Piave from Valdobbiadene to the Priula Bridges and the *Armeé Isonzo* proceeding from there to the Adriatic (Maps 42 and 43 for geography). Battalion-size assault units were being trained in the Adige River Valley for the Piave crossing. It was the intention of the A.O.K. to train all infantry as assault troops. Among the war booty captured in October and now used by the Habsburg troops was the Fiat Villar-Perosa machine pistol (double barrel) firing 1000 rounds per minute per barrel. Later the troops were given the Schwarzlose M 7/12.

Practicing for the June offensive, assault units used live ammunition. Their equipment included a helmet, gas mask, knapsack, a haversack which contained a mess kit with food, eating utensils, tobacco, bread and two canteens around the neck. Grenades were carried in a shoulder bag as were two bags of dirt to use as protection when the terrain afforded none. For men who were armed with carbines sixty rounds went into the haversack, while twenty were in the knapsack. A dagger was in a belt holster, while platoon leaders had star shell-launching pistols. Every other man carried a pick axe or trowel.[34] For good performance be it in throwing grenades to good performance prizes totalling two hundred Crowns per month were awarded.[35] In many areas, the earth's surface was limestone and could not be dug up to form a fox-hole, common in the Second World War. Lacking drinking water in the mountains Habsburg troops melted snow, adding lemon for taste. With Serbia and Russia defeated, the only combat sector for the Habsburg army was the Italian Front. The *Jagdkompanien* were raised from seven in 1917 to thirteen in 1918. Due to equipment lack only two-thirds of the planned number were able to go into action. In May, 1918, men fighting there numbered 2,818,000 with 946,000 combat troops. Even if the number of troops were increased there was no equipment for the new troops, so the number remained at that figure.[36] Morale was very high since the Habsburgs (with German help) had defeated Russia and Serbia. Only France, Britain and Italy remained with Italy having been dealt an almost knockout blow.[37] Dividing Boroevic's and Conrad's (Eleventh and Tenth Armies), forces was a line running east of M. Grappa. A rift now developed within the A.O.K. One group was of the mobile warfare persuasion which had worked so successfully at Caporetto. The other were the more conservatives who did not want to see much of this mobile warfare. Krauss admitted that he had had erred in not requesting cavalry and armored cars. His pursuit speed was limited by the leg power of his men in the mountains.

The Austro-Hungarian Army was still an excellent fighting machine, but it had two problems. First was the lack of food and clothes, while the second was the Bolshevik political philosophy that now started to permeate the empire. Strange as it may seem, Austro-Hungarian morale on the Italian Front remained high. Cramon who was a keen observer, noted that the Habsburg fighting man was equal to any in the world, but the officers left much to be desired. The emperor was constantly agitated, making trips via his train, often without any reason, and keeping Arz with him. Thus both men were often out of contact when immediate critical decisions had to be made. Regarding GM von Waldstätten the Chief of Operations, Cramon noted, he was capable but had a position too elevated for his capabilities. He would often get offended with minimal criticism and surrounded himself with "yes" men. Thus was the shape of the A.O.K. in the spring of 1918, which would have to handle problems on the Home and Battle Fronts. Troops on the Austro-Italian Front were southern Slavs which fought well against Italy. The army had sixty-six three-regiment infantry divisions with increased artillery and machine guns.[38] Each division also had two artillery regiments and a mortar battalion.

Having noted the actions of German troops up close, Charles made a decision to change the composition and formations of his army. As noted, assault troops were being trained in special tactics.

These units were to infiltrate behind enemy lines and capture the enemy artillery. Machine guns were increased augmenting the lethal power of each division enabling the A.O.K. to decrease manpower in each unit. All cavalry divisions were now on foot, calculated as half an infantry division. Mountain brigades were abolished. Field artillery was increased at a divisional level adding howitzers.[39] The Central Powers now realized that the battle for air superiority started on the drawing boards and in the factories resulting in who would produce the best planes to win the battle.[40] In a harbinger of the massive aerial bombings of the Second World War, Naples was bombed on March 10, 1918 by planes flying from Albania and Montenegro.

In a politico-military move, to avoid German claims to a share of the captured province of Venezia, it was administered as a Line of Communication area, not an occupied territory. A small number of German troops remained in the sector whose officers would eventually present themselves to the Italian Armistice Commission in 1918, and not be recognized.[41]

In the first semester of 1918, meat rations to the army were again reduced. Combat troops were allowed two hundred grams of meat per week, while non-combatants were allowed 100 grams.[42] There are 456 grams per pound. On the Home Front were similar difficulties. On June 16, Vienna decreed that the daily flour ration would be 82.5 grams per day,(about one fifth of a pound).[43] As the food crisis increased, so did the workers' strikes.

Artillery fire was now coordinated with the infantry so that as the last shells fell on the enemy, the infantry arrived in enemy trenches. Shelling was now in the computed mode, picking out specific targets, as the Germans had done in Oct. 1917 at Caporetto.

The influence of Charles and his Empress Zita (of Bourbon-Parma) was being felt in the diplomatic, military and home fronts. Until June 29, 1914 Charles was a young man in his twenties, who had no idea that he was the heir apparent. He had had no time to learn how to rule, and was thrust into a cauldron of diplomatic and military events which he was unable to control. Beginning with their reign the use of poison gas shells as well as planes dropping incendiary bombs on civilian targets was forbidden. Tremendous military pressure resulted in altering of these orders.[44] Charles was constantly at odds with the A.O.K., as his aim was to make peace and to decrease casualties. Aerial strategic bombing was prohibited unless ordered by imperial sanction, as were bombing of railways (may hit civilians). With heavy army pressure, these orders were rescinded.[45]

Known and Little Known Diplomatic Moves and Countermoves

With the surrender of Russia, things looked grim for Britain and France.

Toward the end of 1917, the Allies were losing the war. However, things really were not going that well for the Central Powers. On December 7, the U.S.A. declared war on Austria-Hungary. After the Russian collapse in October 1917, both Wilson and Lloyd George no longer had faith in an Allied victory, and thought that perhaps now was the time to make peace.[46] The first nation approached was Austria-Hungary. Had negotiations with Vienna been successful the interests of Italy, Romania and Serbia would be affected. The reader will recall the Treaty of London between the Allies (Great Britain, Russia and France), and Italy. The hundreds of thousands of Italian dead would go by the way side if these negotiations went to fruition. At Brest-Litovsk, Foreign Minister Ottokor Czernin noted that Vienna was ready to make peace without asking for annexations or indemnities.[47] In his meeting in May with Wilhelm Charles had sworn not to pursue a separate peace but early in October, overtures were made to the British Legation in Stockholm and Berne.[48] The diplomatic ballet continued. Who was to approach whom first? London proposed that the opposing diplomats would meet at a Red Cross office in Berne ostensibly for Red Cross business.[49] Opposing nations provided the Red Cross with lists of prisoners so these could be forwarded to the enemy nation and then to the families. Other overtures took place in the Hague.[50] These moves were significant because even with the smashing victory at Caporetto, Vienna was still looking to disassociate herself from Berlin and make a separate peace. Everything was in the most secret of circumstances. Simultaneously, Berlin was making approaches to the Allies in Madrid.[51] In a circular telegram on November 3, 1917 sent to its ambassadors in the capitals of its allies, London noted that Czernin was ready to send an agent to Switzerland to let England know *officieusement* that he is prepared to have *officieuse* conversations on the subject of peace.[52] Vienna was willing to give up all conquered Italian territory which was substantial.[53] The first Viennese pseudo-diplomat to arrive in Switzerland was Count Kàrolyi who was a Hungarian noble anxious for the independence of Hungary. He wished to unite Hungary to Poland forming a bloc which would oppose German domination even proposing to sabotage the war effort by refusing to ship Hungarian foodstuffs to Germany. So far, all discussions with him had been unofficial with official meetings to follow. On November 17 the British Ambassador at the Hague requested the Foreign Office to give him permission to meet with Vienna's representative.[54] Initially, London agreed, but then changed its mind.[55] Finally on November 18 Lord Bertie, the British Ambassador in Paris telegraphed London, that the French Cabinet had decided that if Vienna had any proposals to make regarding peace, it should do so through official channels to the Entente.[56] At a British War Cabinet meeting on the following day, a hand-written minutes noted "It does not seem worthwhile to pursue the subject."[57] Thus ended the beginning parleys hoping to lead to peace for the Austro-Italian Front.

London had proposed to Vienna, that Austria-Hungary would become a federation, while Italy would receive only the Trentino. Learning about this, Rome became very upset. Hundreds of thousands of Italian men had died on the Isonzo for what it felt were iron-clad agreements, which were about to be changed by the Allies. Throughout the series of diplomatic cables from London to its ambassadors, ran one constant thread, Vienna's request for absolute secrecy. The Habsburgs were afraid that Germany would learn of the unilateral negotiations. The Foreign Office felt that the meetings could never be kept secret and might embarrass the Allies.[58] Toward the end of November, it seemed that Vienna was ready to include German occupied territories in the negotiations (without having notified Germany).[59] Finally in December, 1917 Lloyd George sent General Jan Smuts to Berne to get a read on the situation from Count Albert von Mensdorff, former Habsburg Ambassador to London. The information he received was that Vienna would never yield an inch of territory to its "hereditary enemy," after Italy's refusal to enter the war on the side of the Central Powers. This information was contradictory to that contained in previous notes received.[60] This was just after Caporetto, when Italy was prostrate, while Vienna militarily was riding high. There obviously was severe infighting within Vienna's power structure as to what terms would be acceptable. Other emissaries from Vienna had noted that it was ready to return to the pre-war boundaries after having advanced deep into Italian territory as noted. Someone was not being truthful.

On December, 19 in the Commons Lloyd George's Government declared that there would be a simple rearrangement of territory favoring Italy. At the Labor Party Congress on January 5, he stated that what Britain wanted was for people to choose their own government. He did not wish to partition Austria-Hungary. People should be united to the government of the language they spoke. This was all an elastic declaration. Naturally Alsace Lorraine would be returned to France, and the territorial integrity of Serbia and Belgium guaranteed. These words did not make Sonnino happy. To make Washington and Vienna happy London would sacrifice those clauses in the Treaty of London which gave Italy territories inhabited by non-Italian speaking peoples. Sonnino protested but to no avail. It is odd that Britain and France both colonial powers would not listen to Italy's claim to colonies in Asia Minor. Both nations felt that Italy had not pulled it weight in the war.[61] After the British Prime Minister's January 5, speech Sonnino got ready for constant Allied criticisms. With Italy's recent military disaster it was felt that she would be ready to accept a scaling down of her war aims.[62] Simultaneously, the Bolshevik Russian Government published many Czarist Government documents, among them the Treaty of London. The Southern Slavs notified of this while signing documents on the island of Corfu giving birth to the Kingdom of Yugoslavia were greatly disturbed by its terms.

During all these negotiations Bad Kreuznach was asking Vienna to send troops to the Western Front being held off for two reasons. It hoped that negotiations would soon start while it was logistically difficult to supply the troops. Germany could not supply munitions because of different calibers.

Another nation entered the diplomatic equation when the U.S. issued the famous Wilson Fourteen Points. Point Number Nine called for the changing of Italy's frontiers along the lines of nationalities, while Number Ten called for the autonomous development of the people of Austria-Hungary. Italy, it was felt would be amenable to this due to her pressing economic needs and recent military disasters.[63] Meanwhile, Pope Benedict XV in a note to all belligerents called for an end the "useless slaughter."[64]

The Prisoner of War Issue

In the past, prisoners of war had been at the mercy of the victor, to be killed or sold into slavery at the whim of the victor. At the 1864 conventions at Geneva and the 1867 convention at the Hague, rules were formulated for the victor nations. Prisoners were entitled to food, lodging, and medical assistance. Officers were separate from the enlisted men and not required to work. All would be controlled by the International Red Cross operation operating from Geneva.

Italian Prisoners in Austria-Hungary

Until recently, official figures concerning prisoner of war dead did not exist, because they had either been buried or not looked for. To place things in perspective, there were 600,000 French prisoners of war, 350,000 German, 200,000 British and so far 400,000 Italian. Figures for the Austro-Russian Front are unavailable.

Italian prisoners of war were declared "a shame and a disgrace" by Gabriele D'Annunzio who felt that they should have died fighting. For over seventy years, all information regarding the prisoners had been suppressed by the army, the government, and finally, the Fascist dictatorship. Returning prisoners of war believed the propaganda which denounced them. Exact figures on mortality in these prisoners had either been buried or not sought for a long time. Finally in 1993 the dead turned out to be over 100,000.[65] It is strange that this figure had been ignored. It is directly from the "Inquiry Commission on the Violations of the Rights of Man Committed by the Enemy."[66] All prisoners of the Central Powers suffered shortages of food. In 1915 when the French Government realized this, it started to send food packages and requesting families and charitable organizations to do likewise. By 1916, an accord had been reached with the German government for the reception of these. French food packages amounted to over 75 million, while clothing packages were 625,000.

When Italian families became aware of the food situation in the camps, they started to send food packages which amounted to a total of over eighteen million. However, both the Comando Supremo and the *Consulta* did everything to frustrate the shipment of packages. They did not wish the Italian military in combat to consider becoming a prisoner of war as an option. Attempting to cancel this option an anxious army and government halted family food shipments (via the Red Cross), being sent to their starving loved ones in Austro-German prisoner of war camps. They must either fight or die. At the front, it was made known to the *fanti* that prisoners of war were starving. Italian prisoners of war in the Habsburg domains wrote home via the International Red Cross in Geneva, Switzerland. They were confused and disheartened but happy that they were away from the carnage on the Isonzo.[67] Everything was done to harass the shipment of these very important packages. In April 1918, seventeen tons of food packages, held up at the frontier were destroyed. This was not made public. *The Comando Supremo knew that this food was important yet held it up.* In retrospect it must be noted that Italy was fighting for its very life. Newspaper articles had already appeared in Vienna calling for the dismemberment of Italy.[68] In the 1918 Battle of the Montello there had been 4,000 Italians taken prisoners by the Austro-Hungarians.[69] The A.O.K. noted the high rate of desertions particularly by southern Italians, the oft mentioned illiterate infantryman.[70] Basically the Cabinet and Comando Supremo wanted the men to fight and die for their country but *not surrender.* In the June 1918 Habsburg offensive the Comando Supremo was very concerned at the large number of Italian soldiers taken prisoner.[71] In Austria-Hungary the camps were at Mauthausen, Sigmundsherberg as well as Theresienstadt in Bohemia, while in Germany they were in Celle in Hanover and Rastatt in Baden. In the camps were men who had voluntarily surrendered along with those who had involuntarily surrendered. In this latter group the men were mostly bored and angry they had been captured and anxious to return to serve the *Patria.*[72] Prisoners were forced to do manual labor for 12 hours daily, on a diet of less than 1,000 calories, and sometimes ate grass, just to fill their stomachs. Prisoners who were amputees or had tuberculosis were repatriated but often Death greeted the latter first with many being buried in the camps. At Mauthausen, between November, 1917 and April, 1918, 500 men died from enteritis. At Sigmundsherberg in Lower Austria, 491 Italian prisoners died in 1917 from pneumonia, while in 1918 there were 1779 deaths.

Austro-Hungarian Prisoners of War in Italy and Russia

According to official sources, these were 168,898, with deserters amounting to 5,513.[73] They were spread throughout the peninsula and Sicily. Originally, they did not work and were well-fed because Orlando did not want any problems with the unions. Czech prisoners volunteered to fight in the Italian Army (25,000 did) while there was also a Romanian legion to fight against Vienna.[74] These men were part of the large minority in Hungary. In all, there were 415,116 soldiers and 10,658 officers as prisoners. Of these, 40,947 died in captivity. Of these, 13,217 died of combat wounds, while 27,740 died of other causes. Finally, a last word would be describe the fate of the Italian-speaking Austro-Hungarian soldiers which were over 60,000. Taken prisoner on the Russian Front (30,000) they were given the option of fighting in the Italian Army which thousands did. Little is known of the remainder, although it is known that after Brest-Litovsk, they proceeded toward the Orient ((Siberia and China).[75] More information is available in Vol. III. In the convoluted diplomatic situation of the era, on August 3, the U. S. issued a communiqué that U. S. troops would go to Russia "to render such protection and help as is possible to the Czech-Slovaks against the armed Austrian and German prisoners who are attacking them."[76] No one understood that there were Czechs who were long-time residents in Russia fighting in its army in a special unit called the *Druzhina*. There were also Czechs and Slovaks formerly in the Austro-Hungarian Army (as well as Italian-speaking soldiers) who were prisoners of war in Russia. Both groups were proceeding along the Trans-Siberian Railway to Vladivostok intermittently harassed by the Bolsheviks who saw them as enemies. All the ex-soldiers wanted to do was either go home or fight in France, yet this U.S. bulletin had really confused the situation.

After the peace treaty with Russia about 500,000 men were repatriated to Austria-Hungary. They were politically suspect because they had been exposed to Boshevism which had destroyed the monarchy in Russia. Relatively few succumbed to Bolshevik propaganda but those that did scared the Danubian monarchy as well as other European monarchies.[77] The returnees were to return to field units, receiving leave and back pay. With classic bureaucratic bungling they received neither leading to mutinies.

Over 900,000 Russian prisoners were sent home leaving a large void in the work force.

The Economics of the War

No one had forseen the length of the war which impacted as a big drain on the economies of the nations involved. As in every war, there was inflation with the Lire losing about 20% of its purchasing power.[78]

In agriculture, with the men away fighting, grain cultivation terrain decreased from 5,767,000 hectares in 1913, to 4,366,000 in 1918.(One hectare is 2.47 acres). Grain that used to be imported from Russia was now coming from the U.S.A. With the submarine threat, full supply was always a problem. Grain shortages led to riots in Torino in August 1917. During the period of 1913-19, military expenses rose to 76 percent of public expenditures.[79] All of this contributed to inflation. The war was expensive for all nations concerned (See Table II).

TABLE II

Government expenses (billions of 1914-1918 dollars) by the warring nations in the war.[79]

	Expenses.	Normal Expenses.	War Expenses
Allies			
	France	5.0	28.2
	Great Britain	4.7	43.8
	British Empire		5.8
	Italy	2.9	14.7
	Russia	5.9	16.3
	United States	2.9	36.2
	Other allies.	3.3	2.0
Central Powers			
	Germany	3.3	47.0
	Austria-Hungary	5.4	13.4
	Turkey, Bulgaria	1.4	1.1

Important Social Changes

For the first time, women left the hearth to do work outside the home. They now became tram workers, mail carriers, bank tellers, telephone operators, much to the consternation of the Latin *machismo* mentality.

Citizen Control

The population was placed under severe control when speaking about the war and its outcome. For too long, men had been preaching against the war, while sons of Italy were dying, as happened in the U.S.A. during the Vietnam War. This was something new, and was put in place by Premier Vittorio Emanuele Orlando who was also Interior Minister. This was a big about-face for him, as previously, he had allowed all types of public opinions. A propaganda office was also instituted to give reasons for the war and boost the morale of the populace.

Armament Production

By early 1918, all the equipment lost in October had been replaced. The Italian munitions industry was humming along at a good rate. Men who worked in these factories were mostly forty-five or older. Production was as follows:

Table III Italian Armament Production[81]

	In Army Possession	*Monthly*	*Total Production*
Production	1915-1918		
Rifles	1,260,000	3,900/day	3,135,34
Machine Guns	24,934	1,200/mo.	37,029
bombards	4,864	100/mo.	7,000/mo.
various calib. cannons	9,021	540/mo.	over 16,000
6.5 cal. munit.	364,497,000	3,400,000/day	3,616,000,000
bombard munit.	3,389,000	357,000/day	7,300,000
shells for cannon	20,972,000	88,400/day	70,000,000
hand grenades	9,000,000	45,000/day	22,360,000

Changes in the Comando Supremo with new Operating Aims

Diaz reorganized the Comando Supremo according to the needs of war of the time. He increased the Information Office (Intelligence) headed by Col. Odoardo Marchetti. The Operations Office was headed by Col. Ugo Cavallero. Among those who served in his office was Major Giovanni Gronchi, future President of Italy from 1955-1962. Paper work ran smoothly now compared to the previous regime where all papers had to go through Cadorna or his operations chief a huge task.[82] Porro had been more of a public relations man and no use as a Vice Chief. Twice Gatti mentioned that the office ran smoothly.[83] After Caporetto the Italian Army was dispirited, disorganized, apathetic and tired, but now the entire nation demanded resistance and victory. Morale had to be lifted and tactics had to be changed. The Comando Supremo felt that the "discipline of coercion" had failed and that now the "discipline of persuasion" should be used. A Propaganda Office was started *(Ufficio P)* with the task of teaching the troops as well as the nation the "right" slant of events. This had worked successfully for the Allies, especially Great Britain's efforts headed by Lord Northcliffe. Officers were sent throughout the front giving speeches, passing out cigars and cold cuts which most troops had never seen in their lives.[84] In tactics, no longer would there be massed infantry attacks up the slopes of a mountain against hidden machine gun nests. *Fanti* no longer would be massed in the front line trenches to be annihilated by enemy artillery. This was a new philosophy but old ways die hard as the same old tactics where used in the Italian offensive of October 1918 (see vol. III). The new Italian Army Chief of the General Staff was in sharp contrast with Cadorna who was an aristocrat and seldom had contact with the troops while he came from the bourgeois and fully understood the illiterate peasant. When talking to them, he would call them *guaglion*, a Neapolitan dialect term of endearment, which means "boy." He had served in Libya, then as First Assistant to Gen. Pollio who was Chief of the General Staff, and later to Cadorna. After being promoted to Lt. Gen. he had asked for and received a field command. Appointed Chief of the General Staff he weekly met with Orlando which his predecessor had never done.

The class of 1899 was mixed in with units at the end of 1917. Italian Army food rations were raised to pre-war levels. Furloughs were increased to almost one month per year.[85] Troops no longer were left in trenches for long periods of time, but were rotated to the rear for real rest and relaxation. British officers arriving on the scene in November 1917 reported (justly so) that Italian troops milled about, dispirited, apathetic sullen and dog tired. They had neither arms nor food. Often raiding local farms for sustenance periodically they would cut up an animal for raw food.[86] Up to October, 1917, there had been 217 generals, 255 colonels and 335 battalion commanders dismissed.[87] A few weeks after Diaz was installed, he established a commission to review the dismissals of senior officers. Of the 206 cases reviewed, the commission exonerated 95 generals, while of 669 cases down to Lt. Col. 262 were exonerated.

On December 17, the Stefani News Agency reported (after three years of war), "The Cabinet and the Comando Supremo, in consideration of the changing needs of our army which undertakes operations even in winter, therefore needing more energy, has undertaken to increase the food supply to the soldiers in the field." This was *Circolare* (Bulletin) No. 6288. Pasta was now 150 grams daily, coffee 20 grams, sugar 30 grams, with wine being 25 centiliters daily. As has been reported, there are 456 grams in a pound. The bulletin continued, "To afford our troops a variety in food, the meat ration shall be changed to codfish, 200 grams, or salami, 266 grams. The daily allotment was now 90 *centesimi* daily. With these changes the Comando Supremo hoped that the military strike would cease, and men would be willing to fight.[88] *Circolare* No. 170 (May 4, 1918) stated that monetary subsidies were to be paid by the soldier's army corps directly to the needy family at home. Illiterate peasant women who went to the post office to collect monies due by law were told that there was no money due them. The local post master was lending money out at usurious rates.[89] The circle of abuse of the illiterates traveled from the front to the *padroni* to the few locals that could read and write. Having no means to fight with the illiterates could not fight back. The women at home went to the parish priest to write letters to their husbands or fiancé at the front. The men at the front would ask the assistance of one of the few in the trench who was literate. Thus there would be two people between a married couple writing to each other. Deserters arriving at the peasant villages, were badly received. Why were they living, while the brothers, sons, husbands of others who had done their duty were not? The infantry man in the trench would often send one post card to his family with the date and two words *Sto Bene* (I am well). This was his way of stating that as of that date, he was alive. The enemy was now twenty miles from Venice. The whole nation knew that the enemy was approaching the heartland of the nation, Milano, Venezia and Bologna. Lt. Gen. Fayolle, the French commander, sent a report to the CIGS, previously noted, which is summarized in the OBARI and is recorded in the PRO. He noted the same issues that British officers had raised and which have been previously discussed here. Italian staff officers had no organizational capacity and could not adapt themselves to new situations. There was no coordination between artillery and infantry, while the latter did not understand the principles of the counterattack. He felt that the Italian Army not being trained in the type of warfare they faced, could possibly yield in its present condition. The army situation now was grave but slowly getting better. There were 80,000 men returning from leave as well as the 300,000 who had been separated from their units.[90] The report noted that the III Army had good morale and was undergoing training while the IV Army was exhausted after withdrawing and deploying on the cruel and cold Grappa and could not train as all energies were needed simply to survive. The I Army deployed from the Brenta River to Lago di Garda was in bad shape and was in no condition to undergo training (Map 43 for geography).[91] The II Army with two corps had neglected training while the V Army deployed near Parma was seriously training its troops. Serious concerns were addressed to British and French officers to treat their Italian counterparts gingerly as they would be easily offended. Schools were instituted to teach Italian officers, while French officers would be attached to Italian units with Italian officers going to French units. Again for the nth time, the Comando Supremo reiterated that positions should be defended in depth by not placing most of the troops in the front lines. Rear defense points had to be adequately manned in order to have troops ready for a counterattack.[92] It concluded that the Italian Army was imperfectly trained and could yield with an enemy attack. The best source for the events in the Italian Army was the diary of Col. Angelo Gatti, the Army historian. On June 27, 1917, he noted that many corps commanders had been Lieutenant Colonels at the start of the war, and still had the mind of Lt. Cols.[93] Throughout history military officers during wartime gain promotion. However, the mind must develop along with the increase in rank and responsibility.

Italian divisions still retained four regiments consisting in 2,600 men and 81 officers, but had three machine gun companies plus twelve units of machine gun pistols, one of 12 flamethrowers, and three of Stokes grenade throwers. There was also a battery of 37 mm. cannon and an assault platoon. Renault tanks were to arrive in 1919. Specially trained assault detachments were instituted even though there were assault divisions with special equipment. The army also acknowledged that new tactics were in order on the battle front.[94] There had been little communication between artillery and the infantry. When the latter moved, the artillery remained. This would now change. Diaz expostulated that the division was the tactical unit of the army. It should not be broken up and transferred piece meal as had happened in the past.[95]

Toward the end of the war, there was one officer for every 26 soldiers.[96] As of March 1, the Comando Supremo was now at Abano near Padua housed in the Hotel Trieste. In April the II Corps (Lt. Gen. Albericco Albericci) entrained for France. On February 14, Fayolle was rotated back to France soon to be replaced.

On March 1,1918 the Comando Supremo announced the following physical requisites: Height requirements were decreased to 150 cm.(five feet). By the end of the war combat fatalities numbered 500,000 while in the prisoner of war camps there were 100,000 from starvation and 100,000 from sickness. One of the first orders of the new Comando Supremo. One of the first orders of the new Comando Supremo was to the Italian First and Fourth Armies, ordering them to hold the line from M. Caldiera to the other side of the Val Brenta. The First Army responded that it had been previously ordered to withdraw and thus could not execute the new order.[97] (Maps 1,31,35,40).[98]

Italian troop deployments now were:

VII Army: (Gen. Tassoni) deployed from the Passo Stelvio to the western shore of Lago di Garda (Map 1, Vol. I for geography). Deployed here were the III (Lt. Gen. Vittorio Camerana) and XIV Corps (Lt. Gen. Pier Luigi Sagromoso).

I Army: (Lt. Gen. Guglielmo Pecori-Giraldi) deployed from the eastern shore of the Garda to the knot of M. Cengio on the Asiago Plateau where the Ghelpach and Assa Gorges meet with the XXIX (Lt. Gen. Vittorio De Albertis), V (Lt. Gen. Giovanni Chersis) and X Corps (Lt. Gen. Enrico Caviglia). See Maps 29,31,42.

VI Army:(Lt. Gen. Luca Montuori) deployed on the Altopiano dei Sette Communi-(confluence of the Ghelpach-Assa-Gorges Assa Valley) to the Brenta River. It consisted of the the XIV Corps (Lt. Gen. Lord Cavan), the French XII Corps (Lt. Gen. Jean Cèsar Graziani) and the Italian XX Corps (Lt. Gen. Giuseppe Francesco Ferrari) (Maps 14A,31,35,40).

IV Army:(Lt. Gen. Paolo Morrone) Deployed from but not including the Brenta to Pederobba located where the Piave breaks out past the Grappa into the plains. It contained the IX Corps (Lt. Gen. Emilio De Bono), the VI (Lt. Gen. Stefano Lombardi), the XVIII Corps (Lt. Gen. Luigi Basso) and the I Corps (Lt. Gen. Settimio Piacentini) (Map 40)[99]

II Army:—(Lt. Gen. Giuseppe Pennella) deployed from Pederobba to Spresiano. It contained the XXVII Corps (Lt. Gen. Antonio DiGiorgio) and the VIII Corps (Lt. Gen. Asclepio Gandolfo). The XIII Corps (Lt. Gen. Ugo Sani) was in reserve (Maps 42 for geography, 40).

III Army: (Lt. Gen. Duke of Aosta) with the XI (Lt. Gen. Giuseppe Paolini), XXVIII (Lt. Gen. Giovanni Croce) and XXIII Corps (Lt. Gen. Carlo Petiti di Roreto) deployed from Spresiano to the Adriatic (Map 42 for geography)

V Army:(Lt. Gen. Nicolis di Robilant) with the II Corps (Lt. Gen. Albericco Albricci) and the XII Corps (Lt. Gen. Giovanni Cattaneo) in reserve with four cavalry divisions in reserve at Brescia southwest of Lago di Garda (Map 14A). On March 23, allied divisions started to return to the Western Front. These were the French Sixty-fourth, Sixty-fifth Divisions as well as the Forty-sixth and Forty-seventh *Chasseurs des Alpes* with the British Fifth and Forty-first, all of which were on the Western Front by April 11. Remaining were the French Twenty-third and Twenty Fourth Infantry Divisions, as well as the British Seventh, Twenty-third and Forty-eighth Infantry Divisions. On April 13, the Comando Supremo issued orders to Generals Maistre and Plumer regarding their troops. By Jan. 1918, Italy had over 3 million men under arms.[100] Men called to arms had been 5,903,000. There were 145,000 who went into the navy, 282,000 remained at home due to the special needs of the nation, and 437,000 exonerated due to industrial and public administration needs (e.g. railroad conductor). Over 452,000 wounded invalids received a pension.[101]

TABLE IV*

	Total Armed Forces.		Total Mobilized Armed Forces	
	Officers:	Troops.	Officers.	Troops.
JULY 1, 1915.		1,556,000	31,000	1,058,000
Jan. 1, 1916.	90,000	2,059,000	38,000	1,154,000
Jul. 1, 1916		2,347,000	51,000	1,585,000
Jan. 1,1917	118,000	3,042,000	60,000	1,867,000
Oct. 1,1917		3.103,000	79,000	2,352,000
Jan. 1, 1918	147,000	2,809,000	71,000	1,989,000
Jul. 1, 1918		3,026,000	80,000	2,237,000
Oct. 1,1918.	186,000	2,941,000	84,000	2,207,000

* Figures have been rounded off to the nearest thousand. These were men deployed on the Italian Front and other minor fronts outside of Italy's borders. Quadripeds were 228,000 in July 1915, 374,000 in Oct. 1917, 312,000 in Oct. 1918. Of these, 70,000 were saddle horse, the rest were beasts of burden.

Further Allied Troop Deployments

Allied troops deployed on the Piave would be replaced by Italian troops as the former would be sent to the Asiago Front. On March 19 the British Twenty-third Division received orders to relieve the Italian Eleventh Infantry Division in the line. To its right was the French XII Corps while to its left was the Italian Twelfth Infantry Division (X Corps). The British Seventh Division was also sent to the sector with the Forty-eighth in reserve. Known also as the Altopiano dei Sette Communi, the first line trenches were twelve miles from the Plain of Lombardy line.

During the war, there were 45,000 families with four or more men wearing the uniform of the infantry. Since in most instances, this meant almost certain death, further sons were exonerated from military service. During the war, 304,000 men returned from abroad to serve in the Italian Armed Forces. Of these, 155,000 were from the Americas. In all, the draft dodgers were about 12 percent, mostly living abroad. When one eliminated them, it was about 4 percent.[102] In 1919, the government of Francesco Nitti pardoned all the draft dodgers.

Allied Help was on the Way

The Austro-Germans had advanced so rapidly that it took almost one week to obtain an adequate picture of the developments. Britain and France sent troops. Both nations knew that with Serbia, Russia and Romania out of the war, the Central Powers would have about five million men to send to the Western Front. Sending troops to the Italian Front for the Allies was an act of self-preservation. It would take many months before the American soldiers would arrive. Robertson was against sending anyone complaining to Lloyd George, that Italy had plenty of men and that there was no military reason to send troops. After communicating with the Prime Minister he finally realized that this was for political, not military reasons.[103] Lloyd George told him that Germany was also helping its allies so Britain had to do more than lecture at conferences.[104] Four French divisions began to entrain on October 27 and arrived in Italy in four days. It was finally agreed that they should deploy between Brescia and Verona to guard against any possible attack west of Lago di Garda (Map 14 A). As noted their commander was Lt. Gen. Denis Auguste Duchêne. These were the French Sixty-fourth and Sixty fifth Infantry Divisions. The French Forty-seventh Infantry Division arrived later and was deployed in Val Canonica. On October 29, Cadorna suggested that the French troops should deploy in the Montebelluna, Castelfranco and Treviso area to stop any advance by the Austro-German XIV Army across the Piave between Vidor and Ponte di Priula.[105] Justifiably so, Allied troops were leery of deploying next to the Italians. There was always the fear of the military equivalent of a strike by Italian troops allowing the enemy to pierce the line endangering the flanks of adjoining Allied troops. Since the Italians had no reserves the newcomers considered themselves reserves. The French requested that one of their generals command Allied troops on their eastern frontier. They also wanted American troops under their command to which Pershing responded "That is not even remotely possible."[107] Thus the plan was shelved. French troops would not be deployed under Italian command but as reserves to guard against an enemy breakthrough.[108] After thorough inspections, Robertson and Foch drew up a memorandum to the effect that they felt that the Italian Army was sound and that it should hold at the Piave.[109] The second British commander chosen was Lt. Gen. the Earl of Cavan, with Plumer being rotated back to the Western Front. Prior to returning to France, on January 13, he issued a report declaring that more training was necessary for the Italian troops. On January 20, another report was sent to London noting that the Italian General Staff needed much improvement.[110] While still in Britain Cavan was asked where he would deploy his troops choosing Mantua on the Mincio River (Map 14A).[111] He arrived in Italy on November 5, accompanied by aides that would become prominent in future years. One was Brigadier H.L. (later Field Marshal) Alexander with the other being the future King Edward VIII, at the time the Prince of Wales. On November 6 when Cavan met with Cadorna, the latter was surprised that some troops would be as far back as Milan-Lodi. It was agreed to deploy on the west bank of the Mincio River.[112] This was satisfactory to both as the French were deployed near Lago di Garda. Logistics were a nightmare for the Allied troops. After the Rome conference of 1916-1917, a British Military Mission had been sent to Italy to study transportation on the Franco-Italian frontier which the reader is reminded was not the best. One division required seventy trains for men and artillery. There were two railway entrances to Italy. The first was via Nice to Genoa, crossing at Ventimiglia. The second was via the Modane tunnel to Torino. At the time, Genoa could only handle sixteen trains daily. Modane could handle twelve. For sixty miles beyond Ventimiglia, transportation was only single track. Thus with Italian good will and typical British steadfastness, the details were worked out to transport and deploy 200,000 men.[113] By November 10, using both routes, the four French divisions had detrained. British troops started to arrive via the same modality at Mantua by November 12. The divisions had their own four wheeled transportation in three ton lorries which would be used to transport food and ammunition. In the mountains these were useless and had to be discarded for Fiat trucks which could climb the steep slopes.

On November 10, Cavan sent his report to London. He felt that should the Piave be crossed, it would take two to three weeks for the enemy to bring up its heavy guns by which time the British divisions would be arriving. He hoped to deploy along the Mincio River keeping in contact with the French division west of Lago di Garda refusing to move eastward as the roads were clogged with refugees and soldiers.[114]

Diaz met with the Anglo-French military leaders on November 9 the day after his appointment declaring that he intended to hold at the Piave. The generals responded that Anglo-

French divisions would be deployed near Vicenza ready to rush forward either to the Piave or the Asiago plateau which the Italians called the *Altopiano dei Sette Communi.*[115] At another meeting of the threesome on November 11, Diaz noted that these troops were too far to the rear. This would not be good for Italian public opinion which was noting that Allied troops were not going in harm's way.[116] Finally it was decided to deploy the French troops between Vicenza and Valdagno to its north (Map 43 for geography). The British troops would be deployed south of Vicenza behind the Bacchiglione River (Map 35).

The Comando Supremo now started to analyze why the debacle of Caporetto had occurred. First was the thought of going on the defensive which to Italians was shameful and weakened their morale. They had no training in defensive maneuvers and were tired after thirty months of constant offensives. Senior officers constantly kept most of their men in front line positions where they were liable to be easily captured or killed. Finally there was the question of reserves which shall be further discussed in chapter XV.

In the beginning of 1918, the newly arrived allied troops started to install schools in Italy to train their own troops as well as Italian officers and NCOs in the latest methods and techniques developed on the Western Front. On May 29 the Italians notified the Anglo-French military that there would be no more Italian military attending the schools.

The author feels that the Italians were embarrassed to attend these schools. Their training was quite inferior to that of their allies, and this would show if they attended these schools. With Italian infantry units approaching 90% illiteracy in some units would have difficulty understanding the complex maneuvers which the literate Western Front armies easily performed. As noted Fayolle and Plumer had made out accurate, lengthy, detailed and precise reports on the Italian army.[117] The Anglo-French Armies had long histories, including fighting abroad, while Italy had been a nation for less than 50 years with an impoverished, illiterate population and no military tradition. Fayolle noted inefficient staffs, lack of cohesion between the infantry and artillery as well as units constantly moving about resulting in no permanent cohesion with neighboring troops.[118] This was the case of the debacle in October on the Isonzo and would be the case with the British Fifth Army in June 1918 on the Western Front. Plumer noted that the worse Italian defect was that the troops lacked serious training. Commanders did not give it while troops did not appreciate it. Of the five Italian armies, only three were in the first line. He noted that Italian officers and men had no confidence in themselves nor in each other. Officers had not been taught the responsibilities of leadership. Plumer further reiterated that the Italian officers had only theoretical knowledge of staff work, not understanding the practical difficulties of the orders. This was due to a lack of experience as an army. Officers did not check (like Cadorna at Caporetto) to see if the orders had been carried out. He also reported that Italian engineers failed to apply their technical knowledge for military purposes. Italian defenses had many faults. While the front line troops were almost elbow to elbow, there was no defensive depth, artillery was used ineffectively and inaccurate deployment of reserves made none available when needed. The front line massing of troops went back to the episode with Lt. Gen. Roberto Brusati of the First Army and was part of the reason for his dismissal. Communication equipment in Italy was still rudimentary as noted by the arriving British. A phone call to a location 160 miles away took ten hours to get through.[119] Disciplinary measures were also changed under Diaz. Under Cadorna, as one commander testified at the Commission of Inquiry, "It was a well known principle. Enemy trenches lost or not taken, dismiss a commander of a brigade or a division."[120]

January 18, 1918

Diaz ordered the British XI Corps to relieve the Italian VIII Corps in the Arcade sector of the Piave to the right of the British XIV Corps.[121] Losses in the Twelfth Isonzo Battle for the Boroevic Group were 2,353 dead, 12,343 wounded and 5,700 missing (between Oct. 24 & Dec. 1). The XIV Army lost 16,400 Austria-Hungarians and about 15,000 Germans. The Conrad Group reported 878 dead, 6,614 wounded and 599 missing between Nov. 10 and Dec 24.

Allied Troop Deployment in Italy

After the noted November 11 conference among Diaz, Foot and Wilson, the new British Commander, Lt. Gen. Sir Herbert Plumer, arrived in Italy. His orders were to give the Commando Supremo all the support possible, but not endanger his troops.[122] After inspecting the sectors in Italy, Plumer recommended that two more British divisions as well as a cavalry division be sent to Italy. Robertson reluctantly approved.[123] Foch now noted that the Italians started to give an account of themselves. On November 23 he returned to France leaving Lt. Gen. M. Fayolle commander of French forces in Italy. On November 27, the new French commander requested that British troops be placed under his command.[124] Robertson refused his request but as noted above on February 18, 1918 would be replaced by Lt. Gen. Sir Henry Wilson.[125, 126] Agreements had been reached to deploy Anglo-French troops relieving Italian troops in the sector from M. Tomba on the Grappa eastward to Nervesa on the Montello (Maps 24,32,40). There was now a conflict regarding taking orders from Diaz. On November 26, Plumer requested Diaz to order British divisions to enter the line, a request which was granted. Faced with this, Fayolle had to follow suit.[127] Operational Order No. 1 was issued by Cavan on November 23, whereby the British Twenty-third and Forty-first Infantry Divisions would replace the Italian First and Thirtieth Infantry Divisions between Crocetta and Nervesa on the Montello and Piave with the British Seventh Infantry Division in reserve. The British Forty-eighth and Fifth Infantry Divisions were placed in reserve behind the Italian IV and I Armies. The Italian divisions to the left of the British were relieved by the French Forty-seventh (M. Tomba to Pederobba at the Piave) and the

Sixty-fifth Infantry Divisions on the Piave from Pederobba to Crocetta. The Anglo-French forces now decided between themselves on a plan to block the exits from the Astico and Brenta Valleys to the plains (Map 35).

Fayolle now proposed to take the offensive northwards on the Asiago Plateau in the general direction of Trento. It was vital to halt the enemy from descending onto the Plains of Lombardy a few miles away. Enemy lines were ten miles from the plains while an advance of only three miles would allow the enemy to overlook the plains.

In substance the Anglo-French divisions were sent from the Piave to the Asiago Plateau which was a key defensive point. On April 7, 1918, the French Forty-seventh Infantry Division returned to the Western Front leaving the French XII Corps (Lt. Gen. Graziani), constituted by the Twenty-third, Twenty-fourth and Forty-seventh Infantry Divisions. In Dec. 1917, these troops successfully attacked M. Tomba. An hour before the assault, aerial photographs of enemy positions taken by Italian aviators, were given to the French commandant.[128]

A contemporary account of events from the eyes of a British soldier is recorded by Pvt. Norman Gladden in the 11 Battalion of the Northumberland Fusiliers with the Twenty-third Infantry Division. He reported that troops were met with fanfare by the civilian population.[129] As the reader will remember, Italy was constantly requesting more divisions from the allies, and now from the Americans. Lt. Gen. John J. Pershing, Commander of the American Expeditionary Force, refused to place his forces under French or British command. He wished to be given a certain sector, for which American troops would be responsible. Diaz asked for twenty-five divisions and was to receive none.[130] Due to Italian-American pressure on June 19, one regiment was finally sent.[131] This was the 332° which crossed the Tagliamento on Nov. 4, 1918. Plumer had been rotated back to France on March 10, 1918, while Fayolle had been rotated back to France, being replaced by Lt. Gen. Maistre. The stragglers assembled as the Italian II Army still retained old corps names the II, XII (Carnia

Command) and XIV, later being broken up and reformed as the VI Army.

The Battle of Tre Monti (Map 26)

January 6, 1918

Pecori-Giraldi notified the Comando Supremo that the new commander of the C.T.A., Lt. Gen. Gaetano Zoppi, had been presented with a new offensive plan. This involved retaking the line M. Valbella-Col del Rosso-Col d'Echele. It was to keep the enemy as far as possible from the edge of the altipiano and above all, Col. d'Astiago, which was the hinge of defenses on the right.

The reader is reminded of the defensive line reached by the Italians during the Christmas season of 1917. It ran from the stronghold of C. Eckar to Busa del Termine and M. Melago then to V. Chiama in the rear (Map 31).

January 26, 1918

The I Army transmitted to the Comando Supremo documentation regarding the feinting action to be started on the morrow with the real attack starting on January 28. Other subsidiary actions would be undertaken by the Fifty-seventh Infantry Division toward M. Sisemol and the Ronco Carbon Basin. Artillery of the XXVI Corps would start firing on positions known as Zocchi and Stellar, south east of Asiago. This was in pseudo-preparation for the offensive that never would be (in that sector). The IV Bersaglieri Brigade (Maj. Gen. Pio Caselli) would be attached to the Thirty-third Division to concentrate all efforts on M. Valbella. On the left flank, in V. Frenzela, the Fifty-second Infantry Division (XX Corps) would undertake a feinting action on Sasso Rosso and Croce di S. Francesco. Zoppi acknowledged that it would be difficult, but felt that he needed something to boost the morale of his troops.

The major thrust would be undertaken by the XXII Corps (Thirty-third Infantry Division) which also included the already noted Bersaglieri which remained in position while the Fifty-second Infantry Division was to feint an action on the line M. Sisemol-Ronco Carbon. While this was done, the Thirty-third Infantry Division deployed getting ready for action.

The II Assault Unit and the 5° Bersaglieri were to take M. Valbella deploying on Costalunga and C. Eckar. To the rear of C. Eckar were two battalions of the 14° Bersaglieri which would rush in when the crests were taken.

The I Assault Unit and the *Sassari* deployed between M. Melago and C. Cischietto would attempt to take Col del Rosso and Col d'Echele. In reserve south of the Busa del Termine, between C. Eckar and Col del Rosso were the IV Assault Units with five machine gun companies. The *Liguria* would man the defenses in these positions after they were taken. The *Bisagno* was farther to the south ready to give support if needed. The *Sassari* would attack C. Eckar from the west while some alpine troops would do likewise from the east.

Artillery deployment consisted of seven batteries of large caliber, 105 of medium and one hundred of small caliber plus 12 batteries of bombards, nine hundred mouths in all. There were provisions of 400,000 shells per small caliber and 50,000 shells for medium and large caliber. Some shells carried phosgene which would be used in V. Frenzela. Troop morale was high.

Opposing the attackers would be troops of the *Gruppe Kletter* which were very tired after the battles on the Melette. These units would be the VI and XVIII Brigades plus the CLXXIX Mountain Brigade which had received information from Italian deserters of the impending assault. The Twenty-first Infantry. replaced the Sixth Infantry Division.

January 27, 1918

In a feinting action at 1200 artillery began firing on enemy positions between Canove and M. Sisemol. Large holes were made in the barbed wire. Strong patrols from the *Pavia* (XXVI

Corps) attracted enemy attention and interdiction fire in an area where actually there would be no infantry assault.

January 28, 1918

At 0330 units of the IX *Gruppo Alpini* attempted to take the bastion of Croce di S. Francesco which dominated the whole V. Frenzela up to where the Brenta River Valley breaks out near Valstagno (Map 31). Climbing during the night with the assistance of ropes, they surprised and occupied the position. However, it was dominated by positions to the rear, so a counterattack pushed them off the mountain.

At 0630, Italian interdiction fire began in V. Frenzela and destructive fire in the trenches of the Sisemol (Map 31) and Col d'Echele (Map 25). There was enemy shelling from well hidden positions in Col Gallio (Map 25).

At 0800 units of the *Pavia* started their feinting action toward Canove, while others of the IV Bersaglieri proceeded toward M. Sisemol and Ronco Carbon. Machine gun units positioned themselves on the north west slopes of Costalunga to support the attack on M. Valbella. Further to the west the 14° Infantry feinted from Pennar to the hamlets of Zocchi and Stellar.

At 0930 with three columns the 5° Bersaglieri aimed for the summit of M. Valbella. Lateral columns proceeded upward via trenches resulting from shelling. The central column proceeded straight up. Unfortunately, a mistaken red rocket launched by the Austro-Hungarians was misinterpreted by Italian artillery as a request to lengthen the shelling arc resulting in the attackers no longer having artillery support. The defenders took advantage of this repulsing and threatening the attackers with encirclement. The 14° and 20° Bersaglieri along with some *Arditi* units were almost surrounded and forced to withdraw.

From M. Melago, units of the I Assault Unit with the *Sassari* proceeded in three columns. On the left were two companies of *Arditi* and the II and III/151° and advanced on the western side of Col del Rosso actually arriving near Malga Melaghetto.

The right column with the III/152° with a company of Arditi proceeded from C. Cischietto toward Col d'Echele. Machine gun nests on the east side of the mountain halted them near the saddle of Case Caporai. The central column (I/151° & II/152°) was also unsuccessful.

To the right, the *Alpini* Bassano, Tirano, and M. Baldo Battalions isolated the stronghold of Pizzo Razea occupying Case Echele. However efforts to take the overhanging Col d'Echele was blocked by enemy defenses on Case Ruggi. In the afternoon, the Italians started another attack, so that the *Sassari* and assault units were unable to occupy Col del Rosso while the *Alpini* Bassano Battalion overcoming Case Ruggi's defenses finally occupied Col d'Echele. By 1600 the Italians held the line Pizzo Razea-Col d'Echele-Col del Rosso, but made another unsuccessful assault on M. Valbella (Maps 26,31). Gen. Sani (Thirty-Third Infantry Division) assigned the I/58° placing this sector under the direct command of promoted Lt. Gen. Piola Casella who soon received the Thirty-third Division to supplement his IV Bersaglieri. At 2130 units of the 152° and 157° vainly tried to occupy Casa Caporai.

The C.T.A. now realized that more troops would be needed for tomorrow's Valbella assault. It assigned the XVI Assault Unit and the *Bergamo* to the XXII Corps. The *Ligurie, Bisagno* and *Ancona* would be made ready for any eventuality.

January 29, 1918

Heavy Austro-Hungarian interdiction fire rained on the pathways to the new Italian positions at 0400. This was followed by a heavy counterattack with hand-to-hand fighting with the enemy repulsed except at Casa Caporai.

At 0830 Italian troops readied for the assault on M. Valbella with the usual three columns. First, the IV Brigade was preceded by the IV and XVI Assault Units, freshly arrived in the line. These were all repulsed before they got to the objective. Caselli now reinforced the central column with the I and II/209°. The right column also started to retreat, so the commander of the 209° gave it one of his battalions so that by 1300 the right column reached the summit. In the heavy fighting, Col. Redaelli, commander of the central and right columns was killed. By evening, the IV Bersaglieri Brigade tried to link up with the *Sassari* at Col del Rosso while the 210° arrived on the summit of M. Valbella the *Bergamo* (25°).

January 30, 1918

At dawn, units of the *Sassari* and *Liguria* descended in a pincer maneuver from Col del Rosso onto Casa Caporai, surprising the garrison and taking all prisoner (Map 26). Patrols were immediately sent toward Stoccaredo to test the enemy's defenses. Zoppi now ordered the linkup between Col del Rosso and M. Valbella to halt any enemy infiltration toward Busa del Termine and V. Melago (Map 26).

At 0530, the XXIV Assault Unit surprised the garrison at Malga Melaghetto descending onto Portecche and captured Hill 1193. However, the lack of flanking support and reinforcements forced the troops to retreat southward.

Moving slowly from M. Valbella the II/209° was almost destroyed by enemy interdiction shelling.

In another attempt, the C.T.A. sent the 130° (already sent to Busa di Termine) and the 69° Infantry (deployed in V. Chiama) to assist the Thirty-third Infantry Division. The attack was to take place in darkness but when Zoppi realized that it would be too difficult, it was cancelled. The battle ended with a small territorial gain, which would assist the troops fighting on the Altopiano dei Sette Communi. Italian casualties were 45 officers dead, 185 wounded, and 38 missing. There were 534 troop dead, 3,162 wounded, and 2,686 missing. As the Austro-Hungarians reported capturing 15 officers, and 660 soldiers, one must deduce that 23 officers were killed plus 660 men missing.

Official Austro-Hungarian figures are not available. The Thirty-third Infantry Division had captured 199 officers and 2,500 men. The Eleventh Army was now in critical condition. In the *Gruppe Kletter,* one regiment was reduced to 50 rifles.

The survivors of the *Sassari* were taken to Vicenza by truck and officially greeted by Pecori-Giraldi and the Italian First Army Staff, as well as civil and religious leaders. In the photos taken, one can see that many officers and men wore bandages on the head and arms. On another day, there was a similar showing of appreciation for the Bersaglieri. It seemed that the Italians had been reinvigorated and were willing to fight.

Events on the Piave early in 1918.

Due to the winter cold and swift current activity was limited to patrolling to the islands in the middle of the river. Wearing straw or felt shoes to obviate noise, stripped to the buff (well rubbed with oil) the troops encountered none of the enemy while by March 1, the Piave became impassable due to heavy rains.[132]

On Jan. 14, the Comando Supremo initiated *Operations to enlarge the Bridgehead at Capo Sile.* in the lower Piave. The plan was to have British troops cross the river in their sector, establish and hold a bridgehead for forty-eight hours, then withdraw. Simultaneously the III Army would attack from the Sile bridgehead to drive the enemy away from Venice. This task was entrusted to the 2° *Granatieri.* Engineers drove piles into the water at the bridge sites which did not show above the water. Nonetheless enemy aerial photography spotted them.

At 0730 Italian infantry successfully assaulted the enemy at Agenzia Zuliani (Map 34). At dawn on January 16, Vienna's troops counterattacked with the *Honvéd* 12° plus one battalion each from the 31° and 20°. These units pushed on the Italian right forcing it to evacuate Agenzia Zuliani and retreat to the right bank of the Piave. By 0900 the Italians counterattacked retaking the lost positions. In the meantime the river rose four feet washing away the piers of the projected bridges causing further action to be cancelled.

A few months later on May 27 *Arditi* of the XXIII Corps broke through three lines of the enemy defenses. Thus the bridgehead was enlarged to the north, (Casa Bressanin) capturing seven officers, and 433 Hungarian soldiers.

Events on the Grappa Early in 1918 (Map 24)

On January 29, in a letter to Orlando Diaz mentioned an offensive on the Grappa. Since January 4, the IV Army had been planning an offensive action entrusted to the VI and IX Corps. Objectives would be the retaking of the Col Caprile, Col della Berretta, M. Pèrtica and Osteria del Forcelletto. All this would be predicated on taking the Asolone first.

The task was entrusted to the Sixty-sixth Infantry Division (VI Corps) composed of the *Cremona, Pesaro, Massa Carrara,* the 94° and 139° as well as the XIV *Gruppo Alpini.* On January 10 Lt. Gen. Carmelo Squillace ordered an assault on the Asolone pushing westward to the line between Hills 1440, 1472 and Cason delle Fratte. Having done this, V. Cesilla up to Hill 1309 would be blocked.

Other units of the IX and VI Corps would assist the action keeping an aggressive deployment. Units of the Fifty-Sixth Infantry Division (XVIII Corps) would attack in the sector of Solaroli-Spinoncia especially M. Valderòa. On January 13, taking advantage of the lack of snow, Italian artillery started its preparatory shelling. By 0700 of the next day destructive shelling from the IX Corps as well as the XX and XXII on the adjacent Altopiano dei Sette Communi. Enemy shelling was very effective, so Squillace delayed the infantry attack from 1300 to 1400. However, the infantry had already gone on the attack so that by darkness the Sixty-sixth Infantry Division, occupied Hills 1440 and 1486 of M. Asolone. To the right, the *Massa Carrara* proceeded in V. Cesilla while on the left the 140° (Eighteenth Infantry Division) reached Casara Celotti. At 1800, the *Calabria* (Eighteenth Infantry Division) was ordered to link up with the 140° proceeding to the dorsum of the Colli Alti toward Casara Cestarotta which it failed to occupy. As darkness arrived, Squillace ordered the *Cremona* to attack at 2300 reaching the line at Hill 1440 and 1472-Cason delle Fratte. The battle ended on Hill 1520 which the 22° had occupied on January 15. One hour later, the Austro-Hungarians launched a violent counterattack climbing from V. Saline onto Hill 1486 taking it before the Italian artillery could assist the defending 140°.With this, Hill 1520 had to be evacuated.

About 1500, knowing the conditions of the troops, and trying to avoid useless shedding of blood, Squillace requested of the VI Corps a halt to the action which was granted. Later DiRobilant informed the Comando Supremo that it would be useless to continue the attacks on the Asolone. He would assign a methodical advance to regiments deployed on the internal wings of the IX and VI Corps.

A Pertinent Aviation Event

On December 25-26, 1917, occurred the Battle of Istrana where unauthorized bombing of German airfields took place on Christmas with a heavy German return on the next day. The is fully discussed in chapter XVI.

Chapter XV Endnotes

Post Caporetto Non Military and Small Military events.

1 Julius Pratt, *A History of United States Foreign Policy,* Prentice-Hall, 1955, p. 442

2 Gordon Craig, *The Politics in the Prussian Army,* Oxford University Press, 1956, p. 334.

3 Trevelyan, George, *Scene della guerra d'Italia,* Bologna, 1919

4 PRO: WO 106/808

5 *La Grande Guerra Aerea 1915-1918, ed.* Paolo Ferrari, Gino Rossato, Valdagno 1994, p. 40.

6 F. Martini, *Diario 1914-18,* Edited by Gabriele DeRosa, Mondandori, Milano 1966

[7] Julius W. Pratt, *A History of United States Foreign Policy,* Prentice-Hall, 1955, p.486

[8] A. Bailey, *Woodrow Wilson and the Lost Peace* (New York, The Macmillan Company, 1944), p. 25.

[9] R. S. Baker, and W.E.Dodd eds., *the Public Papers of Woodrow Wilson: War and Peace,* 2 Volumes, (New York: Harper and Brother, 1927 I passim.

[10] A.Bailey, op. cited, p. 502-504

[11] Ibid.

[12] PRO: WO/256/28 which is Haig's Diary; E. Greenhalgh, *The Journal of Military History,* Vol. 68, No. 3, July 2004, page 771 clearly illustrates that there were two Haig diaries the written one and the typed one, the latter differing from the original. Moreover there is no record in the War Office Telegram Section of any such telegrams having been sent to Gen. Wilson at the time indicated by Haig.

[13] PRO: FO 371/2948,French troops amounted to 103,000 in Dec. 1917, and 45,000 in April 1918. The British troops were 120,000 and 80,000 in the same periods. Letter sent to Minister Balfour, dated Dec. 14, 1917. The signature is illegible

[14] Encyclopedia Britannica, 1998, Chicago, Ill. Vol. II, p. 503

[15] Lloyd George speech to the Commons on Dec. 20, 1917, ZHC 2/609, Motion for Adjournment, p. 2218.

[16] Speech given by Briand to French Chamber of Deputies on Jan. 2, 1917.

[17] PRO: Minutes of the House of Commons, Vol. 100, Christmas Recess, Dec. 20, 1917, p. 2218.

[18] R. Bachi, *L'Alimentazione e la Politica Annonaria in Italia in serie Storia Economia e Sociale della Guerra Mondiale,* Bari, 1926, p. 98, p. 123

[19] OBARI: op. cit., p. 119; House of Lords Library, Imperiale to Lloyd George, Dec. 13, 1917, F/55/4/3, 13/12, S/81

[20] Idem, p. 120

[21] The London Times Nov. 8, 1917. 9f.

[22] Speech given to Italian Parliament by Deputy Claudio Treves, July 12, 1917

[23] House of Lords Library, Rodd to Balfour, Dec. 16, 1917, F/56/1/64, No. 29, Folder 2 Box 95.

[24] Kriegsarchiv, Vienna : KA MKSM 1917 69-2/7, Rudolf Stöger, *Memoire über die Möglichkeit des Durchhalten im Winter 1917/18,*"

25 Glaise von Horstenau, Edmond, *Die Katastrophe, Die Zertrümmerung Österreich-Ungarns und das Werden der Nachfolgestaagten,* Zurich, 1929, p. 112

26 Gunther E. Rothenberg, *The Army of Francis Joseph,* Purdue University Press, West Lafayette, Indiana, 1976, p. 209-210.

27 Arz, op. cit., p. 213

28 Kriegsarchiv, Vienna : Glaise-Horstenau, op. cit., p. 141-42; KA MKSM 1918 69-3/17-22; Arz, op. cit. p. 223-24,

29 Arz, op. cit., p. 136

30 ÖStA-KA, MKSM 69-6/26. *Die militärische Lage im Frühjahr 1918.* However, the date on this document was Nov. 3, 1917, Kriegsarchiv, Vienna

31 Kriegsarchiv, Vienna : KA MKSM 1918 25-1/9, Report of A.O.K 119083

32 Peter Fiala, *Die letze Offensive Altösterreichs. Fûhrungsprobleme und Fûhreverant-wortlichkeit bei öst-ung. Offensive in Venetien, Juni 1918,* Boppard am Rhein: Harald Boldt Verlag, 1967, p. 12.

33 Kriegsarchiv, Vienna, Anton Pitreich, *Die K.u.k. Piavefront,* part III, I/ 1918/18

34 Massignani, Alessandro, *Le Truppe D'Assalto Austro-Ungariche Nella Grande Guerra,* Gino Rossato Editore, Valdagno, 1996, p. 119

35 Kriegsarchiv Vienna :KA, Neue Feld Akten, 11th AK, (Gstb.) Karton 831, K.u.k., A.O.K., No. 316/5, Jan. 31, 1917.

36 Richard Gustav Gratz-Schüller, *Der Wirtschafliche Zusammenbruch* Österreich *Ungarns* Vienna, 1930, p. 160.

37 Edmund Glaise von Horstenau, op. cit., p. 256.

38 Arz, op. cit. p. 259-260.

39 Kriegsarchiv, Vienna: *Neuorganisation während des Kriegs, Orientierungsbehelf* k.k.Hof-und Staatsdrucerei, 1917); Arz, *Zur Geschichte,* op. cit. p. 258-59.

40 OULK: Vol. VII op, cit., p. 75-6

41 Idem, p. 177

42 Edmund Glaise von Horstenau, op. cit., p. 247

43 Richard Gustav Gratz-Schüller, op. cit. p. 78.

44 Kriegsarchiv, Vienna, MKSM 1916 11-2/16-2; Cramon op. cit., pp. 95-97

45 Kriegsarchiv, Vienna :KA MKSM 1916 11-2/16-2 Regele, p. 124-125; Cramon op. cit., p. 95-97

46 The British government informed Col. House that it was willing to engage in peace discussions if Germany would agree to "reasonable" terms. Confident of victory Germany would not have accepted any terms that the Allies considered reasonable; *A History of United States Foreign Policy,* Julius W. Pratt, op. cit., footnote, p. 479.

47 Piero Pieri, *L'Italia nella Prima Guerra Mondiale,* Einaudi Editore, 1965, p. 178

48 PRO: FO:371-12864 : Telegram from "Sand" for Mr. Campbell. An informal urgent request was put forward by Sil Vara (previous British correspondent for *Neue Freie Presse),* to initiate contacts with British diplomats. At the same time, moves had been made in Berne.

49 PRO: FO 371-12864: Telegram No. 680, Ct. 13, 1917, from Berne to A. Balfour, M.P.

50 PRO: FO 371-12864: Telegram No. 3050, Nov. 15, 1917, Foreign Office to British Amb.at the Hague.

51 PRO: FO 371 /2864 :Nov. 15, 1917, Telegram No. 3050.

52 PRO: FO 371-/2864: Circular Telegram from London to Paris, (No. 2631), Rome (1884) Petrograd (2252), Washington (4706) and Tokyo (533).

53 PRO: FO 371/2864, Telegram No. 208754, Nov. 1, 1917, Czernin was willing to draw the boundary Italy-Austria, as it was before the war right after Caporetto.

54 PRO: FO 371-/2864, Telegram from Brit. Ambassador at the Hague to Foreign Office. No. 3816, Nov. 17, 1917

55 PRO: FO 371/2864: Telegram from FO to Brit. Amb. at the Hague, No. 3098, Nov. 1917

56 PRO: FO 371/2864: Telegram from Lord Bertie, (Paris) to FO. No. 1293, Nov. 18, 1917

57 PRO: FO 371/2864: Handwritten notes of cabinet meetings, Nov. 19, 1917, signed G.P.C.

58 PRO: FO 371/2864: Handwritten minutes of cabinet meetings, Nov. 19, 1917

59 PRO: FO 371/2864, Circular Telegram FO to Allies, and British Ambassadors in Allied capitols, Nov. 16, 1917; Vienna was ready to discuss the total evacuation of Belgium, and northern France, restoration of Serbia to her condition before 1912, discuss Alsace-Lorraine, and return to the

boundaries of Italy-Austria before the war. This proposal was only good until November 20.

60 PRO : FO 371/2864/134202/246162, Report of General Smuts' Mission, 18-19 December 1917

61 D.D. I. 5 X 61 and 74, Sonnino to Imperiale, 8 and 11 January 1918 ; Sonnino, *Diario d1916-1922*, Conversation with Rodd, 9 January 1918.

62 PRO: FO Cab 28.31. C. 33, Minutes of Anglo-American Conference, Nov. 20, 1917 Albert Thomas to Lloyd George, 13 January 1918; House of Lords Library F/50/2/7

63 National Archives: United States States Dept., Paris Peace Conference I, Inquiry Dept. Document 887, Dec. 22, 1917, p. 48.

64 *Civiltà Cattolica,* Rome, Sept. 1, 1917, p. 1

65 Giovanna Procacci, *Soldati e prigionier italiani nella Grande Guerra. Con una raccolta di lettere inedite.* Roma, Editori Riuniti 1993

66 USSME: Relazione Ufficiale, *L'Esercito Italiano nella Grande Guerra (1915-18)* Vol. V. Tomo II, *Narrazione* p.1081-1082; Ibid. Tomo II *Documenti,* Roma, 1988, p. 1482-86; Memorandum of Italian Army Chief of Staff, April 28, 1936.

67 Leo Spitzer, *Italienische Kriegsgefangennbriefe Materielien zu einter Charakteristik der volkstumlichen italienischen Korrespondenz,* Bonn, Peter Hanstein, 1921.p. 227. Sptizer was a linguistic interested in the correspondence of prisoners of war. He collected much of it and wrote a book.

68 Vienna Reichpost, Nov. 9 p. 4

69 USSME: Relazione Ufficiale, Vol. V, Tomo 2, *La Conclusione del Conflitto,* op. cit., 1988,p.90.

70 Kriegsarchiv, Vienna: *Armeeoberkomando Secret Operations No. 1740/I* Jansa Report, p. 1,(547)

71 USSME :Relazione Ufficiale, Vol. V, Tomo 2, op. cit., p. 966

72 Carlo Emilio Gadda, *Giornale di Guerra e di Prigionia,* Einaudi, 1965, p. 291-292.

73 USSME:, Relazione Ufficiale, op. cit. Vol. V, Tomo 2 bis, op. cit., Memorandum of Italian Army Chief of Staff, April 28, 1936

74 USSME: Relazione Ufficiale, Vol. V, Tome 2 bis, op. cit., Memorandum of Chief of Staff, April 28, '1936

75 M. Rossi, *I prigionieri dello Zar, Soldati italiani dell'esercito austro-ungarico nei lager della Russia* (1914-1918) Milano, Mursia, 1997 Idem. *Irredenti giuliani al fronte russo,* Udine, Del Bianco 1998

76 *Papers relating to the Foreign Relations of the United States, 1918, Russia,* Volume II, p. 328. U.S. Government Printing Office, Washington.

77 George Kennan, *The Decision to Intervene,* Princeton University Press, 1958, p. 71

78 Istituto Centrale di Statistica, Rome,

79 Franco Angeli, *Storia dell'economia italiana negli ultimi cento anni,* Milano 1969 Vol. II pp. 216-217

80 Gerd Hardach, *La Prima Guerra Mondiale,1914-18;* Etas books 1982, p. 182

81 Andrea Curami, *L'Artiglieria Italiana nella Grande Guerra,* Valdagno Rossato, 1998, p. 7-8. Figures given are those by the War Ministry in 1924.

82 Gatti, op. cit. p. 146-48.

83 Gatti, op. cit. p. 403

84 Personal Communication

85 P. Melograni, *Storia Politica della Grande Guerra,* Bari, 1972 p. 501

86 Barnett, G.H. *With the 48th Division in Italy,* London, 1923, p. 5

87 Mario Silvestri, *Isonzo 1917,* Giulio Einaudi Editore, Torino, 1965, p. 103

88 Alessandro Luzio, *Il Comando Supremo con Armando Diaz,* Vercelli, 1920, p. 7.

89 Personal Communication.

90 RICC, Vol. I, op. cit., p. 374

91 OBARI, op. cit., p. 144

92 USSME: Relazione Ufficiale, Vol V. Tome 1, Doc. p. 60

93 A. Gatti, *Caporetto, Diario.* Bologna, 1965, p. 147

94 USSME: Relazione Ufficiale, Vol. VI, Tomo 2, *Le istruzioni tattiche del Capo di Stato Maggiore dell'Esercito,* Roma, 1980, Enc.No. 92, pp.430-31, No. 146 of April 20, 1918, "Safety Precautions."

95 Note divisions of Lt. Gen. Luigi Basso on Oct. 24, and of Lt. Gen. Pier Luigi Sagramoso on Oct. 25, all transferred with generals having no more troops.

96 Giorgio Rochat, *Gli Ufficiali italiani nella prima guerra mondiale,* in Id. *L'esercito italiano in pace e in guerra,* Milano, Rara, 1991.

97 Diaz's order was Order No. 5468. I Army responded it could not comply, USSME Relazione Ufficiale, Vol. IV. Tome 3, op. cit., p. 544

98 USSME : Relazione Ufficiale, Vol. V, Tome I op. cit., p 320-344.

99 Lt. Gen. Gaetano Giardino would soon take over the Italian IV Army

100 Fulvio Zugaro, *La Forza dell'esercito. Statistica dello sforzo militare italiano nella Guerra Mondiale.* Ufficio Statistico del Ministero della Guerra, Roma, 1927.

101 Diaz's order was Order No. 5468. I Army responded it could not comply, USSME Relazione Ufficiale, Vol. IV. Tomo 3, op. cit., p. 544

102 Piero del Negro, *La leva militare in Italia dall'unita' alla Grande Guerra,* in Idem. *Esercito, stato, società*, Bologna, Cappelli, 1979.

103 W.R. Robertson, *The Military Correspondence of Field Marshal Sir William Robertson*, editor D.R. Woodward, Army Records Soc. London, 1989. p.239

104 Idem, p. 240

105 FAR, op. cit., Tome VI, Vol. I Annexe 37.

106 E.E. Herbillon, *Du Général en chef au Gouvernement* 2 volumes, Paris, 1930, p. 156

107 J.J. Pershing, *My Experiences in the World War,* 2 vol. New York 1931, Vol. I p. 261

108 *Les Armée,* op. cit., p. 97

109 Ibid, p. 97

110 OBARI, op. cit., p. 134

111 OBARI, op. cit., p. 59

112 Ibid p. 90

113 Ibid p. 91

114 PRO WO79/67

115 FAR, Tome VI, Vol. I, op. cit., 1931, Annexe 68

116 Ibid. p. 103

117 PRO WO 106/805, Report of Gen. M. Fayolle, No. 638, dated Dec 26, 1917, as well as Report No 1078 dated Jan. 15, 1918, total of eleven pages.

118 OBARI: op. cit., p. 132-37; Gen. Plumer's reports dated January13, and January 20.

119 OBARI, op. cit., p. 129

120 USSME; *Relazione della Commissione d'Inchiesta, Dall'Isonzo al Piave,* Rome, 1919, Vol II, p. 326.

121 OBARI, op. cit., p. 138

122 Ibid. p. 424

123 W. R. Robertson, *Military Correspondence etc,* op. cit., Army Records Soc. London, 1989, p. 257

124 FAR, Ministre de la défense, Paris, tome VI, Vol. I p. 23.

125 OBARI Op. Cit. p. 99

126 Idem footnote, p. 148

127 *USSME:* Relazione Ufficiale, Vol. V Tomo I Doc. op. cit., p.140

128 Paolo Ferrari, *La Grande Guerra Aerea, 1915-18,* Editore Rossati-Valdagno, 1994, p39

129 Norman Gladden, *Across the Piave,* London 1971.

130 Pershing, op. cit. Vol. II p. 256; USSME: Relazione Ufficiale, Vol V, Tomo 2, Doc. 297

131 Telegram to Gen. Pershing from Chief of the General Staff, Army U.S.A., 19 June 1918. No. 1580. Documents of Military History, U.S. Army War College, Carlisle Pa.

132 OBARI, op. cit., p. 131

CHAPTER XVI

THE NEW WEAPONS OF WAR THAT SHOCKED, PANICKED AND AWED ENEMY INFANTRY

When the Great War broke out it had only been about ten years since the Wright brothers took their historic flight. Some military personnel realized the potential of air power, while others thought of it as a toy. When in 1909 Louis Blériot crossed the English Channel most European military staffs started to think of ways of using this possible new weapon. Both the Habsburgs and the Kingdom of Italy lacked air power and initially had to turn to their allies for men and machines. When planes strafed deployed infantry unaccustomed to aerial attack and with no defense they panicked. In 1917 flying as an observer on reconnaissance missions Lt. Heinz Guderian future tank commander in the Second World War appreciated the potential of air power.[1] *Krauss the great Habsburg commander on the Italian Front lamented the fact of the lack of political and military foresight in using this weapon.*[2] *Armoured cars (but not tanks) made their debut on the Italian Front fighting in cavalry regiments which they would replace while the perfected machine gun became the queen of the battle field.*

Off We go into the Wide Blue Yonder
Flying High Into the Skies

AS THE AUTHOR investigated, researched and finally wrote this work, it was realized that toward the end of the conflict air power had become a potent and *deciding* factor.

At the outbreak of the war the use of airpower was on a learning curve with everyone from the plane designers to the factories to the pilots being students and improving as they went along. In the first two years of warfare on the Austro-Italian Front, planes were mostly used for artillery spotting and reconnaissance while later they mounted machine guns which fired through the propeller blades or were above the wings or to the rear of the plane for the observer to fire. Later planes were used as bombers and to strafe ground troops. Naturally their primary target was each other.

Machine guns had been used for some time but were perfected to a rapid rate of fire by 1911. Haig, Kitchener and Cadorna felt that this weapon was overrated. British battalions received only two to four such weapons. Only the Germans used the force-multiplier concept to good advantage.

To counteract this new gun menace Winston Churchill, First Lord of the Admiralty, proposed the construction of an armoured vehicle with guns and caterpillar treads to cross enemy trenches. During its experimental phase to avoid enemy knowledge of its development and resembling a washing machine, it was given the name 'tank.' The name stuck. First used in 1916 the vehicles outpaced the accompanying infantry and were destroyed.

Hindenburg felt that there was no need for such a vehicle. He felt that by concentrating anti-tank guns and light artillery the tank's armor could be pierced. Instead Colonel Bauer chief of the Prussian Army dept. dealing with artillery technical problems realized the significance and potential of this weapon. A model was shown to representatives of the High Command but was rejected. On his own responsibility Bauer directed Krupp's to produce plans for a light fast model while the allies had gone into mass production.[3] Shortage of materials prohibited Germany from doing likewise. Finally in 1918 German tank formations appeared which were really captured British tanks. On the Italian Front development did not go beyond rubber-wheeled armoured cars.

ITALIAN AVIATION

Prior to the war Italy had the brains but no industrial base or factories to mass produce planes. Swiftly adapting and setting up facilities after May 1915, it did produce about 12,000 planes during the war with a peak production of 541 aircraft per month in 1918. In 1909 Gianni Caproni had built a factory and had an airfield at Vizzola Ticino in northern Italy. For his work eventually he was made a count.

After the Italo-Turkey War in 1911 a commission was appointed to examine the question of aviation. In that war Italy was the first nation to use air power in a war. To head the commission were General Giuseppe Valleris and Rear Admiral Enrico Presbiterio. The commission felt that national plane production should be encouraged with a national contest which became law on June 27, 1912 and finally took place in 1913.[4] The reader will remember that in Volume I, chapter V it was noted that on July 12, 1914 the War Minister issued a decree constituting a *Battaglione Aviatori* which incidentally was temporarily commanded by Major Giulio Douhet of future aviation theory fame.

None of the planes constructed were usable forcing him to write a memorandum that since the Caproni plant depended on military contracts it should not be allowed to go bankrupt. Aware of this Col. M. M. Moris, Inspector General of Aviation purchased the factory and employed Caproni. By August 1913 Douhet was very upset, wanting twelve squadrons but had to be happy with eight. He wanted to increase Italian plane construction but there was difficulty in obtaining qualified personnel plus he was afraid that the public thought that constructing a plane was easy with a tremendous profit.[5] On January 27, 1914 he asked the War Minister for L. 15,000 to proceed with the construction of a plane which was approved. Apparently the plane was tested without a government representative present which annoyed many resulting in Douhet being transferred and Caproni's dismissal. However the plane flew so well that he was rehired.[6] Also watching the flight was *Commendatore* Mercanti who represented an industrial group.

Attempts to build the plane in military factories were unsuccessful so the task was given to Mercanti who then rented the Vizzola factory from the government. Finally in 1914 twelve were built and sold to the government at a cost of L 135,000 each. Toward the middle of 1915 Douhet had made out a report criticizing all the planes available. Of note was the fact that *FIAT* planes did not produce the requested 100 h.p. in flight but only 80. After the conflict the major wrote a classic on airpower declaring that heavily armed bombers could get through to the target bombing military and civilian targets to destroy enemy civilian morale.[7]

With no increase in plane production, in 1915 a parliamentary commission reported that not only was Italian aviation in serious difficulty but its very existence had been compromised. It was hoped that Italian industry would come to the forefront of plane construction but in the meantime foreign planes would have to do. Planes for the *Battaglioni Aviatori* were not ready for combat flying forcing plane purchases in France and Britain or constructed in Italy under foreign licenses. Farmans, Nieuports, Blériots and Bristols were purchased abroad and later constructed in Italy under patent agreements. Italy used French fighter planes built under licenses while it was dominant in bomber design with its planes being built under license in France as well as exported to the U.S.A.

There would soon be many Italian aircraft manufacturing companies, among them the *Caproni, Società Italiana Transaerea, Savoia Macchi, Pomilio* and *FIAT*. Starting with next to nothing these companies eventually produced enough planes either original or foreign models to defend Italian skies. As Italy entered the conflict the Comando Supremo realized that it would need many aircraft mechanics and crews. It requested that interested army personnel would apply via the familiar *Carta Bollata* (a government form which had to be purchased) thus even making money on those would applied.

Parachutes were available only to crews serving on the balloons. Pilots thought them uncomfortable and always thought that if in trouble they could land in some meadow, hence never used them.

Josef Kiss flying over the Alps in July 1917 in his
Oeffag-built Albatross D III (53.33)
Courtesy of Bruce Robertson

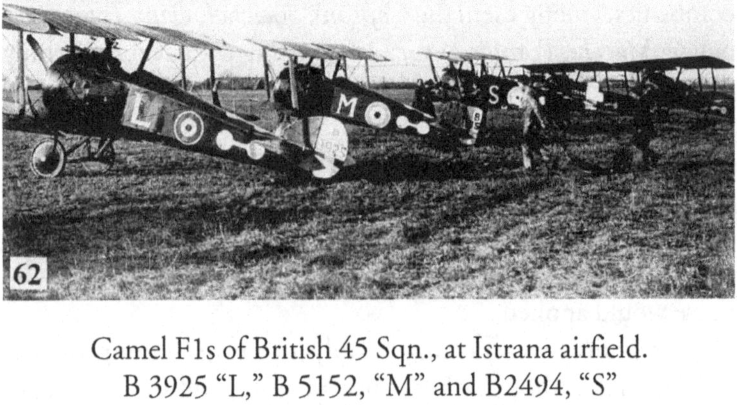

Camel F1s of British 45 Sqn., at Istrana airfield.
B 3925 "L," B 5152, "M" and B2494, "S"
can easily be recognized.

63

Deployment of Habsburg Phoenix fighters Flik 55 J at the Cire di Pergine airfield on July 24, 1918. Note the personal insignias. Fourth from the right is the "M" of its commander *Hauptmann* Joseph von Maier, while first on the left with the white-lined heart belongs to *Zugsführer* Alexander Kasza and the third from the left with the "L" belongs to *Feldwebel* Franz Lahner *Courtesy of Museo di Guerra, Rovereto*

64

The Macchi M 5 the best Italian flying boat fighter of the war

An Austrian Lohner L 127 flying boat captured at Ancona in June 1918. Note German (on fuselage) and Habsburg (on tail section) insignia. It is now in the Italian Air Force Museum *Courtesy Andrea Curami*

ITALIAN AIRCRAFT

Ansaldo S.V.A. 5,9,10[7]

The Savoia Verduzio Ansaldo single seat biplane Type 5 appeared in mid-1917. It had a 220 h.p. SPA 6A motor with a flat upper wing and inversely tapered ailerons. The engine had a car-type radiator with six stub-outlets carrying its exhaust gases away to starboard. The fuselage was configured so as to allow the pilot a good view to the rear and front. The lower wing was shorter and slightly dihedral. Twin synchronized Vickers guns were mounted in the grooves on top of the cowling. Unsuitable as a fighter it was used as a long range reconnaissance and bomber plane. It was used to bomb Innsbrück and Bolzano on October 29, 1918. Almost 1300 S.V.A. 5s were constructed with the machines being flown by the *Sezione 1-6*, the *56a, 57a, 87a, 89a, 111a* and *116a Squadriglia*, the naval *242a Squadriglia* and part of the naval *San Marco* and *103a Squadriglia.*[8] A two-seater version was constructed, the S.V.A. 9. On August 2, 1918 it was used by Gabriele D'Annunzio and his pilot Capt. Natale Palli of the *87a Squadriglia* along with five S.V.A. 5 bombers to drop leaflets on Vienna returning via Graz and Ljubljana, a distance of 625 miles. This model was also used by the navy. An S.V. A. 10 was also built which in 1920 flew from Rome to Tokio, 11,250 miles in 109 hours of flying time.

Aviatik (Italian version)

The *Società Anonima Meccanica Lombarda* (S.A.M.L.) produced copies of the German Aviatik B-1 in their factory in Monza during 1915-1916. The wings, fuselages and empennages resembled the original while the engine was a water-cooled 140 h.p. Canton-Unné.[9] A total of 570 of these were produced. Subsequently it was powered by FIAT, Isotta-Fraschini or Le Rhône engines and was mostly used for training purposes. Later the S.A.M.L. 1 was developed using a FIAT A 12 motor with 260 h.p. with a box radiator in front of the cabane-trestle. The fuselage had flat sides with a rounded top. The observer had a Revelli gun on a pivoting mount while the wings were strut-braced from below. This model was used for bombing as well as artillery observation. Another model the S.A.M. L. 2 was produced with a second Revelli gun fixed on top of the upper wing firing above the propeller and to be fired by the pilot. Any problems with the gun with had to be fixed in flight by the observer. By October 1918 only twenty-six of these craft were available. In all there were twenty-three produced in 1916, 448 in 1917 and 186 in 1918. Flying S.A.M.L. 1 planes were the *21a, 39a, 72a, 74a, 75a, 111a, 112a, 113a, 114a, 115a, 116a, 117a, 118a, 120a,* and *122a Squadriglia.*[10] Flying S. A. M.L 2 craft on the Italian Front were the *121a Squadriglia* and part of the *115a* and *120a Squadriglia.*

Caproni[11]

These three-engined bombers with a crew of four first went into action in August 1915 flying from Pordenone to bomb Aisovizza. It was a tactical bomber with a bomb load of 1,000 lb. used against railway junctures and troop concentrations. The first significant sortie was against Ljubljana with seven planes on February 18, 1916. Of the six returning planes one was piloted by Capt. Oreste Salamone whose whole crew had been killed. For this heroic act he was awarded the *Medaglia d'Oro.* There were also raids against Cattaro in Albania. The Ca. 33 was introduced in 1917 with a 450 h.p. engine also flying with the Italian Navy as a torpedo bomber. *Escadrilles CAP 115* and 130 of the French *Group de Bombardement 2* used these craft. There were several American pilots flying these planes on the Italian Front. The Italian XVII Group flying Capronis started serving in France from February 1918 until the Armistice with the *3a, 14a, 15a Squadriglie.*

The Caproni Ca.40 using three Isotta Fraschini engines with a total of 600 h.p. was a stupendous plane for its time. It was a triplane bomber with a wing-span of almost 100 feet with struts and wires. It had the double nose-wheels of the Ca. 3 and a nacelle with a vertical profile. There were two pilots sitting side-by-side with gunners in the front and rear of the fuselage. A total of twenty three were built being used by the Italian Army and Navy in October 1918.

Models developed were the Ca 41 with a pointed nacelle and no nose-wheels and the Ca 42 with more powerful engines and carrying the bomb load between the landing wheels. The thick maize of struts and wires slowed it down making it a good target for enemy fighters forcing it to be used in night bombing runs only. The British Royal Naval Air Service purchased six of the latter model. The Ca 42 was modified to to carry torpedoes in the Naval Air Arm and called a Ca 43. The Ca 44 had three 200/300 FIAT h.p. engines fitted with frontal radiators with the radiator of the pusher engine being in the nacelle. The Ca 45 had a pointed nacelle and separate box-radiators and the Ca 46 was identical except for its Liberty engines and frontal radiators. The Ca 45s were built in France under Italian license while the Ca 46s were built in the U.S.A., Italy and France.

The Ca 5 series provided greater lifting power and round-sectioned nacelles. These were to replace the Ca 3 with five being available for the October 1918 offensive. A total of 255 were constructed in Italy with some being flown on the Western Front by the Italian XVIII Group of night bombers. Post war due to complicated maintenance these planes were discarded.

Macchi Parasol

Prior to the war the *Società Anonima Nieuport-Macchi* in Varese obtained the license to manufacture the Macchi two seater Parasol which was manufactured in 1913. It had a speed of 78 m.p.h. but climbed poorly. Its motor was a Gnôme 80 h.p. rotary. During the first three Isonzo battles it was used for artillery spotting. Due to its defects such as stalling and spinning, it was replaced.

Pomilio PC, PD, PE and PY

The Torino-based firm of *O. Pomilio & Co.* (founded in March 1916) put out a two seater reconnaissance biplane which was introduced in the beginning of 1917. Called the PC it was powered by a FIAT 260 h.p. A 12 engine with its cylinders protruding. In front of the top wing was the radiator. There were two Revelli machine guns, one for the observer, the other mounted above the upper wing firing over the revolving propeller. Its top speed was over 100 m.p.h. but it was unstable especially in bad winds which led it to fall in disfavor with pilots.[12] In 1918 the PD model was introduced with a cowled-in engine and a frontal radiator. Another improvement was the PE which an enlarged tailplane and slightly enlarged rudder fin. These models proved to be very efficient so much so that by October in the Battle of Vittorio Veneto almost sixty-percent of the Italian planes were Pomilios with a synchronised gun for the pilot and a Lewis gun on a Scarff ring.[13] Slightly over 1,600 Pomilios were built, with seven being PYs with the type being flown by the *22a, 23a, 27a, 31a, 32a, 33a, 36a, 38a, 39a, 48a, 61a, 62a, 111a, 112a, 113a, 114a, 115a, 116a, 117a, 118a, 120a, 131a, 132a, 133a, 134a, 135, 136a,* and the *139a Squadriglia.* The company was sold to Ansaldo (a FIAT subsidiary at the time) with the Pomilio brothers going to the United States where they developed the Pomilio BVL-12 two seater and the FVL-8 single seater samples of which were purchased by the U.S. government.

Savoia-Pomilio, (S.P. 2,3,4)

This craft used *FIAT* A 12 motors with 260 h.p. It had twin radiators to cool it fixed on each side of the nacelle. The observer sat in the nose of the nacelle armed with a Revelli gun. Sometimes a gun was mounted between the cockpits to fire back over the upper wing.[14] The S.P. 2 established the world altitude record in 1917 reaching 21,113 feet. The pilot had a blind spot thus this plane was not favored by the crews. Often the men note that the S.P. stood for *Siamo Perduti* (We are lost), while the S.P. 2 meant *Sepultura per due* (A grave for two). They were still flying in October 1918. In 1916, there were 128 S.P. 2s built while in 1917 there were 274 built. Flying these craft were the *21a, 22a,23a,24a, 26a, 27a,28a, 31a, 32a, 33a, 35a, 37a, 38a, 39a, 40a, 41a, 45a, 61a, 74a, 114a, 116a,* and *120a Squadriglie.*

S.I.A. 7B 1, 7B2, and 9B

Another *FIAT* subsidiary was the *Società Italiana Aviazione.* This company had two craft designers, the Majors Savoia and Verduzio whose name together with Ansaldo produced the initials SVA. Several types of craft were produced in its factories. The 7 B-1 had a car-type radiator for its 260 h.p. FIAT A 12 motor with six stub outlets to carry exhaust fumes to starboard. The pilot's front view was partially obscured by the cowling top which came well above the fuselage. There were two guns with one on top of the upper wing to be fired by the pilot with the other to be fired by the observer. This plane broke the world's record for climb at 22,147 feet as well as making non-stop flights such as roundtrip Torino to Naples and Torino to London each a distance of 750 miles. The 7 B 2 was introduced in May 1918, climbed higher than the 7 B 1 with the front view problems of the pilot being eliminated. Even though having its wing struts strengthened it had the same problem as its predecessor. All 7 Bs were withdrawn from service. The SIA 9 B was fitted with a 700 h.p. FIAT A 14 motor.[15] This model with D'Annunzio as a passenger bombed the Pola Naval Air Station on July 17.

A view of the Crocco-Ricaldoni flying bomb during a test flight on June '5, 1918

Francesco Baracca with his Spad XIII biplane.
Note the prancing horse on the fuselage later to be used by the Ferrari auto racing stable as its insignia.

Gabriele D'Annunzio (center), with fellow flyers after his flight in a S.V.A. 9 dropping leaflets over Vienna
Courtesy Carlo Lucchini

Major Fiorello LaGuardia of the U.S. Signal Service served as a Caproni bomber pilot on the Italian Front. He later was Mayor of the City of New York

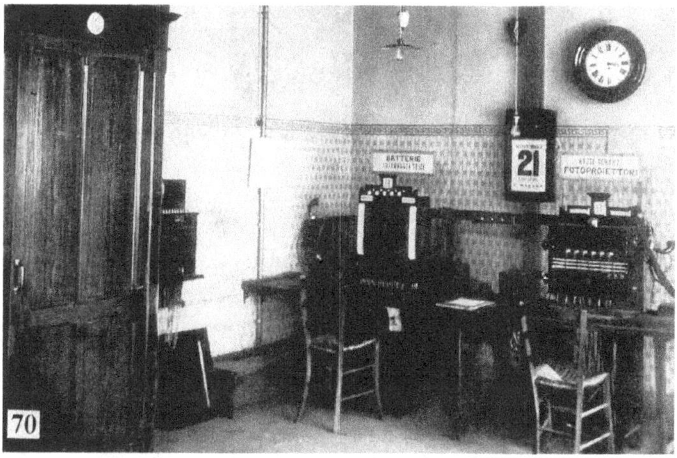

The City of Milano's Air Defense Command Center
Courtesy Carlo Lucchini

German Gotha G-II bomber used against London
as well as on the Italian Front.

A captured Italian armoured car

Rare photo of the newly arrived Nieuport 17s delivered to the Aces *91a Squadriglia.* In the foreground on the fuselage we see the star of Sgt. Poli, further to the rear the skull and crossbones of Lt. Ruffo di Calabria while to the far rear is the plane of Capt. Francesco Baracca. Subsequently the Bongiovanni list dropped Poli from the list of aces. *Courtesy Maurizio Longoni*

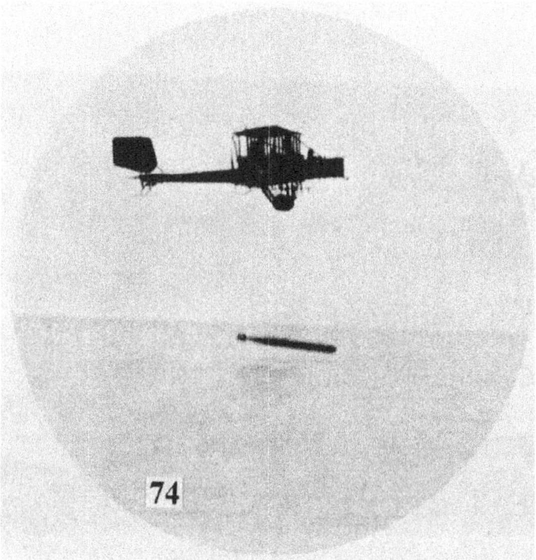

A Caproni bomber launching a torpedo while in flight over the Adriatic.

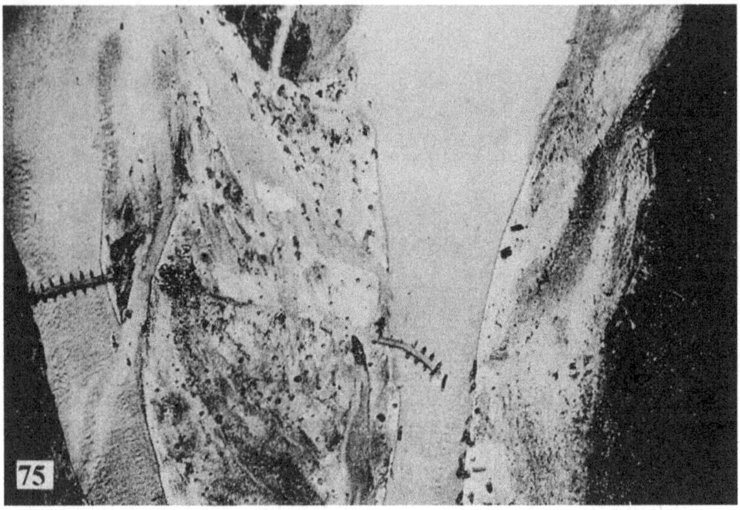

Note the destruction wrought by Italian bombers on this bridge over the Piave in June 1918. The new weapon of war was asserting itself

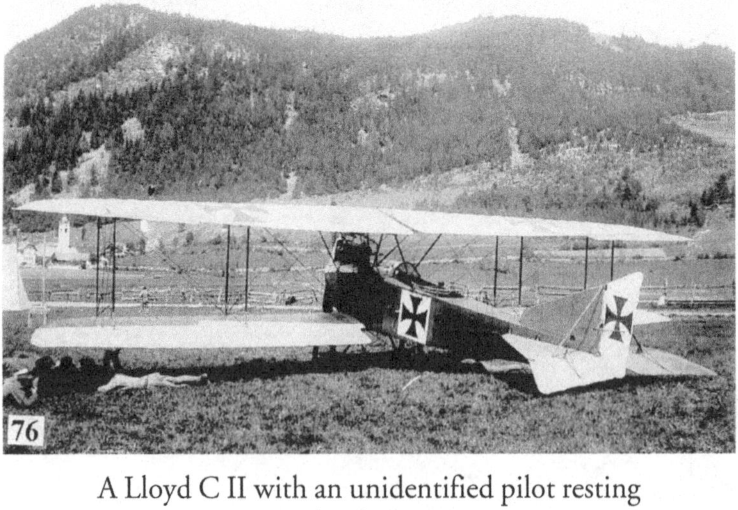

A Lloyd C II with an unidentified pilot resting under the wings.

77

Oeffag-built Albatross D III (153.45) of Austrian Air Ace Goodwin Brumowski shot up on February 1, 1918. Enemy fire punctured the plane's fuel tank and ignited the spilling contents. Note the burned wing fabric.

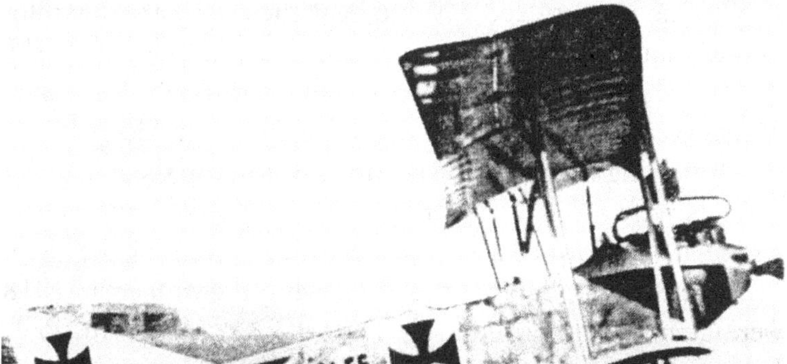

78

Albatross Series 24 with box-type radiator.

AIR ACES

At the outbreak of the war French pilots coined the phrase "ace" defining a fighter pilot who had downed more than one enemy plane.[16] In Germany the name *Kanone* was used for a pilot who had downed four planes similar to Top Gun used today. On both sides these men were worshiped with special events to put them on public display. Lt. Silvio Scaroni one of Italy's best air aces wrote that the first thing one should do is never lose sight of the enemy pilot but as larger numbers of planes were involved in dogfights, this became difficult. In the Austrian Air Service, each member of the crew that defeated an enemy plane (not necessarily destruction) received full credit for one downed plane. In the British Service it was difficult to certify a downed plane as most of the air combat was over German-held territory. Therefore a "competent" witness had to certify that the enemy plane was downed. In the U.S. Signal Corps (predecessor of the Army Air Corps) only confirmed victories were accredited, not a plane probably destroyed. German air combat was over friendly territory so all could be certified. It had to be witnessed by another pilot or creditable witness from the ground. On both sides of the sky there were several characteristics which ran through all the aces. They were daring, had nerves of steel and often reckless.

Appearing strange in today's times Air Aces in the Italian Air Services were offered monetary rewards by different business entities if they downed enemy planes. In 1917 winning the Pirelli Prize were Piccio, Baracca and Ruffo while the winners in 1918 were Cerutti, Scaroni and Reali. The *Officine di Savigliano* Prize (where parts for dirigibles were built) offered varying sums to pilots and mechanics. Winners of this prize were two future Chiefs of Staff of the *Regia Aeronautica*, Francesco Pricolo and Giuseppe Valle.[17] Also giving monetary prizes in Italy were the magazines *Il Secolo Illustrato* and its rival *Domenica del Corriere*. Austro-Hungarian officialdom also offered prizes of up to 3,000 *Kronen* if an allied plane were destroyed or downed within friendly lines.[18]

After the war the Italian Air Service issued a list of Air Aces and their recognized kills.

Allied Planes flown on the Italian Front

Blériot

Louis Blériot crossed the English Channel in 1909. Single and two-seaters were built many of which were flown in Italy. With the passage of time these craft were gradually eclipsed by faster planes.

Farman

Henry Farman established a aircraft producing factory which eventually was two miles long producing ten aircraft per day.[19] These planes were also eclipsed by faster and better fighters.

Hanriot[20]

René Hanriot was a pioneer name in French aviation. He was a driver of Darracq cars as well as an airplane designer. After designing and flying an airplane in 1907 he opened a factory at Reims in 1910. In May 1910 a British company, the Hanriot Monoplane, Ltd. was established. In May 1912 the British government set up a contest which was won by a plane which was eventually useless with the second award going to the Hanriot. He withdrew from aviation in 1913 while his company continued to produce planes. Re-entering the industry in 1915 he opened a factory at Billancourt producing Sopwith 1½ Strutters. Pierre Dupont joined him as a designer with a new plane appearing in 1916.

This new plane was called the HD-1, having a single-seat, powered by a 110 h.p. Le Rhône 9J rotary engine. Many pilots thought it resembled the Sopwith Camel. The wings (upper twenty-eight feet, lower twenty-four feet fuselage nineteen were heavily staggered and of uneven length with the cockpit immediately behind the cabane. The upper wing had four degrees of dihedral, being almost level with the pilot's eyes giving him an unobstructed view. The lower wing had no dihedral. The only armament it had was a Vickers mounted above the port upper longeron. It had a maximum speed of 110 m.p.h. and could climb to 20,000 feet. Its autonomy was three hours. Coming in production about the same time as the Spad VII which had been enthusiastically accepted by French aviation, it had no chance in the French Air Arm.

However Italian military in France were enthusiastic about it seeing it could replace the older Nieuport single-seaters. Checked out by Italian pilots, it was adopted for their *Squadriglie di Caccia* to be produced by the Macchi factory at Varese. It became operational on the Italian Front in mid-1917 joining the *76a squadriglia.*[21] Instantly it won approval by Italian pilots as it was similar to the Nieuport 17 (both had the same type of engine). Scaroni who would become an aide to the king was the most brilliant exponent of the HD-1. He had twin guns installed, but other pilots refused this as the extra weight would decrease the maneuverability of the plane.

It is unknown exactly how many were flown on the Italian Front, but it hovers about 1,000. One source declares that 831 craft were sent to the Italian Front.[22] The HD-2 a seaplane version was used by the French and U.S. navies. With all its uses and accolades it was not even acknowledged by *Jane's All the World's Aircraft* up to 1966.

Macchi and Nieuport

The *Società Anonima Nieuport-Macchi* (Varese) started to manufacture these monoplanes under license in 1912 which continued into the war period. On May 27, 1915 an Austro-Hungarian Lohner seaplane fell into Italian hands with the Varese factory commissioned to produce a copy. Several were produced through the years culminating in the M-5 which appeared early in 1918. It had a 150 hp. Isotta-Fraschini V4B engine with a speed of 118 mph at sea level. Carrying a Lewis or Vickers machine gun its autonomy was four hours while the operational ceiling was 15,000 feet. The Macchi was mostly used by the Naval Air Arm.

SPAD

This series of planes were popular on the Italian Front. They were constructed in France by the Société *Anonyme pour l'Aviation et ses Derives,* commonly known as SPAD. The designer was Louis Béchereau while Marc Birkigt developed the Hispano-Suiza engines.

Spad XII

This was a variant of the Spad XIII which had a 37 mm. Pureaux cannon with a shortened barrel which could fire through a hollow propeller shaft. It also had a single Vickers machine gun and could reach the maximum ceiling of 23,000 feet with a speed of 137 m.p.h.[23] However, it was difficult for the average pilot to fly the plane and fire the cannon which had to be manually loaded so most pilots relied on the Vickers.

Spad XIII

Powered by a Hispano-Suiza engine 8 B engine, it could reach a top speed of 124 m.p.h., climbing to 13,000 feet. With twin 0.303.-in Vickers machine guns with 380 rounds apiece it was a deadly weapon. In October 1917, these planes were delivered to Italian pilots. They were flown by the *10°* Gruppo (*70a Squadriglia)* and the *17°* Gruppo (*71a, 77a, 91a Squadriglie).* The latter was the famed "Aces Squadron."

Voisin

The oldest aircraft firm in the world was that founded by the Brothers Voisin in 1905. Producing single and two-seater craft it was eclipsed by faster and more rapidly climbing aircraft.[24]

ALLIED AIR ACTIVITY ON THE ITALIAN FRONT

British Air Aces

Britain had formed the Royal Naval Air Service on July 1, 1914 and the Royal Air Force on April 1, 1918. Naval squadrons were renumbered: No. 1 (Naval) squadron became No. 201 Squadron, R.A.F.; and so on. After the Caporetto debacle several British divisions were sent to the Italian Front. To support them five squadrons (28, 42, 34,45 and 66) were sent to support them being attached to the Italian Sixth Army. The planes (Camels) were dismantled, crated and shipped. Arriving in Milano the pilots found no one to greet them nor anyone who spoke English. Finally someone was found, the planes were assembled and the citizens of Milano given a view of aerial acrobatics by Capt. William Barker commander of the 28 Squadron.[25] Later in July, 1918 Squadron 139 arrived flying Bristol F2B which would perform reconnaissance and air combat missions.

All squadrons arrived in Italy in November, 1917 and returned to France at varying times while the 28 squadron remained in Italy for the duration of the conflict. The pilots soon realized that flying on this front was quite different. There were deep valleys with high mountains with fog and strong winds sometimes making flying very dangerous. The achievements of British Air Aces on the Italian Front are listed below. Space limitations oblige the author to list only a short biography of several aces (in alphabetical order).

Lt. Gordon Frank Mason Apps was born in Kent in 1899 and commissioned in the RFC in August 1977. Flying in Italy in the 66 Squadron he claimed nine victories.[26]

Major William George Barker (9, 4,15,28,66,139,201 Squadrons) was born on November 3, 1894 in Dauphin, Manitoba. He joined the second contingent of the Canadian Expeditionary Force (First Regiment of the Canadian Mounted Rifles) shipped to France where he served in a quiet sector of the front. By January 1916 he applied to the RFC taking his first flight in March 1916. Planes had a wireless which could send but not receive. By April 1916 he was commissioned as a second Lt. in the RFC assigned to Squadron No. Four flying a BE2c. He even flew the Prince of Wales about in his plane numbered D8063. In November, 1917 with Squadron 28 which he commanded he was transferred to the Italian Front where he increased his number of victories. On October 27, 1918 finding himself fighting alone against a large Fokker formation he destroyed four craft, flaming three. This brought his victory score up to fifty. In that action he was wounded in both legs and suffered a shattered left arm. He managed to crash-land in friendly territory and recovered from his wounds. He was well-known for constantly breaking regulations of all types as well as taking unauthorized flights.[27] In all he had fifty victories and was personally awarded the Victoria Cross by King George V on November 30, 1918 for the feats of October 27, 1918.

Classic of his exploits was the escapade with Capt. William Wedgewood-Benn MP who often went on spy missions. The captain wished to carry an Italian agent deep into enemy territory where the agent would parachute down. Originally a Ca 3 was thought as the plane to use but in trials with a mannequin both it and the parachute were chewed up by the propeller of the third motor mounted in the back of the fuselage. Instead a converted Savoia-Pomilio SP-4 was used with a built in trapdoor with the release mechanism in the observer's cockpit. Navigation would also be a problem so a series of anti-aircraft lights were placed in series all pointing to destination. Benn was an excellent telegrapher so via wireless he would query Italian Army field wireless units (each with a distinct call sign) stationed near the lights to distinguish them from other lights. Firing ground red Verey flares would indicate that the mission should be aborted while motorcycle couriers stood by to transport messages should the wireless break down. After several delays they flew the Italian agent, *Alpini* Lt. Alessandro Tandura, who parachuted behind enemy lines communicating with headquarters via passenger pigeons. Tandura received the *Medaglia d'Oro al Valore Militare* while Barker received the *Medaglia d'Argento al Valore Militare.*[28] He was killed on March 12, 1930 in a flying accident in Canada.

Capt. Hilliard Brooke Bell of the 66 Squadron was born in Toronto, Canada in 1897, initially serving with the Field Artillery then joining the RFC in July 1917. After training he was posted to Italy where he flew with the 66 Squadron from October 1917. He claimed ten victories, with eight destroyed and two out of control.[29] He was awarded the MC and the *Medaglia di Bronzo al Valore Militare.* He died on September 16, 1960.

Lt. Gerald Alfred Birks (66 Squadron) was also a Canadian. Born in Montreal he joined the RFC in 1917 and by March, 1918 was in Italy with the 66 Squadron. He was awarded an MC and Bar in September 1918 and credited with twelve planes destroyed.[30] On May 24, 1918, while flying with Birks and Apps over Grigno they engaged three enemy planes. Engaging them he was given credit for downing *Offizierstellvertreter* Josef Kiss of Flik 55J the fifth-ranking Austro-Hungarian Air Ace. He died at the age of 96.

Lt. Francis Stephen Bowles flew in the 66 Squadron. He was born on October 30, 1899 in Thornton Heath, Surrey. He flew with the 66 Squadron in Italy, later returning to France. On November 3, 1918 he failed to return from a patrol having been shot down by Lt. Karl Romeis of Jasta 80.[31] Taken prisoner he was released with the signing of the armistice. In the Second World War he served as an account officer, promoted to Flight Lieutenant. He is credited with five victories.[32]

In all there were forty-three British Air Aces on the Italian Front which compiled a total of 420 victories. Following is a list of British Air Aces flying on the Italian Front.[33]

Name	*Total Victories*	*Victories in Italy*	*Squadron*
Lt. Gordon Apps	10	10	66
Maj. Wm. Barker	50	43	28, 66, 139
Capt. Hilliard Bell	10	10	66
Lt. Gerald Birks	12	12	66
Lt. Francis Bowles	5	5	45
Lt. Howard Boysen	5	5	66
Capt. Peter Carpenter	24	19	66
Lt. Charles Catto	6	6	45
Lt. James Child	5	2	45

Lt. Arnold Cooper	7	5	58
Capt. Jack Cottle	13	11	45
Capt. Richard Dawes	9	8	48
Lt. James Dewhirst	7	6	45
Lt. Harold Eycott	8	8	66
Capt. John Firth	11	2	45
Capt. Matthew Frew	23	23	45
Lt. Harry Goode	15	15	66
Lt. Alfred Haines	6	6	45
Capt. Joseph Hallonquist	5	5	58
Capt. Earl Hand	5	4	58
Capt. William Hillborn	7	7	66, 28
Capt. Cedric Howell	19	19	66, 28
Lt. Harold Hudson	13	13	28
Capt. James Mansell	11	11	45
Lt. Arthur Jarvis	5	5	28
Capt. Norman Jones	9	9	28, 45
Lt. James Lennox	5	5	66
Lt. Hector MacDonald	8	8	66
Capt. John MacKereth	7	7	28
Lt. Ernst Masters	8	8	45
Capt. Charles Maud	11	11	66
Capt. Christopher McEvoy	9	9	66
Lt. Clifford McEwan	27	27	28
Capt. James Mitchell	11	8	28
Capt. Kenneth Montgomery	12	2	45
Capt. Henry Moody	8	4	45
Lt. Augustus Paget	6	6	66
Capt. Stanley Stanger	13	12	66, 28
Capt. Francis Symondson	13	13	66
Capt. Thomas Williams	14	10	45, 28
Capt. Percy Wilson	7	7	28

French Air Activity on Italian Front

ESCADRILLE N92, N392, N561, SPA 561

Commanded by *Capitaine* Challeronge known as *l'Escadrille de Venise'* and flying Nieuports, SpAD VIIs and SPAD XIII it was entrusted with the defense of Venice. Throughout its stay its designation changed constantly as noted above. Early in 1917 it was equipped with one Spad, one Sopwith and sixteen Nieuports.[34] In all this unit had sixteen victories on the Italian Front with one Air Ace.[35]

Sergent André Robert Lévy was born in Paris on June 6, 1893, on September 2, 1914 he was mobilized with the 164°. By July 14, 1916 he had reached the rank of *Sergent*. Transferring to the aviation service he was sent to Juvisy for pilot training on November 1, 1916. On March 4, 1917 he received Military Pilot's Brevet No. 5542. First flying Farmans, but later flying Sopwith 1.A2 he shared credit for downing an enemy plane over Berry-au-Bac on April 7 1917. On May 16, 1917 he was assigned to Escadrille N561 in Italy which was charged with the protection of Venice. Together with MdL Edmond Corniglion they shot down an Austro-Hungarian floatplane on November 16. Using a dog as his personal insignia on the fuselages of Spads and Nieuports he scored victories on June 21, July 20 and August 5, 1918.

On September 16 flying a Spad XIII Lévy burned a balloon of *Ballonkompagnie 3* west of Ceggia, but was also downed by anti-aircraft fire from *Luftfahrzeug-Abwehrbatterie* 6/146. Taken prisoner he was imprisoned at Mulbach prison camp on November 2. After two attempts he escaped, climbed an 8,000 ft. mountain to return to his base on November 6.

He was made a *Chévalier de la Légion d'Honneur, the Médaille Militaire* and *Croix de Guerre* with two É*toiles de bronze.* He was also awarded the Italian *Croce di Guerra,* two *Medaglie d'Oro* and two *Medaglie da Bronzo al Valore Militare.* He passed away on March 12, 1973.

AUSTRIAN PLANE PRODUCTION

Unlike Italy Vienna had a fairly good industrial base but a military hierarchy which with rare exceptions felt that airplanes were play things called *Tauben* (Doves). The Hungarian portion of the army had no aviation component. Aviation had been used by FM Radetzky in Italy during the nineteenth century when he used a balloon for reconnaissance purposes. During the war it built 5,180 planes less than half of Italian plane production. By 1907 using their own funds technicians and interested officers were building and flying planes. To demonstrate these in action on Sept. 10, 1910 Conrad arranged for the emperor to see these planes flying out of the airport at Wiener-Neustadt after which he asked for 200 planes and 400 pilots.

By 1915 the aviation forces were placed into a separate unit under the *Kommando der K.u.k. Luftfahrtruppen* all under orders of the War Minister. Initially commanding the *Kuk LFT* was Col. Emil Uzelac whose background was not in aviation. Nonetheless he took pilot training becoming one of the best and even his own test pilot. Throughout the war he was plagued by lack of planes and the official policy of using fighters only for defense. Missions for the planes would be ordered by the Aeronautical Headquarters (*Stoluft*) in the A.O.K. By the outbreak of the war there were only 85 pilots deployed in nine *Fliegerkompanien.* The number of aircraft available varied according to which report one reads but it was about 40 airplanes, one dirigible and ten balloons. One source reported that with German help at the war's outbreak there were 147 available aircraft.[36] Others noted that at the outbreak of the conflict Conrad had four aircraft (Vol. I, p.35). Initially unable to produce planes itself Vienna looked to Germany for planes. Initially they were used only for reconnaissance and artillery spotting while later they were utilized for ground support.

In 1912 a collection was undertaken by a committee with 1.5 million *Kronen* assembled. Handing the sum over to the *Militärkanzlei*, one committee member noted that it was not to make factory owners richer.[37] Many factories were heavily in debt and looked to these sums to better their financial position. Aware of these criticisms Archduke Francis Ferdinand as Inspector General of the Armed Forces on June 9, 1914 sent a memorandum to the War Ministry asking that the situation be clarified. Naturally in bureaucratese the ministry stated that there was no corruption. Conrad entered the arena noting that monies collected never arrived to destination. With this background the only factory in the empire which was involved in plane production was the Jakob Lohner & Co, while motors were only constructed by *Österreichisch-Ungarische Daimler-Motoren AG.* With ineffective Habsburg planes Vienna was forced to purchase German planes and accept German production on its territory. Albatross and

Aviatik established production facilities in Vienna. Aviation cooperation between the two Central Powers Allies was very close.

By the end of 1914 Vienna had 1,400 aircraft production workers which rose to over 12,000 by the war's end. It produced 4,900 motors, 413 naval aviation planes and 4,768 planes for the armies. The Viennese banker Camillo Castiglioni in partnership with aircraft designer Ludwig Lohner owned the *Motor Luftfahrzeug Gesellschaft* and became prominent in aircraft production. Notwithstanding his Italian name the banker would become a major player in airplane manufacturing. In 1909 Jakob Lohner & Co., an automobile manufacturer had started to assemble planes. Its technical director was Ferdinand Porsche who left in 1909 to go to the *Österreichische Daimler Motoren AG.* In September 1912 Lohner and Castiglioni through their companies established a flying school at their expense at Wiener Neustadt which was the only civil aviation school in the empire. The German manufacturers of the Albatross and the Aviatik created Austro-Hungarian subsidiaries. Castiglioni purchased the German plane producer Brandenburg from Igo Etrich eventually molding it into a new company the *Hansa und Brandenburg Flugzeugwerke.*

Used in reconnaissance were the Lohner B-category, the Phöenix-built Albatross B-1 and the Austrian Aviatik B I, B II and B-III as well as the Lloyd C II. An 8 mm. Schwarzlose MO& /12 machine gun mounted behind the rear cockpit was usually carried for the observer. Another gun was placed on the middle of the upper wing firing over the propeller. Castiglioni later purchased the Albatross factory in Vienna renaming the plane the Phöenix. This company was called the *Österreichisch-Ungarische Albatross-Flugzeugwerke GmbH* with production facilities at Stadlau. In January 1915 the *Luftfahrtruppen* accepted the first plane. In October 1915 it started to produce Brandenburg C-1 showing the Castiglioni link with its initial.

The UFAG was founded by Castiglioni and Jakob Lohner, and the Hungarian companies Ganz & Co. and Manfred Weiss in November 1912. The new company was called *Ungarische Luftschiff und Flugmaschinen AG* with production facilities on the Danube south of Budapest. It started to produce Brandenburg C I in January 1916 reaching thirty-five per month in 1918.

The last pillar of the Castiglioni empire was the *Automobil und Aviatik AG.* Apparently there was to be some financial support by the Hungarian Ministry of Commerce which was not forthcoming. Finally in July, 1914 the *Aviatik und Weiser & Sohn AG* was founded in Vienna. The planes had many technical difficulties notwithstanding the hiring of a new production director Julius von Berg. Eventually per pilot request Albatross production was replaced by the Fokker D VIII.

Under Charles' protection seeing the way the war was going Castiglioni started to move his fortune to Switzerland.[38] Showing his quick agility to adapt to a situation post-war he became an Italian citizen in the Fascist period and a financier of note.[39] During the war he was criticized by Uzelac for monopolizing the industry however it must be noted that only such a great enterprise could easily shift personnel to where needed to make production run smoothly.

Another production facility was established at Aszòd using imprisoned inmates in Hungary. This was the *Deutsche Flugzeug Werke* (DFW), which would produce 279 Lloyds from February 1915 to the end of the conflict. Uzelac's emissary visited the factory in August 1918 noting no quality controls in the factory.[40]

The *Österreichische Flugzeugfabrik AG* (Oeffag) was a subsidiary of the *Österreichische Daimler Motoren AG* which in December, 1913 obtained permission from the municipal authorities in Wiener-Neustadt to establish a factory there. The principal stockholders were the Creditsbank, Ferdinand Porsche and Karl von Skoda. Porsche was the automobile (and plane) motor genius. In July 1915 the facility received orders for twenty-five planes being fully employed in producing type K seaplanes for the navy. In 1916, it finally obtained the rights to produce the Albatross D III. Ideally this plane should have been produced by the *Phoenix Flugzeugwerke AG* but since the War Minister wished to establish competition to Castiglioni's empire, the production was established here where it already produced the Brandenburg fighter. The Albatross D III was the best Habsburg fighter of the conflict. The plant was scheduled to also start producing the German Friedrichshafen G IIIa but the conflict ended before this model's production could start.

The *Ungarische Allemeine Maschinenfabrik AG* (MAG), was founded in 1866 to produce agricultural motors. In 1914 it was entrusted with the task of producing Daimler motors. In 1916 in Màtyàsfòld on the outskirts of Budapest a factory was established in partners with Anthony Fokker to manufacture his planes. Quality was poor with only 56 planes being produced in 1917. Later it was to produce Fokker D VII but none were accepted before the end of the conflict. In September 1917, balloon units in the empire were renamed *Ballonkompagnie.*[41] They were also given a distinctive uniform. In 1915 War Minister Krobatin had recommended to the emperor that aviation personnel wear a different uniform. As of 1918 the problem had not been solved but as of September 2, 1912 pilots were wearing a pilot identification badge.

Austrian military airplanes had four individual serial numbers painted on the sides of the fuselage. Mostly these consisted of numbers including a decimal point.

AUSTRIAN AIRCRAFT IDENTITY CODES[42]

Code No.		*Abbreviation*
1	Jakob Lohner & Co	Lo.
2	Phöenix Flugzeugwerke A G	Ph
3	Automobil und Aviatik A G	Av
4	Ungarische Lloyd Flugzeug und Motorenfabrik	Ll
5	Österreichische Flugzeugfabrik A G	Oef
6	Ungarische Luftschiff und Flugmaschinen A G	U
7	Naval Air Arsenal, Fischamend	Fd
8	Wiener Karosserie und Flugzeugfabrik	WKF
9	Ungarische Allemeine Maschinenfabrik A G	MAG

The numbers on the fuselage signified as follows:

A. The first digit represented the name of the factory, e.g. 3 would signify the Aviatik factory.

B. The second digit denoted the type of aircraft. There was a code for this with each plane manufacturer which the author feels is beyond the scope of this text.[43]

C. The digits to the right of the decimal point signified the number in the series of production, e.g. 02 would be the second craft, 31 would be the thirty-first plane etc.

D. Sometimes this system became confused. If a company subcontracted, e.g. 84.01, the first machine, Aviatik D I (WKF) built by Vienna Carriage Factory (code no. 8)

B-III known as the "Gondola"

Berg single-seater used for aerial photography

Hansa-Brandenburg C-1 Series 26

Ansaldo ISVA seaplane

UFAG C-I 161.15 with balanced rudder 1

Lohner-built Knoller C-II 19.04

SVA 5 single-seater today in Museum of Science, Milan. Note post-war rudder markings

Caproni 33 flown by American pilots. Note anterior and posterior machine guns

Pomilio two seater PC with frontal radiator and lower fin

Two-seater SAML used for bombing and reconnaissance. Note machine gun above wing.

SIA 7 B 1 which flew non-stop from London to Turin. Note stack-exhaust and overload tanks

Twin-engined SP-4 with its bathtub-style fuselage flown by RFC pilots Capt. William Barker and Capt. William Wedgewood-Benn from which Italian agent *Tenente* Alessandro Tandura parachuted behind enemy lines in May 1918

By 1917 the *LFT* was reorganized as follows:

Fliegerkompanie : the basic front-line combat unit usually of six planes. By war's end there 77 Flik.
Fliegertappenpark (Flep): responsible for supplying the Fliks with planes, motors, guns cameras. Each Flep was responsible for a segment of the front.
Fliegersatzkompanie (Flek) : supplied Fliks with men, mechanics and orderlies. It also trained pilots.
Fliegerarsenal (Flars) : obtained equipment, tested it and passed it on to the Flik.

By 1917 Flik units were assigned a letter in addition to the unit numbers as follows:

D was *Divisionfliegerkompanie*) : short range reconnaissance and artillery spotters attached to a division.
F *Fernaufklärerkompanie* long range reconnaissance
G *Grossflugzeugkompanie*) bomber unit

J (*Jagkfliegerkompanie*) fighter unit
K (*Korpsfliegerkompanie*) short range reconnaissance unit attached to a corps
P was a *Photoeinsitzerkompanie* single seat photo-reconnaissance unit
Rb was a *Reihenbildaufklärerkompanie* a map-making photography unit
S was a *Schlachtfliegerkompanie* ground attack and close support unit

On October 1, 1918, Major General Otto Ellison von Nidlef (he of Pasubio fame), was appointed as *Chef des Luftfahrwesens.* On the Tyrolean Front he had been awarded the Order of Maria Theresa. The reader should realize that the *Luftfahrtruppen* was fighting a war on three fronts with a maximum of 550 planes.

PLANES FLOWN BY THE CENTRAL POWERS ON THE ITALIAN FRONT

Bombers

In the early days of the war bombing missions were performed by two seater Lohner or Lloyds. Milan was bombed on February 14, 1916 by these planes.[44] Two engined Brandenburgs were also used. In 1918, German-built Gotha G-IV were used by Vienna's forces.[45]

Gotha G. IV (LVG) Series (08)

Needing bombers the *LFT* purchased six Gotha G. IV (LVG) bombers powered by 230 hp Hiero engines. More were purchased later. In March 1918 the Flik 101/G, 102/G and 103 G (bombing squadrons) received the planes which were plagued with excessive engine vibration, unsuitable propellers and piping leaks. Used as tactical bombers once the bombs were launched it was impossible to synchronize the engine revolutions to maintain a straight course.[46] Most of the planes were downed due to engine failure so that by September 1918, they were no longer in service. The wings had a span of over 71 feet, with a fuselage length of 41 feet. Powered by a Hiero 2x 240 hp. its top speed was 87 m.p.h. With four machine guns they were a difficult target for enemy fighters. Their bomb load was about 600 lbs. These planes could not maneuver on the mountainous front in Italy with its deep valleys. As the war progressed bomber squadrons preferred the Brandenburg C.I. (U) series 169 and 369 bomber. Additional variations were produced. With an autonomy of seven hours these planes bombed London on June 13, 1917 in a formation of fourteen led by Hauptmann Brandenburg.[47]

FIGHTERS

Albatross[48]

Four series of two-seater reconnaissance biplanes were flown by the *Luftfahrtruppen* all based on the B-type produced by the German parent company. The first model (Series 21) resembling the German version produced by the Phoenix Flugzeugwerke. The engine was the 145 h.p. Hieronymus (Hiero) and not the German Mercedes. Radiators were fixed to the fuselage. When Professor Richard Knoller came onto the scene a Knoller-Albatross (Series 22) with a 160 h.p. Austro-Daimler engine was produced. Some of these were equipped with a 37 mm. cannon in a special turret in the observer's position. This model proved popular with pilots with a second batch of machines going into production with the serial no. 23. Instead the company was obliged to build the new two-seater Brandenburg C-I (later this craft had the serial no. 23). Another Albatross series was the Series 24 which carried no guns, had a 145 h.p. Hiero engine which eventually had a box radiator. Bracing struts were vertical. Albatross planes were later being used as training planes or transferred to the Balkans.

Austrian-Aviatik (B-II, B-III)

During the first half of the war, this two-seater plane arrived on the scene along with the previous two. The series 32 Aviatik (military designation B-II) had a 120 h.p. Austro-Daimler engine but no mounted machine guns.[49] The series 33 (B-III), had a larger 160 h.p. Austro-Daimler engine had one Schwarzlose mounted on a semi-circular ring for the observer. In gusty weather it would sway being nicknamed "The Gondola." By 1916 this plane was relegated to training duties.

When Professor Julius Berg came on the scene another model was produced the Berg (C-I). Uzelac was the one of the first to fly this machine. This was a two seater with a 185 h.p. Austro-Daimler engine. Strength was sacrificed for speed. It had a synchronizing gear for the Schwarzlose which due to urgent production needs was abandoned. The gun was mounted above the top wing to fire over the propeller with the plane to be built by five plane manufacturers.

Aviatik	37	had a Austro-Daimler 200 h.p. engine
Lloyd	47	had a 185 h.p. Austro-Daimler engine
WKF	83	" " " " " "
MAG	91	" " " " " "
Lo	114	had an Austro-Daimler 200 h.p. engine

It is doubtful whether all orders were completed. Lightly built and fragile it was abandoned by pilots who favored the Brandenburg C-I. In the war's last year some planes were equipped with a 200 h.p. Austro-Daimler engine and a movie camera inside the fuselage. Parachutes were also provided.[50] The Aviatik D-I was the most extensively built single-seater.

Fokker B, B-1 and B-III (German)[51]

Anthony Fokker a resident of the Netherlands produced plane models which were sold to the Central Powers. A Fokker M-7 two-seater biplane with a long upper wing braced from above by inverted—V-kingposts was successfully tested in 1914. This model was sold to Austria-Hungary and called the B-type Fokker. An improved version the M.10E with a 80 h.p. Oberursel rotary engine. The improved version the M.10E was accepted by Vienna in 1915. Officially it was called the B-I, but unofficially it was known as "Sardine Oil" because of the spray of castor oil thrown off by its engine.

In the spring of 1916 Fokker sold his M.16Z (two-seater) and M.17K single seater to Vienna. The prototype of the M.16Z had a 160 h.p. Mercedes engine with a "comma" shaped rudder. The Habsburg model had a 200 h.p. Austro-Daimler engine and a rectangular rudder. Of this model about thirty planes were purchased from Germany and called B-III. Some were built by MAG of Budapest and were serialled about 0430.

Hansa-Brandenburg C-I[52]

This two-seater was the mainstay of the *Luftfahrtruppen* for nearly three years. Originally designed and built by Ernest Heinkel in the *Hansa und Brandenburg Flugzeuwerke* it was built under license by the Ufag and Phöenix companies. Its main attribute was that as larger engines were developed it could use them and improve its performance. As noted above one could tell in which factory the plane was manufactured so as engines became more powerful serial numbers changed.

Austro-Daimler 160 h.p.
- Phöenix series 23. (part) and 26, Phöenix series 29.5 and 229
- Ufag series 61,64,67 and 68

Mercedes 160 h.p.
- Ufag series 63

Austro-Daimler 185 h.p.
- Phöenix series 27, Austro-Daimler 200 h.p.
- Ufag series 269

Austro-Daimler 210 h.p.
- Phöenix series 29

Hiero 200 h.p.
Phöenix 29.5 and 229
Ufag series 69
Hiero 200 h.p. (Austrian built FIAT)
Phöenix series 129 and 329
Benz 220 h.p. (Marta built)
Ufag series 169
Hiero 230 h.p.
Ufag series 369
Hiero 230 (FIAT)
Phöenix 429

Box-radiators in front of the leading edge became standard. The interplane struts sloped up and inward when viewed from the front. The tailplane was triangular. A Schwarzlose machine gun on a semi-circular ring mounting was operated by the observer while in later models there was a complete ring. The Brandenburg D-I KD single-seater *Kamf-Doppeldecker* (Fighter Biplane)with a 185 h.p. Daimler engine, built both by Ufag series 65) and Phöenix (series 28) had the characteristic 'Star-Strutter' configuration when viewed from the front. This was the favorite machine of *Hauptmann* Godwin Brumowski who had the ammunition belt on his aeroplane (65. 53) disengaged from its drum and spread in layers inside the casing to reduce jamming due to condensation.

On May 14, 1916 Ufag-built planes attacked the Ponte di Piave (Map 42). They carried a 176 lb load, two 22 lb. bombs, a machine-gun as well as a camera. Pilots loved this machine because it could climb had a good rate of speed and was stable.

Knoller C-I and C-II

Knoller who was on the faculty of the Imperial and Royal Technical School in Vienna designed these planes which were manufactured by Lohner and Aviatik companies. During the first test flight the machine collapsed, killing the crew. All production was halted and it was never used.

Lohner[53]

Produced by the already-mentioned firm of Jakob Lohner of Vienna the *Pfeil* (Arrow) biplane had been used by the *Luftfahrtruppen* since 1913. The military designation was B-I of the plane which had a 100 h.p. Austro-Daimler engine with swept back wings. The Lohner "C" (B-II) had a Hiero 85 h.p. engine and was used as a trainer. The Lohner "I" (B-VII) with a 150 h.p. Austro-Daimler engine bombed Milan on February 14, 1916. Finally there was the "H" (B-VI) series with the 145 h.p. Rapp engine. Some planes were built by at the Fischamend Government Arsenal.

Lohner 'B' (B-I)
  Built by Lohner :series 11
  Built by Fischamend Government Arsenal : series 73
Lohner 'C' (B-II)
  Built by Lohner : series 12
  Built by Fischamend: series 74
Lohner 'E' (B-IV)
  Built by Lohner: series 15
  Built by Ufag : series 15.5
Lohner 'H' (B-VI)
  Built by Lohner: series 16.1
Lohner 'I' (B-VII)
  Built by Lohner: series 17
  Built by Ufag: series 17.5
Lohner 'K' (C-1)
  Built by Lohner : series 18

Lloyd C-1, C-11, C-111, C-IV and C-V

In 1914 a two-seater plane produced by the Ungarische Lloyd Flugzeug und Motorenfabrik (C-1) reached a height of 20,243 feet. Other improved versions soon followed. The C-II (series 42) had a Hiero 145 h.p. engine with a box-type radiator mounted in front of the cabane trestle. The C-II series (42.50-99) Initially it was unarmed but later a Schwarzlose was installed for the observer. This was a great airplane for 1915. The C-III (series 43) has a 160 h.p. Austro-Daimler engine. This model was stable, could glide easily in the mountainous topography of the Italian Front and was well-liked by the pilots. The models C-IV and C-V nicknamed (Cock-a-doodle-doo) had swept-back wings and high fin and rudder but were flimsy for operational use.[54]

Oeffag C-II

The original plane of this series was the C-I a two-seater reconnaissance biplane produced in 1915 by the *Öesterreichische Flugzeug A.G.* in Wiener Neutstadt (Oeffag).

With its series no. of 51 it was not accepted by the pilots so the factory switched production to Albatross tow-seater machines. In 1917 the C-II (series 52.) appeared. The engine was an Austro-Daimler with its radiator fixed in front of the top plane. This model was used on the Russian Front and was replaced by the Brandenburgs.

Phöenix C-1[55]

Many aircraft designers feel that this plane had its ancestor in the Hansa-Brandenberg C-1. Tested in 1918 together with the Ufag C-I, it was difficult to decide which was the better craft. Both could climb to about 16,000 feet. They were both ordered with the C-1 in series 121 and the Ufag C-1 in series 161 and 123 (Phöenix-built). The pilot had the use of a Schwarzlose mounted under the port engine-cowling. A second gun was employed by the observer. About 110 were built.

Ufag C-1

As noted above this craft had a 230 h.p. Hiero engine and could climb to 16,000 feet. Both the observer and pilot had Schwarzlose guns available, the former on a ring platform, and the later under the engine cowling firing through the propeller arc. The top speed was 118 m.p.h.[56] This craft was used in artillery spotting and reconnaissance. Later the empennage was modified, to give better directional stability. In addition to the original 161 Ufag series a second series 123 was constructed by the rival Phöenix firm.

ITALIAN AIRFIELDS

The first Italian airfield was at Centocelle (See Vol. I, p.108) near Rome where in April, 1907 Wilbur Wright flew a plane which would eventually be sold to the Club Aviatori of Rome for the price of L. 50,000. After giving flying lessons for about two weeks, Wright left Italy. At the time airports were defined as being near a cemetery on the outskirts of a city. As noted above in October 1911, Italy undertook the first military air action in the world in Libya taking off near the "Cemetery of the Jews" southwest of the City of Tripoli.[57, 58]

At the outbreak of the war Italy had only twenty-seven airports including naval air stations. During the negotiations of the Treaty of London frantic searches were made along the future Austro-Italian Front for airport locations. One of the first and in existence to this day was the area known as Malpensa, north of Milano where cavalry regiments performed their maneuvers. In 1910 Gianni Caproni the plane designer had requested of the *Direzione del Genio Militare di Milano* permission to use the area to test his planes[59] In January 1915 planning for a war against the ex-partners of the Triple Alliance the *Direzione Generale dell'Aeronautica del Ministero della Guerra* entrusted Second Lt. Giulio Laureati to reconnoiter the Friuli-Cadore regions for the possibility of military airfields.[60] Since many of the planes on the Italian Front were French, emergency airfields were established along the path of Torino-Pordenone. These would be simple fields about 300 ft. by 1500 ft. and had no infrastructure. Farmers would be compensated for any loss of crops.

As on the Habsburg side initially planes were used only for reconnaissance and artillery spotting. By the beginning of the Third Battle of the Isonzo there were mostly bombers and reconnaissance craft with only the *8a Squadriglia* based at S. Caterina to defend Udine. By early 1917 each army had its own attached air formation. By the time of the armistice the Royal Italian Air Force (*Aeronautica del Regio Esercito)* had sixty-eight squadrons.

The Naval Air Service *(Aeronautica della Regia Marina),* consisted of nine fighter and thirty-seven reconnaissance squadrons in addition to fifteen dirigible airships, as well as the naval *Squadriglia 'San Marco'*, a mixed unit of Capronis, S.I.A. 9Bs and SVA 5s.[61] (see vol. I).

AUSTRIAN AIRFIELDS

Martin O'Conner has the best description of Habsburg airfields.[62] On the Italian Front there were 34 airfields. The classic field was that of Ciré di Pergine (Map 35). Technical and logistical support (*Fliegertappenpark* or *Flep*) for planes of the Eleventh Army was located here being established in 1915, with a landing-takeoff runway of over one mile. Flik 55J located here had the honorary title of *Kaiserstaffel.* All nearby inhabitants from the ages of fifteen to eighteen were inducted into military service. When fully operational in 1916 there were six hangars and 47 buildings. The premier air ace stationed there was Josef Kiss who was shot down over Valsugana on May 25,1918. For the following fifty-two years, his fiancé Enrica Bonecker who never married daily placed flowers on his tomb. By 1970 the military cemetery there was closed with the remains being transported to the large cemetery at Rovereto. In 1985 a planned new highway was to obliterate the old airport. However in a historical showing of unity, that September 15, Aero Clubs of Trento as well as some in Austria held a *Ultimo Volo dal Ciré* (last flight from Ciré) as eight Piper Cubs showing the Black Cross insignia landed at the old airport.[63] Kiss was very well respected but in an illustration of the social differences between officers and men despite his accomplishments he was only promoted to an officer rank the day after his death. Not much is known in detail about the other fields except for that at Gardolo which was described as the worse airport in the Habsburg air service. A descending wind every afternoon made takeoffs there difficult.

NAVAL AIR STATIONS ON THE AUSTRO-ITALIAN FRONT

Important in defending the long coasts of Italy was the naval air arm. With its long coast line the eastern shores of the peninsula was dotted with naval air stations which eventually would house American and British pilots. In these bases there were two types of planes used. The first was called a flying boat which meant its fuselage landed in the water like a boat and took off likewise. The second was called a seaplane which meant that under the wings there were pontoons which allowed it to land in water and take off.

Austrian Naval Air Service

Via an Imperial Decree on May 30, 1914 the *K.u.k. Seeflugleitung* came into being with the task of performing reconnaisance and support naval units as well as defend the coast of the empire. The direct commander was the commanding admiral at Pola while technical and support services were provided by the *Kriegsministerium.* In 1909 several naval officers had gone to France and Britain to learn how to fly, among them being Lt. Cdr. Viktor Klobucar Rukavina de Bunic who later designed and built a seaplane on the island of S. Caterina in Pola harbour achieving a speed of 56 m.p.h. In all the empire produced 413 for the service others being purchased in Germany.

The *Kriegsmarine* pre-war commander was Admiral Rudolph Graf Montecuccoli who himself went aloft a number of times on Klobucar's plane, a first by naval commanders.[64] In 1914 the Naval Air Service had twenty-two aircraft mostly purchased from Curtiss and Donnet-Lévêque.[65] In 1916,Habsburg seaplanes successfully bombed and sunk a French submarine the *Foucault*, in the open sea.[66] Planes were used so often that there were two motors always available as well as spare parts. Placed in service were 662 planes while at the conflict's end there were 232. Lack of raw materials for plane construction as well as bomb manufacture drastically cut down on flights. There were 256 in 1915, 1,217 in 1916, 1,225 in 1917 and 614 in 1918. In 1917 there were 797 missions flown using 153 planes while in 1918 there were only 245 using 53 planes.

Planes used were the Lohner-L flying boat, and Type-A and Type-G Phöenix planes. Its superb superior plane was the two seater Lohner L produced at Pola with a velocity of seventy m.p.h., and a Habsburg Daimler engine of 165 h.p. On the right was emplaced a Schwarzlose 8 mm. with a wide range of fire. During 1917 seventy-nine Hansa-Brandenburg two seater Type-A and eighty-two Type K biplanes were delivered. These craft had only one machine gun.[67] Other planes used by the service were the Hansa-Brandenburg W 13 or K-type which initially was a-seater seaplane bomber and later was converted to three seats. It had a Habsburg-Daimler motor of 350 h.p. It had up to three Schwarzlose and could carry up to 1000 lbs in bombs. Manufacturers were the Jakob Lohner & Co., the Oeffag, the Phöenix-Flugzeugwerke A.G. and the UFAG. During 1916-1917 the Brandenburg KDW *Kampf-Doppeldecker Wasser* (Aquatic Fighter Biplane) the sister of the land plane made its appearance but then was replaced by the Phöenix A boat. Finally there was a Hansa-Brandeburg CC (the initials of the owner). It was a single seater with a Schwarzlose machine gun which could reach the speed of 160 m.p. h.

Austrian Naval Air Stations

The naval air arsenal was located on the island of S. Caterina just off the shore from Pola.[68]

Countering the Italian naval air presence, the A.O.K. placed naval air stations all along the eastern coast of the Adriatic at Trieste, Cosada near Pola to the north and Cattaro (today Kotor in Montenegro) and Durazzo (Albania). The latter base was bombed forty-one times by the Italians who lost 114 aircraft in the process. Gottfried Banfield the premier air ace commanded the Trieste base later writing a book describing how he had established the base.[69] At the end of the war the naval planes were destroyed except two which were taken to the U.S.A.

Aircraft used by the Austrian Navy were designated as follows:[70]

A. Type landplanes were single-seater fighters mostly Phoenix D IIs with a 200 h.p. Hiero or 220 h.p. Austro-Daimler engine. This also included some Fokker DIII and E IIIs. Serials A 1-60 were allocated.

A. Type flying boats (single-seater), built under license from Hansa-Brandenburg, Types CC and W.18 (about sixty were built). There were also forty-five Phöenix built designed by Mickl.

E. Flying Boats which were Lohners with a 85 h.p. Hiero engine.

G. Flying Boat, three-engined carrying a crew of three, with 160 h.p. Austro-Daimler engine. There were two machine guns one in the nose the other in the rear gun position. These craft were never perfected, never flown in anger and destroyed at war's end. The only evidence available are photos. Even the Naval War Archives gives no information on this craft. The documentation is all photographic.

J Type landplanes (Phoenix D III) with a Hiero 230 h.p. engine.

K Type flying boats (Hansa-Brandenburg) Type W 13 license built by Oeffag, Ufag and Phöenix. The first figure of the serial number designated the series.

100 series—acquisitions from Germany of floatplanes
200s built only by Phoenix
300s built by Phoenix and Ufag
400s built by Oeffag

KG Type flying boats were large K Type built by Ufag and Phoenix.
L Type flying boats were Lohner with Hiero or Austro-Daimler engines of 140 h.p.
M Type were L type built at the Naval Arsenal at Pola.
R Type flying boats were Lohner reconnaissance flying boats with no provision for bombs.
S Type flying boats were Lohner trainers with smaller engines.

Austrian Naval Air Aces:[71]

Leutnant Freiherr Gottfried von Banfield was born in Castelnuovo on the Gulf of Cattaro (Montenegro), on February 6, 1890 the son of a naval officer. All his service was in the Trieste Naval Air Station eventually commanding the base. In 1905 he entered the Austro-Hungarian Naval Academy graduating in 1909. He was awarded the rank of *Freggattenleutnant in May 1912* following which he started pilot training at Wiener-Neustadt. A plane accident almost cost him his right foot. As a pilot and commander at Trieste he was engaged in many exploits. On May 16, 1918 attacking two Italian motor boats his left tibia was shattered and he almost passed out but managed to return to the base.

He received the Knight's Cross of the Order of Léopold with the War Decoration and Swords, the Order of the Iron Crown, Third Class with War Decoration and Swords.

Emperor Francis Joseph himself presented him with the Knight's Cross of the Military Order of Maria Theresa thus allowing him to use the title of *Freiherr* (Baron). Another award was presented by the emperor was the Great Military Bravery Medal. After the conflict he married and took over his father-in-law's shipping salvage company in Trieste.[72] He died on September 23, 1986

Fregattenleutnant Friedrich Lang was born an Austrian joining the navy in 1912 by 1915 attaining the rank of ensign. While serving on the destroyer *Balaton* he was awarded the Silver Bravery Medal Second Class. In March 1916 he transferred to the Naval Air Service receiving his pilot's wings the following month after which he was assigned to the Naval Air Station at Kumbor (today Kotor in Montenegro).[73] Subsequently he was stationed at Durazzo flying Lohner flying boats. In January 1917 he was stationed at Pola from which he won Military Merit Cross, Third Class, with War Decoration and Swords, in addition to the Silver Military Merit Medal with Swords. He left the navy in 1919 having achieved a total of five victories.

91

Macchi-built Hanriot HD 1 of the
82a Squadriglia, X Grupppo

92

Members of the *91a Squadriglia.* From left to right, *Tenente* Gastone Novelli, *Tenente* Ferruccio Ranza, *Capitano* Fulco Ruffo di Calabria, *Capitano* Bortoli Constanti and *Maggiore* Francesco Baracca

93

Italian Macchi M-5

94

Lohner Type S trainer

95

Italian-built Nieuports on the Italian Front in 1916

96

POMILIO PE : Note the machine gun with a cooling jacket above the wing. This model did not fire through the propeller

97

King Vittorio Emanuele III (right) visiting the U.S.A. flying school at Foggia. Caproni pilots were trained here.

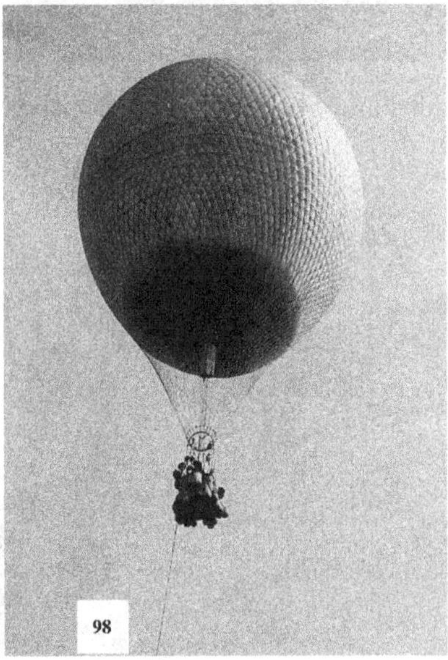

98

Observation balloon used to direct artillery shelling and observe enemy troop movements.

99

Experimental Austrian Lohner D fighter.

100

An American pilot (left) training on a Caproni bomber *(Courtesy C. Lucchini).*

British Naval Air Activity in the Adriatic

In May 1916 Rear Admiral C.K. Kerr who had a pilot's license was given command of the British Adriatic Squadron. The admiral thought that aircraft would be of great use in hunting submarines. Requesting aircraft from London to carry out this task he was turned down. Instead two naval air stations with two squadrons each were set up at Otranto and Taranto on the heel of the Italian boot. Commanding the Otranto base was Commodore (later Rear Admiral) Murray Sueter not a pilot who initially was given Short 826 and 184 seaplanes. Sueter's main targets were Pola where submarines were being assembled with parts sent from Germany, Fiume scene of torpedo manufacturing and Cattaro a large naval base. Limited by the short range of his planes which could not fly the width of the Adriatic he devised the strategy of towing the planes to within striking distance of the target, then taking off. A heavy storm cancelled these plans. After the Royal Naval Air Service and the Royal Flying Corps were combined to form the Royal Flying Corps they were designated as the 224 and 225 Squadrons (Otranto) while the 226 and 227 Squadrons were at Taranto. The latter base was later opened and used Sopwith Baby floatplanes as well as Sopwith 1 ½ Strutters and De Havilland DH 4 and DH-9 craft. The main target of these planes were submarines in the Adriatic Sea as well as the enemy submarine bases at Cattaro and Durazzo, involving flights of hundreds of miles.[74] In June 1917 air patrols looking for submarines were started which dramatically decreased sinkings of allied shipping. Sueter's work was finally recognized by the Admiralty toward the end of 1917. Recently members of a local flying club in Capo Leuca declared they would use the *Idroscalo Molo degli Inglesi* (British seaplane pier), resuscitating interest in local history relating to the Great War.[75] Hopefully this interest will spread to other actions that occurred on the Italian boot in the Great War (see volume I).

Italian Naval Air Stations

When Wilbur Wright arrived in Rome in 1909 Mario Calderara a naval lt. (*tenente)* was chosen to be his first flying student. In 1911 he designed a floatplane taking off in a powered version. In 1912 a flying school was established at Venice for naval pilots. In 1912 Capt. Alessandro Guidoni took a Farman removed the wheels and successfully replaced them with pontoons. The Italian Navy purchased seven Curtiss flying boats plus fifteen as trainers. By May 15, 1915, the Naval Air Service had eleven airplane pilots, six dirigible pilots and 354 personnel to maneuver the craft.[76]

Dirigibles were entrusted to the Naval Air Service with an impressionable round-trip flight by the *P 1* (piccolo or small) from Rome to Naples in 1909. By 1911 the Italian Navy purchased *P 2* and *P 3* establishing Brindisi as their base of operations. In the Italo-Turkey War, dirigibles were used for topography and observation. On May 30, 1915 the *P 4* bombed the enemy naval air station at Pola. In the beginning of the war the Italians had nothing to compete with the Habsburg Lohner plane, but this was soon rectified when on May 27,1915 due to motor failure a Lohner plane set down in the Adriatic. It was captured by the Italians and copied by the Macchi-Nieuport factory in only thirty-three days. The new Italian seaplane would be the Macchi L. 1, similar to the Lohner L, differing by having one less bay of struts on either side of the wing. Planes produced there soon reached all the naval air stations at Porto Corsini, Venice, Taranto, Ancona, Brindisi, S. Maria di Capo Leuca and Grado. The Leuca station was transferred to the British in May 1918. Planes increased from thirty-nine in 1915 to 467 in 1917.

Venice the most important Italian naval air station was bombed by the enemy on thirty-six occasions. The leading naval air aces were Guido Janello, Luigi Bologna, Giuseppe Miraglia who had many encounters with Goodwin Brumzowski the Habsburg air ace. Orazio Pierozzi scored most of his victories in a Macchi M.5, while Bologna subsequently raced in the Schneider cup races. Most of the naval air action was between Venezia and Trieste with the enemy base at Pola being a top target.

Italy finally realized that its naval air activity was inadequate requesting allied help. A conference was held in Malta in March,

1916. Britain was given permission to install naval air stations in Brindisi, Otranto, S. Maria di Leuca and Valona (today Albania) to halt enemy submarine incursions into the Adriatic. In a fine example of strategic bombing of the era on October 5, 1917 fourteen Caproni Ca 3 took off at dusk from Gioia del Colle near Bari to bomb Cattaro. Commanded by Major Armando Armani and having as part of the crew the poet-warrior Gabriele D'Annunzio it crossed the dark Adriatic guided by the lights of torpedo boats anchored along the way. Five tons of bombs rained down on the submarine pens with all the planes returning to base after a five hour flight. Landing in the dark was facilitated by two huge floodlights which crossed their beams indicating the runways and red and white lights indicating the southern and northern limits of the coast approaches. The warrior-poet wanted to use Ca 5s torpedo bombers to attack ships anchored in the enemy naval base at Pola but the conflict's end halted any further planning. Shades of Pearl Harbour! One of the planes had been purchased by donations of Italian-speaking *émigrés* of Vienna's territories.

By the summer of 1917 Italy had deployed twenty one seaplanes at Porto Corsini, forty-six at Grado, thirteen at Ancona, eighty-seven at Venice, nine at Leuca, forty-two in Valona, seventeen in Pescara fifty-one in Varano and seventy-eight in Brindisi.[77] Toward the end of the war the service was using the S.V.A. 5 on floats as well as the Sopwith Baby. Allied naval air service pilots received medals for valor with twenty-one silver and twenty-five bronze medals given to French pilots, fourteen silver to the British and two silver to American fliers.

Italian Naval Air Aces

Tenente di Vascello Orazio Pierozzi (*255a Squadriglia,*— Brindisi, *Gruppo Idrocaccia Venezia)* was born in San Casciano Val di Siena on December 8, 1884. He entered the Naval Academy at Livorno on November 8, 1908. Joining the flying service he was awarded a pilot license on October 14, 1916 being posted to the Brindisi station where he obtained his first victory eventually rising to command the station. Awarded three *Medaglie d'Argento* and a *Medaglia di Bronzo* during 1917, he was transferred to the Venice station as commander of a new fighter (Macchi M-5) group there. Almost at war's end (November 3, 1918), he was transferred to the Trieste station. The Official Naval History awarded him seven confirmed victories. On March 17, 1919 taking off in poor weather from Venice in a Macchi M.-9 carrying HRH *Tenente di Vascello* Aimone di Savoia his plane was thrown against the dam protecting the harbour's entrance. Rescued he died the next day. Posthumously he was awarded the *Medaglia d'Argento* for his bravery and efforts to protect the prince.

Number two Italian Naval Air Ace was *Sottotenente di Vascello* Umberto Calvello who flew in the *260a Squadriglia* He was born in Pistoia on May 28, 1897 serving in aviation initially as an observer, later becoming a pilot. Originally his duties included flying behind the lines to supply informants with carrier pigeons. Always flying an M-5 his first victory was against a Lohner TL onApril 22, 1918, followed by others on May 4, 1918 when he downed several Hansa B.W. 18 in shared victories. The official postwar Naval Aviation list describes him as a five victory ace. He was awarded two Silver Medals and a Bronze. He died on August 18, 1919.

Third on the Naval Air list was *Tenente di Vascello* Federico Martinengo (*260a Squadriglia*) who was born in Rome on July 18, 1897. He attended the naval academy at Livorno. After serving on the battleship *Cavour* he transferred to the Naval Air Service in Venice. In December 1917 he became commander of the *260a Squadriglia* a position which he held until June 1918. He has been credited with five victories in the official Navy list. After the conflict he remained in the navy holding a number of posts including that of commander of the Tien Tsin naval detachment in 1931-1933. He rose to rear admiral rank becoming the commander of the anti-submarine unit at La Spezia. On Sept. 9, 1943 he was killed in air combat against a large German air group. Posthumously he was awarded the *Medaglia d'Oro* as well as two *Medaglie d'Argento* and a War Cross while he lived.

Tenente di Vascello Eugenio Casagrande was nominated Marchese di Villaviera after his multiple flights ferrying agents in and out of enemy territory in a sector called by that name.

American Naval Air Activity on the Italian Front

On July 24, 1918 at Porto Corsini near Ravenna on the Adriatic Coast the U.S. established a naval air station. The very next day it was bombed by Austro-Hungarian forces showing that they were aware of the American presence there. The base was fifty miles south of Venice and about fifty miles from the Austrian naval air station at Pola a base which also contained submarines and large surface vessels all defended by 114 anti-aircraft guns. Flown out of here were Macchi M-5 fighters which rendezvoused over the Adriatic with Italian bombers proceeding to bomb Pola. On August 21, the unit carried out its first mission of dropping propaganda leaflets over the city. The A.O.K. had declared that anyone caught doing this would be treated as a spy and executed. Flying escort for the bombers was Ensign George Ludlow who was shot down by an Albatross, landing in the choppy waters not far from the port. Setting down next to him was Ensign Charles H. Hamman in his M 5 which was built for one person. Ludlow opened the port in the bottom of the hull, kicked holes in the wings to make the plane sink faster and jumped onto Hamman's plane getting behind the pilot's seat under the motor holding the struts to keep from being swept into the propeller or the sea. The question now was whether the plane would take off with the extra weight. It did arriving at the base a feat for which Hamman received the Congressional Medal of Honor while Ludlow was awarded the Navy Cross. Subsequently Hamman received the *Medaglia d'Argento al Valore Militare* while Ludlow was awarded the *Medaglia d'Oro al Valore Militare.* Tragically, Hamman was killed in an accident with an M-5 almost a year later on June 24, 1919. After an inspection on November 10, 1918, Admiral H. T. Mayo declared that the base was the most heavily engaged unit of the U. S. Navy in Europe.

101

Group photo of famous Austrian pilots; From the left are *Stabsfeldwebel* Stefan Fejes (15 victories), *Oberleutnant* Michael Dorcie, *Oberleutnant* Benno Fiala Ritter von Fernbrugg (29 victories), *Leutnant* Franz Rudorfer (10 victories) and *Feldwebel* Eugene Bonsch (15 victories).

102a

Habsburg Air Ace Julius Arrigi

Habsburg Naval Air Ace Gottfried Fr. Von Banfield

Habsburg Number One Air Ace Goodwin Brumowski

Habsburg Air Ace Josef Kiss

Italian Air Ace *Tenente* Silvio Scaroni

RFC Air Ace Capt. William Barker

Austrian Air Aces

Vienna had its own method of rating aces. If a two seater downed an enemy plane, both the pilot and the observer were credited with a kill. The enemy plane did not have to be destroyed. Likewise if two single seaters downed an enemy plane each pilot was credited for one kill.

Most of the Habsburg Air Aces were on the Italian Front simply because there was more air action there. Pilots would be rotated from the Eastern to the Italian to the Western Fronts (the latter to obtain more experience). A glaring defect in the service was the fact that no one was promoted from NCO (Non-Commissioned Officer) to officer. Classic of the Austro-Hungarian Forces as well as the Air Arm was the clear distinction between officers, non-coms and troops. Often the pilot was a non-com or lesser rank while the observer was an officer. The lone exception being that of Josef Kiss being promoted from *Offizierstellvertreter* to *Leutnant der Reserve* posthumously after he was shot down and killed. In the two seater the pilot was expected to be a sergeant while the observer was always an officer. There was even a rank for such a task, *Apparatchauffeur.*

Offizierstellvertreter Julius Arigi flying in Flik 6, 55J and IJ was born in Tetschen (later Czechoslovakia) on October 3, 1895. In 1913 he volunteered for the artillery and later was transferred to the airship service of the Habsburg Army.[78] This was followed by pilot training arriving at the rank of *Zugsführer-Feldpilot* (sergeant). Assigned to *Flik* 6 in southern Dalmatia using Lohner biplanes he started his deadly work. Due to engine trouble he had to land and was taken prisoner. He escaped driving Prince Nikolous of Montenegro's car returning to *Flik 6.*[79] On August 22, 1916 he noted six Italian Farmans heading for Durazzo. Demonstrating initiative and recklessness, even though lacking permission he took off to engage them. There were no available officer-observers so he took an NCO with him. Engaging the Farmans they shot down five, capturing all the crews.[80] Subsequently he was transferred to the Italian Front in Linke-

Crawford's *Flik 60* where he flew an Albatross DIIIs. In April 1918 he returned to the Albanian Front. By the war's end his victory total was thirty-two. He received the Silver Medal for Bravery, First Class, four times as well as a recipient of the *Glodene Tapferkeitsmedailles* (Gold Medal for Bravery) and was the most decorated NCO in the *Luftfahrtruppen.* Many of his superiors unsuccessfully attempted to have him promoted to commissioned rank but failed. Post-war together with Benno Fiala, another air ace, he founded the Wiener-Neustadt Airport Management Association. During the Second World War he was a flying instructor for the *Luftwaffe* with two of his pupils Nowotny and Marseille becoming top scoring aces. He died on August 1, 1981.

A stellar example of these aces was Hauptmann Goodwin Brumowski who was the highest ranked air ace with thirty five confirmed and eight unconfirmed kills.[81] He was born in the Galician (today Poland) town of Wadowice on July 26, 1886. After graduating from the Technical Military Academy near Vienna he joined the *Feld-Artillerie Regiment Nr. 6* fighting on the Eastern Front. Soon after he applied to the *Luftfahrtruppen* where he served as an officer-observer in *Flik 1* stationed at Czernowitz commanded by *Hauptmann* Otto Jindra. Flying with his commander he had his first kill at Chotin. On April 12, 1916 while the Tsar and General Brusilov were attending a military review Jinda appeared with six planes to bomb the airfield where Brumowski shot down two planes. The following May 2, flying in an Albatross B I with *Zugsführer* Kurt Gruber he downed another Morane-Saulnier Parasol-wing fighter.

He never received any formal pilot training but learned to fly as an observer. He joined *Flik 1* on July 3, 1916 as a *Feldpilot.* His fourth kill was on December 3, flying a Hansa-Brandenburg D I (65. 53) when he downed a Caproni Ca-1 assisted by *Linienschiffsleutnant* (Lieutenant Commander) Gottfried Banfield of the Trieste naval air station and *Zugsführer* Karl Cislagi of the *Flik 28.* His fifth and ace-qualification kill was on January 2, 1917 flying a Hansa-Brandenburg C I when he downed a Farman two seater near Lake Doberdò. His plane was always painted all-red having a white skull against a black shroud on the fuselage. In mid-1917 his plane was an Albatross D III (OEF) with two synchronized guns whose barrels extended beyond the front of the engine to prevent muzzle flashes from igniting petrol fumes. All his group had their fuselage painted red with a skull badge in imitation of Richtofen's Circus. His idea was to use the *Massa di Caccia* (fighter mass) favored by the Italians toward the end of the war and often used on the Western Front. Fighter mass maneuvers were used in the Austro-German offensive of October 1917. Unfortunately he was not given material support by his superiors. He was killed in an air crash in Holland in 1937.

Feldwebel Eugen Bönsch of Flik 51J was born on May '1, 1897 in Gross-Aupa a village in northern Bohemia.[82] After schooling as a mechanic and machine manufacturing he volunteered for the army, then requested a transfer to the Air Service where he was assigned to Fliegerersatzkompanie (Flek) 6 as a mechanical engineer. In 1917 he requested pilot training, was accepted and trained at *Flek 8* qualifying as a pilot in June and promoted to *Korporal.* In August 1917 he was posted to *Flik 51J* in northern Italy flying Oeffag-built Albatross Scouts. His first kill was a Nieuport on September 1. On September 28 he attacked and downed a balloon despite desperate opposition by two Italian fighters. For this he was awarded the Gold Medal for Bravery. On January 3, 1918 he was brought down by ground fire but survived. In May he received a second Gold Medal for Bravery. Performing low-level attacks against enemy infantry during the Battle of the Piave brought him another Gold Medal for Bravery. On October 29, he was shot down in flames but using his parachute survived. During the Second World War due to his awards he was awarded a commission (*Hauptmann*) in the Luftwaffe commanding the Oschatz aerodrome in Saxony. He died on July 24, 1951

Feldwebel Julius Busa was born on February 18, 1891 in Budapest joining up at the outbreak of the conflict. He completed his pilot training in December 1915 and was assigned to the

Russian Front. Soon he earned the ranks of *Korporal* and *Feldwebel,* being awarded the Silver Bravery Medal 2nd Class and two 1st Class. In October 1916 he was rotated to the Italian Front where on May 13, 1917 with his pilot, *Oberleutnant* Hermann Grösser he was shot down by Italian Air Ace Francesco Baracca, the Italian's tenth victory. Busa was credited with five victories.

Oberleutnant Benno Fiala Ritter von Fernbrugg flying in Flik 1,19,12,56 and 51 was the third ranking Habsburg Air Ace. In addition to being a great pilot he was also a good administrator, a talent which he would use in a career spanning over forty years. Born in Vienna, he graduated from the Technical University there with a degree in engineering. Enlisting in the army in 1910 he was assigned to the artillery. Transferring to the *Luftfahrtruppen* he was posted to *Fliegerkompanie* I as a technical officer. On the Galician Front he realized that planes could be used as artillery observers and outfitted a plane with a radio transmitter as well as photographic equipment. Flying about he had a *Apparatchauffeur* (non-com pilot) while he was entrusted with more important task (or so it was thought at the time) of observer. Showing his resourcefulness, at one point riding on a train ambushed by Russian soldiers he ran toward the controls of the locomotive in the cab and took the train out of danger. Later he was assigned to *Flik 19* on the Isonzo Front. Most planes in this unit there were two-seaters. Fiala obtained his first victory on April 29, 1916 downing an Italian plane near San Daniele. His second victory was on May 4, 1916 flying in a Hansa-Brandenburg C-I piloted by Hauptmann Adolf Heyrowsky when they downed an Italian dirigible near Gorizia. Soon after flying in a bombing mission he was severely wounded almost losing his right arm after which he decided to become a pilot. Accomplishing this he joined *Flik 12 D.* His favorite airplane was the Hansa-Brandenburg D I which was very difficult to fly. On August 10 he downed a Caproni near Auzza while the next day he downed a SAML two-seater. On August 15, he downed a Caproni which crashed at Fajti Hrib. With these victories he was now an Air Ace. With his large number of victories he became eligible to fly the single seaters so that by the spring of 1917 he was flying Brandenburg D Is (Ph.) Series 28 at the Aidussina air base. Eventually he commanded *Flik 51J*. He received the Order of the Iron Crown, third class, with War Decorations and Swords, as well as the Knight's Cross of the Order of Leopold with Ward Decorations and Swords, the German Iron Cross 1st Class and the Gold Medal of Merit.

Several times he clashed with British pilots of the 14 Wing. In actions on March 3, 1918, he shot down a British plane whose pilot received a Victoria Cross for feats that day. Flying at 13,000 feet four Habsburg scouts were attacked by three Camels of the 66 Squadron.[83] During the clash Fiala arrived on the scene with a large group of fighters. Flying in the British formation was Capt. P. Carpenter with a B 7387, Lt. H.R. Eycott-Martin in B7283 as well as Lt. A. Jerrard in his B 5648 'E' who became separated. Jerrard flamed two of the enemy with his twin Vickers before he went down under Fiala's guns. Fortunately he was able to land his plane receiving only minor injuries. For his actions the downed British pilot was awarded the Victoria Cross. Fiala ended the war as Inspector General of the LFT. He had had twenty-eight confirmed and five unconfirmed kills. In later years he was involved in airline and plane manufacturing positions. In commemoration of his service the Austrian Air Force base at Aigen in Ennstal was named "Fiala-Fernbrugg." He died on October 29, 1964.

Oberleutnant Josef Friedrich was born on September 12, 1893 in Zwiken, Bohemia of German Sudenten parents. At the outbreak of the conflict he was an engineering student but enlisted in the military serving in Kaiser-Schützen No. 1. Later he volunteered for the Air Service, was promoted to *Leutnant* as an observer and posted to the Carinthian front flying with Flik 16. As an observer flying with pilot Raoul Stojsavljevic he scored four victories. Taking pilot instructions he received his pilot's badge in January 1917. Flying as a pilot his observer downed an enemy aircraft which under Habsburg rules certified him as an

Air Ace. That July he was assigned to *Flik 24* flying escort and protection where flying an Albatross D III he had multiple scores. After a short stint at *Flik 51J* he returned to *Flik 24* serving until June 1918.

Promoted to *Oberleutnant der Reserve* he was awarded the Silver Military Merit Medal and a second award of the Military Merit Cross, third class, with War Decoration and Swords. When he left Flik 24 he went to Jastaschule at Pergine, then was appointed the Commanding Officer at the Jastaschule at Neumarkt. Completing his engineering studies after the war he settled in Czechoslovakia.

Zugsführer and *Feldpilot* Josef Kiss was born on January 26, 1896 in Hungary.[84] Upon the war's outbreak he volunteered for the aviation service, qualifying for an N.C.O. pilot in 1916. Initially he flew with Brumowski who taught him a great deal but in 1917 he was transferred to the Trentino where he started to achieve fame as a great fighter pilot. His first victory was an Albatross D III (OEF) which had a black nose and struts. Later he used the Albatross D III series 153 which was all-black marked with a large white "K" on the fuselage sides. Kiss always desired to be promoted to officer rank and wore his medals on his tunic even when flying. He was wounded in action for the second time on January 25, 1918 during an encounter with Italian ace Silvio Scaroni after which a section of his intestine was removed. Even though he was not fully recovered he took to the air again and was shot down on May 25, 1918 over Valsugana by Lt. Gerald Birks of the RFC.

Oberleutnant Frank Linke-Crawford known as the "Falcon of Feltre" was born in Cracow, Poland on August 18, 1893. Initially he was a *Leutnant* in *Dragoner Regiment No. 6*, then transferred to the infantry in February 1916 after which he went to the air services in April. Completing his training as a pilot he was sent to the Italian Front where he was assigned to Brumowski's *Flik 41*. Here he flew the Brandenburg D I (Ufag 65.54) and a late Phöenix-built model of the 28 series adopting a red helmet becoming known as the "The Red-Head." His number of victories rose dramatically competing with Brumowski. In 1917 at the age of twenty-four he was given command of *Flik 60* at Feltre. Flying over the Montello on July 31, 1918 he fell in flames. It is not certain whether he was a victim of Capt. Cottle (RFC Squadron No. 45) or Canadian Ace Capt. William Barker of Squadron No. 28 and three Italian pilots. Coincidentally his father (*Major* Adalbert Linke Crawford) and brother were to visit him that day with both being visibly shaken by the news. He was buried near Marburg-Drau (today Maribor) but after the conflict was buried in Salzburg, Austria.

A complete Official List of Austrian Air Aces was never published but the most authoritative sources to provide good information.[85]

Austrian Air Aces

Names	*Total Victories*	*Victories in Italy*
Hauptman Godwin Brumowski	35	33
Offizierstellvertreter Julius Arrigi	32	32
Oberleutnant der Reserve		
Benno Fiala Ritter von Fernbrugg	28	26
Oberleutnant Frank Linke-Crawford	27	27
Leutnant der Reserve Josef Kiss	19	19
Leutnant der Reserve Franz Gräser	18	18
Feldwebel Eugen Bönsch	16	16
Stabsfeldwebel Stefan Fejes	16	16
Oberleutnant der Reserve		
Ernest Strohschenider	15	15
Hauptmann Adolf Heyrowsky	12	10
Offizierstellvertreter Kurt Gruber	11	8
Oberleutnant Franz Rudorfer	11	11
Oberleutnant Friedrich Navratil	10	10
Hauptmann Raoul Stojsavljevic	10	10
Linienschiffsleutnant		
Godfried von Banfield	9	9
Hauptmann Otto Jindra	9	-
Oberleutnant Georg Kenzian	9	9

Offizierstellvertreter Karl Kaszala	8	5
Hauptmann Heinrich Kostrba	8	8
Oberleutnant Alexander Tahy	8	8
Stabfeldwebel Ferdinand Udvardy	8	8
Oberleutnant der Reserve Josef Friedrich	7	7
Oberleutnant der Reserve Ludwig Hautzmayer	7	7
Oberleutnant der Reserve Otto Jäger	7	1
Hauptmann Josef Von Maier	7	7
Stabfeldwebel Johann Risztics	7	7
Stabfeldwebel Andreas Dombrowski	6	1
Hauptmann Johann Frint	6	6
Feldwebel Alexander Kasza	6	6
Hauptmann Karl Nikitsch	6	6
Oberleutnant Franz Peter	6	6
Oberleutnant Josef Pürer	6	6
Oberleutnant Roman Schmidt	6	3
Oberleutnant Rudolf Weber	6	5
Feldwebel Julius Busa	5	-
Offizierstellvertreter Friedrich Hefty	5	4
Offizierstellvertreter Julius Kowalczik	5	5
Feldwebel Franz Lahner	5	5
Fregattenleutnant Friedrich Lang	5	5
Stabfeldwebel Johann Lasi	5	5
Oberleutnant der Reserve Bela Macourek	5	5
Oberleutnant der Reserve Kurt Nachod	5	-
Feldwebel Augustin Novak	5	5
Oberleutnant Karl Paltzel	5	4
Leutnant der Reserve Alois Rodlauer	5	5
Oberleutnant Rudolf Szepessy-Sokol	5	3
Feldwebel Karl Teichmann	5	5
Offizierstellvertreter Karl Urban	5	1
Offizierstellvertreter Franz Wognar	5	5

Italian Air Aces

During the Tenth Battle of the Isonzo, the *91a Squadriglia* was formed from the best pilots of the *71a Squadriglia* eventually being known as the Aces Squadron. Used was the French scoring system. Planes strafed on the ground were not counted, neither partial nor probable victories were allowed while sharing was not automatic. Judgment was made at the squadron level as to whom it was that determined the fall of the foe. Upon landing pilots were expected to fill out a report before talking with anyone. Italian military aviation records of the Great War were disorganized and often skimpy. Sometimes one could obtain information from the War Bulletins which indicated the performance of a pilot. On February 1, 1919, the *Comando Generale di Aeronautica* (*5a sezione),* published a list of allowed and disallowed victories of all pilots. This was the so-called Bongiovanni List (he of Caporetto), which aroused the ire of many pilots who were given little time to protest when they thought that the list had not treated them fairly.

Major Francesco Baracca (*1a,70a,91a Squadriglia)* was born in Lugo di Romagna in the province of Ravenna, on May 9, 1888. Against his father's wishes he entered the Military Academy at Modena graduating after two years as a *sottotenente* and was posted to the *Piemonte Reale* Cavalry. Volunteering for aviation duty he soon had French and Italian pilot licenses. In 1914 he was seconded to the *Battaglione Aviatori.* Italy's first air (his) victory took place in a Nieuport 11 on April 7, 1916 earning him a Silver Medal. A second victory followed on May 16, a third on May 24, 1917 and a fourth on September 16 after which he received the second Silver Medal. On Sept. 16 he was promoted to captain. That April he adopted the personal insignia of the black prancing horse to be placed on the left side of the fuselage while on the right side was painted the insignia of the *91a Squadriglia* the griffon, a lion with the head of a hawk. The horse was the insignia of his old cavalry unit. His mechanic was the brother of Enzo Ferrari (automobile racing) who later asked the Baracca family for permission to use the insignia on his racing stable. On May 1, 1917 he transferred to the new *91a Squadriglia.* By November 1917 he had achieved the fifth kill thus being eligible (according to Italian classification) for the nomination to

Air Ace. Kills followed quickly so that by December he already achieved the thirtieth kill. Baracca was happy only when in the air. He had been offered desk jobs but refused them all. It seemed that his only activities were flying and writing to his mother. Air Aces on opposing sides wrote to their mother daily.[87] The text of his letters persist to this day.[88]

He was killed flying over the Montello on June 19, 1918 his body being found four days later. It is not definitely known how he died. Postwar review awarded him thirty-four victories. The king decreed that the *91a Squadriglia* be named after Baracca. In all he was awarded a *Medaglia d'Oro al Valore Militare,* as well as three *Medaglie d'Argento al Valore Militare.* He also received the British Military Cross, the Officer's Cross of the Belgian Crown, the French Croix de Guerre with Palms and was made an Officer of the Military Order of Savoy.

Tenente Flavio Torello Baracchini flying in the *7a, 26a, 81a 76a Squadriglia* often flew with Baracca. He was born on July 28, 1895 in Villafranca Lunigiana in the province of Massa Carrara. Joining the army by December 1915 he had earned a pilot's license. Initially he flew Voisins being posted to the *7a Squadriglia,* then the *26a Squadriglia,* later being converted to Nieuports and flying with the *81a Squadriglia* where he scored eight victories and was awarded the *Medaglia d'Oro al Valore Militare.* Later he flew in the *76a Squadriglia* where on August 8 he was wounded in the jaw. Rejoining the *81a Squadriglia* he was wounded in the abdomen after which he never saw action again. Initially he was credited with thirty-three victories which were reduced to twenty-one by Bongiovanni which left his family very upset. After a chemical explosion in his laboratory in July 1928, he died on the following August 18.

Capitano Costantini Bortolo was born in Vittorio Veneto (Prov. of Treviso) on February 14, 1889. His birthplace was the site of the last Italian offensive of the war.[89] Joining the Regular Army he reached the rank of *tenente* in the engineers after which he decided to join the Air Service.

Trained as a pilot at the *Campo Scuola Militare d'Aviazione* at Aviano (near Udine), on September 13, 1912 he passed the test on Blériots receiving Brevet No. 177. After the war's outbreak he joined the *70a Squadriglia* with Baracca, both later departing to join the Air Aces squadron the *91a Squadriglia.* During the Caporetto debacle he started to pile up victories often flying with Baracca. On June 19, 1918 responding to a call for help from the Italian Forty-eighth Infantry Division near the Montello he flew in a trio of Spads together with Baracca and another pilot. Baracca never returned. In all Bortolo had six confirmed kills before the war's end.

Sergente Guido Nardini was born in Florence on March 13, 1883. Going to France he obtained a pilot's license in Betheny (Pilot Brevet No. 590, on August 22, 1911). Flying in the *91a Squadriglia* he achieved six victories.

Tenente Luigi Olivari arrived at the *70a Squadriglia* with the rank of *Aspirante Ufficiale* in April 1917. In May he joined the *91a Squadriglia* which transferred to the aerodrome at Istrana.[90] In August 1917 he had his first victory followed by many others. By September he was in third place in the Italian aces pecking order. On October 13 while climbing steeply his Spad stalled and plunged into the ground making him the first casualty of the *91a Squadriglia.*

Tenente Giuliano Parvis (real name Giorgio Pessi) served in the *91a Squadriglia* first tasting success on October 25, 1917. Often flying with Baracca he achieved a score of six kills.

Tenente Colonello Pier Ruggero Piccio (*3a,5a, 70a, 77a, 91a Squadriglia)* was born in Rome on September 27, 1880. It seems that aviation was in his genes as both his son and grandson have achieved significant rank in the Italian Air Forces. Graduating from the Modena Military Academy on September 8, 1900 he was posted to the 43°. After three years he was seconded to the Foreign Affairs Ministry which sent him to Africa until February 17. 1907. From March 1908 to July 31, 1909 he served as an officer in the 2 Mixed Company in Crete. Returning to the infantry during the Turkish-Italian War he served in Libya from December 11, 1911 for a year. In February 1912 he was awarded the *Medaglia di Bronzo* as commander of a machine gun section. In March 1913 he was promoted to *Capitano.* Picked as one of Italian aviation pioneers he attended flying school at Somma Lombardo in the Province of Varese. He was awarded his wings on July 12, 1913. He was a pioneer in advocating the use of the airplane as an artillery observer when on June 2, 1914 accompanied by *Tenente Tacchini* (later commander of the *91a Squadriglia*), he conducted a trial with the Officer Commanding the 17° Artillery. The trial was successful but there was still resistance in the artillery officer corps which led to tremendous casualties in future infantry attacks. In July 1913 he obtained a license to pilot Nieuport monoplanes and Caproni bombers the following October. Soon after he was made commander of the *5a Squadriglia.* For reconnaissance flights during mid-1915 he was awarded the *Medaglia di Bronzo.* After renewed training on Caproni bombers he was nominated commander of the *3a Squadriglia* from October 1915 to February 1916. In May 1916 he went to Paris for training on Nieuports returning to command the newly formed *77a Squadriglia.* That May he was awarded the *Medaglia d'Argento* for downing a balloon. Promoted major on January 26, 1917, he left the *77a Squadriglia* to command the *10 Gruppo* splitting operational duties with the *77a Squadriglia* and the *91a Squadriglie.* Due to his steady build-up of victories he was awarded a *Medaglia d'Oro al Valore Militare* on May 15, 1918. After promotion to Lt. Col. he became commander of the *Massa di Caccia* (fighter mass). In all he had twenty-four confirmed victories. Another *Medaglia d'Argento* was awarded in June 1918. On December 25, 1923 he became a full general later becoming Italian Air Attaché in Paris. He died in Rome on July 31, 1965.

Tenente Fulco Ruffo di Calabria (*1a, 4a, 42a, 44a, 72a, 76a Squadriglia*) was born in Napoli on August 12, 1884. One of his ancestors was Cardinal Fabrizio Ruffo who led 25,000 men against the French in Calabria in 1797.[91] Volunteering for the army in 1904 he slowly rose in rank until he was commissioned *sottotenente* on February 18, 1906. Assigned to the *Battaglione Aviatori* he received his pilot's license on December 20, 1914.[92] He was in the *4a Squadriglia Artiglieria* (later *44a*), then the *42a*. His personal insignia was a black skull and bones. Planes he flew were Nieuports 11 and 17, and Spad VII. On June 28, 1916 he was posted to the *70a Squadriglia.* In March 1917 he was promoted to *tenente*, while in May he followed Baracca to the newly-formed *91a* Squadriglia or the Aces Squadron. On May 5, 1918 he received the *Medaglia d'Oro al Valore Militare.*

His first victory was on August 23, 1916 when he downed a Brandenburg C-I over Gorizia, his second on Sept. 16, downing a Lloyd C. III over Staro Selo. These victories were followed by a total of twenty victories confirmed by post-war review. He earned a total of three Bronze Medals, two Silver Medals as well as the already mentioned Gold. He was made a Knight of the Military Order of Savoy. Following Baracca's death he became commander of the *91a Squadriglia* but after a nervous breakdown relinquished it to Lt. Ranza.[93] He died on August 23, 1946. His daughter Paola Ruffo di Calabria married Prince Albert of Belgium and became Queen on September 9, 1993.

Tenente Ferruccio Ranza was one of the founding members of the *91 Squadriglia* often flying with Baracca and succeeded Ruffo di Calabria as commander of the *91a Squadriglia.* He was born in Fiorenzuola d'Arda (Piacenza), on September 9, 1892. Commissioned as a *sottotenente* in the First Engineers Regiment he was posted to the *43 Squadriglia.* Starting in October 1915 he engaged in reconnaissance duties for which he was awarded a *Medaglia di Bronzo al Valore Militare.* After pilot training he was trained on Nieuports posted to the *77a Squadriglia.* By early June 1917 his talents were recognized and he was posted to the *91a Squadriglia* the Aces Squadron. He soon was awarded two *Medaglia d'Argento al Valore Militare* having a total of twenty victories. He received four War Crosses (one for Valour, one for Merit, a French one with palms and a Belgian one with crossed swords), the Serb Star of Karageorgevich. After the conflict served in ever more-responsible positions abroad retiring on January 29, 1945 with the rank of general. He died in Bologna on April 25, 1973. His total victories amounted to seventeen.

Tenente Giovanni Sabelli was born in Naples on September 23, 1886. He was one of the pioneers of Italian aviation. Going to Britain to take his pilot training earning his pilot's wings (No. 178) from the Royal Aero Club on January 30, 1912 No. 178). Prior to the war he was a racing auto driver in England. At the end of October 1912 he went to Bulgaria to establish that nation's Air Service for the war against Turkey. When Italy entered the war he returned home becoming one of the first members of the *91a Squadriglia.* After scoring five victories he was killed in action on October 25, 1917. One of his last victories was over German Ace *Leutnant* Ahenfeld.

Tenente Silvio Scaroni of the *4a, 44a,44a, 76a Squadriglia* was born in Brescia on May 12, 1893. He was serving in the Second Field Artillery Regiment as a corporal when he volunteered for pilot training in March 1915. His basic pilot training was at the San Giusto school earning a license to fly Blériots on August 28, 1916. His initial assignment was with the *4a Squadriglia* as an artillery observer, later flying with the *44a Squadriglia* doing similar duty. On October 8 he flew his first operational mission later earning a Bronze Medal. In January 1917 he was posted to the *43a Squadriglia.* Later in June he was posted to Malpensa to be pilot-trained on the newly arrived Nieuports. His next assignment was with the *86a Squadriglia* but due to the Caporetto retreat he was sent to the *76a Squadriglia* a Nieuport 17 squadron. During November he had four victories but reported only three. On one day, December 26, 1917 in the Battle of Istrana he downed three planes. This was an encounter which started with a prank. Capt. William Barker (RFC), bombed a German airfield on Christmas Day, 1917. The next day German bombers attacked his airfield but upon returning to their home base were assaulted by British and Italian fighters with severe losses for the Germans.

By now his plane was a HD 1 with concentric white and black squares on the fuselage. During November he was awarded the Second Silver Medal. By July 1918 he had scored his thirtieth victory and seriously wounded would fly no longer.

After the war he held various military positions abroad as well as ADC to King Vittorio Emanuele III always rising in rank retiring from the military after the September 1943 armistice. After writing several books on his experiences (see complete bibliography vol. III) and serving the king as ADC he died in Milan on February 16, 1977.

ITALIAN ACES[94]

Score	*Rank and Name*	*Squadriglia*	*Particular Notes*
34	Maj. Francesco Baracca	*5a, 70a, 91a*	Killed in action, 6-18-18
26	Lt. Silvio Scaroni	*4a, 44a, 76a*	
24	Lt. Col. Pier Ruggiero Piccio	*5a, 91a*	
21	Lt. Flavio Torello Baracchini	*76a*	
20	Capt. Fulco Ruffo di Calabria	*70a,91a*	
17	Sgt. Marziale Cerutti	*79a*	
17	Lt. Ferruccio Ranza	*70a, 91a*	
12	Lt. Luigi Olivari	*70a, 91a*	Killed in action 10-13-17
11	Lt. Giovanni Ancillotto	*77a, 91a*	
11	Sgt. Antonio Reali	*78a*	
8	Lt. Flaminio Avet	*70a*	
8	Second Lt. Ernesto Cabruna	*77a,91a*	
8	Second Lt. Alvaro Leonardi	*80,91a*	
8	Lt. Carlo Lombardi	*77a*	
8	Sgt. Giovanni Nicelli	*79a, 91a*	Killed in action 5-5-18
8	Gastone Novelli	*91a*	
7	Sgt. Maj. Guglielmo Fornagiari	*78a*	
7	Lt. Mario Fucini	*78a, 91a*	
7	Insegna Orazio Pierozzi	*San Marco*	
7	Sgt. Maj. Cosimo Renella	*78a*	
7	Capt. Antonio Riva	*78a*	
7	Lt. Leopoldo Eleuteri	*70a*	
6	Capt. Bertoldo Constantini	*70,91a*	
6	Lt. Luigi Olivi	*76a*	Killed in action 7-17-17
6	Lt. Giuliano Parvis	*91a*	
6	Sgt. Attilio Imolesi	*79a*	Killed action, 3-3-17
6	Sgt. Mario Stoppani	*76a*	
6	Sgt. Guido Nardini	*91a*	
6	Sgt. Aldo Bocchese	*70a*	
6	Sgt. Romolo Ticconi	*76a*	

6	Sgt. Cesare Magistrini	*91a*	
6	Sgt. Cosimo Rizzotto	*76a*	
6	Sgt. Giulio Lega	*76a*	
5	Lt. Giovanni Sabelli	*70a, 91a*	Killed in action, 10-25-17
5	Lt. Alessandro Buzio	*81a*	
5	Lt. Guido Masiero	*78a,91a*	
5	Lt. Sebastiano Bedendo	*71a*	
5	Lt. Amedeo Mecozzi	*78a*	
5	Lt. Giorgio Michetti	*76a*	
5	Sec.Lt. Michele Allasia	*77a,91a*	Killed in action, 7-20-18
5	Sec. Lt. Antonio Amantea	*71a*	
5	Sec. Lt. Alessandro Resch	*70a*	

German Air Activity on the Italian Front[95]

The significant air battle involving German pilots on the Italian Front was known as the Battle of Istrana. On December 25, Capt. William Barker of the British 45 Squadron accompanied by Lt. Harold Byrne Hudson strafed and bombed the German air base at San Fior. Upset at this intrusion on their Christmas holiday, the next day the Germans reacted by bombing the Italian air base at Istrana during which Italian pilots took off to engage the enemy. All German pilots were still either drunk or tired from lack of sleep resulting in poor bombing and twelve German planes being downed. One plane forced to land after which its pilot fell asleep.[96]

Jagdstaffel (Jasta)[97]

To help its Austro-Hungarian Ally Germany sent three Jastas (1,31, and 39) to the Italian Front. By Spring 1918, they were rotated back to the French Front.

Jasta 1 (Royal Prussian)

It was formed at Bertincourt, on the Somme, August 22, 1916. In September 1917, it was transferred to Italy (Jagdgruppe 14), to support the XIV Army. Flying mostly Albatross Scouts, it flew from Aviano, Campoformidi and Possanerio. In March 1918 it returned to France.

Jasta 31 (Royal Prussian)

This unit was formed in Breslau on December 14, 1916. On September 11, 1917 it departed for Italy where it was credited with fourteen victories. In February 1918 it returned to the French Front.

Jasta 39 (Royal Prussian)

This unit was formed at Hanover on June 30, 1917 and sent to the Italian Front in September 1917. There it scored forty-one victories returning to France in March 1918.[98] In Italy it flew Albatross DIII and DV Scouts. Flying Albatross D III from October 1917 to March 1918 and using bases such as San Fior, Aviano and Campoformido German aces had eighty victories on the Italian Front.

GERMAN AIR ACES ON THE ITALIAN FRONT:[99]

Leutnant Hans von Freden started his career as an observer in a two-seater. He finished the artillery observer school at Juterbog arriving on August 21 at *Feldflieger-Abteilung 48* where he spent ten months. In June 1917 he started pilot's training later joining *Jasta 1* in Italy where he had three victories all balloons. By March 25, 1918 he was back in France again with *Jasta 1.* On June 11 he was appointed *Staffelführer* of *Jasta 50* where he remained for the duration of the conflict. He claimed sixteen victories in all. He had been awarded the prestigious *Pour le Mérite* which many observers thought he had not earned. Others thought it was due to slow paper-work processing of his victories.[100]

Offizierstellvertreter Wilhelm Hippert flew in the *FAA 227* and *Jasta 39,74.*[101] Known as Willi he served as a pilot in France. Transferring to *Jasta 39* as a *Vizefeldwebel* he became one of the German Air Aces on the Italian Front. In mid-1918 he was transferred back to France being promoted to *Offizierstellvertreter* and flying a Fokker DVII with a blue nose and a black and white checkered fuselage with the name "Mimmi" on the top wing.

He received the Iron Cross First Class. He was given recognition for eight victories.[102]

Vizefeldwebel Ludwig Gaim of *Jasta 39* was born in Daggendorf on April 1, 1892. Joining the army in August 1914 he served in the artillery until July 1916 winning the Iron Cross 2nd Class. He transferred to the Air Service flying with the *FA (A) 293* until he was wounded.[103] After single-seater training he was assigned to *Jasta 39* in Italy where he gained five victories, the last being on December 30 when he was wounded. Rotated back to France he was promoted to *Vizefeldwebel* on May 25, 1917 receiving the Military Verdeinst Cross 3rd Class with Swords on April 7, the Iron Cross 1st Class on November 8 and the Austrian Silver Medal on December 31.

Leutnant Alwin Thurm flying in *Jasta 24* and *31* was born on April 10, 1894 in Windhausen. He served with *Jasta 24* from July 6 to August 4, 1917. During this period he had one victory. Soon after he was transferred to *Jasta 31* in Italy where he gained four more victories. He was shot down and killed on December 30, while attacking Italian balloon lines near Asolo. His victors were the Lieutenants R. J. Brownell and H.M. Moody flying Camels of the 45 Squadron RFC.

Leutnant Werner Wagener (*Jastas 38,21* and *39, Kest 1,5,SS 14*), was born on November 13, 1894 in Desau. At the outbreak of hostilities he volunteered for military duty. Wounded by shrapnel he was hospitalized returning to duty on March 1, 1915 when he volunteered for aviation duty. During training he was promoted to *Unteroffizier*, completing observer and pilot school after which he was sent to *Kagohl 7, Staffel 38* on July 24, 1916 on the Bulgarian front. One victory was obtained while flying a Fokker Eindekker. That October 22 he was promoted to *Vizefeldwebel* transferring to *Jasta 21* received a commission on June 26. In August he was transferred to the Italian Front serving in *Jasta 39*. There he scored three confirmed victories. On November 25 he was wounded after which he returned to the Western Front.[104]

A summary of German Air Aces on the Italian Front follows:[105]

Name	*Total Victories*	*Victories in Italy*	*Unit*
Oblt. Kummetz, Hans	7	2	Jasta 1
Ltn. Schroeder, Herbert	5	3	"
Ltn. Von Freden, Hans	16	3	"
Ltn. Thurm, Alwin	5	4	Jasta 31
Uffz. Hippert, Wilhelm	8	5	Jasta 39
Vzfw. Gaim, Ludwig	5	5	"
Ofstlv. Ultsch, Bernhard	12	3	"
Ltn. Wagener, Werner	5	3	"

The German Air Service (*Luftstreitkräfte*) emerged from the conflict with more sophisticated tactics than its opponents. By 1916 a quasi-independent Air Service was emplaced by the High Command with General Erich von Höppner as the commander and Chief of Staff Col. Hermann von der Lieth-Thomsen. Lt. Gen. William Mitchell (U.S.A.) noted that Fokkers were easily transportable via railroad flatcar with wings off against the fuselage, gas tanks full, then immediately assembled and ready for combat.[106] Plans were being made for 100-plane assaults on British cities using Goth G4s which would eventually carry 1,800 kg.(3960 lbs) of explosives.

Fighting in the British 28 Squadron was Lt. George Fordrer, a native of Chicago.[106] It has been reported that there were about eight Americans flying in the RFC on the Italian Front. On May 11, 1918, he was shot down by Austro-Hungarian Air Ace Frank Linke-Crawford, the *Falcon of Feltre*. Luckily he survived and was visited in the prisoner of war camp by Crawford. There were also American Naval Air pilots at Porto Corsini on the Adriatic (See elsewhere in this chapter).

Already mentioned has been Major Fiorello Laguardia, future Mayor of the City of New York, congressman and Director of the United Nations Relief and Rehabilitation Agency after the Second World War. Killed in action on October 27, 1918 and receiving a posthumous award of the *Medaglia d'Oro al Valore Militare* was bomber pilot and U. S. citizen Coleman deWitt Fenafly whose

Caproni bomber was attacked by five enemy fighters.[107] Most of the air activity took place in the naval air station although there were some Americans flying land-based planes on the Italian Front. Aviation would prove to be a vital factor for the victors in the coming battles on the Italian Front as shall be noted in the next volume.

Chapter XVI Endnotes

The New Weapons of War that Shocked, Panicked and Awed Enemy Infantry

1 Heinz Guderian, *Panzer Leader*, DaCapo Press, New York 1966. p. *viii*

2 A. Krauss, *Die Ursachen unserer Niederlage*, op. cit., p. 89

3 Walter Goerlitz, *History of the German General Staff*, op. cit., p. 189

4 *USMMA: Cronistoria dell'aeronautica militare italiana*, 8 volumes, Rome, 1989,Vol. VI, pp. 3-4

5 USSMA: A. Curami, G. Rochat, *Giulio Douhet, Scritti 1901-1915*, Rome, 1993; This regarded a report, *Relazione sullo stato attuale dell'aviazione militare 1 dicembre 1913*.

6 Andrea Curami, *I Primi Passi dell'Industria Aeronautica Italiana* in *La Grande Guerra Aerea, 1915-1918*, Editor, Paolo Ferrari, Gino Rossato Editore, Valdagno, (VI), 1994, p110

7 Douhet, Giulio, *The Command of the Air*, trans. Dino Ferrari (1942); New printing Washington, D.C., Office of Air Force History, 1983, p. 34

8 *Reconnaissance and Bomber Aircraft of the 1914-1918 War*, Editor, E.F. Cheesman, Harleyford Publications Ltd. Letchworth Herts, England, 1962, p.162

9 Idem, p. 170

10 Idem, p. 170

11 Idem, p. 164-66

12 Idem, p. 168

13 Idem, p. 168

14 Idem, p. 174

15 Idem, p. 172

16 Maurizio Longoni, *Gli "Assi" Sul Fronte Italiano* in *La Grande Guerra Aerea 1915-1918*, op. cit. 292,

17 Idem, p. 303

18 Manfried Rauchensteiner, *Der Tod des Doppeladlers. Österreich-Ungarn und der Erste Weltkrieg*, Graz, Styria, 1993, p. 572.

19 *Jane's Fighting Aircraft of World War I,* Military Press, 1990, p. 111

20 J.M. Bruce, *The Hanriot HD-1,*Profile Publications, Surrey, No. 109, p. 3-14

21 Idem, p. 7

22 *Jane's Fighting Aircraft,* op. cit., p. 114

23 Jon Guttman, *Spad XII/XIII Aces of World War I,* Osprey Publishing, 2002, p. 18

24 *Jane's Fighting Aircraft,* op. cit., p. 122

25 *Barker V C,* Ralph Wayne, Grub Street, London, 1999, p. 85

26 *Above the Trenches,* Christopher Shores, Norman Franks, Russell Guest, 1990, Grub Street, p. 52

27 Idem, p. 62

28 Wayne Ralph, *Barker, VC,* Grub Street, London, 1999, p. 151

29 Christopher Shores et al, see above, p. 73

30 Idem p. 76

31 *Above the Trenches,* Supplement, Christopher Shores, Norman Franks & Russell Guest, Grub Street, London, 1996, p. 12

32 Idem, p. 83 and supplement p. 11

33 *Above the Trenches,* Norman L.R. Franks, C. Shores, Grub Street, 1991.

34 *Over the Front,* Norman L. R. Franks, Frank W. Bailey, Grub Street, London, 1990 p. 109

35 Maurizio Longoni, op. cit. p.,306

36 John H. Morrow Jr., *The Great War in the Air. Military Aviation from 1909 to 1921,* London, Airlife, 1993,p. 84

37 Fabio degli Esposti, *L'Industria Aeronautica degli Imperi Centrale,* in *La Grande Guerra Aerea 1915-1918,* op. cit., p. 147

38 Ibid, p. 172

39 Valerio Castronovo, *Dizionario biografico degli italiani,* Roma, Istituto dell'Enciclopedia Italiana 1979, Vol. XXII, p. 133-137

40 P.M. Grosz, G. Haddow and P. Schiemer, *Austro-Hungarian Army Aircraft of World War I,* Flying Machines Press, Montainview, California, 1993, p. 191. This is an excellent work on planes and production facilities of the Habsburg Empire.

41 Georg Gasser, *Die Österreichisch-ungarische Fliegertruppe an der Südwestfront 1915-1918* Ph.D. thesis, University of Vienna, 1980, p. 57

42 Adapted from *Austro-Hungarian Army Aircraft,* op. cit., p. 200

43 For further information please see Peter Grosz et al, *Austro-Hungarian Army Aircraft of World War I,* Appendix 1, *Austro-Hungarian Army Aircraft Designation System,* pages 505-506; also Appendix 2, *Checklist of Austro-Hungarian Army Aircraft,* pages 507-510

44 *Reconnassiance & Bomber Aircraft of the 1914-1918 War,* Edit. E.F. Chessman, Aero Publishers Inc., Los Angeles, 1962, p. 13

45 *Reconnassiance & Bomber Aircraft of the 1914-1918 War,* op. cit., p. 148

46 Idem, p. 20

47 Grosz, Haddow, Schiemer, op. cit., p. 448

48 *Reconnassiance & Bomber Aircraft,* op. cit., p. 18

49 Idem p. 20-21

50 Lamberton, W.M., Chessman, E.F. *Reconnaissance & Bomber Aircraft of the 1914-1918 War,* Aero Publishers, Los Angeles,1962 p. 22

51 Jane's Fighting Aircraft of World War I, op. cit., pp. 148-151;

52 Reconnassiance & Bomber Aircraft *Reconnaissance,* op. cit., p. 24

53 Idem, op. cit., p. 28

54 Idem

55 Idem, p. 30

56 Jane's Fighting Aircraft of World War I, op. cit., p. 32

57 That cemetery was bulldozed by Qadhafi when he took over and made into a residential area.

58 USSMA : *Cronistoria dell'Aeronautica Militare Italiana,* 1928, (reprinted 1989), Vol. III, pp. 28, 51, 53

59 Gregory Alegi, *I Campi d'Aviazione sul Fronte Italiano, La Grande Guerra Aerea, 1915-1918* op. cit., p. 252

60 AUSSME: Carta 53 contains a lithograph entitled *Aviazione I Armata*

61 *Air Aces of the 1914-1918 War,* Edited by Bruce Robertson, Harleyford Publications 1959, D.A.S. McKay, D.F.M., *The Italian Section,* p. 119

62 Martin O'Connor, *Air Aces of the Austro-Hungarian Empire,* Mesa, Champlin Fighter Museum Press, 1986, p.8

63 *L'aeroporto di Pergine rivivrà per un giorno; Alto Adige* Sept. 13, 1985; *Le CroceNeri di nuovo in volo,* Alto Adige, Sept. 17, 1985

64 Layman, R.D., *Naval Aviation in the First World War,* Naval Institute Press, Annapolis, 1996, p. 42

65 Heinz J. Nowarra, *Marine Aircraft of the 1914-1918 War,* Harleyford Publications Ltd., 1966, p. 9

66 Layman, R.D. op. cit., p. 83

67 *Marine Aircraft of the 1914-1918 War,* Compiled by Heinz Nowarra, Harleyford Publications Ltd, Letchworth, Herts, England, 1966, p. 9

68 P. Grosz et al, op. cit., p. 511

69 Gottfried de Banfield, *L'Aquila di Trieste,* Trieste, Lint, 1984

70 Nowarra, op. cit., p. 21

71 *Air Aces of the 1914-1918 War,* Edited by Bruce Robertson, Harleyford Publication, 1959, W.M. Lamberton, p. 172

72 Ibid., p. 172

73 Ibid, p. 190

74 See *British Aeroplanes 1914-1918,* J.M. Bruce, London: Putnam, 1957 See *Squadron Histories,* Peter Lewis, London : Putnam, 1959

75 Also see vol. I; information taken from tourist brochure

76 Giancarlo Garello, *L'Aviazione della Regia Marina* in *La Grande Guerra Aerea, 1915-1918,* op. cit., p. 65

77 *Marine Aircraft,* op. cit., p. 15

78 *Air Aces of the 1914-1918 War,* Edit. Bruce Robertson, Garden City Press, 1959 p. 172

79 Idem, p. 172

80 Idem p. 272

81 Christopher Chant, *Austro-Hungarian Air Aces of World War I,* Osprey Publishing, 2001, p. 50

82 *Air Aces of the 1914-1918 War, op. cit., p. 174*

83 Idem, p. 205

84 Ibid,

85 Riccardo Caviglioli, *L'aviazione austro-ungarica sulla fronte italiana 1915-1918,* Castiglioni & Archenti, Milano, reprinted 1993, Albertelli, p. 296; Martin O'Connor, *Air Aces* op. cit.

86 Pilots are listed in descending number of victories

87 Along with Major Francesco Baracca of the Regio Aeronautica, the German Air Ace *Rittmeister* Manfred von Richtofen also daily wrote to his mother.

88 Vincenzo Manca, *L'Idea Meravigliosa di Francesco Baracca,* Roma, Edizione dell'Ateneo 1980

[89] *Air Aces of the 1914-1918 War,* op. cit., D.A.S. McKay p. 128 Xcii See Above

[91] Idem, pp. 125-126

[92] Norman Franks, Russell Guest, Gregory Alegi *Above the War Fronts,* Grub Street, London, 1997 p. 158

[93] Idem p. 158.

[94] This is a mixture of the so-called Bongiovanni List, (he of Caporetto), issued on February 1, 1919, *La Grande Guerra Aerea,* op. cit., p. 309, and the naval list; Information was also taken from *Air Aces in the 1914-1918 War,* op. cit., p. 131

[95] Neal O'Connor, *Aviation Awards of Imperial Germany in World War I and the Men Who Earned Them,* Six volumes, Volume II, *The Aviation Awards of the Kingdom of Prussia,* Foundation for Aviation World War I, Princeton, NJ, 1990

[96] S. F. Wise, *Canadian Airman and the First World War,* The Official History of the Royal Canadian Air Force, Volume I, University of Toronto Press, 1980, pp. 449-478; Gregory Alegi *La Battaglia Aerea di Istrana, 26 dicembre, Storia Militare,* February 1994, No. 5 pp. 41-48

[97] *Above the Lines,* Norman Franks, Frank W. Bailey and Russell Guest, Grub Street London, 1993, p. 29

[98] Idem p. 44.

[99] Norman Franks, Frank W. Bailey, Russell Guest, *Above the Lines,* Grub Street, London, 1993, p. 29

[100] Aviation Awards of Imperial Germany, Vol. II, op. cit., Neal O'Connor

[101] Ibid

[102] Different ranks in the German Air Service are listed as follows:
Feldwebel: Company Sergeant Major in the infantry, or engineers.
Vizefeldwebel : Vice Sergeant Major
These ranks were non-commissioned officers.
Offizierstellvertreter: Acting officer (non-commissioned) (Listed as a Regimental Officer), Walter Goerlitz, *History of the German General Staff,* op. cit., p. p. 185 calls this rank a hybrid officer. Sergeants would behave as officers with the understanding that they would revert to sergeants at the end of the conflict. Other source, *German Army Handbook, April 1918,* 1977, Hippocrene Books, N.Y. and Arms and Armour Press, London.

[103] An Addendum to the ranks of the military reveals the following terms: FAA (*Fliegerabteilung), (A),* or reconnaissance flight, artillery. Earlier it was called *Feldfliegerabteilung* (FFA). Later it changed to FA and FA(A). These were planes used to provide adjustment to an artillery barrage. KEST: *Kampf Einsitzer Staffel,* literally Single Seater Flight for Battle. These planes assigned to cities, munitions factories, railway centers etc. for protection. *SchutzStaffel:* (Schusta) Protection Flight. These were used in conjunction with reconnaissance flights as escorts. *Insegna* in the list of Italian aces refers to the naval rank of ensign.

[104] *Air Aces of the 1914-1918 War,* op. cit.

[105] Alessandro Massignani, *La Guerra Aerea sul Fronte Italiano, La Grande*

[106] William Mitchell, *Memoirs of World War I,* New York, Random House, 1960, p. 306

[107] *Barker VC,* Ralph Wayne, Grub Street, London, 1997, p. 107

[108] Achille Rastelli, *I Bombardamenti Sulle Città, La Grande Guerra Aerea 1915-1918,*op. cit., p. 231

CHAPTER XVII

THE SAGA OF THE PASUBIO (CONT'D)

Both sides had decided to conduct mining warfare on the Pasubio. More and more complex tunnels were dug with explosions causing extensive damage. The Epic Battle of the Pasubio is now known in Austria as the Thermopylae of the Tyrol.

Ah ! nerver shall the land forget
How gushed the life-blood ofher brave,-
Gushed, warm with hope and courage yet,
Upon the soil they fought to save.
William Cullen Bryant, The Battlefield

The Italian Third Mine

ITALIAN ENGINEERING UNITS now worked to connect the Zero and Belluno tunnels (Map 39). The objective now was to force the enemy to continue its mining war north of the Dente Italiano thus not damaging Italian positions. The only tunnel available for this project was the Napoli tunnel from which tunnels were dug at right angles and then at a right angle again, thus obligating the enemy to dig deeper ever deeper in a countermining operation. By January 19, excavation had proceeded forty-five feet as seismograph equipment indicated that the enemy had infiltrated between two tunnels. Suddenly no more sounds emanated from the enemy sector making one suspect that an explosion was imminent.

The only strategy now was to do likewise as 600 kg. of explosives were exploded at 1335 on January 21. This resulted in minimal damage to the Habsburg tunnels.

The Third Habsburg Mine

As the Napoli tunnel approached enemy engineers detonated four tons of explosives on February 3, 1918 at 0300 resulting in much damage to the Belluno and Zero tunnel (Map 39). So great was the explosion that men were lifted off their feet and thrown against the wall.

The Fourth Italian Mine

February 13 was the day of the commemoration of the founding of the Italian Army Engineering Corps. There were two mining tunnels about thirty feet apart. Suddenly at 1645 there occurred an enormous explosion with flaming vapors invading the Napoli tunnel burning six miners alive and seriously wounding eight. Neither the amount of explosive nor the reason for the explosion are known. Some observers felt that the Italian explosives had detonated from an underlying Habsburg tunnel which had been full of dense smoke which could have set off the Italian explosives. The A.O.K. admitted that it never found out the cause of the explosion.[1]

The Fifth Italian Mine

Another explosion was detonated by the Italians on March 5, 1918 at 1730, with some of the poison gases entering the Ellison tunnel. Instead good ventilation cleaned them out as work there progressed to the final Habsburg detonation.

The Fourth and Decisive Habsburg Mine.

The A.O.K. now changed its strategy. It decided to blow off the top of the *Dente Italiano*. Two explosion chambers were set up with the eastern one containing twenty tons and the western one having thirty tons of explosives. Feinting was part of the strategy as another tunnel in an opposite direction was constructed to confuse Italian Army engineers listening with seismograph equipment. The Ellison proceeded under the *Dente Austriaco* ending under the Dente Italiano (Map 39). On March 3, the detonation chambers were almost ready. Now was the time to deceive the Italian engineers. Small charges of explosives were detonated near Italian tunnels. Deceived by these detonations on March 5, the Italians set off their charge deluding themselves in thinking that the Austro-Hungarian tunnels would be destroyed. After all quieted down, Italian equipment picked up only the false indicators of a tunnel far away from the dangerous one. The time for the explosion was set at 0430 on March 13 hoping to find the entire Italian garrison within the tunnels. Detonation occurred that morning at 0430 ripping off the top of the *Dente Italiano* resulting in a huge crater. Flames reached the *Dente Austriaco* and entered the Ellison tunnel. The Belluno, Siena and Reggio tunnels collapsed while there were large cracks in the Napoli. Fortunately, most of the Italian garrison was away from the *Dente Italiano.* Italian deaths were thirty-seven, wounded twenty-five, missing three. As a result of the detonation the Comando Supremo decided to halt all mining operations.

During the summer the *Piceno* was replaced by the *Catania* (145° and 146°) but on September 10 returned to the mountain. On October 20, 1918 attempting to halt the spread of politically damaging news from the Home Front, the distribution of newspapers and mail was stopped.

• • •

October 31, 1918

Col. Brig. von Eccher who had replaced Col. Brig. Ellison was called to divisional headquarters where he was ordered to withdraw his troops from the Pasubio. Isolated on the mountain the garrison could not understand why they had to withdraw. Political news had not reached them. On Nov. 3, the troops started to withdraw thinking that the armistice was signed on that date. Instead, Italian troops coming from Val Astico and Tonezza captured the whole division without firing a shot. No one had informed the Kaiserjäger of the twenty four hour delay. Thus the men who had not been beaten finally became prisoners of war.[2]

Chapter XVII Footnotes

The Saga of the Pasubio (Cont'd)

1 Gianni Pieropan, *Guida della Zona Sacra del Pasubio,* Gino Rossato Editore, 1993

2 AUSSME: *Diario storico del 236 reg. fant.,* Reperterio b 1, Vol. 1557f; Same sources *Diario storico 55a Div. Fanteria,* Reperterio b 1, Vol. 148 g

APPENDIX I

INSTRUCTIONS BY THE CHIEF OF THE IMPERIAL GENERL STAFF TO GENERAL SIR HERBERT PLUMER WHEN LEAVING FOR ITALY

9th November 1917

(1) You are appointed to command the British Forces now in course of dispatch to Italy and will take over this duty, from Lt. Gen. Lord Cavan, who is now in command, as soon as possible after your arrival in the country. Lord Cavan will revert to the command of an Army Corps.

(2) The immediate object of dispatching British troops to Italy is to assist the Italians in defending their country against invasion, and to give time and opportunity to reorganize their Armies and generally to restore them to an efficient condition. The Prime Minister desires me to add that, in view of the low morale and poor fighting qualities of the Austrian troops, he trusts you will bear in mind the desirability of exploiting to the full any favourable opportunity for doing so what may arise.

(3) His Majesty's Government attach great importance to the early achievement of the above-mentioned object and, as information regarding the state of affairs is obscure and somewhat unreliable, you will , as soon as possible after reaching Italy,forward to me a report on the situation, with special reference to the amount and nature of reinforcements, if any,which you consider to be required, in addition to those which have already been dispatched or are under orders, namely, 4 British and 4 French divisions with a due proportion of heavy artillery.

(4) In pursuance of the object specificed in paragraph 2 and in order to effectively cooperate with the French and Italian Armies, you will be good enough to conform to the wishes of the Italian Commander in Chief with respect to the dispositions and employment of your troops and to give him all the assistance in your power.

Subject to the above you will regard yourself as an independent commander and will be responsible to His Majesty's Government for ensuring that your troops are not placed in a compromising position. If at any time , you are requested by the Italian Commander-in-Chief to carry out operations which in your opinion would unduly endanger the safety of your troops you should make the requisite representations to Italian General Headquarters, and if necessary ,refer to me for instructions of the War Cabinet.

No part of your force should be detached from your Command except as a temporary and urgent measure and then only with your concurrence. The British troops are likely to render much more valuable assistance if kept together in a compact body than if disseminated amongst Italian or French troops.

(5) The supply and maintenance of your force will be controlled by the War Office. Major General Grey who is G.O.C. Mediterranean L.of C. (Cherbourg-Taranto) had been appointed to act as D.G.T. to the Froce in in this capacity will be under your orders. The Base of the force in Italy is Arquata. The force is now concentrating at Mantua , but as the Italians are pressing for a more forward concentration, Lieut. Gen. Wilson has been ordered by the Supreme War Council to examine the matter and consult with Lord Cavan in regard to it. You will report direct to me regarding operations and to the Secretary, War Office , on other necessary matters. You will send me a report of progress of events at least once daily and more frequently when engaged in more important operations.

Paris, 9th November 1917

W.R.Robertson
C.I.G.S.

The greater part of paragraph 4 was communicated to the Italian Government with the addition after "in order effectively to cooperate "of the words " and then only with your concurrence."

MAPS

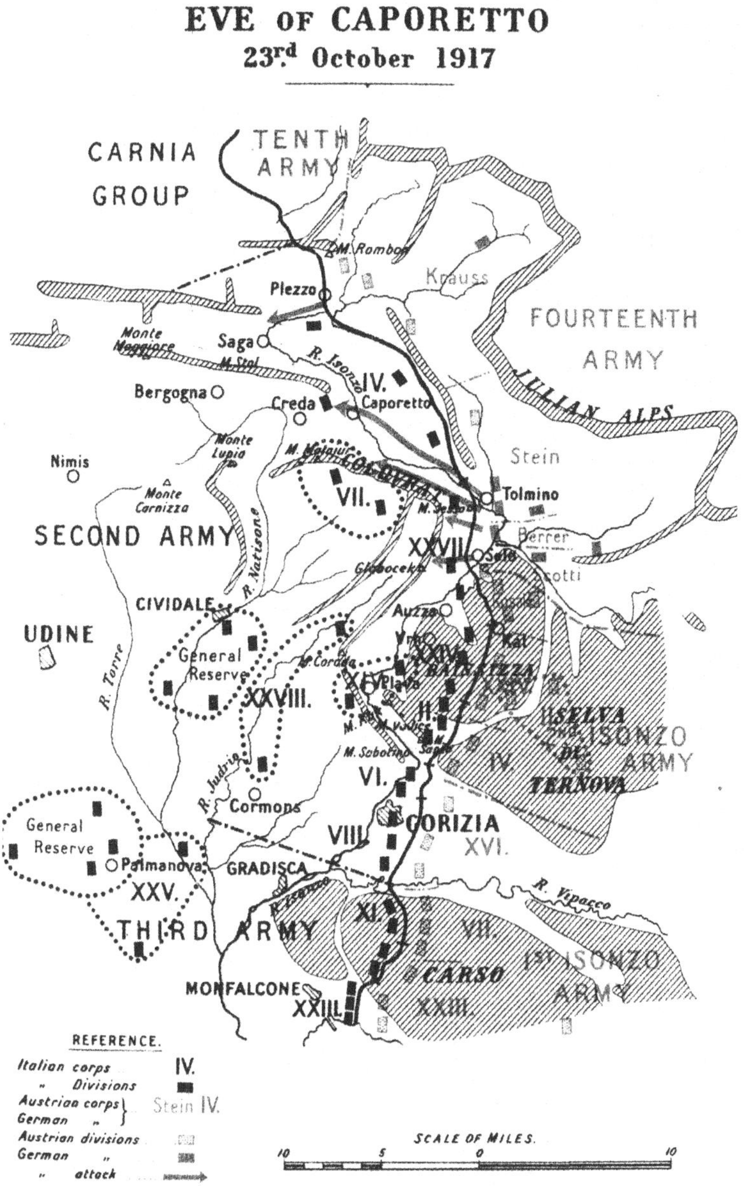

Map 13 G Troop deployment, Oct. 23, 1917.

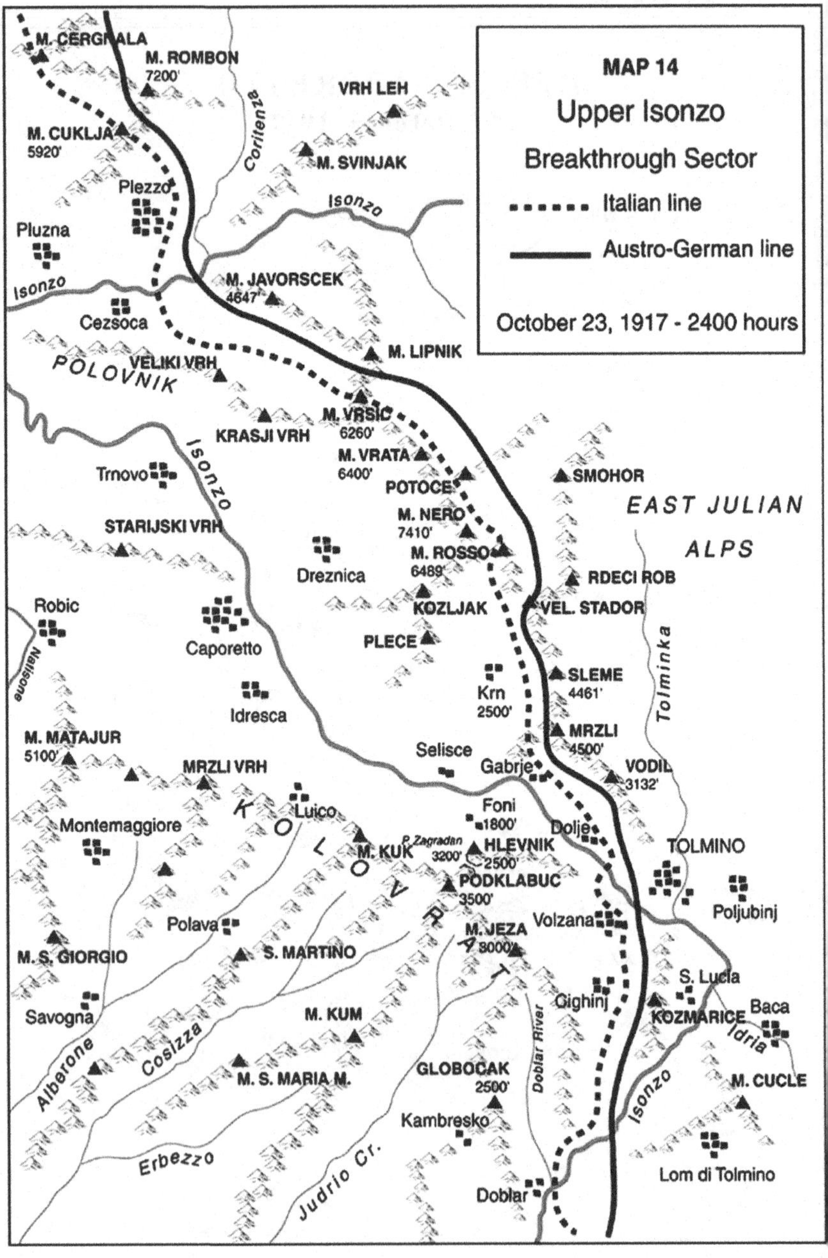
MAP 14
Upper Isonzo
Breakthrough Sector
Italian line
Austro-German line
October 23, 1917 - 2400 hours
M. CERGNALA
M. ROMBON
7200'
VRH LEH
M. CUKLJA
5920'
Coritenza
M. SVINJAK
Plezzo
Isonzo
Pluzna
Isonzo
M. JAVORSCEK
4647'
Cezsoca
M. LIPNIK
POLOVNIK
VELIKI VRH
M. VRSIC
6260'
KRASJI VRH
Isonzo
M. VRATA
6400'
Trnovo
POTOCE
SMOHOR
EAST JULIAN
ALPS
M. NERO
7410'
STARIJSKI VRH
M. ROSSO
6489'
Dreznica
RDECI ROB
KOZLJAK
VEL. STADOR
Robic
Caporetto
PLECE
Natisone
Tolminka
Krn
2500'
SLEME
4461'
Idresca
M. MATAJUR
5100'
MRZLI
4500'
Selisce
Gabrje
VODIL
3132'
MRZLI VRH
Luico
Foni
1800'
KOLOVRAT
Montemaggiore
Dolje
TOLMINO
M. KUK
P. Zagradan
3200'
HLEVNIK
2500'
PODKLABUC
3500'
Poljubinj
Polava
Volzana
M. JEZA
3000'
M. S. GIORGIO
S. MARTINO
S. Lucia
Savogna
Gighinj
KOZMARICE
Baca
Idria
M. KUM
Alberone
Cosizza
Doblar River
M. S. MARIA M.
GLOBOCAK
2500'
Isonzo
M. CUCLE
Kambresko
Erbezzo
Judrio Cr.
Lom di Tolmino
Doblar

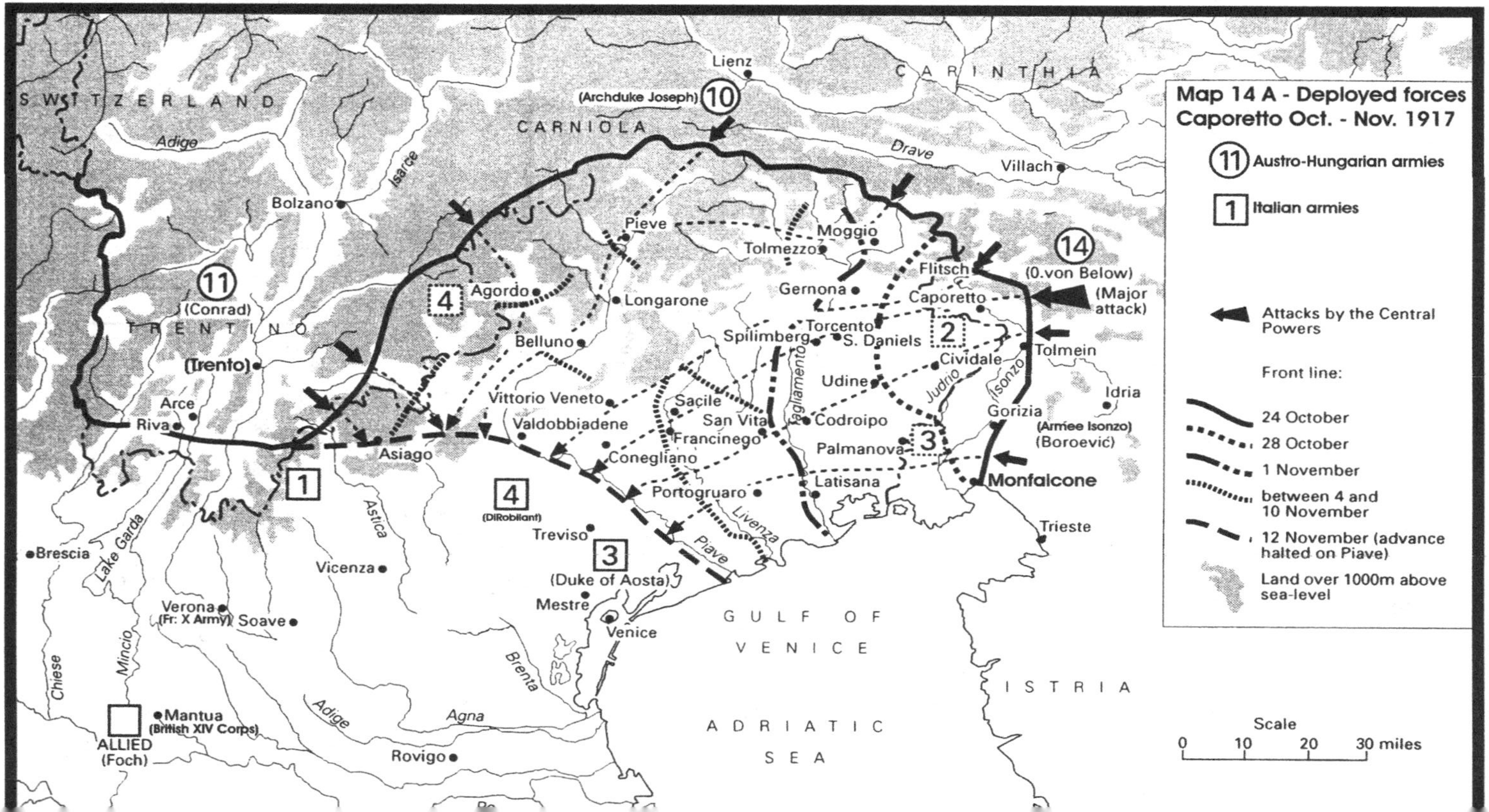
Map 14 A - Deployed forces
Caporetto Oct. - Nov. 1917
11 Austro-Hungarian armies
1 Italian armies
Attacks by the Central Powers
Front line:
24 October
28 October
1 November
between 4 and 10 November
12 November (advance halted on Piave)
Land over 1000m above sea-level
Scale
0 10 20 30 miles
SWITZERLAND
CARINTHIA
CARNIOLA
TRENTINO
Lienz
(Archduke Joseph) 10
Adige
Isarce
Drave
Villach
Bolzano
Pieve
Moggio
Tolmezzo
Flitsch
14
(0.von Below)
(Major attack)
11
(Conrad)
Agordo
4
Longarone
Gernona
Caporetto
Torcento
2
Spilimberg
S. Daniels
Tolmein
Belluno
Cividale
(Trento)
Isonzo
Idria
Judrio
Udine
Vittorio Veneto
Tagliamento
Sacile
Arce
Riva
San Vita
Codroipo
Gorizia
Valdobbiadene
(Armée Isonzo)
(Boroević)
Francinego
3
Palmanova
Asiago
Conegliano
Monfalcone
1
Latisana
Portogruaro
4
(DiRobilant)
Livenza
Astica
Trieste
Treviso
Piave
3
Brescia
Lake Garda
Vicenza
(Duke of Aosta)
Verona
(Fr: X Army)
Soave
Mestre
Venice
GULF OF VENICE
Brenta
Chiese
Mincio
ISTRIA
Mantua
(British XIV Corps)
Adige
Agna
ADRIATIC SEA
ALLIED
(Foch)
Rovigo

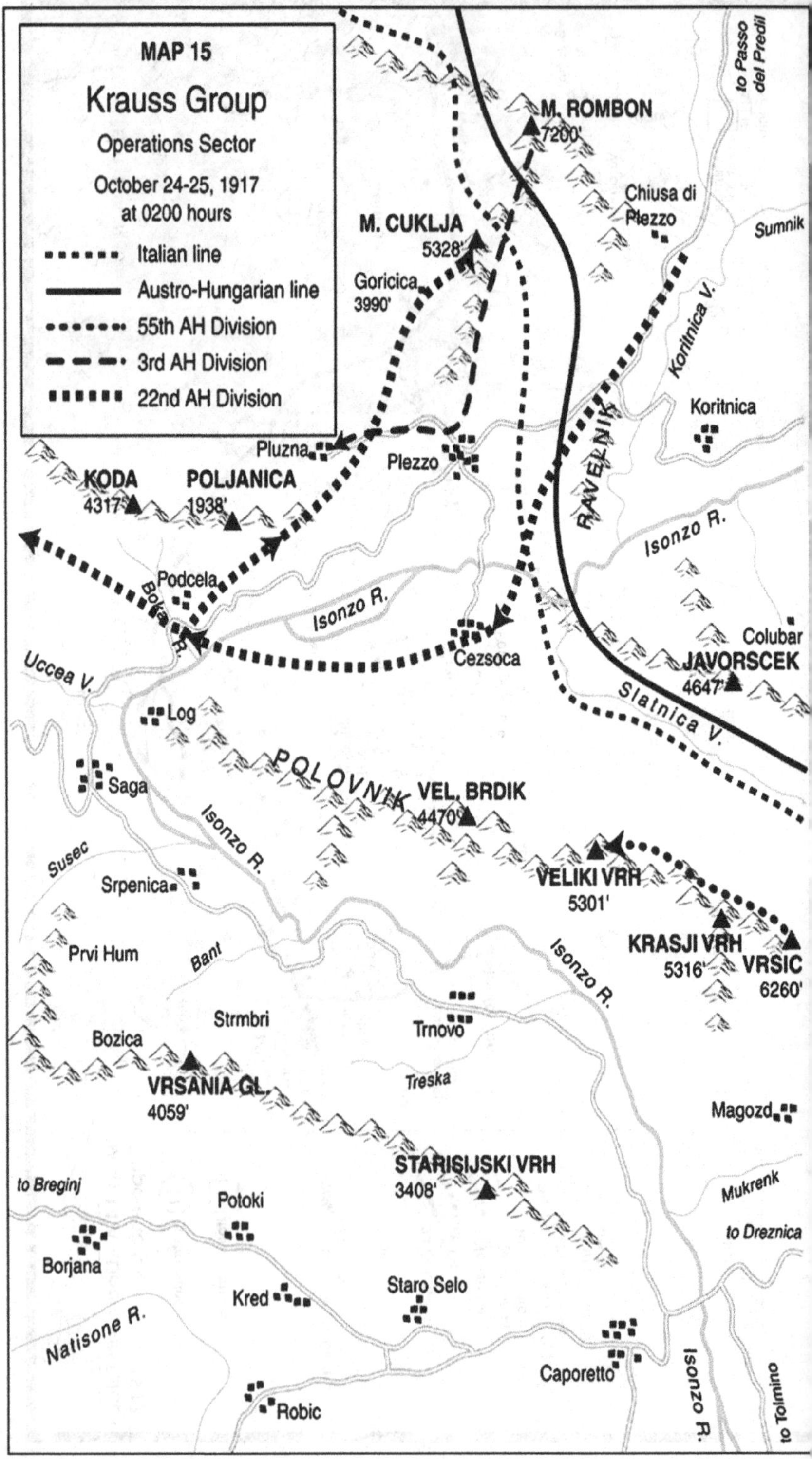
MAP 15
Krauss Group
Operations Sector
October 24-25, 1917
at 0200 hours
Italian line
Austro-Hungarian line
55th AH Division
3rd AH Division
22nd AH Division
to Passo del Predil
M. ROMBON
7200'
Chiusa di Plezzo
Sumnik
M. CUKLJA
5328'
Goricica
3990'
Koritnica V.
RAVELNIK
Koritnica
Pluzna
Plezzo
KODA
4317'
POLJANICA
1938'
Isonzo R.
Podcela
Boka R.
Isonzo R.
Cezsoca
Colubar
JAVORSCEK
4647'
Uccea V.
Slatnica V.
Log
Saga
POLOVNIK
VEL. BRDIK
4470'
Isonzo R.
Susec
Srpenica
VELIKI VRH
5301'
KRASJI VRH
5316'
VRSIC
6260'
Prvi Hum
Bant
Isonzo R.
Strmbri
Trnovo
Bozica
VRSANIA GL.
4059'
Treska
Magozd
STARISIJSKI VRH
3408'
to Breginj
Mukrenk
Potoki
to Dreznica
Borjana
Staro Selo
Kred
Natisone R.
Caporetto
Isonzo R.
Robic
to Tolmino

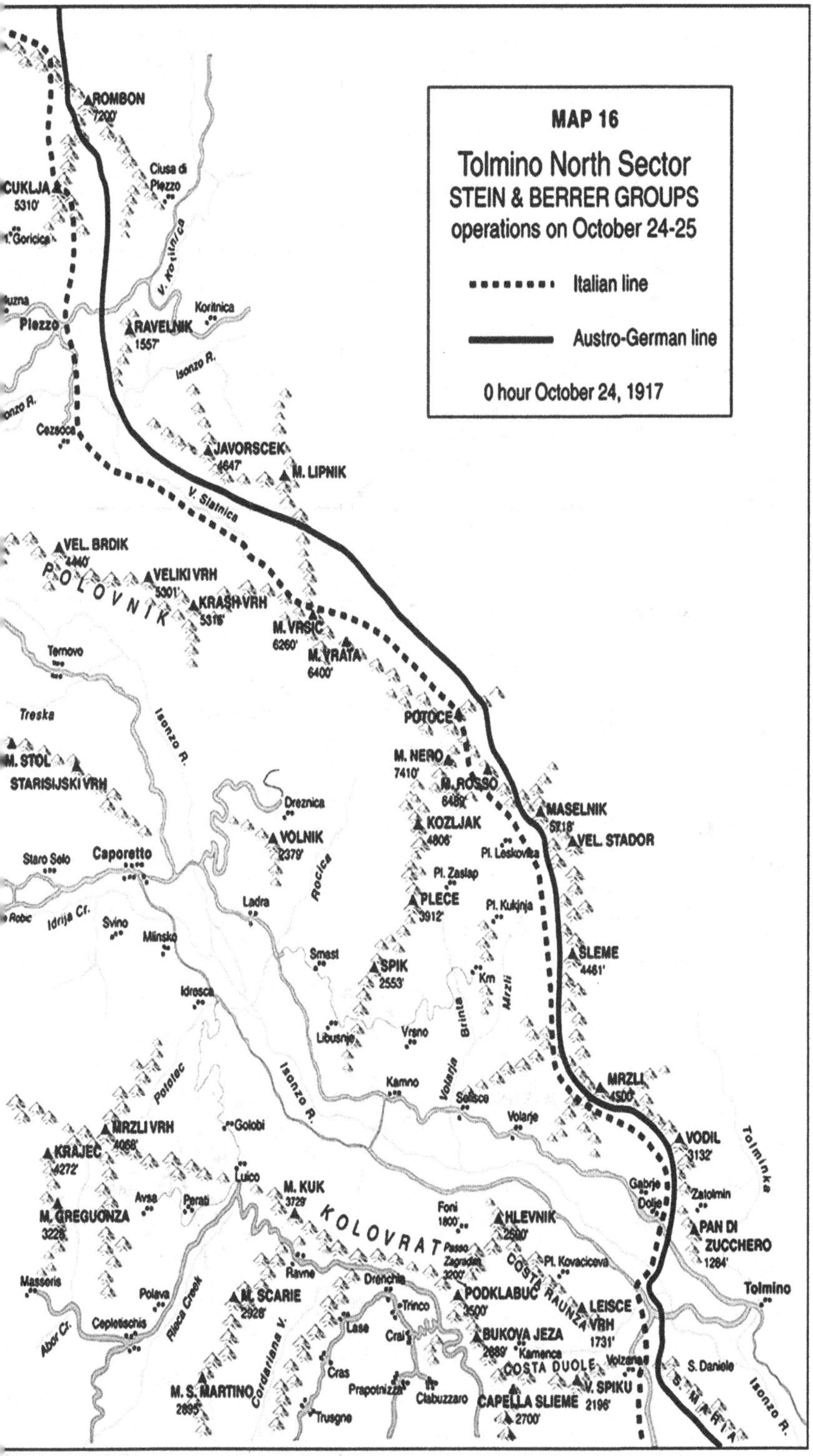
MAP 16
Tolmino North Sector
STEIN & BERRER GROUPS
operations on October 24-25
Italian line
Austro-German line
0 hour October 24, 1917
ROMBON
7200'
Clusa di Plezzo
CUKLJA
5310'
V. Koritnica
Koritnica
Plezzo
RAVELNIK
1557'
Isonzo R.
Cezsoca
JAVORSCEK
4647'
M. LIPNIK
V. Slatnica
VEL. BRDIK
4440'
POLOVNIK
VELIKI VRH
5301'
KRASJI VRH
5316'
M. VRSIC
6260'
M. VRATA
6400'
Ternovo
Treska
Isonzo R.
POTOCE
M. STOL
STARISIJSKI VRH
M. NERO
7410'
M. ROSSO
Dreznica
MASELNIK
KOZLJAK
4806'
VOLNIK
2379'
VEL. STADOR
Pl. Leskovica
Staro Selo
Caporetto
Pl. Zaslap
Rocica
Idrija Cr.
Ladra
PLECE
3912'
Pl. Kukjnja
Svino
Mlinsko
Smast
SPIK
2553'
SLEME
4461'
Km
Mrzli
Idrosca
Brinta
Libusnje
Vrsno
Isonzo R.
Kamno
Volarja
MRZLI
4500'
Pototec
Selisce
Volarje
Golobi
MRZLI VRH
4068'
VODIL
3132'
KRAJEC
4272'
Tolminka
Luico
M. KUK
3729'
Gabrje
Zatolmin
Dolje
Avsa
Perati
M. GREGUONZA
3226'
KOLOVRAT
Foni
1800'
HLEVNIK
2590'
PAN DI ZUCCHERO
1284'
Passo Zagradan
3200'
Pl. Kovacicova
Ravne
COSTA RAUNZA
Masseris
Drenchia
Tolmino
M. SCARIE
2926'
PODKLABUC
3500'
LEISCE VRH
1731'
Polava
Trinco
Abor Cr.
Cepletischis
Rieca Creek
Lase
Cras
BUKOVA JEZA
2680'
Kamenca
Volzana
S. Daniele
Cras
COSTA DUOLE
V. SPIKU
2196'
Cosiarlana V.
S. MARIA
Isonzo R.
M. S. MARTINO
2895'
Prapotnizza
Clabuzzaro
CAPELLA SLIEME
2700'
Trusgne

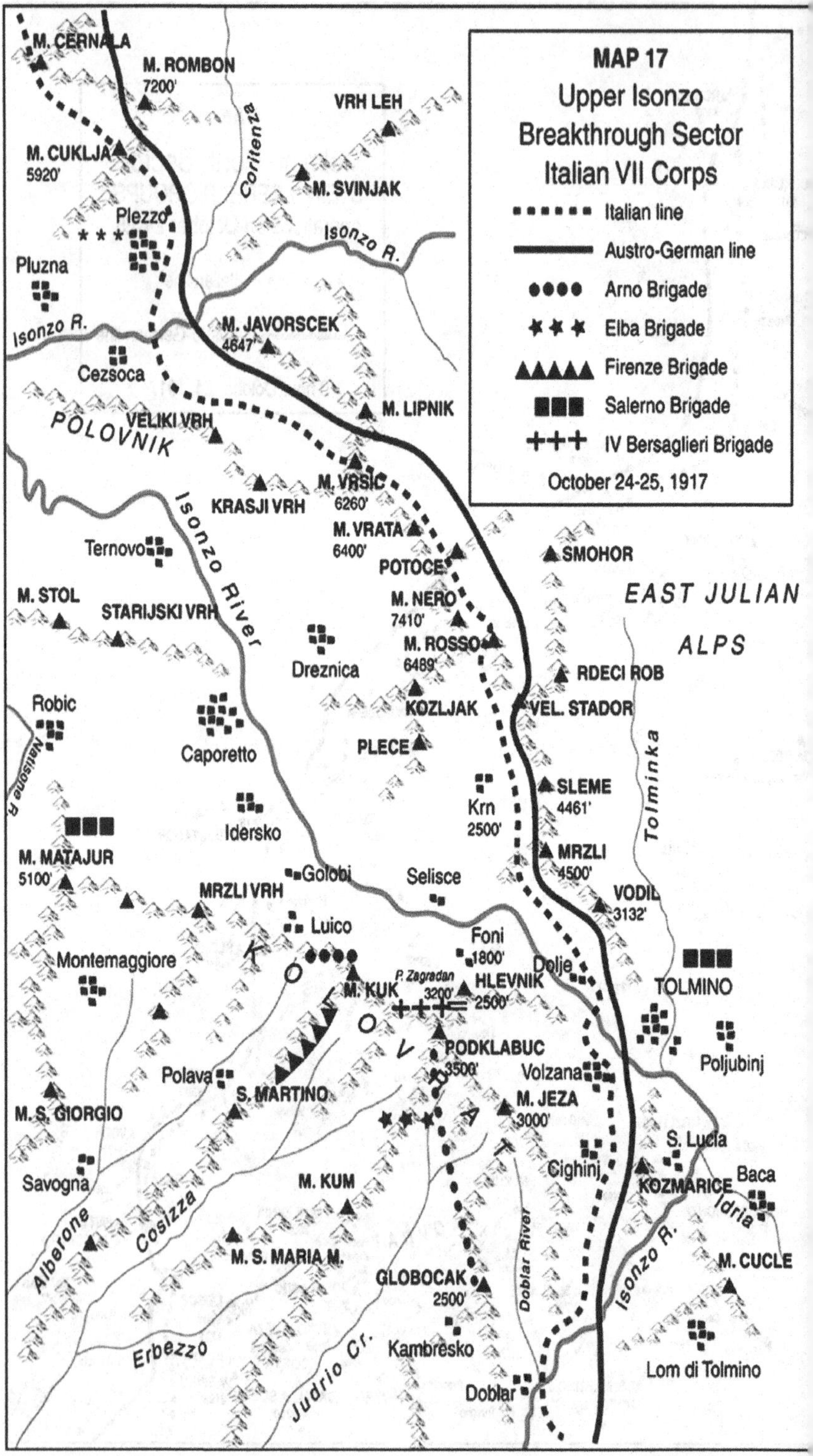
MAP 17
Upper Isonzo
Breakthrough Sector
Italian VII Corps
Italian line
Austro-German line
Arno Brigade
Elba Brigade
Firenze Brigade
Salerno Brigade
IV Bersaglieri Brigade
October 24-25, 1917
M. CERNALA
M. ROMBON
7200'
VRH LEH
Coritenza
M. CUKLJA
5920'
M. SVINJAK
Plezzo
Isonzo R.
Pluzna
Isonzo R.
M. JAVORSCEK
4647'
Cezsoca
M. LIPNIK
POLOVNIK
VELIKI VRH
M. VRSIC
6260'
KRASJI VRH
Isonzo River
M. VRATA
6400'
Ternovo
POTOCE
SMOHOR
M. STOL
STARIJSKI VRH
M. NERO
7410'
EAST JULIAN
ALPS
M. ROSSO
6489'
Dreznica
RDECI ROB
Robic
KOZLJAK
VEL. STADOR
Natisone R.
Caporetto
PLECE
Tolminka
SLEME
4461'
Krn
2500'
Idersko
M. MATAJUR
5100'
MRZLI
4500'
Golobi
Selisce
MRZLI VRH
VODIL
3132'
Luico
Foni
1800'
Montemaggiore
KOLOVRAT
Dolje
TOLMINO
M. KUK
P. Zagradan
3200'
HLEVNIK
2500'
PODKLABUC
3500'
Poljubinj
Polava
Volzana
S. MARTINO
M. JEZA
3000'
M. S. GIORGIO
S. Lucia
Savogna
Cighinj
KOZMARICE
Baca
M. KUM
Idria
Alberone
Cosizza
M. S. MARIA M.
Doblar River
Isonzo R.
M. CUCLE
GLOBOCAK
2500'
Erbezzo
Kambresko
Judrio Cr.
Lom di Tolmino
Doblar

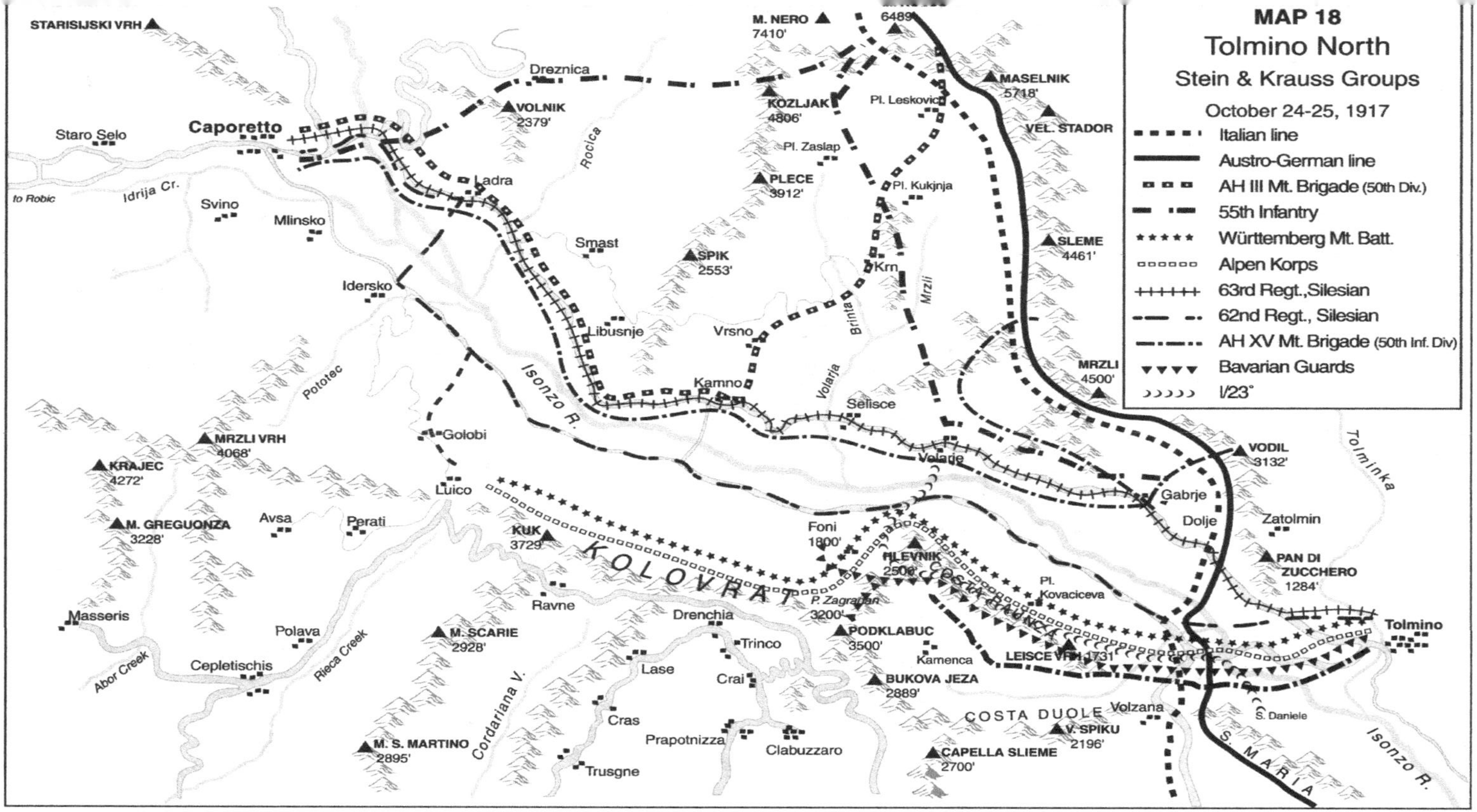
MAP 18
Tolmino North
Stein & Krauss Groups
October 24-25, 1917
Italian line
Austro-German line
AH III Mt. Brigade (50th Div.)
55th Infantry
Württemberg Mt. Batt.
Alpen Korps
63rd Regt., Silesian
62nd Regt., Silesian
AH XV Mt. Brigade (50th Inf. Div)
Bavarian Guards
I/23°
STARISIJSKI VRH
M. NERO 7410'
6489'
MASELNIK 5718'
VEL. STADOR
Dreznica
VOLNIK 2379'
KOZLJAK 4806'
Pl. Leskovic
Pl. Zaslap
Pl. Kukjnja
PLECE 3912'
SLEME 4461'
Caporetto
Staro Selo
to Robic
Idrija Cr.
Svino
Mlinsko
Ladra
Rocica
Smast
SPIK 2553'
Krn
Mrzli
Idersko
Libusnje
Vrsno
Brinta
Volaria
Kamno
Selisce
MRZLI 4500'
Isonzo R.
Pototec
Golobi
MRZLI VRH 4068'
KRAJEC 4272'
Luico
Volarje
VODIL 3132'
Tolminka
Gabrje
Dolje
Zatolmin
PAN DI ZUCCHERO 1284'
M. GREGUONZA 3228'
Avsa
Perati
KUK 3729'
KOLOVRAT
Foni 1800'
HLEVNIK 2500'
COSTA RAUNZA
Pl. Kovaciceva
P. Zagradan 3200'
PODKLABUC 3500'
Kamenca
LEISCE VRH 1731'
Tolmino
Masseris
Ravne
Drenchia
Trinco
Polava
M. SCARIE 2928'
Lase
Crai
BUKOVA JEZA 2889'
Abor Creek
Cepletischis
Rieca Creek
Cordariana V.
Cras
COSTA DUOLE
Volzana
V. SPIKU 2196'
S. Daniele
Prapotnizza
Clabuzzaro
CAPELLA SLIEME 2700'
M. S. MARTINO 2895'
Trusgne
S. MARIA
Isonzo R.

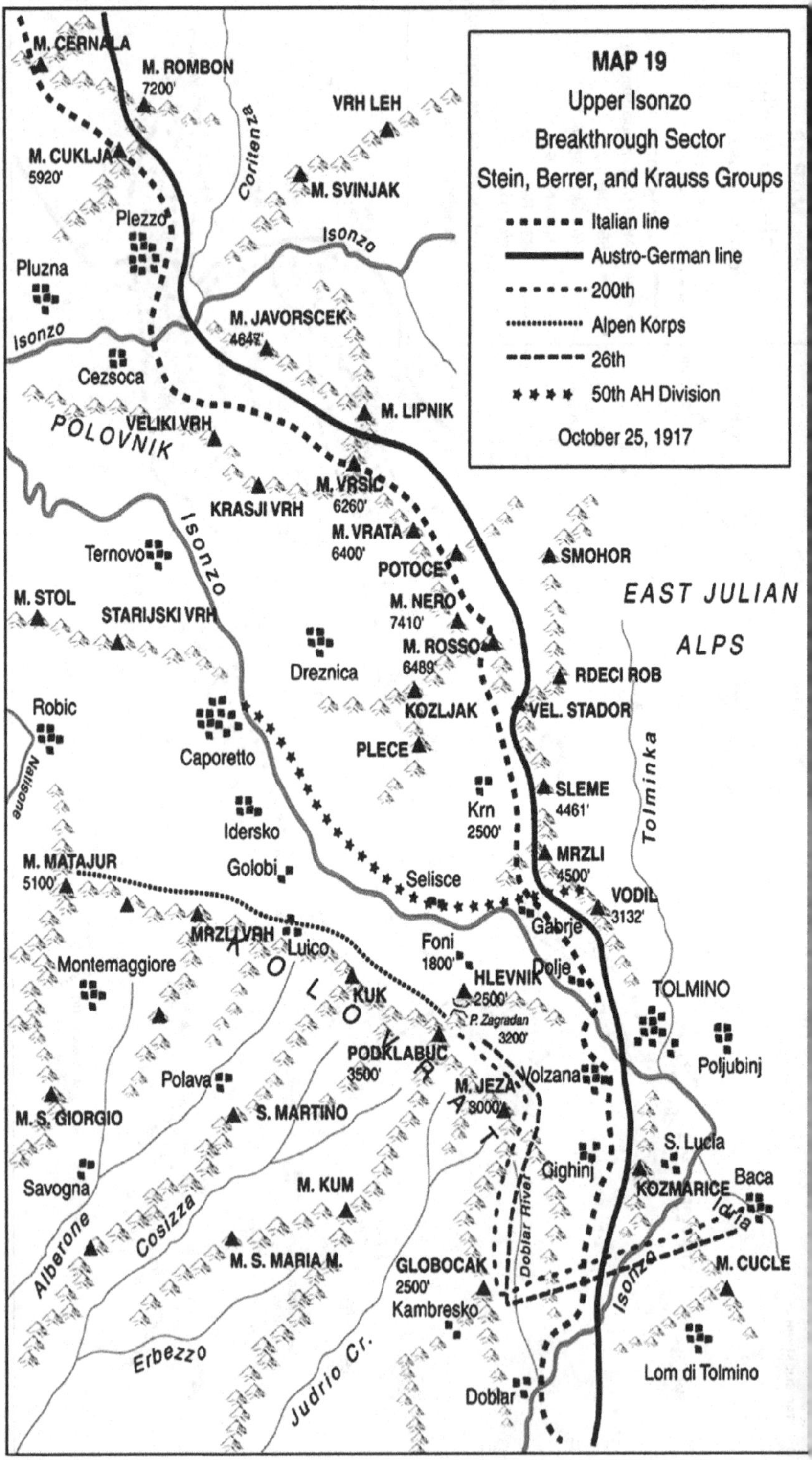
MAP 19
Upper Isonzo
Breakthrough Sector
Stein, Berrer, and Krauss Groups
Italian line
Austro-German line
200th
Alpen Korps
26th
50th AH Division
October 25, 1917
M. CERNALA
M. ROMBON
7200'
VRH LEH
Coritenza
M. CUKLJA
5920'
M. SVINJAK
Plezzo
Isonzo
Pluzna
M. JAVORSCEK
4647'
Cezsoca
M. LIPNIK
POLOVNIK
VELIKI VRH
M. VRSIC
6260'
KRASJI VRH
M. VRATA
6400'
Ternovo
POTOCE
SMOHOR
EAST JULIAN
ALPS
M. STOL
STARIJSKI VRH
M. NERO
7410'
M. ROSSO
6489'
Dreznica
RDECI ROB
Robic
KOZLJAK
VEL. STADOR
Caporetto
PLECE
Natisone
SLEME
4461'
Krn
2500'
Tolminka
Idersko
M. MATAJUR
5100'
Golobi
Selisce
MRZLI
4500'
VODIL
3132'
Gabrje
MRZLI VRH
Luico
Foni
1800'
KOLOVRAT
Montemaggiore
HLEVNIK
2500'
Dolje
KUK
TOLMINO
P. Zagradan
3200'
PODKLABUC
3500'
Polava
Volzana
Poljubinj
M. S. GIORGIO
S. MARTINO
M. JEZA
3000'
S. Lucia
Savogna
M. KUM
Gighinj
KOZMARICE
Baca
Idria
Alberone
Cosizza
Doblar River
M. S. MARIA M.
GLOBOCAK
2500'
Kambresko
Isonzo
M. CUCLE
Erbezzo
Judrio Cr.
Lom di Tolmino
Doblar

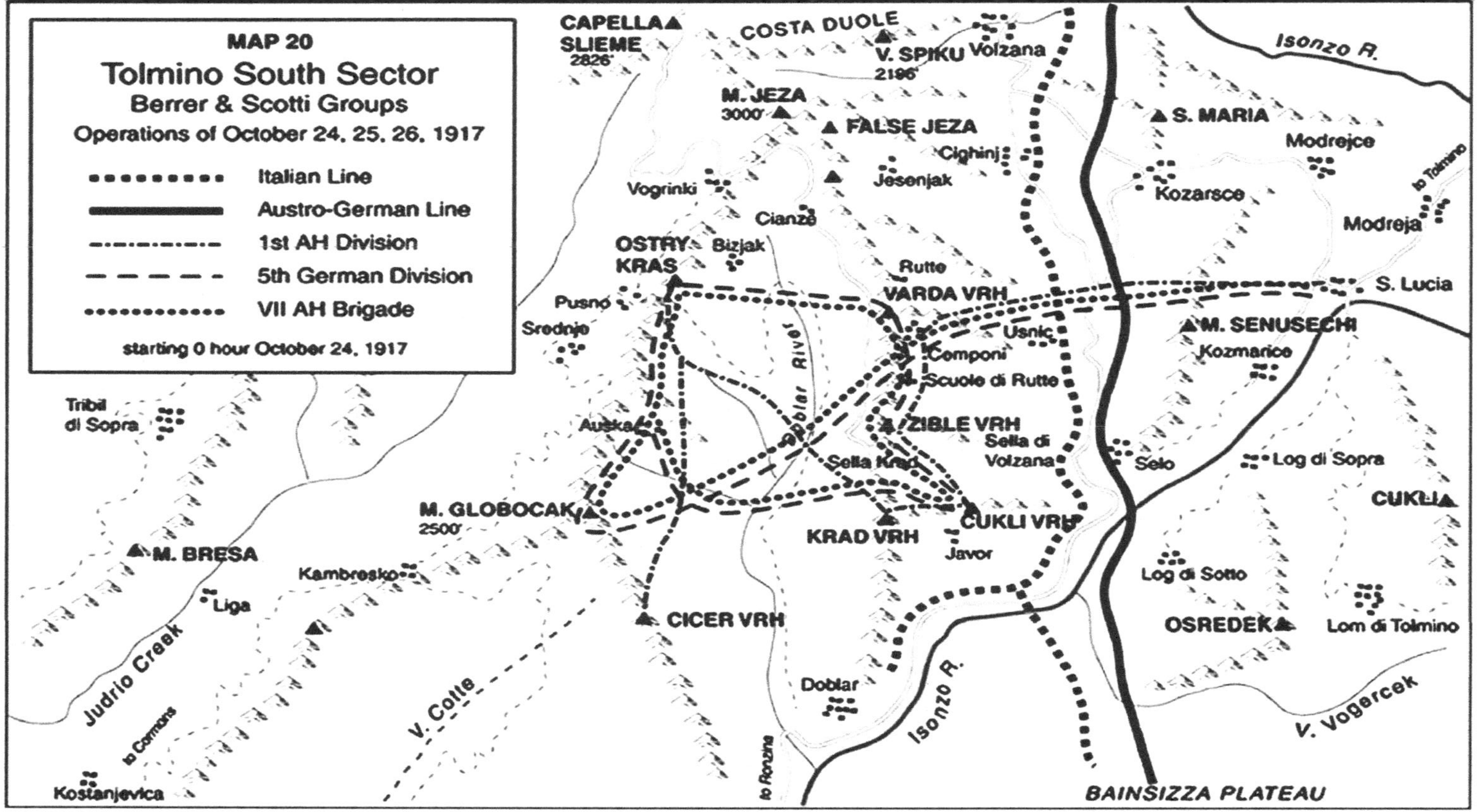

MAP 20
Tolmino South Sector
Berrer & Scotti Groups
Operations of October 24. 25. 26. 1917
Italian Line
Austro-German Line
1st AH Division
5th German Division
VII AH Brigade
starting 0 hour October 24. 1917
CAPELLA
SLIEME
2826'
COSTA DUOLE
V. SPIKU
2196'
Volzana
Isonzo R.
M. JEZA
3000'
FALSE JEZA
S. MARIA
Modrejce
Cighinj
Jesenjak
Kozarsce
to Tolmino
Vogrinki
Cianze
Modreja
OSTRY
KRAS
Bizjak
Rutte
VARDA VRH
S. Lucia
Pusno
Srednje
Usnic
M. SENUSECHI
Componi
Kozmarico
Scuole di Rutte
Tribil
di Sopra
Dolbar River
Auska
ZIBLE VRH
Sella di
Volzana
Sella Krad
Selo
Log di Sopra
CUKLI
M. GLOBOCAK
2500'
CUKLI VRH
KRAD VRH
Javor
M. BRESA
Kambresko
Log di Sotto
Liga
CICER VRH
OSREDEK
Lom di Tolmino
Judrio Creek
V. Colle
Doblar
Isonzo R.
V. Vogercek
to Cormons
Kostanjevica
to Ronzina
BAINSIZZA PLATEAU

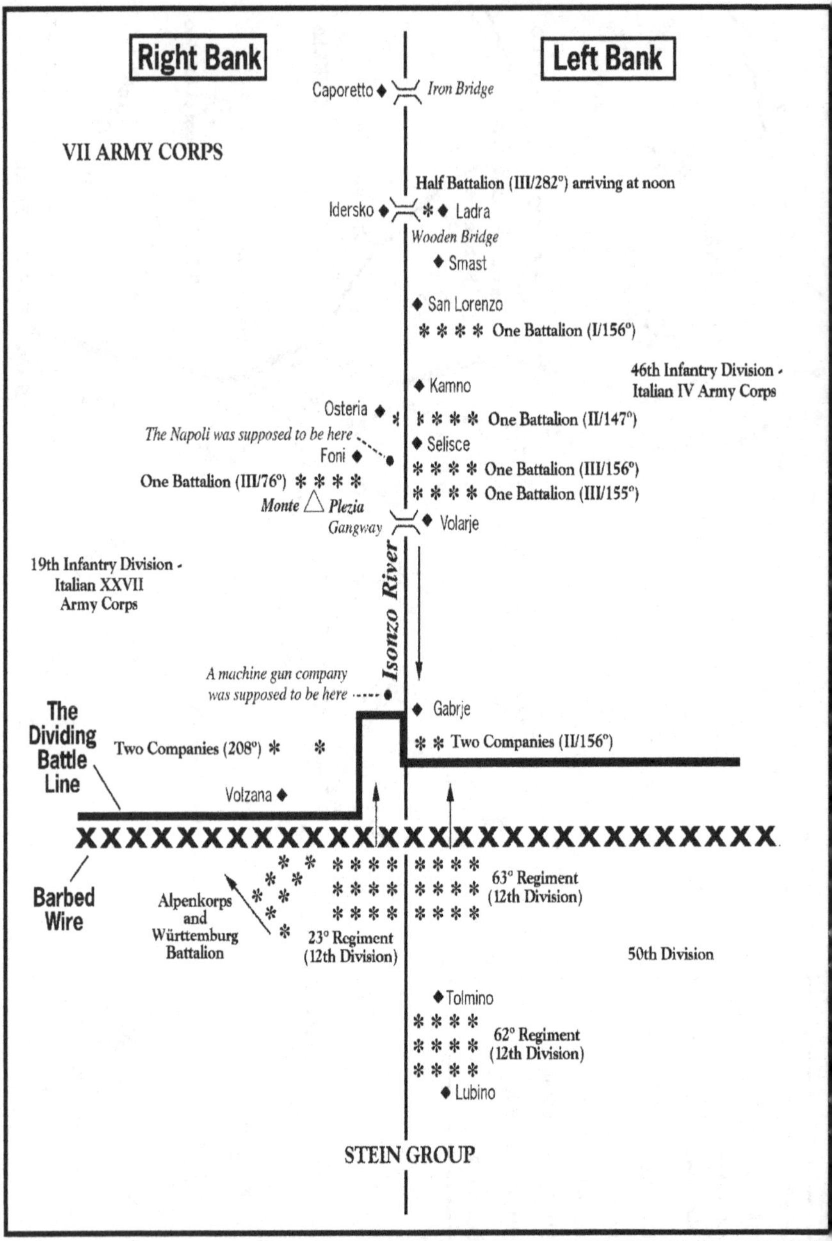

Map 21:
Schematic of the 12th Silesian up the Isonzo River

Advance of the 12th Silesian from Tolmino to Caporetto on October 24, 1917.
Each asterisk (*) represents a company. Four companies are in a battalion (except the Württemburg Battalion).
Actually, a battalion of the 23° Infantry advanced along the left bank of the Isonzo and crossed via the gangway at Volarie.

One Battalion (III/155°) means One Battalion (the III of the 155th Infantry Regiment).
53° Infantry means 53rd Infantry Regiment.

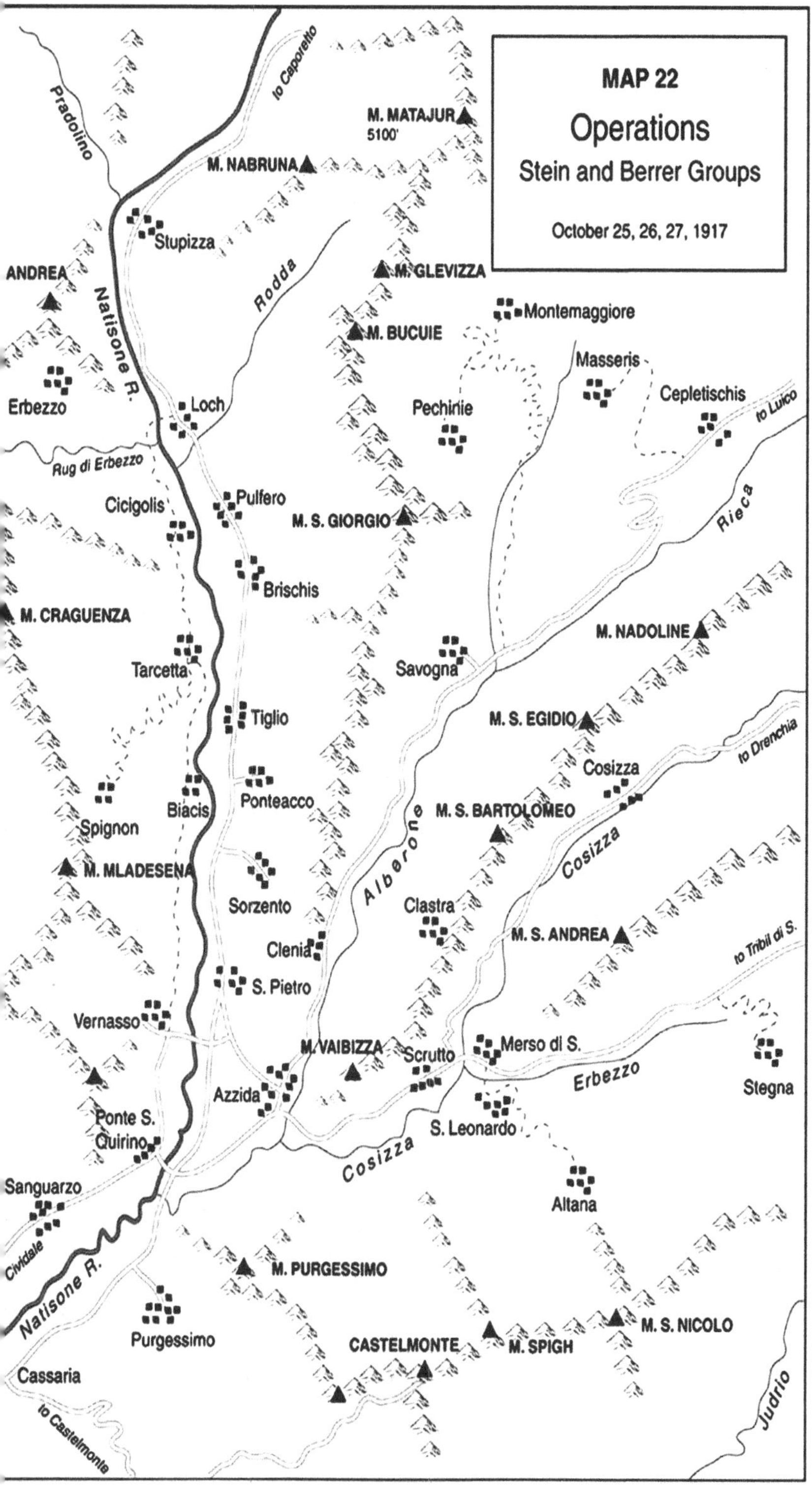
MAP 22
Operations
Stein and Berrer Groups
October 25, 26, 27, 1917
to Caporetto
Pradolino
M. MATAJUR
5100'
M. NABRUNA
Stupizza
Rodda
ANDREA
Natisone R.
M. GLEVIZZA
Montemaggiore
M. BUCUIE
Masseris
Erbezzo
Loch
Pechinie
Cepletischis
to Luico
Rug di Erbezzo
Cicigolis
Pulfero
M. S. GIORGIO
Rieca
Brischis
M. CRAGUENZA
M. NADOLINE
Tarcetta
Savogna
Tiglio
M. S. EGIDIO
to Drenchia
Cosizza
Spignon
Biacis
Ponteacco
M. S. BARTOLOMEO
Alberone
M. MLADESENA
Cosizza
Sorzento
Clastra
M. S. ANDREA
Clenia
S. Pietro
to Tribil di S.
Vernasso
M. VAIBIZZA
Scrutto
Merso di S.
Erbezzo
Stegna
Azzida
Ponte S.
Quirino
S. Leonardo
Cosizza
Sanguarzo
Altana
Cividale
M. PURGESSIMO
Natisone R.
M. S. NICOLO
Purgessimo
CASTELMONTE
M. SPIGH
Cassaria
Judrio
to Castelmonte

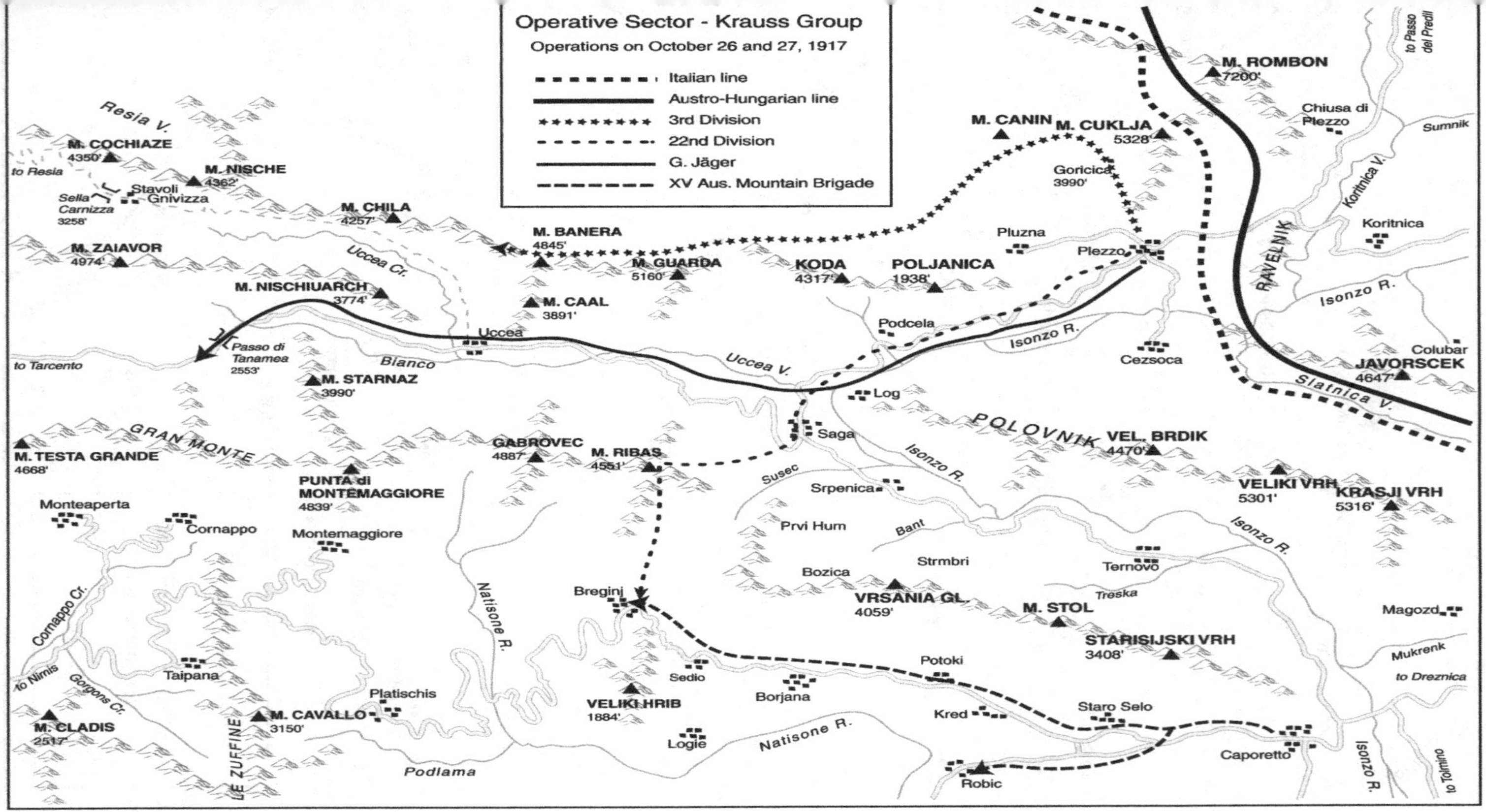
Operative Sector - Krauss Group
Operations on October 26 and 27, 1917
Italian line
Austro-Hungarian line
3rd Division
22nd Division
G. Jäger
XV Aus. Mountain Brigade
Resia V.
M. COCHIAZE
4350'
to Resia
M. NISCHE
4362'
Stavoli
Gnivizza
Sella Carnizza
3258'
M. CHILA
4257'
M. BANERA
4845'
M. ZAIAVOR
4974'
Uccea Cr.
M. GUARDA
5160'
KODA
4317'
POLJANICA
1938'
M. NISCHIUARCH
3774'
M. CAAL
3891'
Uccea
Passo di Tanamea
2553'
to Tarcento
Bianco
Uccea V.
M. STARNAZ
3990'
M. CANIN
M. CUKLJA
5328'
Goricica
3990'
Pluzna
Plezzo
Podcela
Isonzo R.
Cezsoca
M. ROMBON
7200'
Chiusa di Plezzo
Sumnik
to Passo del Predil
Koritnica V.
Koritnica
RAVELNIK
Isonzo R.
Colubar
JAVORSCEK
4647'
Slatnica V.
Log
POLOVNIK
VEL. BRDIK
4470'
Saga
GRAN MONTE
M. TESTA GRANDE
4668'
GABROVEC
4887'
M. RIBAS
4551'
PUNTA di MONTEMAGGIORE
4839'
Isonzo R.
Susec
Srpenica
VELIKI VRH
5301'
KRASJI VRH
5316'
Monteaperta
Cornappo
Montemaggiore
Prvi Hum
Bant
Isonzo R.
Strmbri
Bozica
Ternovo
Natisone R.
Breginj
VRSANIA GL.
4059'
Treska
M. STOL
Magozd
Cornappo Cr.
STARISIJSKI VRH
3408'
Mukrenk
Taipana
Potoki
to Nimis
Gorgons Cr.
Sedio
Borjana
to Dreznica
Platischis
VELIKI HRIB
1884'
Kred
Staro Selo
M. CLADIS
2517'
M. CAVALLO
3150'
LE ZUFFINE
Logie
Natisone R.
Caporetto
Isonzo R.
to Tolmino
Podlama
Robic

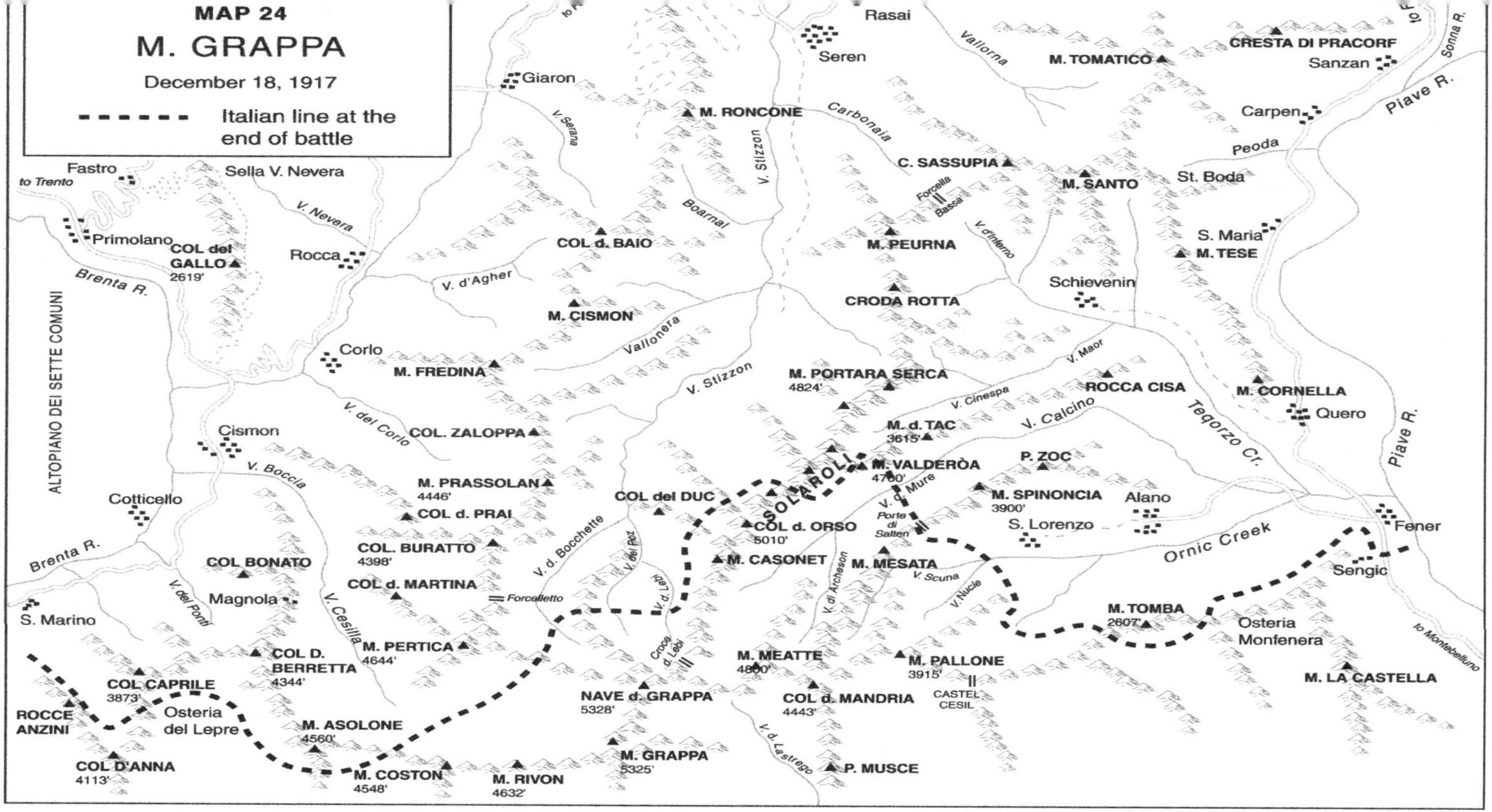
MAP 24
M. GRAPPA
December 18, 1917
Italian line at the end of battle
Fastro
to Trento
Sella V. Nevera
Primolano
COL del GALLO 2619'
Rocca
V. Nevera
Brenta R.
ALTOPIANO DEI SETTE COMUNI
Corlo
Cismon
V. Boccia
Cotticello
Brenta R.
S. Marino
Giaron
V. Serana
COL d. BAIO
V. d'Agher
M. CISMON
M. FREDINA
V. del Corlo
COL. ZALOPPA
M. PRASSOLAN 4446'
COL d. PRAI
COL. BURATTO 4398'
COL d. MARTINA
Forcelletto
COL BONATO
Magnola
V. del Ponti
V. Cesilla
M. PERTICA 4644'
COL D. BERRETTA 4344'
COL CAPRILE 3873'
ROCCE ANZINI
Osteria del Lepre
COL D'ANNA 4113'
M. ASOLONE 4560'
M. COSTON 4548'
M. RIVON 4632'
M. GRAPPA 5325'
NAVE d. GRAPPA 5328'
Croce d. Lebi
V. d. Lebi
V. del Poz
V. d. Bocchette
COL del DUC
M. RONCONE
Boarnal
V. Stizzon
Vallonera
V. Stizzon
Rasai
Seren
Carbonaia
Vallorna
C. SASSUPIA
Forcella Bassa
M. PEURNA
V. d'Inferno
CRODA ROTTA
M. PORTARA SERCA 4824'
M. d. TAC 3615'
SOLAROLI
M. VALDERÒA 4760'
COL d. ORSO 5010'
M. CASONET
V. d. Mure
Porte di Salten
M. MESATA
V. di Archeson
M. MEATTE 4800'
COL d. MANDRIA 4443'
V. d. Lastrego
P. MUSCE
M. PALLONE 3915'
CASTEL CESIL
V. Scuna
V. Nucie
M. TOMATICO
CRESTA DI PRACORF
Sanzan
Sonna R.
Carpen
Piave R.
Peoda
M. SANTO
St. Boda
S. Maria
M. TESE
Schievenin
V. Maor
ROCCA CISA
V. Cinespa
V. Calcino
M. CORNELLA
Quero
Teqorzo Cr.
Piave R.
P. ZOC
M. SPINONCIA 3900'
Alano
S. Lorenzo
Fener
Ornic Creek
Sengic
M. TOMBA 2607'
Osteria Monfenera
to Montebelluno
M. LA CASTELLA

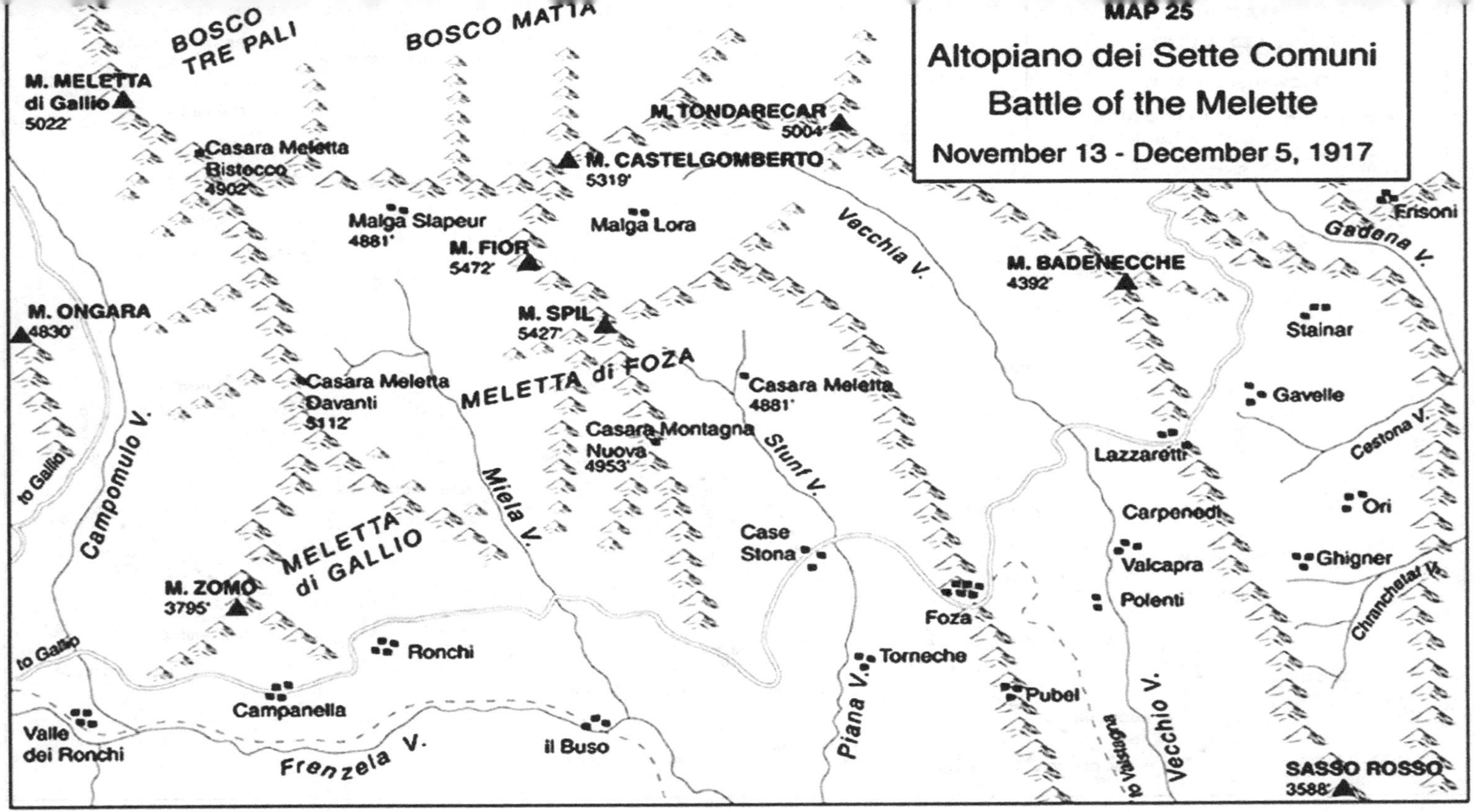

MAP 25

Altopiano dei Sette Comuni
Battle of the Melette
November 13 - December 5, 1917

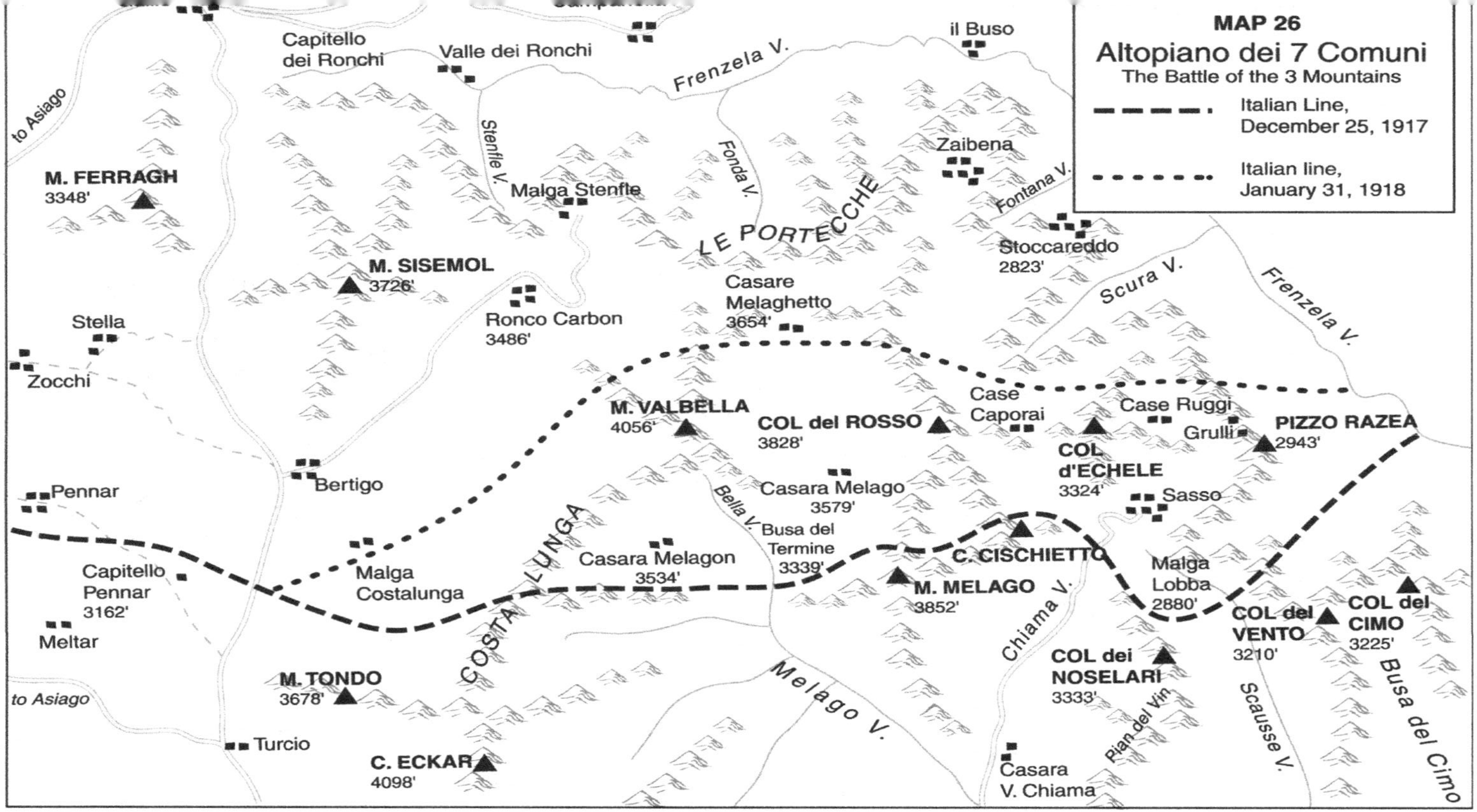
MAP 26
Altopiano dei 7 Comuni
The Battle of the 3 Mountains
Italian Line, December 25, 1917
Italian line, January 31, 1918
il Buso
Capitello dei Ronchi
Valle dei Ronchi
Frenzela V.
to Asiago
Stenfle V.
Fonda V.
Zaibena
Fontana V.
M. FERRAGH 3348'
Malga Stenfle
LE PORTECCHE
Stoccareddo 2823'
M. SISEMOL 3726'
Casare Melaghetto 3654'
Scura V.
Frenzela V.
Stella
Ronco Carbon 3486'
Zocchi
M. VALBELLA 4056'
COL del ROSSO 3828'
Case Caporai
Case Ruggi
Grulli
PIZZO RAZEA 2943'
COL d'ECHELE 3324'
Bertigo
Pennar
Casara Melago 3579'
Sasso
Bella V.
Busa del Termine 3339'
C. CISCHIETTO
Malga Lobba 2880'
COSTA LUNGA
Casara Melagon 3534'
Capitello Pennar 3162'
Malga Costalunga
M. MELAGO 3852'
Chiama V.
COL del VENTO 3210'
COL del CIMO 3225'
Meltar
COL dei NOSELARI 3333'
M. TONDO 3678'
to Asiago
Melago V.
Scausse V.
Busa del Cimo
Pian del Vin
Turcio
C. ECKAR 4098'
Casara V. Chiama

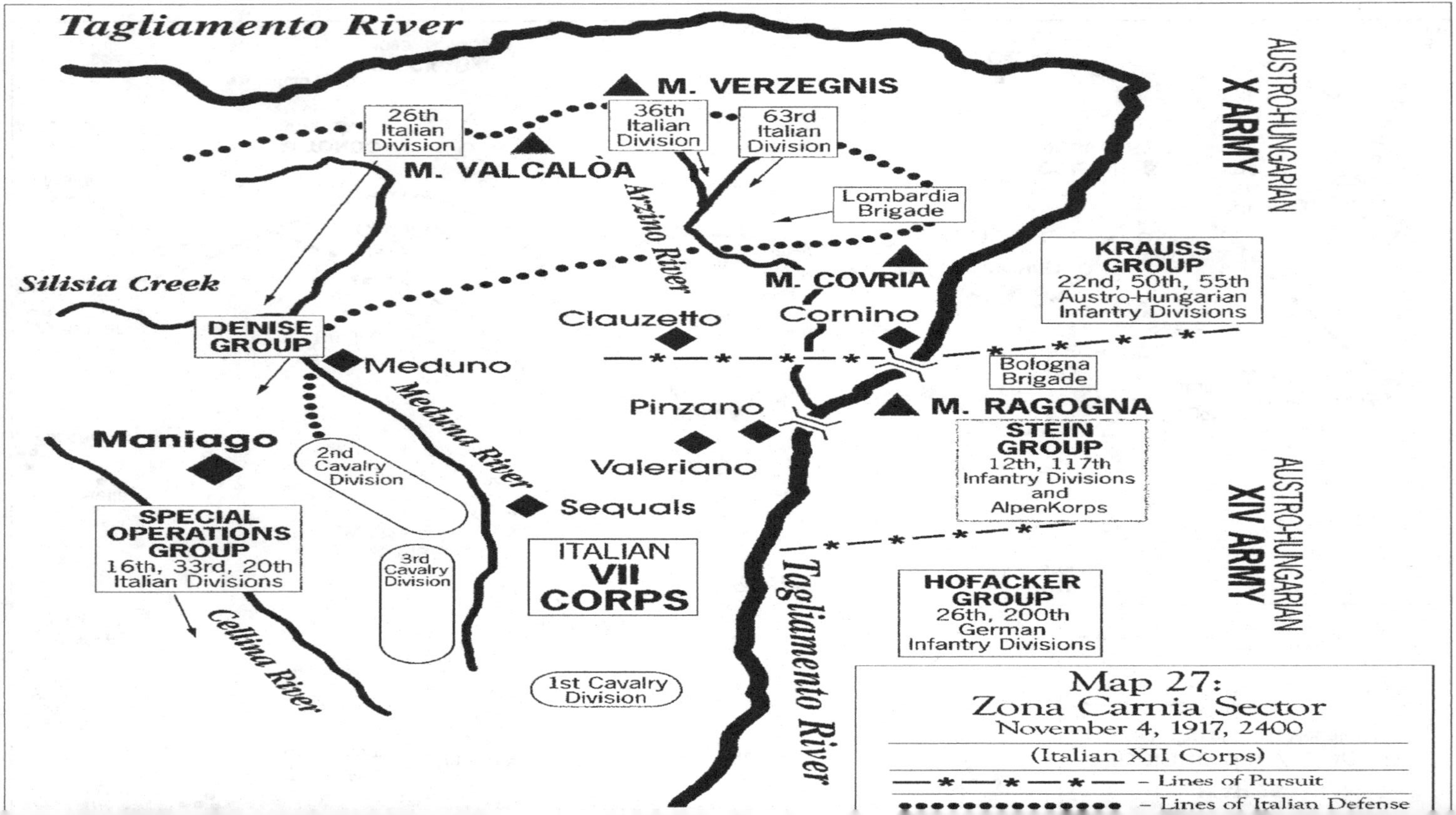
Tagliamento River
M. VERZEGNIS
26th Italian Division
36th Italian Division
63rd Italian Division
M. VALCALÒA
Arzino River
Lombardia Brigade
AUSTRO-HUNGARIAN
X ARMY
KRAUSS GROUP
22nd, 50th, 55th Austro-Hungarian Infantry Divisions
M. COVRIA
Silisia Creek
Clauzetto
Cornino
DENISE GROUP
Meduno
Bologna Brigade
Meduna River
Pinzano
M. RAGOGNA
STEIN GROUP
12th, 117th Infantry Divisions and AlpenKorps
Maniago
2nd Cavalry Division
Valeriano
Sequals
AUSTRO-HUNGARIAN
XIV ARMY
SPECIAL OPERATIONS GROUP
16th, 33rd, 20th Italian Divisions
3rd Cavalry Division
ITALIAN
VII
CORPS
Tagliamento River
HOFACKER GROUP
26th, 200th German Infantry Divisions
Cellina River
1st Cavalry Division
Map 27:
Zona Carnia Sector
November 4, 1917, 2400
(Italian XII Corps)
– Lines of Pursuit
– Lines of Italian Defense

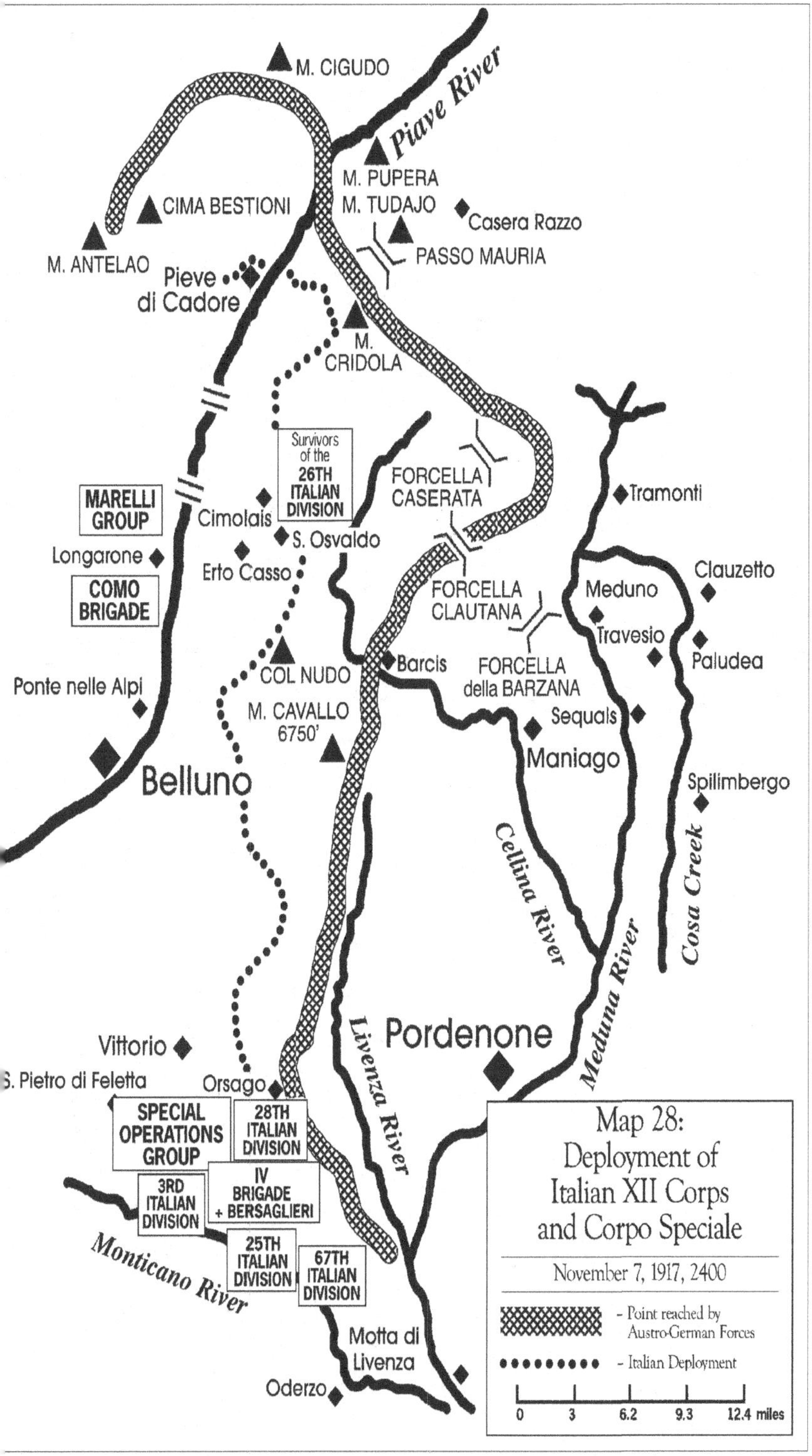
M. CIGUDO
Piave River
M. PUPERA
M. TUDAJO
CIMA BESTIONI
Casera Razzo
PASSO MAURIA
M. ANTELAO
Pieve di Cadore
M. CRIDOLA
Survivors of the 26TH ITALIAN DIVISION
FORCELLA CASERATA
MARELLI GROUP
Cimolais
Tramonti
S. Osvaldo
Longarone
Erto Casso
COMO BRIGADE
FORCELLA CLAUTANA
Clauzetto
Meduno
Travesio
Paludea
COL NUDO
Barcis
FORCELLA della BARZANA
Ponte nelle Alpi
M. CAVALLO 6750'
Sequals
Maniago
Belluno
Spilimbergo
Cellina River
Cosa Creek
Meduna River
Pordenone
Livenza River
Vittorio
S. Pietro di Feletta
Orsago
SPECIAL OPERATIONS GROUP
28TH ITALIAN DIVISION
3RD ITALIAN DIVISION
IV BRIGADE + BERSAGLIERI
25TH ITALIAN DIVISION
67TH ITALIAN DIVISION
Monticano River
Motta di Livenza
Oderzo
- Point reached by Austro-German Forces
- Italian Deployment
0 3 6.2 9.3 12.4 miles

Map 28:
Deployment of
Italian XII Corps
and Corpo Speciale

November 7, 1917, 2400

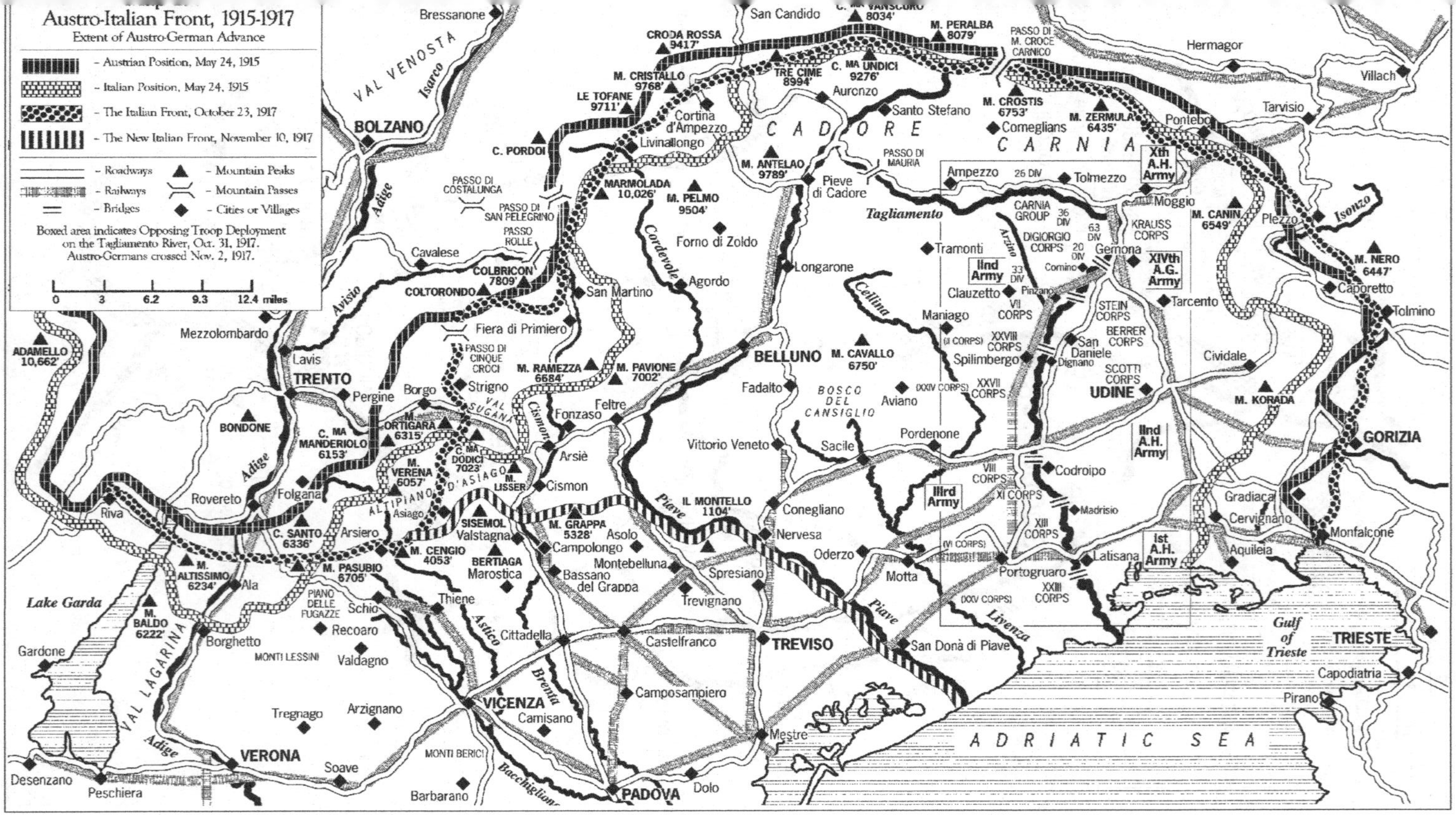

Austro-Italian Front, 1915-1917
Extent of Austro-German Advance
- Austrian Position, May 24, 1915
- Italian Position, May 24, 1915
- The Italian Front, October 23, 1917
- The New Italian Front, November 10, 1917
- Roadways
- Railways
- Bridges
- Mountain Peaks
- Mountain Passes
- Cities or Villages
Boxed area indicates Opposing Troop Deployment on the Tagliamento River, Oct. 31, 1917. Austro-Germans crossed Nov. 2, 1917.
0 3 6.2 9.3 12.4 miles
Bressanone
VAL VENOSTA
Isarco
BOLZANO
Adige
Avisio
Cavalese
Mezzolombardo
Lavis
TRENTO
Pergine
Borgo
ADAMELLO 10,662'
BONDONE
Rovereto
Riva
Folgaria
C. SANTO 6336'
Arsiero
C. MA MANDERIOLO 6153'
M. ORTIGARA 6315'
M. VERENA 6057'
C. MA DODICI 7023'
M. LISSER
ALTIPIANO D'ASIAGO
Asiago
SISEMOL
Valstagna
M. CENGIO 4053'
M. PASUBIO 6705'
BERTIAGA
Marostica
M. ALTISSIMO 6234'
Ala
Lake Garda
M. BALDO 6222'
VAL LAGARINA
Borghetto
Gardone
PIANO DELLE FUGAZZE
Schio
Thiene
Recoaro
Valdagno
MONTI LESSINI
Tregnago
Arzignano
Astico
Cittadella
Brenta
VICENZA
Camisano
VERONA
Soave
MONTI BERICI
Barbarano
Bacchiglione
PADOVA
Desenzano
Peschiera
PASSO DI COSTALUNGA
PASSO DI SAN PELEGRINO
PASSO ROLLE
COLBRICON 7809'
COLTORONDO
San Martino
Fiera di Primiero
PASSO DI CINQUE CROCI
Strigno
VAL SUGANA
Cismon
M. RAMEZZA 6684'
M. PAVIONE 7002'
Fonzaso
Feltre
Arsiè
M. GRAPPA 5328'
Asolo
Campolongo
Montebelluna
Bassano del Grappa
IL MONTELLO 1104'
Piave
Spresiano
Trevignano
Castelfranco
Camposampiero
TREVISO
Mestre
Dolo
C. PORDOI
MARMOLADA 10,026'
M. PELMO 9504'
Forno di Zoldo
Cordevole
Agordo
LE TOFANE 9711'
M. CRISTALLO 9768'
CRODA ROSSA 9417'
Cortina d'Ampezzo
Livinallongo
TRE CIME 8994'
C. MA UNDICI 9276'
San Candido
8034'
M. PERALBA 8079'
Auronzo
Santo Stefano
CADORE
M. ANTELAO 9789'
Pieve di Cadore
PASSO DI MAURIA
Longarone
BELLUNO
M. CAVALLO 6750'
Fadalto
BOSCO DEL CANSIGLIO
Aviano
Vittorio Veneto
Sacile
Pordenone
Conegliano
Nervesa
Oderzo
Motta
San Donà di Piave
Livenza
PASSO DI M. CROCE CARNICO
M. CROSTIS 6753'
M. ZERMULA 6435'
Comeglians
CARNIA
Ampezzo
26 DIV
Tolmezzo
Xth A.H. Army
Tagliamento
CARNIA GROUP
36 DIV
63 DIV
DIGIORGIO CORPS
20 DIV
KRAUSS CORPS
Moggio
Gemona
Comino
XIVth A.G. Army
Tramonti
Arzino
IInd Army
33 DIV
Clauzetto
Pinzano
VII CORPS
Cellina
Maniago
(II CORPS)
XXVIII CORPS
Spilimbergo
Dignano
San Daniele
STEIN CORPS
BERRER CORPS
SCOTTI CORPS
UDINE
Tarcento
(XXIV CORPS)
XXVII CORPS
IIIrd Army
VIII CORPS
XI CORPS
Codroipo
Madrisio
XIII CORPS
(VI CORPS)
Portogruaro
(XXV CORPS)
XXIII CORPS
Latisana
Ist A.H. Army
IInd A.H. Army
Hermagor
Villach
Tarvisio
Pontebba
M. CANIN 6549'
Plezzo
Isonzo
M. NERO 6447'
Caporetto
Tolmino
Cividale
M. KORADA
GORIZIA
Gradiaca
Cervignano
Aquileia
Monfalcone
Gulf of Trieste
TRIESTE
Capodiatria
Pirano
ADRIATIC SEA

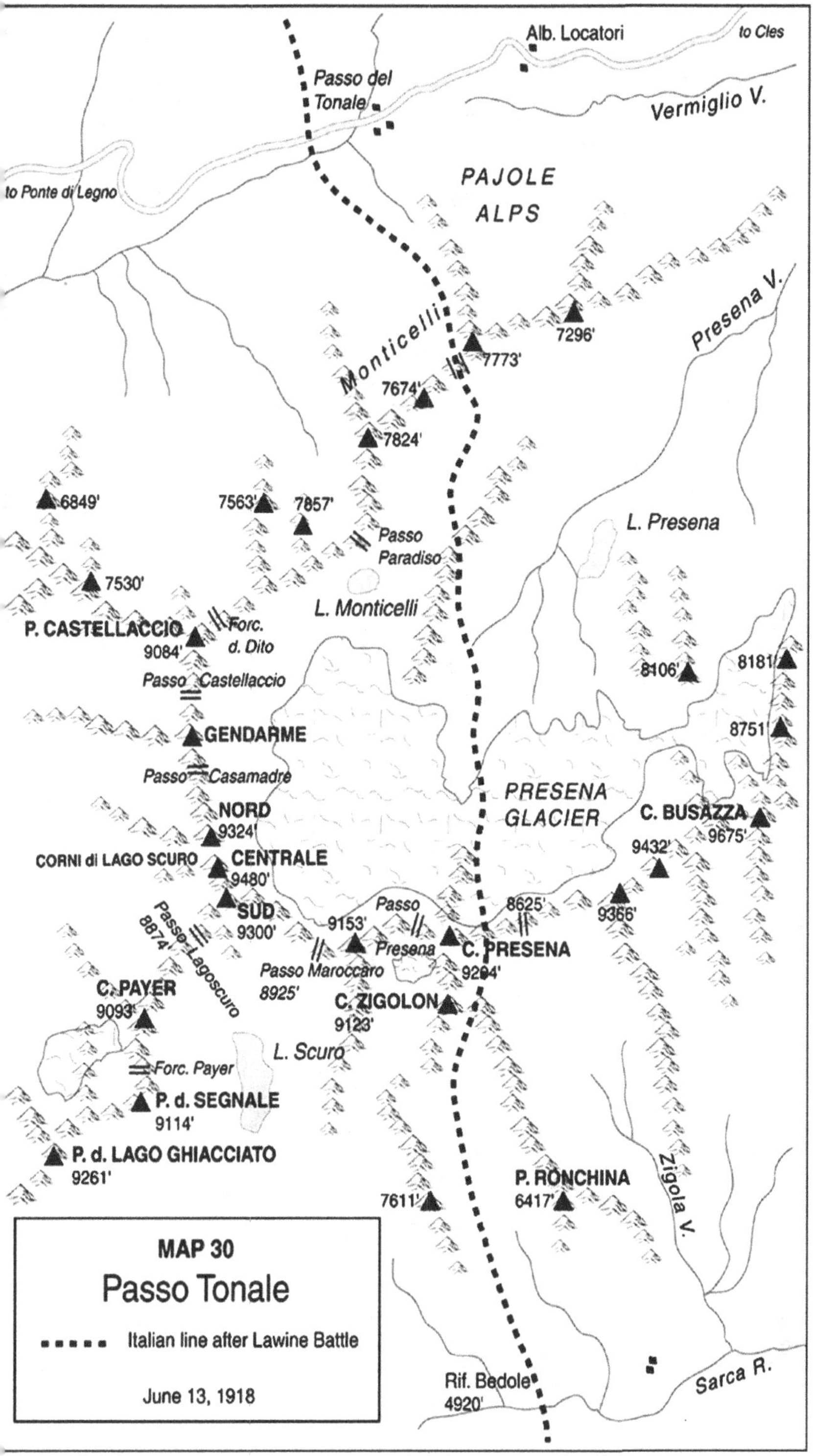

MAP 30
Passo Tonale

Italian line after Lawine Battle

June 13, 1918

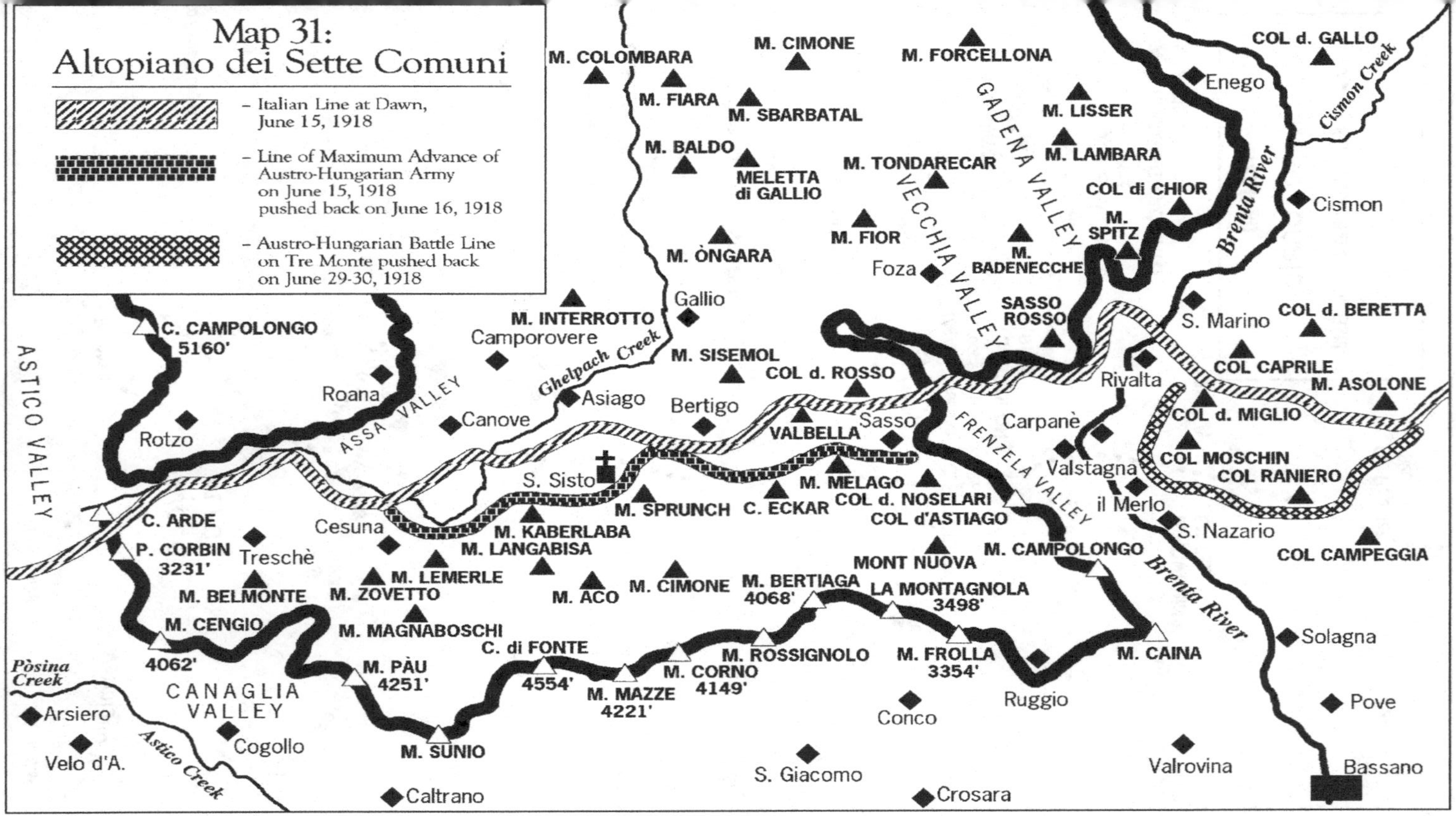

Map 31:
Altopiano dei Sette Comuni
– Italian Line at Dawn, June 15, 1918
– Line of Maximum Advance of Austro-Hungarian Army on June 15, 1918 pushed back on June 16, 1918
– Austro-Hungarian Battle Line on Tre Monte pushed back on June 29-30, 1918
M. COLOMBARA
M. CIMONE
M. FORCELLONA
COL d. GALLO
Enego
Cismon Creek
M. FIARA
M. SBARBATAL
M. LISSER
GADENA VALLEY
M. BALDO
MELETTA di GALLIO
M. TONDARECAR
M. LAMBARA
Brenta River
VECCHIA VALLEY
COL di CHIOR
Cismon
M. FIOR
M. SPITZ
M. ÒNGARA
Foza
M. BADENECCHE
Gallio
SASSO ROSSO
S. Marino
COL d. BERETTA
M. INTERROTTO
C. CAMPOLONGO
5160'
Camporovere
Ghelpach Creek
M. SISEMOL
COL CAPRILE
ASTICO VALLEY
Roana
COL d. ROSSO
Rivalta
M. ASOLONE
Asiago
Bertigo
Sasso
Carpanè
COL d. MIGLIO
ASSA VALLEY
Canove
VALBELLA
FRENZELA VALLEY
Rotzo
COL MOSCHIN
Valstagna
COL RANIERO
S. Sisto
M. MELAGO
COL d. NOSELARI
il Merlo
M. SPRUNCH
C. ECKAR
C. ARDE
COL d'ASTIAGO
S. Nazario
Cesuna
M. KABERLABA
M. CAMPOLONGO
COL CAMPEGGIA
P. CORBIN
3231'
Treschè
M. LANGABISA
MONT NUOVA
Brenta River
M. LEMERLE
M. BELMONTE
M. ZOVETTO
M. ACO
M. CIMONE
M. BERTIAGA
4068'
LA MONTAGNOLA
3498'
M. CENGIO
4062'
M. MAGNABOSCHI
Solagna
C. di FONTE
4554'
M. ROSSIGNOLO
M. FROLLA
3354'
M. CAINA
Pòsina Creek
M. PÀU
4251'
M. CORNO
4149'
CANAGLIA VALLEY
M. MAZZE
4221'
Ruggio
Pove
Arsiero
Conco
Cogollo
Velo d'A.
Astico Creek
M. SUNIO
S. Giacomo
Valrovina
Bassano
Caltrano
Crosara

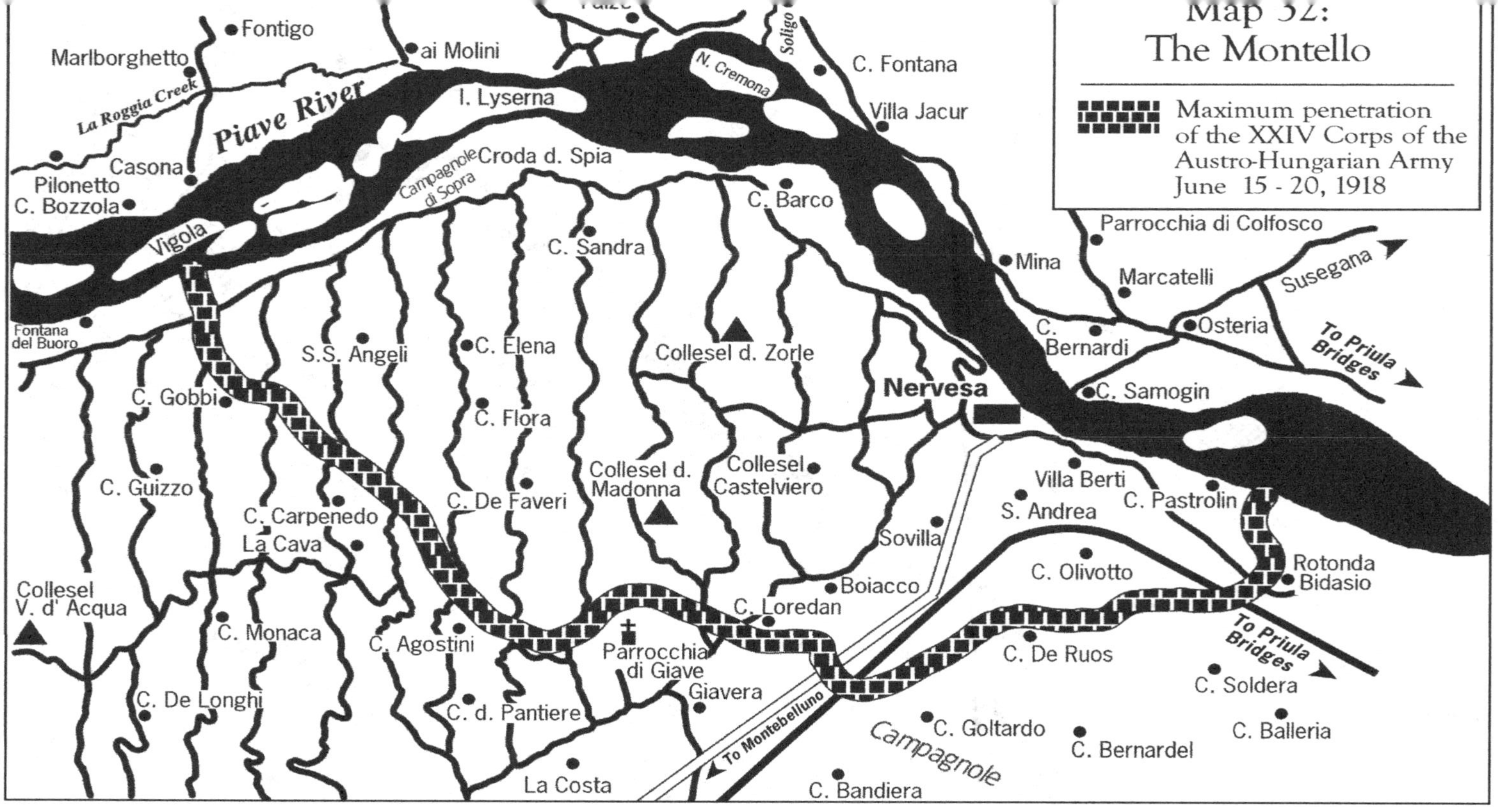
Map 32:
The Montello
Maximum penetration of the XXIV Corps of the Austro-Hungarian Army June 15 - 20, 1918
Fontigo
Marlborghetto
ai Molini
La Roggia Creek
Piave River
I. Lyserna
N. Cremona
Soligo
C. Fontana
Villa Jacur
Casona
Pilonetto
C. Bozzola
Campagnole di Sopra
Croda d. Spia
C. Barco
Vigola
C. Sandra
Parrocchia di Colfosco
Mina
Marcatelli
Susegana
Osteria
To Priula Bridges
C. Bernardi
Fontana del Buoro
S.S. Angeli
C. Elena
Collesel d. Zorle
Nervesa
C. Samogin
C. Gobbi
C. Flora
Collesel d. Madonna
Collesel Castelviero
Villa Berti
C. Pastrolin
S. Andrea
C. Guizzo
C. Carpenedo
La Cava
C. De Faveri
Sovilla
C. Olivotto
Rotonda Bidasio
Collesel V. d' Acqua
C. Monaca
C. Agostini
Parrocchia di Giave
Boiacco
C. Loredan
C. De Ruos
To Priula Bridges
C. Soldera
C. De Longhi
C. d. Pantiere
Giavera
To Montebelluno
Campagnole
C. Goltardo
C. Bernardel
C. Balleria
La Costa
C. Bandiera

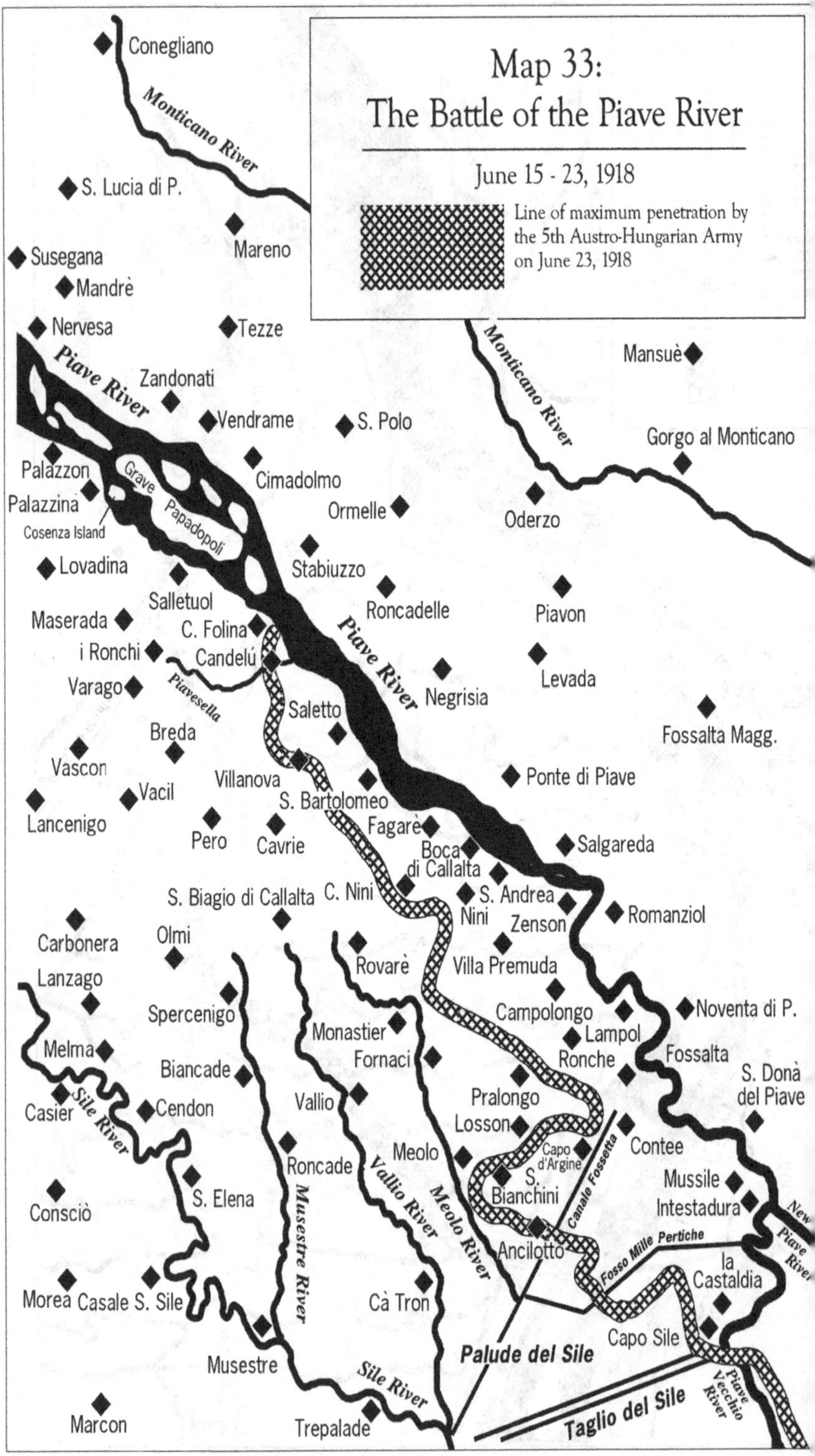

Map 33: The Battle of the Piave River

June 15 - 23, 1918

Line of maximum penetration by the 5th Austro-Hungarian Army on June 23, 1918

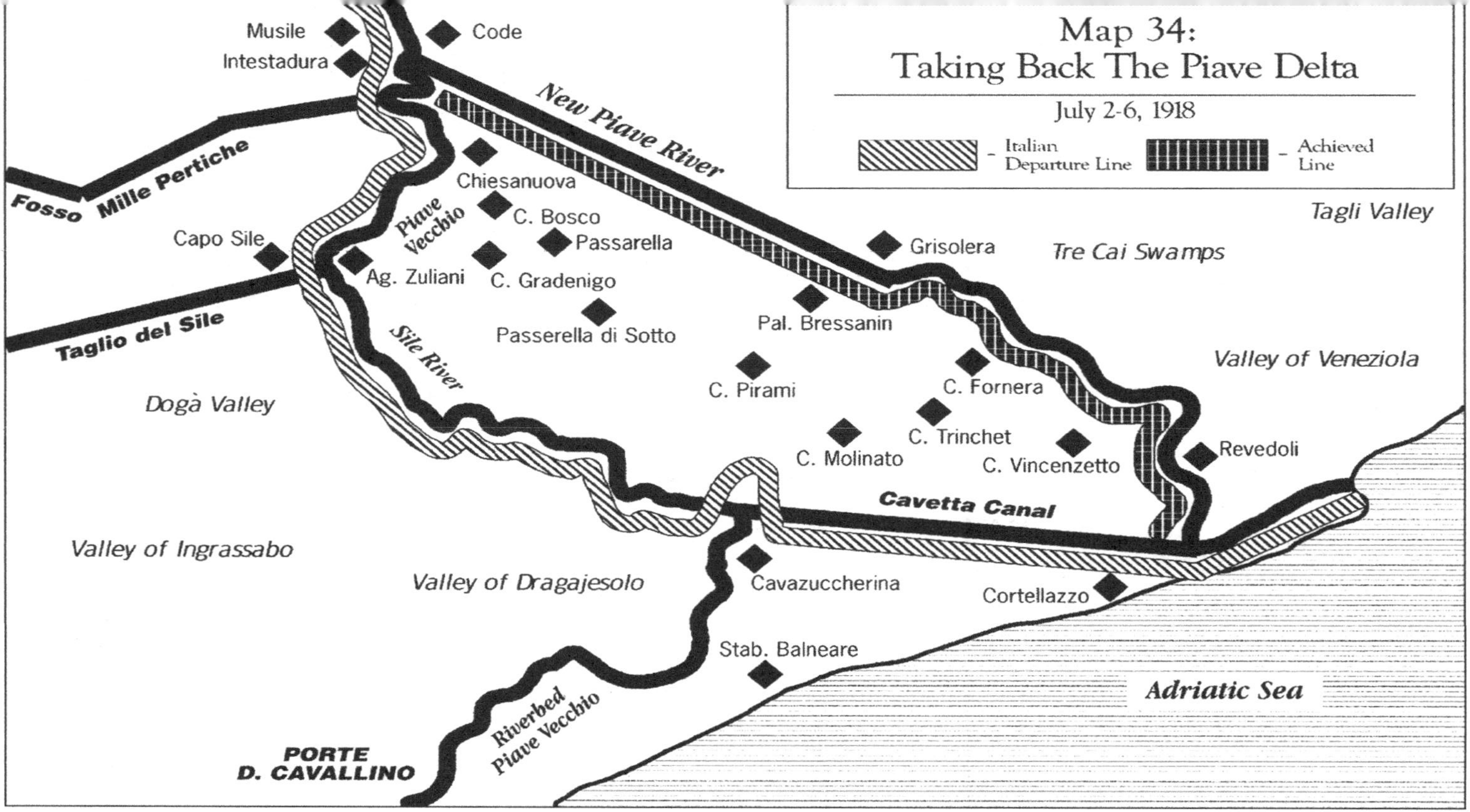
Map 34:
Taking Back The Piave Delta
July 2-6, 1918
- Italian Departure Line
- Achieved Line
Musile
Intestadura
Code
New Piave River
Fosso Mille Pertiche
Chiesanuova
C. Bosco
Passarella
Capo Sile
Piave Vecchio
Ag. Zuliani
C. Gradenigo
Taglio del Sile
Passerella di Sotto
Sile River
Dogà Valley
Grisolera
Tagli Valley
Tre Cai Swamps
Pal. Bressanin
Valley of Veneziola
C. Pirami
C. Fornera
C. Trinchet
C. Molinato
C. Vincenzetto
Revedoli
Cavetta Canal
Valley of Ingrassabo
Valley of Dragajesolo
Cavazuccherina
Cortellazzo
Stab. Balneare
Adriatic Sea
Riverbed Piave Vecchio
PORTE D. CAVALLINO

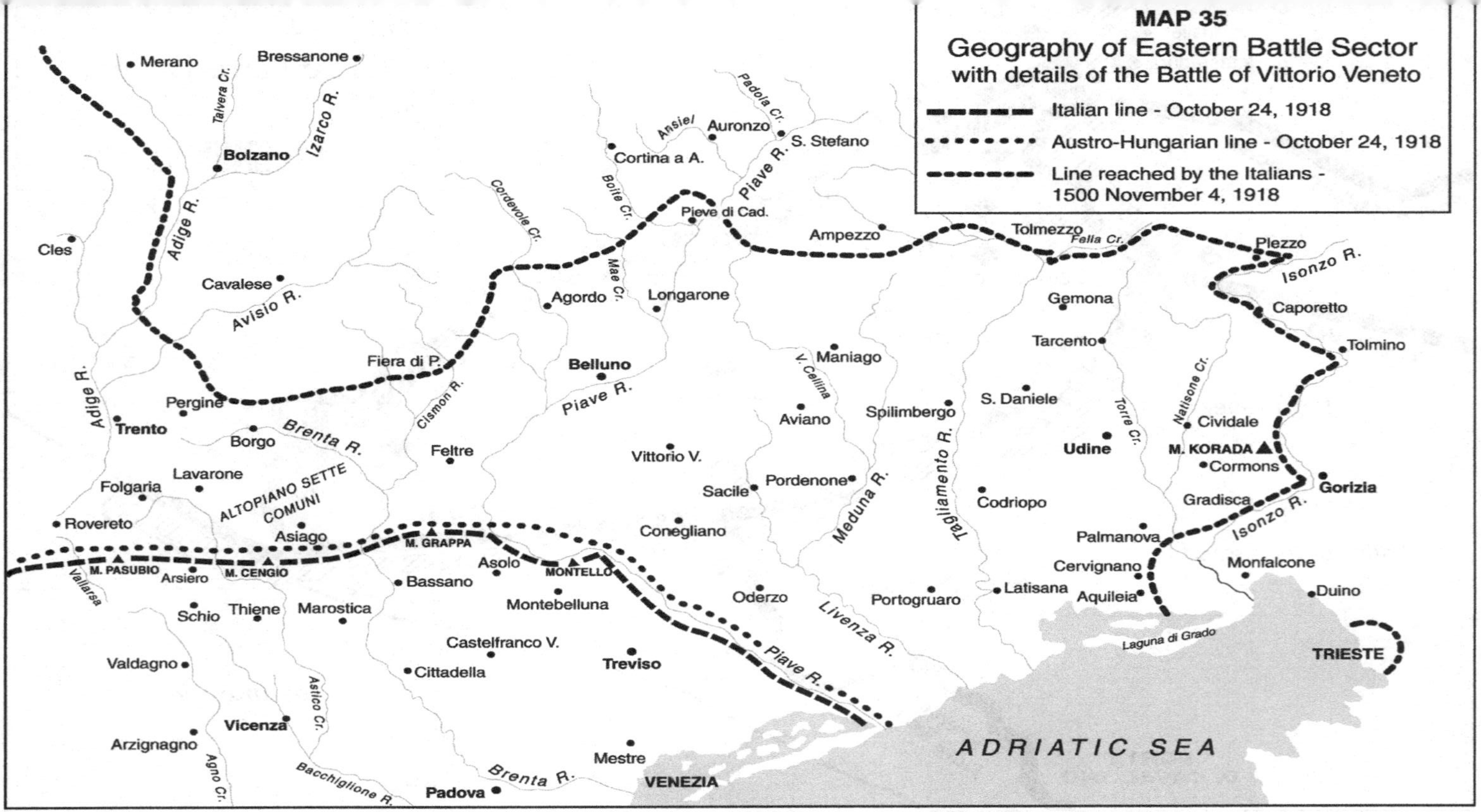
MAP 35
Geography of Eastern Battle Sector
with details of the Battle of Vittorio Veneto
Italian line - October 24, 1918
Austro-Hungarian line - October 24, 1918
Line reached by the Italians -
1500 November 4, 1918
Merano
Bressanone
Talvera Cr.
Izarco R.
Bolzano
Adige R.
Cles
Cavalese
Avisio R.
Trento
Pergine
Borgo
Brenta R.
Folgaria
Lavarone
Rovereto
ALTOPIANO SETTE COMUNI
Asiago
M. PASUBIO
Arsiero
M. CENGIO
Vallarsa
Schio
Thiene
Marostica
Valdagno
Vicenza
Astico Cr.
Arzignagno
Agno Cr.
Bacchiglione R.
Padova
Brenta R.
Mestre
VENEZIA
Fiera di P.
Cismon R.
Feltre
M. GRAPPA
Bassano
Asolo
MONTELLO
Montebelluna
Castelfranco V.
Cittadella
Treviso
Cordevole Cr.
Agordo
Belluno
Piave R.
Boite Cr.
Mae Cr.
Longarone
Cortina a A.
Ansiel
Auronzo
Padola Cr.
S. Stefano
Piave R.
Pieve di Cad.
Ampezzo
Vittorio V.
Conegliano
Sacile
Pordenone
Oderzo
Piave R.
Livenza R.
Maniago
V. Cellina
Aviano
Spilimbergo
Meduna R.
Tagliamento R.
Portogruaro
Latisana
Tolmezzo
Fella Cr.
Gemona
Tarcento
S. Daniele
Codriopo
Udine
Torre Cr.
Natisone Cr.
Cividale
M. KORADA
Cormons
Gradisca
Palmanova
Cervignano
Aquileia
Laguna di Grado
Plezzo
Isonzo R.
Caporetto
Tolmino
Gorizia
Isonzo R.
Monfalcone
Duino
TRIESTE
ADRIATIC SEA

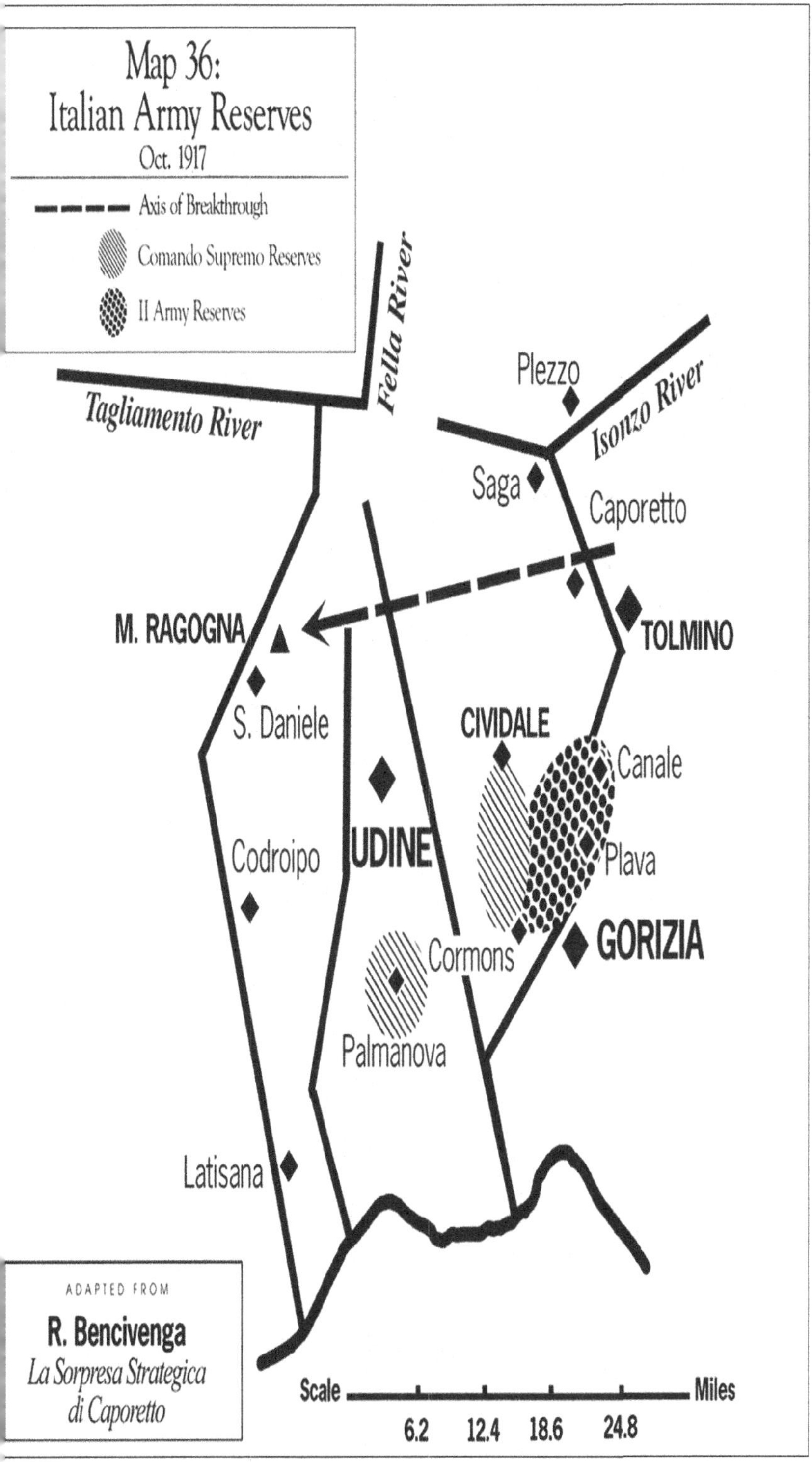

Map 36:
Italian Army Reserves
Oct. 1917
Axis of Breakthrough
Comando Supremo Reserves
II Army Reserves
Fella River
Tagliamento River
Isonzo River
Plezzo
Saga
Caporetto
TOLMINO
M. RAGOGNA
S. Daniele
CIVIDALE
Canale
UDINE
Plava
Codroipo
GORIZIA
Cormons
Palmanova
Latisana
ADAPTED FROM
R. Bencivenga
La Sorpresa Strategica di Caporetto
Scale
Miles
6.2
12.4
18.6
24.8

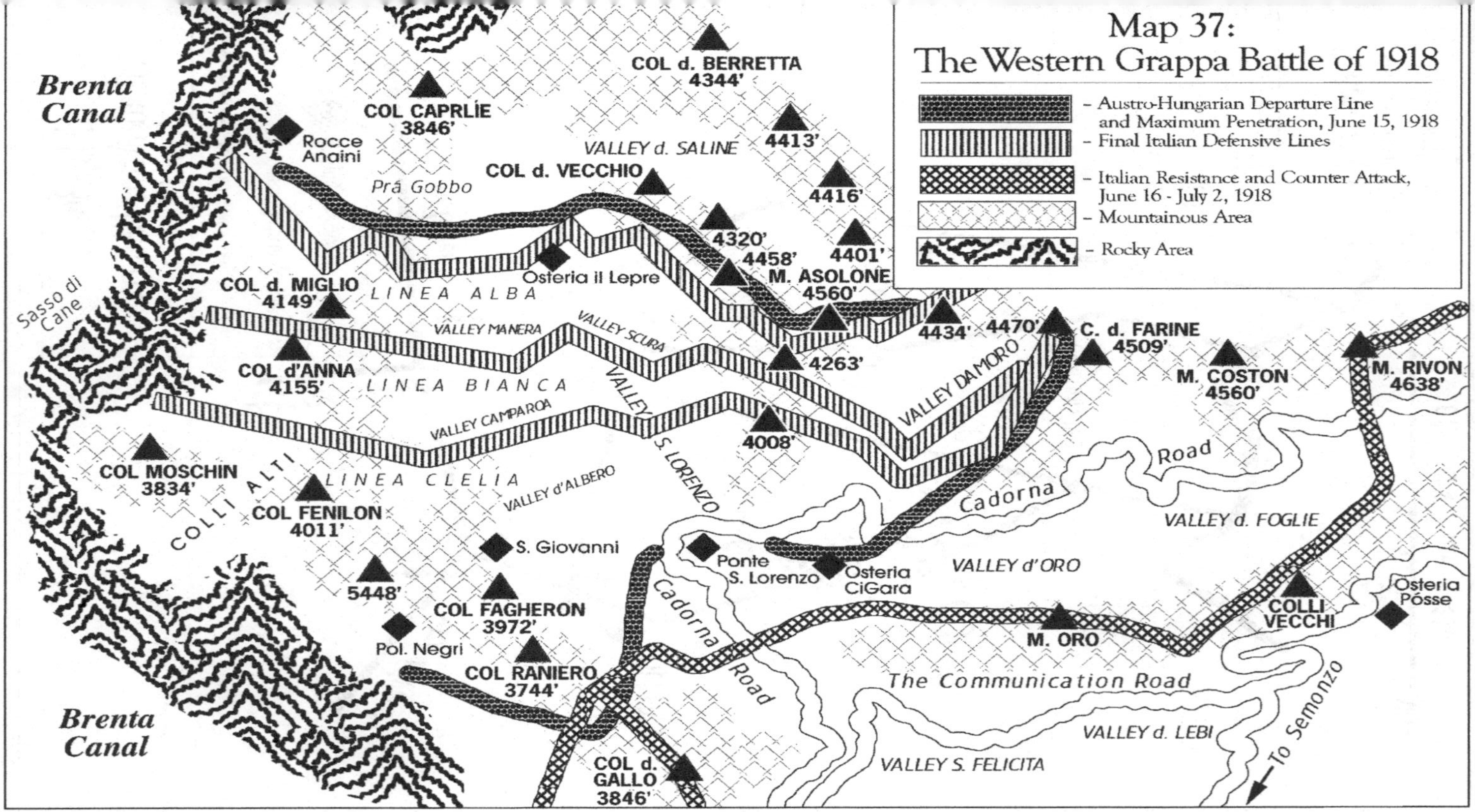
Map 37:
The Western Grappa Battle of 1918
- Austro-Hungarian Departure Line and Maximum Penetration, June 15, 1918
- Final Italian Defensive Lines
- Italian Resistance and Counter Attack, June 16 - July 2, 1918
- Mountainous Area
- Rocky Area
Brenta Canal
COL CAPRLÍE 3846'
COL d. BERRETTA 4344'
Rocce Anaini
Prà Gobbo
VALLEY d. SALINE
4413'
COL d. VECCHIO
4416'
4320'
4401'
4458'
M. ASOLONE 4560'
Osteria il Lepre
Sasso di Cane
COL d. MIGLIO 4149'
LINEA ALBA
VALLEY MANERA
VALLEY SCURA
4434'
4470'
C. d. FARINE 4509'
COL d'ANNA 4155'
LINEA BIANCA
4263'
VALLEY DA MORO
M. COSTON 4560'
M. RIVON 4638'
VALLEY CAMPAROA
VALLEY S. LORENZO
4008'
COL MOSCHIN 3834'
COLLI ALTI
LINEA CLELIA
VALLEY d'ALBERO
COL FENILON 4011'
Cadorna Road
VALLEY d. FOGLIE
S. Giovanni
Ponte S. Lorenzo
Osteria CiGara
VALLEY d'ORO
5448'
COL FAGHERON 3972'
Pol. Negri
COL RANIERO 3744'
Cadorna Road
M. ORO
COLLI VECCHI
Osteria Pósse
The Communication Road
Brenta Canal
COL d. GALLO 3846'
VALLEY d. LEBI
VALLEY S. FELICITA
To Semonzo

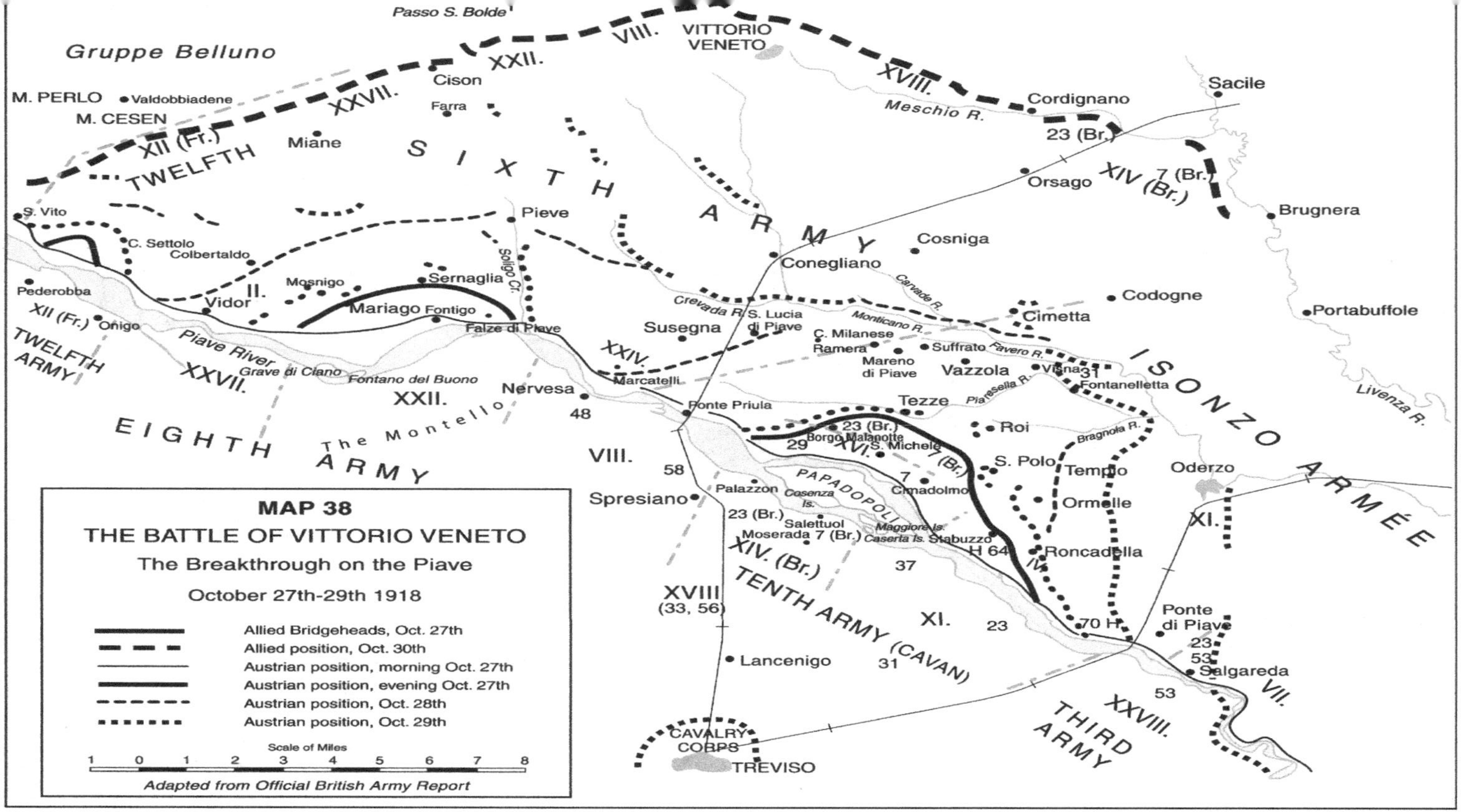
MAP 38
THE BATTLE OF VITTORIO VENETO
The Breakthrough on the Piave
October 27th-29th 1918
Allied Bridgeheads, Oct. 27th
Allied position, Oct. 30th
Austrian position, morning Oct. 27th
Austrian position, evening Oct. 27th
Austrian position, Oct. 28th
Austrian position, Oct. 29th
Scale of Miles
1 0 1 2 3 4 5 6 7 8
Adapted from Official British Army Report
Passo S. Bolde
Gruppe Belluno
M. PERLO
Valdobbiadene
M. CESEN
VITTORIO VENETO
Cison
Farra
Miane
Sacile
Cordignano
Meschio R.
Orsago
Brugnera
Cosniga
Conegliano
Codogne
Portabuffole
Cimetta
Pieve
Soligo Cr.
S. Vito
C. Settolo
Colbertaldo
Mosnigo
Sernaglia
Pederobba
Vidor
Mariago
Fontigo
Falze di Piave
Onigo
Piave River
Grave di Ciano
Fontano del Buono
Nervesa
Susegna
Crevada R.
S. Lucia di Piave
C. Milanese
Ramera
Mareno di Piave
Monticano R.
Carvade R.
Suffrato
Favero R.
Vazzola
Visna
Fontanelletta
Livenza R.
Marcatelli
Ponte Priula
Tezze
Piavesella R.
Roi
Bragnola R.
Borgo Malanotte
S. Michele
S. Polo
Tempio
Oderzo
Palazzon
Cosenza Is.
PAPADOPOLI
Cimadolmo
Ormelle
Spresiano
Salettuol
Moserada
Maggiore Is.
Caserta Is.
Stabuzzo
Roncadella
Ponte di Piave
Salgareda
Lancenigo
CAVALRY CORPS
TREVISO
The Montello
TWELFTH
TWELFTH ARMY
SIXTH ARMY
EIGHTH ARMY
TENTH ARMY (CAVAN)
THIRD ARMY
ISONZO ARMÉE
VIII.
XXII.
XXVII.
XVIII.
XII (Fr.)
23 (Br.)
XIV (Br.)
7 (Br.)
II.
XXIV.
XXII.
48
58
VIII.
XVI.
29
23 (Br.)
7 (Br.)
7
31
23 (Br.)
7 (Br.)
XIV. (Br.)
37
XVIII
(33, 56)
XI.
23
31
H 64
70 H
XI.
23
53
53
XXVIII.
VII.

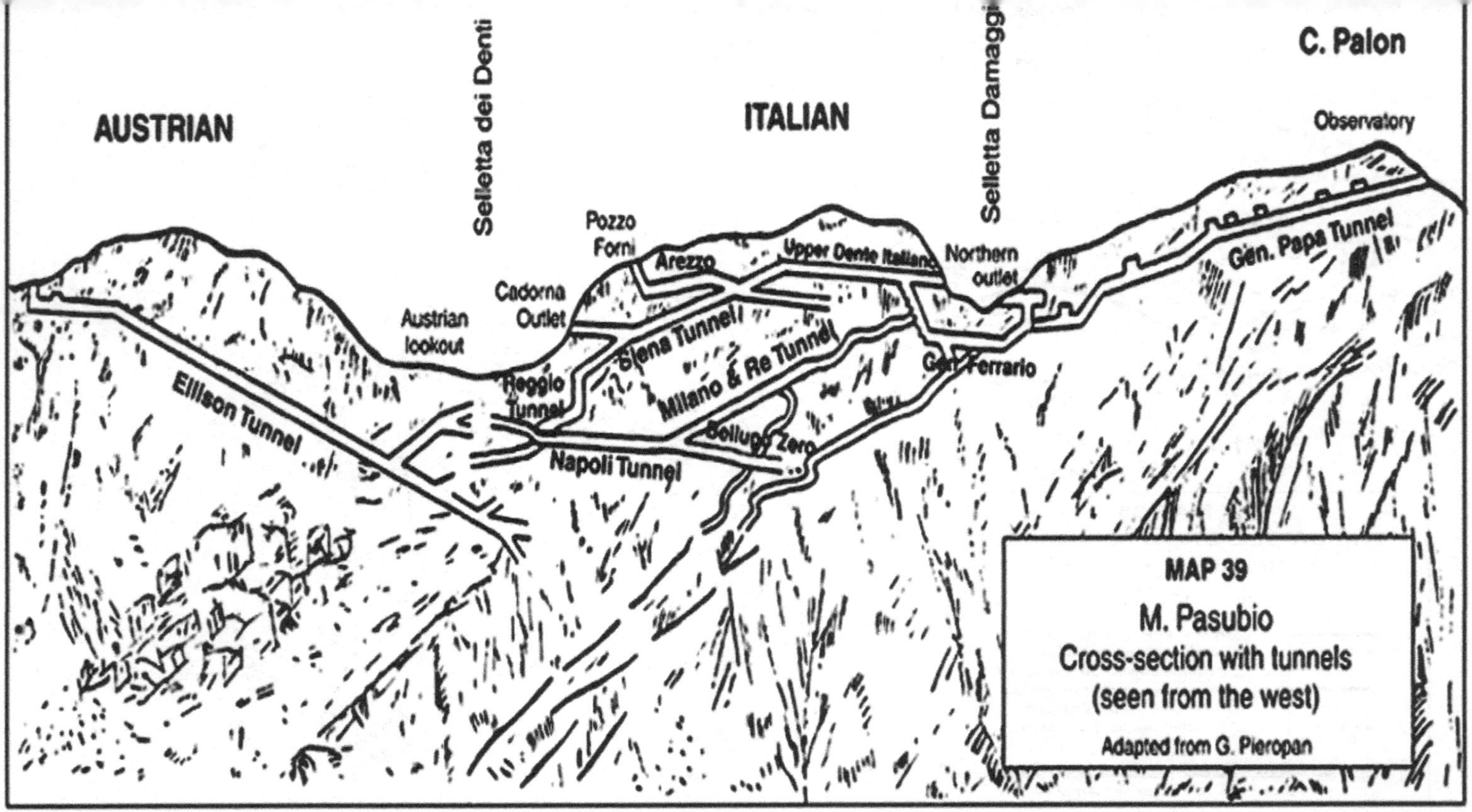

MAP 39
M. Pasubio
Cross-section with tunnels
(seen from the west)
Adapted from G. Pieropan

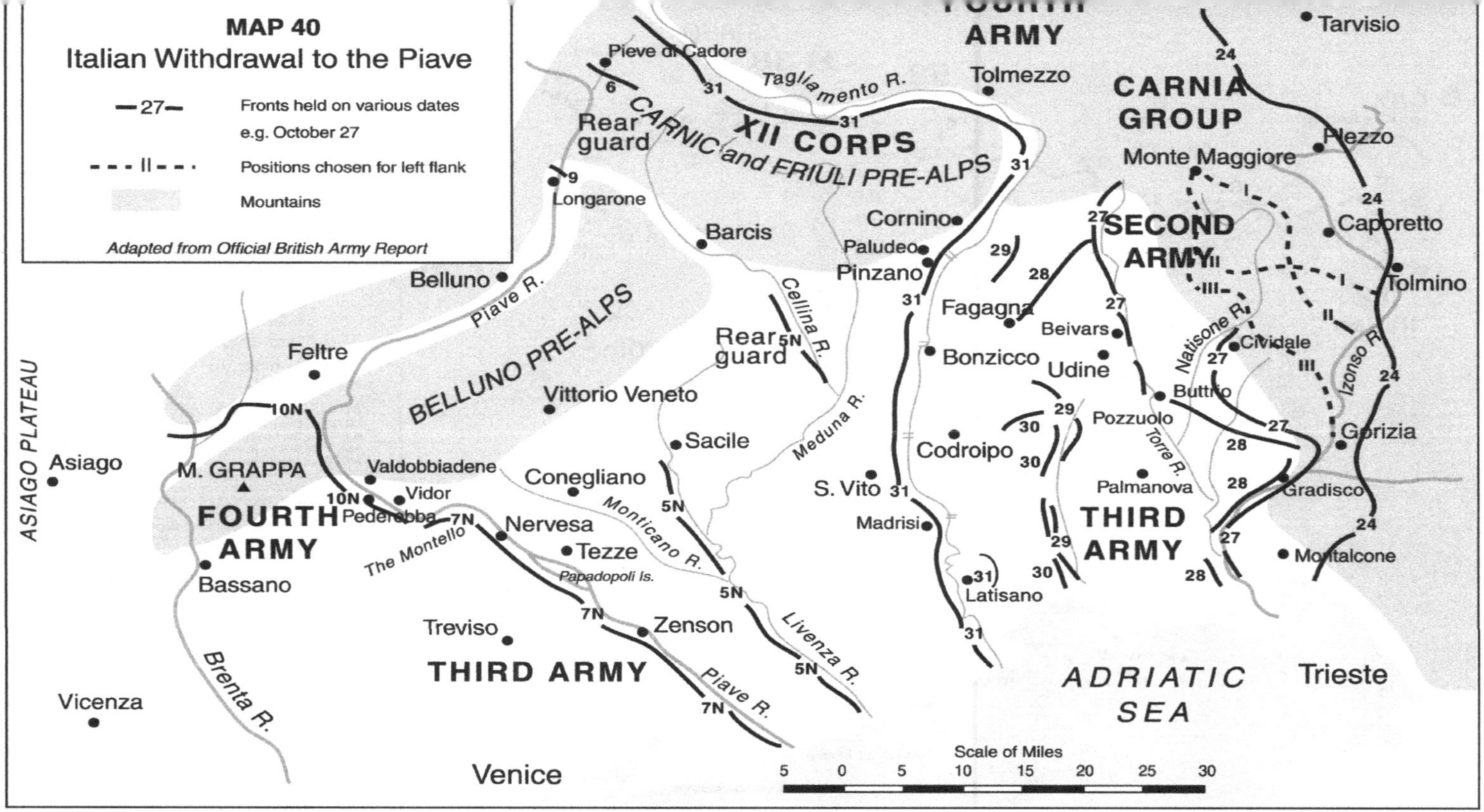
MAP 40
Italian Withdrawal to the Piave
—27— Fronts held on various dates e.g. October 27
- - - II - - - Positions chosen for left flank
Mountains
Adapted from Official British Army Report
FOURTH ARMY
Tarvisio
Pieve di Cadore
Tagliamento R.
Tolmezzo
CARNIA GROUP
Plezzo
Monte Maggiore
Rear guard
XII CORPS
CARNIC and FRIULI PRE-ALPS
Longarone
Cornino
Caporetto
SECOND ARMY
Barcis
Paludeo
Pinzano
Tolmino
Belluno
Piave R.
Cellina R.
Fagagna
Beivars
Natisone R.
Cividale
Izonso R.
Feltre
BELLUNO PRE-ALPS
Rear guard
Bonzicco
Udine
Buttrio
Vittorio Veneto
Meduna R.
Pozzuolo
Gorizia
Sacile
Codroipo
Torre R.
Asiago
M. GRAPPA
Valdobbiadene
Conegliano
S. Vito
Palmanova
Gradisco
ASIAGO PLATEAU
Vidor
Pederobba
FOURTH ARMY
Nervesa
Monticano R.
Madrisi
THIRD ARMY
Montalcone
The Montello
Tezze
Latisano
Bassano
Papadopoli Is.
Treviso
Zenson
Livenza R.
ADRIATIC SEA
Trieste
THIRD ARMY
Piave R.
Vicenza
Brenta R.
Venice
Scale of Miles
5 0 5 10 15 20 25 30

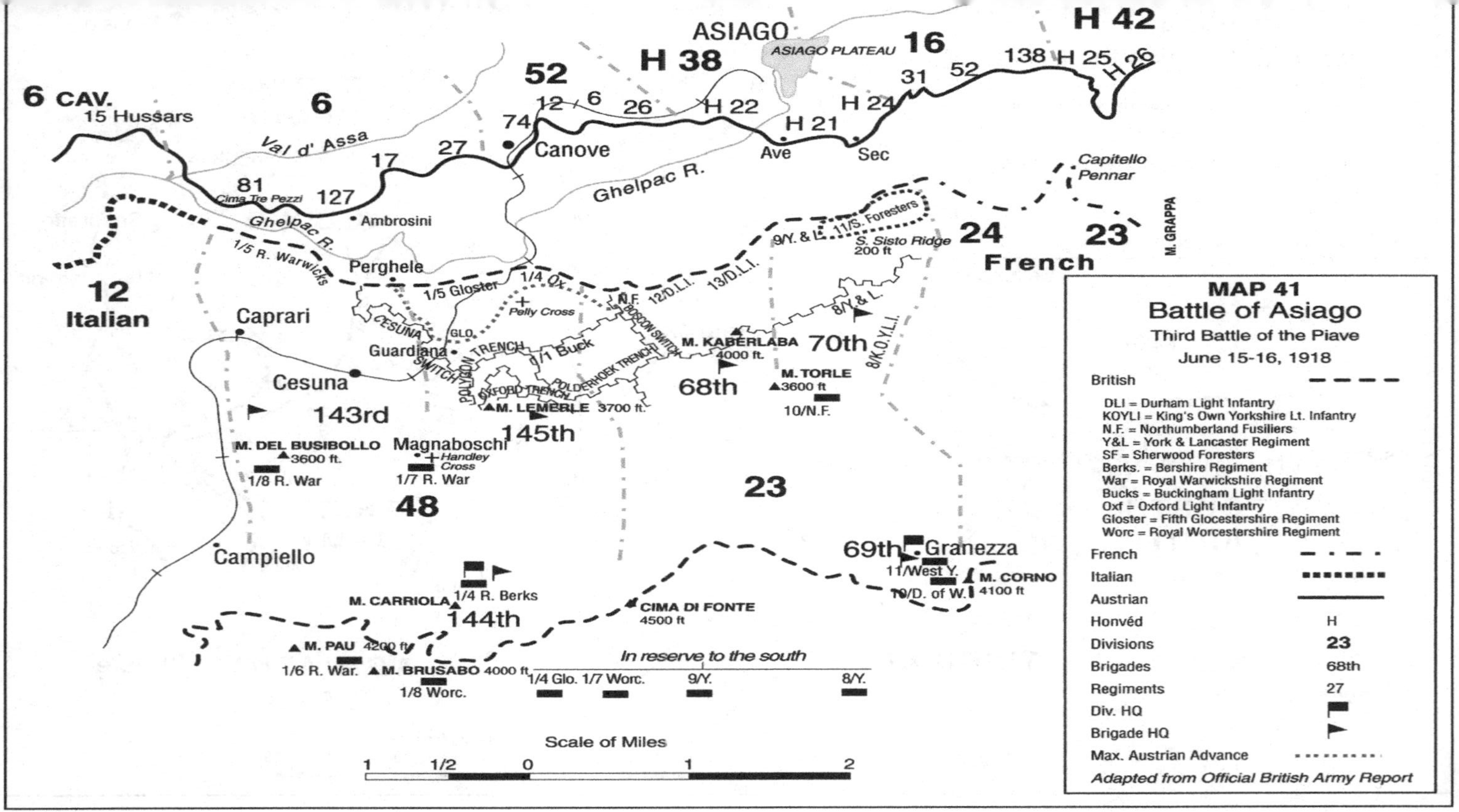
MAP 41
Battle of Asiago
Third Battle of the Piave
June 15-16, 1918
British
DLI = Durham Light Infantry
KOYLI = King's Own Yorkshire Lt. Infantry
N.F. = Northumberland Fusiliers
Y&L = York & Lancaster Regiment
SF = Sherwood Foresters
Berks. = Bershire Regiment
War = Royal Warwickshire Regiment
Bucks = Buckingham Light Infantry
Oxf = Oxford Light Infantry
Gloster = Fifth Glocestershire Regiment
Worc = Royal Worcestershire Regiment
French
Italian
Austrian
Honvéd H
Divisions 23
Brigades 68th
Regiments 27
Div. HQ
Brigade HQ
Max. Austrian Advance
Adapted from Official British Army Report
6 CAV.
15 Hussars
6
Val d' Assa
52
H 38
ASIAGO
ASIAGO PLATEAU
16
H 42
138 H 25
H 26
31
52
H 24
H 22
H 21
26
12
6
74
Canove
Ave
Sec
27
17
81
Cima Tre Pezzi
127
Ambrosini
Ghelpac R.
Ghelpac R.
Capitello Pennar
24
23
French
M. GRAPPA
1/5 R. Warwicks
Perghele
12
Italian
1/5 Gloster
1/4 Ox.
Pelly Cross
N.F.
12/D.L.I.
13/D.L.I.
9/Y. & L.
11/S. Foresters
S. Sisto Ridge
200 ft
8/Y. & L.
8/K.O.Y.L.I.
Caprari
CESUNA
GLO.
Guardiana
SWITCH
POLYGON TRENCH
1/1 Buck
BOSCON SWITCH
POLDERHOEK TRENCH
OXFORD TRENCH
M. KABERLABA
4000 ft.
70th
68th
M. TORLE
3600 ft
10/N.F.
Cesuna
143rd
M. LEMERLE 3700 ft.
145th
M. DEL BUSIBOLLO
3600 ft.
1/8 R. War
Magnaboschi
Handley Cross
1/7 R. War
48
23
69th
Granezza
11/West Y.
10/D. of W.
M. CORNO
4100 ft
Campiello
1/4 R. Berks
M. CARRIOLA
144th
CIMA DI FONTE
4500 ft
M. PAU 4200 ft
1/6 R. War.
M. BRUSABO 4000 ft
1/8 Worc.
In reserve to the south
1/4 Glo.
1/7 Worc.
9/Y.
8/Y.
Scale of Miles
1 1/2 0 1 2

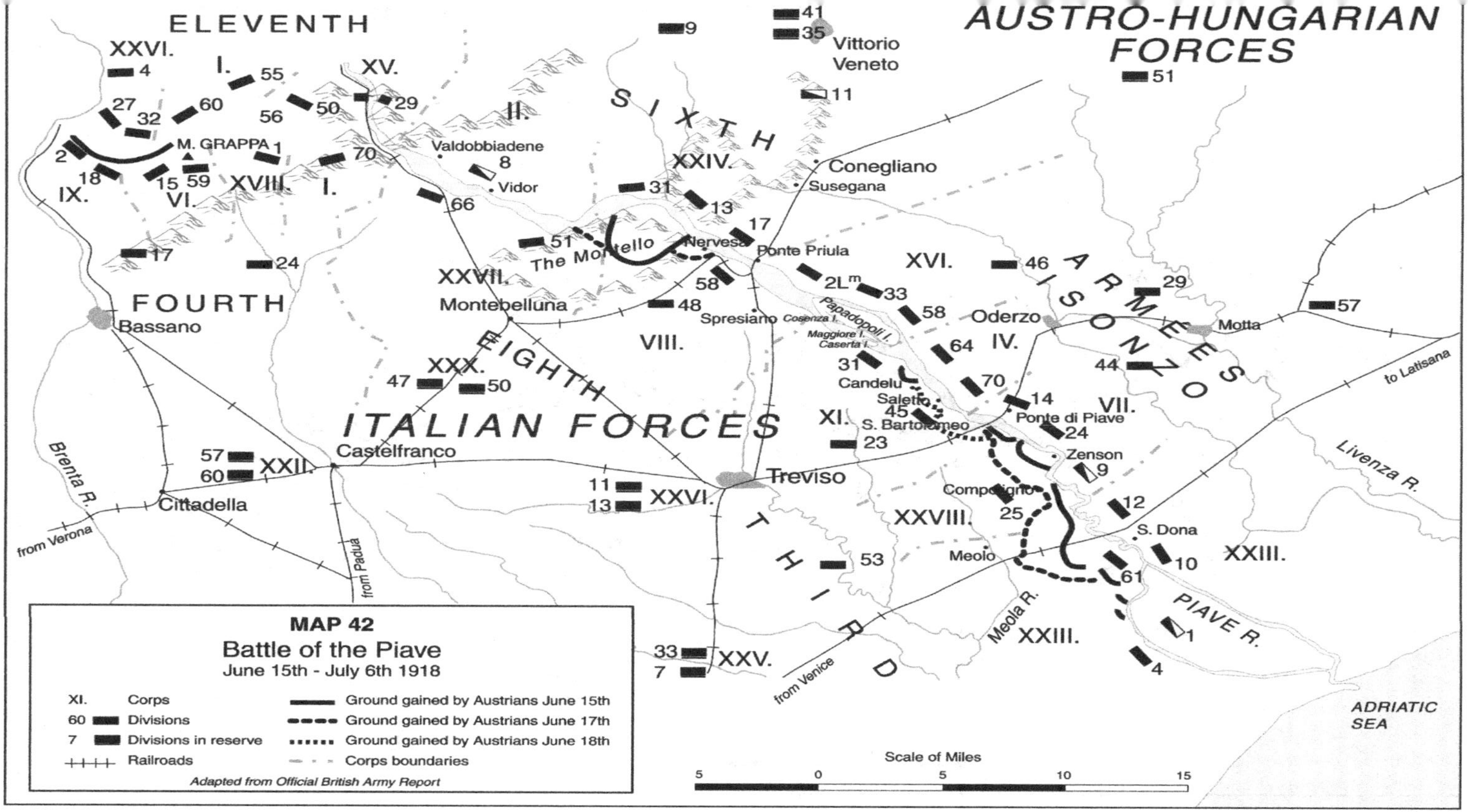

MAP 42
Battle of the Piave
June 15th - July 6th 1918

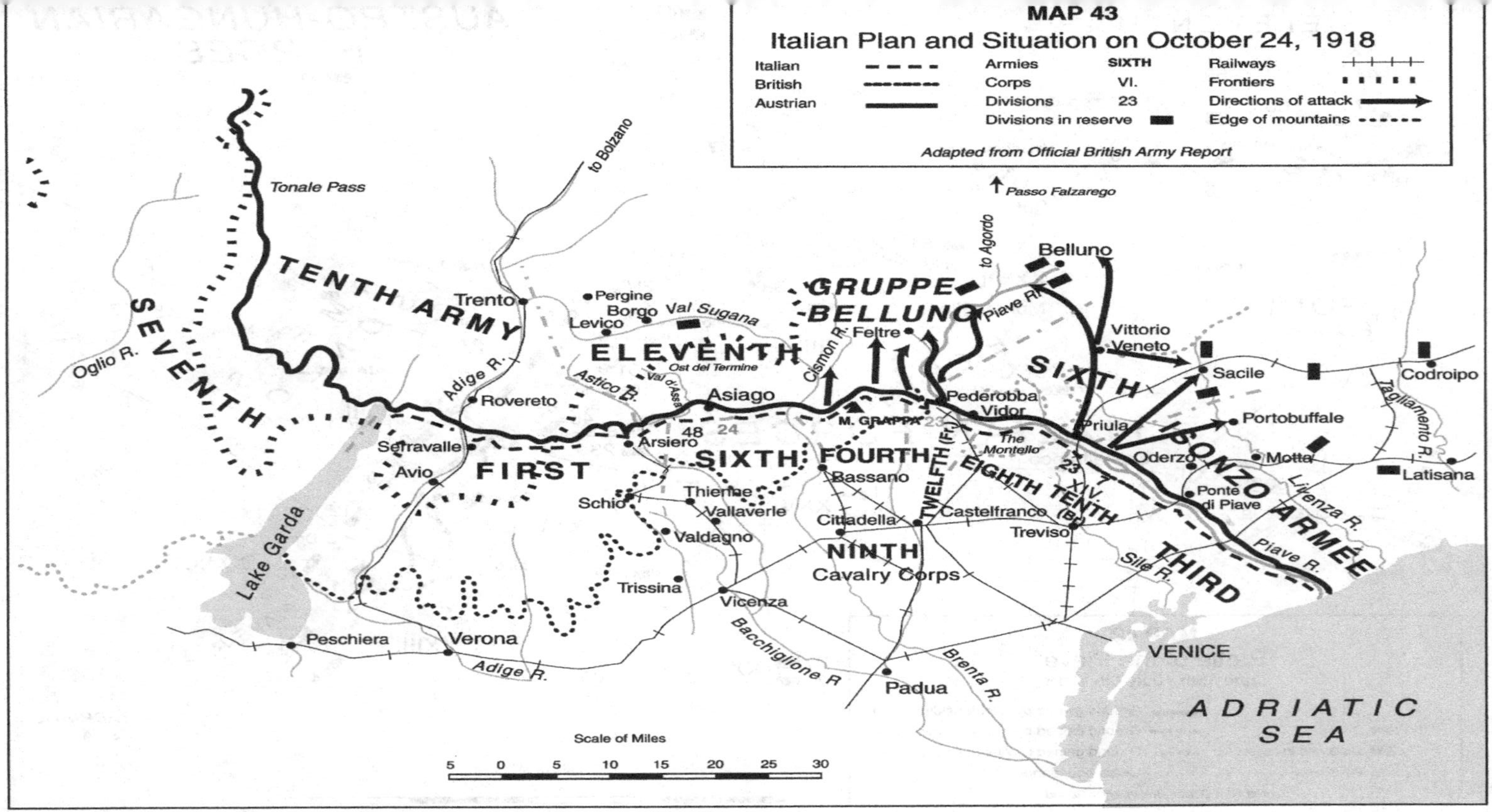
MAP 43
Italian Plan and Situation on October 24, 1918
Italian
British
Austrian
Armies SIXTH
Corps VI.
Divisions 23
Divisions in reserve
Railways
Frontiers
Directions of attack
Edge of mountains
Adapted from Official British Army Report
Passo Falzarego
Tonale Pass
to Bolzano
to Agordo
TENTH ARMY
SEVENTH
ELEVENTH
GRUPPE BELLUNO
FIRST
SIXTH
FOURTH
TWELFTH (Fr.)
EIGHTH
TENTH (Br.)
ISONZO ARMEE
THIRD
NINTH
Cavalry Corps
SIXTH
Trento
Pergine
Borgo
Val Sugana
Levico
Ost del Termine
Val d'Assa
Oglio R.
Adige R.
Rovereto
Astico R.
Asiago
Cismon R.
Feltre
Piave R.
Belluno
Vittorio Veneto
Sacile
Codroipo
Tagliamento R.
Pederobba
Vidor
M. GRAPPA
23
48
24
Arsiero
Serravalle
Avio
Schio
Thiene
Vallaverle
Valdagno
Trissina
Bassano
Cittadella
Castelfranco
The Montello
Treviso
Priula
Oderzo
Portobuffale
Motta
Latisana
Ponte di Piave
Livenza R.
Piave R.
Sile R.
23
7
XIV.
Lake Garda
Peschiera
Verona
Adige R.
Vicenza
Bacchiglione R
Padua
Brenta R.
VENICE
ADRIATIC SEA
Scale of Miles
5 0 5 10 15 20 25 30

INDEX

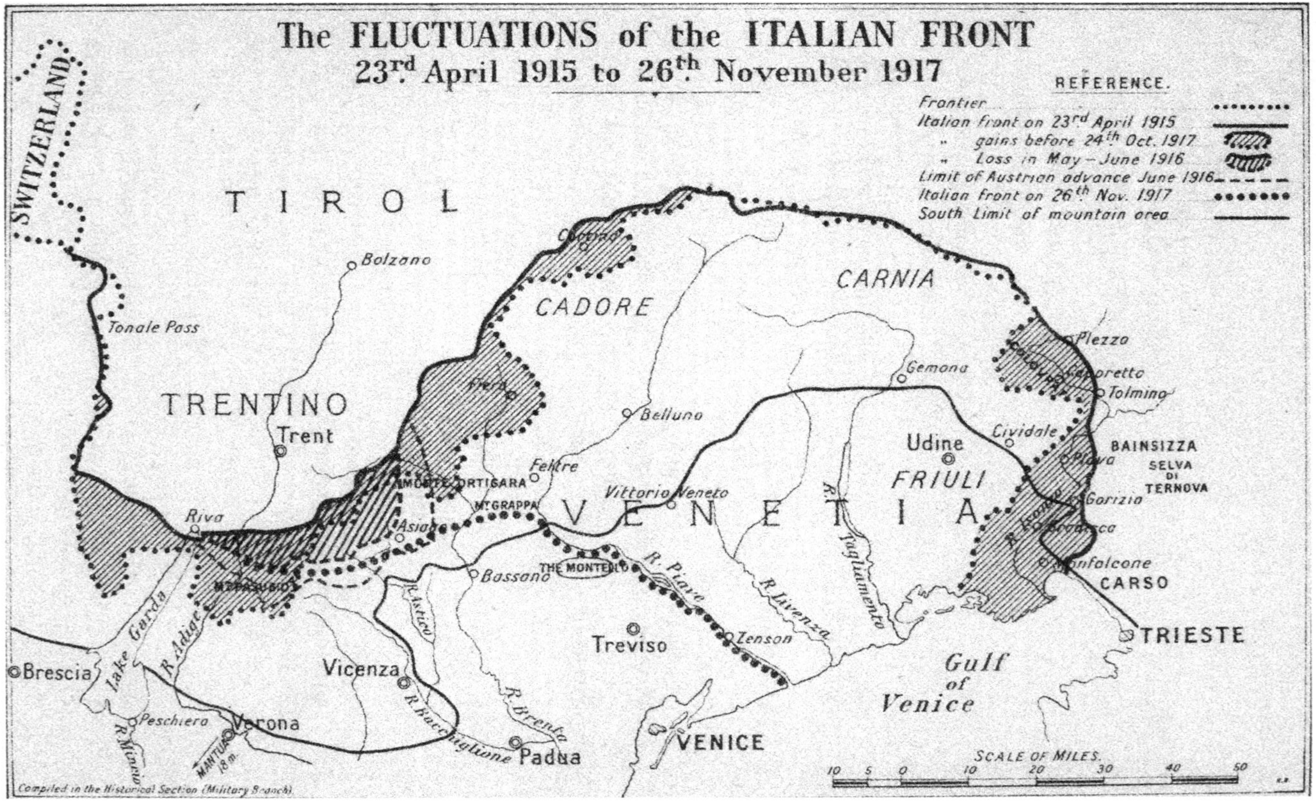
The FLUCTUATIONS of the ITALIAN FRONT
23rd. April 1915 to 26th. November 1917
REFERENCE.
Frontier
Italian front on 23rd April 1915
" gains before 24th Oct. 1917
" Loss in May – June 1916
Limit of Austrian advance June 1916
Italian front on 26th Nov. 1917
South Limit of mountain area
SWITZERLAND
TIROL
Bolzano
Tonale Pass
TRENTINO
Trent
Riva
CADORE
CARNIA
Belluno
Feltre
MONTE ORTIGARA
MT GRAPPA
Asiago
Vittorio Veneto
VENETIA
FRIULI
Udine
Gemona
Plezzo
Tolmino
Cividale
BAINSIZZA
SELVA DI TERNOVA
Gorizia
CARSO
TRIESTE
Bassano
THE MONTELLO
R. Piave
R. Livenza
R. Tagliamento
Zenson
Treviso
Gulf of Venice
VENICE
Padua
R. Brenta
R. Bacchiglione
Vicenza
R. Astico
Verona
Peschiera
R. Mincio
MANTUA 18 m.
Brescia
Lake Garda
R. Adige
SCALE OF MILES.
10 5 0 10 20 30 40 50
Compiled in the Historical Section (Military Branch).

FINISH VOLUME II

COMPLETE BIBLIOGRAPHY AT END OF VOLUME III